25 Years 2025-2001

ICSE

CHAPTERWISE TOPICWISE QUESTION BANK

Physics

Class 10

Author
Rahul Kumar

arihant
SUCCESS AND NOTHING LESS

arihant

SUCCESS AND NOTHING LESS

ARIHANT PRAKASHAN

(School Division Series)

ADMINISTRATIVE & PRODUCTION OFFICES

Regd. Office

'Ramchhaya' 4577/15, Agarwal Road, Darya Ganj, New Delhi -110002

Tele: 011- 47630600, 43518550

Head Office

Kalindi, TP Nagar, Meerut (UP) - 250002, Tel: 0121-7156203, 7156204

SALES & SUPPORT OFFICES

Agra, Ahmedabad, Bengaluru, Bareilly, Chennai, Delhi, Guwahati, Hyderabad, Jaipur, Jhansi, Kolkata, Lucknow, Nagpur & Pune.

PO No : TXT-XX-XXXXXXX-X-XX

Published By Arihant Publications (India) Ltd.

For further information about the books published by Arihant, log on to www.arihantbooks.com or e-mail at info@arihantbooks.com

PRICE ₹260.00

Follow us on

Achieving 99+
Marks in Board Exams

Achieving 99+ marks in board exams is definitely an ambitious goal, but with the right approach and these 7 tips from toppers, you can definitely increase your chances of success!

Here are the 7 Topper Tips to ace your board exams:

1. Master the art of consistency

Consistency builds understanding and confidence, both crucial for excelling in exams.

2. Build a winning study strategy

Create a personalised timetable that prioritises subjects based on your strengths and weaknesses.

3. Befriend the syllabus

Focus on high-weightage topics and prioritise mastering core concepts before moving on to advanced ones.

4. Embrace active learning

Explain concepts to yourself or in study groups to solidify understanding.

5. Conquer the past

Solve Past years' papers and Sample Papers under timed conditions to practice time management and understand paper pattern.

6. Seek help, when needed!

Don't hesitate to clarify doubts with teachers, tutors, or study groups. Asking questions strengthens your understanding and prevents confusion.

7. Prioritise well-being

Eat nutritious meals, get enough sleep, regular exercise and practice stress management techniques like meditation to stay calm and focused during exams.

These tips are just a starting point, and you can personalise them to fit your learning style and preferences.

Description of

Newly Added Features

01

Force

TREND ANALYSIS 4 YEARS

Average No. of Questions Across all Sets

Topic	Types of Questions	2024	2023	2020	2019
TOPIC 01 Types of Forces and Turning Forces Concept	1 Mark	1	1	–	–
	2 Marks	1	1	1	1
	3 Marks	1	–	–	1
	4 Marks	–	–	–	–
TOPIC 02 Uniform Circular Motion	1 Mark	1	–	–	–
	2 Marks	–	–	–	–
	3 Marks	–	–	–	–
	4 Marks	–	–	–	–

Trend Analysis

At the start of each chapter, Trend Analysis is given to indicate the types of questions asked from different topics of the chapter. This feature helps students to know the importance of different topics of the given chapter from exam point of view and helps them to prepare accordingly.

10. If the moment of F about the centre of a wheel O is 6 N-m, then calculate the moment of F about A. **(ICSE SQP 2023)**

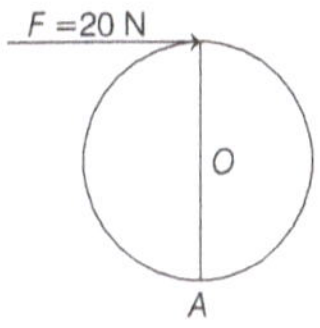

KEY idea

To calculate moment of force or torque about any point, first identify point about which the body rotates, then by knowing perpendicular distance between point of rotation and the direction of force, we calculate torque by using

$$\tau = \text{force} \times \text{perpendicular distance}$$

Key Idea

'Key Idea' is given with selected questions with the purpose to help students to get the approach 'to answer the question'. This feature help students to develop the systematic approach to answer difficult/complex questions.

10. Moment of force, $\tau = 6$ N-m point at O.

Force, $F = 20$ N

As we know, $\tau = r \times F$

$$r = \frac{\tau}{f} = \frac{6}{20}\text{m} = 0.3 \text{ m}$$

When the rotation occur at point A, then $r' = 2r$

$$= 2 \times 0.3 \text{ m}$$

$$r' = 0.6 \text{ m}$$

Hence, the moment of force about A,

$$\tau = r' \times F = 20 \times 0.6 = 12 \text{ N-m}$$

Concept Enhancer When a force is applied on the rim of a wheel angentially, then torque produced in the wheel will be maximum.

Concept Enhancer

Concept Enhancer gives the brief description of the concept, which has been used to answer the question. This feature provides revision of important concept along with practice of question solving.

Dream, Believe, Achieve

Insights from ICSE Toppers

"Board exams are way easier than you think. It's easy to score if you study regularly for even an hour. Consistency is key,"

DIVYANSH AGARWAL

ICSE Topper (99.40%)

He dedicated time to solving topic-wise papers from the last 10 years, providing valuable practice before his final revision. A planned approach and schedule help to prepare and cover the syllabus better.

ANONDEE SAHA

ICSE Topper (99.6%)

Before the boards, my school had given all students a month to study and I tried my best to study 8-9 hours every day.

I relied on revising the syllabus of each subject at least twice during this period and went through past years' question papers and extra questions that my teachers had sent.

For excelling in the boards I would like to advice students to study regularly from DAY 1. They should refer to previous years Board question papers and should always have a positive attitude and should be confident. But not overconfident

MUSKAN PATHAN

ICSE Topper (99.4%)

"I studied everything independently, which gave me a better understanding of what topics I needed to improve. I studied only 1.5 to 2 hours daily but stayed consistent and regular,"

MIHIKA SANJANWALA

ICSE Topper (99%)

NILOTMA SINGH

ICSE Topper (99.6%)

"I had started preparing, chapter by chapter, right from the beginning of the academic session as we had weekly tests on every topic that was covered in class. However, the hard-core preparation started only in late November 2022 which was about three months prior to the board examination.,"

Previous Years Papers guide me to a great extent as they helped me understand the scope and area of the questions that could be asked. The specimen papers were extremely helpful as we had undergone a change in examination pattern this year.

"While my primary schooling in Shanghai (China) taught me to be a global citizen, my higher secondary schooling at Greenwood High (Bannerghatta) elevated my inquisitiveness and curiosity on various subjects,"

"Personally, POMODORO technique, a time-management method based on 25-minute stretches of focused work broken by five-minute breaks, helped me immensely not only to organise myself better but also to cover a vast syllabus with the least fatigue,"

SHIVANI NEELAMRAJU

ICSE Topper (99.40%)

Please Note that all the information is collected from different websites.

Most Important Topics

from each Chapter

On the basis of analysis of last 5 Years' Board Examination Papers, we have identified Important Topics from each chapter.

Chapter Name	Important Topics	Weightage in Last 5 Years' Boards				
		2025	2024	2023	2020	2019
Force	Types of Forces and Turning Forces Concept	1M(2Q), 2M(1Q), 3M(1Q)	1M, 2M, 3M	1M, 2M	2M	2M, 3M
	Uniform Circular Motion	–	1M	-	-	-
Work, Power and Energy	Work	1M(1Q)	1M(2Q)	-	-	-
	Power and Energy	1M(1Q), 4M(1Q)	2M	2M(2Q), 4M(1Q)	-	2M
	Energy Sources and Conservation of Energy	–	1M, 3M	1M	2M, 4M	3M
	Machines	1M(1Q), 3M(2Q)	1M(2Q), 2M, 4M	-	2M, 3M	4M
Refraction of Light	Refraction of Light at Plane Surfaces	1M(2Q), 3M(2Q)	3M(2Q), 4M	-	2M(3Q), 3M	2M, 3M
	Total Internal Reflection	2M(1Q), 1M(1Q), 3M(1Q)	3M	1M, 3M(3Q)	3M	2M
Lenses	Lenses	1M(1Q), 3M(1Q), 4M(1Q)	1M(2Q), 2M, 3M	1M, 2M 3M(2Q)	4M	2M, 3M, 4M
Spectrum of Light	Spectrum of Light	1M(1Q), 4M(Q)	1M, 3M	1M, 4M(2Q)	2M	2M
Sound	Sound Waves and Vibrations	4M(1Q),3M(1Q)	1M, 2M, 3M, 4M	1M(2Q), 2M3M, 4M	2M(2Q), 4M	3M
	Characteristics of Sound	1M(1Q),2M(1Q)	-	1M	3M	2M(3Q), 3M
Current Electricity	Electricity and Resistance	1M(3Q), 2M(1Q),	1M(2Q), 2M, 3M, 4M	1M, 3M, 4M	2M, 4M	2M(2Q), 4M
	Electrical Power and Energy	4M(1Q)	-	1M, 2M	2M, 3M	-
	Domestic Circuits	2M(1Q), 3M(1Q)	1M, 2M	-	2M	-
Magnetic Effect of Current	Magnetic Effect of Current	2M(1Q), 1M(1Q), 4M(1Q)	2M, 3M	1M, 2M, 4M	2M(2Q)	-
	Electromagnetic Induction	1M(1Q), 2M(1Q)	1M, 3M	-	-	2M
Heat	Specific Heat Capacity	1M(2Q), 3M(1Q)	1M	2M	2M(2Q), 3M	2M(2Q), 3M
	Latent Heat	1M(Q), 2M(1Q), 3M(1Q)	1M, 2M, 3M(2Q)	3M	3M(2Q), 4M	2M, 3M, 4M
Radioactivity and Nuclei	Radioactivity and Nuclei	1M(2Q), 3M(2Q)	1M(2Q), 2M(2Q), 3M	2M, 3M(2Q)	1M, 2M, 4M	1M, 2M(2Q)

Contents

ICSE Chapterwise Topicwise Question Bank 2025-2001

Latest Syllabus

*There will be **one** paper of **two hours** duration carrying 80 marks and Internal Assessment of practical work carrying 20 marks.*

*The paper will be divided into two sections, **Section I** (40 marks) and **Section II** (40 marks).*

***Section I** (compulsory) will contain short answer questions on the entire syllabus.*

***Section II** will contain six questions. Candidates will be required to answer any four of these six questions.*

***Note:** Unless otherwise specified, only S I. Units are to be used while teaching and learning, as well as for answering questions.*

Force, Work, Power and Energy

(i) Turning forces concept; moment of a force; forces in equilibrium; centre of gravity; [discussions using simple examples and simple numerical problems].

Elementary introduction of translational and rotational motions; moment (turning effect) of a force, also called torque and its cgs and SI units; common examples - door, steering wheel, bicycle pedal, etc.; clockwise and anti-clockwise moments; conditions for a body to be in equilibrium (translational and rotational); principle of moment and its verification using a metre rule suspended by two spring balances with slotted weights hanging from it; simple numerical problems; Centre of gravity (qualitative only) with examples of some regular bodies and irregular lamina.

(ii) Uniform circular motion

As an example of constant speed, though acceleration (force) is present. Differences between centrifugal and centripetal force.

(iii) Work, energy, power and their relation with force.

Definition of work. $W = FS\cos\theta$; special cases of $\theta = 0^0, 90^0$. $W = mgh$. Definition of energy, energy as work done. Various units of work and energy and their relation with SI units.[erg, calorie, kW h and eV]. Definition of Power, $P = W/t$; SI and cgs units; other units; kilowatt (kW), megawatt (MW) and gigawatt (GW); and horse power (1hp=746W) [Simple numerical problems on work, power and energy].

(iv) Different types of energy (e.g. chemical energy, Mechanical energy, heat energy, electrical energy, nuclear energy, sound energy, light energy).

Mechanical energy: potential energy $U = mgh$ (derivation included) gravitational PE, examples; kinetic energy $K = \frac{1}{2}mv^2$ (derivation included); forms of kinetic energy: translational, rotational and vibrational - only simple examples. [Numerical problems on K and U only in case of translational motion]; qualitative discussions of electrical, chemical, heat, nuclear, light and sound energy, conversion from one form to another; common examples.

(v) Machines as force multipliers; load, effort, mechanical advantage, velocity ratio and efficiency; simple treatment of levers, pulley systems showing the utility of each type of machine.

Functions and uses of simple machines: Terms- effort E, load L, mechanical advantage $MA = L/E$, velocity ratio $V_R = V_E/V_L = dE/dL$, input (W_i), output (W_o), efficiency (h), relation between h and MA,VR (derivation included); for all practical machines h < 1; $MA < VR$.

Lever: principle. First, second and third class of levers; examples: MA and VR in each case. Examples of each of these classes of levers as also found in the human body.

Pulley system: single fixed, single movable, block and tackle; MA, VR and h in each case.

(vi) Principle of Conservation of energy.

Statement of the principle of conservation of energy; theoretical verification that $U + K$ = constant for a freely falling body. Application of this law to simple pendulum (qualitative only); [simple numerical problems].

Light

(i) Refraction of light through a glass block and a triangular prism - qualitative treatment of simple applications such as real and apparent depth of objects in water and apparent bending of sticks in water. Applications of refraction of light.

Partial reflection and refraction due to change in medium. Laws of refraction; the effect on speed (V), wavelength (λ) and frequency (f) due to refraction of light; conditions for a light ray *to pass undeviated. Values of speed of light (c) in vacuum, air, water and glass; refractive index $\mu = c/V$, $V = f\lambda$. Values of μ for common substances such as water, glass and diamond; experimental verification; refraction through glass block; lateral displacement; multiple images in thick glass plate/mirror; refraction through a glass prism simple applications: real and apparent depth of objects in water; apparent bending of a stick under water. (Simple numerical problems and approximate ray diagrams required).*

(ii) Total internal reflection: Critical angle; examples in triangular glass prisms; comparison with reflection from a plane mirror (qualitative only). Applications of total internal reflection.

Transmission of light from a denser medium (glass/water) to a rarer medium (air) at different angles of incidence; critical angle (C) $\mu = 1/\sin C$. Essential conditions for total internal reflection. Total internal reflection in a triangular glass prism; ray diagram, different cases - angles of prism (60°60°60°, (60°30°90°, (45°45°90°; use of right angle prism to obtain d = 90° and 180° (ray diagram); comparison of total internal reflection from a prism and reflection from a plane mirror.

(iii) Lenses (converging and diverging) including characteristics of the images formed (using ray diagrams only); magnifying glass; location of images using ray diagrams and thereby determining magnification.

Types of lenses (converging and diverging), convex and concave, action of a lens as a set of prisms; technical terms; centre of curvature, radii of curvature, principal axis, foci, focal plane and focal length,; detailed study of refraction of light in spherical lenses through ray diagrams; formation of images - principal rays or construction rays; location of images from ray diagram for various positions of a small linear object on the principal axis; characteristics of images. Sign convention and direct numerical problems using the lens formula are included.(derivation of formula not required).

Scale drawing or graphical representation of ray diagrams not required.

Power of a lens (concave and convex) – [simple direct numerical problems]: magnifying glass or simple microscope: location of image and magnification from ray diagram only [formula and numerical problems not included]. Applications of lenses.

(iv) Using a triangular prism to produce a visible spectrum from white light; Electromagnetic spectrum. Scattering of light.

Deviation produced by a triangular prism; dependence on colour (wavelength) of light; dispersion and spectrum; electromagnetic spectrum: broad classification (names only arranged in order of increasing wavelength); properties common to all electromagnetic radiations; properties and uses of infrared and ultraviolet radiation. Simple application of scattering of light e.g. blue colour of the sky.

Sound

(i) Reflection of Sound Waves; echoes: their use; simple numerical problems on echoes.

Production of echoes, condition for formation of echoes; simple numerical problems; use of echoes by bats, dolphins, fishermen, medical field. SONAR.

(ii) Natural vibrations, Damped vibrations, Forced vibrations and Resonance - a special case of forced vibrations.

Meaning and simple applications of natural, damped, forced vibrations and resonance.

(iii) Loudness, pitch and quality of sound:

Characteristics of sound: loudness and intensity; subjective and objective nature of these properties; sound level in dB (as unit only); noise pollution; interdependence of: pitch and frequency; quality and waveforms (with examples).

Electricity and Magnetism

(i) Ohm's Law; concepts of emf, potential difference, resistance; resistances in series and parallel, internal resistance.

Concepts of pd (V), current (I), resistance (R) and charge (Q). Ohm's law: statement, V=IR; SI units; experimental verification; graph of V vs I and resistance from slope; ohmic and non-ohmic resistors, factors affecting resistance (including specific resistance) and internal resistance; super conductors, electromotive force (emf); combination of resistances in series and parallel and derivation of expressions for equivalent resistance. Simple numerical problems using the above relations. [Simple network of resistors].

(ii) Electrical power and energy.

Electrical energy; examples of heater, motor, lamp, loudspeaker, etc. Electrical power; measurement of electrical energy, $W = QV = VIt$ from the definition of pd. Combining with Ohm's law $W = VIt = I^2 Rt = (V^2/R)t$ and electrical power $P = (W/t) = VI = I^2R = V^2/R$. Units: SI and commercial; Power rating of common appliances, household consumption of electric energy; calculation of total energy consumed by electrical appliances; $W = Pt$ (kilowatt × hour = kW h), [simple numerical problems].

(iii) Household circuits – main circuit; switches; fuses; earthing; safety precautions; three-pin plugs; colour coding of wires.

House wiring (ring system), power distribution; main circuit (3 wires-live, neutral, earth) with fuse / MCB, main switch and its advantages - circuit diagram; two-way switch, staircase wiring, need for earthing, fuse, 3-pin plug and socket; Conventional location of live, neutral and earth points in 3 pin plugs and sockets. Safety precautions, colour coding of wires.

(iv) Magnetic effect of a current (principles only, laws not required); electromagnetic induction (elementary); transformer.

Oersted's experiment on the magnetic effect of electric current; magnetic field (B) and field lines due to current in a straight wire (qualitative only), right hand thumb rule – magnetic field due to a current in a loop; Electromagnets: their uses; comparisons with a permanent magnet; Fleming's Left Hand Rule, the DC electric motor- simple sketch of main parts (coil, magnet, split ring commutators and brushes); brief description and type of energy transfer(working not required): Simple introduction to electromagnetic induction; frequency of AC in house hold supplies , Fleming's Right Hand Rule, AC Generator - Simple sketch of main parts, brief description and type of energy transfer(working not required). Advantage of AC over DC. Transformer- its types, characteristics of primary and secondary coils in each type (simple labelled diagram and its uses).

Heat

(i) Calorimetry: meaning, specific heat capacity; principle of method of mixtures; Numerical Problems on specific heat capacity using heat loss and gain and the method of mixtures.

Heat and its units (calorie, joule), temperature and its units (°C, K); thermal (heat) capacity $C' = Q/\Delta T$... (SI unit of C): Specific heat Capacity $C = Q/m\Delta T$ (SI unit of C) Mutual relation between Heat Capacity and Specific Heat capacity, values of C for some common substances (ice, water and copper). Principle of method of mixtures including mathematical statement. Natural phenomenon involving specific heat. Consequences of high specific heat of water. [Simple numerical problem].

(ii) Latent heat; loss and gain of heat involving change of state for fusion only.

Change of phase (state); heating curve for water; latent heat; specific latent heat of fusion (SI unit). Simple numerical problems. Common physical phenomena involving latent heat of fusion.

Modern Physics

(i) Radioactivity and changes in the nucleus; background radiation and safety precautions.

Brief introduction (qualitative only) of the nucleus, nuclear structure, atomic number (Z), mass number (A).Radioactivity as spontaneous disintegration. α, β and γ - their nature and properties; changes within the nucleus. One example each of α and β decay with equations showing changes in Z and A. Uses of radioactivity - radio isotopes. Harmful effects. Safety precautions. Background radiation.

Radiation: X-rays; radioactive fallout from nuclear plants and other sources.

Nuclear Energy: working on safe disposal of waste. Safety measures to be strictly reinforced.

(ii) *Nuclear fission and fusion; basic introduction and equations.*

Analysis of Pupil Performance: ICSE Physics

The document 'Analysis of Pupils' Performance' in ICSE Class 10 Examination, is prepared by Research Development and Consultancy Division (RDCD) of the Council for the Indian School Certificate Examination (CISCE). The purpose of this document is to provide feedback to schools in terms of strengths and weaknesses of the candidates in handling the examination.

TOPICS FOUND DIFFICULT BY STUDENTS

- Work done when a body moves in a circular path.
- Diagram of refraction from denser to rarer medium to show the formation of an image.
- Completing the path of a ray through 30°,60° and 90° prism.
- Scattering of light
- Refraction through any refracting medium when opposite faces are parallel and when they are not parallel.
- Numerical problems based on light using sign convention.
- Graphs on calorimetry.
- Numerical problems based on Heat.
- Numerical problems based on Electricity, especially in finding the current in parallel branches.
- Completing the nuclear reactions in reverse order.

CONCEPTS IN WHICH STUDENTS GOT CONFUSED

- Meaning of 'without changing the length of the lever'.
- Frequency being constant when a wave enters from one medium to another.
- Maximum force experienced by a current carrying coil and a straight conductor when placed in a magnetic field.
- 'Dispersion of light and scattering of light'.
- The appearance of an object when viewed from a denser medium.
- The path of light through a right isosceles prism and a 30°, 60° and 90° prism.
- Reason-based questions related to heat capacity and specific heat capacity.
- Giving reasons for a loud sound in both resonance and non-resonance cases.
- Drawing a graph between displacement from mean position and time for a body executing free vibration in a vacuum.
- Using formula to decide whether sound is audible in air.
- Semiconductor and Superconductor.
- Diagram of a D.C. motor and a D.C. generator.

SUGGESTIONS FOR STUDENTS

- Try to understand the concept and try to apply it to the immediate surrounding.
- Try to relate the concepts from Mathematics with Physics and vice-versa.
- Avoid rote learning. Answer in your own words and then verify whether you have covered all points.
- Watch related videos on YouTube and try to make some projects/models which work on the principles which you have learnt.
- Pay equal attention to all chapters.
- Take out time for self-study.
- Periodic revision of the topics completed should be done.
- Practice previous years; question papers.
- Analyse your errors during practice papers and work accordingly.
- Use the reading time of 15 minutes judiciously to decide the questions that you are going to attempt.
- Keep your answer paper presentable by keeping your handwriting legible and by avoiding unnecessary scratching and striking off.
- Write the formula in the beginning while solving numerical.
- Definitions along with key words must be practiced.
- Practice conversion of CGS units to SI units and vice-versa.
- Practice drawing block and tackle system of pulleys, by drawing string straight, showing rigid support and tension in the string opposite to the direction of load.
- Practice ray diagrams with arrows marked.
- Show virtual images by dotted lines.
- Do not leave the answer in fractional form. Express it in decimal form.

01

Force

TREND ANALYSIS 4 YEARS

Average No. of Questions Across all Sets

		Types of Questions	2024	2023	2020	2019
TOPIC 01	Types of Forces and Turning Forces Concept	1 Mark	1	1	–	–
		2 Marks	1	1	1	1
		3 Marks	1	–	–	1
		4 Marks	–	–	–	–
TOPIC 02	Uniform Circular Motion	1 Mark	1	–	–	–
		2 Marks	–	–	–	–
		3 Marks	–	–	–	–
		4 Marks	–	–	–	–

A **force** is any external effort that causes an object to undergo a certain change, either concerning its movement direction or geometrical shape and size. In simple terms, it is a push or pull acting upon an object. It has both magnitude and direction, so it is a **vector quantity**.

In SI unit, it is measured as **newton** and in CGS, it is measured as **dyne**.

$$1 \text{ dyne} = 10^{-5} \text{ N}$$

$$1 \text{ kgf} = 9.8 \text{ N}$$

$$1 \text{ gf} = 980 \text{ dyne}$$

Force applied on an object can do three things

(i) It can make objects move faster or slower.

(ii) It can change the shape and size of an object.

(iii) It can change the direction of motion of a moving object.

TOPIC 1

Types of Forces and Turning Forces Concept

Contact Forces

These forces represent the result of contact between the two bodies, one by which force is exerted and the other one on which force is exerted. e.g. Stretching of a coiled spring, pulling of a cart, frictional forces, normal reaction forces, forces in collisions, etc.

Some contact forces are discussed below

Friction

It is the force resisting the relative motion between two solid surfaces, fluid layers and material elements sliding against each other. There are four types of friction

(i) **Static friction** The friction that exist between the two surfaces in contact when there is no relative motion but a tendency of relative motion between them is called static friction.

(ii) **Limiting friction** The maximum friction that can be generated between two static surfaces in contact with each other.

(ii) **Kinetic friction** The friction that exist between a surface sliding on another surface is called kinetic friction.

(iv) **Rolling friction** When a body rolls on the surface of another body, the friction that exist between the surfaces is known as rolling friction.

Normal Reaction Force

It is the force acting perpendicular to the surfaces which are in contact with each other.

Tension as Applied Through Strings

When a body is suspended from a string, the body pulls the string vertically downward due to its weight (w). As a reaction force, the string pulls the body vertically upward by an equal and opposite force. The reaction force balances the weight of the body and is known as **tension force**.

Force Exerted during Collision

When two bodies are collide with each other, equal and opposite forces come into play and act on each other. As a result of these forces, the two bodies move apart after the collision.

Non-Contact Forces

These forces do not involve in any physical contact between the two objects but act through the space between them. These forces are also called as **action at a distance**. e.g. Gravitational force, electrostatic force, magnetic force, etc.

Gravitational Force

In universe, each body attracts the other body due to its mass. This force of attraction between them is called gravitational force. The force on a body due to earth's attraction is called the pull of gravity or the force of gravity.

The magnitude of gravitational force between two masses m_1 and m_2 situated at distance r,

$$F = \frac{G m_1 m_2}{r^2}$$

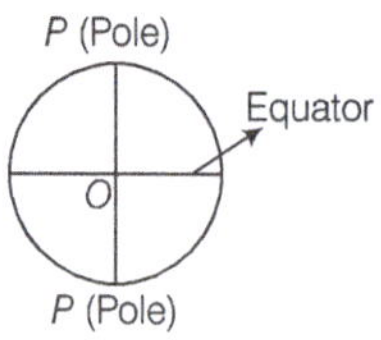

where, G is gravitational constant.

Acceleration due to gravity, $g = \frac{G M_e}{R_e^2}$

where, M_e = mass of earth and R_e = radius of earth.

(i) Acceleration due to gravity is maximum at equator.

(ii) Acceleration due to gravity is minimum at poles.

(iii) At the centre of the earth, g becomes zero.

Electrostatic Force

The force between two charged bodies when placed at a separation is called electrostatic force. The force between unlike charges is attractive and between like charges is repulsive.

Magnetic Force

The force between two magnetic poles placed at a separation is called magnetic force. The force between two unlike poles is attractive in nature and like poles repel each other.

Rigid Body

Every material object is made up of a large number of particles. A rigid body is one whose shape and size remains the same whatever force be applied to different parts of it.

A rigid body has two types of motion

(i) **Translational Motion** When a force is applied on a stationary rigid body, the body starts moving in a straight path in the direction of applied force, this type of motion is called translational motion.

e.g. On pushing a ball lying on a floor, it starts moving.

(ii) **Rotational Motion** When a force is applied on fixed point of a body which is pivoted at a point, then the body starts rotating about that point. This is called a rotational motion.

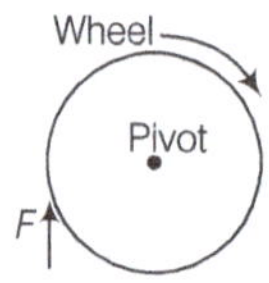

e.g. If a wheel is pivoted at its centre and a force is applied tangentially on its rim as shown in figure, the wheel rotates about its centre.

Moment of a Force

The turning effect produced by a force on a rigid body about a point, pivot or fulcrum is called **moment of a force** or **torque**. It is the product of the magnitude of the force and the perpendicular distance of the line of action of force from the axis of rotation.

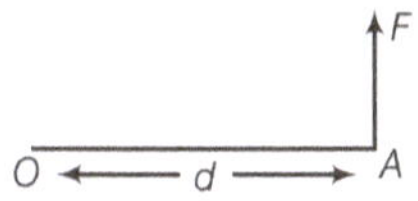

Torque (Moment of force) = Perpendicular distance × Force

or $$\tau = \mathbf{d} \times \mathbf{F}$$

where, d is the perpendicular distance.

It is a **vector** quantity.

Its SI unit is **newton-metre (N-m)** and CGS unit is **dyne-cm**.

$$1 \text{ N-m} = 10^7 \text{ dyne-cm}$$
$$\text{kgf} \times \text{m} = 9.8 \text{ N-m}$$
$$1 \text{ gf} \times \text{cm} = 980 \text{ dyne-cm}$$

Forces in Equilibrium

If an object is in equilibrium, then the sum of the forces acting on it and the sum of the moments of the forces (torque) on it, is equal to zero.

Principle of Moment

If a body is in equilibrium under the action of a number of forces, then the algebraic sum of the moments of the forces about any point is equal to zero.

It can be expressed as,

$$\text{Load} \times \text{Load arm} = \text{Effort} \times \text{Effort arm}$$
$$L \times d_L = E \times d_E$$

Clockwise and Anti-Clockwise Moments

The direction of turning (or sense of rotation) produced on the body depends on the point of application of force and on the direction of force. If the turning effect on the body is anti-clockwise or positive, then the moment of force is called **anti-clockwise moment**. On the other hand, if the turning effect on the body is clockwise or negative, then the moment of force is called **clockwise moment**.

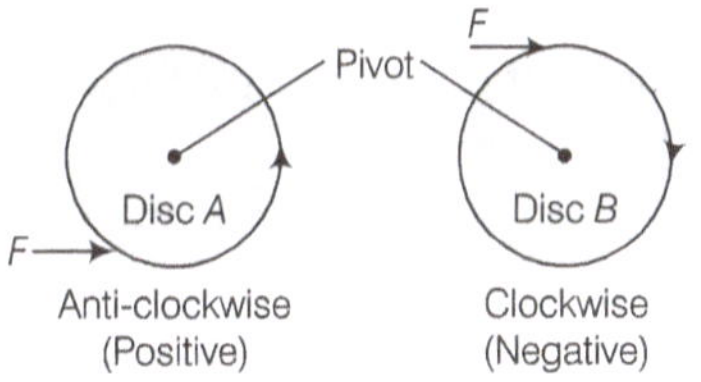

Centre of Gravity

The centre of gravity of a body is the point about which the algebraic sum of the moments of weights of all the particles constituting the body is zero. The entire weight of the body can be considered to act at this point, however the body is placed.

Centre of gravity of some regular objects

Object	Position of centre of gravity
Rod	Mid-point of rod
Circular disc	Geometric centre
Solid or hollow sphere	Geometric centre of the sphere
Solid or hollow cylinder	Mid-point on the axis of cylinder
Solid cone	At a height $h/4$ from the base, on its axis (where, h = height of cone)
Hollow cone	At a height $h/3$ from the base on its axis
Circular ring	Centre of ring
Triangular lamina or scalene triangle	The point of intersection of medians
Parallelogram, rectangular lamina, square or rhombus	The point of intersection of the diagonals

PYQs Previous Years Questions

1 Mark Questions

1. A door lock is opened by turning the level (handle) of length 0.2 m . If the moment of force produced is 1 N-m, then the minimum force required is **(ICSE 2024)**

   (a) 5 N (b) 10 N (c) 20 N (d) 0.2 N

2. Clockwise moment produced by a force about a fulcrum is considered to be **(ICSE 2023)**

   (a) positive (b) negative
   (c) zero (d) None of these

3. SI unit of moment is **(ICSE SQP 2023)**

   (a) kgf-m (b) N-m (c) gf-m (d) N-cm

4. The relation between CGS and SI unit of moment of force is **(ICSE 2022 Sem-I)**

   (a) 1 N-m = 10^5 dyne-cm
   (b) 1 N-m = 10^5 dyne
   (c) 1 N-m = 10^7 dyne-cm
   (d) 1 dyne-cm = 10^7 N-m

5. The diagram below shows the balanced position of a meter scale.

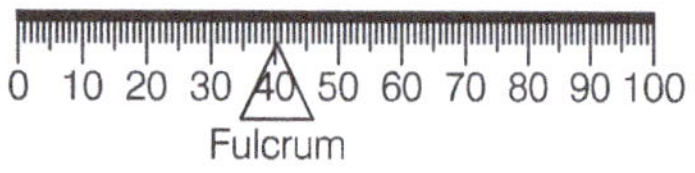

   Which one of the following diagrams shows the correct position of the scale when it is supported at the centre? **(ICSE 2022 Sem-I)**

(a)
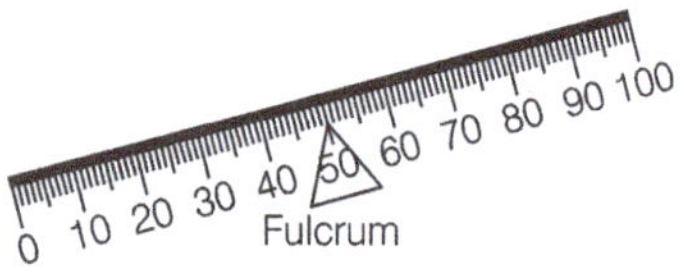

(b)
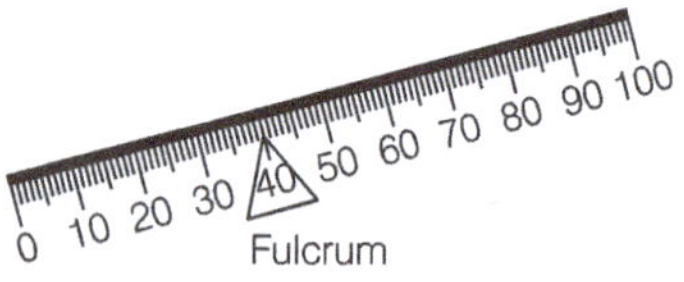

(c)
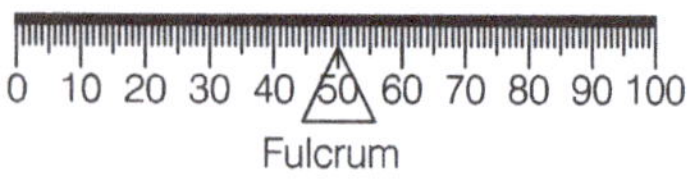

(d)
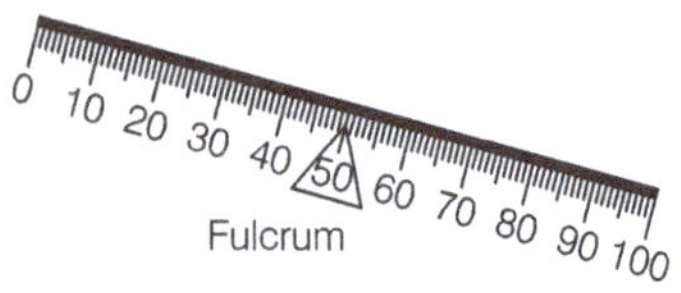

6. If the centre of gravity of a meter scale of mass 80 g lies at the 45 cm mark, then which one of the following diagrams will show the balanced position of the scale? **(ICSE SQP 2022 Sem-I)**

(a)
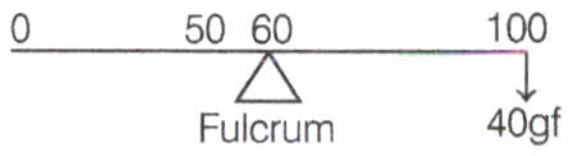

(b)
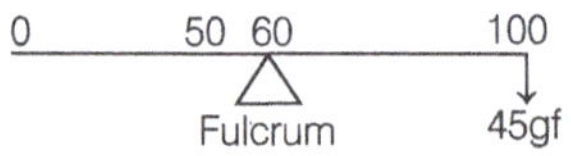

(c)
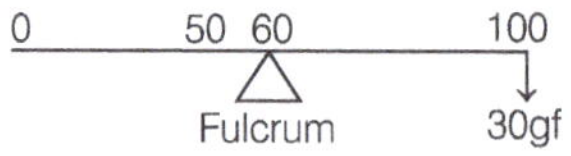

(d)
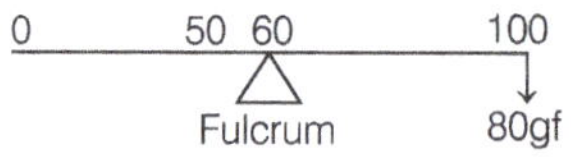

7. What is the weight of a body placed at the centre of the earth? **(ICSE 2014)**

2 Marks Questions

8. A non - uniform beam of weight 120 N pivoted at one end is shown in the diagram below.

   Calculate the value of *F* to keep the beam in equilibrium. **(ICSE 2024)**

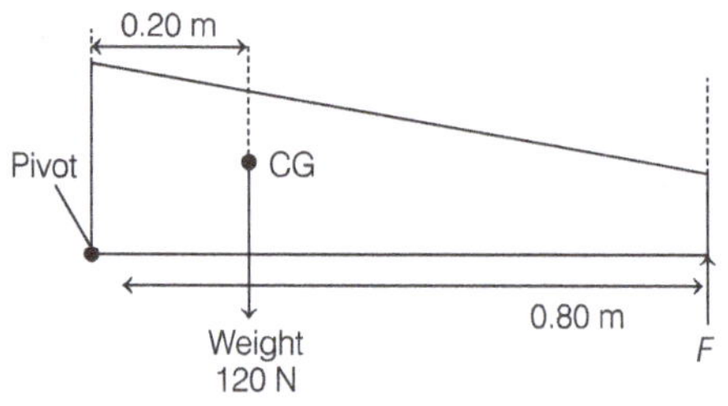

9. (i) What is the position of centre of gravity of a triangular lamina?

   (ii) When this triangular lamina is suspended freely from any one vertex, what is the moment of force produced by its own weight in its rest position? **(ICSE 2023)**

10. State two factors that affects the centre of gravity of the body. **(ICSE SQP 2023)**

11. If the moment of F about the centre of a wheel O is 6 N-m, then calculate the moment of F about A. **(ICSE SQP 2023)**

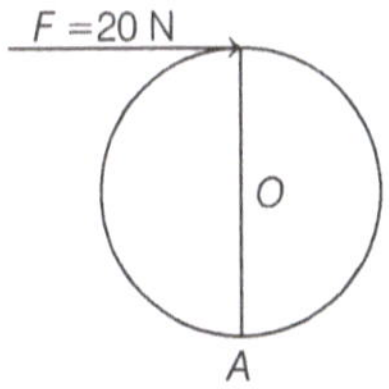

KEY idea

To calculate moment of force or torque about any point, first identify point about which the body rotates, then by knowing perpendicular distance between point of rotation and the direction of force, we calculate torque by using

τ = force × perpendicular distance

12. (i) Name the force which produces maximum moment about.

(ii) Calculate this moment in SI unit. **(ICSE SQP 2023)**

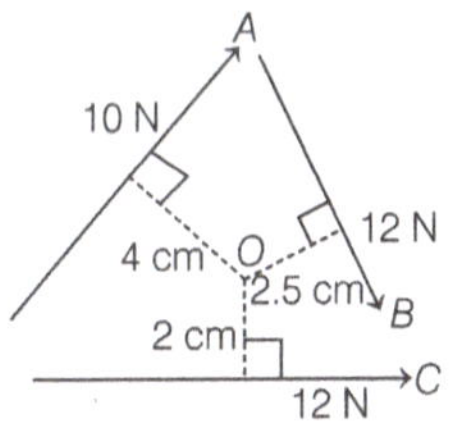

13. (i) Define moment of force.

(ii) Write the relationship between the SI and CGS unit of moment of force. **(ICSE 2020)**

14. (i) Define couple.

(ii) State the SI unit of moment of couple. **(ICSE 2019)**

15. A brass ball is hanging from a stiff cotton thread. Draw a neat labelled diagram showing the forces acting on the brass ball and cotton thread. **(ICSE 2017, 14)**

16. The distance between two bodies is doubled. How is the magnitude of gravitational force between them affected? **(ICSE 2017)**

17. Why is a jack screw provided with a long arm? **(ICSE 2017)**

18. A uniform meter scale is in equilibrium position. Calculate the mass of the ruler. **(ICSE SQP 2017)**

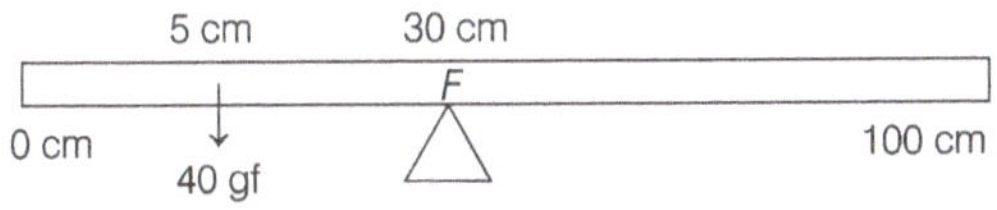

19. Derive the relation between CGS and SI unit of force. **(ICSE SQP 2017)**

20. Classify the following into contact and non-contact forces **(ICSE 2017)**

(i) Tension (ii) Friction

(iii) Gravitational force (iv) Magnetic force

21. Where is the centre of gravity of the following objects situated? **(ICSE SQP 2017)**

(i) Ring (ii) Rhombus

(iii) Scalene triangle (iv) Cylinder

22. Calculate the resultant torque from the following diagram. **(ICSE SQP 2017)**

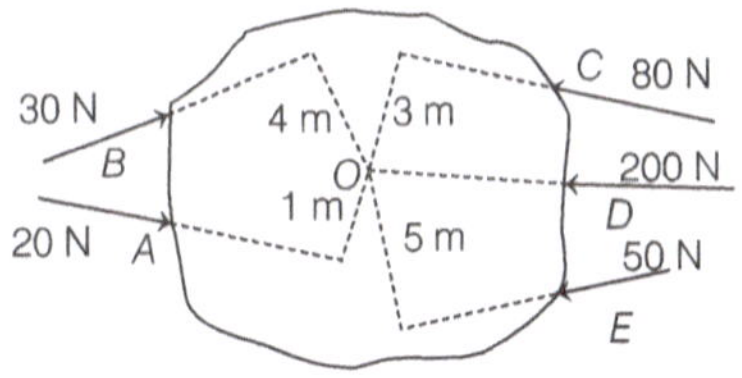

KEY idea

Calculate the resultant torque with the formula

τ_{net} = Clockwise torque – Anti-clockwise torque and Torque due to 200 N as zero because it is passing through point O.

23. (i) Give an example of a non–contact force which is always of attractive nature.

(ii) How does the magnitude of this non–contact force on the two bodies depend on the distance of separation between them? **(ICSE 2016)**

24. (i) Define equilibrium.

(ii) In a beam balance, when the beam is balanced in a horizontal position, it is in_____equilibrium. **(ICSE 2015)**

25. When a body is placed on a table top, it exerts a force equal to its weight downwards on the table top but does not move or fall.

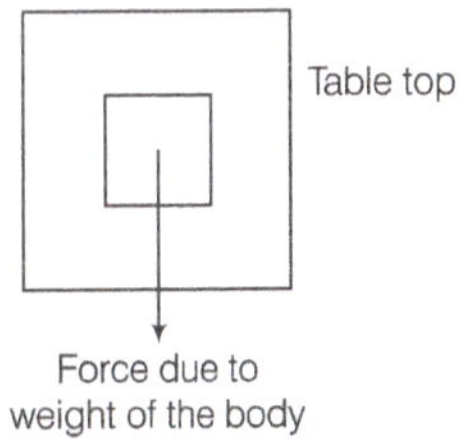

(i) Name the force exerted by the table top.

(ii) What is the direction of the force? **(ICSE 2015)**

26. (i) On what factor does the position of the centre of gravity of a body depend?

(ii) What is the SI unit of the moment of force? **(ICSE 2015)**

27. Name the factors affecting the turning effect of a body. **(ICSE 2015)**

28. A nut is opened by a wrench of length 20 cm. If the least force required is 2N, find the moment of force needed to loosen the nut. **(ICSE 2015)**

29. A force is applied on

(i) a rigid body and (ii) a non-rigid body.

How does the effect of the force differ in the above two cases? **(ICSE 2014)**

30. (i) Where is the centre of gravity of a uniform ring situated?

(ii) The position of the centre of gravity of a body remains unchanged even when the body is deformed. State whether the statement is true or false. **(ICSE 2013)**

31. One end of a spring is kept fixed while the other end is stretched by a force as shown in the diagram.

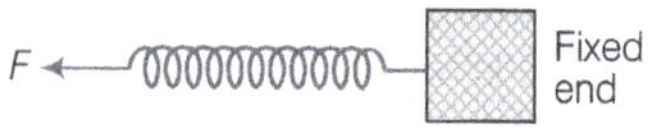

(i) Copy the diagram and mark on it the direction of the restoring force.

(ii) Name one instrument which works on the above principle. **(ICSE 2013)**

32. Give any two effects of a force on a non-rigid body. **(ICSE 2013)**

33. A boy of mass 30 kg is sitting at a distance of 2 m from the middle of a see-saw. Where should a boy of mass 40 kg sit, so as to balance the see-saw? **(ICSE 2012)**

34. (i) What is meant by the term moment of force?

(ii) If the moment of force is assigned a negative sign, then will the turning tendency of the force be clockwise or anti-clockwise? **(ICSE 2012)**

35. (i) What are non-contact forces?

(ii) How does the distance of separation between two bodies affect the magnitude of the non-contact force between them? **(ICSE 2012)**

36. (i) Define 1 kgf.

(ii) How is it related to the SI unit of force? **(ICSE 2012)**

37. A man can open a nut by applying a force of 150 N by using a lever handle of length 0.4 m. What should be the length of the handle, if he is able to open it by applying a force of 60 N? **(ICSE 2011)**

38. Where does the position of centre of gravity lie for

(i) a circular lamina?

(ii) a triangular lamina? **(ICSE 2011)**

39. (i) Define one newton.

(ii) Write the relation between SI unit and CGS unit of force. **(ICSE 2011)**

3 Marks Questions

40. (a) Define centre of gravity.

(b) A hollow icecream cone has height 6 cm.

I. Where is the position of its centre of gravity from the broad base?

II. Will its position change when it is filled completely with honey. Write **yes** or **no**. **(ICSE 2024)**

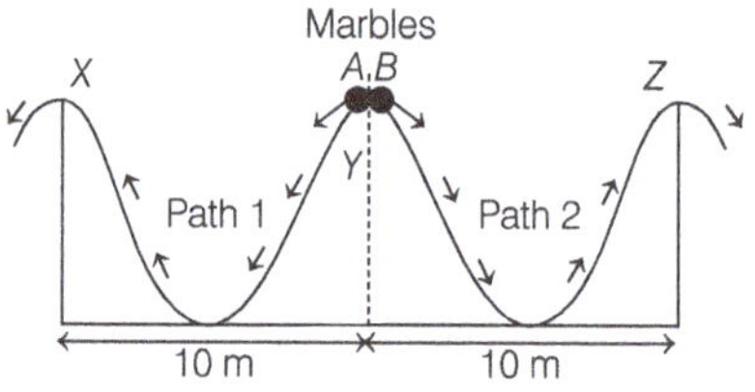

41. A uniform meter scale is in equilibrium as shown in the figure given below.

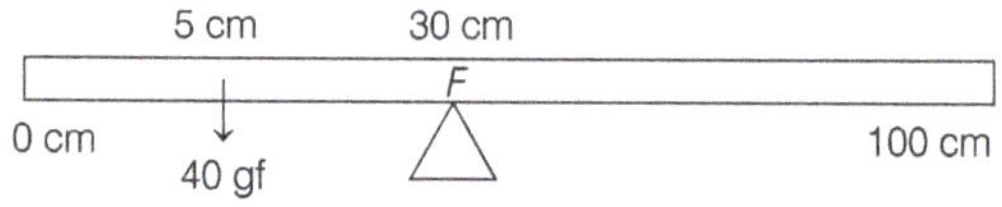

(i) Calculate the weight of the meter scale.

(ii) Which of the following option is correct to keep the ruler in equilibrium, when 40 gf-wt is shifted to 0 cm mark? *F* is shifted towards 0 cm or *F* is shifted 100 cm. **(ICSE 2019)**

4 Marks Question

42. Two forces each of 5 N act vertically upwards and downwards, respectively. On the two ends of a uniform meter rule which is placed at its mid-point as shown in the diagram. Determine the magnitude of the resultant moment of these forces about the mid-point. **(ICSE 2014)**

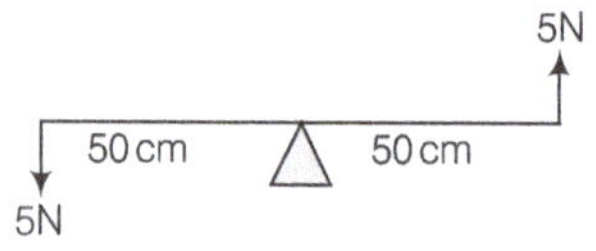

Explanations

1. (a) Given, $\tau = 1$ N-m

$d = 0.2$ m

The moment of force is given by

$\tau = F \times d$

$1 = F \times 0.2$

Minimum force, $F = \frac{1}{0.2} = \frac{10}{2} = 5$ N

2. (b)

3. (b)

4. (c) We know that,

1 newton $= 10^5$ dyne

1 N-m $= 10^5 \times 10^2$ dyne-cm

1 N-m $= 10^7$ dyne-cm

5. (a)

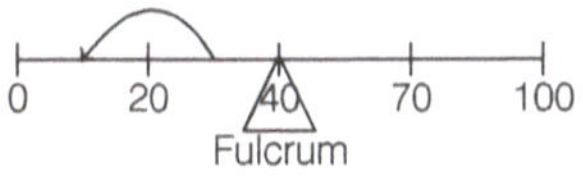

6. (c)

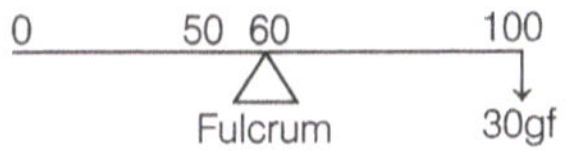

80 gf $\times (60 - 45)$ cm $= 30$ gf $\times (100 - 60)$ cm

7. The weight of a body placed at the centre of the earth is zero, because the value of g at the centre of the earth is zero.

8. By principle of moments above O,

$$F_1 d_1 = F_2 d_2$$

$$120 \times (0.20) = F_2 \times (0.80)$$

$$F_2 = \frac{120 \times 0.20}{0.80} = 30 \text{ N}$$

9. (i) Refer to text on page No 3 (Centre of gravity)

(ii) The moment of force produced by the weight of the triangular lamina in its rest position when suspended freely from any one vertex is equal to the torque produced by the weight of the lamina.

10. The factors that affects the centre of gravity of the body depends upon

(i) shape of the body

(ii) distribution of mass

11. Moment of force, $\tau = 6$ N-m point at O.

Force, $F = 20$ N

As we know, $\tau = r \times F$

$$r = \frac{\tau}{f} = \frac{6}{20} \text{m} = 0.3 \text{ m}$$

When the rotation occur at point A, then $r' = 2r$

$= 2 \times 0.3$ m

$r' = 0.6$ m

Hence, the moment of force about A,

$$\tau = r' \times F = 20 \times 0.6 = 12 \text{ N-m}$$

Concept Enhancer When a force is applied on the rim of a wheel tangentially, then torque produced in the wheel will be maximum.

12. (i) The force $F = 10$ N which produces maximum moment about O.

(ii) Moment of force A,

$F = 10$N, $d = 4$ cm $= 0.04$ m

$\tau = 10 \times 0.04 = 0.4$ N-m

Moment of force B,

$F = 12$ N, $d = 2.5$ cm $= 0.025$ m

$\tau = 12 \times 0.025 = 0.3$ N-m

Moment of force C,

$F = 12$ N, $d = 2$ cm $= 0.02$ m

$\tau = 12 \times 0.02 = 0.24$ N-m

13. (i) Refer to text on page no . 3. (Moment of a force).

(ii) Refer to text on page No. 3. (Moment of a force)

14. (i) A couple is a pair of forces equal in magnitude, oppositely directed and displaced by perpendicular distance or moment. The simplest kind of couple consists of two equal and opposite force whose lines of action do not coincide. This is called a simple couple.

(ii) The moment of couple is defined as the product of either force and the perpendicular distance between the line of action of forces.

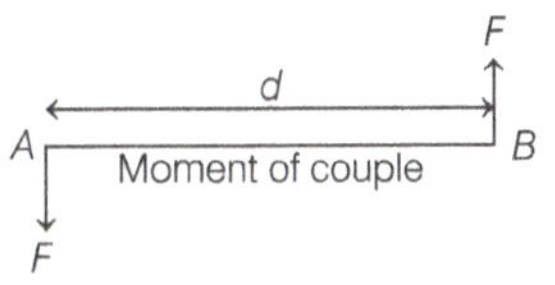

The SI unit of moment of couple is N-m.

Concept Enhancer Couple does not produce translational motion because net resulting force on the body is zero.

15. Diagram showing the forces on the ball is given below

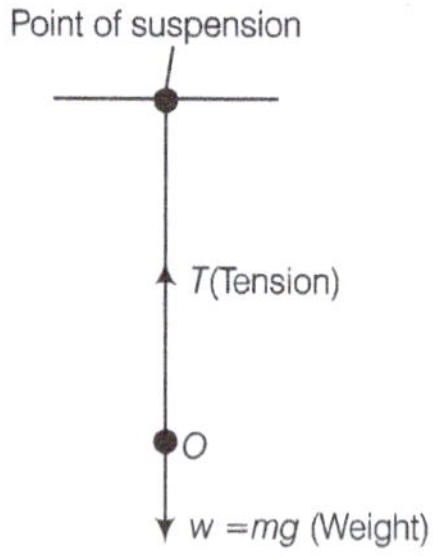

The forces acting on the brass ball are

(i) Weight (mg) of the brass ball is acting vertically downwards.

(ii) Tension (T) along the string.

16. Let m_1 and m_2 are the two bodies separated by a distance r. Gravitational force between them is

$$F = \frac{Gm_1 m_2}{r^2} \quad \ldots(i)$$

where, G = Gravitational constant.

If the distance between two bodies is doubled, then new gravitational force between them will be

$$F_1 = \frac{Gm_1 m_2}{(2r)^2} = \frac{Gm_1 m_2}{4r^2} \quad \ldots(ii)$$

Now, if we divide Eq. (i) by Eq. (ii), we get

$$\frac{F}{F_1} = \frac{\frac{Gm_1 m_2}{r^2}}{\frac{Gm_1 m_2}{4r^2}} = 4$$

$$\Rightarrow \quad F_1 = \frac{F}{4}$$

$\therefore$ Gravitational force will become one-fourth, if the distance between two bodies is doubled.

17. In order to produce maximum turning effect of the screw jack by a force, the force is applied at a point on the body for which the distance from the axis is maximum. So that, the given force provides maximum torque to turn the screw jack.

Numerically, Moment of force (torque, which is responsible for turning effect of the body)

= Force applied $\times$ perpendicular distance of force from axis of rotation.

Therefore, the longer arm of the jack screw, the more torque it can apply.

18. Let m be the mass of scale in gram.

$\therefore$ Weight of scale = mgf

By principle of moment, we get

$40 \times (30 - 5) = m \times (50 - 30)$

[$\therefore$ centre of gravity of scale is 50 cm]

$\Rightarrow \quad 40 \times 25 = m \times 20 \Rightarrow m = 50\text{ g}$

19. The CGS unit of force is dyne.

The SI unit of force is newton, then

$$\begin{aligned} 1\text{ newton} &= 1\text{ kg} \times 1\text{ m/s}^2 \\ &= 1000\text{ g} \times 100\text{ cm/s}^2 \\ &= 10^5\text{ g} \times \text{cm/s}^2 \\ &= 10^5\text{ dyne} \end{aligned}$$

Therefore, the relation betwen CGS and SI unit of force is 1 newton $= 10^5$ dyne.

20. Contact Force $\longrightarrow$ (i) Tension (ii) Friction

Non-contact force $\longrightarrow$ (iii) Gravitational force

(iv) Magnetic force

21. Refer to text on page 3 (Centre of gravity).

22. Total torque acting in clockwise direction

$= -(30 \times 4 + 50 \times 5) = -(120 + 250) = -370$ N-m

Total torque acting in anti-clockwise direction

$= +(20 \times 1 + 80 \times 3)$

$= +(20 + 240) = +260$ N-m

Resultant torque $= (-370 + 260)$ N-m

$= -110$ N-m (clockwise direction)

23. (i) The examples of non-contact force, which are attractive in nature are

(a) Gravitational force

(b) Electrostatic force between two opposite charges.

(ii) **Gravitational force** It is given by

$$F = \frac{GMm}{r^2}$$

[symbols have their usual meanings]

$$F \propto \frac{1}{r^2}$$

Force is inversely proportional to the square of distance between the masses.

24. (i) A body is said to be in equilibrium, if

(a) sum of forces on the body is zero. i.e. $\sum \mathbf{F} = 0$

(b) sum of torques on the body is zero, i.e. $\sum \tau = 0$

Due to this, no change in its state of rest or motion of the body.

(ii) In a beam balance, when the beam is balanced in a horizontal position, it is in **static** equilibrium.

25. (i) Since, the body is at rest on the table top, so the weight of the body is balanced by normal reaction.

(ii) Normal reaction acts in vertically upward direction to the top of the table.

26. (i) The position of centre of gravity of a body depends upon the shape and size of that body.

(ii) The SI unit of moment of force or torque is N-m, i.e. newton-metre.

27. The factors that affect the turning effect of a body by a force are

(i) The magnitude of the force applied.

(ii) The distance of line of action of the force from axis of rotation.

28. Here, $F = 2\text{ N}$, $d = 20\text{ cm} = 0.2\text{ m}$

We know, moment of force or torque

$$= F \times d = 2 \times 02 = 0.4\text{ N-m}$$

29. A force when applied on a rigid body does not change the inter-spacing between its constituent particles and therefore it does not change the dimensions of the object, but causes motion in it.

On the other hand, a force when applied on a non-rigid body, it changes the inter-spacing between its constituent particles and therefore causes a change in its dimensions.

30. (i) The centre of gravity of a uniform ring is situated at the centre of ring.

(ii) The statement is false, because it changes its position when the body is deformed.

Concept Enhancer It is not necessary that the centre of mass of a body should lie inside the body. It can also lie outside the body. For example, in circular ring.

31. (i)

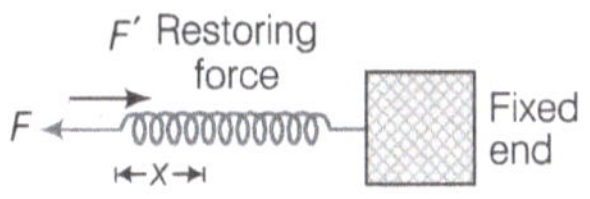

i.e. $F' = -kx$ [where, x = displacement, and k = spring constant]

(ii) Spring balance works on the above principle.

32. The two main effects of a force on a non-rigid body are

(i) It can change the state of rest or motion of the body.

(ii) It can change the size or shape of the body.

33. Let the distance of boy of mass 40 kg from the mean position be x metre. Using principle of moments,

$$30 \times 2 = 40 \times x \Rightarrow x = 1.5\text{ m}$$

So, the boy of mass 40 kg should sit at a distance 1.5 m from the middle of see-saw.

34. (i) The turning effect produced by a force on a rigid body about a point, pivot or fulcrum is called the moment of force.

(ii) If moment of the force is negative, then the turning tendency of the force is clockwise.

35. (i) The forces which are applied from a distance without actually touching the body are known as non-contact forces.

(ii) When the distance of separation between the two bodies increases, the magnitude of non-contact force decreases.

36. (i) 1 kgf is the force with which the earth pulls an object of mass 1 kg towards its centre.

(ii) It is related by, $1\text{ kgf} = mg = 9.8\text{ N}$

[Given, $m = 1\text{ kg}$, $g = 9.8\text{ m/s}^2$]

37. Given, load $L = 150\text{ N}$

Load arm $d_L = 0.4\text{ m}$, Effort arm $d_E = ?$

Effort $E = 60\text{ N}$

By principle of moments,

$$L \times d_L = E \times d_E$$

$$\Rightarrow \quad d_E = \frac{L \times d_L}{E}$$

$$= \frac{150 \times 0.4}{60} = 1\text{ m}$$

38. (i) The position of centre of gravity for a circular lamina lie at the centre of the circle.

(ii) The position of centre of gravity for a triangular lamina is at the centroid or the point of intersection of the medians.

39. (i) One newton is the amount of force required to produce an acceleration of 1 m/s^2 in a body of mass 1 kg.

(ii) The relation between SI unit and CGS unit of force is $1\text{N} = 1\text{kg} \times 1\text{ m/s}^2$

$$= 10^3\text{g} \times 10^2\text{cm/s}^2$$

[$1\text{ kg} = 10^3\text{ g}$, $1\text{ m} = 10^2\text{ cm}$]

$\therefore \quad 1\text{N} = 10^5$ dyne

40. (i) Refer to text centre of gravity on page 3.

(ii) I. At the height $\left(\frac{h}{3}\right)$ from the broad base.

II. Yes

41.

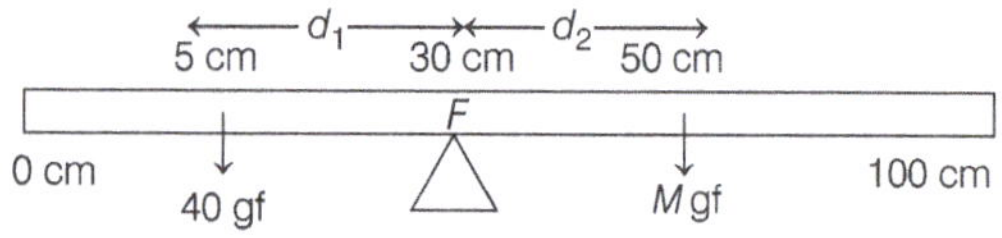

(i) At 50 cm,

Mass of meter scale = Mgf

Now, $F_1 d_1 = F_2 d_2$

$$(40\text{gf})(30-5) = F_2(50-30)$$
$$F_2 = 50\text{ gf}$$
$$F_2 = 0.49\text{ N}$$
$$\therefore \quad F_2 = Mg$$
$$0.49 = M \times 9.8$$
$$M = \frac{0.49}{9.8} = 0.05\text{ kg}$$

Common Mistake In solution of such type of problems, sometimes, students assume mass to gram force (gf).

(ii) F is shifted towards 0 cm.

42. Given, forces $F_1 = F_2 = 5\text{ N}$

Distances $d_1 = d_2 = 50\text{ cm} = 0.5\text{ m}$

Resultant moment = Torque $\tau = ?$

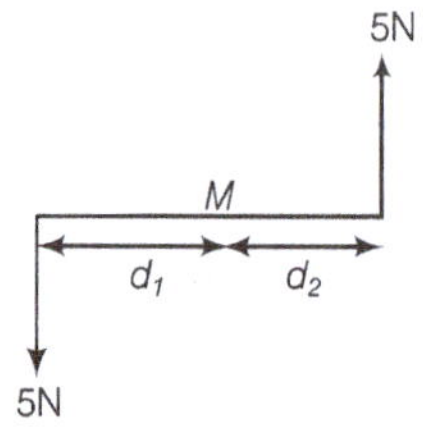

$$\therefore \quad \tau_1 = F_1 \times d_1 = 5 \times 0.5 = 2.5\text{ N-m}$$
$$\text{and} \quad \tau_2 = F_2 \times d_2 = 5 \times 0.5 = 2.5\text{ N-m}$$
$$\therefore \quad \tau = \tau_1 + \tau_2 = 2.5 + 2.5 = 5\text{ N-m}$$

TOPIC 2

Uniform Circular Motion

When a body moves with a constant speed in a circular path, its motion is known as uniform circular motion.

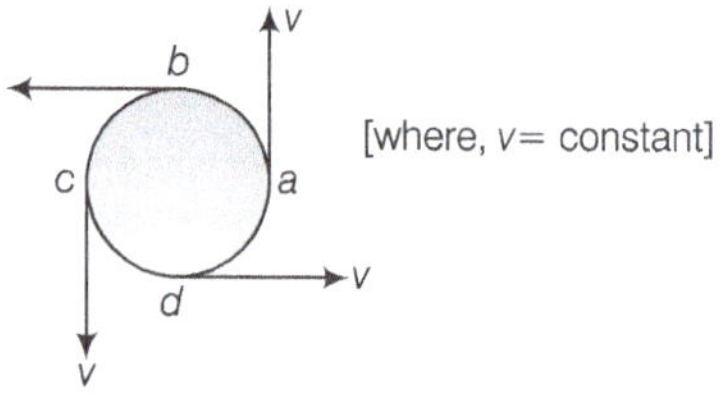

e.g. When the body travels equal distances along with the circular path in equal intervals of time, then the speed of the body is uniform. However, the direction of motion of the body changes at every point of the circular path. Due to this continuous change in the direction of motion, the velocity is no longer uniform, i.e. the motion is an **accelerated motion**. In a uniform linear motion, the velocity is constant and the acceleration is zero.

Centripetal Acceleration

The acceleration which causes a uniform circular motion in a body is called centripetal acceleration. This acceleration is always directed towards the centre of the circle.

$$a_c = \frac{v^2}{r}$$

where, v = speed of the body

and r = Radius of the circular path.

Centripetal Force

A force which keeps a body moving with a uniform speed along a circular path and is directed along the radius towards the centre. The magnitude of the centripetal force on an object of mass m moving at tangential speed v along a path with radii of curvature r is given by

$$F = ma_c = \frac{mv^2}{r} \quad \left[a_c = \frac{v^2}{r} = \text{Centripetal acceleration}\right]$$

where, a_c is centripetal acceleration.

Centrifugal Force

It is the apparent force that draws a rotating body away from the centre of rotation. It is caused by the inertia of the body as the body's path is continually redirected. The centrifugal force is in the direction opposite to the direction of centripetal force. It is not the force of reaction of centripetal force and it is not the real force but it is a fictitious force.

PYQs Previous Years Questions

1 Mark Questions

1. Why is the motion of a body moving with a constant speed around a circular path said to be accelerated? **(ICSE 2018)**

2. How does uniform circular motion differ from uniform linear motion? **(ICSE 2017)**

3. Is it possible to have an accelerated motion with a constant speed? Explain **(ICSE 2014)**

2 Marks Question

4. Explain the motion of a planet around the sun in a circular path. **(ICSE 2015)**

3 Marks Questions

5. A stone of mass *m* is rotated in a horizontal circular path with a uniform speed by tying a strong string with the help of your hand. Answer the following questions:
   (i) Is the stone moving with a uniform or variable speed?
   (ii) Is the stone moving with a uniform acceleration? In which direction does the acceleration act?
   (iii) What kind of force acts on the hand and state its direction? **(ICSE 2016)**

6. With reference to their direction of action, how does a centripetal force differ from a centrifugal force? **(ICSE 2013)**

7. (i) Which of the following remains constant in a uniform circular motion, speed or velocity or both?
   (ii) Name the force required for a uniform circular motion. State its direction. **(ICSE 2012)**

Explanations

1. In a circular motion with constant speed, linear velocity changes in terms of direction, therefore it is said to be accelerated motion.

2.

Uniform circular motion	Uniform linear motion
When a body moves in a circular path with uniform speed (constant speed). e.g. A stone tied to a thread.	When a body travels equal distance in equal intervals of time, no matter how small the intervals may be. e.g. A car moving with a constant speed 10 km/h and *s*-*t* graph is a straight line.
Acceleration of a moving body in a circle is v^2/r.	Acceleration of the body is zero.
Direction changes continuously	Direction of motion does not change

3. Yes, the velocity of a particle in a uniform circular motion is variable or the circular motion is accelerated even through the speed of particle is constant.

4. A planet moves around the sun in a nearly circular path under the action of centripetal force provided by the gravitational force of attraction on the planet by the sun.

5. (i) The stone is moving with a uniform speed and variable velocity.
   (ii) No, the stone is not moving with a uniform acceleration, because the direction of acceleration changes. Acceleration always acts towards the centre of the circular path.

   Concept Enhancer As per Newton's third law of motion, the force of action and reaction occur on two different bodies. Centripetal force and centrifugal force act on the same body. So, centrifugal force is not the reaction of centripetal force.

   (iii) Reaction force of centripetal force, radially in outwards direction from the centre of the circle.

6. With reference to their direction of action, centripetal force is directed towards the centre of circle, whereas centrifugal force is opposite to the centripetal force (i.e. radially outward).

7. (i) Speed remains constant in a uniform circular motion.
   (ii) Centripetal force is required for a uniform circular motion. It is directed towards the centre.

CHAPTER TEST

01 Mark Questions

1 Which of the following is an example of non-contact force?
(a) Tension
(b) Friction
(c) Magnetic
(d) Normal reaction

2 The moment of a force about a given axis depends
(a) only on the magnitude of force
(b) only on the perpendicular distance of force from the axis
(c) Neither on the force nor on the perpendicular distance of force from the axis
(d) Both on the force and its perpendicular distance from the axis

3 Name the force required for this circular motion.
(a) Centrifugal force
(b) Force of gravity
(c) Frictional force
(d) Centripetal force

4 A body is pivoted at a point. A force of 20 N is applied at a distance of 20 cm from the pivot. Find the moment about the pivot.
(a) 4 N-m (b) 0.6 N-m
(c) 0.04 N-m (d) 2 N-m

5 A body is acted upon by two unequal forces in opposite directions, but not in same line. The effect is that
(a) the body will have only the rotational motion
(b) the body will have rotational as well as translational motion
(c) the body will have only the translational motion
(d) the body will have neither the rotational motion nor the translational motion

02 Marks Questions

6 (i) Define one newton.
(ii) Write the relation between SI unit and CGS unit of force.

7 What is meant by moment of force?

8 Give any two effects of a force on a non-rigid body.

9 Define force. Explain any two examples of contact and non-contact forces.

10 Where does the position of centre of gravity lie for
(i) a circular lamina
(ii) a triangular lamina

Structured Questions

11 (i) Write the differences between centripetal and centrifugal force. **(3)**
(ii) What do you meant by clockwise and anti-clockwise moments of force. Explain with the diagram. **(3)**
(iii) Explain the moment of a force with diagram and formula for
(a) the steering wheel of a car
(b) the pedal and the rear wheel of a bicycle **(4)**

12 (i) A man can open a nut by applying a force of 150 N by using a lever handle of length 0.4 m. What should be the length of the handle, if he is able to open it by applying a force of 60 N? **(3)**
(ii) What is uniform circular motion? Draw a diagram to explain it. **(4)**
(iii) Define couple, prove that
Moment of couple = Force × Couple **(3)**

Answers

1. (c) **2.** (d) **3.** (d) **4.** (a) **5.** (c)
12. (i) 1 m

02

Work, Power and Energy

TREND ANALYSIS 4 YEARS

Average No. of Questions Across all Sets

Topic	Types of Questions	2024	2023	2020	2019
TOPIC 01 Work	1 Mark	2	–	–	–
	2 Marks	–	–	–	–
	3 Marks	–	–	–	–
	4 Marks	–	–	–	–
TOPIC 02 Power and Energy	1 Mark	–	1	–	–
	2 Marks	1	2	–	1
	3 Marks	–	–	–	–
	4 Marks	–	1	–	–
TOPIC 03 Energy Sources and Conservation of Energy	1 Mark	1	1	–	–
	2 Marks	–	–	1	–
	3 Marks	1	–	–	1
	4 Marks	–	–	1	–
TOPIC 04 Machines	1 Mark	2	–	–	–
	2 Marks	1	–	1	–
	3 Marks	–	–	1	–
	4 Marks	1	–	–	1

TOPIC 1

Work

It is said to be done when a force produces displacement in the direction in which it acts. e.g. A man pulling a car, a horse pulling a cart, a cyclist while pedaling a bicycle, etc. *It is expressed as*

$$\mathbf{W} = \mathbf{F} \cdot \mathrm{s} \quad \text{or} \quad \boxed{W = Fs\cos\theta}$$

where, F = Force applied on the body, s = Displacement produced and θ = Angle between direction of force and direction of displacement.

The SI unit of work is **joule** (J) and CGS unit is **erg.** It is a **scalar quantity**.

- 1 joule of work is said to be done when a force of 1 newton, displaces an object by 1 metre along with the direction of force.
- 1 erg of work is said to be done when a force of 1 dyne displaces an object by 1 centimetre along with the direction of force.

Different Cases

- If θ is 0°, then $\cos 0° = 1$ $\therefore$ $W = Fs$
  Thus, work done is positive.
- If θ is 90°, then $\cos 90° = 0$ $\therefore$ $W = 0$
  Thus, work done is zero.
- If θ is 180°, then $\cos 180° = -1$ $\therefore$ $W = -Fs$
  Thus, work done is negative.

Bigger Units of Work

1 kJ (kilo-joule) $= 10^3$ J, 1 MJ (mega-joule) $= 10^6$ J

1 GJ (giga-joule) $= 10^9$ J

Relation between Joule and Erg

$$1 \text{ joule} = 1 \text{ newton} \times 1 \text{ metre}$$

$$\Rightarrow \quad 1 \text{ joule} = 10^5 \text{ dyne} \times 10^2 \text{ centimetre}$$

$$\therefore \quad 1 \text{ joule} = 10^7 \text{ erg}$$

Different Formulae for Work Done

- Work done in terms of initial and final velocity,
$$W = F \cdot s = m\frac{v^2 - u^2}{2}$$
$$[\because v^2 = u^2 + 2as \text{ and } F = ma]$$
where, u is the initial velocity and v is the final velocity.
- Work done by the force of gravity, i.e. $(F = mg)$ on a body, acting vertically downwards and the displacement is in the direction of the force, i.e. $(s = h)$ is expressed as $W = Fs = mgh$

PYQs Previous Years Questions

1 Mark Questions

1. A force F moves a load from A to C as shown in the figure below. For the calculation of the work done, which of the these lengths would you use as the displacement ? **(ICSE 2024)**

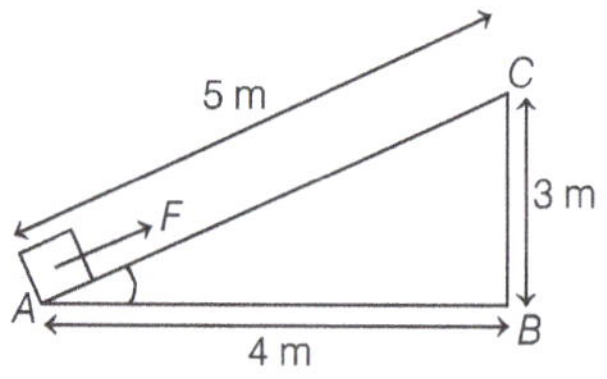

(a) 3 m (b) 4 m
(c) 5 m (d) 7 m

2. 1 J = ... erg. **(ICSE 2022 Sem-I)**

(a) 10^9 (b) 10^7
(c) 10^5 (d) 10^6

3. A coolie raises a load upwards against the force of gravity, then the work done by the load is **(ICSE 2022 Sem-I)**

(a) zero (b) positive work
(c) negative work (d) None of the above

4. Work done by a body moving on a circular track is zero at every instant because **(ICSE SQP 2022 Sem-I)**

(a) displacement is zero
(b) displacement is perpendicular to the centripetal force
(c) there is no force acting
(d) reason is not mentioned in the other options

5. A coolie carrying a load on his head and moving on a frictionless horizontal platform does no work. Explain the reason, why? **(ICSE 2011)**

> **KEY idea**
> Always, remember that work is done when the displacement is in the direction of applied force.

2 Marks Questions

6. (i) When a stone tied to a string is rotated in a horizontal plane, the tension in the string provides .... force necessary to circular motion.
(ii) Work done by this force at any instant is .... **(ICSE 2024)**

7. What is the work done by a force when the force is
(i) normal to the displacement produced
(ii) in the same direction as the displacement produced **(ICSE SQP 2018)**

> **KEY idea**
> Always try to understand the angle between the force and the displacement.

8. Explain briefly, why the work done by a fielder when he takes a catch in a cricket match, is negative? **(ICSE 2015)**

9. How is work done by a force measured when the force
(i) is in the direction of displacement?
(ii) is at an angle θ to the direction of displacement? **(ICSE 2015)**

10. (i) When does a force do work?

(ii) What is the work done by the moon when it revolves around the earth? **(ICSE 2014)**

11. A man having a box on his head, climbs up a slope and another man having an identical box walks the same distance on a levelled road. Who does more work against the force of gravity and why? **(ICSE 2014)**

12. A force is applied on a body of mass 20 kg moving with a velocity of 40 ms^{-1}. The body attains a velocity of 50 ms^{-1} in 2 s. Calculate the work done by the body. **(ICSE 2013)**

13. A body is acted upon by a force. State two conditions under which the work done could be zero. **(ICSE 2010)**

14. State the amount of work done by an object when it moves in a circular path for one complete rotation. Give your reason to justify your answer. **(ICSE 2006)**

3 Marks Questions

15. (i) Derive a relationship between the SI and CGS unit of work.

(ii) A force acts on a body and displaces it by a distance s in a direction at an angle θ with the direction of force. What should be the value of θ to get the maximum positive work? **(ICSE 2018)**

15. Define joule. Give the SI unit of work and establish a relationship between the and CGS unit of work. **(ICSE 2008)**

Explanations

1. (c) Work done of the object, $W = F \cdot d$

where, d is the displacement of object, when the load is moved along the slope, the displacement is 5m. So it will be depend on 5m.

2. (b) The relation between joule and erg is

$$1 \text{ J} = 10^7 \text{ erg}$$

3. (c) The coolie raises load in the upward direction and the force of gravity is in downward direction.

So, work done $= |\mathbf{F}|\,|\mathbf{s}|\cos 180° = -|\mathbf{F}|\,|\mathbf{s}|$

$\therefore$ negative work

4. (b) Displacement is perpendicular to the centripetal force.

5. A coolie carrying a load on his head and moving on a frictionless horizontal platform does no work, because the angle between the applied force and displacement of load is 90°.

As, $W = Fs\cos\theta$

$= Fs\cos 90°$

$= 0$ $\quad [\because \cos 90° = 0]$

6. (i) centripetal

(ii) zero

7. (i) Work done is defined as the product of force and displacement.

$$W = F \times s$$

Work done in this case is zero because both force and displacement are perpendicular to each other.

$$W = Fs\cos 90° = 0 \quad [\because \cos 90° = 0]$$

(ii) Work done is said to be positive.

Concept Enhancer The work done by a body can be negative, if the force acts opposite to the direction of displacement. Magnitude of work done always positive

8. When a fielder catches a ball in a cricket match, then he applies force in the opposite direction of displacement of ball. So, work done by the fielder on the ball is negative.

9. (i) Work done by an external force is given by

$$W = \mathbf{F} \cdot \mathbf{s} = Fs\cos\theta$$

When the force is in the direction of displacement, then θ will be 0°. So, $W = Fs$

(ii) Work done by a force when it is at an angle to the direction of displacement is given by $W = Fs\cos\theta$.

10. (i) When the force is applied on a body and it makes the body to move some distance, then work is said to be done.

(ii) The work done by the moon when it revolves around the earth is zero, because the force on the moon is directed towards the centre of its circular path and the displacement at all instants is along the tangent to the circular path, i.e. angle between force and displacement is 90°.

$\therefore \quad W = F \cdot s\cos 90° = F \cdot s \times 0 = 0$

11. A man having a box on his head, climbs up a slope does more work, because the work done by the man walking on a levelled road is zero as the angle between displacement and force is 90°.

Common Mistake Some students could not understand the direction of force and displacement.

12. Given, mass $m = 20$ kg,

Initial velocity $u = 40$ m/s

Final velocity $v = 50$ m/s

Time $t = 2$s, Work done $W = ?$

Using third equation of motion, $v^2 - u^2 = 2as$

$$\Rightarrow \quad as = \frac{v^2 - u^2}{2} \quad \ldots(i)$$

$\therefore$ Work done, $W = F \times s = mas$ $[\because F = ma]$

$$= m \times \frac{v^2 - u^2}{2} \quad \text{[From Eq. (i)]}$$

$$= \frac{20 \times [(50)^2 - (40)^2]}{2}$$

$$= 10 \times (2500 - 1600)$$

$$= 9000 \text{ J}$$

13. There are two conditions under which the work done can be zero

(i) displacement is zero.

(ii) angle between the force and displacement is 90°.

14. The amount of work done will be zero, because when a body moving in a circular path, the force on the object is directed towards the centre of the circular path and the displacement at all instant is along the tangent to the circular path, so the angle between the force and the displacement is 90°.

15. (i) The SI unit of work is joule.

$$1\text{J} = 1\text{N} \times 1 \text{ m} = 10^5 \text{ dyne} \times 100 \text{ cm}$$

$$1\text{J} = 10^7 \text{ dyne-cm} = 10^7 \text{ erg}$$

(ii) For maximum work done, the angle should be 0°. i.e.

$$W_{max} = \mathbf{F} \cdot \mathbf{s} = |F||s| \cos 0° = Fs \quad [\because \cos 0° = 1]$$

16. One joule is defined as the work done when a force of one newton displaces a body through a distance of one metre in its own direction.

The SI unit of work is joule.

$$1 \text{ J} = 1 \text{ N} \times 1 \text{ m} = 10^5 \text{ dyne} \times 100 \text{ cm}$$

$$= 10^7 \text{ dyne-cm}$$

$$= 10^7 \text{ erg}$$

TOPIC 2

Power and Energy

Power

The rate of doing work or the rate of transfer of energy into work is called the power. The power of a source is measured as the amount of work done per second by the source or energy transfer per second.

If work W is done in time t, then power can be expressed as

$$\boxed{P = \frac{W}{t}}$$

It is a **scalar quantity**. The SI unit of power is **watt** (W) and CGS unit is **erg/s**.

The power depends on the two factors such as

(i) the amount of work done and

(ii) the time taken to perform that work.

Expressions of Power

When a constant force F acts on a body and it moves the body through a distance d along the direction of applied force in time t, then power (P) is given by

$$P = \frac{W}{t} = \frac{Fd}{t} \quad [\because W = Fd]$$

If $\frac{d}{t} = v$, where v is the average speed of the body.

So, power $\quad P = Fv$

If in case displacement (s) and force has some angle θ, then power,

$$P = \frac{Fs\cos\theta}{t} = Fv\cos\theta = \mathbf{F} \cdot \mathbf{v} \quad \left[\because v = \frac{s}{t}\right]$$

Multiple Units of Power

1 kW (kilo-watt) $= 10^3$ W

1 MW (mega-watt) $= 10^6$ W

1 GW (giga-watt) $= 10^9$ W

Sub-multiple Units of Power

1 mW (milli-watt) $= 10^{-3}$ W

1 μW (micro-watt) $= 10^{-6}$ W

Relationship between SI and CGS Unit

$$1\ \text{W} = 1\ \text{J/s} = 10^7\ \text{erg/s}$$

NOTE Horse power is a common unit of power; 1 HP = 746 W = 0.746 kW

Energy

The energy of a body is its ability to do work. A body capable of doing work is said to possess energy. Work and energy are directly related to each other. The SI unit of energy is **joule** (J) and in CGS unit is **erg**. It is a **scalar quantity**.

The larger units of energy are watt hour (Wh) and kilowatt hour (kWh)

$$1\ \text{Wh} = 3600\ \text{J}$$

$$\Rightarrow \quad 1\ \text{kWh} = 3.6 \times 10^6\ \text{J}$$

Other unit of energy are calories and eV.

$$1\ \text{cal} = 4.18\ \text{J}$$

$$1\ \text{eV} = 1.6 \times 10^{-19}\ \text{J}$$

The energy possessed by a body due to its position and state of motion is called **mechanical energy**.

It has two types

(i) Kinetic energy and

(ii) Potential energy

The total mechanical energy of a body is equal to the sum of its kinetic energy and potential energy.

Kinetic Energy

It is defined as the energy possessed by a body by virtue of its state of motion.

e.g. A swinging pendulum, a roaring rocket, running water, moving air, etc. It is generally denoted by KE. It is expressed as

$$\boxed{\text{KE} = \frac{1}{2} mv^2}$$

where, m = mass of the body, v = speed of the body.

- Kinetic energy K and momentum $p\,(= mv)$ are related as $K = p^2/2m$.
- **Work-Energy Theorem** If initial speed (velocity) of a body is u and final speed (velocity) of a body is v, then according to work-energy theorem,

Work done by all the forces acting on the body (ΔW)

= Change in kinetic energy of the body

$$(\Delta K) = \frac{1}{2} mv^2 - \frac{1}{2} mu^2$$

Forms of Kinetic Energy

A moving body can have three types of motions namely the translational, rotational and vibrational.

There are three forms of kinetic energy as mentioned below

(i) **Translational Kinetic Energy** This energy comes in act when a force applied on a body causes a displacement in a straight line in its own direction. e.g. A car moving in a straight path, freely falling body, molecule of a monoatomic gas, etc.

(ii) **Rotational Kinetic Energy** If a body rotates about an axis, the motion is called rotational motion and the energy possessed due to rotational motion is called rotational kinetic energy. e.g. A rotating wheel, a spinning top, etc.

(iii) **Vibrational Kinetic Energy** This energy comes in act when a body vibrates to and fro about its mean position. e.g. A wire clamped at both ends when plucked at the middle vibrates.

Potential Energy

The energy possessed by a body by virtue of its specific position (configuration) is called the potential energy. e.g. A body placed at a height above the ground, a wound up watch spring. It is usually denoted by the symbol U.

Forms of Potential Energy

Mainly there are two types of potential energy such as

(i) **Gravitational Potential Energy** It is the amount of work done in raising a body from the ground to a point at height h, against gravity.

It is expressed by

$$\boxed{U = mgh}$$

where, m is the mass of the object, g is acceleration due to gravity and h is the height through which the object is raised.

(ii) **Elastic Potential Energy** The energy possessed by a body in the deformed state due to change in its shape and size is called elastic potential energy. e.g. Energy possessed by a compressed spring.

Different Forms of Energy

We get energy in various forms. Some of these forms are

(i) **Chemical energy** It is the energy possessed by fossil fuels such as coal, petroleum and natural gases. A battery has chemical energy in it.

(ii) **Mechanical energy** It is the energy possessed by a body due to its position and state of motion. A moving ball, a body at rest, etc., have mechanical energy.

(iii) **Heat energy** The energy released on burning fuels such as coal, oil, gas, etc., is called heat energy.

(iv) **Electrical energy** The energy the possessed by a charged body due to movement of free electrons is called electrical energy.

(v) **Nuclear energy** It is the energy released during the process of nuclear fission and fusion. We use nuclear energy in nuclear reactor to produce electrical energy.

(vi) **Sound energy** The energy possessed by a vibrating body producing sound is called sound energy. Sound energy is sensed by our ears.

(vii) **Light energy** A form of energy in presence of which we can see the object around us is called light energy. Sun is the natural source of light energy.

PYQs Previous Years Questions

1 Mark Questions

1. When the speed of a moving object is doubled, then its kinetic energy **(ICSE 2023)**

(a) remains the same
(b) decreases
(c) is doubled
(d) becomes four times

2. Which of the following is the correct expression for gain in kinetic energy, if initial velocity is not zero? **(ICSE SQP 2023)**

(a) $K = \frac{1}{2}mv^2$ (b) $K = \frac{mv^2}{4}$

(c) $K = \frac{mv^2}{2t}$ (d) $K = \frac{1}{2}m(v^2 - u^2)$

3. The usable form of mechanical energy is **(ICSE SQP 2022 Sem-I)**

(a) elastic potential energy
(b) kinetic energy
(c) gravitational potential energy
(d) none of the given options

4. The conversion of part of the energy into an undesirable form is called? **(ICSE 2014)**

5. What is nuclear energy? **(ICSE 2014)**

6. A body is thrown vertically upwards, its velocity keeps on decreasing. What happens to its KE, as its velocity becomes zero? **(ICSE 2014)**

7. By what factor, does the kinetic energy of a moving body change when its speed is reduced to half ? **(ICSE 2002)**

8. What do kilowatt hour measure? **(ICSE 2002, 01)**

2 Marks Questions

9. Sumit does 600 J of work in 10 min and Amit does 300 J of work in 20 min. Calculate the ratio of the powers delivered by them. **(ICSE 2024)**

10. Calculate the power spent by a crane, while lifting a load of mass 2000 kg, at velocity of 1.5 ms^{-1}. (Take, $g = 10 ms^{-2}$) **(ICSE 2023)**

> **KEY idea**
> In this case, power can be calculated by using $p = F \cdot v$, where F is force and v is the velocity of the object.

11. (i) What should be the angle between the direction of force and the direction of displacement, for work to be negative?
(ii) Name the physical quantity obtained using the formula $\frac{u}{h}$, where U is the potential energy and h is the height. **(ICSE 2023)**

12. If kinetic energy of a moving body is 40 J, then what will be its kinetic energy when its velocity is doubled? **(ICSE SQP 2023)**

13. A light body A and a heavy body B have the same momentum. **(ICSE 2022 Sem-I)**

(i) Choose a correct statement from the given options.

(a) Kinetic energy of body A and body B will be the same.

(b) Kinetic energy of body A is greater than kinetic energy of body B.

(c) Kinetic energy of body B is greater than kinetic energy of body A.

(d) Unless we know the velocity, we cannot find which body has greater kinetic energy.

(ii) If the ratio of kinetic energies of A and B is 5 : 2, then which one of the following gives the mass ratio of the bodies respectively?

(a) 5 : 2 (b) 25 : 4

(c) 2 : 5 (d) 4 : 24

14. A body has kinetic energy 2500 J. If the mass of the body is 500 g, **(ICSE SQP 2022 Sem-I)**

(i) the velocity of the body is

(a) $\sqrt{10}$ m/s

(b) 10 m/s

(c) 20 m/s

(d) 100 m/s

(ii) the momentum of the body will be

(a) 10 kg-m/s

(b) $500\sqrt{10}$ kg-m/s

(c) 50 kg-m/s

(d) 4. 5 kg-m/s

15. Two bodies A and B have masses in the ratio 5 : 1 and their kinetic energies are in the ratio 125 : 9. Find the ratio of their velocities. **(ICSE 2019)**

16. (i) State and define the SI unit of power.

(ii) How is the unit horse power related to the SI unit of power? **(ICSE 2018)**

17. State the energy changes in the following cases while in use

(i) an electric iron.

(ii) a ceiling fan. **(ICSE 2018)**

18. Name the unit of physical quantity obtained by the formula $\frac{2K}{v^2}$, where K is kinetic energy and v is linear velocity. **(ICSE 2018)**

19. A metal ball of mass 60 g falls on a concrete floor from a vertical height of 2.8 m and rebounds to a height of 1.3 m. Find the change in KE in SI units. **(ICSE SQP 2018)**

20. If the power of a motor be 100 kW, at what speed can it raise a load of 50000 N? **(ICSE 2017)**

21. A boy weighing 40 kgf climbs up a stair of 30 steps each 20 cm high in 4 min and a girl weighing 30 kgf does the same in 3 min. Compare

(i) the work done by them.

(ii) the power developed by them. **(ICSE 2016)**

22. State the energy changes in the following while in use

(i) burning of a candle.

(ii) a steam engine. **(ICSE 2015)**

23. Rajan exerts a force of 150 N in pulling a cart at a constant speed of 10 m/s. Calculate the power exerted. **(ICSE 2015)**

24. Calculate the change in the kinetic energy of a moving body, if its velocity is reduced to (1/3)rd of the initial velocity. **(ICSE 2014)**

25. A girl of mass 35 kg climbs up from the first floor of a building at a height 4 m above the ground to the third floor at a height 12 m above the ground. What will be the increase in her gravitational potential energy? (Take, $g = 10\ \text{ms}^{-2}$) **(ICSE 2013)**

26. A ball is placed on a compressed spring. When the spring is released, the ball is observed to fly away.

(i) What form of energy does the compressed spring possess?

(ii) Why does the ball fly away? **(ICSE 2012)**

27. A body of mass 0.2 kg falls from a height of 10 m to a height of 6 m above the ground. Find the loss in potential energy taking place in the body. (Take, $g = 10\ \text{ms}^{-2}$) **(ICSE 2012)**

28. A moving body weighing 400 N possesses 500 J of KE. Calculate the velocity with which the body is moving. (Take, $g = 10\ \text{m/s}^2$) **(ICSE 2012)**

KEY idea

Here, velocity of moving body is determine by

$$v = \sqrt{\frac{KE \times 2 \times g}{w}}$$

29. A body of mass 5 kg is moving with a velocity of 10 ms^{-1}. What will be the ratio of its initial kinetic energy and final kinetic energy, if the mass of the body is doubled and its velocity is halved? **(ICSE 2009)**

30. What is the SI unit of energy? How is the electron volt (eV) related to it? **(ICSE 2009, 05)**

31. Two bodies *A* and *B* of equal mass are kept at heights 20 m and 30 m, respectively. Calculate the ratio of their potential energies. **(ICSE 2007)**

32. The work done by the heart is 1 joule per beat. Calculate the power of the heart, if it beats 72 times in one minute. **(ICSE 2005)**

33. If the power of a motor is 40 kW, at what speed does it raises a load of 20000 N? **(ICSE 2003)**

34. A body *P* has a mass of 20 kg and is moving with a velocity of 5 m/s. Another body *Q* has a mass of 5 kg and is moving with a velocity of 20 m/s. Calculate
   (i) the ratio of the momentum of *P* and *Q*.
   (ii) the kinetic energy of *P* in SI unit. **(ICSE 2000)**

KEY idea

Apply the formula of momentum for both the bodies ($p = mv$) and then to calculate kinetic energy, apply formula $\left(KE = \frac{p^2}{2m}\right)$.

3 Marks Questions

35. A body of mass 50 kg has a momentum of 3000 kg-ms^{-1}. Calculate
   (i) the kinetic energy of the body.
   (ii) the velocity of the body. **(ICSE 2010)**

36. 6.4 kJ of energy causes a displacement of 64 m in a body in the direction of force in 2.5 s. Calculate (i) the force applied (ii) power in horse power (HP). (Take, 1 HP = 746 W) **(ICSE 2009)**

37. (i) Define one kilowatt hour. How is it related to the joule?
   (ii) How can the work done be measured when force is applied at an angle to the direction of displacement? **(ICSE 2007)**

38. Define power and energy. **(ICSE 2002)**

39. An engine can pump 30000 L of water to a vertical height of 45 m in 10 min. Calculate the work done by the machine and its power. (Take, $g = 9.8\ m/s^2$, density of water $= 10^3\ kg/m^3, 1000\ L = 1\ m^3$) **(ICSE 2000)**

4 Marks Question

40. A car of mass 120 kg is moving at a speed 18 km/h and it accelerates to attain a speed of 54 km/h in 5 s. Calculate **(ICSE 2023)**
   (i) the work done by the engine.
   (ii) the power of the engine.

Explanations

1. (d) If v becomes 2 v, then

$$KE = \frac{1}{2} m (2v)^2 = \frac{4}{2} mv^2 = 4 \text{ times the initial kinetic energy.}$$

2. (d) Gain in kinetic energy

$$= \frac{1}{2} mv^2 - \frac{1}{2} mu^2 = \frac{1}{2} m(v^2 - u^2)$$

3. (b)

4. The conversion of part of the energy into an undesirable form is called dissipation of energy.

5. The energy released during the process of nuclear fission or fusion is known as nuclear energy.

6. If a body is thrown vertically upwards, its velocity decreases continuously, so its KE also decreases and its PE increase due to increase in height. When the velocity becomes zero, kinetic energy will also be zero.

7. KE of moving body, $KE = \frac{1}{2} mv^2$ ...(i)

If speed is reduced to half, i.e. $v_1 = \frac{v}{2}$

$$\therefore \quad KE_1 = \frac{1}{2} m \left(\frac{v}{2}\right)^2 = \frac{1}{2} mv^2 \times \frac{1}{4}$$

$$KE_1 = \frac{1}{4} KE \quad \text{[From Eq. (i)]}$$

So, KE becomes $\frac{1}{4}$th of the original KE.

8. The kilowatt hour measures electrical energy. It is the unit of electrical energy and $1\ kWh = 3.6 \times 10^6$ J.

9. For Sumit,

Work, $W = 600\text{ J}$

Time, $t = 10\text{ min} = 10 \times 60 = 600\text{ s}$

$$\text{Power} = \frac{W}{t} = \frac{600}{600}$$

$$P_S = 1\text{ W}$$

For Amit,

Work, $W = 300\text{ J}$

Time, $t = 20\text{ min} = 20 \times 60 = 1200\text{ s}$

$$\text{Power} = \frac{W}{t} = \frac{300}{1200}$$

$$P_A = (1/4)\text{ W}$$

Ratio of the powers,

$$\frac{P_S}{P_A} = \frac{1}{1/4} = 4$$

10. $\text{Power} = F \cdot v = mgv = 2000 \times 10 \times 1.5$

$$= 30000\text{ W}$$

11. (i) The angle should be $180°$ between force and displacement for the work to be negative.

(ii) This formula gives the amount of potential energy possessed by an object per unit height above a reference point due to the gravitational force between the object and the earth. This quantity is the weight of the object.

12. $$\frac{K_1}{K_2} = \frac{v_1^2}{v_2^2} \Rightarrow \frac{40}{K_2} = \left(\frac{v_1}{2v_1}\right)^2 = \frac{1}{4}$$

$$\Rightarrow \quad K_2 = 160\text{ J}$$

13. (i) (b) $\text{Kinetic energy} = \dfrac{(\text{Momentum})^2}{2 \times \text{Mass}}$

$$(\text{KE})_A = \frac{(p)^2}{2M_A}, (\text{KE})_B = \frac{(p)^2}{2M_B}$$

Here, $M_A < M_B$

So, $(\text{KE})_A > (\text{KE})_B$

(ii) (c) Given, $\dfrac{(\text{KE})_A}{(\text{KE})_B} = \dfrac{5}{2}$

$$\therefore \quad \frac{(\text{KE})_A}{(\text{KE})_B} = \frac{M_B}{M_A}$$

$$\frac{M_B}{M_A} = \frac{5}{2} \Rightarrow \frac{M_A}{M_B} = \frac{2}{5}$$

14. (i) (d) $\text{KE} = \dfrac{1}{2}mv^2$

$$\Rightarrow \quad v^2 = \frac{2\text{KE}}{m}$$

$$\Rightarrow \quad v^2 = \frac{2 \times 2500}{0.5}$$

$$\Rightarrow \quad v = \sqrt{10000}$$

$$\Rightarrow \quad v = 100\text{ m/s}$$

(ii) (c) $\text{KE} = \dfrac{p^2}{2m}$

$$\Rightarrow \quad p^2 = \text{KE} \times 2m$$

$$\Rightarrow \quad p^2 = 2500 \times 2 \times 0.5$$

$$\Rightarrow \quad p^2 = 2500$$

$$\Rightarrow \quad p = \sqrt{2500}$$

$$\Rightarrow \quad p = 50\text{ kg-ms}^{-1}$$

15. Let mass of body A be m_A and mass of body B be m_B.

Given, $\dfrac{m_A}{m_B} = \dfrac{5}{1}$ ...(i)

and $\dfrac{(\text{KE})_A}{(\text{KE})_B} = \dfrac{125}{9}$ ...(ii)

We know that, kinetic energy, $\text{KE} = \dfrac{1}{2}mv^2$

$$\therefore \quad \frac{(\text{KE})_A}{(\text{KE})_B} = \frac{\frac{1}{2}m_A v_A^2}{\frac{1}{2}m_B v_B^2}$$

From Eqs. (i) and (ii), we get

$$\Rightarrow \quad \frac{125}{9} = \frac{5}{1}\left(\frac{v_A}{v_B}\right)^2$$

$$\Rightarrow \quad \frac{25}{9} = \left(\frac{v_A}{v_B}\right)^2$$

$$\Rightarrow \quad \frac{v_A}{v_B} = \frac{5}{3}$$

Hence, ratio of their velocities is 5 : 3.

16. (i) The rate of doing work is called the power and the SI unit of power is watt(W).

(ii) 1HP = 746 W

17. (i) An electric iron converts electrical energy into heat energy.

(ii) A ceiling fan converts electrical energy into mechanical energy.

18. We know that,

Kinetic energy $(K) = \frac{1}{2}mv^2$ ...(i)

Given, $m = \frac{2K}{v^2} = \frac{2}{v^2} \times \left(\frac{1}{2}mv^2\right)$ [From Eq. (i)]

$= m$ (mass)

Hence, the physical quantity is mass.

19. Potential energy of ball at height $h_1 = 2.8$ m

$$PE_1 = mgh_1 = \frac{60}{1000} \times 10 \times 2.8 = 1.68 \text{ J}$$

∴ Kinetic energy just before striking the ground

$= KE_1 = 1.68$ J

Potential energy at height $h_2 = 1.3$ m

$$PE_2 = mgh_2 = \frac{60}{1000} \times 10 \times 1.3 = 0.78 \text{ J}$$

KE_2 just after rebounding $= 0.78$ J

∴ Change in KE $= KE_1 - KE_2$

$= 1.68 - 0.78 = 0.9$ J

20. Given, power of the motor, $P = 100$ kW

$= 100 \times 1000 \text{ W} = 10^5$ W

and force $F = 50000$ N

Now, from the definition of power,

$$P = \frac{\text{Work done}}{\text{Time}} = \frac{F \times s}{t}$$

[$\because W =$ Force × Displacement]

$\Rightarrow \quad P = F \times \frac{s}{t} = F \times v$

Substituting the given values, we get

$100000 = 50000 \times v$

$\Rightarrow \quad v = \frac{100000}{50000} = 2 \text{ ms}^{-1}$

Hence, the motor can lift the load with a speed of 2 ms^{-1}.

21. (i) According to question,

Weight of boy,

$w_b = 40$ kg f $= 40 \times 10 = 400$ N

Weight of girl ,

$w_g = 30$ kgf$= 30 \times 10 = 300$ N

Time taken by boy,

$t_b = 4$ min $= (60 \times 4)$ s

Time taken by girl ,

$t_g = 3$ min $= (60 \times 3)$ s

Total height of the stairs

$= 30 \times 20 = 600$ cm$= 6$ m

Now, work done

$W_b = mgh = 400 \times 6$ [$\because mg = 400$N]

Work done by girl

$W_g = 300 \times 6$ [$\because mg = 300$ N]

$\therefore \frac{W_b}{W_g} = \frac{400 \times 6}{300 \times 6} = \frac{4}{3} \Rightarrow W_b = \frac{4}{3}W_g$

Work done by the boy is 4/3 times of work done by the girl.

(ii) Power developed by boy, $P_b = \frac{W_b}{t_b} = \frac{400 \times 6}{60 \times 4}$ W

Power developed by girl, $P_g = \frac{W_g}{t_g} = \frac{300 \times 6}{60 \times 3}$

So, $\frac{P_b}{P_g} = \frac{400 \times 6 \times 60 \times 3}{60 \times 4 \times 300 \times 6} = 1$

$P_b = P_g$

They both developed equal power to do the different works.

22. (i) **Burning of a candle**

Chemical energy is converted into heat energy and light energy.

i.e. Chemical energy → Heat energy + Light energy

(ii) **A steam engine**

Chemical energy → Heat energy + Mechanical energy

23. Given, $F = 150$ N, $v = 10$ m/s

∴ Power, $P = F \times v = 150 \times 10 = 1500$ W

24. Let, initial velocity $= v$

Hence, final velocity $= \frac{v}{3}$

Change in kinetic energy,

$\Delta KE = KE_1 - KE_2$

Initial kinetic energy $KE_1 = \frac{1}{2}mv^2$ ...(i)

Final kinetic energyKE_2

$$= \frac{1}{2}m\left(\frac{v}{3}\right)^2 = \frac{1}{2}\frac{mv^2}{9} \qquad \left[\text{As, } v_1 = \frac{v}{3}\right]$$

Thus, $\Delta KE = KE_1 - KE_2$

$$= \frac{1}{2}mv^2 - \frac{1}{2}\frac{mv^2}{9} = \frac{1}{2}mv^2\left(1 - \frac{1}{9}\right)$$

$$= \frac{8}{9} \times \frac{1}{2}mv^2 = \frac{8}{9}KE_1 \quad \text{[From Eq. (i)]}$$

Concept Enhancer The change in KE of a particle equal to the work done on it by the net force if force acting on it is conservative.

25. Given, mass $m = 35$ kg

Height of first floor, $h_1 = 4$ m

Height of third floor, $h_2 = 12$ m

Increase in gravitational PE = ?

Gravitational PE at first floor,

$PE_1 = mgh_1 = 35 \times 10 \times 4 = 1400$ J

Gravitational PE at third floor,

$PE_2 = mgh_2 = 35 \times 10 \times 12 = 4200$ J

$\therefore$ Increase in PE $= PE_2 - PE_1 = 4200 - 1400 = 2800$ J

26. (i) The compressed spring possesses elastic potential energy.

(ii) The ball flies away, because potential energy is converted into kinetic energy and is also transferred to the ball.

27. Given, mass $m = 0.2$ kg

Height $h_1 = 10$ m , Height $h_2 = 6$ m

and $g = 10 \text{ m/s}^2$

$\therefore$ Loss in PE $= mg(h_1 - h_2)$

$= 0.2 \times 10\,(10 - 6) = 8$ J

28. Given, weight $w = 400$ N

Kinetic energy KE = 500 J

Velocity $(v) = ?$ and $g = 10 \text{ m/s}^2$

$$\therefore \quad KE = \frac{1}{2}mv^2 = \frac{1}{2}\frac{w}{g}v^2 \qquad \left[\because m = \frac{w}{g}\right]$$

$$500 = \frac{1}{2} \times \frac{400}{10} \times v^2$$

$$\Rightarrow \quad v = \sqrt{\frac{500 \times 20}{400}} = 5 \text{ m/s}$$

29. Given, mass, $m_1 = 5$ kg

$m_2 = 2m_1 = 2 \times 5 = 10$ kg

Velocity, $v_1 = 10$ m/s, $v_2 = \frac{v_1}{2} = \frac{10}{2} = 5$ m/s $\quad \frac{KE_1}{KE_2} = ?$

$$\therefore \quad KE_1 = \frac{1}{2}m_1v_1^2 = \frac{1}{2} \times 5 \times (10)^2 = 250 \text{ J}$$

$$\text{and } KE_2 = \frac{1}{2}m_2v_2^2 = \frac{1}{2} \times 10 \times (5)^2 = 125 \text{ J}$$

$$\therefore \quad \frac{KE_1}{KE_2} = \frac{250}{125} = \frac{2}{1}$$

$\therefore$ Ratio $KE_1 : KE_2$ is 2:1.

30. The SI unit of energy is joule.

The relation between the joule and electron volt is

$$1 \text{ eV} = 1.6 \times 10^{-19} \text{ J}$$

31. Given, height of A, $h_A = 20$ m

Height of B, $h_B = 30$ m, $\frac{PE_A}{PE_B} = ?$

$$\frac{PE_A}{PE_B} = \frac{mgh_A}{mgh_B} = \frac{20}{30} = \frac{2}{3}$$

$\therefore$ Ratio $PE_A : PE_B$ is 2 : 3.

Concept Enhancer Potential energy depends on the force acting on the two objects and given by PE = mgh.

32. Given, work done in 1 beat = 1 J

Work done in 72 beats = 72 J, $t = 1$ min $= 60$ s

$$\therefore \text{ Power} = \frac{\text{Work done}}{\text{Time}} = \frac{72}{60} = 1.2 \text{ W}$$

33. Given, power of the motor

$$P = 40 \text{ kW} = 40 \times 10^3 \text{ W}$$

Average speed $v = ?$, Load $F = 20000$ N

$\therefore$ Power P = Force $\times$ Average speed

$$\Rightarrow \text{Average speed } v = \frac{P}{F} = \frac{40 \times 10^3}{20000} = 2 \text{ m/s}$$

34. Given, masses $m_P = 20$ kg, $m_Q = 5$ kg

Velocity, $v_P = 5$ m/s, $v_Q = 20$ m/s

$\therefore$ Momentum of the body P,

$$p_P = m_P v_P = 20 \times 5 = 100 \text{ kg-m/s}$$

and momentum of the body Q,

$$p_Q = m_Q v_Q = 5 \times 20 = 100 \text{ kg-m/s}$$

(i) Ratio of momentum $= \frac{p_P}{p_Q} = \frac{100}{100} = 1:1$

(ii) KE of $P = \frac{(\text{Momentum of } P)^2}{2 \times \text{Mass of } P} \qquad \left[\because KE = \frac{p^2}{2m}\right]$

$$= \frac{100 \times 100}{2 \times 20} = 250 \text{ J}$$

35. Given, mass $m = 50$ kg

Momentum $p = 3000 \text{ kg ms}^{-1}$

(i) KE = ? (ii) $v = ?$

We know that, momentum $p = m \times v$

$$\Rightarrow \quad v = \frac{p}{m} = \frac{3000}{50} = 60 \text{ m/s}$$

[where, v = Velocity of the body]

$$\therefore \quad KE = \frac{1}{2}mv^2 = \frac{1}{2} \times 50 \times 60 \times 60$$

$$= 90000 \text{ J} = 90 \text{ kJ}$$

36. Given, energy $E = 6.4 \text{ kJ} = 6400 \text{ J}$,

Time $t = 2.5 \text{ s}$

Displacement $s = 64$ m, Force $F = ?$,
Power in HP = ?

(i) Energy = Work done = $F \cdot s$

$$\therefore \quad E = F \cdot s$$

$$\Rightarrow \quad F = \frac{E}{s} = \frac{6400}{64} = 100 \text{ N}$$

(ii) $\therefore$ Power $P = \dfrac{E}{t} = \dfrac{6400}{2.5} = 2560 \text{ W}$

$$= \frac{2560}{746} = 3.43 \text{ HP} \quad [\because 1 \text{ HP} = 746 \text{ W}]$$

37. (i) One kilowatt hour is defined as the amount of electric energy consumed in an electrical circuit when an electric appliance of power 1 kW works for an hour.

$$1 \text{ kWh} = 1000 \text{ W} \times 3600 \text{ s} = 1000 \text{ J/s} \times 3600 \text{ s}$$

$$= 36 \times 10^5 \text{ J} = 3.6 \times 10^6 \text{ J}$$

(ii) When a force F is applied at an angle θ to the direction of displacement s, then work done is given by

$$W = Fs\cos\theta$$

38. The rate of doing work or the rate of conversion of energy is called power. The power of a source is measured as the amount of work done per second by the source or energy change per second. If work W is done in time t, then power can be expressed as

$$P = \frac{W}{t}$$

It is a **scalar quantity**. The SI unit of power is watt (W) and in CGS unit is erg/s. The power depends on the two factors such as

(i) the amount of work done and

(ii) the time taken to perform that work.

The energy of a body is its ability to do work. A body capable of doing work is said to possess energy. Work and energy are directly related to each other. The SI unit of energy is joule(J) and CGS unit is erg.

39. Given, volume of water, $V = 30000 \text{ L} = \dfrac{30000}{1000} = 30 \text{ m}^3$

$$[\because 1000 \text{ L} = 1 \text{ m}^3 \text{ and } 1 \text{L} = \frac{1}{1000} \text{m}^3]$$

Height $h = 45$ m

Time $t = 10 \text{ min} = 10 \times 60 = 600 \text{s}$

Acceleration due to gravity $g = 9.8 \text{ m/s}^2$

Density of water $\rho = 10^3 \text{ kg/m}^3$

Work done = ?, Power = ?

$$\therefore \text{ Density } \rho = \frac{m}{V} \Rightarrow m = \rho V \quad \ldots\text{(i)}$$

$\therefore$ Work done by the machine = mgh

$$= V \times \rho \times g \times h \quad \text{[From Eq. (i)]}$$

$$= 30 \times 10^3 \times 9.8 \times 45$$

$$= 13230 \times 10^3 = 1.3230 \times 10^7 \text{ J}$$

$$\therefore \text{ Power } P = \frac{\text{Work done}}{\text{Time}} = \frac{1.3230 \times 10^7}{600}$$

$$= 22.05 \times 10^3 \text{ W}$$

$\therefore$ Power = 22.05 kW

40. (a) Given, $m = 120 \text{ kg}$, $v_1 = 18 \text{ km/h}$

$$= \frac{18 \times 1000}{60 \times 60} \text{ m/s}$$

$$v_1 = 5 \text{ m/s}$$

$$v_2 = 54 \text{ km/h} = 15 \text{ m/s}$$

and $t = 5 \text{ s}$

Work done = Change is KE $= \dfrac{1}{2} m (v_2^2 - v_1^2)$

$$= \frac{1}{2} \times 120 \times (15^2 - 5^2) = 12000 \text{ J}$$

(b) Power $= \dfrac{\text{Work done}}{\text{Time}} = \dfrac{12000}{5} = 2400 \text{ W}$

TOPIC 3

Energy Sources and Conservation of Energy

Conversion of Energy from One Form to Another

The process of the conversion of energy from one form to the other form is known as **transformation of energy**. In our daily life, we require energy in various forms.

Production of electricity from different forms of energy are illustrated as below

Production of Electricity from Solar Energy

The sun is the most vast and direct source of energy. The energy obtained from the sun is called **solar energy**. The two devices **solar cell** and **solar power plant** are used for generating electricity.

Solar Cell

Solar cells are usually made from semiconductors like silicon and gallium. At ordinary temperature, a semiconductor has a very low conductivity but its conductivity increases either with the rise in temperature or when some impurities are added to it.

If the sunlight is made to incident on an impurity added semiconductor, a potential difference is produced between its surfaces.

Due to this potential difference, a current flows in the circuit connected between the opposite faces of the semiconductor. Thus, electricity is produced.

Solar Power Plant

It consists of a number of concave reflectors, at the focus of which, there are black painted water pipes.

The reflectors concentrate the heat energy of the sun rays on the pipes due to which water inside the pipes starts boiling and produces steam. The produced steam is used to rotate a steam turbine which drives a generator to produce electricity.

Production of Electricity from Wind Energy

Wind energy is used in a wind generator to produce the electricity by making use of two drive and a wind generator. In wind generator, a small electric generator (or dynamo) is placed at the top of a pillar. The armatue of the connected is connected to the shaft attached with the blades of a wind mill.

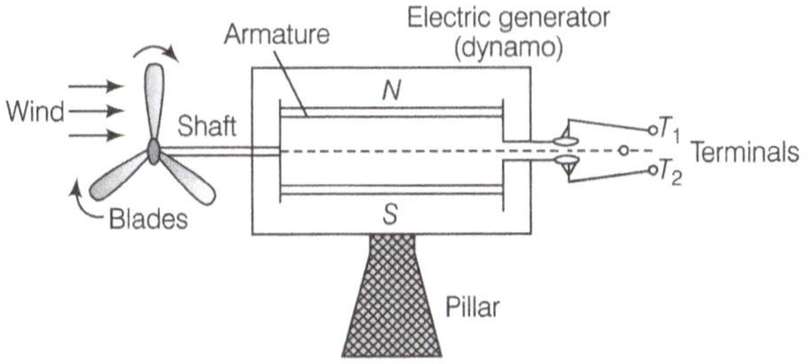

When the blowing wind strikes the blades of the wind mill, the translational KE of wind changes into rotational KE of the blades. The rotation of blades of the turbine rotates the armature of the dynamo. Due to rotation of the armature, the magnetic flux linked with it changes between the poles N and S of a strong magnet, an emf is produced between the terminals T_1 and T_2, which leads to the production of electricity.

Production of Electricity from Water or Hydro Energy

The kinetic energy possessed by the flowing water is called the water (or hydro) energy. A high rise dam is constructed on the river to obstruct the flow of water and thereby collect water in large reservoirs.

Due to rise in water level, the kinetic energy of flowing water gets converted into potential energy. The water from the high level is carried through the pipe to turbine located near the bottom of the dam, which is connected to the electric generator.

When the water turbine rotates, then the armature of the generator also rotates rapidly and produce electricity.

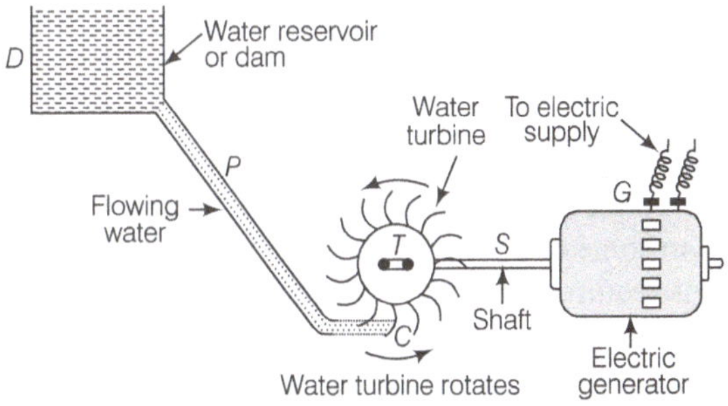

Nuclear Power Plant

The most important use of nuclear energy is generation of electricity. This is done by using a s et up called nuclear power plant.

Nuclear energy of U^{235} → Heat energy of steam → Kinetic energy of turbine → Electrical energy

Connection of nuclear effects into electrical energy

Principle The heat produced in a controlled nuclear fission reaction is utilised for producing steam. This steam is used to run turbines connected to the generators and electricity is generated.

Components of a Nuclear Power Plant

A nuclear power plant consists of the following components

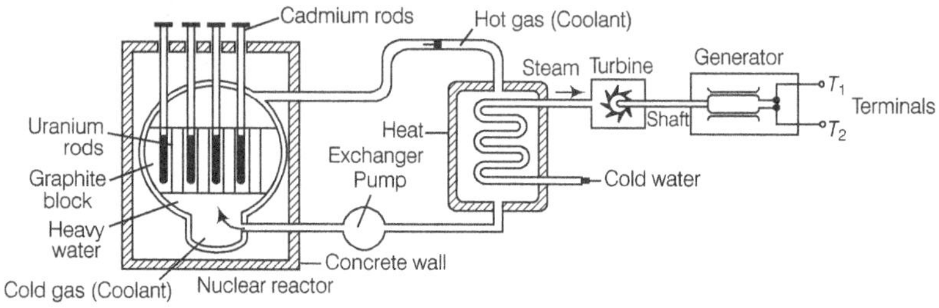

A schematic view of nuclear power plant

(i) **Nuclear Reactor** Here, a controlled nuclear fission of a fissionable fuel such as ${}_{92}U^{235}$ is carried out.

(ii) **Heat Exchanger** The reactor is connected to a heat exchanger. Here, the heat produced in the reactor is transferred to water by circulating a **coolant** through a coiled pipe. The water gets converted into steam. The coolant is pumped back to the reactor.

(iii) **Steam Turbine** The steam generated in the heat exchanger is used to run the steam turbine. The spent steam is sent back as hot water to the **heat exchanger**.

(iv) **Electric Generator** (or dynamo) The shaft of the steam turbine is connected to an electric generator (or dynamo) electricity, so produced is sent for transmission.

Sources of Energy

We require energy in every activity of our life. e.g. Energy is required to light homes, to cook food, to move vehicles, to run TV, etc. To meet these requirements the energy is generally needed in some of the forms like heat, electricity, etc. Heat energy is required for cooking food. Electricity is required for running electric motors, fans, etc.

A source of energy provides adequate amount of useful energy at a steady rate over a longer period of time. From the availability point of view, *th*e energy sources are divided into following two groups

(a) Renewable sources of energy

(b) Non-renewable sources of energy

Law of Conservation of Energy

According to this law, energy can neither be created nor be destroyed, it can only be transferred from one form to another form.

Conservation of Mechanical Energy

The total mechanical energy of a system remains constant, if the internal forces involved are non-dissipative (not frictional) and the external forces do not work. This is called the **principle of conservation of energy**.

If kinetic energy of the system is K and potential energy is U, then from conservation of mechanical energy,

$$\text{Mechanical energy} = K + U = \text{constant}$$

Example of conservation of mechanical energy is a free falling body, as it falling the potential energy gets converted to kinetic energy such that

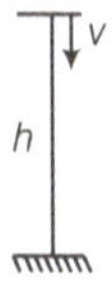

$$mgh + \frac{1}{2}mv^2 = \text{constant}$$

where, h is height and v is speed of the body.

- The law of conservation of energy can also be applied to a simple pendulum as shown in the figure.

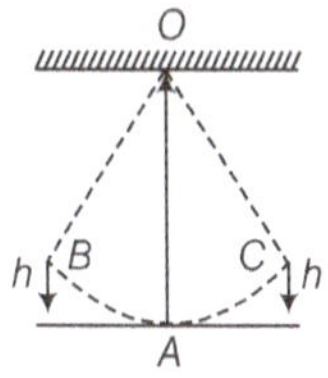

- The particle is having mass m when it goes from A to B or B to C. We can apply conservation of mechanical energy as $(KE)_A = (PE)_C$ or $\frac{1}{2}mv^2 = mgh$

PYQs Previous Years Questions

1 Mark Questions

1. When a bell fixed on a cycle rings, then the energy conversion that takes place is **(ICSE 2024)**
   (a) gravitational potential energy to sound energy
   (b) kinetic energy to sound energy
   (c) sound energy to electrical energy
   (d) sound energy to mechanical energy

2. The energy conversion in washing machine is from **(ICSE 2023)**
   (a) magnetic to electrical (b) electrical to mechanical
   (c) electrical to magnetic (d) magnetic to electrical

3. The energy conversion, when an oscillating pendulum moves from mean to extreme position is **(ICSE SQP 2023)**
   (a) kinetic to potential
   (b) potential to kinetic
   (c) potential to kinetic to potential
   (d) kinetic to potential to kinetic

4. The energy change during photosynthesis in plants is **(ICSE 2022 Sem-I)**
   (a) heat to chemical
   (b) light to chemical
   (c) chemical to light
   (d) chemical to heat

5. In an electric cell while in use, the change in energy is from **(ICSE SQP 2022 Sem-I)**
   (a) chemical to mechanical
   (b) chemical to electrical
   (c) electrical to mechanical
   (d) electrical to chemical

2 Marks Questions

6. The diagram below shows a pendulum having a bob of mass 80 g. A and C are extreme positions and B is the mean position. The bob has velocity 5 m/s at position B. [Take, $g = 10\text{N}/\text{kg}$] **(ICSE SQP 2022 Sem-I)**

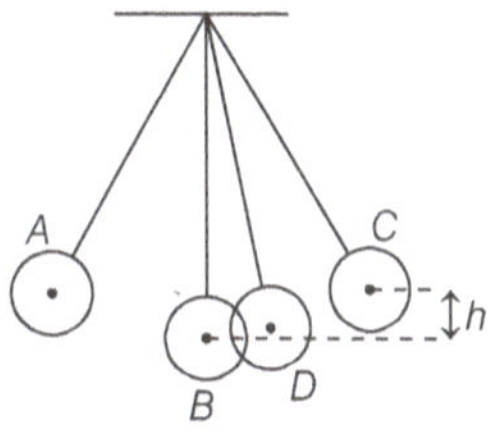

   (i) Which one of the following statements is correct?
   (a) At point A, the bob has only kinetic energy.
   (b) At point B, the bob will have only potential energy.
   (c) At point B, the bob will have maximum kinetic energy.
   (d) At point D, the bob will have more potential and less kinetic energy.
   (ii) The height h is
   (a) 1.25 cm (b) 125 m
   (c) 1.25 m (d) 0.125 m

7. Give one example of each, when **(ICSE 2020)**
   (i) chemical energy changes into electrical energy.
   (ii) electrical energy changes into sound energy.

8. Write the energy conversions in the following. **(ICSE SQP 2018)**
   (i) Microphone
   (ii) Lighted candle

9. State the energy changes in the following devices while in use
(i) a loudspeaker
(ii) a glowing electric bulb. **(ICSE 2014)**

10. State one important advantage and disadvantage each of using nuclear energy for producing electricity. **(ICSE 2014)**

11. (i) State the energy conversion taking place in a solar cell.
(ii) Give one disadvantage of using a solar cell. **(ICSE 2012, 02)**

12. A ball of mass 200 g falls from a height of 5 m. What will be its kinetic energy when it just reaches the ground? (Take, $g = 9.8\,m/s^2$) **(ICSE 2011)**

13. A spring is kept compressed by a small trolley of mass 0.5 kg lying on a smooth horizontal surface as shown in the figure given below.

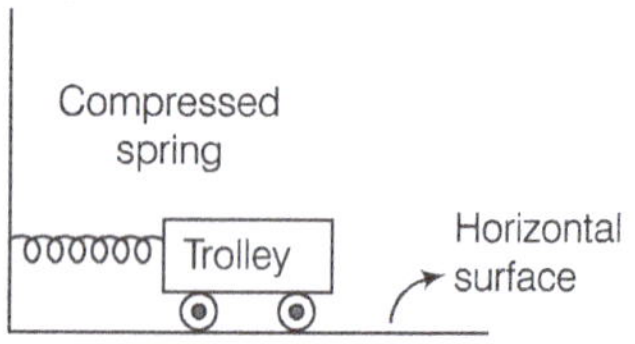

When the trolley is released, it is found to move at a speed of 2 ms^{-1}, what potential energy did the spring possess when compressed? **(ICSE 2010)**

> **KEY idea**
> Apply conservation of energy, i.e. PE of spring is equal to KE imparted to the trolley.

14. State the energy changes that takes place in the following when they are in use
(i) a photovoltaic cell.
(ii) an electromagnet. **(ICSE 2009)**

15. When an arrow is shot from a bow, it has a kinetic energy in it. Explain briefly from where does it get its kinetic energy? **(ICSE 2008)**

16. What energy conversions take place in the following when they are working
(i) Electric toaster?
(ii) Microphone? **(ICSE 2008)**

17. What is the main energy transformation that occurs in
(i) photosynthesis in greenhouse?
(ii) charging of a battery? **(ICSE 2007)**

18. A ball of mass 0.20 kg is thrown vertically upwards with an initial velocity of 20 m/s. Calculate the maximum potential energy it gains as it goes up. **(ICSE 2004)**

3 Marks Questions

19. Two identical marbles A and B are rolled down along path 1 and path 2, respectively. Path 1 is frictionless and path 2 is rough. **(ICSE 2024)**
(a) Which marble will surely reach the next peak ?
(b) Along which path(s), the mechanical energy will be conserved'?
(c) Along which path(s) is the law of conservation of energy obeyed'.

20. A body of mass 10 kg is kept at a height of 5 m. It is allowed to fall and reach the ground. **(ICSE 2019)**
(i) What is the total mechanical energy possessed by the body at the height of 2 m assuming it is a frictionless medium?
(ii) What is the kinetic energy possessed by the body just before hitting the ground? (Take, $g = 10\,m/s^2$)

21. Draw a diagram to show the energy changes in an oscillating simple pendulum. Indicate in your diagram how the total mechanical energy in it remains constant during the oscillation. **(ICSE 2011)**

22. State the law of conservation of energy. **(ICSE 2005)**

4 Marks Questions

23. A body of mass 200 g falls freely from a height of 15 m. (Take, $g = 10\,ms^{-2}$) **(ICSE 2022 Sem-I)**
(i) When the body reaches 10 m above the ground, its potential energy will be
(a) 20000 J (b) 10 J
(c) 10000 J (d) 20 J
(ii) The gain in kinetic energy of the body when it reaches 10 m above the ground is
(a) 20 J (b) 10 J (c) 30 J (d) 25 J
(iii) The total mechanical energy it will possess, when it is just about to strike the ground is
(a) 30000 J (b) 20000 J
(c) 30 J (d) 20 J
(iv) The velocity in ms^{-1} with which the body will hit the ground is
(a) 30 (b) 10 (c) $10\sqrt{3}$ (d) $10\sqrt{2}$

24. The figure below shows a simple pendulum of mass 200 g. It is displaced from the mean position A to the extreme position B. The potential energy at the position A is zero. At the position B, the pendulum bob is raised by 5 m. **(ICSE 2020)**

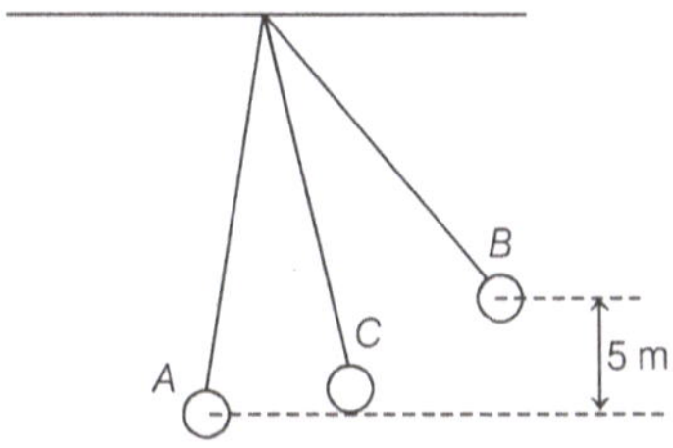

(i) What is the potential energy of the pendulum at the position B?
(ii) What is the total mechanical energy at point C?
(iii) What is the speed of the bob at the position A when released from B?
(Take $g = 10\ ms^{-2}$ and there is no loss of energy)

25. An object of mass m is allowed to fall freely from point A as shown in the figure. Calculate the total mechanical energy of the object at

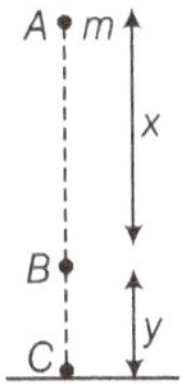

(i) Point A
(ii) Point B
(iii) Point C
(iv) State the law which is verified by your calculations in parts (i), (ii) and (iii). **(ICSE 2009)**

26. (i) A stone of mass 64.0 g is thrown vertically upward from the ground with an initial speed of 20.0 m/s. The gravitational potential energy at the ground level is considered to be zero. Apply the principle of conservation of energy and calculate the potential energy at the maximum height attained by the stone. (Take, $g = 10\ ms^{-2}$)
(ii) Using the same principle, state what will be the total energy of the body at its half-way point? **(ICSE 2008)**

Explanations

1. (b) When a bell fixed on a cycle rings, then the energy conversion that takes place is kinetic energy to sound energy.
2. (b)
3. (a) When pendulum goes from mean position to extreme position, its velocity becomes zero and kinetic energy changes to potential energy.
4. (b) During photosynthesis, solar energy is trapped by leaves and gets converted into chemical energy.
5. (b)
6. (i) (c) At point B, the bob will have maximum kinetic energy.
(ii) (c)
7. (i) Dry cell (ii) Loudspeaker
8. (i) Sound energy to electrical energy.
(ii) Chemical energy is converted into heat and light energy.

Concept Enhancer Energy transformation is used when energy changes from one form to another, whether the energy transfered or transformed.

9. (i) In loudspeaker, electrical energy is converted into sound energy.
(ii) In a glowing electric bulb, electrical energy is converted into light and heat energy.
10. (i) The advantage of nuclear energy is that a very small amount of nuclear fuel can produce a tremendous amount of energy.
(ii) The disadvantage of nuclear energy is that a very harmful nuclear radiations are produced in the process which are highly energetic and penetrating.
11. (i) In solar cell, solar energy is converted into electrical energy.
(ii) The main disadvantage of solar cell is that it is not a constant source of energy.
12. Given, mass $m = 200\ g = 0.2\ kg$

Height $h = 5\ m$

Kinetic energy, KE = ?

and $g = 9.8\ m/s^2$

According to law of conservation of energy,
KE at the lowest point = PE at the highest point

$$= mgh = 0.2 \times 9.8 \times 5 = 9.8\ J$$

13. Given, mass $m = 0.5$ kg, speed $v = 2$ m/s,

Potential energy PE = ?

When the spring is compressed, then

PE = KE (kinetic energy of the trolley when released)

$$= \frac{1}{2}mv^2 = \frac{1}{2} \times 0.5 \times (2)^2 = 1\text{ J}$$

14. (i) In photovoltaic cell, light energy is converted into electrical energy.

(ii) In electromagnet, electrical energy is converted into magnetic energy.

15. A stretched bow possesses potential energy on account of change in its shape. The potential energy of the bow is converted into the kinetic energy of the arrow.

16. (i) In electric toaster, electric energy is converted into heat energy.

(ii) In microphone, sound energy is converted into electrical energy.

17. (i) In photosynthesis in greenhouse, light energy is converted into chemical energy.

(ii) In charging of a battery, electrical energy is converted into chemical energy.

18. Given, mass $m = 0.20$ kg

Initial velocity $u = 20$ m/s

Potential energy $PE_{max} = ?$

According to the principle of conservation of energy,

Maximum PE gain = Initial KE

$$= \frac{1}{2}mu^2 = \frac{1}{2} \times 0.20 \times (20)^2 = 40\text{ J}$$

19. (a) Marble A

(b) Along path 1, the mechanical energy will be conserved.

(c) Along path 1, the law of conservation of energy is obeyed.

20. (i) Given, mass of body , $m = 10$ kg

Height, $h = 5$ m

So, potential energy at height of 5 m

$$= mgh = 10 \times 10 \times 5 = 500\text{ J}$$

If it falls to a height of 2 m, the increase in kinetic energy will be equal to the decrease in potential energy, so the total mechanical energy will equal to potential energy. Hence, total mechanical energy 500 J.

(ii) From principle of energy transformation when body is about to reach the ground, potential energy will be converted to kinetic energy. So, kinetic energy (KE) = 500 J.

21. Refer to text on page 27.

22. The law of conservation of energy states that energy can neither be created nor be destroyed but can be transferred from one form to the other.

23. (i) (d) Mass of the body

$$= 200\text{ g} = 0.2\text{ kg}$$

Height = 15 m

Potential energy = mgh

$$= 0.2 \times 10 \times 10 = 20\text{ J}$$

(ii) (b) Gain in kinetic energy

$$= \text{Loss in potential energy}$$
$$= \text{mass} \times g \times \text{loss in height}$$
$$= 0.2 \times 10 \times 5 = 10\text{ J}$$

(iii) (c) $(\text{Total mechanical energy})_{\text{at bottom}}$

$$= (KE)_{\text{at top}} + (PE)_{\text{at top}}$$
$$= 0 + mgh$$
$$= 0 + 0.2 \times 10 \times 15 = 30\text{ J}$$

(iv) (c) Kinetic energy which hits the ground

$$= \frac{1}{2}mv^2$$

$$\Rightarrow \quad 30 = \frac{1}{2}mv^2$$

$$\Rightarrow \quad 30 \times 2 = 0.2v^2$$

$$\Rightarrow \quad \frac{60}{0.2} = v^2$$

$$\therefore \quad v = \sqrt{300} = 10\sqrt{3}\text{ m/s}$$

24. Mass of simple pendulum, $m = 200$ g = 0.2 kg.

(i) Since, B is extreme position, so total energy at B is extreme position, hence total energy at B is present in the form of its potential energy.

Potential energy, $U = mgh$

$$= 0.2 \times 10 \times 5 = 10\text{ J}$$

(ii) Since, total mechanical energy (E) remains conserved, hence total mechanical energy at C is

$$E = U = 10\text{ J}$$

(iii) At point A, whole of the potential energy of the bob is converted into its kinetic energy.

So, $\frac{1}{2}mv^2 = U$

$$\Rightarrow \frac{1}{2} \times 0.2 \times v^2 = 10$$

$$\Rightarrow \quad v^2 = \frac{10}{0.1} = 100$$

$$\Rightarrow \quad v = \sqrt{100}$$

$$\Rightarrow \quad v = 10\text{ m/s}$$

25. (i) Mechanical energy at point A,

$$(\text{ME})_A = (\text{KE})_A + (\text{PE})_A$$
$$= 0 + mg(x + y)$$
$$= mg(x + y)$$

(ii) Mechanical energy at point B will be same as A

$$= mg(x + y)$$

(iii) Mechanical energy at point C will be same as A

$$= mg(x + y)$$

(iv) **For conservation of energy** Refer to page 26 (Conservation of mechanical energy).

26. (i) Given, mass $m = 64.0\text{ g} = 0.064\text{ kg}$

Velocity $v = 20.0\text{ m/s}$, $g = 10\text{ m/s}^2$

According to principle of conservation of energy, PE at the maximum height will be the same as the KE imparted from the ground.

$$\therefore \quad \text{PE} = \text{KE}$$
$$= \frac{1}{2}mv^2$$
$$= \frac{1}{2} \times 0.064 \times (20)^2$$
$$= 12.8\text{ J}$$

(ii) According to principle of conservation of energy, the total energy of the body at its half-way point remains same.

So, $\quad \text{TE} = 12.8\text{ J}$

TOPIC 4

Machines

It is a device which helps us to do the work at one point and deliver it at another point with a view of accomplishing the work conveniently.

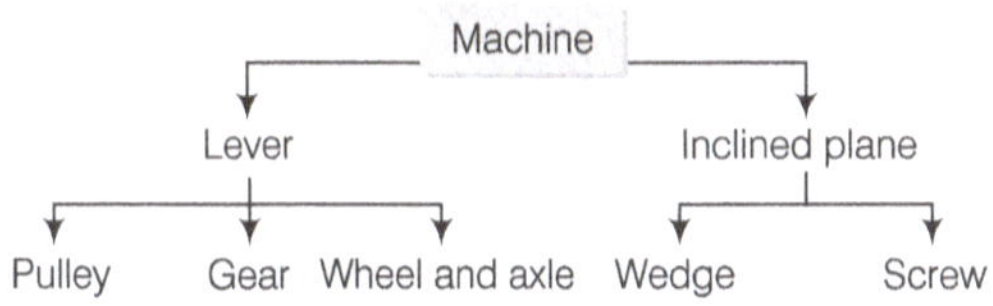

Classification of machine

Uses of Machines We use machines to

(i) multiply force
(ii) to change the direction of the force
(iii) to increase or decrease the speed

Terms Related to Machine

Load It is the resistive or opposing force against which the machine does the work. It is denoted by L.

Effort It is the force applied on the machine to overcome the load. It is denoted by E.

Mechanical Advantage (MA) It is the ratio of the load to the effort. It is denoted by MA. It is expressed as

$$\text{MA} = \frac{L}{E}$$

Being a ratio, it has no unit.

If MA > 1, then it works as force multiplier.

If MA < 1, then it gains speed.

If MA = 1, then it changes the direction of effort.

Velocity Ratio (VR) It is the ratio of the distance moved by the effort d_E to the corresponding distance moved by the load d_L.

It is denoted by VR. It is expressed as

$$\text{VR} = \frac{\text{Velocity of effort } (v_E)}{\text{Velocity of load } (v_L)} = \frac{d_E}{d_L}$$

Efficiency (η) It is the ratio of the work done on the load by the machine to the work put into the machine by the effort. It is denoted by η.

It is expressed as

$$\eta = \frac{\text{Work done on the load}}{\text{Work done by the effort}} = \frac{W_{\text{output}}}{W_{\text{input}}}$$

It is expressed in percentage,

$$\eta = \frac{W_{\text{output}}}{W_{\text{input}}} \times 100$$

Relation between η, MA and VR If η is expressed as efficiency percentage, then

$$\eta = \frac{\text{MA}}{\text{VR}} \times 100$$

Ideal Machine For an ideal machine, η is 100%. For practical purpose, the efficiency of a machine is less than 100% that is because practical MA is always less than theoretical VR due to friction and the weight of the moving parts.

Lever

It is a rigid body capable of rotating about a fixed axis. It is one of the commonest and simplest of all machines.
According to principle of lever,
Movement of load about the fulcrum = Movement of effort about the fulcrum

$$L \times d_L = E \times d_E$$

Kinds of Levers

There are following three types of levers
(i) Class I Lever
(ii) Class II Lever
(iii) Class III Lever

Class I Lever

In this type of lever, the effort (E) and the resistance load (L) are situated on either side of the fulcrum (F). e.g. A pair of scissors, handle of water pump, a catapult and the nodding of the human head, etc.

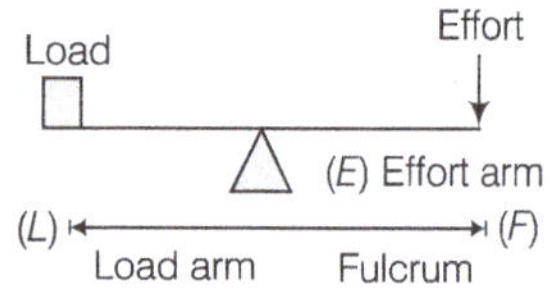

$$\text{MA of class I lever} = \frac{\text{Effort arm}}{\text{Load arm}},$$

$$\text{VR of class I lever} = \frac{d_E}{d_L}$$

If MA = 1, then load arm = effort arm
If MA > 1, then effort arm > load arm
If MA < 1, then effort arm < load arm

Class II Lever

In this type of lever, the load is situated between fulcrum and effort. e.g. A bottle opener, a wheel barrow, a paper cutter, raising the weight of the human body on toes, etc. As effort arm is always greater than the load arm, then MA and VR are always more than 1.

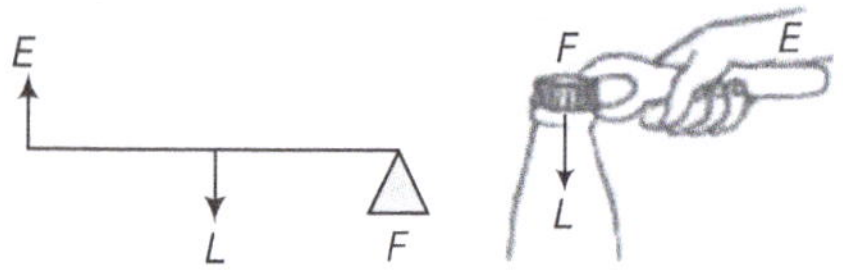

(a) (b) Bottle opener

Class III Lever

In this type of lever, effort is situated between the load and the fulcrum. e.g. Sugar tongs, the forearm used for lifting a load (**or action of the bicep muscle**), foot treadle, spade lifting a load. As effort is situated between the load and the fulcrum, then MA and VR is always less than 1.

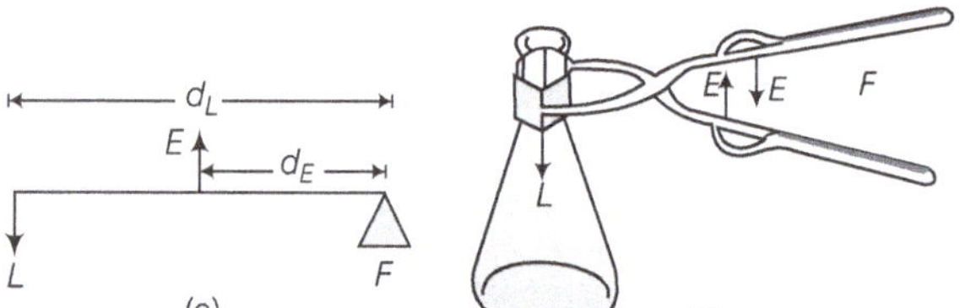

(a) (b)

Inclined Plane

The inclined plane is a sloping surface that behaves like a simple machine whose mechanical advantage is always greater than 1.

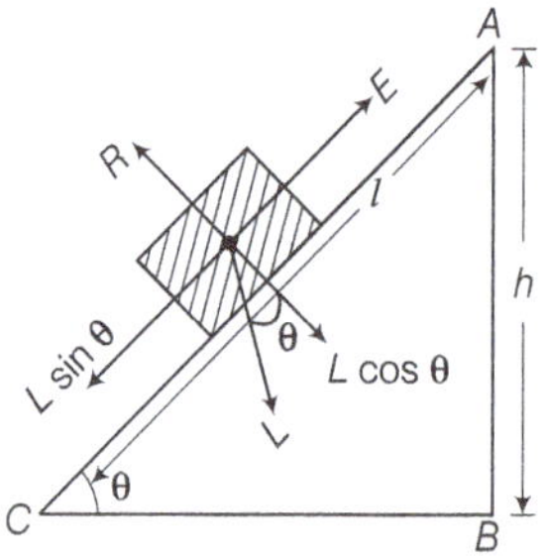

$$\text{Mechanical Advantage (MA)} = \frac{\text{Load}\,(L)}{\text{Effort}\,(E)} = \frac{L}{L\sin\theta}$$

$$\because \quad \sin\theta = \frac{h}{l}$$

$$\therefore \quad \text{MA} = \frac{l}{h} = \frac{1}{\sin\theta}$$

The velocity ratio of an inclined plane

$$\text{VR} = \frac{d_E}{d_L} = \frac{AC}{BC} = \frac{l}{h}$$

Gears

A gear is a wheel with teeth around its rim. A gear wheel closer to the source of power is called the **driver** (or the **driving gear**), while the gear wheel which receives motion from the driver is called the **driven gear**.

Let r_A and r_B be the radii of the driver and driven wheels and N_A and N_B be the number of teeth in the driving gear and driven gear respectively.

The ratio of number of teeth in the driving wheel to the number of teeth in the driven wheel is called the **gear ratio**.

$$\text{Gear ratio} = \frac{N_A}{N_B}$$

The ratio of number of teeth in driven gear to the number of teeth in driving gear gives the gain in torque (or tunning effect).

$$\text{Gain in torque} = \frac{N_B}{N_A} = \frac{r_B}{r_A}$$

The gain in speed is equal to the ratio of speed rotation of driven wheel to the speed of rotation of the driving wheel.

$$\text{Gain in speed} = \frac{n_B}{n_A} = \frac{N_A}{N_B}$$

Pulley

It is a wheel on an axle that is designed to support movement and change the direction of a cable or belt along its circumference.

A set of pulleys assembled, so that they rotate independently on the same axle to form a block is called **pulley system**.

Single Fixed Pulley

A pulley which has its axis of rotation fixed in position is called single fixed pulley.

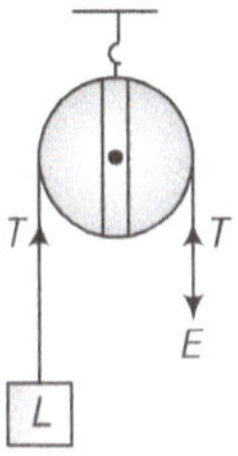

Mechanical Advantage

$$(\text{MA}) = \frac{\text{Load}}{\text{Effort}} = \frac{T}{T} = 1$$

[$\because$ Load $L = T$, Effort $E = T$, if pulley is not rotating]

$$\text{Velocity Ratio (VR)} = \frac{d_E}{d_L} = \frac{d}{d} = 1$$

[$\because d_E = d$ and $d_L = d$]

$$\text{Efficiency } (\eta) = \frac{\text{MA}}{\text{VR}} = 1 \text{ or } 100\%$$

Single Movable Pulley

A pulley whose axis of rotation is not fixed in position is called a movable pulley.

$$\text{Mechanical Advantage (MA)} = \frac{\text{Load}}{\text{Effort}} = \frac{2T}{T} = 2$$

[$\because L = T + T = 2T$ and $E = T$]

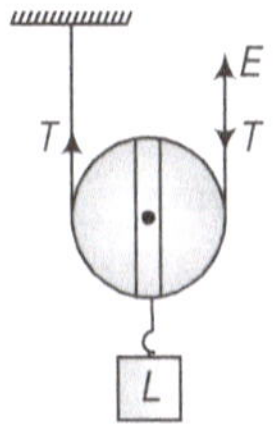

$$\text{Velocity Ratio (VR)} = \frac{d_E}{d_L} = \frac{2d}{d} = 2 \quad [\because d_E = 2d \text{ and } d_L = d]$$

$$\text{Efficiency } (\eta) = \frac{\text{MA}}{\text{VR}} \times 100 = \frac{2}{2} \times 100 = 100\% \text{ or } 1$$

Combination of Pulleys

The combination can be made in two ways

(i) Using one fixed pulley and several movable pulleys.

(ii) Using several fixed pulleys in two blocks known as **block and tackle system**.

Using one fixed pulley and other movable pulley

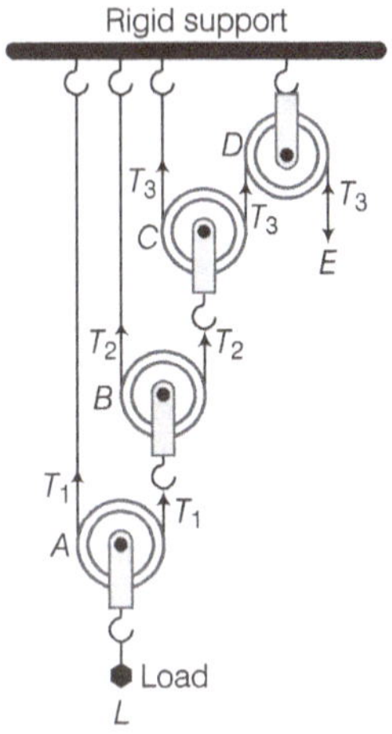

If there are n movable pulleys with one fixed pulley, then the mechanical advantage of this system is $\text{MA} = 2^n$

So, mechanical advantage of system which has one fixed pulley and three movable pulleys $= 2^3 = 8$

If there are n movable pulleys connected to a fixed pulley, the velocity ratio of this system is $\text{VR} = 2^n$

So, velocity ratio of system which has one fixed pulley and three movable pulleys $= 2^3 = 8$

Using several fixed pulleys in two blocks (block and tackle system)

If the total number of pulleys used in both the blocks is n and the effort is being applied in the downward direction. In this case, Load $= nT$ and Effort $= T$

$$\text{Mechanical Advantage (MA)} = \frac{\text{Load}}{\text{Effort}} = n$$

Velocity ratio

In a block and tackle system, if the load moves up through a distance d, the effort end moves through a distance nd, because each section of the string supporting the load is loosened by a length d. i.e.

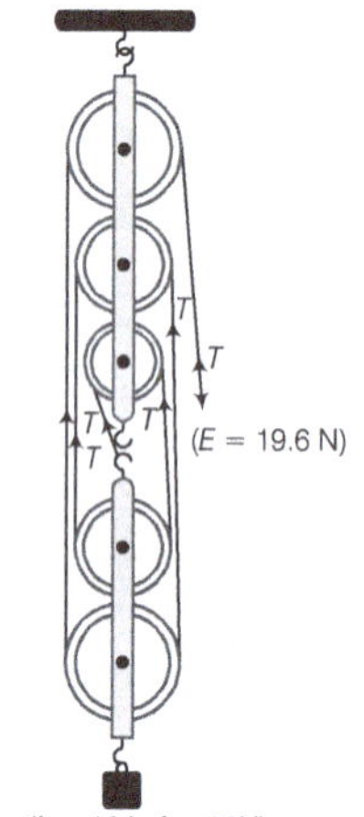

Block and tackle for five pulleys

if $d_L = d$, then $d_E = nd$

$\therefore$ Velocity ratio $= \dfrac{nd}{d} = n$

But, if total weight of pulleys in the lower block be W,

$$L + w = nT$$

$$E = T$$

Mechanical Advantage (MA)

$$= n - \frac{w}{E}, \quad \text{VR} = n$$

Efficiency, $\eta = \dfrac{\text{MA}}{\text{VR}}$

$$= \frac{(n - W/E)}{n}$$

$$= 1 - \frac{W}{nE}$$

PYQs Previous Years Questions

1 Mark Questions

1. Which of the following is a class III lever? **(ICSE 2024)**
   (a) Pair of scissors
   (b) Wheelbarrow
   (c) Crowbar
   (d) Human forearm

2. Name the class of the lever shown in the picture below. **(ICSE 2024)**

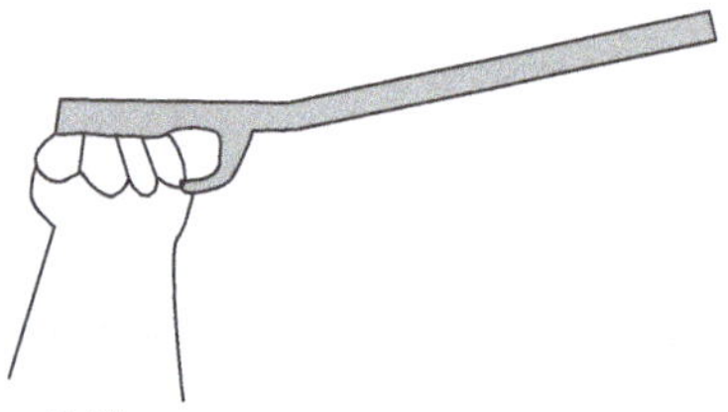

3. A single fixed pulley is used because **(ICSE 2022 Sem-I)**
   (a) it changes the direction of applied effort conveniently
   (b) it multiplies speed
   (c) it multiplies effort
   (d) its efficiency is 100%

4. In the diagram shown below, the velocity ratio of the arrangement is rigid support **(ICSE 2022 Sem-I)**

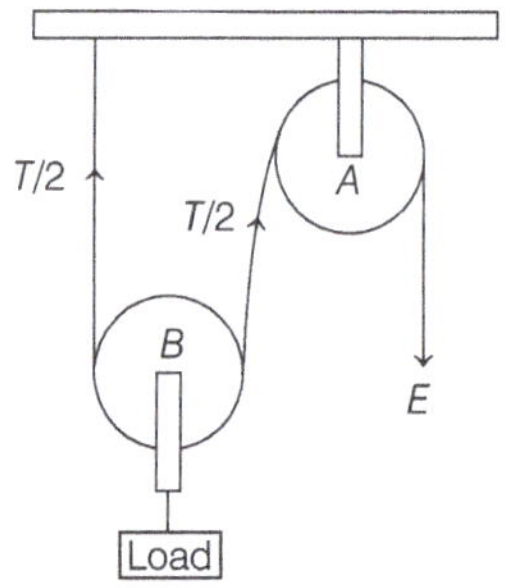

   (a) 1 (b) 2
   (c) 3 (d) 0

5. A woman draws water from a well using a fixed pulley. The mass of the bucket and the water together is 10 kg. The force applied by the woman is 200 N. The mechanical advantage is (Take $g = 10\ \text{m/s}^2$) **(ICSE 2022 Sem-I)**
   (a) 2 (b) 20
   (c) 0.05 (d) 0.5

6. Mechanical Advantage (MA), load (L) and effort (E) are related as **(ICSE SQP 2022 Sem-I)**
   (a) $\text{MA} = L \times E$ (b) $\text{MA} = E/L$
   (c) $\text{MA} \times E = L$ (d) $\text{MA} \times L = E$

7. Which one of the following statements is correct?
   (a) A machine is used to have more output energy as compared to input energy. **(ICSE SQP 2022 Sem-I)**
   (b) Mechanical advantage of a machine can never be greater than 1.
   (c) If a machine gives convenience of direction, then its mechanical advantage should be greater than 1.
   (d) For a given design of a machine, even if the mechanical advantage increases, the velocity ratio remains the same.

8. If a block and tackle system with convenient direction has 3 movable pulleys, then its velocity ratio **(ICSE SQP 2022 Sem-I)**
   (a) is either 6 or 7
   (b) should be 6
   (c) should be 7
   (d) is 3

9. A boy uses a single fixed pulley to lift a load of 50 kgf to some height. Another boy uses a single movable pulley to lift the same load to the same height. Compare the effort applied by them. Give a reason to support your answer. **(ICSE 2017)**

2 Marks Questions

10. Meera choose to use a block and tackle system of 9 pulleys instead of a single movable pulley to lift a heavy load **(ICSE 2024)**
   (a) What is the advantage of using a block and tackle system over a single movable pulley?
   (b) Why should she connect more number of pulleys in the upper fixed block ?

11. Crane *A* lifts a heavy load in 5s, whereas another crane *B* does the same work in 2s. Compare the power of crane *A* to that of crane *B*. **(ICSE 2020)**

12. The diagram below shows a lever in use **(ICSE 2018)**

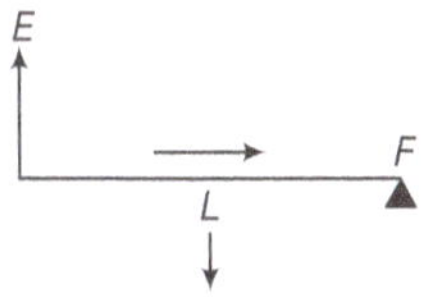

   (i) To which class of levers does it belong?
   (ii) Without changing the dimensions of the lever, if the load is shifted towards the fulcrum, what happens to the mechanical advantage of the lever?

13. Explain why a single fixed pulley is used despite no gain in mechanical advantage. **(ICSE SQP 2018)**

14. Which class of lever will always have MA > 1 and why? **(ICSE 2017)**

15. With reference to the terms mechanical advantage, velocity ratio and efficiency of a machine, name and define the term that will not change for a machine of a given design. **(ICSE 2016)**

16. (i) Give an expression for mechanical advantage of an inclined plane in terms of the length of an inclined plane.
   (ii) Name a common device, where a gear train is used. **(ICSE 2015)**

17. Draw a simplified diagram of a lemon crusher, indicating direction of load and effort. **(ICSE 2015)**

18. Draw a diagram to show how a single pulley can be used, so as to have its ideal MA = 2. **(ICSE 2014)**

19. A type of single pulley is very often used as a machine even though it does not give any gain in mechanical advantage
   (i) Name the type of pulley used.
   (ii) For what purpose is such a pulley used? **(ICSE 2013)**

20. Under what condition will a set of gears produce
   (i) a gain in speed?
   (ii) a gain in torque? **(ICSE 2012)**

21. (i) What is meant by an ideal machine?
   (ii) Write a relationship between the mechanical advantage (MA) and velocity ratio (VR) of an ideal machine? **(ICSE 2011)**

22. The diagram below shows a lever in use.

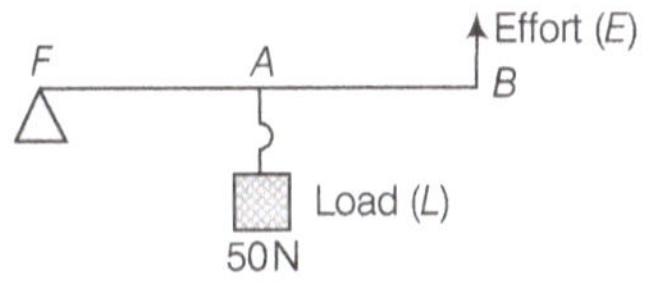

   (i) To which class of lever does it belong?
   (ii) If *FA* = 40 cm, *AB* = 60 cm, then find the mechanical advantage of the lever. **(ICSE 2011)**

23. Name a machine which can be used to
   (i) multiply force.
   (ii) change the direction of force applied. **(ICSE 2011)**

24. (i) Why is the mechanical advantage of a lever of the second order always greater than one?
   (ii) Name the type of single pulley that has a mechanical advantage greater than one. **(ICSE 2010)**

25. (i) With reference to the terms mechanical advantage, velocity ratio and efficiency of a machine, name the term that will not change for a machine of a given design.

(ii) Define the term stated by you in part (i). **(ICSE 2009)**

26. Copy the diagram of the forearm given below, indicate the positions of load, effort and fulcrum.

(ICSE 2008)

27. Write an expression to show the relationship between mechanical advantage, velocity ratio and efficiency for a simple machine. **(ICSE 2007)**

28. Which class of levers has a mechanical advantage always greater than one? What change can be brought about in this lever to increase its mechanical advantage? **(ICSE 2007)**

29. A woman draws water from a well using a fixed pulley. The mass of the bucket and water together is 6.0 kg. The force applied by the woman is 70 N. Calculate the mechanical advantage. (Take, $g = 10 \text{ m/s}^2$) **(ICSE 2004)**

30. Give two reasons why the efficiency of a single movable pulley system is not 100%. **(ICSE 2003)**

31. What is the relationship between the mechanical advantage and the velocity ratio for

(i) ideal machine?

(ii) practical machine? **(ICSE 2002)**

32. To use a machine as a force multiplier, what types (class) of lever should preferably be used? Draw a sketch of such a lever. **(ICSE 2001)**

3 Marks Questions

33. A block and tackle system of pulleys has velocity ratio 4. **(ICSE 2020)**

(i) Draw a neat labelled diagram of the system indicating clearly the points of application and direction of load and effort.

(ii) What will be its velocity ratio, if the weight of the movable block is doubled?

34. A uniform half meter rule balances horizontally on a knife edge at 29 cm mark when a weight of 20 gf is suspended from one end.

(i) Draw a diagram of the arrangement.

(ii) What is the weight of the half meter rule? **(ICSE 2017)**

> **KEY idea**
>
> When a body is balanced, the total clockwise moment about a point is equal to total anti-clockwise moment about same point.

35. From the diagram given below, answer the questions that follow:

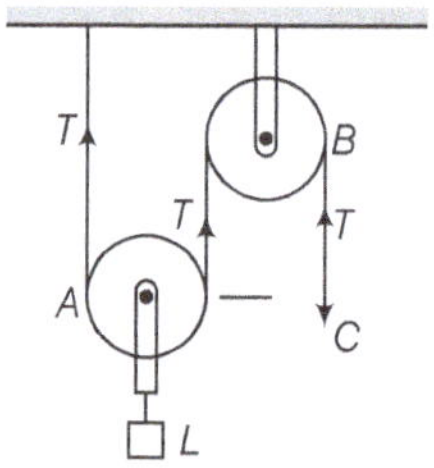

(i) What kind of pulleys are A and B?

(ii) State the purpose of pulley B.

(iii) What effort has to be applied at C to just raise the load $L = 20$ kgf?

(Neglect the weight of pulley A and friction) **(ICSE 2016)**

36. Derive a relationship between MA, VR and η of a machine. **(ICSE 2014)**

37. A coolie is pushing a box weighing 1500 N up an inclined plane 7.5 m long onto a platform, 2.5 m above the ground.

(i) Calculate the mechanical advantage of the inclined plane.

(ii) Calculate the effort applied by the coolie.

(iii) In actual practice, the coolie needs to apply more effort than what is calculated. Give one reason, why you think the coolie needs to apply more effort? **(ICSE 2013)**

38. (i) State the class of levers and the relative positions of load (L), effort (E) and fulcrum (F) in each of the following cases:

(a) A bottle opener (b) Sugar tongs

(ii) Why is less effort needed to lift a load over an inclined plane as compared to lifting the load directly? **(ICSE 2012)**

39. A pulley system comprises two pulleys, one fixed and the other movable.

(i) Draw a labelled diagram of the arrangement and show clearly the directions of all the forces acting on it.

(ii) What change can be made in the movable pulley of this system to increase the mechanical advantage of the system? **(ICSE 2009)**

40. A pulley system has a velocity ratio of 4 and an efficiency of 90%. Calculate

(i) the mechanical advantage of the system.

(ii) the effort required to raise a load of 300 N by the system. **(ICSE 2006)**

> **KEY idea**
> To obtain the effort (E), first calculate the mechanical advantage and then effort (E).

41. Name the type of single pulley that can act as a force multiplier. Draw a labelled diagram of the above named pulley. **(ICSE 2006)**

42. (i) Define an inclined plane.

(ii) Draw a labelled sketch of a class II lever. Give one example of such a lever. **(ICSE 2005)**

43. A cook uses a fire tong of length 28 cm to lift a piece of burning coal of mass 250 g. If he applies his effort at a distance of 7 cm from the fulcrum, what is the effort in SI unit? (Take, $g = 10\ \text{m/s}^2$) **(ICSE 2002)**

44. A pair of scissors and a pair of pliers belong to the same class of levers.

(i) Which one has mechanical advantage less than one?

(ii) State the usefullness of such a machine whose mechanical advantage is less than 1. **(ICSE 2001)**

4 Marks Questions

45. Given are two pulleys. **(ICSE 2024)**

(a) Copy and complete the labelled diagram connecting the two pulleys with a tackle to obtain velocity ratio = 2.

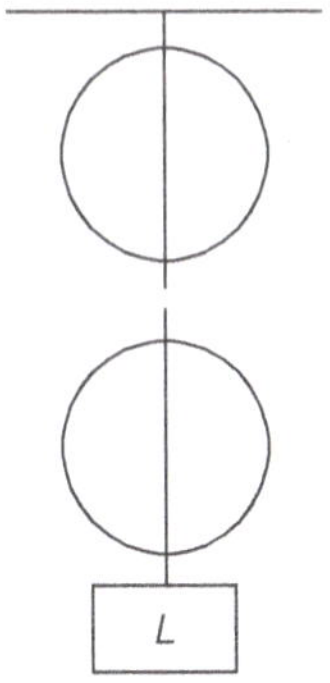

(b) It load is 48 kgf and efficiency is 80%, then calculate

I. Mechanical advantage

II. Effort needed to lift the load

46. The figure below shows a pulley arrangement. **(ICSE 2019)**

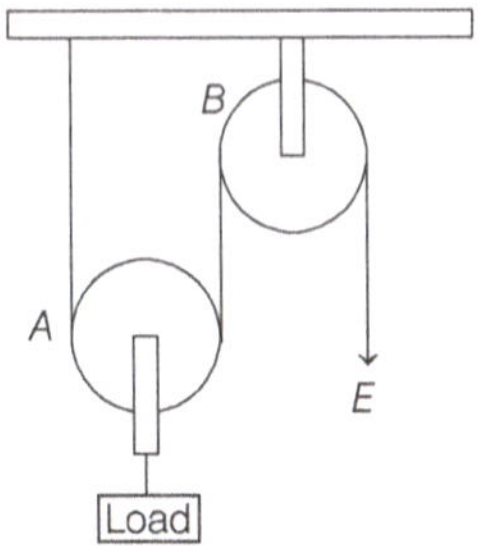

(i) Copy the figure and mark the direction of tension on each strand of the string.

(ii) What is the velocity ratio of the arrangement?

(iii) It the tension acting on the string is T, then what is the relationship between T and effort E?

(iv) If the free end of the string moves through a distance x, then find the distance by which the load is raised.

47. (i) Draw a diagram to show a block and tackle pulley system having a velocity ratio of 3 marking the direction of load (L), effort (E) and tension (T).

(ii) The pulley system drawn lifts a load of 150 N. When an effort of 60 N is applied, find its mechanical advantage.

(iii) Is the above pulley system an ideal machine or not? **(ICSE 2018)**

48. A pulley system with VR = 4 is used to lift a load of 175 kgf through a vertical height of 15 m. The effort required is 50 kgf in the downward direction. (Take, $g = 10\ \text{m/s}^2$). Calculate

(i) distance moved by the effort.

(ii) work done by the effort.

(iii) MA of the pulley system.

(iv) efficiency of the pulley system. **(ICSE 2017)**

49. (i) An effort is applied on the bigger wheel of a gear having 32 teeths. It is used to turn a wheel of 8 teeths. Where is it used?

(ii) A pulley system has three pulleys. A load of 120 N is overcome by applying an effort of 50 N. Calculate the mechanical advantage and efficiency of this system. **(ICSE 2016)**

50. A block and tackle system has VR = 5

(i) Draw a neat labelled diagram of a system indicating the direction of its load and effort.

(ii) Rohan exerts a pull of 150 kgf. What is the maximum load he can raise with this pulley system, if its efficiency –75%? **(ICSE 2015)**

51. A block and tackle system of pulleys has a velocity ratio 4.

(i) Draw a labelled diagram of the system indicating clearly the points of application and directions of load and effort.

(ii) What is the value of the mechanical advantage of the given pulley system, if it is an ideal pulley system? **(ICSE 2013)**

52. A uniform meter scale can be balanced at the 70.0 cm mark when a mass of 0.05 kg is hung from the 94.0 cm mark.

(i) Draw a diagram of the arrangement.

(ii) Find the mass of the meter scale. **(ICSE 2011)**

53. (i) Write a relation expressing the mechanical advantage of a lever.

(ii) Write an expression for the mechanical advantage of an inclined plane.

(iii) Give two reasons as to why the efficiency of a single movable pulley system is always less than 100%. **(ICSE 2010)**

54. (i) Draw a labelled diagram of a block and tackle system of pulleys with two pulleys in each block. Indicate the directions of the load, effort and tension in the string.

(ii) Write down the relation between the load and the effort of the pulley system. **(ICSE 2008)**

55. A block and tackle pulley system has a velocity ratio 3.

(i) Draw a labelled diagram of this system. In your diagram, indicate clearly the points of application and the directions of the load and effort.

(ii) Why should the lower block of this pulley system be of negligible weight? **(ICSE 2007)**

56. The below figure shows the combination of a movable pulley P_1 with a fixed pulley P_2 used for lifting up a load w.

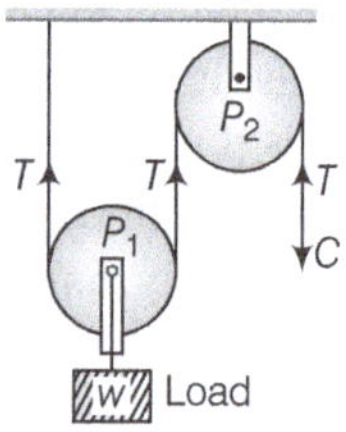

(i) State the function of the fixed pulley P_2.

(ii) If the free end of the string moves through a distance x, find the distance by which the load w is raised.

(iii) Calculate the force to be applied at C to just raise the load $w = 20$ kgf, neglecting the weight of the pulley P_1 and friction. **(ICSE 2005)**

Structured Questions (10 Marks)

57. (i) The diagram below shows a block and tackle system.

(a) Copy and redraw the labelled diagram showing the correct connection of tackle, direction of the forces involved to obtain the maximum VR and convenient direction. **(3)**

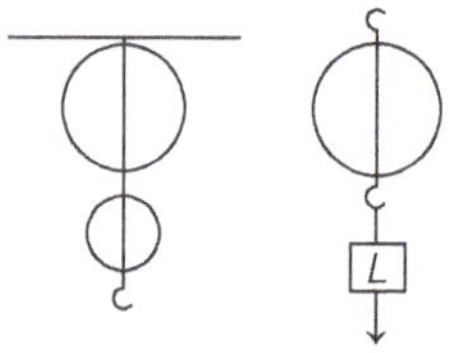

(b) Calculate the MA of this pulley system, if its efficiency is 80%.

(ii) The adjacent diagram shows a wheel of diameter 40 cm fixed on a wall capable of rotating around its centre O. If the wheel rotates in an anti-clockwise direction, then

(a) Calculate the clockwise moment.

(b) State whether $X = 100$ gf or $X < 100$ gf or $X > 100$ gf.

(c) Give a reason for your answer. **(3)**

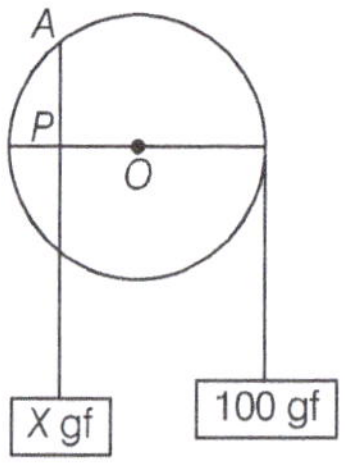

(iii) A cocount of mass 450 g falls from the top of an 80 m high tree.

(a) Calculate the potential energy possessed by the cocount when it is at the top of the tree.

(b) Without calculation, state the kinetic energy with which it strikes the ground and state the principle involved to arrive at the answer in (a). Use, $g = 10\,\text{ms}^{-2}$ **(ICSE SQP 2023) (4)**

58. (i) Show how the energy of a freely falling object remains conserved. **(3)**

(ii) A uniform metre rod is balanced at the 70 cm mark by suspending a weight of 50 gf at the 40 cm mark and 200 gf at the 95 cm mark. Draw a diagram of the arrangement and calculate the weight of the metre rod. **(3)**

(iii) Draw a diagram of a pulley system of velocity ratio 4. Calculate its mechanical advantage, if its efficiency is 90%. **(ICSE SQP 2018) (4)**

Explanations

1. (d) In third class lever, effort is situated between the load and the fulcrum. Human forearm is a class III - lever.
2. Second class lever
3. (a) A single fixed pulley is used to lift load by changing the direction of the lifting force. Even through a single fixed pulley has no mechanical gain in that, the effort applied is greater than the load.
4. (b) Velocity Ratio (VR) $= \frac{d_E}{d_L} = \frac{2d}{d} = 2$
5. (d) Given load = weight of water

$$L = 10 \times 10 = 100 \text{ N}$$

Effort = force applied

$$E = 200 \text{ N}$$

Now, $\text{MA} = \frac{\text{Load}}{\text{Effort}} = \frac{100}{200}$

$\text{MA} = 0.5$

6. (c) $\text{MA} \times E = L$

$\text{MA} = \frac{L}{E}$

$\therefore \text{MA} \times E = L$

7. (d) For a given design of a machine, even if the mechanical advantage increases, the velocity ratio remains the same.
8. (d)
9. Effort applied will be in the ratio 2 : 1 as MA of single fixed pulley is 1 whereas MA of single movable pulley is 2.
10. (a) Block and tackle systems can reduce the effort.

(b) She connect more number of pulleys in the upper fixed block because in case of a block and tackle system, the mechanical advantage increases with increase in the number of pulleys.

11. Time taken to lift load by crane A, $t_1 = 5\text{s}$

Time taken to same work by crane B, $t_2 = 2\text{s}$

$$\therefore \quad \frac{\text{Power of crane } A}{\text{Power of crane } B} = \frac{W_1 / t_1}{W_2 / t_2}$$

$$\frac{P_A}{P_B} = \frac{t_2}{t_1} \Rightarrow \frac{P_A}{P_B} = \frac{2}{5} \quad [\because W_1 = W_2]$$

$$\Rightarrow \quad P_A = \frac{2}{5} P_B$$

Thus, power of crane A is two-fifth of crane B.

12. (i) It belongs to class II lever because load is situated between fulcrum and effort.

(ii) If load is shifted towards the fulcrum, then mechanical advantage will increase.

13. There is no gain in mechanical advantage in the case of a single fixed pulley. A single fixed pulley is used only to change the direction of the force applied that is with its use, the effort can be applied in more conveninent direction. To raise a load directly upwards is difficult.
14. In second class lever (class II lever), an effort arm is always greater than the load arm and the load is situated between fulcrum and effort. In this lever, the mechanical advantage and velocity ratio are always more than 1. The sketch of such lever is shown below

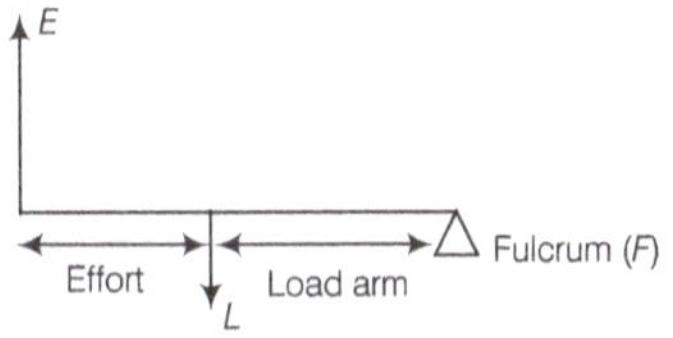

15. From the given variables, velocity ratio of a machine will not change for a machine of a given design. It is the ratio of the velocity of effort to the velocity of load.
16. (i) The expression for the mechanical advantage of an inclined plane is given by

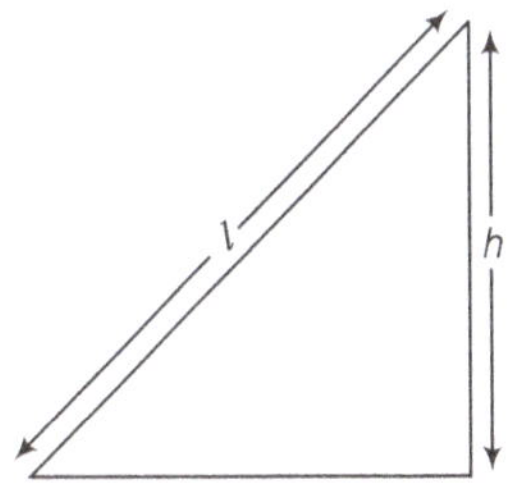

$$\text{MA} = \frac{l}{h}$$

where, l is the length of inclined plane, h is the height of inclined plane.

(ii) A gear train is used in clocks.

17.

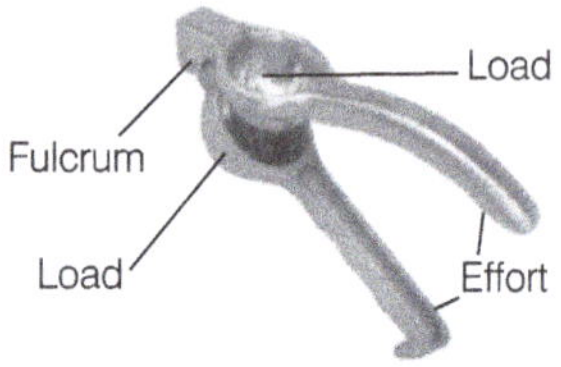

18.

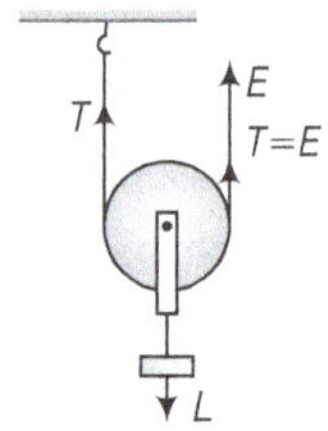

19. (i) The pulley which is used in the arrangement of single fixed pulley.

(ii) Single fixed pulley is used only to change the direction of the force applied.

20. (i) The set of gears gain its speed when the number of teeth in driving gear is more than as in the driven gear.

(ii) The set of gears gain its torque when the number of teeth in driving gear is less than as in the driven gear.

21. (i) A machine having 100% efficiency is called an ideal machine.

(ii) The relation between MA and VR is given by

$$\text{MA} = \text{VR} \qquad [\because \eta = 100\%]$$

22. (i) It belongs to class II lever.

(ii) Effort arm $FB = FA + AB$

$$= 40 + 60 = 100 \text{ cm}$$

Load arm $= FA = 40$ cm

$$\therefore \quad \text{MA} = \frac{\text{Effort arm}}{\text{Load arm}} = \frac{FB}{FA} = \frac{100}{40} = 2.5$$

23. (i) Inclined plane is a machine used to multiply force.

(ii) Pulley is a machine which can change the direction of force applied.

24. (i) The effort arm is always greater than the load arm, so the mechanical advantage of class II lever is always greater than one.

(ii) Single movable pulley is the type of pulley whose mechanical advantage is greater than unity.

25. (i) Velocity ratio will not change for a machine of a given design, because the distance moved by load in the same time is equal to the distance moved by the effort.

(ii) Velocity ratio is defined as the ratio of the velocity of effort (v_E) to the velocity of load (v_L).

$$\text{VR} = \frac{v_E}{v_L} = \frac{d_E}{d_L}$$

26. The below diagram shows the position of load (L), effort (E) and fulcrum (F).

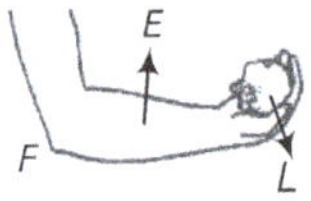

27. The expression showing the relationship between mechanical advantage (MA), velocity ratio (VR) and efficiency (η) for a simple machine is given by

$$\eta = \frac{\text{MA}}{\text{VR}} \times 100$$

28. In class II lever, effort arm is always greater than load arm. Therefore, mechanical advantage (MA = effort arm/load arm) is always greater than one. To increase its MA, we need to decrease its load arm.

29. Given, load $L = mg = 6 \times 10 = 60$ N

Effort $E = 70$ N

Mechanical advantage, MA = ?

$$\therefore \quad \text{MA} = \frac{L}{E} = \frac{60}{70} = 0.857$$

30. In single movable pulley system, efficiency is not 100%, because

(i) the weight of the movable pulley with its frame is not negligible as compared to the effort.

(ii) the frictional force between the pulley wheel and the string used is not negligible.

(iii) the string is not inextensible and massless.

31. (i) For an ideal machine, the work done by the machine is equal to the work done on the machine. Therefore, mechanical advantage is equal to velocity ratio.

i.e. MA = VR.

(ii) For practical machine, mechanical advantage is less than velocity ratio as efficiency is less than 1.

32. Lever of II type (class) is used as a force multiplier in a machine.

The sketch of such lever is as shown below

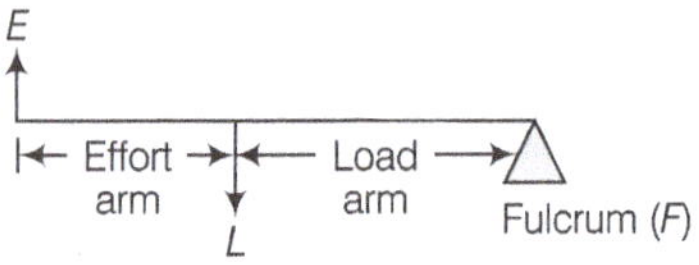

The effort arm is always greater than the load arm, so mechanical advantage of class II lever is always greater than 1.

33. (i) The labelled diagram of the system is shown below

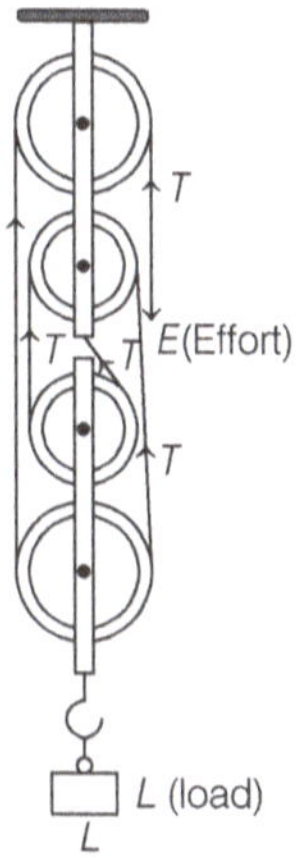

(ii) Given, velocity ratio (VR) = 4

$$\text{Efficiency}, \eta = \frac{\text{MA}}{\text{VR}} = \frac{\text{MA}}{4}$$

$$\Rightarrow \quad \eta = \frac{\text{MA}}{4} \quad \text{...(i)}$$

When movable load is doubled, then MA is also increased to double, i.e. 2 MA.

$$\text{Efficiency}, \eta = \frac{2\text{MA}}{\text{VR}} \quad \text{...(ii)}$$

From Eqs. (i) and (ii), we have

$$\frac{2\text{MA}}{\text{VR}} = \frac{\text{MA}}{4} \Rightarrow \text{VR} = 8$$

34. (i) Diagram of the given arrangement is shown below

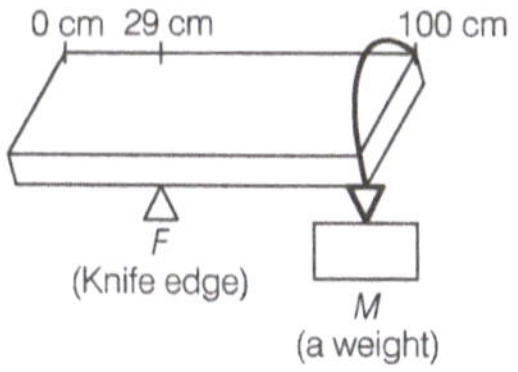

(ii) Given, load $L = 20$ gf

Effort arm, $d_f = 29$ cm

Weight of $M = w_m = 20$ gf

$$\text{Total length} = \frac{1}{2}\text{ m} = 50 \text{ cm}$$

Load arm, $d_L = 50 - 29 = 21$ cm

According to principle of moment,

$L \times d_L = E \times d_E \Rightarrow w_m \times d_L = E \times d_E$

where, E = Effort

Substituting the given values, we get

$$20 \times 21 = E \times 29 \Rightarrow E = \frac{20 \times 21}{29}$$

$\therefore$ Effort = 14.48 gf

35. (i) According to question, A is a movable pulley while B is a fixed pulley.

(ii) The purpose of pulley B is to change the point of application of effort and load in the same direction.

(iii) Given, load = 20 kgf, MA = 2

and we know that,

$$\text{MA} = \frac{\text{Load}}{\text{Effort}} \Rightarrow \text{Effort} = \frac{\text{Load}}{\text{MA}} = \frac{20}{2} = 10 \text{ kgf}$$

36. Let a machine overcome a load L by the application of an effort E. In time t, the displacement of effort is d_E and the displacement of load is d_L.

Work input = Effort × Displacement of effort = $E \times d_E$

Work output = Load × Displacement of load

$= L \times d_L$

$$\therefore \text{Efficiency } \eta = \frac{\text{Work output}}{\text{Work input}}$$

$$= \frac{L}{E} \times \frac{d_L}{d_E} = \frac{L}{E} \times \frac{1}{d_E/d_L}$$

But $\frac{L}{E} = \text{MA}$ and $\frac{d_E}{d_L} = \text{VR}$

$$\therefore \quad \eta = \frac{\text{MA}}{\text{VR}}$$

37. Given, length $l = 7.5$ m, height $h = 2.5$ m,

Load $L = 1500$ N

(i) $\text{MA} = \frac{l}{h} = \frac{7.5}{2.5} = 3$

(ii) $\text{Effort} = \frac{\text{Load}}{\text{MA}} = \frac{1500}{3} = 500 \text{ N}$

(iii) In actual practice, due to some friction between the plane and the bottom face of the body which is pulled over it, the effort needed is certainly more than $L \sin \theta$ (θ is inclination of the plane), so that MA is always less than $\frac{l}{h}$, hence efficiency is less than one.

38. (i) (a) A bottle opener is a class II lever. In this case, the load is in between the fulcrum and the effort.

(b) Sugar tongs is a class III lever. In this case, the effort is in between the fulcrum and the load.

(ii) Less effort is needed to lift a load over an inclined plane as compared to lifting the load directly, because mechanical advantage increases.

39. (i) The labelled diagram of the above arrangement is shown below

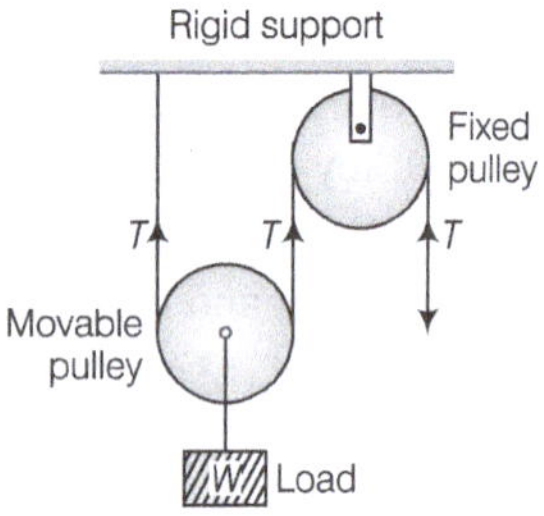

(ii) To increase the mechanical advantage of the system, we need to reduce the friction between the string and the movable pulley.

40. Given, Velocity Ratio VR = 4

Efficiency $\eta = 90\%$

(i) Mechanical advantage,

$$\therefore \quad \text{MA} = \text{VR} \times \frac{\eta}{100} \qquad \left[\text{as } \eta = \frac{\text{MA}}{\text{VR}}\right]$$

$$= 4 \times \frac{90}{100} = 3.6$$

(ii) Effort $E = ?$, Load $L = 300\text{ N}$

$$\therefore \quad E = \frac{L}{\text{MA}} \qquad \left[\text{MA} = \frac{L}{E}\right]$$

$$= \frac{300}{3.6} = 83.33$$

41. The single pulley that can act as a force multiplier in single movable pulley. The labelled diagram of single movable pulley is shown below

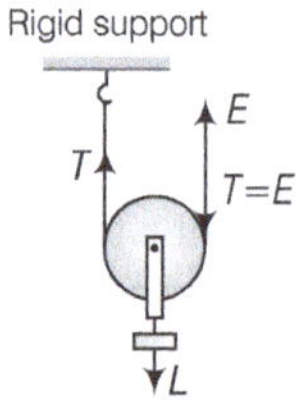

where, E = Effort = T and L = Load = $2T$

42. (i) An inclined plane is a sloping surface kept inclined to the horizontal at an angle θ. Its mechanical advantage is always greater than unity.

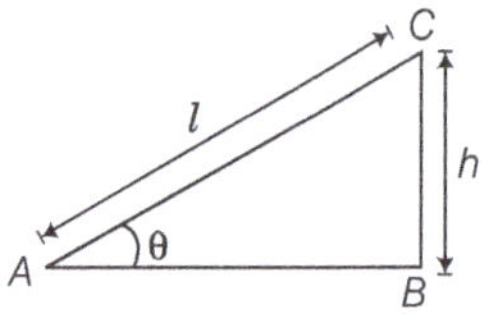

(ii) The labelled sketch of class II lever are

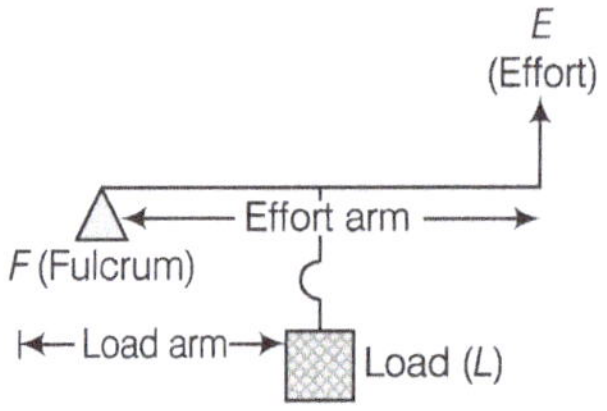

Example of a class II lever
(Nut cracker)

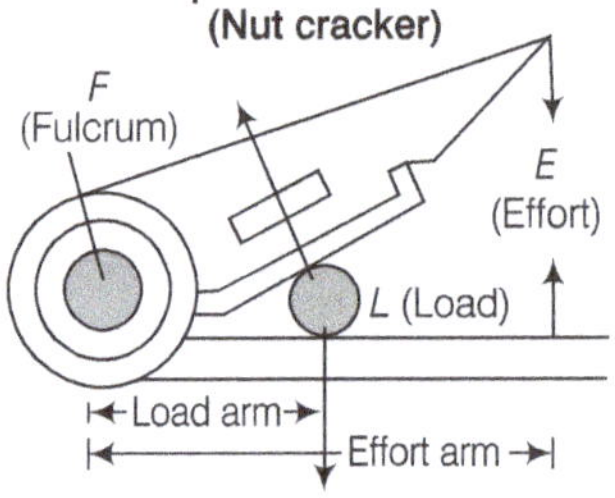

43. Given, mass $m = 250\text{ g} = 0.25\text{ kg}$

Load $L = 0.25 \times 10\text{ N} = 2.5\text{ N}$

Distance of load $L_d = 28\text{ cm} = 0.28\text{ m}$

Distance of effort $E_d = 7\text{ cm} = 0.07\text{ m}$

Effort $E = ?$

According to the principle of moment, we have

$$E \times E_d = L \times L_d$$

$$\Rightarrow \quad E = \frac{L \times L_d}{E_d} = \frac{2.5 \times 0.28}{0.07} = 10\text{ N}$$

44. (i) A pair of scissors has mechanical advantage less than one, because the blades are longer than its handles which is used to cut a piece of paper or cloth, so that the blades move longer on the cloth or paper when the handles are moved a little.

(ii) A machine such as a single fixed pulley whose MA < 1 is useful because it is easy and comfortable to apply effort (E) in the downward direction rather than upward direction. We can also use own body weight while applying effort in the downward direction.

45. (a)

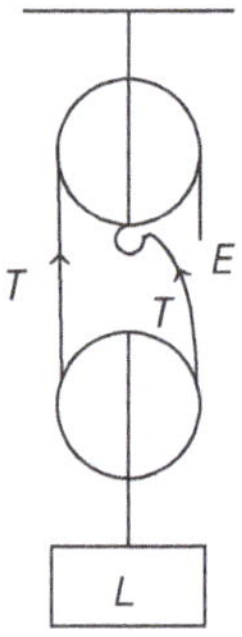

(b) (i) Mechanical advantage,

$$MA = VR \times \eta$$

$$= 2 \times \frac{80}{100} = \frac{160}{100} = 1.6$$

(ii) $\text{Effort} = \frac{\text{Load}}{\text{MA}} = \frac{48}{1.6} = 30\text{ kgf}$

46. (i)

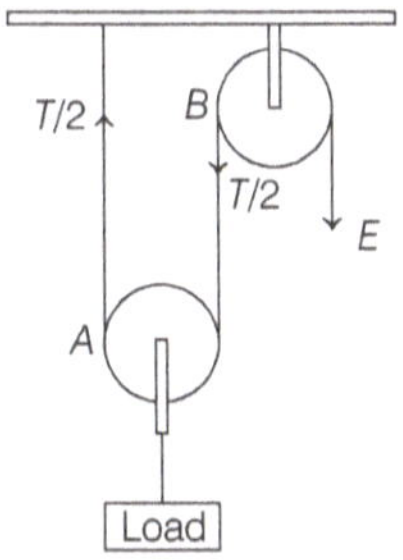

(ii) The system has one fixed pulley and one movable pulley. Thus, the velocity ratio is given by

$$VR = 2^1 = 2$$

(iii) The relation between T and effort E is given by

$$\frac{T}{2} = E$$

$$T = 2E$$

(iv) If the free end of the string moves through a distance x, then the load is raised by $\frac{x}{2}$ distance.

47. (i) The labelled diagram of the system is shown below

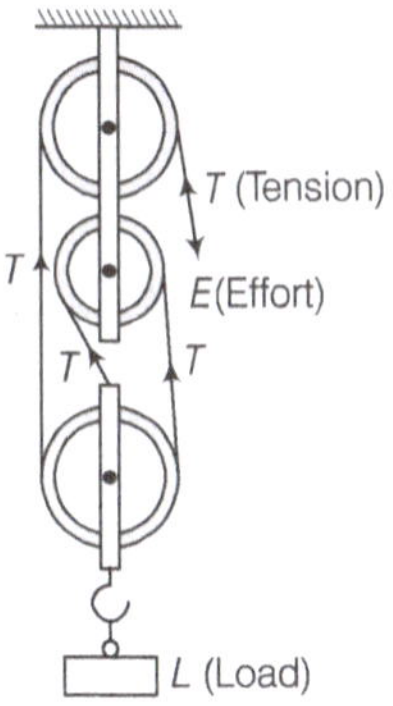

(ii) Given, load $L = 150\text{ N}$

Effort $E = 60\text{ N}$

We know that,

Mechanical Advantages,

$$MA = \frac{\text{Load}}{\text{Effort}} = \frac{150}{60} = 2.5$$

(iii) No, the above pulley system is not an ideal machine, because velocity ratio (VR = 3) is not equal to mechanical advantage.

48. Given, VR = 4, load = 175 kgf,

Load arm = 15 m, Effort = 50 kgf

Applying the formula, $L \times d_L = E \times d_E$

where, L = Load, d_L = Load arm,

E = Effort and d_E = Effort arm.

Also, $VR = \frac{\text{Distance moved by effort}}{\text{Distance moved by load}} = \frac{d_E}{d_L} \Rightarrow 4 = \frac{d_E}{15}$

(i) Distance moved by the effort,

$$d_E = 15 \times 4 = 60\text{ m}$$

(ii) Work done, $W = F \times s = 50 \times 60$

$$= 3000\text{ J}$$

(iii) $MA = \frac{\text{Load}}{\text{Effort}} = \frac{175}{50} = 3.5$

(iv) Efficiency, $\eta = \frac{MA}{VR} \times 100$

$$= \frac{3.5}{4} \times 100 = 8.75\%$$

49. (i) If an effort is applied on the bigger wheel of gear having 32 teeths to turn a wheel of 8 teeths, it acts as speed multiplier. And it is used in bicycles and car to gain speed.

(ii) According to question,

Load = 120 N, Effort = 50 N

So, mechanical advantage $= \frac{\text{Load}}{\text{Effort}} = \frac{120}{50} = 2.4$

$$\% \text{ efficiency} = \frac{MA}{VR} \times 100$$

$$\Rightarrow \quad \frac{2.4}{3} \times 100 \Rightarrow 80\%$$

50. (i) Velocity ratio is always equal to the number of strands of tackle supporting the load. For velocity ratio 5, there will be 5 strands supporting the load.

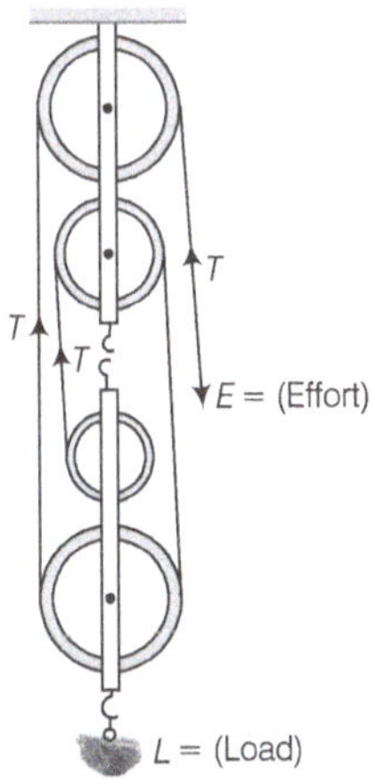

(ii) Here, $E = 150$ kgf, $\eta = 75\% = 0.75$,

$VR = 5$

$MA = L/E = VR \times \eta = 5 \times 0.75 = 3.75$

$L/150 = 3.75$

$L = 3.75 \times 150 = 562.5$ kgf

51. (i) The labelled diagram of the system is shown below

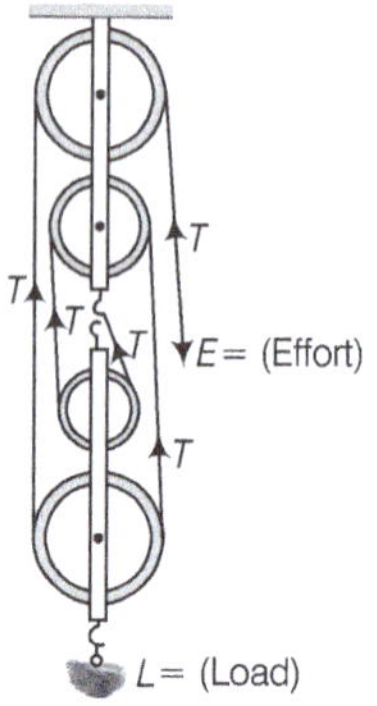

(ii) Given, VR = 4, Load $L = 4T$, Effort $= T$

$$\therefore \quad MA = \frac{\text{Load}}{\text{Effort}} = \frac{4T}{T} = 4$$

52. (i) The diagram of the above arrangement is shown below

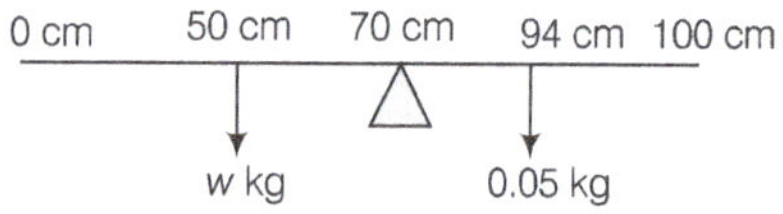

(ii) Let w be the weight of the scale.

By principle of moments, we get

$$w \times (70 - 50) = 0.05\ (94 - 70)$$

$$\Rightarrow \quad w \times 20 = 0.05 \times 24$$

$$\Rightarrow \quad w = \frac{0.05 \times 24}{20} = 0.06 \text{ kg}$$

53. (i) The relation expressing mechanical advantage of a lever is given by

$$MA = \frac{\text{Effort arm}}{\text{Load arm}}$$

(ii) The expression for the mechanical advantage of an inclined plane is given by

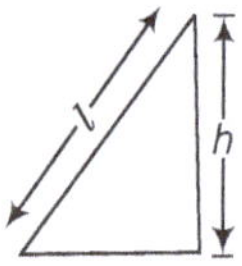

$$MA = \frac{l}{h}$$

where, l is the length of inclined plane,

h is the height of inclined plane.

(iii) (a) The weight of movable pulley with its frame is not negligible.

(b) The frictional force between pulley and string is not negligible. [$\because \eta = 100\%$]

54. (i) The labelled diagram of a block and tackle system of pulleys is shown below

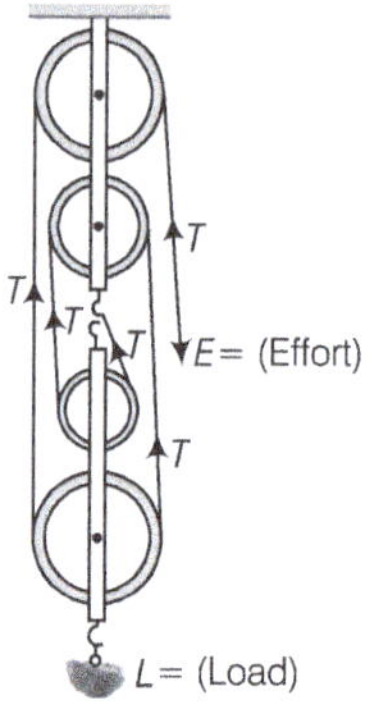

(ii) Given, Load $L = 4T$, Effort $E = T$

$$\therefore \quad \frac{\text{Load}}{\text{Effort}} = \frac{4T}{T}$$

$$\therefore \quad L = 4E$$

55. (i) The labelled diagram of the system is shown below

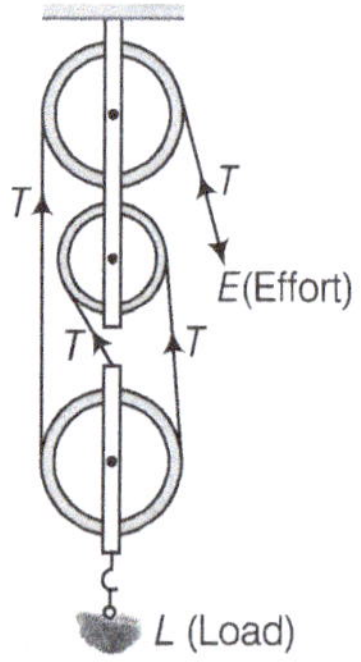

(ii) If the total weight (w) of pulleys in the lower block is in the balanced position, then

$$\text{Efficiency, } \eta = \frac{MA}{VR} = \frac{n - \frac{w}{E}}{n} = 1 - \frac{w}{nE}$$

From the expression, it is clear that for greater efficiency $\frac{w}{nE}$ should be negligible.

Thus, the pulleys in the lower block should be as light as possible.

56. (i) The fixed pulley (P_2) helps us to apply the effort in a convenient direction.

(ii) If the free end of the string moves through a distance x, then the load is raised by a distance of $\frac{x}{2}$.

(iii) Force, $F = ?$

Load, $w = 20\,\text{kgf} = 20 \times 10$

$= 200\,\text{N}$ $\quad [\because g = 10\,\text{m/s}^2]$

$\therefore \quad F \times x = w \times \frac{x}{2}$

$\Rightarrow \quad F = \frac{200}{2} = 100\,\text{N}$

$= 10\,\text{kgf}$

57. (i) (a)

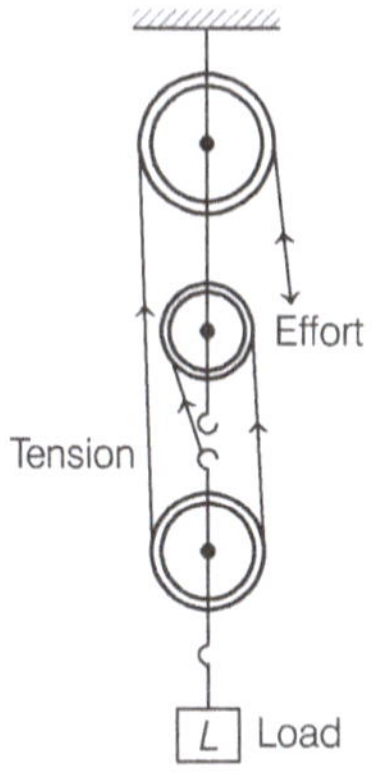

(b) Efficiency $= \frac{\text{MA}}{\text{VR}} \times 100\%$

$\Rightarrow \quad \frac{80}{100} = \frac{\text{MA}}{3}$

$\Rightarrow \quad \text{MA} = \frac{240}{100}$

$\Rightarrow \quad \text{MA} = 2.4$

(ii) (a) Clockwise moment

$= 100\,\text{gf} \times \frac{40}{2}\,\text{cm} = 2000\,\text{gf cm}$

(b) If wheel rotates in anti-clockwise direction, then

$X \times OP > 100 \times 20$

Since, $OP < 20\,\text{cm}$

$\therefore \quad X > 100\,\text{gf}$

(c) because $OP < 20$ cm

(iii) (a) Potential energy

$= mgh = 450 \times 10 \times 80$

$= 360000$ J or 360 kJ

(b) By law of conservation of energy kinetic energy of coconut at the time of striking ground $= 360000$ J or 360 kJ

58. (i)

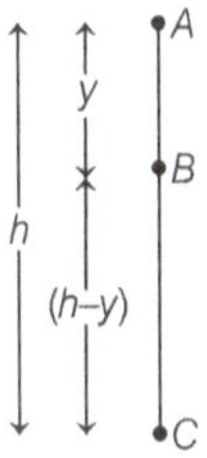

Consider a body of mass m be dropped from A

Case I (At A)

PE $= mgh$

KE $= 0$

Total energy $= mgh$

Case II (At B)

Applying, $v^2 = u^2 + 2as$

Velocity at B can be obtained as

$v^2 = (0)^2 + 2gy$

$\text{KE} = \frac{1}{2}mv^2 = \frac{1}{2}m \times 2gy$

$\text{KE} = mg \times y$

$\text{PE} = mg(h - y)$

$\text{TE} = mgy + mg(h - y)$

$= mg(y + h - y)$

$\text{TE} = mgh$ ...(ii)

Case III (At C)

Velocity can be obtained as

$v^2 = (0)^2 + 2gh$

$$KE = \frac{1}{2}mv^2 = \frac{1}{2}m(2gh)$$

$$KE = mgh$$

$$PE = 0$$

$$TE = mgh \quad ...(iii)$$

From Eqs. (i), (ii) and (iii), we can conclude that total energy of a freely falling body remains same.

(ii)

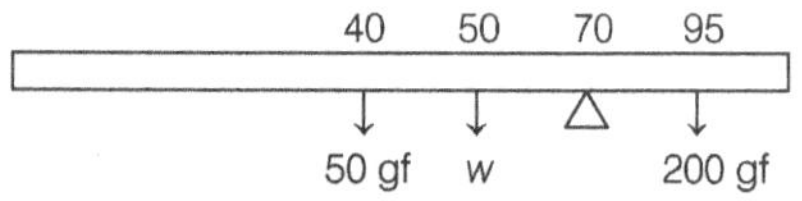

Let the weight of metre rod be w gf.

Applying principle of moments,

Clockwise moment = Anti-clockwise moment

$$200(95-70) = 50(70-40) + w(70-50)$$

$$200 \times 25 = 50 \times 30 + w \times 20$$

$$5000 = 1500 + w \times 20$$

$$20 \times w = 3500$$

$$w = \frac{3500}{20} = 175 \text{ gf}$$

(iii) Given, VR = 4

Efficiency, $\eta = 90\%$

Mechanical Advantage (MA)

$$= \eta \times VR = \frac{90}{100} \times 4 = 3.6$$

MA = 3.6

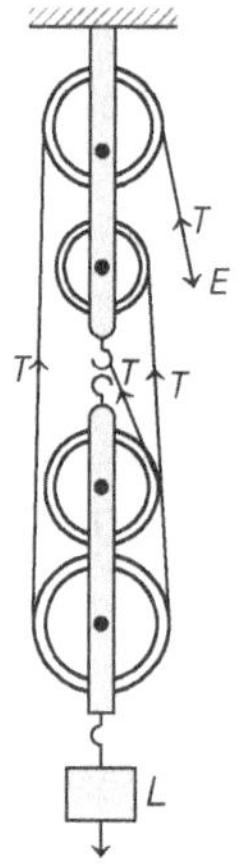

CHAPTER TEST

01 Mark Questions

1 If the angle between force and displacement is 0°, then work done is

(a) 0 (b) $F \cdot s$

(c) F/s (d) None of these

2 A body of mass 50 kg has a momentum of 3000 kg-m/s. Calculate its kinetic energy and velocity.

(a) 90000 J and 60 m/s

(b) 900 J and 60 m/s

(c) 90000 J and 6 m/s

(d) 6000 J and 630 m/s

3 An electric heater of power 3 W is used for 10 h, how much energy does it consume?

(a) 300 kWh (b) 1.08×10^5 J

(c) Both a and b (d) 30 erg

4 Mechanical advantage of a machine is

(a) effort × load (b) load × effort

(c) load × effort (d) None of these

5 A pump of 200 W power is lifting 2 kg water per second from an average depth of 10 m. The velocity with which water comes out of the pump is (Take, $g = 9.8\ \text{ms}^{-2}$)

(a) 2 ms^{-1} (b) 2.5 ms^{-1}

(c) 4 ms^{-1} (d) 10.2 ms^{-1}

02 Marks Questions

6 Define work and state its SI unit.

7 Write a relation among mechanical advantage, velocity ratio and efficiency.

8 How can you define the term power? State its SI unit.

9 Give two reasons why the efficiency of a single movable pulley system is not 100%.

10 A body is dropped from a height h above the ground. Draw a graph showing variation of both kinetic energy and potential energy with height.

Structured Questions

11 (i) Differentiate between the potential energy and the kinetic energy **(3)**

(ii) Write transformation of energy in

(a) solar cell

(b) electric iron

(c) induction cooker **(3)**

(iii) A boy X can run with a speed of 8 ms^{-1} against the frictional force of 10 N and another Y can move with a speed of 3 ms^{-1} against the frictional force of 20 N. Find the ratio of powers of X and Y. **(4)**

12 (i) Explain, how do the work is related to direction of force and displacement. **(3)**

(ii) Mention the name of three forms of kinetic energy and give one example of each form. **(3)**

(iii) A fire tongs has its arms 30 cm long. It is used to lift a coal of weight 2 kgf by applying an effort at distance 20 cm from the fulcrum. Find the following

(a) the mechanical advantage of fire tongs and

(b) the effort needed. **(4)**

Answers

1. (b) **2.** (a) **3.** (b) **4.** (b) **5.** (a)

11. (iii) 4 : 3

12. (iiii) (a) 0.66 (b) 3 kgf

03

Refraction of Light

TREND ANALYSIS 4 YEARS

		Average No. of Questions Across all Sets				
		Types of Questions	2024	2023	2020	2019
TOPIC 01	Refraction of Light at Plane Surfaces	1 Mark	–	–	–	–
		2 Marks	–	–	3	1
		3 Marks	2	–	1	1
		4 Marks	1	–	–	–
TOPIC 02	Total Internal Reflection	1 Mark	–	1	–	2
		2 Marks	–	–	–	–
		3 Marks	1	3	1	–
		4 Marks	–	–	–	–

TOPIC 1

Refraction of Light at Plane Surfaces

The change in direction of light when it passes from one medium to another obliquely is called **refraction of light**.

It has been found that

(i) When a ray of light travels from a rarer medium to a denser medium, it bends towards the normal.

i.e. $\angle r < \angle i$

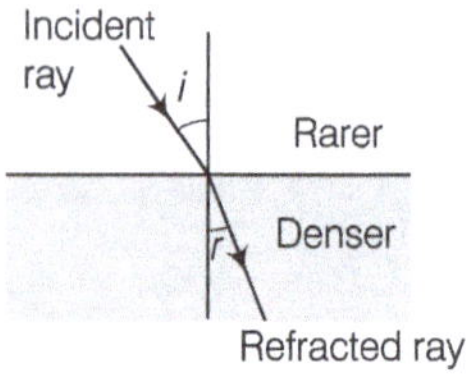

(ii) When a ray of light travels from a denser medium to rarer medium, it bends away from the normal.

i.e. $\angle r > \angle i$

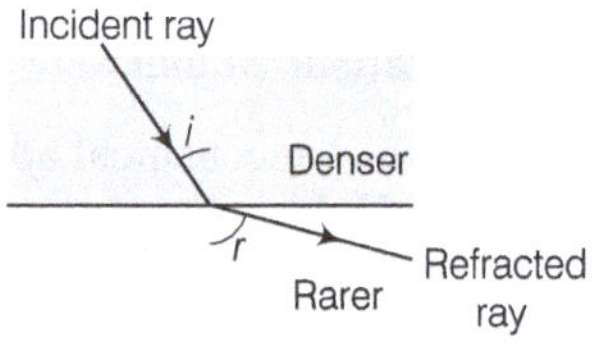

(iii) The ray of light which is incident normally on the surface separating the two media, passes undeviated.

i.e. $\angle i = \angle r = 0°$

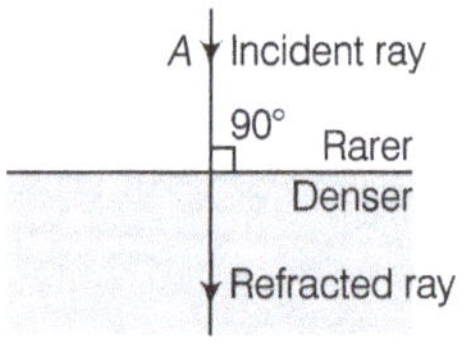

Causes of Refraction

The speed of light is different in different media. It is lesser in denser medium and greater in rarer medium. So, when light enters a denser medium, its speed reduces and it bends towards the normal and when it enters rarer medium, its speed increases and it bends away from the normal.

Refracted Beam has Change in Speed v, Direction and Wavelength λ, While its Frequency ν Remains Constant

- When a ray of light passes through a rarer to a denser medium, the speed of light (c) decreases, while if it passes from a denser to a rarer medium, the speed of the light increases.
- Due to change in speed of light is passing from one medium to another, the direction of ray of light changes except for $\angle i = 0$.
- The frequency of light depends on the source of light, so it does not change on refraction.
- Due to refraction of light, the wavelength also changes, because its frequency remains unchanged.
- The relation between speed of light (c), frequency (f) and wavelength (λ) is given by

$$\boxed{c = f\lambda}$$

Value of speed of light in air/vacuum $= 3 \times 10^8$ m/s
Value of speed of light in water $= 2.25 \times 10^8$ m/s
Value of speed of light in glass $= 2.00 \times 10^8$ m/s

Laws of Refraction

(i) **First law** The incident ray, the refracted ray and the normal at the point of incidence, all lie in the same plane.

(ii) **Second law** The ratio of sine of angle of incidence to the sine of angle of refraction is constant for a given pair of media. This constant is known as refractive index of the second medium w.r.t. first medium. It is expressed as ${}_1\mu_2 = \frac{\sin i}{\sin r} = \text{constant}$

This is also known as **Snell's law.**

Relation between Refractive Index and Velocity of Light

The refractive index of the medium is the ratio of the velocity of light in vacuum (or air) to the velocity of light in that medium.

$$\mu = \frac{\text{Velocity of light in vacuum } (c)}{\text{Velocity of light in medium } (v)}$$

Relation between Refractive Index and Wavelength

$$\mu = \frac{\text{Speed of light in air } (c)}{\text{Speed of light in medium } (v)} = \frac{f\lambda_0}{f\lambda}$$

$$\Rightarrow \quad \mu = \frac{\lambda_0}{\lambda} \Rightarrow \lambda = \frac{\lambda_0}{\mu}$$

or $$\lambda \propto \frac{1}{\mu} \text{ or } \mu \propto \frac{1}{\lambda}$$

where, λ = wavelength of the light in air

and μ = refractive index of medium.

Principle of Reversibility of Light

This principle states that, the path of light ray is reversible.

For light ray moving from rarer medium 1 to denser medium 2, incidence angle is i and angle of refraction is r.

According to Snell's law,

$${}_1\mu_2 = \frac{\sin i}{\sin r} \quad \ldots \text{(i)}$$

Suppose a plane mirror is placed perpendicular to the path of ray OB. This reverses the ray along its own path in this case, angle of incidence is r and angle of refraction is i.

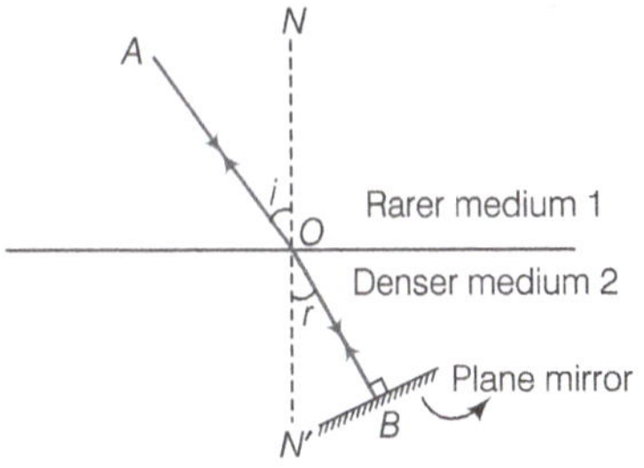

According to Snell's law,

$${}_2\mu_1 = \frac{\sin r}{\sin i} \quad \ldots \text{(ii)}$$

On multiplying Eqs. (i) and (ii), we get

$${}_1\mu_2 \times {}_2\mu_1 = \frac{\sin i}{\sin r} \times \frac{\sin r}{\sin i} = 1$$

$$\therefore \quad {}_1\mu_2 = \frac{1}{{}_2\mu_1}$$

This is known as reversibility principle.

Refraction of Light Through a Glass Slab

When a light ray enters in a glass slab, then the emergent ray is parallel to the incident ray but it is shifted sideward slightly. In this case, refraction takes place twice, first when ray of light enters glass slab from air and second when ray of light exits from glass slab to air.

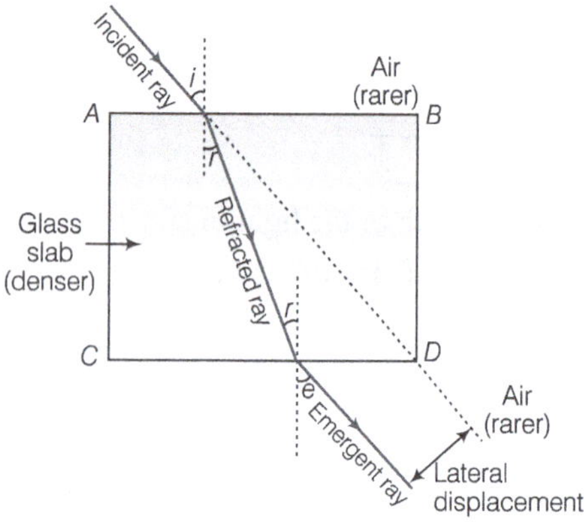

So, the ray emerges parallel to incident ray but shifted sideward slightly.

where, i = Angle of incidence, r = Angle of refraction and e = Angle of emergence.

Lateral Displacement

The perpendicular separation between the incident ray and the emergent ray is called lateral displacement. The lateral displacement depends on

(i) the thickness of the glass block.

(ii) the angle of incidence.

(iii) the refractive index of glass.

Multiple Images in Thick Glass Plate/Mirror

If a pin A is placed in front of a thick plane glass plate/thick mirror and is viewed obliquely, a number of images are seen. Out of all these images, the second image A_2 is the brightest while others are of diminishing brightness.

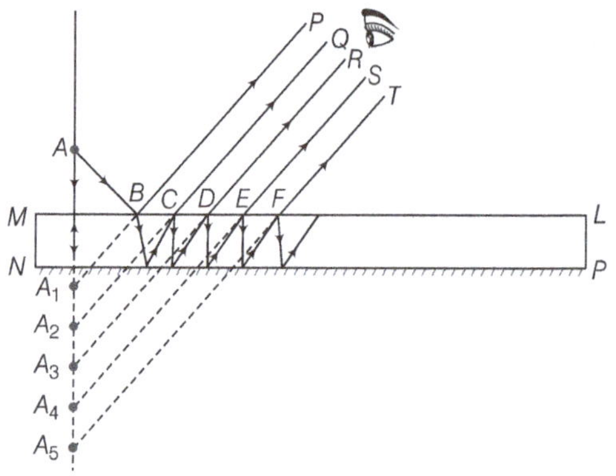

Refraction of Light Through a Prism

Prism is a transparent refracting medium bound by two plane surfaces, inclined to each other at certain angle (60° or 45°) as shown in the adjacent figure.

It has two triangular bases and three rectangular lateral surfaces. The angle between two lateral surfaces is called **angle of prism** (A).

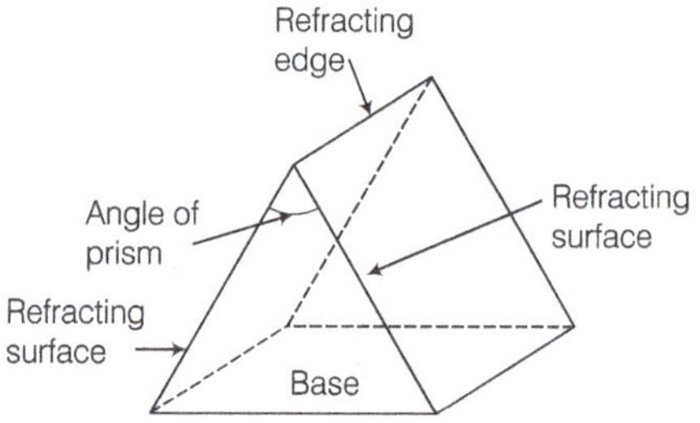

The figure below shows refraction through a prism.

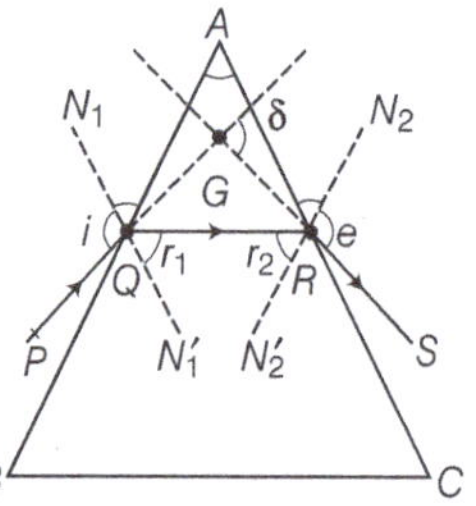

Sectional view of a prism

where, PQ = Incident ray,

QR = Refracted ray

RS = Emergent ray, $\angle A$ = Angle of prism

$\angle i_1$ = Angle of incidence, $\angle r_1$, $\angle r_2$ = Angles of refraction

$\angle e$ = Angle of emergence

and $\angle \delta$ = Angle of deviation.

NOTE When a ray of light passes through a prism, it bends towards the thicker part of the prism.

Angle of Deviation (δ)

It is the angle by which the emergent ray (produced backward) makes with the incident ray (produced forward). It depends upon the angle of prism.

Different Relations of Angle in the Prism

The different relations of angle in the prism are as follows

(i) $\delta = (i + e) - (r_1 + r_2)$

(ii) $i + e = A + \delta$

(iii) $r_1 + r_2 = A$

where, i = Angle of incidence,
e = Angle of emergence,
δ = Angle of deviation,
A = Angle of prism and
r_1, r_2 = Angles of refraction.

The relation between angle of incidence and angle of deviation can be represented through the graph as given below.

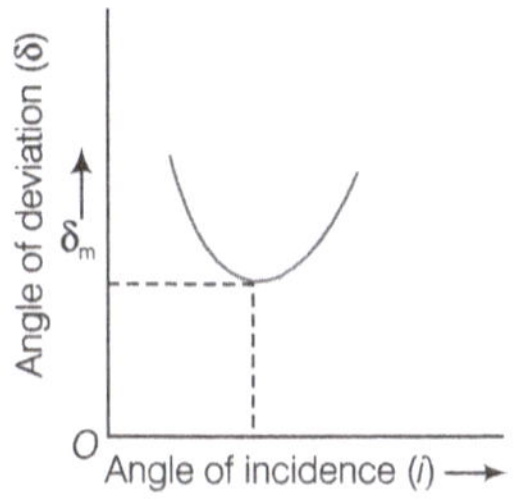

Angle of Minimum Deviation

In the position of minimum deviation, the refracted ray inside the prism travels parallel to its base, if the prism is equilateral.

Thus, the position of minimum deviation is

$$\delta = \delta_{min}, i = e = i$$

Then, the equation is $i + e = A + \delta$

$$\therefore \quad \boxed{\delta_{min} = 2i - A}$$

Relation between deviation angle (δ) and refractive index of prism material (μ)

$$\boxed{\delta = (\mu - 1) A}$$

Simple Applications

Real and Apparent Depth of Objects in Water

According to the situation shown in the figure,

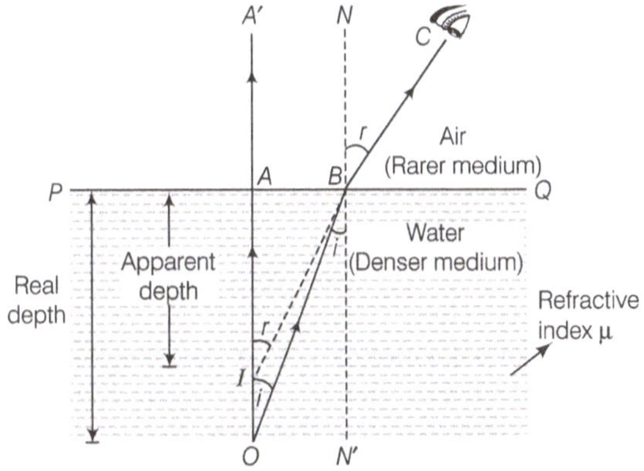

$$\text{Refractive index } \mu = \frac{OA}{IA} = \frac{\text{Real depth}}{\text{Apparent depth}}$$

$$\Rightarrow \text{Apparent depth} = \frac{\text{Real depth}}{\mu}$$

$$\text{Shift } (OI) = \text{Real depth} - \text{Apparent depth}$$

$$\Rightarrow \text{Shift} = \text{Real depth} \times \left(1 - \frac{1}{\mu}\right)$$

Apparent Bending of a Stick Under Water

Consider a straight stick ABO, which is placed obliquely in water. The portion of the stick OB under water appears to be shortened and raised up as LB. This is due to refraction of light passing from water to air.

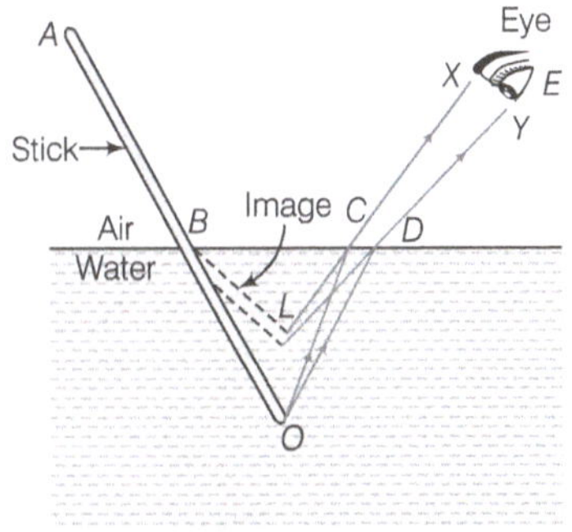

The rays of light coming from tip O of the stick when passing from water to air, bend away from the normal and appear to be coming from a point L, which is the virtual image of the point O. It is true for every point of the stick inside the water.

PYQs Previous Years Questions

1 Mark Questions

1. When a ray of light travels normal to the given surface, then the angle of refraction is **(ICSE SQP 2023)**
   (a) 180° (b) 90°
   (c) 0° (d) 45°

2. While entering from medium *A* to medium *B* if light slows down, then **(ICSE SQP 2023)**
   (a) $\angle i < \angle r$ (b) $\angle i = \angle r$
   (c) $\angle i > \angle r$ (d) $\angle i \leq \angle r$

3. The ratio of velocities of light of wavelength 400 nm and 800 nm in a vacuum is **(ICSE 2022 Sem-I)**
   (a) 1 : 1 (b) 1 : 2
   (c) 2 : 1 (d) 1 : 3

4. The refractive index of a diamond is 2.4. It means that, **(ICSE 2022 Sem-I)**
   (a) the speed of light in vacuum is equal to $\frac{1}{2.4}$ times the speed of light in diamond
   (b) the speed of light in diamond is 2.4 times the speed of light in vacuum
   (c) the speed of light in vacuum is 2.4 times the speed of light in diamond
   (d) the wavelength of light in diamond is 2.4 times the wavelength of light in vacuum

5. A ray of light *IM* is incident on a glass slab *ABCD* as shown in the figure. The emergent ray for this incident ray is **(ICSE 2022 Sem-I)**

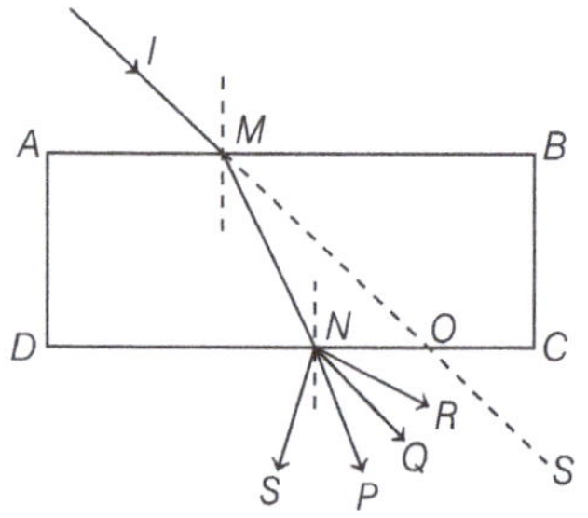

   (a) *NQ* (b) *NR*
   (c) *NP* (d) *NS*

6. Choose the correct statement with respect to refraction of light. **(ICSE SQP 2022 Sem-I)**
   (a) The frequency always changes when light enters from one optical medium to another.
   (b) Absorption of light when it strikes the surface of a medium is refraction.
   (c) Speed of light changes when it enters from one optical medium to another of different optical density.
   (d) Speed of light does not change when it enters from one optical medium to another of different optical density.

7. When a light ray enters from a denser medium to a rarer medium **(ICSE SQP 2022 Sem-I)**
   (a) The light ray bends towards the normal.
   (b) Angle of incidence is less than angle of refraction.
   (c) Speed of light decreases.
   (d) Speed of light remains unchanged.

8. In the diagram shown below **(ICSE SQP 2021)**

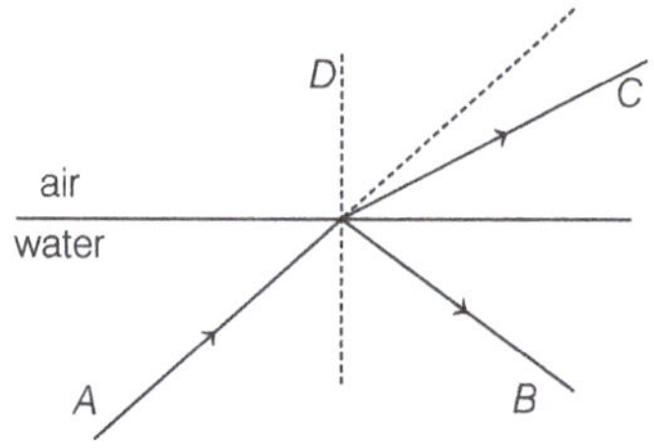

   (a) *B* is incident ray and *C* is refracted ray.
   (b) *A* is incident ray and *B* is refracted ray.
   (c) *C* is incident ray and *B* is refracted ray.
   (d) *A* is incident ray and *C* is refracted ray.

9. Name one factor that affects the lateral displacement of light as it passes through a rectangular glass slab. **(ICSE 2015)**

10. Does the depth of a tank of water appear to change or remain the same when viewed normally from above? **(ICSE 2012)**

11. How does the speed of light in glass change on increasing the wavelength of light? **(ICSE 2007)**

2 Marks Questions

12. A pond appears to be 2.7 m deep. If the refractive index of water is $\frac{4}{3}$, find the actual depth of the pond. **(ICSE 2020)**

13. Complete the path of the monochromatic light ray *AB* incident on the surface *PQ* of the equilateral glass prism *PQR* till it emerges out of the prism due to refraction. **(ICSE 2020)**

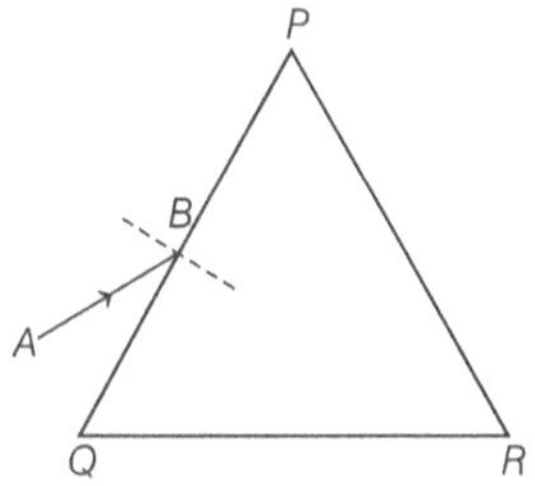

14. A ray of light falls normally on a rectangular glass slab. Draw a ray diagram showing the path of the ray till it emerges out of the slab. **(ICSE 2020)**

15. (i) What is the relation between the refractive index of water with respect to air ($_a\mu_w$) and the refractive index of air with respect to water ($_w\mu_a$)?
    (ii) If the refractive index of water with respect to air ($_a\mu_w$) is $\frac{5}{3}$. Calculate the refractive index of air with respect to water ($_w\mu_a$). **(ICSE 2019)**

16. (i) Why is the ratio of the velocities of light of wavelengths 4000 Å and 8000 Å in vacuum 1 : 1 ?
    (ii) Which of the above wavelengths has a higher frequency? **(ICSE 2018)**

17. How is the refractive index of a material related to
    (i) real and apparent depth?
    (ii) velocity of light in vacuum or air and the velocity of light in a given medium? **(ICSE 2017, 11)**

18. Draw a ray diagram to show the refraction of a monochromatic ray through a prism when it suffers minimum deviation. **(ICSE 2017)**

19. Calculate the refractive index of a liquid with respect to air applying Snell's law (use geometric construction).

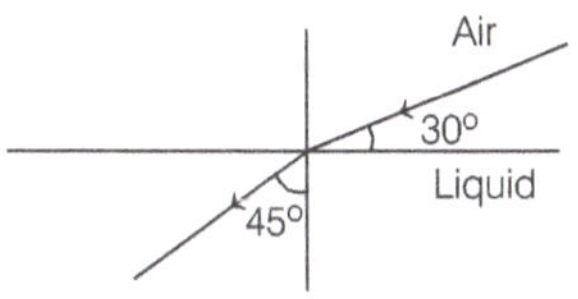

20. When a ray of light passes from air to glass, for what angle of incidence, the ray will not be deviated. **(ICSE SQP 2017)**

21. Draw a ray diagram to illustrate how a ray of light incident obliquely on one face of a rectangular glass slab of uniform thickness emerges. **(ICSE SQP 2017)**

22. A coin at the bottom of a trough containing water to a depth of 15 cm appears to be 3.75 cm raised above from the bottom. Calculate the refractive index of water. **(ICSE SQP 2017)**

> **KEY idea**
> You can find the value of refractive index (μ) with the help of folllowing formula, $\mu = \frac{\text{Real depth}}{\text{Apparent depth}}$

23. State the dependence of angle of deviation
    (i) on the refractive index of the material of the prism.
    (ii) on the wavelength of light. **(ICSE 2016)**

24. The speed of light in glass is 2×10^5 km/s. What is the refractive index of glass? **(ICSE 2015)**

25. Draw the diagram given below and clearly show the path taken by the emergent ray. **(ICSE 2014)**

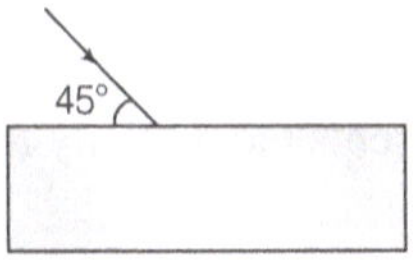

26. (i) A ray of light passes from water to air. How does speed of light change?
    (ii) Which colour of light travels fastest in any medium except air? **(ICSE 2014)**

27. Light passes through a rectangular glass slab and through a triangular glass prism. In what way, does the direction of the two emergent beams differ and why? **(ICSE 2014)**

28. A ray of light is moving from a rarer medium to a denser medium and strikes a plane mirror placed at 90° to the direction of the ray as shown in the diagram.

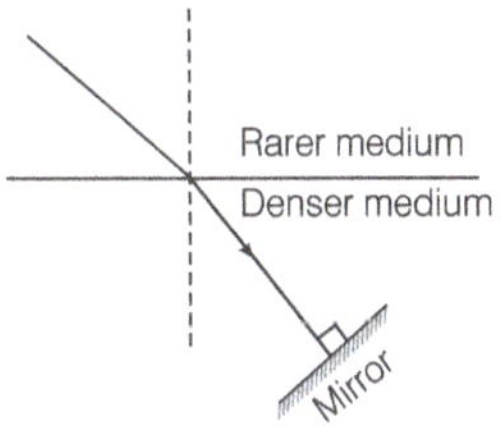

(i) Copy the diagram and mark arrows to show the path of the ray of light after it is reflected from the mirror.

(ii) Name the principle you have used to mark the arrow to show the direction of the ray. **(ICSE 2013)**

29. (i) The refractive index of glass with respect to air is 1.5. What is the value of the refractive index of air with respect to glass?

(ii) A ray of light is incident as a normal ray on the surface of separation of two different mediums. What is the value of the angle of incidence in this case? **(ICSE 2013)**

30. A ray of light incident at an angle of incidence *i* passes through an equilateral glass prism such that the refracted ray inside the prism is parallel to its base and emerges from the prism at an angle of emergence *e*.

(i) How is the angle of emergence *e* related to the angle of incidence *i*?

(ii) What can you say about the value of the angle of deviation in such a situation? **(ICSE 2012)**

31. (i) Define the term refractive index of a medium in terms of velocity of light.

(ii) A ray of light moves from a rarer medium to a denser medium as shown in the diagram alongside. Write down the number of the ray which represents the partially reflected ray. **(ICSE 2012)**

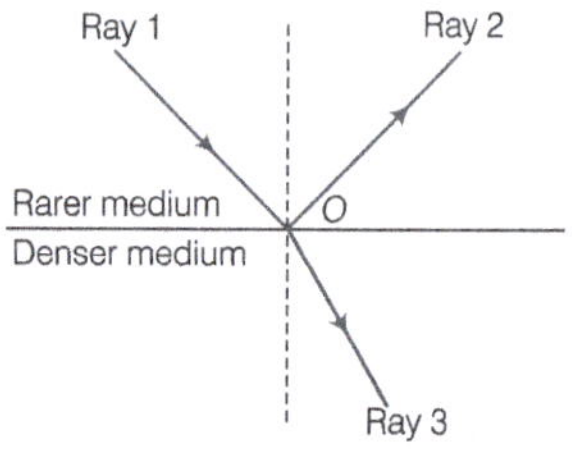

32. A ray of monochromatic light enters in a liquid from air as shown in the diagram given below.

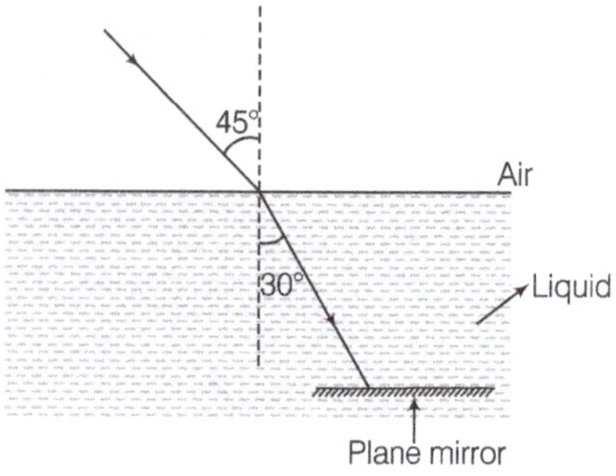

(i) Copy the diagram and show in the diagram the path of the ray of light after it strikes the mirror and re-enters the medium of air.

(ii) Mark in your diagram, the two angles on the surface of separation, when the ray of light moves out from the liquid to air. **(ICSE 2011)**

33. In the given diagram, *PQ* is a ray of light incident on a rectangular glass block.

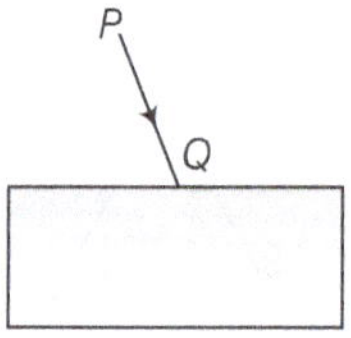

(i) Copy the diagram and complete the path of the ray of light through the glass block. In your diagram, mark the angle of incidence by letter *i* and the angle of emergence by the letter *e*.

(ii) How are the angles *i* and *e* related to each other? **(ICSE 2011)**

34. The refractive index of diamond is 2.42. What is meant by this statement? **(ICSE 2010)**

35. (i) What is meant by refraction of light?

(ii) What is the cause of refraction of light? **(ICSE 2010)**

36. A ray of light strikes the surface of a rectangular glass block such that the angle of incidence is (i) 0° and (ii) 42°. Sketch a diagram to show the approximate path taken by the ray in each case as it passes through the glass block and emerges. **(ICSE 2009)**

37. (i) A monochromatic beam of light of wavelength λ passes from air into a glass block. Write an expression to show the relation between the speed of light in air and the speed of light in glass.

(ii) As the ray of light passes from air to glass, state how the wavelength of light changes. Does it increase, decrease or remain constant? **(ICSE 2008)**

38. The velocity of light in diamond is 121000 km/s. What is its refractive index? (Take, velocity of light in air is 3×10^8 m/s) **(ICSE 2003)**

3 Marks Questions

39. (i) (a) Refractive index of glass with respect to water is $\frac{9}{8}$. Find the refractive index of water with respect to glass.

(b) Name the principle used to find the value in part (a).

(c) If we change the temperature of water, then will the ratio $\frac{9}{8}$ remain the same ? Write Yes or No.

(ii) Light travels a distance of $10x$ units ion time t_1 in vacuum and it travels a distance of x units in time t_2 in a denser medium. Using this information, answer the question that follows.

(a) Light covers a distance of $20x$ units in time t_1 in diamond. State true or false.

(b) Calculate the refractive index of the medium in terms of t_1 and t_2. **(ICSE 2024)**

40. The diagram (not drawn to the scale) below shows the graphical relation between angle of deviation and angle of incidence, when light passes through a triangular prism of angle 62° of a certain glass material.

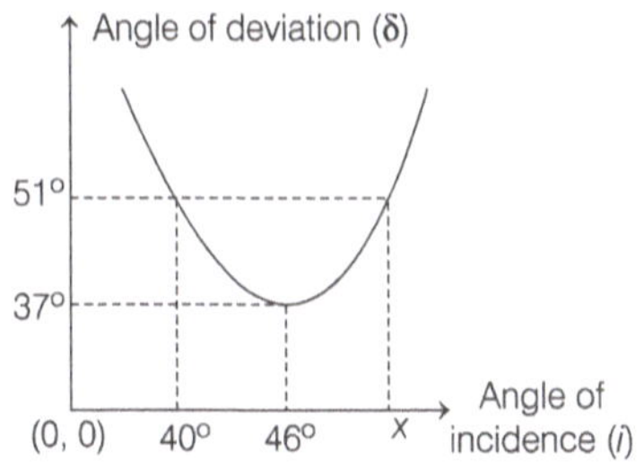

(i) State the angle of minimum deviation of this prism and the corresponding angle of incidence.

(ii) Calculate the value of X. **(ICSE SQP 2023)**

41. A diver in water looks obliquely at an object AB in air.

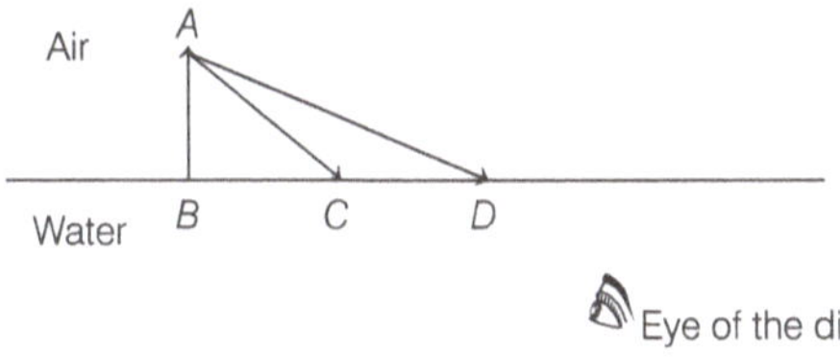

(i) Does the object appear taller, shorter or of the same size to the diver?

(ii) Show the path of two rays AC and AD starting from the tip of the object as it travels towards the diver in water and hence obtain the image of the object. **(ICSE 2020)**

42. How does the angle of deviation formed by a prism change with the increase in the angle of incidence? Draw a graph showing the variation in the angle of deviation with the angle of incidence at a prism surface. **(ICSE 2019)**

43. What is understood by lateral displacement? State two factors on which it depends. **(ICSE 2018)**

44. (i) Write a relationship between angle of incidence and angle of refraction for a given pair of media.

(ii) When a ray of light enters from one medium to another having different optical densities it bends. Why does this phenomenon occur?

(iii) Write one condition, where ray of light does not bend when entering in a medium of different optical density. **(ICSE 2016)**

45. (i) Can the absolute refractive index of a medium be less than one?

(ii) A coin placed at the bottom of a beaker appears to be raised by 4.0 cm. If the refractive index of water is 4/3, then find the depth of the water in the beaker. **(ICSE 2013)**

46. (i) State the laws of refraction of light.

(ii) Write a relation between the angle of incidence (i), angle of emergence (e), angle of prism (A) and angle of deviation (δ) for a ray of light passing through an equilateral prism. **(ICSE 2011)**

47. A stick partly immersed in water appears to be bent. Draw a ray diagram to show the bending of the stick when placed in water and viewed obliquely from above. **(ICSE 2010)**

48. A ray of monochromatic light is incident from air on a glass slab.

(i) Draw a labelled ray diagram showing the change in the path of the ray till it emerges from the glass slab.

(ii) Name the two rays that are parallel to each other.

(iii) Mark the lateral displacement in your diagram. **(ICSE 2010)**

4 Marks Questions

49. A monochromatic ray of light is incident on an equilateral prism placed at minimum deviation position with an angle of incidence 45° as shown an the diagram. **(ICSE 2024)**

(i) Copy the diagram and complete the path of the ray PQ.

(ii) State two factors on which the angle of deviation depends.

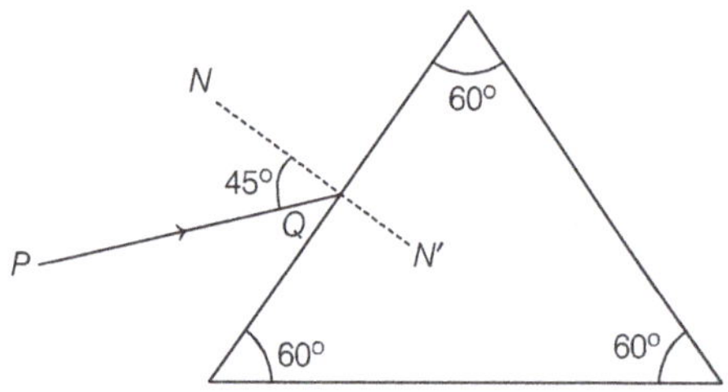

50.

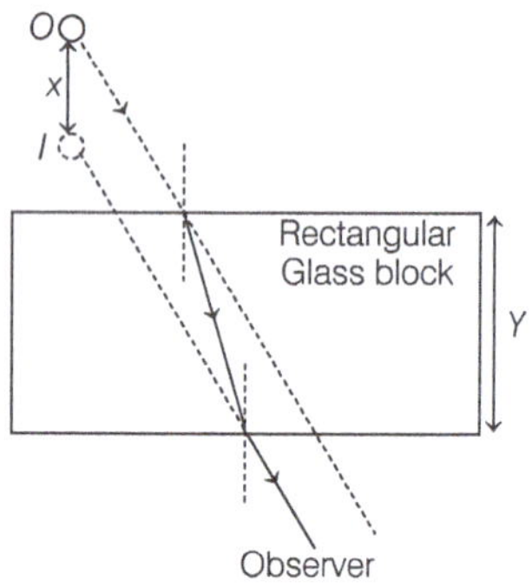

The above diagram shows that an observer sees the image of an object O at I.

(i) Name and define the phenomenon responsible for seeing the image at a different position.

(ii) State the effect on X when

(a) Y increases (b) Y decreases **(ICSE SQP 2023)**

51. Jatin puts a pencil into a glass container having water and is surprised to see the pencil in a different state.

(i) What change is observed in the appearance of the pencil?

(ii) Name the phenomenon responsible for the change.

(iii) Draw a ray diagram showing how the eye sees the pencil. **(ICSE 2015)**

52. The diagram given below shows a ray of light incident on an equilateral glass prism placed in minimum deviation position.

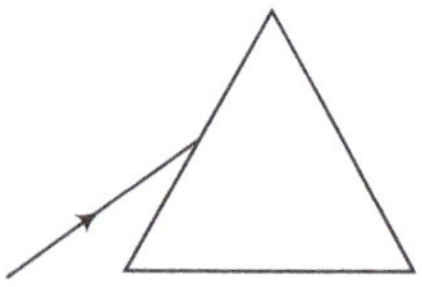

(i) Copy the diagram and complete it to show the path of the refracted ray and the emergent ray.

(ii) How are angle of incidence and angle of emergence related to each other in this position of the prism? **(ICSE 2008)**

53. (i) With the help of a well-labelled diagram, show that the apparent depth of an object such as a coin in water is less than its real depth.

(ii) How is the refractive index of water related to the real depth and the apparent depth of a column of water? **(ICSE 2007)**

54. (i) State Snell's laws.

(ii) Calculate the velocity of light in a glass block of refractive index 1.5. (Take, velocity of light in air $= 3 \times 10^8$ m/s) **(ICSE 2007, 04)**

55. (i) What is meant by refraction?

(ii) Express the refractive index μ of a medium

(a) in terms of the velocity of light.

(b) in terms of the angle of incidence i in air and the angle of refraction r in a denser medium.

(iii) If a ray of light passes from one medium to other medium without any change of direction. What can be said about the refractive indices of these media (angle i is not zero)? **(ICSE 2005)**

Structured Questions (10 Marks)

56. A monochromatic point source of light O is seen through a rectangular glass block $ABCD$. Paths of two rays, in and outside the block, are shown in the figure alongside.

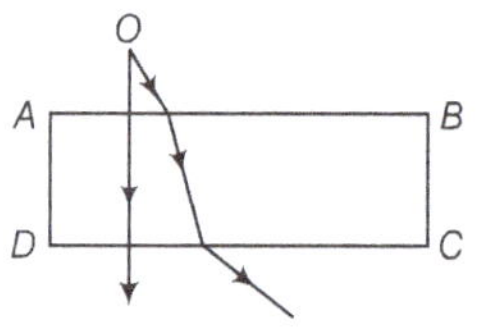

(i) Does the source at point O appear to be nearer or farther with respect to the surface AB? **(2)**

(ii) How does the shift depend on the thickness (AD or BC) of the block? **(2)**

(iii) Justify your answer with the help of an appropriate ray diagram as shown in part (ii). **(3)**

(iv) For the same rectangular glass block, which colour from the visible spectra will produce the maximum shift? **(ICSE 2003) (3)**

Explanations

1. (c) 0°

2. (c) $\angle i > \angle r$

3. (a) Since, light is an EM wave and it is the property of all electromagnetic waves that they travel with same speed equal to 3×10^8 m / s in vacuum.

   So, ratio of velocities of light having wavelength 400 nm and 800 nm in vacuum is 1: 1.

4. (c) We know that, refractive index

$$= \frac{\text{speed of light in air}}{\text{speed of light in medium}}$$

   So, speed of light in vacuum = 2.4 times speed of light in diamond.

5. (a) Here, the emergent ray will be away from the normal but is parallel to the incident ray.

   So, *NQ* will be the emergent ray.

6. (c) Speed of light changes when it enters from one optical medium to another of different optical density.

7. (b) Angle of incidence is less than angle of refraction.

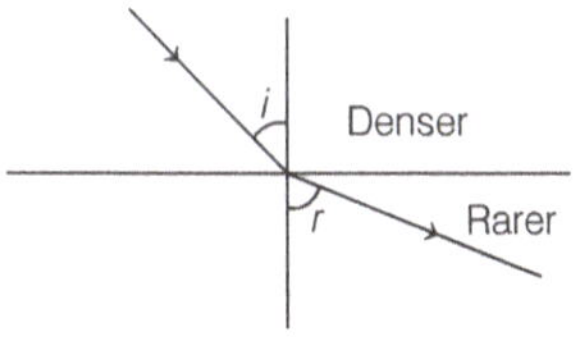

$\therefore \quad \angle i < \angle r$

8. (d) *A* is incident ray and *C* is refracted ray.

9. The lateral displacement of light while passing through a rectangular glass slab depends upon angle of incidence of the incident light.

10. No, when the depth of a tank of water is viewed normally from above, no refraction takes place. Therefore, the depth of the tank remains the same.

11. The speed of light in glass increases on increasing the wavelength of light.

12. Apparent depth of pond, $d = 2.7$ m

   Refractive index of water, $\mu = \frac{4}{3}$

   We know that, $\mu = \frac{\text{Actual depth}}{\text{Apparent depth}}$

$$\Rightarrow \quad \frac{4}{3} = \frac{\text{Actual depth}}{2.7}$$

$$\therefore \text{ Actual depth } = \frac{4}{3} \times 2.7 = 3.6 \text{ m}$$

13. The complete path of a monochromatic light *AB* is incident on the surface *PQ* of the equilateral glass prism *PQR* till it emerges out of the prism due to refraction is given below.

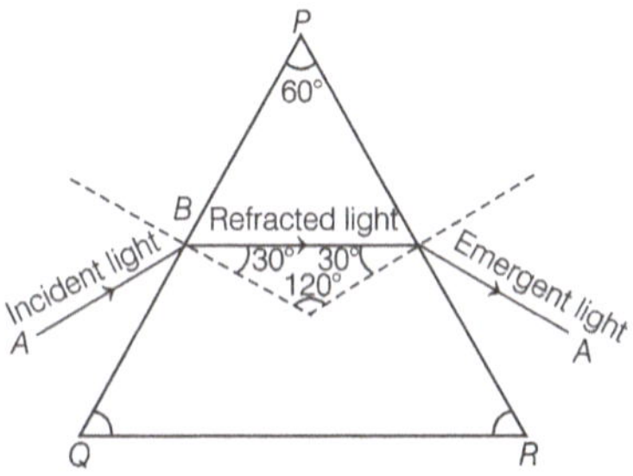

14. When a ray of light falls normally on a rectangular glass slab, then angle of incidence, $i = 0$

$$\therefore \text{ By Snell's law, } {}_a\mu_g = \frac{\sin i}{\sin r}$$

$${}_a\mu_g = \frac{\sin 0^\circ}{\sin r} = \frac{0}{\sin r}$$

$$\Rightarrow \quad {}_a\mu_g \times \sin r = 0$$

$$\therefore \quad {}_a\mu_g \neq 0,$$

$$\therefore \quad \sin r = 0 \Rightarrow r = 0^\circ$$

   Hence, when a ray of light falls normally on a rectangular glass slab, then it emerges out of the slab without any deviation which is shown in the figure.

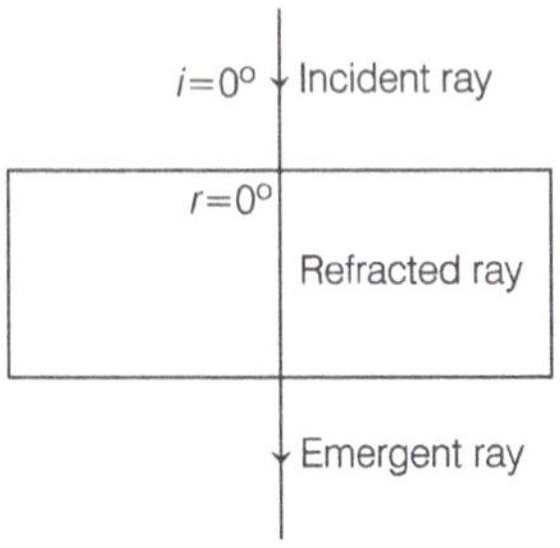

> **Concept Enhancer** A ray of light incident normally on surface separating the medium passes undeviated.

15. (i) Refractive index of water with respect to air,

$${}_a\mu_w = \frac{\mu_w}{\mu_a} \quad \ldots\text{(i)}$$

and refractive index of air with respect to water,

$$_w\mu_a = \frac{\mu_a}{\mu_w} \quad \ldots\text{(ii)}$$

From Eqs. (i) and (ii), we get

$$_a\mu_w = \frac{1}{_w\mu_a}$$

(ii) Refractive index of water with respect to air,

$$_a\mu_w = \frac{1}{\text{Refractive index of air with respect to water } (_w\mu_a)}$$

Given, $_a\mu_w = \frac{5}{3}$

$\therefore$ $_a\mu_w = \frac{1}{_w\mu_a}$

$\therefore$ $_w\mu_a = \frac{3}{5}$

16. (i) The speed of light in vacuum is always constant $(3\times10^8 \text{ m/s})$ and it does not depend on wavelength or frequency.

(ii) As we know that, $v = n\lambda$, $n = \frac{v}{\lambda} \Rightarrow n \propto \frac{1}{\lambda}$

where, n = frequency, v = velocity

and λ = wavelength.

Therefore, frequency is inversely proportional to wavelength. Thus, wavelength of 4000Å will have higher frequency.

17. (i) When an object is placed under water (any denser medium), then observing it from outside the air (or a rarer medium), it appears to be raised above.

The ratio of real depth and apparent depth is equal to the refractive index of the medium.

$$\text{Refractive index, } \mu = \frac{\text{Real depth}}{\text{Apparent depth}}$$

(ii) **Relation between Refractive Index and Velocity of Light**

The refractive index of the medium is the ratio of the velocity of light in vacuum (or air) to the velocity of light in that medium.

$$\mu = \frac{\text{Velocity of light in vacuum } (c)}{\text{Velocity of light in medium } (v)}$$

18. When a ray of light passes through a prism, it bends towards the thicker part of the prism.

Let the incident ray PQ falls on the face AB of prism and emerges out from the face AC as RS.

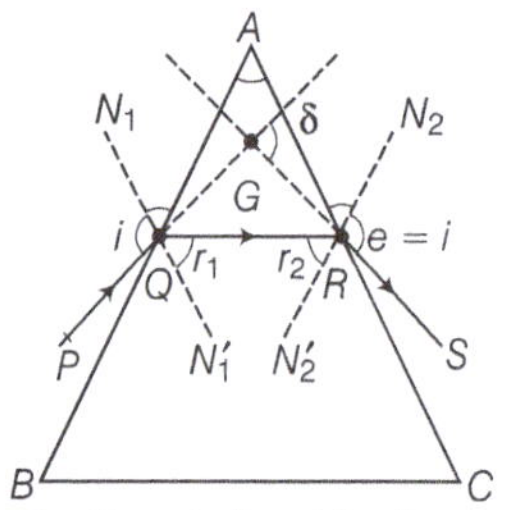

Sectional view of prism

Here,

PQ = Incident ray, QR = Refracted ray,

RS = Emergent ray, $\angle A$ = Angle of prism,

$\angle i_1$ = Angle of incidence,

$\angle r_1, \angle r_2$ = Angles of refraction,

$\angle e$ = Angle of emergence

and $\angle\delta$ = Angle of deviation.

Angle of Deviation (δ) It is the angle which the emergent ray (produced backward) makes with the incident ray (produced forward). It depends upon the angle of prism. When angle of deviation is minimum, the prism is said to be in minimum deviation position.

19. Applying Snell's law,

$$\mu_1 \sin i = \mu_2 \sin r$$

$$1\times \sin 30° = \mu_2 \sin 45°$$

$$\mu_2 = \frac{\sin 30°}{\sin 45°}$$

$$\mu_2 = \frac{1}{2}\frac{2}{\sqrt{2}}$$

$$\mu_2 = \frac{1}{\sqrt{2}}$$

$\therefore$ Refractive index of a liquid with respect to air is $\frac{1}{\sqrt{2}}$.

20. The ray will not be deviated when ray of light coincides with the normal i.e., angle of incidence is 0.

21. Refer to text on page no. 50.

22. $\text{Refractive index} = \frac{\text{Real depth}}{\text{Apparent depth}}$

$\therefore$ Apparent depth of the coin is

$$15 - 3.75 = 11.25 \text{ cm}$$

Now,

$$\text{Refractive index} = \frac{15}{11.25} = 1.33$$

$\therefore$ Refractive index of water is 1.33.

23. (i) Since, refractive index of the prism is directly proportional to the angle of deviation. So, larger the refractive index, larger will be the deviation angle.

(ii) Since, refractive index of material is inversely proportional to the wavelength of light. So, smaller the wavelength of light larger will be the deviation angle.

24. Refractive index of a material is given by

$$\mu = \frac{\text{Speed of light in air}}{\text{Speed of light in medium /material}}$$

$$\text{For glass, } \mu = \frac{3 \times 10^8 \text{ m/s}}{2 \times 10^8 \text{ m/s}} = 1.5$$

25. The emergent ray diagram is shown below

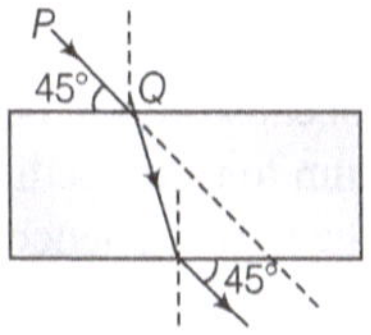

26. (i) When a ray of light passes from water to air, then it bends away from the normal and its speed increases due to increase in its wavelength.

(ii) Red colour of light travels fastest in any medium except air.

27. In a rectangular glass slab, the emergent ray is parallel to the incident ray but they are not along the same line, whereas in a prism, the emergent ray is not parallel to the incident ray. They differ, because in a glass block, the two surfaces at which refraction occurs is parallel to each other.

28. (i) The diagram is redrawn and the path of ray of light is shown below

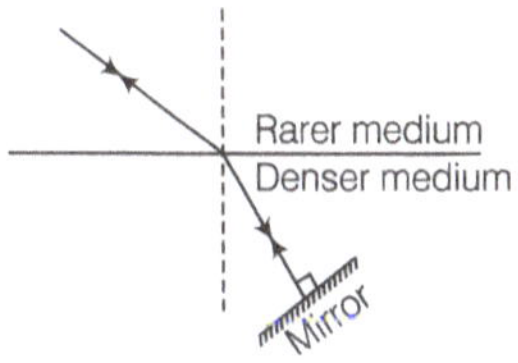

(ii) The principle of reversibility have used to mark the arrow to show the direction of the ray.

29. (i) Given, refractive index of glass w.r.t. air, ${}_a\mu_g = 1.5$. Refractive index of air w.r.t. glass, ${}_g\mu_a = ?$

$$\therefore \qquad {}_g\mu_a = \frac{1}{{}_a\mu_g} = \frac{1}{1.5}$$

$$= \frac{10}{15} = \frac{2}{3} = 0.667$$

(ii) The value of the angle of incidence in this case is zero.

30. (i) The angle of incidence $\angle i$ is equal to the angle of emergence $\angle e$.

$$\therefore \qquad \angle i = \angle e$$

(ii) Inside the prism, the refracted ray is parallel to its base and the angle of deviation is minimum in such a situation.

31. (i) The refractive index of a medium is the ratio of the speed of light in vacuum to the speed of light in that medium.

It is expressed as,

$$\mu = \frac{\text{Velocity (or speed) of light in vacuum } c}{\text{Velocity (or speed) of light in medium } v}$$

(ii) Ray 2 represents the partially reflected ray.

> **Concept Enhancer** Refractive index gives information about the direction of bending of refracted ray.

32. (i) and (ii) The following diagram shows the path of the ray of light after striking on the mirror and the two angles on the surface of separation.

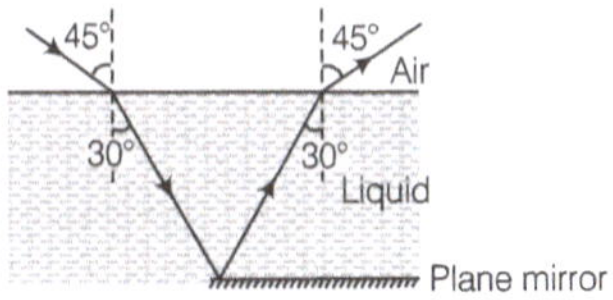

33. (i)

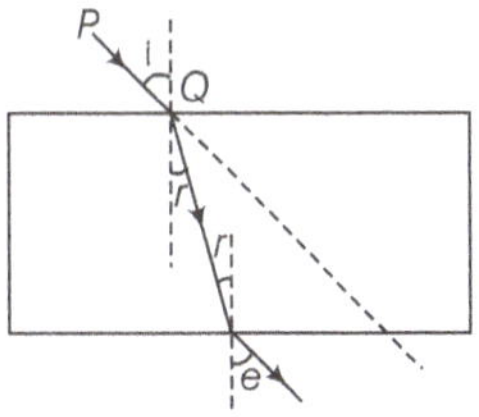

(ii) The angle of incidence $\angle i$ is equal to angle of emergent $\angle e$, i.e. $\angle i = \angle e$.

34. The refractive index of diamond is 2.42 means that the speed of light in air is 2.42 times the speed of light in diamond.

35. (i) Refraction of light is a phenomenon in which a ray of light passing from one transparent medium to another transparent medium changing its direction.

(ii) The main cause of refraction of light is due to different speeds of light in different media.

36. (i) Given, $i = 0°$

$\therefore \quad r = 0°$

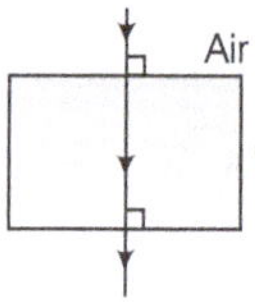

(ii) Given, $i = 42°$, $e = 42°$

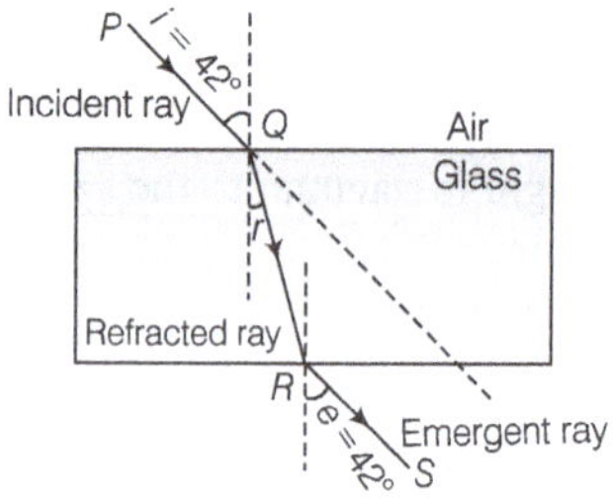

37. (i) The relation is given by

Refractive index

$$\mu = \frac{\text{Speed of light in air } (v_a)}{\text{Speed of light in glass } (v_g)}$$

But wavelength λ changes to λ', $\lambda' = \mu\lambda$

(ii) The refractive index is inversely proportional to wavelength.

i.e. $\mu \propto \frac{1}{\lambda} \Rightarrow \lambda \propto \frac{1}{\mu}$

As the refractive index of glass is more than that of air, so wavelength λ decreases.

38. Given, velocity of light in diamond,

$$v = 121000 \text{ km/s}$$
$$= 121000 \times 10^3 \text{m/s} = 121 \times 10^6 \text{ m/s}$$

Velocity of light in air, $c = 3 \times 10^8$ m/s, refractive index, $\mu = ?$

$$\therefore \quad \mu = \frac{c}{v} = \frac{3 \times 10^8}{121 \times 10^6} = 2.48$$

Common Mistake Sometimes, students use incorrect formula, $\mu = \frac{v}{c}$ in place of correct as $\mu = \frac{c}{v}$

39. (i) (a) Given, ${}^w\mu_g = \frac{9}{8} \Rightarrow {}^g\mu_w = \frac{1}{{}^w\mu_g} = \frac{1}{\frac{9}{8}} = \frac{8}{9}$

(b) Principle of reversibility (c) No

(ii) (a) False

(b) Velocity of light in vacuum, $v_1 = \frac{10x}{t_1}$

Velocity of light in denser medium, $v_2 = \frac{x}{t_2}$

Refractive index of medium, $\mu = \frac{v_1}{v_2} = \frac{\frac{10x}{t_1}}{\frac{x}{t_2}}$

$$\mu = \frac{10x}{t_1} \times \frac{t_2}{x} = \frac{10t_2}{t_1}$$

40. (i) Angle of minimum deviation $= 37°$

Corresponding angle of incidence $= 46°$

(ii) $\delta = i_1 + i_2 - A$

From the graph, $51° = 40° + X - 62°$

$$X = 73°$$

41. (i) When a diver in water looks obliquely at an object AB in air, then object AB appears taller than its actual size, because when the ray coming from denser medium to rarer medium then they deviates away from the normal, hence they make larger image.

(ii)

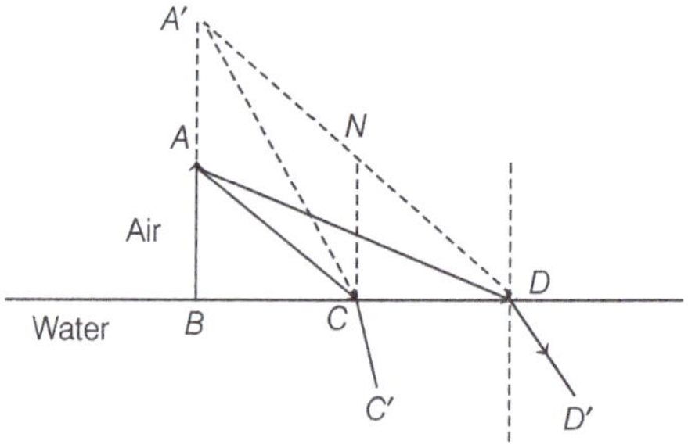

When the rays of light coming from rarer medium to denser medium, then it bends towards normal. Hence, path of rays AC and AD are shown above in figure.

The image of object AB is shown in the figure as $A'B$.

42. If the angle of incidence is increased gradually, then angle of deviation first decreases, attains a minimum value (δ_m) and then again starts increasing.

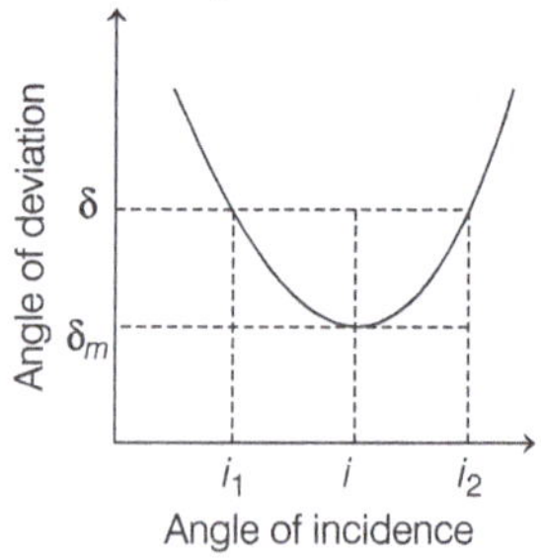

43. Refer to text on page no. 50.

44. (i) For a given pair of media, the relationship between the angle of incidence and angle of refraction is given by ${}_1\mu_2 = \dfrac{\sin i}{\sin r}$

where, i = angle of incidence,

r = angle of refraction,

${}_1\mu_2$ = refraction index of the second medium with respect to the first medium.

(ii) The phenomenon of refraction occurs, because light travels at different speeds in different medium. If a ray of light travels through air and enter a more dense medium, such as water, they slow down and bend towards the normal.

(iii) When a ray of light is incident normally to the surface, then it passes straight from one medium to another medium without any bending.

45. (i) No, the absolute refractive index of a medium can never be less than one, because the speed of light in any medium is always less than that in vacuum.

(ii) Given, shift = 4.0 cm,

Refractive index, $\mu = \dfrac{4}{3}$, real depth = ?

$\therefore \quad \text{Shift} = \text{Real depth} \times \left(1 - \dfrac{1}{\mu}\right)$

$\Rightarrow 4 = \text{Real depth} \times \left(1 - \dfrac{1}{\frac{4}{3}}\right)$

$\Rightarrow 4 = \text{Real depth} \times \left(1 - \dfrac{3}{4}\right)$

$\Rightarrow \quad 4 = \text{Real depth} \times \dfrac{1}{4}$

$\Rightarrow \quad \text{Real depth} = 16 \text{ cm}$

46. (i) The laws of refraction of light

(a) The incident ray, the refracted ray and the normal at the point of incidence all lie in the same plane.

(b) The ratio of sine of angle of incidence to the sine of angle of refraction is a constant for a pair media. This constant is known as refractive index, i.e. $\mu = \dfrac{\sin i}{\sin r}$.

(ii) For a ray of light passing through an equilateral prism have the following relation

$\angle i + \angle e = \angle A + \angle \delta$

where, the symbols have their usual meaning.

47. The ray diagram showing the bending of stick is shown below

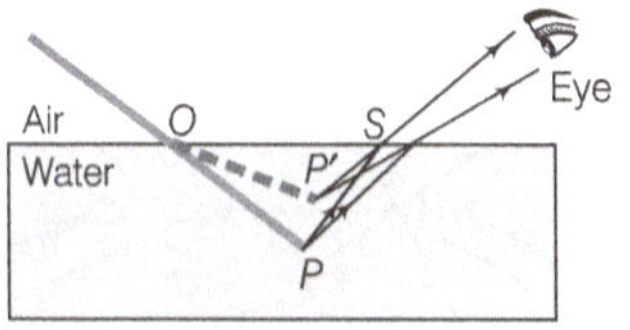

48. (i) The ray diagram is shown below

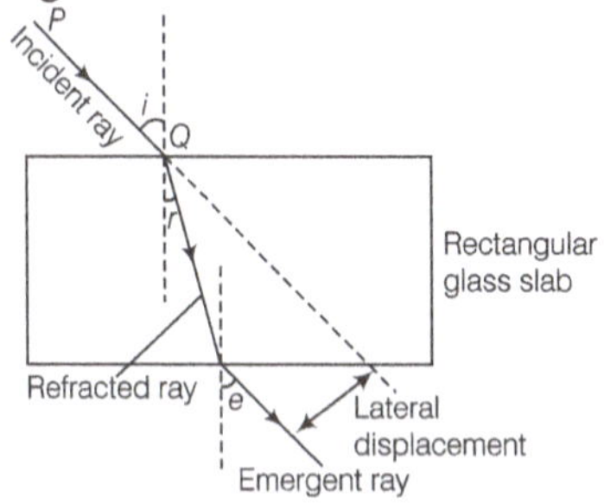

(ii) The incident ray and the emergent ray are parallel to each other.

(iii) The lateral displacement is shown in part (i).

49. (i)

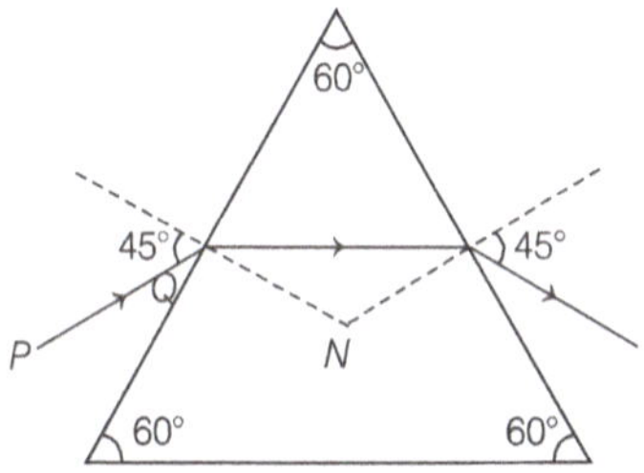

(ii) The angle of deviation depends upon

(i) Angle of incidence

(ii) Angle of prism

50. (i) Lateral displacement and it define as the perpendicular separation between the incident ray and the emergent ray is called lateral displacement.

(ii) (a) Increases (b) Decreases.

51. (i) When a pencil is dipped into a glass container having water, it appears to bend upward.

(ii) This appearance in the shape of pencil when dipped in water is due to refraction of light.

(iii) Ray diagram to show appearance of bending of pencil due to refraction of light.

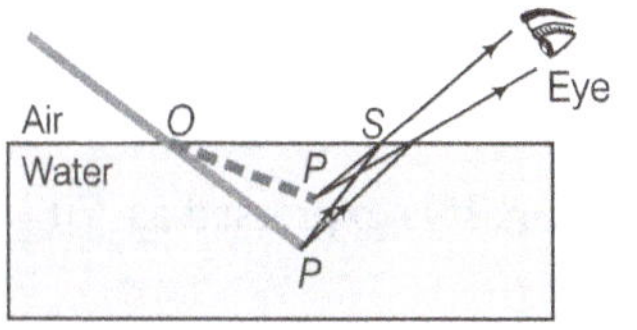

52. (i) The diagram is redrawn to show the path of refracted ray and emergent ray.

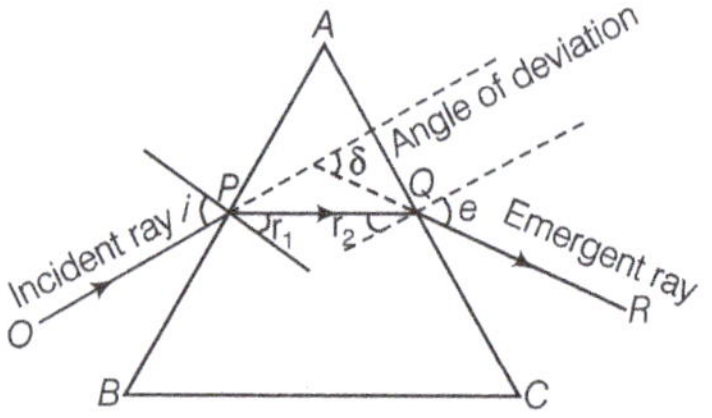

(ii) The angle of incidence $\angle i$ is equal to the angle of emergent $\angle e$.

i.e. $\angle i = \angle e$

Common Mistake In such type of question, some students do not understand the relation between angles.

53. (i) A ray from bottom of the tank A (coin) is striking normally at B goes straight.

Another ray from A striking the interface at C is refracted towards E and when produced back, it appears to come from A'. When BD and CE enter the eye, these form an image of A (coin) at A' (coin). Thus, the depth appears to be at $A'B$ instead of the actual AB.

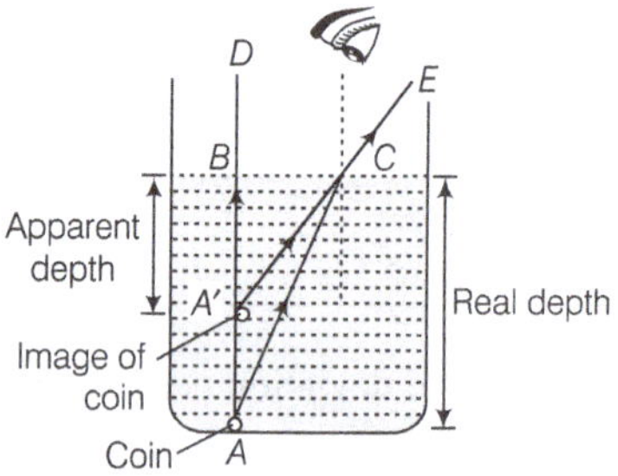

(ii) The refractive index of water related to the real depth and the apparent depth of a column of water is given by

$$\text{Refractive index } \mu = \frac{\text{Real depth}}{\text{Apparent depth}}$$

Common Mistake In such type of question, some students confused between apparent depth and lateral displacement.

54. (i) Snell's law of refraction light states that the ratio of the sine of the angle of incidence i to the sine of the angle of refraction r is always a constant for the same pair of media. This constant ratio is called refractive index of the second medium w.r.t. the first medium. It is expressed as ${}_1\mu_2 = \frac{\sin i}{\sin r}$.

(ii) Given, refractive index, $\mu = 1.5$

Velocity of light in air,

$$c = 3 \times 10^8 \text{ m/s}$$

Velocity of light in glass, $v = ?$

$$\therefore \quad \mu = \frac{c}{v}$$

$$\Rightarrow \quad v = \frac{c}{\mu} = \frac{3 \times 10^8}{1.5}$$

$$= 2 \times 10^8 \text{ m/s}$$

55. (i) When a ray of light passes from one medium to the other medium, it changes its path. This phenomenon is called refraction of light.

(ii) (a) Refractive index of second medium w.r.t. first medium,

$$ {}_1\mu_2 = \frac{\text{Velocity of light in the first medium}}{\text{Velocity of light in the second medium}}$$

(b) Refractive index of second medium w.r.t. first medium, ${}_1\mu_2 = \frac{\sin i}{\sin r}$

(iii) If a ray of light passes from one medium to other medium without any change of direction/path even when angle i is not zero, then the refractive index of two media must be equal.

56. (i) The source of light O appear to be nearer w.r.t. the surface AB.

(ii) The shift is directly proportional to the thickness of glass slab. So, the shift decreases with decrease in the thickness of glass slab.

(iii)

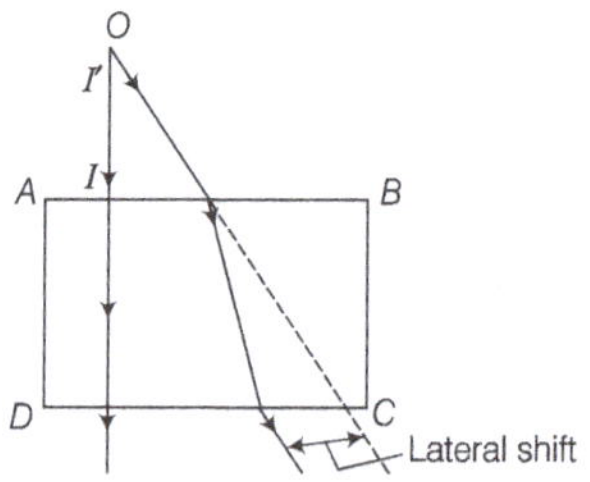

(iv) The refractive index of glass is minimum for red light and maximum for violet light , i.e. $\mu_v > \mu_r$. Therefore, for the same rectangular glass block, violet colour in the visible spectra will produce maximum shift.

TOPIC 2

Total Internal Reflection

Transmission of Light from a Denser Medium (Glass) to a Rarer Medium (Air)

When a ray of light travelling in a denser medium (glass) falls on the surface separating it from the rarer medium (air), it is partly reflected back into the denser medium and partly refracted in the rarer medium. The refracted ray bends away from the normal on the surface at the point of incidence satisfying the laws of refraction.

The following cases arises

***Case* 1 When the angle of incidence is less than critical angle, ($i < i_C$)**

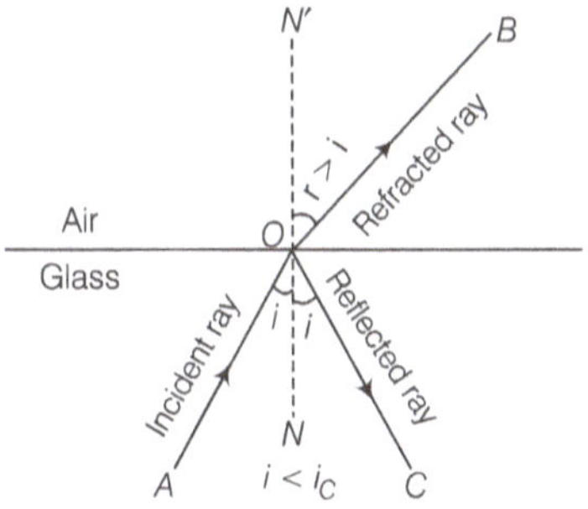

***Case* 2 When the angle of incidence is equal to critical angle, ($i = i_C$)**

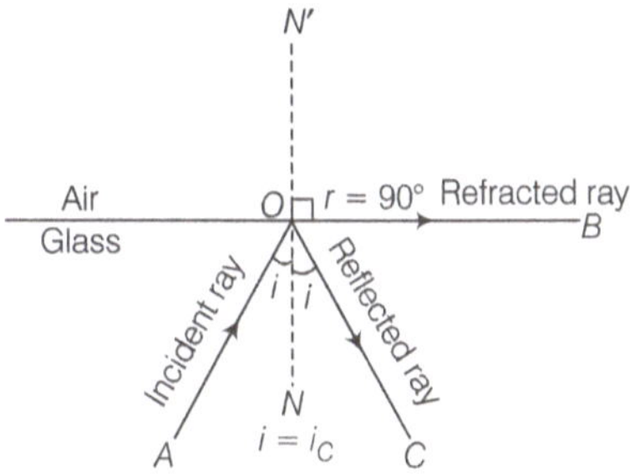

***Case* 3 When the angle of incidence is greater than critical angle, ($i > i_C$)**

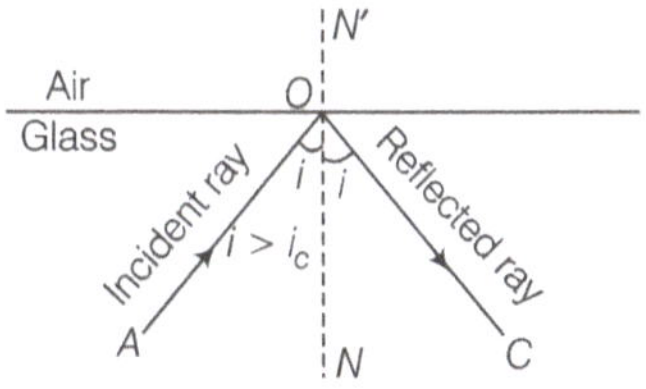

Critical Angle

It is the angle of incidence in the denser medium corresponding to which the angle of refraction in the rarer medium is 90°. It is denoted by i_C.

The critical angle is affected by the following two factors

(i) The colour of the light

(ii) The temperature

Relation between Critical Angle and Refractive Index

We know that, a refractive index of rarer medium w.r.t. denser medium, ${}_d\mu_r = \dfrac{\sin i}{\sin r}$

If $\quad i = i_C$ and $r = 90°$, then ${}_d\mu_r = \dfrac{\sin i_C}{\sin 90°}$

$$\Rightarrow \quad {}_d\mu_r = \sin i_C \Rightarrow {}_r\mu_d = \frac{1}{\sin i_C}$$

where, r is rarer medium and d is denser medium.

Total Internal Reflection

It is the phenomenon due to which a ray of light travelling in a denser medium, is incident at the surface of a rarer medium such that the angle of incidence is greater than the critical angle for the pair of media, the ray is totally reflected back into the denser medium.

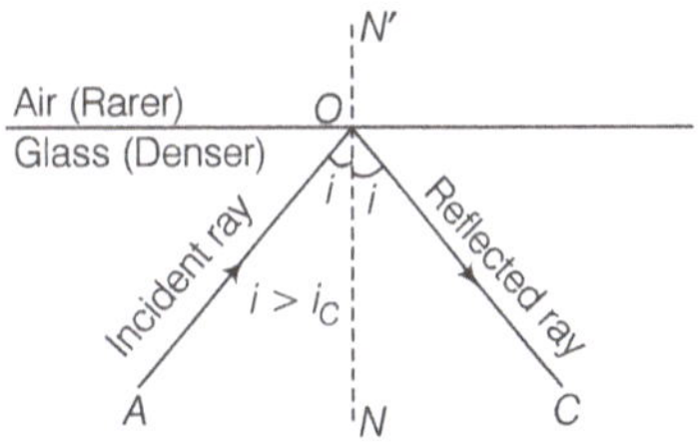

Essential Conditions for Total Internal Reflection

The necessary conditions for the total internal reflection are

(i) The light must travel from a denser medium to a rarer medium.

(ii) The angle of incidence must be greater than the critical angle for the pair of media.

Total Internal Reflection in Triangular Glass Prism

Prism of each angle is 60°, i.e. equilateral prism

A prism of each angle 60° can be used to deviate a light ray through 60° by total internal reflection.

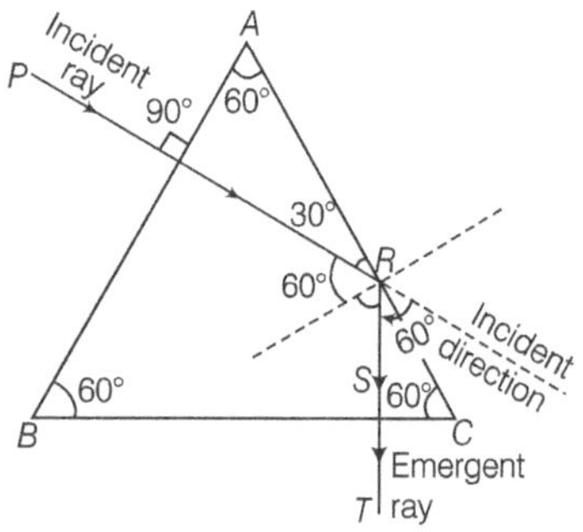

Prism of angles (45°, 45° and 90°), i.e. right angled is isosceles prism

A prism having an angle of 90° between its two refracting surfaces and the two other angles each of 45° suffers total internal reflection inside the prism.

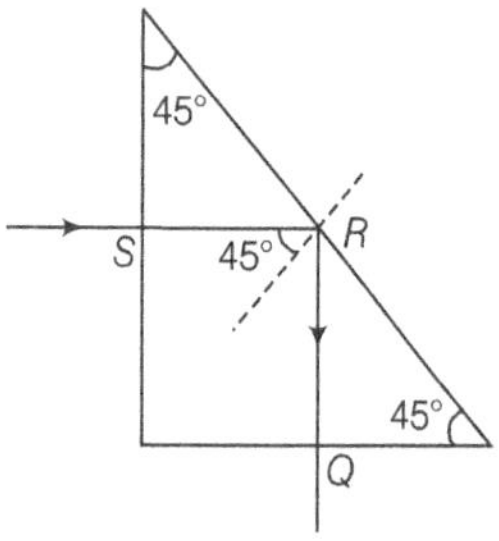

Prism of angles (30°, 60° and 90°), i.e. right angled prism

A 30°, 60° and 90° angled prism can be used to deviate a light ray through an angle less than 60° by total internal reflection.

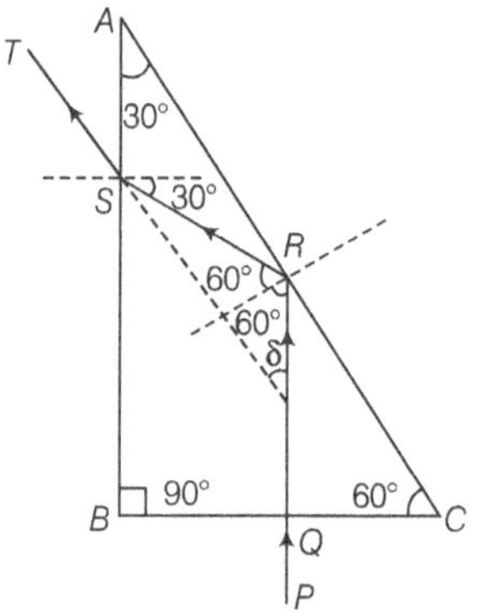

No internal reflection through 30°, 60° and 90°.

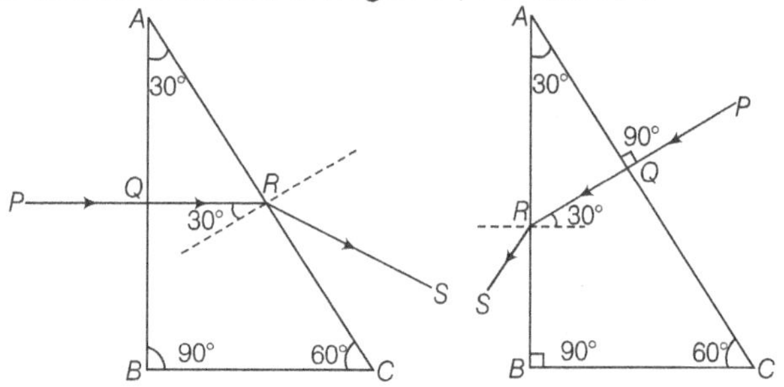

Comparison of Total Internal Reflection from a Prism and Reflection from a Plane Mirror

Total Internal Reflection from a Prism	Total Internal Reflection from a Plane Mirror
It takes place only when light passes from a denser medium to a rarer medium at an angle of incidence greater than the critical angle for that pair of media.	It takes place when light is incident on a plane mirror from any medium at any angle of incidence.
The entire light is reflected.	Only a part of light is reflected while rest is refracted and absorbed.
There is no loss of energy. The energy of reflected ray is same as that of incident ray.	There is a loss of energy. The energy of reflected ray is less than that of the incident ray.

PYQs Previous Years Questions

1 Mark Questions

1. Small air bubbles rising up a fish tank appear silvery when viewed from some particular angle is due to the **(ICSE 2023)**
   (a) reflection (b) refraction
   (c) dispersion (d) total internal reflection

2. The phenomenon of light that causes the diamond to glitter is **(ICSE SQP 2023)**
   (a) refraction (b) total internal reflection
   (c) reflection (d) absorption

3. The diagram below shows the path of light passing through a right-angled prism of critical angle 42°.

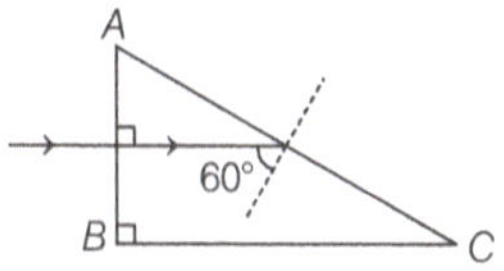

(ICSE 2022 Sem-I)

   (i) The angle C of the prism is
   (a) 45° (b) 60°
   (c) 90° (d) 30°

   (ii) Which one of the following diagrams show the correct path of this ray till it emerges out of the prism?

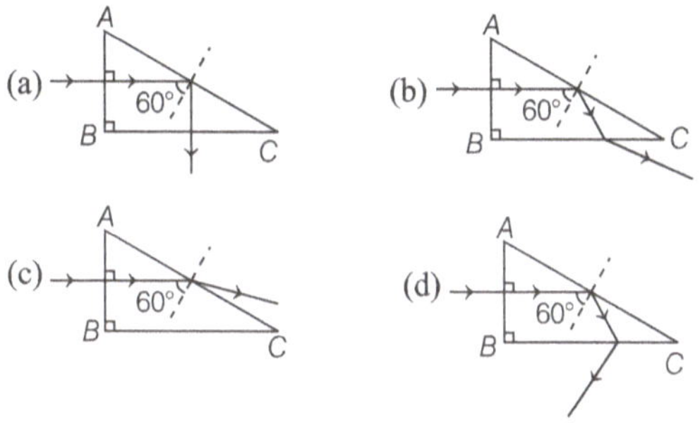

4. Select correct options for total internal reflection in a medium. **(ICSE SQP 2022 Sem-I)**
   (a) Can take place in an optically denser medium as compared to an optically rarer medium.
   (b) Takes place for any angle of incidence greater than 42 degree.
   (c) This reflection does not obey the laws of reflection.
   (d) Can take place if the angle of incidence in a denser medium is less than the critical angle.

5. Diamonds glitter in the dark because **(ICSE SQP 2022 Sem-I)**
   (a) They emit light.
   (b) They have a very small critical angle due to very high refractive index.
   (c) Due to the fluorescence.
   (d) Chemical reaction in the diamond produces light energy.

6. (i) Define critical angle.
   (ii) State one important factor which affects the critical angle of a given medium. **(ICSE 2019)**

7. The diagram below shows a light source P embedded in a rectangular glass block $ABCD$ of critical angle 42°. Complete the path of the ray PQ till it emerges out of the block. [Write necessary angles]. **(ICSE 2019)**

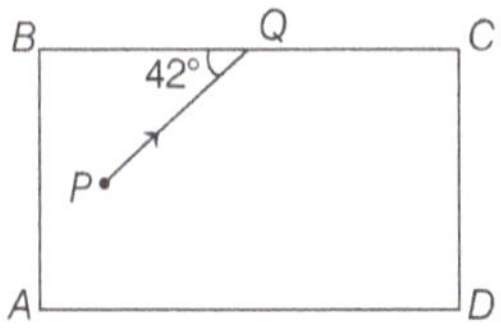

KEY idea

To solve this question, you should use the conditions of total internal reflection.

2 Marks Questions

8. (i) State the relation between the critical angle and the absolute refractive index of a medium.
   (ii) Which colour of light has a higher critical angle? Red light or green light. **(ICSE 2018)**

9. The following diagram shows a 60°, 30°, 90° glass prism of critical angle 42°. Copy the diagram and complete the path of incident ray AB emerging out of the prism marking the angle of incidence on each surface. **(ICSE 2018)**

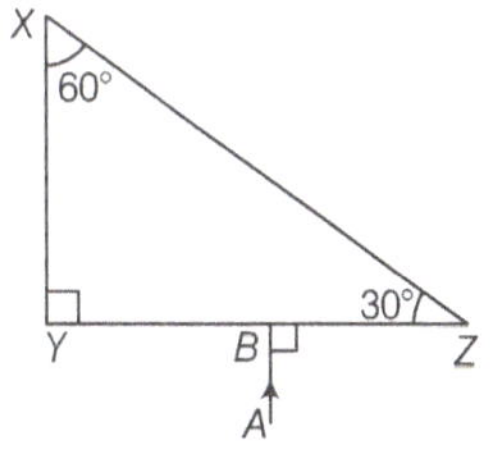

10. State the conditions required for the total internal reflection of the light to take place. **(ICSE 2017, 09)**

11. Copy the diagram given below and complete the path of the light ray till it emerges out of the prism. The critical angle of the glass is 42°. In your diagram, mark the angles wherever necessary. **(ICSE 2016)**

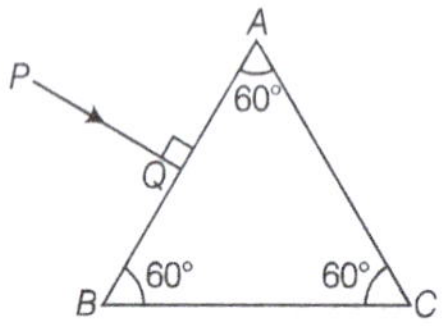

12. Name the factors affecting the critical angle for the pair of media. **(ICSE 2014)**

13. (i) What is meant by the term critical angle?

(ii) How is it related to the refractive index of the medium? **(ICSE 2012)**

14. A ray of light enters a glass slab *PQRS*, as shown in the diagram. The critical angle of the glass is 42°. Copy this diagram and complete the path of the ray till it emerges from the glass slab.

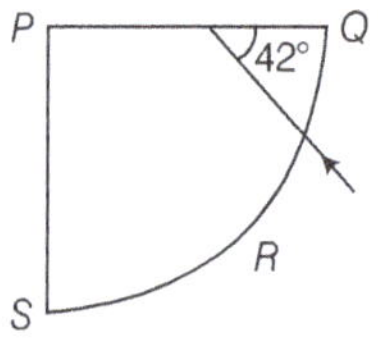

Mark the angles in the diagram wherever necessary. **(ICSE 2010)**

15. Two isosceles right-angled glass prisms are placed near each other as shown in the figure.

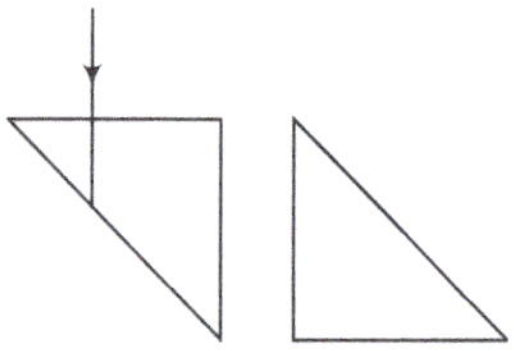

Complete the path of the light ray entering the first isosceles right-angled glass prism till it emerges from the second identical prism. **(ICSE 2008)**

3 Marks Questions

16. The diagram below shows the path of a blue ray through the prism.

(i) Calculate the critical angle of the material of the prism for blue colour.

(ii) What is the measure of the angle of this prism (*A*)?

(iii) Which colour should replace the blue ray, for the ray to undergo total internal reflection ? **(ICSE 2024)**

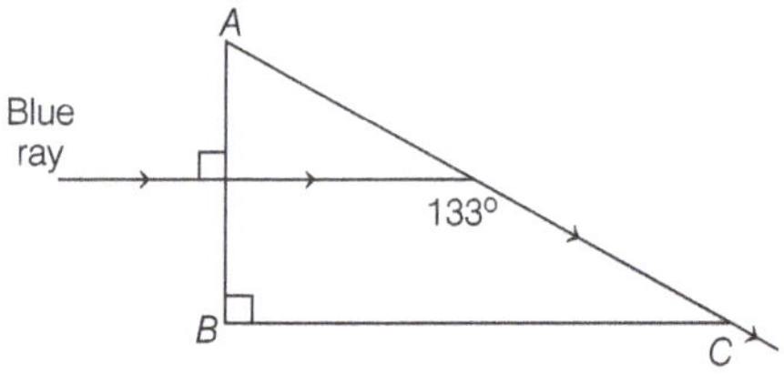

17. The diagram below shows the ray *OP* travelling through an equilateral prism of a certain material.

(i) Calculate the value of i_2, if the angle of deviation is 43°.

(ii) What is the ray *QS* called? **(ICSE 2023)**

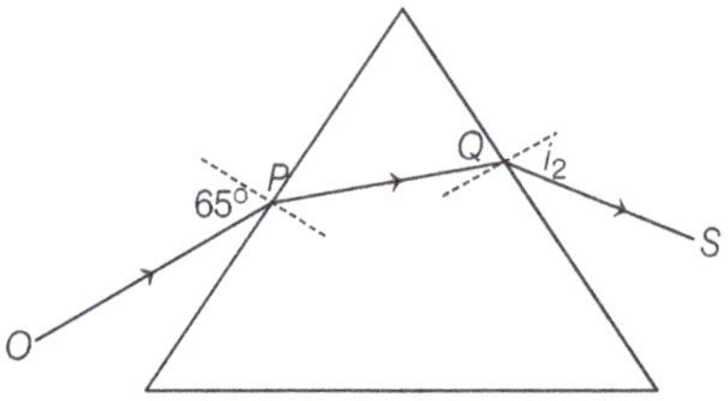

18. (i) A coin kept inside water [$\mu = 4/3$] when viewed from air in a vertical direction appears to be raised by 3.0mm. Find the depth of the coin in water.

(ii) How is the critical angle related to the refractive index of a medium? **(ICSE 2023)**

> **KEY idea**
> To obtain the shift, first calculate the apparent depth and then calcualte the shift.

19. Copy the diagram given below and complete the path of the light ray *PQ*, as it emerges out of the prism by marking necessary angles. The critical angle of glass is 42°. **(ICSE 2023)**

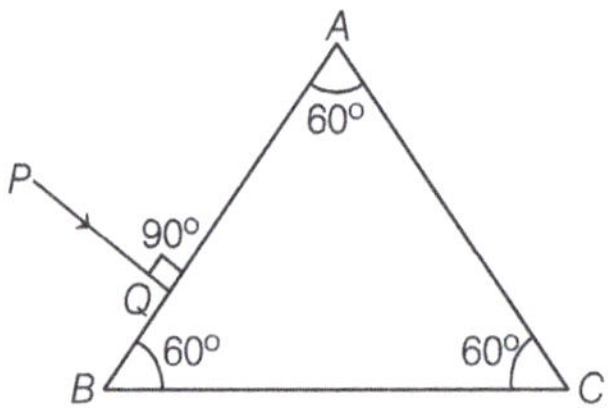

20 Redraw and complete the path of the ray *AB* till it emerges out of the prism of critical angle 42°. **(ICSE SQP 2023)**

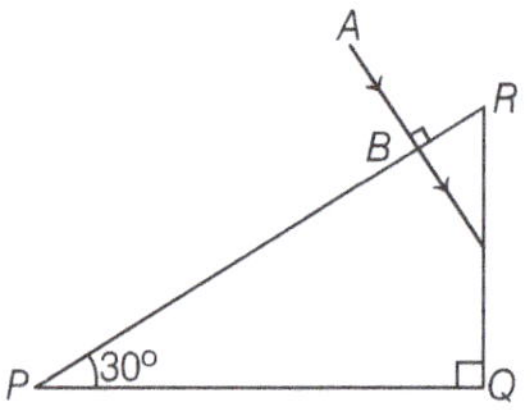

21. Complete the path of the ray AB through the glass prism in PQR till it emerges out of the prism. Given the critical angle of the glass as 42°. **(ICSE 2020)**

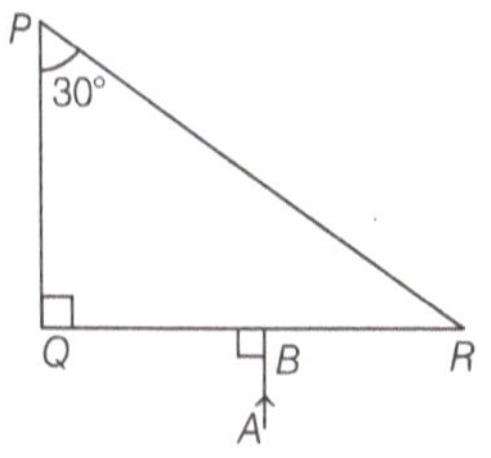

22. A ray of light XY passes through a right angled isosceles prism as shown below

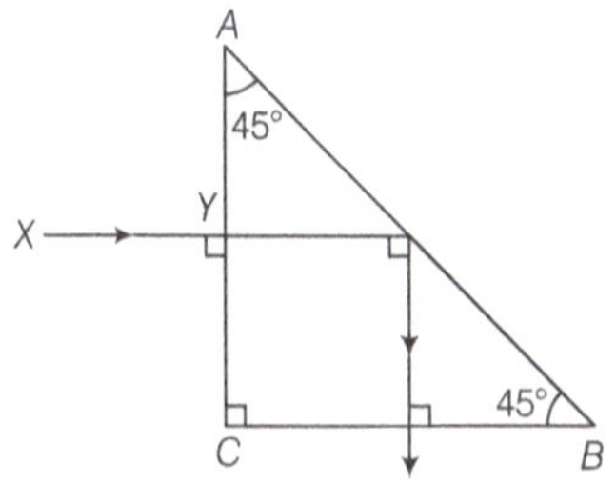

(i) What is the angle through which the incident ray deviates and emerges out of the prism?

(ii) Name the instrument, where this action of prism is put into use.

(iii) Which prism's surface will behave as a mirror? **(ICSE 2018)**

23. Draw the diagram of a right angled isosceles prism which is used to make an inverted image erect. **(ICSE 2018)**

24. A ray of light travels from water to air as shown in the diagram given alongside

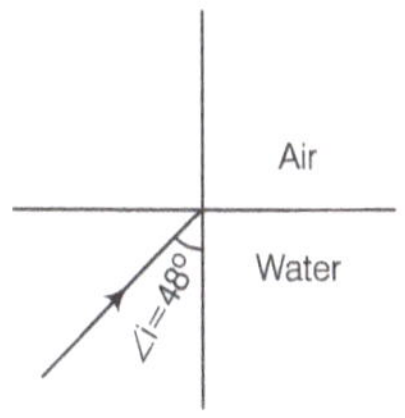

(i) Copy the diagram and complete the path of the ray. Given, the critical angle for water is 48°.

(ii) State the condition, so that total internal reflection occurs in the above diagram. **(ICSE 2017)**

25. A ray of light PQ is incident normally on the hypotenuse of a right angled prism ABC as shown in the diagram given alongside.

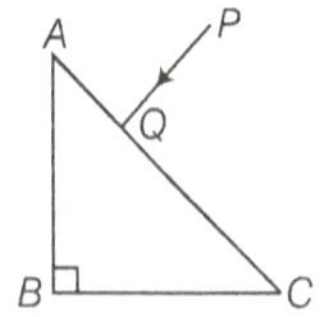

(i) Copy the diagram and complete the path of the ray PQ till it emerges from the prism.

(ii) What is the value of the angle of deviation of the ray?

(iii) Name an instrument, where this action of the prism is used. **(ICSE 2012)**

26. (i) Draw a labelled ray diagram to illustrate (a) critical angle (b) total internal reflection for a ray of light moving from one medium to another.

(ii) Write a formula to express the relationship between refractive index of the denser medium with respect to rarer medium and its critical angle for that pair of media. **(ICSE 2008)**

27. The diagram given alongside shows a right angled prism with a ray of light incident on the side AB.

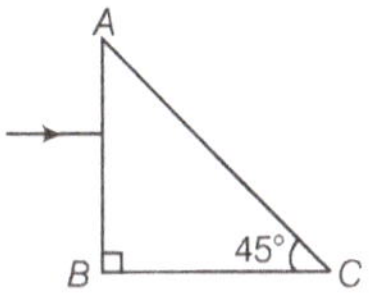

(The critical angle for glass is 42°).

(i) Copy the diagram and complete the path of the ray of light in and out of the glass prism.

(ii) What is the value of the angle of deviation shown by the ray? **(ICSE 2007)**

4 Marks Questions

28. A ray of light travelling from air into a glass material as shown below. Answer the questions that follow. **(ICSE 2022 Sem-I)**

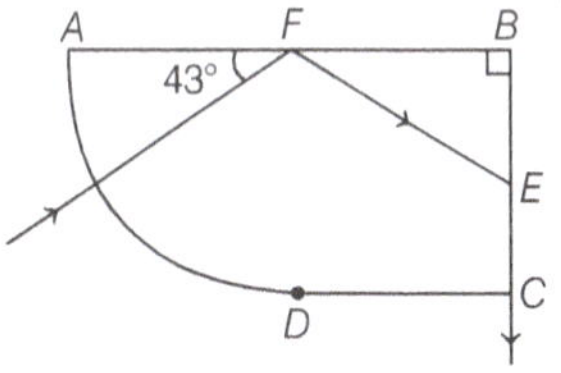

(i) The angle of incidence at the surface AB is

(a) 43° (b) 47° (c) 90° (d) 0°

(ii) Select a correct statement from the following.

(a) The speed of light at the curved surface AD does not change while entering the block.

(b) The ray at the surface AD is not travelling along the radius of the curved part.

(c) The ray at the surface AD is travelling along the radius of the curved part.

(d) Light never refracts when it enters a curved surface.

(iii) The angle of incidence on the surface BC is
(a) 43° (b) 47° (c) 90° (d) 0°

(iv) The critical angle of this material of glass is
(a) 47° (b) 43° (c) 42° (d) 45°

29. The diagram shows the path of light through a right-angled prism of critical angle 42°.

Observe the diagram and answer the questions that follow. **(ICSE SQP 2022 Sem-I)**

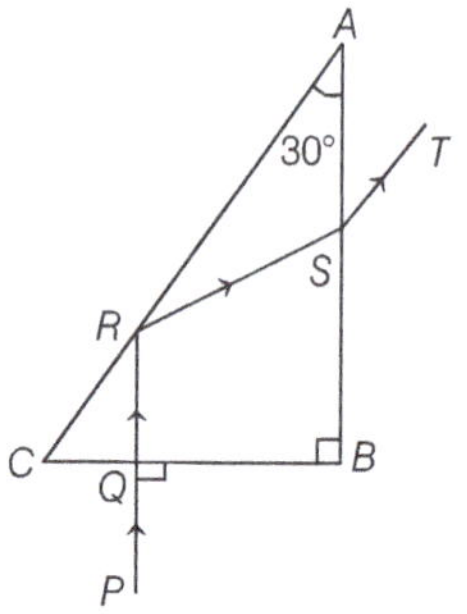

(i) The phenomenon at the surface AC is
(a) refraction
(b) partial reflection
(c) total internal reflection
(d) scattering.

(ii) The angle of incidence at the surface AC is
(a) 30° (b) 45° (c) 60° (d) 90°

(iii) The angle of incidence at the surface AB is
(a) 30° (b) 45° (c) 60° (d) 90°

(iv) Which of the following statement is wrong?
(a) Speed of light ray PQ is equal to the speed of light ray ST.
(b) Speed of light ray QR is equal to the speed of light ray RS.
(c) Speed of light ray PQ is greater than the speed of light ray RS.
(d) Speed of light ray RQ is greater than the speed of light ray ST.

30. The diagram below shows a point source P inside a water container. Four rays A, B, C and D starting from the source P are shown upto the water surface.

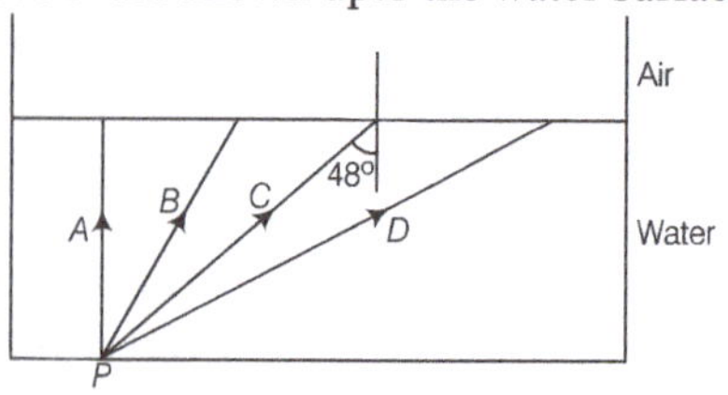

(i) Show in the diagram, the path of these rays after striking the water surface. The critical angle for water-air surface is 48°.

(ii) Name the phenomenon which the rays B and D exhibit. **(ICSE 2017)**

31. PQ and PR are two light rays emerging from the object P as shown in the figure.

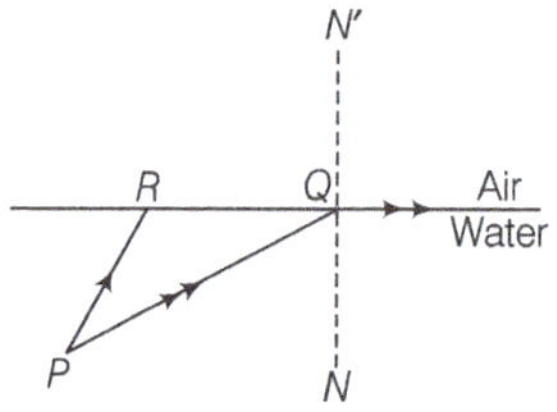

(i) What is the special name given to the angle of incidence ($\angle PQN$) of ray PQ?

(ii) Copy the ray diagram and complete it to show the position of the image of the object P, when seen obliquely from above.

(iii) Name the phenomenon that occurs, if the angle of incidence $\angle PQN$ is increased still further. **(ICSE 2006)**

32. (i) Define critical angle.

(ii) A ray of light passess through a right angled prism as shown in the figure. State the angles of incidence at the faces of AC and BC. **(ICSE 2004)**

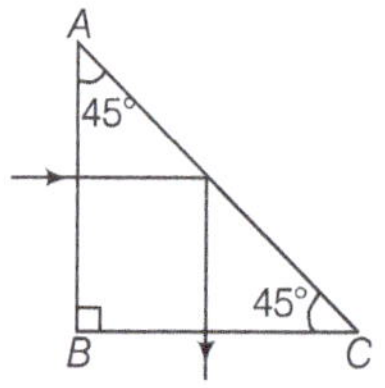

33. (i) In the given diagram, a ray of light PQ is incident normally on one face AB of an equilateral glass prism. What are the angles of incidence at the faces AB and AC?

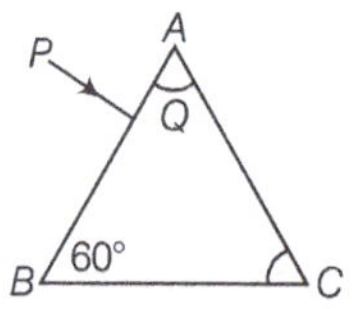

(ii) Complete the ray diagram showing its emergence into air after passing through the prism. **(ICSE 2002)**

Explanations

1. (d) **2.** (b)

3. (i) (d)

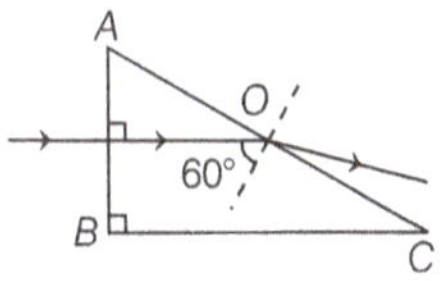

Here, $\angle AOP = \angle C$

Also, $\angle AOP = 90° - 60°$

$\Rightarrow \qquad \angle AOP = \angle C = 30°$

(ii) (b) Given, critical angle, $i_C = 42°$

Here, angle of incidence, $i = 60°$ angle of incidence = angle of reflection.

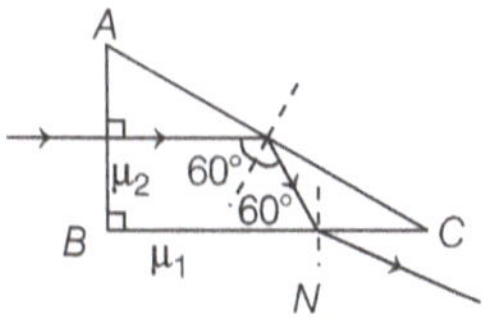

So, $i > i_C$ due to which total internal reflection will occur and the ray gets reflected back in the prism. After that the rays bend away from the normal due to change in medium.

4. (a)

5. (b)

6. (i) Critical angle is the angle of incidence beyond which rays of light passing through a denser medium to the surface of a less dense medium are no longer refracted but totally reflected.

Or

The angle of incidence in denser medium for which angle of refraction in rarer medium is 90° is called critical angle.

(ii) **Temperature** On increasing the temperature of the medium, its refractive index decreases, so the critical angle for that pair of media increases. Thus, the critical angle increases with increase in temperature.

7. Given, critical angle, $i_C = 42°$

At a point Q, $i = 48°$

i.e. $\qquad i > i_C$

When the incident angle i is greater than critical angle, the rays are reflected back into the same medium and laws of reflection are applied.

$\therefore \qquad r = 48°$

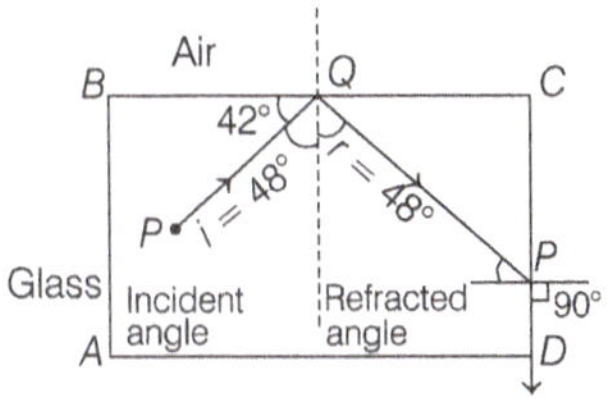

At a point P, $i = 42°$ and $i_C = 42° \Rightarrow i = i_C$

Therefore, $\quad r = 90°$

Hence the refracted ray will graze along CD.

8. (i) The relation between the critical angle i_C and the absolute refractive index (μ) of medium is given by

$$\mu = \frac{1}{\sin i_C} \quad \text{or} \quad \sin i_C = \frac{1}{\mu}$$

(ii) As $\mu_{\text{green}} > \mu_{\text{red}}$

Therefore, critical angle (i_C) for red colour light is higher than green colour light.

9. Given, $i_C = 42°$

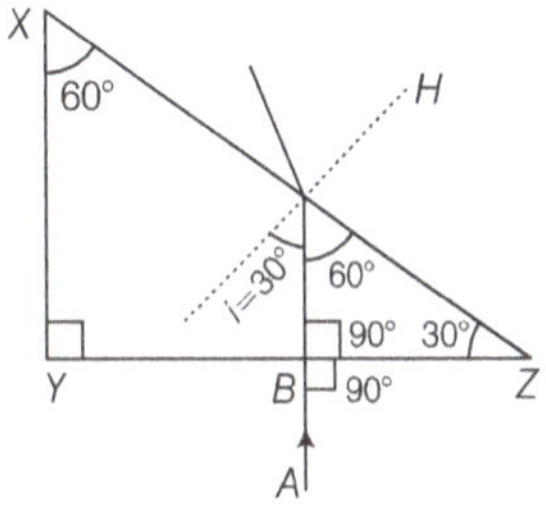

As angle of incidence on face XZ is less than i_C, so ray is refracted.

10. The necessary conditions for the total internal reflection are

(i) The light must travel from a denser medium to a rarer medium.

(ii) The angle of incidence must be greater than the critical angle (i_C) for that pair of media.

11. The ray diagram is given below

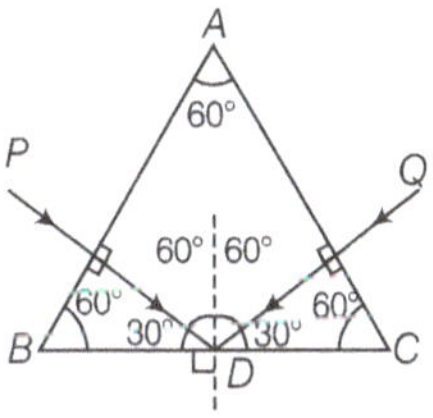

12. The main factors affecting the critical angle for the pair of media are

(i) The colour (or wavelength) of light.

(ii) The temperature.

13. (i) Refer to the sol. Q.6 (i)

(ii) The relation between refractive index of the medium and critical angle is $\mu = \dfrac{1}{\sin i_C}$

14. The diagram is redrawn as

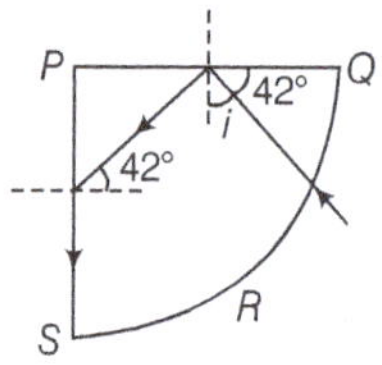

$$i = 90° - 42° = 48°$$

$\because \quad i > i_C$

$\therefore$ Total internal reflection takes place.

15. The complete path of the light ray is shown below

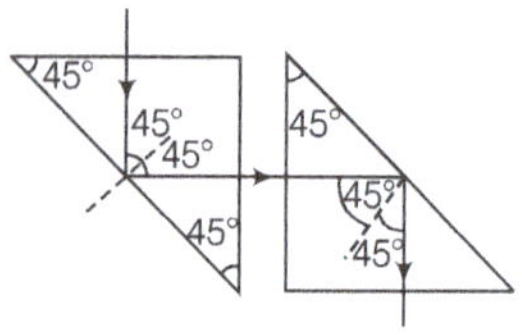

16.

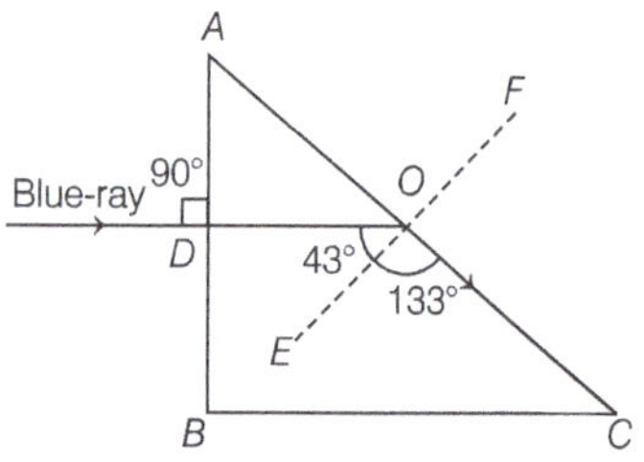

(i) From the figure,

$$\angle EOD = \angle DOC - \angle EOC = 133° - 90°$$

$$\angle EOD = 43°$$

So, the critical angle of the material of the prism for blue colour will be 43°

(ii) From the figure,

$$\angle DOA = \angle EOA - \angle EOD = 90° - 43° = 47°$$

So, $\angle DAO = 90° - 47° = 43°$

The prism angle = 43°

(iii) Violet or indigo

17. (i) We know that angle of deviation is given as

$$\delta = i + e - A$$

where, i = angle of incidence

e = angle of emergence

A = Angle of prism

$A = 60°$ for an equilateral prism

Given, $\delta = 43°, i = 65°$

and $\quad i_2 = e$

Now, $i_2 = \delta + A - i$

$i_2 = 43° + 60° - 65°$

$i_2 = 38°$

(ii) The ray QS is called the emergent ray.

18. (i) Given, $\mu = 4/3$

and the shift = 3 mm

Let the real depth be x mm, then

$$\text{Apparent depth} = \frac{x}{\mu} = \frac{x}{4/3} = \frac{3x}{4}$$

Shift = Real depth − Apparent depth

$\Rightarrow \quad x - \dfrac{3x}{4} = 3 \text{ mm}$

$\Rightarrow \quad 4x - 3x = 12 \text{ mm}$

$\Rightarrow \quad x = 12 \text{ mm}$

(ii) Refer to the sol. 8 (i).

19.

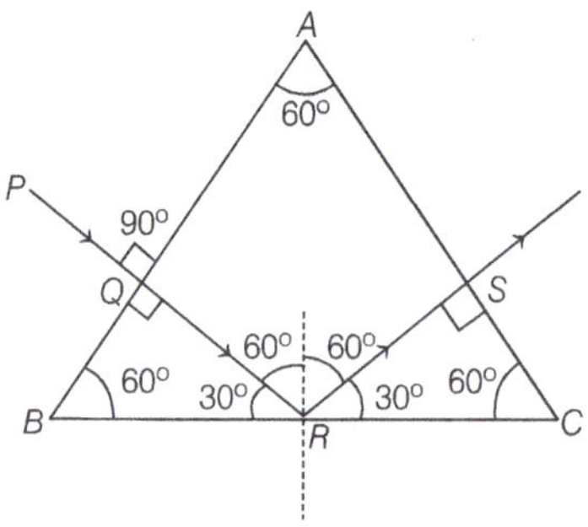

20.

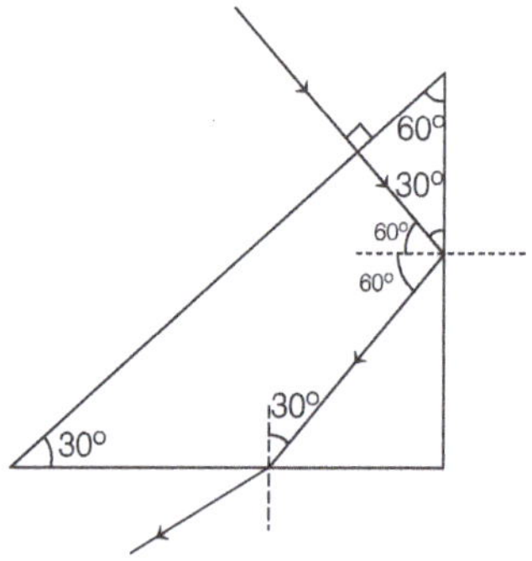

Concept Enhancer Total internal reflection takes place only when angle of incidence is more than critical angle.

21. Refer to sol. Q.9 on page 69.

22. (i) 90°

(ii) Periscope

(iii) Surface AB behaves like a mirror, because on this surface, total internal reflection occurs.

23.

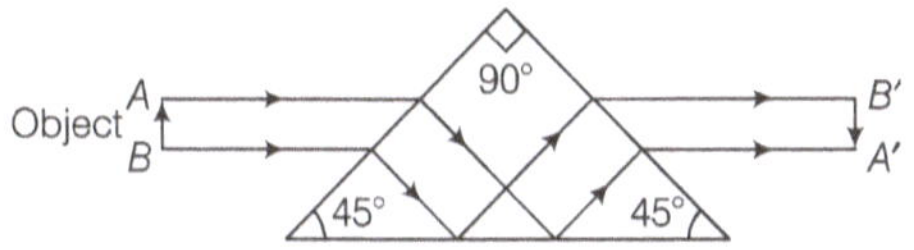

24. (i) When the angle of incidence in water is at critical value, then the refracted ray lies along the boundary, having an angle of refraction is 90°.

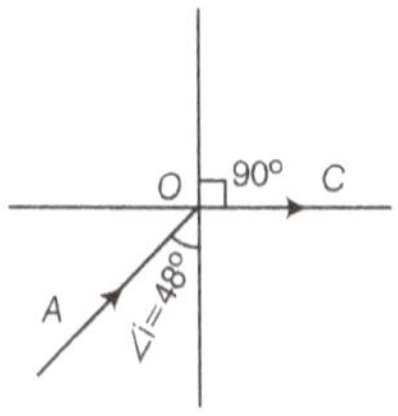

(ii) Necessary conditions for total internal reflection in the above figure are

I. The ray of light must travel from denser medium into a rarer medium.

II. The angle of incidence in the denser medium must be greater than the critical angle for that pair of media.

25. (i) The diagram is redrawn and the complete path of PQ is shown below

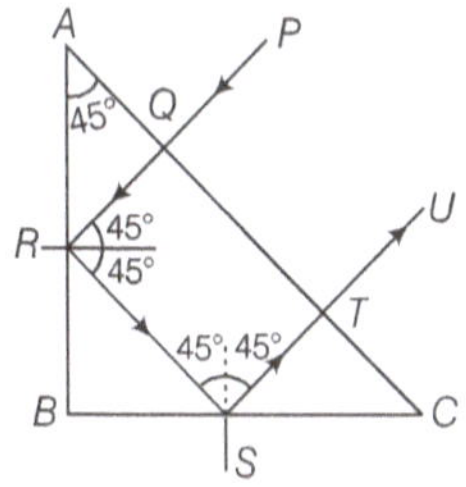

(ii) The value of the angle of deviation of the ray is 180°.

(iii) Prism binocular is an instrument, where this action of prism is used.

26. (i) The labelled diagram of critical angle and total internal reflection is given below

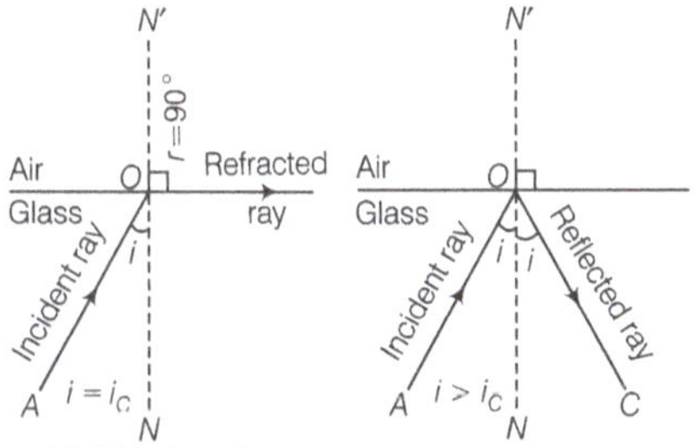

(a) Critical angle (b) Total internal reflection

(ii) The formula to express the relationship between refractive index of the denser medium w.r.t. rarer medium and its critical angle is given by

$$\mu = \frac{1}{\sin i_C} = \text{cosec } i_C$$

27. (i) The diagram below shows the complete path of the ray of light in and out of the glass prism.

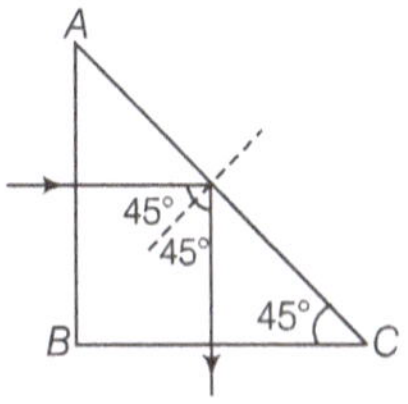

$\because \quad i > i_C$

$\therefore$ Total internal reflection takes place.

(ii) The value of the angle of deviation shown by the ray is 90°.

28. (i) (b)

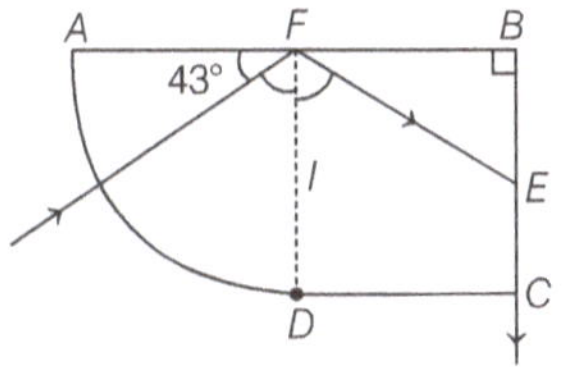

By using law of reflection,

angle of incidence = angle of reflection

$$\angle GFI = 90° - 43°$$

$$\angle FGI = 47°$$

$$\angle GFI = \angle i = 47°$$

(ii) (c) The ray at the surface AD is travelling along the radius of the curved part. So, the correct statement is (c).

(iii) (a) The angle of incidence on surface BC is given by using law of reflection.

$\therefore$ angle of incidence = angle of reflection

$$\angle AFG = \angle BFE = 43°$$

So, angle of incidence on surface

$$BC = 43°$$

(iv) (a) Critical angle of this glass

$$\theta_C = 90° - 43°$$

$$\theta_C = 47°$$

Common Mistake Sometimes, students put the conditions of total internal reflection even through the angle of incidence is less than the critical angle, which gives wrong results.

29. (i) (c)

(ii) (c) 60°

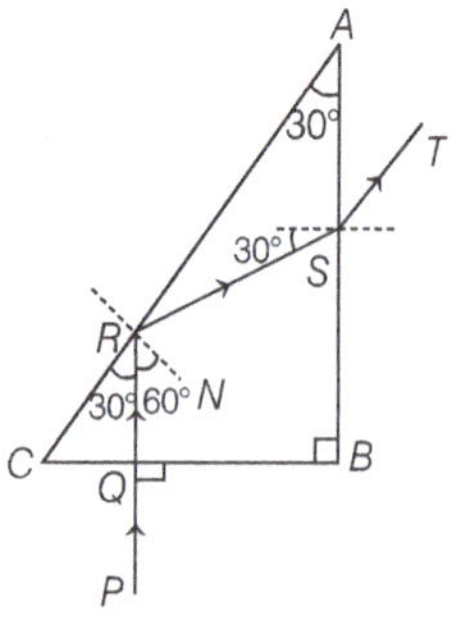

$\angle CRQ = \angle A = 30°$

$\angle ARS = 30°$ $\qquad [\because \angle ARS = \angle CRQ]$

$\angle SRN = 90° - 30° = 60°$

Angle of incidence at surface AC is 60°.

(iii) (a)

(iv) (d) Speed of light rays RS is greater than the speed of light ray ST.

30. (i) Diagram showing total internal reflection

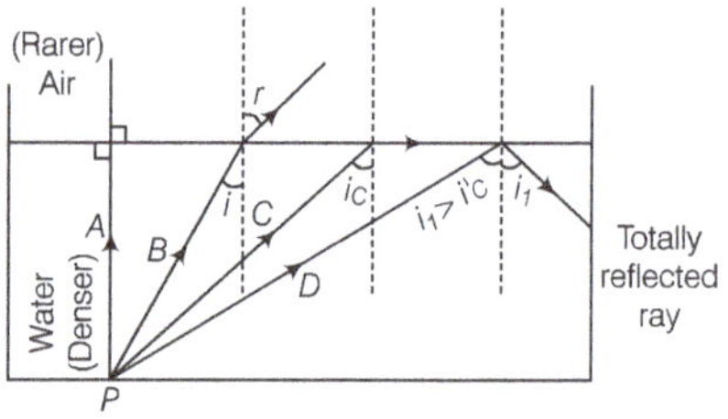

(ii) $B \rightarrow$ exhibits refraction from denser to rarer medium.

$D \rightarrow$ exhibits total internal reflection as $i > 48°$ (i_C) of water.

Concept Enhancer With the increase of temperature of medium, critical angle increases as its refractive index decreases.

31. (i) The special name given to the angle of incidence $\angle PQN$ of ray PQ is critical angle.

(ii) The complete diagram is shown below

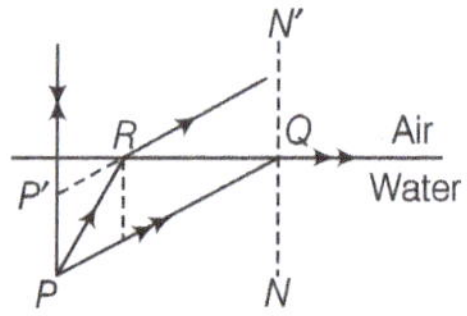

The image of the object P will be formed at P' when seen obliquely from above.

(iii) Total internal reflection occurs, if the angle of incidence $\angle PQN$ is increased still further.

32. (i) Refer to ans. 6 (i).

(ii) Angle of incidence at face $AC = 45°$.

Angle of incidence at face $BC = 0°$.

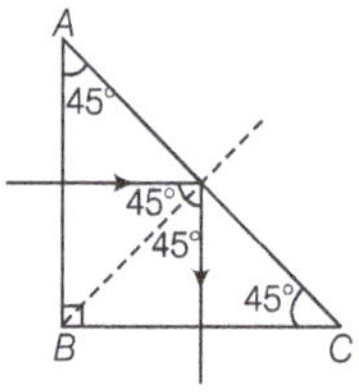

33. (i) The angle of incidence at the face AB is 0°. The angle of incidence at the face AC is 60°.

(ii)

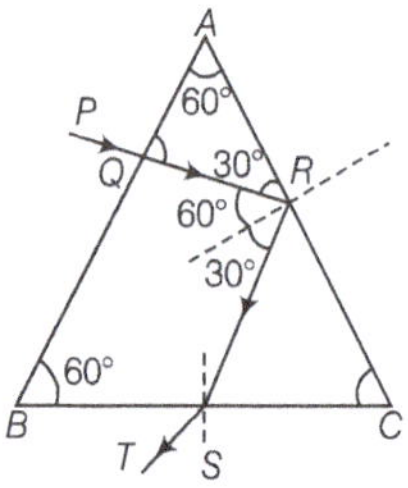

CHAPTER TEST

01 Mark Questions

1 Refraction causes due to

(a) change in wavelength of light
(b) change in frequency of light
(c) change in speed of light
(d) Both (a) and (c)

2 The speed of light in water is 2.25×10^8 m/s, then refractive index of water is

(a) 2.32 (b) 1.03 (c) 1.33 (d) 2.33

3 When angle of incidence and angle of emergence are equal, then angle of deviation is

(a) minimum (b) maximum (c) zero (d) equal

4 A ray of light suffers refraction through an equilateral prism. The deviation produced by prism does not depend on the

(a) angle of incidence (b) colour of light
(c) material of prism (d) size of prism

5 In total internal reflection

(a) angle of incidence is not equal to critical angle.
(b) angle of incidence is greater than the critical angle.
(c) angle of incidence is less than the critical angle.
(d) angle of incidence is equal to critical angle.

02 Marks Questions

6 What do you understand by refraction of light?

7 How is refractive index of a medium related to the speed of light in it?

8 Draw a ray diagram to show the refraction of a monochromatic ray through a prism when it suffers minimum deviation.

9 State the condition required for total internal refraction of light to take place.

10 A water pond appears to be 2.7 m deep. If the refractive index of water is 4/3. Find the actual depth of the pond.

Structured Questions

11 (i) What is lateral displacement? Draw a ray diagram showing the lateral displacement of a ray of light when it passes through a parallel sided glass slab. **(3)**

(ii) A coin at the bottom of a trough containing water to a depth of 15 cm appears to be 3.75 cm raised above from the bottom. Calculate the refractive index of water. **(3)**

(iii) A ray of light strikes the surface at a rectangular glass slab such that the angle of incidence is (i) 0°, (ii) 45°. In each case, draw diagram to show the path taken by the ray as it passes through the glass slab and emerges from it. **(4)**

12 (i) Copy the diagram given below and complete the path of light ray till it emerges out of the prism. The critical angle of glass is 42°. In your diagram mark the angles wherever necessary. **(3)**

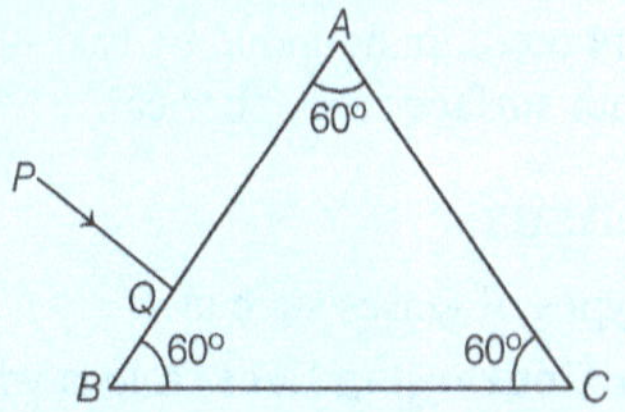

(ii) Light passes through a rectangular glass slab and through a triangular glass prism. In what way does the direction of two emergent beams differ and why? **(3)**

(iii) Draw diagram to show the refraction of light from (i) air to glass, (ii) glass to air.

In each diagram, label the incident ray, refracted ray, the angle of incidence (i) and the angle of refraction (r). **(4)**

Answers

1. (d) **2.** (c) **3.** (a) **4.** (d) **5.** (b)
10. 3.6 m **11.** (b) 1.33

04

Lenses

TREND ANALYSIS 4 YEARS

Average No. of Questions Across all Sets

	Types of Questions	2024	2023	2020	2019
Lenses	1 Mark	2	1	–	–
	2 Marks	1	1	–	1
	3 Marks	1	2	–	1
	4 Marks	–	–	1	1

Lens

It is a transparent medium bounded by two surfaces of which one or both surfaces are spherical.

Types of Lenses

There are two types of lenses such as

(i) **Convex or Converging Lens** A lens which is thicker at the centre and thinner at its periphery is called convex or converging lens.When a parallel beam of light rays passing through it, converges.

(ii) **Concave or Diverging Lens** A lens which is thinner at the centre and thicker at its periphery is called concave or diverging lens. When a parallel beam of light rays passing through it, diverges.

Technical Terms Related to Lens

(i) **Optical Centre** The optical centre is a point within or outside the lens directed to which incident rays refract without any deviation in the path. It is a central point of a lens as shown in the figure.

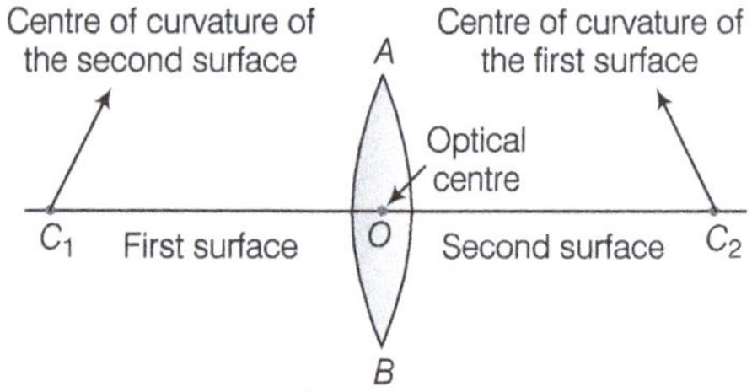

Convex lens

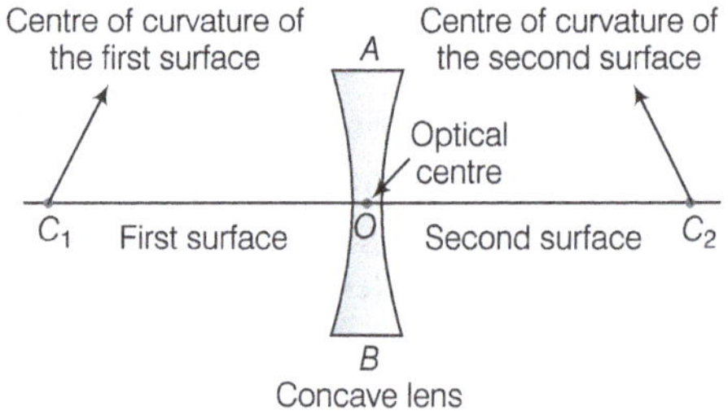

Concave lens

(ii) **Centre of Curvature** The centres of the two imaginary spheres by which the lens is a part are called centre of curvature of the lens. A lens has two centres of curvature with respect to its two curved surfaces.

(iii) **Radii of Curvature** The radii of the two imaginary spheres by which the lens is a part are called radii of curvature of the lens. A lens has two radii of curvature. These may or may not be equal.

(iv) **Principal Axis** The imaginary line joining the two centres of curvature is called principal axis of lens. The principal axis also passes through the optical centre.

(v) **Principal Focus** Lens has two principal foci which are as follows

(a) **First principal focus** It is the point on the principal axis of lens at which the rays starting from or directed to which become parallel to the principal axis after the refraction.

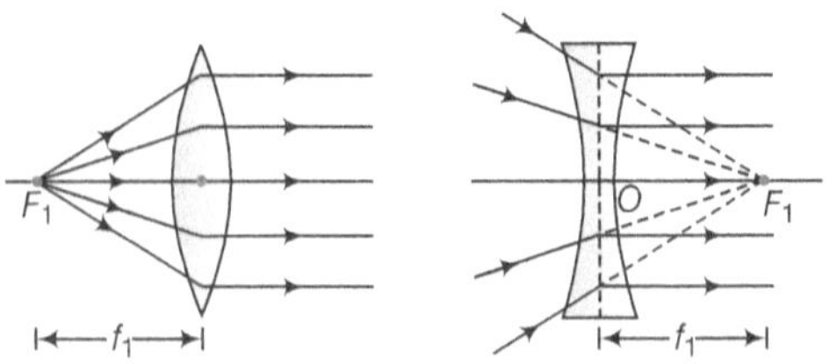

(b) **Second principal focus** It is the point on the principal axis at which the rays coming parallel to the principal axis converge (convex lens) or passing through it appear to diverge from (concave lens) after refraction from the lens. Both the foci of convex lens are real while that of concave lens are virtual.

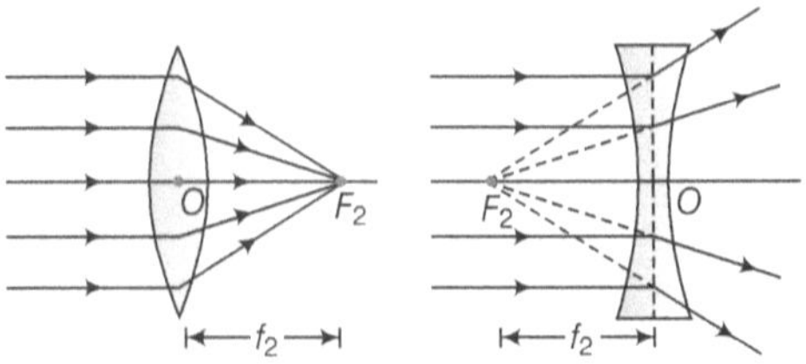

(vi) **Focal Length of Lens** The distance between focus and optical centre of lens is called focal length of lens.

(vii) **Focal Plane** The plane passing through the focus and perpendicular to the principal axis is called focal plane.

(viii) **Aperture** The effective diameter of the circular outline of a spherical lens is called its aperture.

(ix) **Refractive Axis** It is an imaginary axis at the optical centre and perpendicular to the principal axis, which represents the lens.

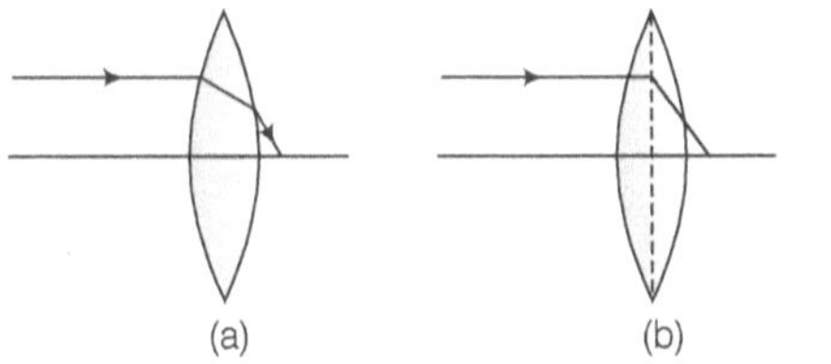

(a) Real path of a ray (b) Path of a ray as shown with reference to refractive axis

Formation of Images

Principal Rays or Construction Rays The position, size and nature of the image of an object formed by a lens can be determined by drawing a ray diagram. The figure shows the path through a convex lens and concave lens separate from each other, for the three principal rays generally used for the construction of the ray diagrams.

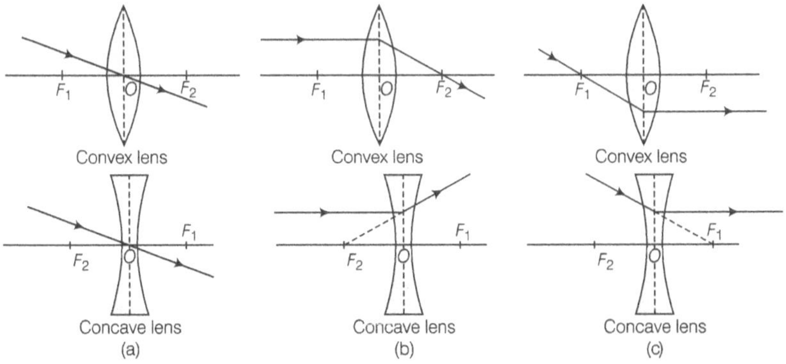

Different images formed by convex and concave lenses

Formation of Images by a Convex Lens for Different Positions of the Object

Position of Object	Figure	Position of Image	Characteristics of Image	Uses
Between the optical centre and first principal focus	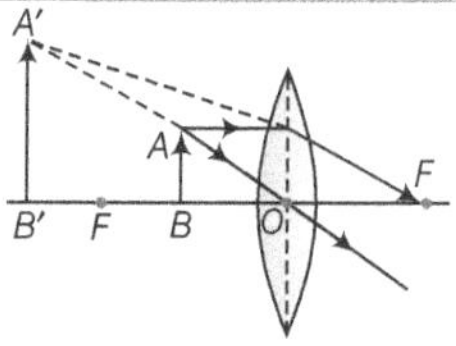	On the same side as that of object	(i) Virtual (ii) Erect (iii) Magnified	Magnifying glass, eye lenses spectacles for long sightedness or hypermetropia
At the first principal focus	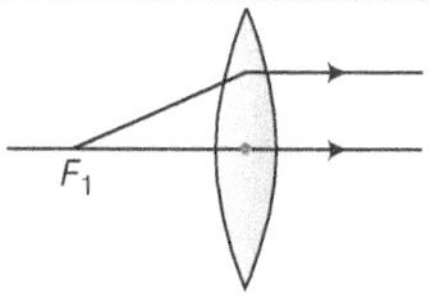	At infinity	(i) Real (ii) Inverted (iii) Extremely magnified	Telescope, camera lens, burning glass
Between F_1 and $2F_1$	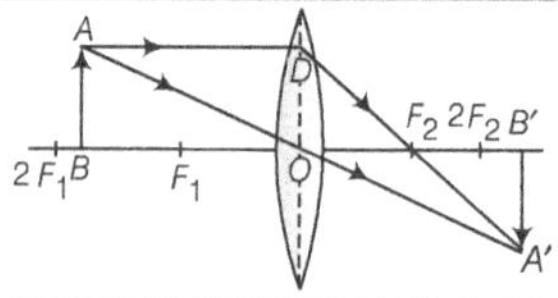	Beyond $2F_2$	(i) Real (ii) Inverted (iii) Bigger than object	Projector, microscope objective
At $2F_1$	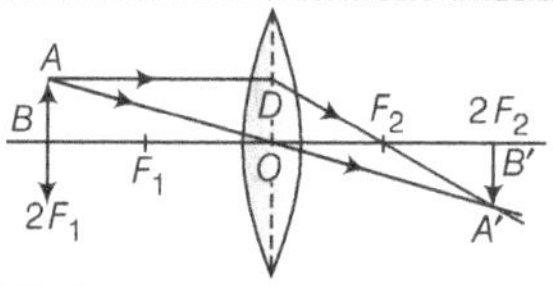	At $2F_2$	(i) Real (ii) Inverted (iii) Equal to the size of the object	Photocopies
Beyond $2F_1$	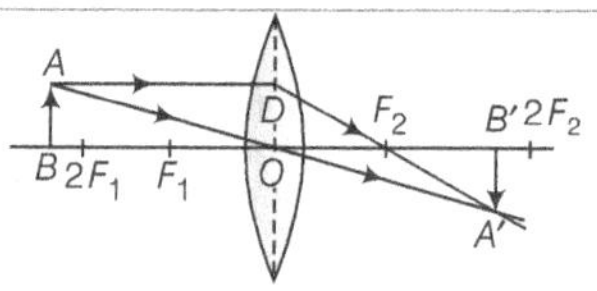	Between F_2 and $2F_2$	(i) Real (ii) Inverted (iii) Diminished	In a camera, in eye while reading
At infinity	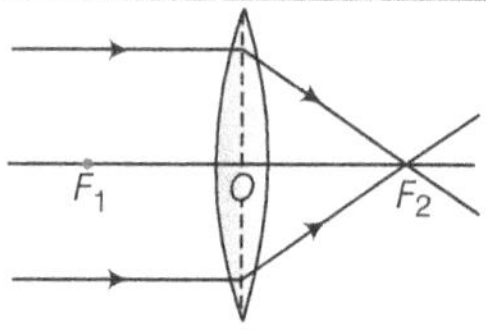	At the second principal focus	(i) Real (ii) Inverted (iii) Highly diminished	Spotlights

Formation of Images by a Concave Lens for Different Positions of the Object

Position of Object	Figure	Position of Image	Characteristics of Image	Uses
At infinity	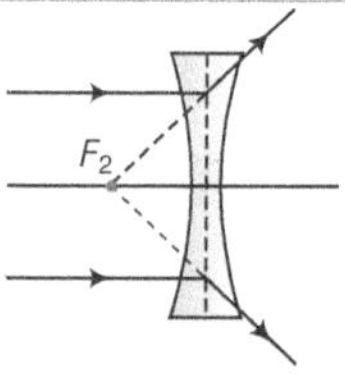	Appears at the second principal focus	(i) Virtual (ii) Erect (iii) Extremely diminished	Spectacles for short sightedness
Between infinity and the optical centre of the lens	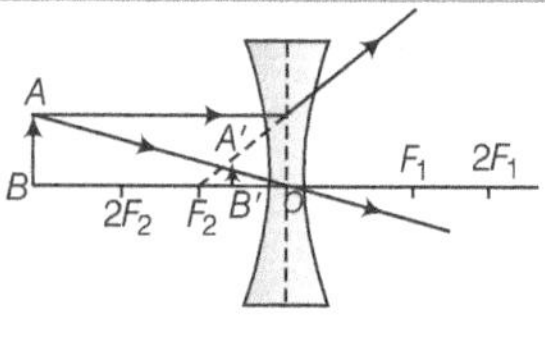	Appears between the second principal focus and the lens	(i) Virtual (ii) Erect (iii) Diminished	Spectacles for short sightedness or myopia

Sign Convention for Spherical Lenses

Sign convention for lenses is as following

Measurements	For Convex Lens	For Concave Lens
Distance of the object	Negative	Negative
Distance of the real image	Positive	N/A
Distance of the virtual image	Negative	Negative
Focal length	Positive	Negative

Lens Formula

This formula gives the relationship between object distance (u), image distance (v) and the focal length (f).

The lens formula is expressed as $\frac{1}{v}-\frac{1}{u}=\frac{1}{f}$

Magnifying Glass or Simple Microscope

When an object AB is placed in front of a convex lens. The position of lens is so adjusted that the object AB lies in between its optical centre O and focus F_1 and the image formed is at the distance of distinct vision (D).

The characteristics of image formed is virtual, magnified and erect.

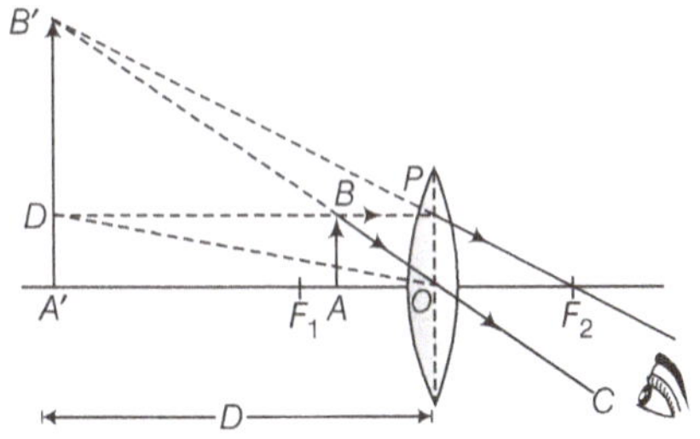

Magnification Using Ray Diagram

The magnifying power of the microscope is defined as the ratio of the $\angle B'OA'$ subtended by the image $A'B'$ at the eye to the $\angle DOA'$ subtended by $A'D$ at the eye. It is expressed as

Magnifying power $M=\frac{\angle B'OA'}{\angle DOA'}=1+\frac{D}{f}$

Power of a Lens

It is defined as the reciprocal of lens's focal length in metres. It is expressed as

Power $P=\frac{1}{f\text{ (in m)}}$

Its unit is dioptre (D). The power of convex lens is positive and that of concave lens is negative.

PYQs Previous Years Questions

1 Mark Questions

1. Linear magnification (m) produced by a concave lens is **(ICSE 2024)**

(a) $m<1$ (b) $m>1$ (c) $m=1$ (d) $m\leq 2$

2. A block of glass is pushed into the path of the light as shown below. Then, the converging point X will **(ICSE 2024)**

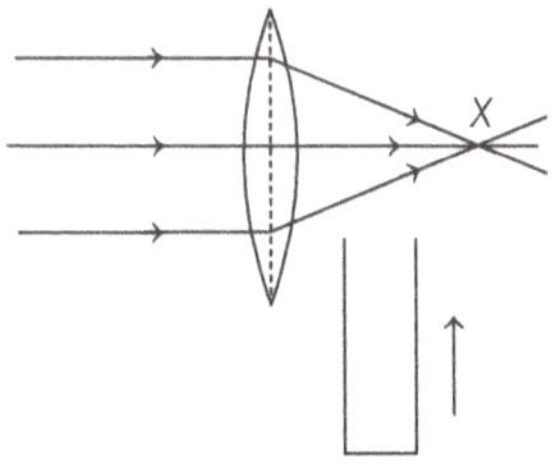

(a) move away from the slab
(b) move towards the slab
(c) not shift
(d) move towards the left side of the lens

3. A concave lens produces only ___ image. **(ICSE 2023)**

(a) real, enlarged
(b) virtual, enlarged
(c) virtual, diminished
(d) real, diminished

4. In which of the following diagrams is the refraction **not** correct? **(ICSE SQP 2023)**

(a)
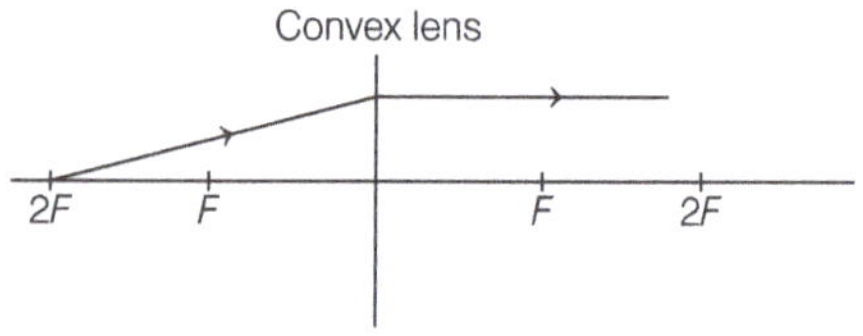

(b)
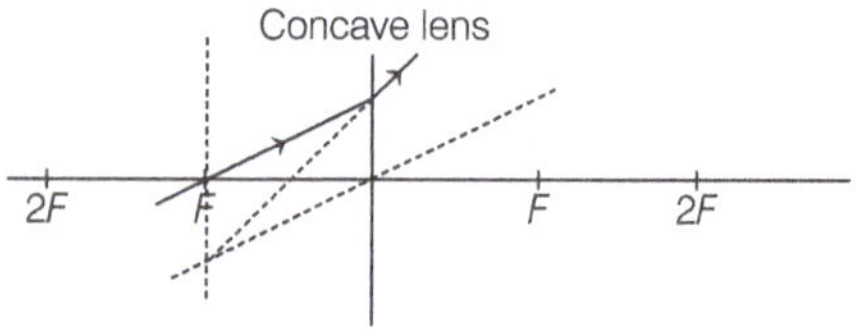

(c)
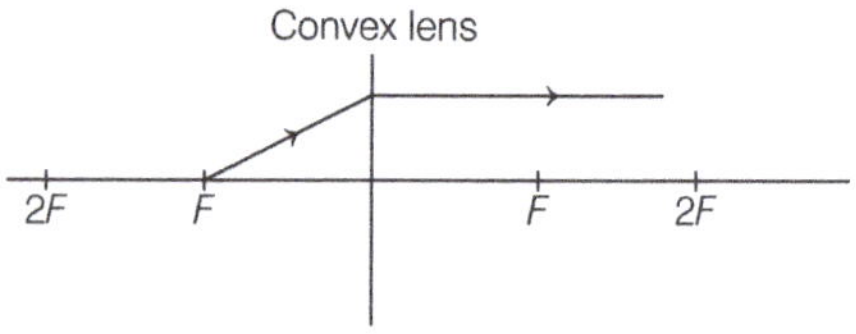

(d)
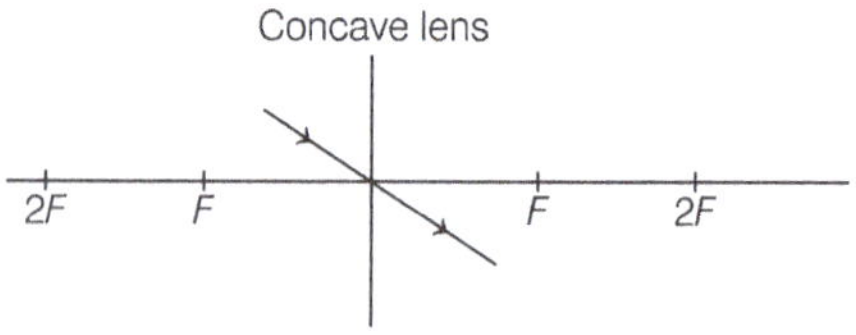

5. An object of height 10 cm is placed in front of a concave lens of focal length 20 cm, at a distance of 25 cm from the lens. Is it possible to capture this image on a screen? Select a correct option from the following. **(ICSE 2022 Sem-I)**

(a) Yes, as the image formed will be real.
(b) Yes, as the image formed will be erect.
(c) No, as the image formed will be virtual.
(d) No, as the image formed will be inverted.

6. From the diagram shown below, identify the characteristics of the image that will be formed. **(ICSE SQP 2022 Sem-I)**

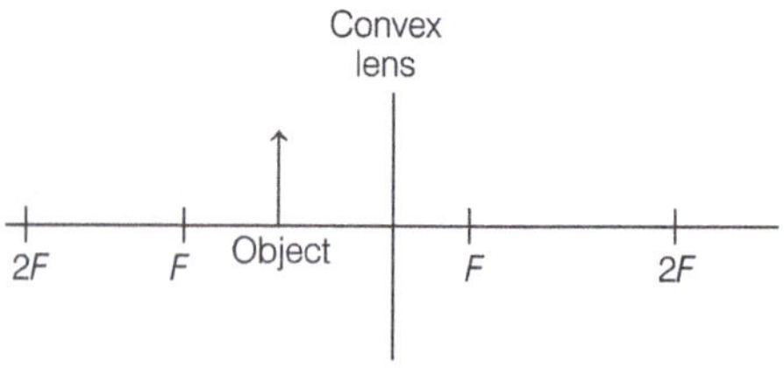

(a) Real
(b) Diminished
(c) Formed within the focal length
(d) Virtual

7. Assuming all lenses shown below are of the same material, state which lens has the maximum power. **(ICSE SQP 2022 Sem-I)**

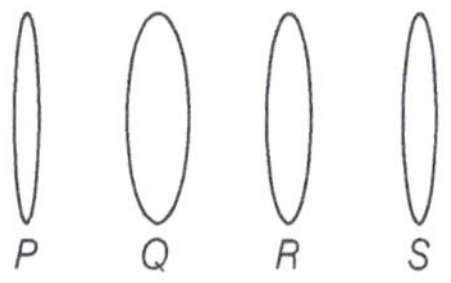

(a) *R* (b) *P* (c) *Q* (d) *S*

8. Ranbir claims to have obtained an image twice the size of the object with a concave lens. Is he correct? Give reason for your answer. **(ICSE 2014)**

9. You are provided with a printed piece of paper. Using this paper, how will you differentiate between a convex lens and concave lens? **(ICSE 2012)**

10. (i) When does a ray of light falling on a lens pass through it undeviated?

(ii) Which lens can produce a real and inverted image of an object? **(ICSE 2011)**

11. We can burn a piece of paper by focussing the sun rays by using a particular type of lens.

(i) Name the type of lens used for the above purpose.

(ii) Draw a ray diagram to support your answer. **(ICSE 2010)**

12. Copy and complete the following table.

Type of Lens	Position of Object	Nature of Image	Size of Image
Convex	At *F*		
Concave	At infinity		

(ICSE 2009)

13. An object is placed in front of a converging lens at a distance greater than twice the focal length of the lens. Draw a ray diagram to the formation of the image. **(ICSE 2007)**

14. An object is placed in front of a convex lens such that the image formed has the same size as that of the object. Draw a ray diagram to illustrate this. **(ICSE 2006)**

2 Marks Questions

15. (i) In a reading glass, what is the position of the object with respect to the convex lens used ?

(ii) Why can we not use concave lens for the same purpose? **(ICSE 2024)**

16. (i) Is it possible for a concave lens to form an image of size two times that of the object? Write Yes or No.

(ii) What will happen to the focal length of the lens, if a part of the lens is covered with an opaque paper? **(ICSE 2023)**

17. (i) If the lens is placed in water instead of air, how does its focal length change?
(ii) Which lens, thick or thin has greater focal length? **(ICSE 2019)**

18. The power of a lens is – 5 D.
(i) Find its focal length.
(ii) Name the type of lens. **(ICSE 2018)**

19. State the position of the object in front of a converging lens, if
(i) it produces a real and same size image of the object.
(ii) it is used as a magnifying lens. **(ICSE 2018)**

20. Draw a ray diagram to show how a convex lens can be used as a magnifying glass. **(ICSE 2018)**

21. Name the lens that always forms a virtual and erect image. **(ICSE 2017)**

3 Marks Questions

22. The image of a candle flame placed at a distance of 36 cm from a spherical lens, is formed on a screen placed at a distance of 72 cm from the lens. Calculate the focal length of the lens and its power . **(ICSE 2024)**

23. A convex lens of focal length 10 cm is placed at a distance of 60 cm from a screen. How far from the lens should an object be placed so as to obtain a real image on the screen? **(ICSE 2023)**

24. An object of height 20 cm is placed in front of a lens at a distance of 50 cm. Its virtual, diminished image is formed at a distance of 15 cm. **(ICSE 2023)**
(i) Identify the type of the lens.
(ii) Calculate the focal length of the lens.

25. A virtual diminished image is formed when an object is placed between the optical centre and the principal focus of a lens.
(i) Name the type of lens which forms the above image.
(ii) Draw a ray diagram to show the formation of the image with the above stated characteristics. **(ICSE 2019)**

26. An object AB is placed between O and F_1 on the principal axis of a converging lens as shown in the diagram.

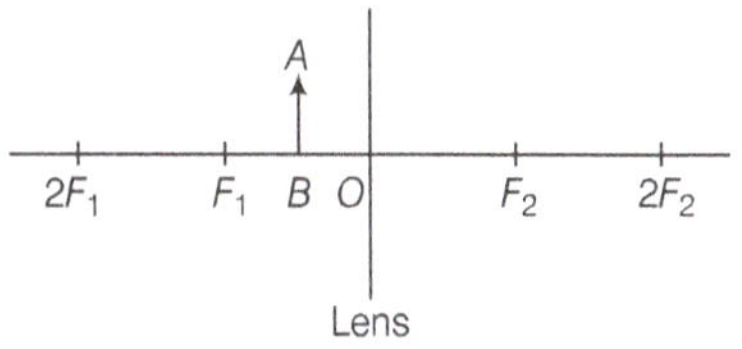

Copy the diagram and by using three standard rays starting from point A, obtain an image of the object AB. **(ICSE 2018)**

27. (i) Define power of a lens.
(ii) A child is using a spectacle with power of – 2.5 D. What is meant by the negative sign?
(iii) Find the focal length of the lens used. **(ICSE 2018)**

28. An object is kept at a distance of 15 cm from a convex lens of focal length 10 cm. Calculate the image distance and state the characteristics of the image formed. **(ICSE 2018)**

KEY idea
Students must learn the concept "formation of image" to make it easy to give answer of this question.

29. A lens forms an upright and diminished image of an object when the object is placed at the focal point of the given lens.
(i) Name the lens.
(ii) Draw a ray diagram to show the image formation. **(ICSE 2017)**

30. A lens produces a virtual image between the object and the lens.
(i) Name the lens.
(ii) Draw a ray diagram to show the formation of this image. **(ICSE 2016)**

31. (i) Where should an object be placed, so that a real and inverted image of the same size as the object is obtained using a convex lens?
(ii) Draw a ray diagram to show the formation of the image as specified in the part (i). **(ICSE 2015)**

32. A lens forms an erect, magnified and virtual image of an object.
(i) Name the lens.
(ii) Draw a labelled ray diagram to show the image formation. **(ICSE 2014)**

33. (i) Define the power of a lens.

(ii) The lens mentioned in Q.31 above is of focal length 25 cm. Calculate the power of the lens. **(ICSE 2014)**

34. (i) Copy and complete the diagram to show the formation of the image of an object *AB*.

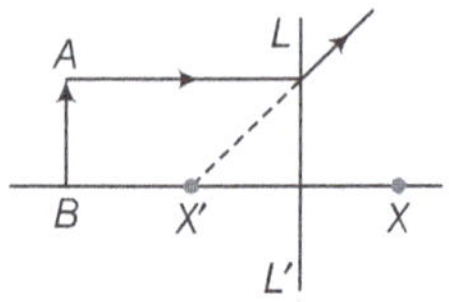

(ii) What is the name given to *X*? **(ICSE 2009)**

35. A linear object is placed on the axis of a lens. An image is formed by refraction in the lens. For all positions of the object on the axis of the lens, the positions of the image are always between the lens and the object.

(i) Name the lens.

(ii) Draw a ray diagram to show the formation of the image of an object placed in front of the lens at any position of your choice except infinity. **(ICSE 2008)**

4 Marks Questions

36. The diagram below shows an object *AB* kept in front of the lens. The path of one ray coming from the object is shown. **(ICSE SQP 2023)**

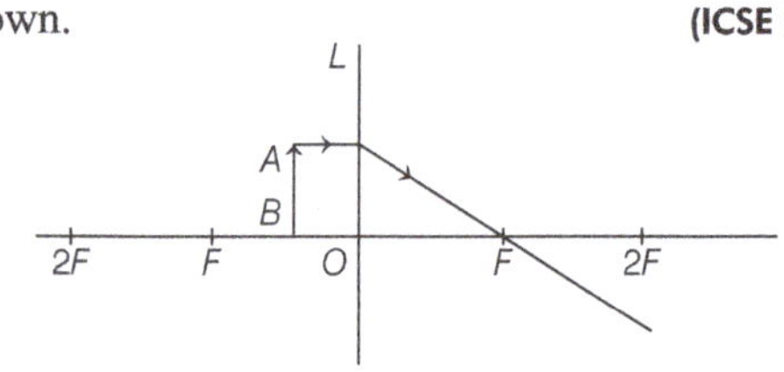

(i) Name the lens *L*.

(ii) Redraw and complete the ray diagram showing the formation of the image.

(iii) In which optical instrument is this kind of image formed?

37. Observe the diagram which shows the path of an incident ray through an optical plane *LL'* of a lens. The focal length of the lens is 20 cm.

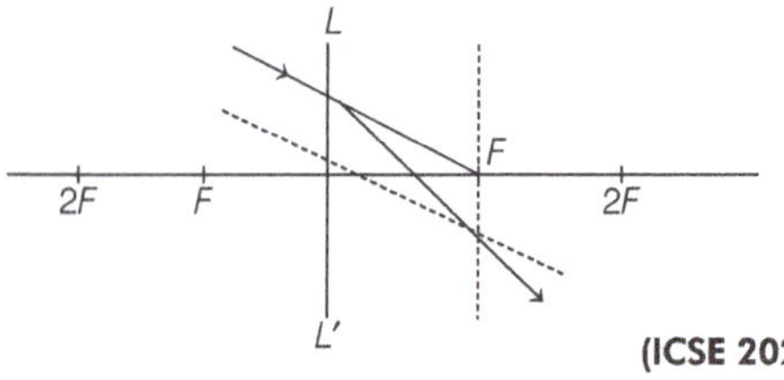

(ICSE 2022 Sem-I)

(i) If an object is placed at a distance of 30 cm in front of this lens, then the image will be

(a) virtual (b) diminished and inverted
(c) diminished (d) real and magnified

(ii) This type of lens can be used

(a) to correct hypermetropia
(b) to correct myopia
(c) to diverge light
(d) in the front door peepholes

(iii) An object is placed in front of this lens at a distance of 60 cm, then the image distance from the lens with proper sign convention is

(a) + 60 cm (b) + 30 cm
(c) − 30 cm (d) + 15 cm

(iv) An object is placed in front of this lens at a distance of 60 cm, then the magnification of the image is

(a) 0.25 (b) 1.25 (c) 0.5 (d) 1

38. The diagram below shows an image formed at a distance 36 cm from the lens *LL'* of focal length 12 cm. With respect to this answer the questions that follow. **(ICSE 2022 Sem-I)**

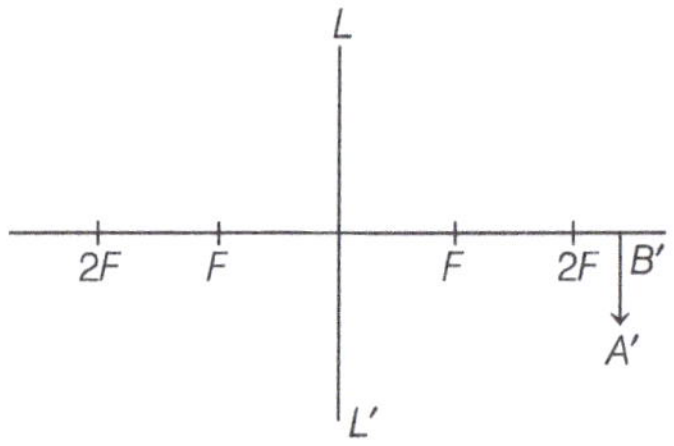

(i) The position of the object on the left-hand side should be

(a) between 12 cm to 30 cm from the lens
(b) beyond 24 cm from the lens
(c) between 12 cm to 24 cm from the lens
(d) within 12 cm from the lens

(ii) Power of this lens is

(a) − 8.33 D (b) + 8.4 D
(c) + 8.33 D (d) − 8.4 D

(iii) The object distance with sign convention is

(a) − 18 cm (b) − 15 cm
(c) − 9 cm (d) + 18 cm

(iv) If the lens *LL'* is replaced by another lens of same type but focal length 15 cm then for the same object distance,

(a) the size of the image decreases
(b) the size of the image increases
(c) the size of the image remains the same
(d) Information is insufficient to conclude

39. A lens of focal length 20 cm forms an inverted image at a distance of 60 cm from the lens. **(ICSE 2020)**

(i) Identify the lens.

(ii) How far is the lens present infront of the object?

(iii) Calculate the magnification of the image.

40. An object is placed at a distance 24 cm in front of a convex lens of focal length 8 cm. **(ICSE 2019)**

(i) What is the nature of the image so formed?

(ii) Calculate the distance of the image from the lens.

(iii) Calculate the magnification of the image.

> **KEY idea**
>
> To calculate the magnification, first calculate the distance of the image from lens (v) and then magnification.

41. An object is placed at a distance of 12 cm from a convex lens of focal length 8 cm. Find **(ICSE 2018)**

(i) the position of the image.

(ii) nature of the image.

42. An object AB is placed between $2F_1$ and F_1 on the principal axis of a convex lens as shown in the diagram.

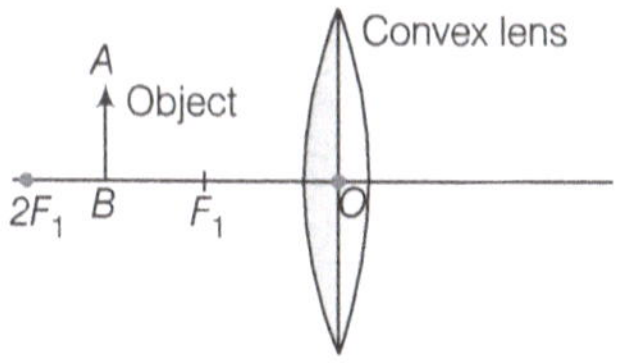

Copy the diagram and using these rays starting from point A, obtain the image of the object formed by the lens. **(ICSE 2013)**

43. A converging lens is used to obtain an image of an object placed in front of it. The inverted image is formed between F_2 and $2F_2$ of the lens.

(i) Where is the object placed?

(ii) Draw a ray diagram to illustrate the formation of the image obtained. **(ICSE 2012)**

44. An object is placed in front of a lens between its optical centre and the focus and forms a virtual, erect and diminished image.

(i) Name the lens which forms this image.

(ii) Draw a ray diagram to show the formation of the image with the above stated characteristics. **(ICSE 2011)**

45. An erect, magnified and virtual image is formed when an object is placed between the optical centre and principal focus of a lens.

(i) Name the lens.

(ii) Draw a ray diagram to show the formation of the image with the above stated characteristics. **(ICSE 2010)**

46. The diagram given alongside shows an object O and its image I. Copy the diagram and draw suitable rays to locate the lens and its focus. Name the type of lens in this case. **(ICSE 2004)**

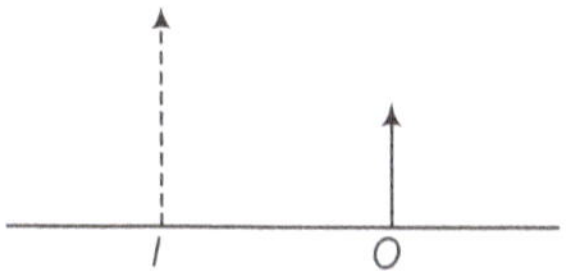

47. An erect, diminished and virtual image is formed when an object is placed in between the optical centre and principal focus of a lens.

(i) Name the type of lens, which forms the above image.

(ii) Draw a ray diagram to show the formation of the image with the above characteristics. **(ICSE 2002)**

48. Draw a ray diagram to illustrate the action of a convergent lens as a reading lens or a magnifying glass. **(ICSE 2000)**

Additional Questions

49. A concave lens of focal length 15 cm forms an image 10 cm from the lens. How far is the object placed from the lens? Draw the ray diagram.

50. An object 5 cm in length is placed 25 cm away from a converging lens of focal length 10 cm. Draw the ray diagram and find position, size and nature of image formed.

> **KEY idea**
>
> To know the size of the image, first calculate the image distance (v), then size of image with the help of formula
>
> $$h_i = h_o \times \frac{v}{u}$$

51. At what distance should an object be placed from a convex lens of focal length 18 cm to obtain an image at 36 cm from it? What will be the magnification produced in this case?

52. The image of an object formed by a lens is of magnification -1. If the distance between the object and its image is 60 cm, what is the focal length of the lens? If the object is moved 20 cm towards the lens, where would the image be formed? State reason and also draw a ray diagram in support of your answer.

53. A 6 cm tall object is placed perpendicular to the principal axis of a convex lens of focal length 25 cm. The distance of the object from the lens is 40 cm.

    By calculation determine
    (i) the position and
    (ii) the size of the image formed.

54. A thin converging lens form a real magnified image and virtual magnified image of an object in front of it.
    (i) Write the positions of the objects in each case.
    (ii) Draw ray diagrams to show the image formation in each part.
    (iii) How will the following be affected on cutting this lens into two halves along the principal axis?
    (a) Focal length
    (b) Intensity of the image formed by half lens

55. One-half of a convex lens of focal length 10 cm is covered with a black paper. Can such a lens produce an image of a complete object placed at a distance of 30 cm from the lens? Draw a ray diagram to justify your answer.

    A 4 cm tall object is placed perpendicular to principal axis of a convex lens of focal length 20 cm. The distance of the object from the lens is 15 cm. Find the nature, position and the size of the image.

Explanations

1. (a) Linear magnification, $m = \frac{v}{u} = \frac{h_i}{h_o}$

   The image formed by concave is virtual and highly diminished.

   i.e. $h_i < h_0$

   So, $m < 1$.

2. (d) Here, the converging point X will move towards the left side of the lens.

3. (c) A concave lens always diverge light rays and it produce virtual diminished image.

4. (a)

5. (c) Given, object size $= h_1 = 10$ cm

   Object distance $= u = -25$ cm

   Focal length $= f = -20$ cm

   By lens formula, $\frac{1}{v} - \frac{1}{u} = \frac{1}{f}$

   $$\frac{1}{v} + \frac{1}{25} = \frac{-1}{20} \Rightarrow \frac{1}{v} = \frac{-1}{25} - \frac{1}{20}$$

   $$\Rightarrow \frac{1}{v} = \frac{-4-5}{100} \Rightarrow \frac{1}{v} = \frac{-9}{100}$$

   $$\Rightarrow v = \frac{-100}{9} \text{ cm}$$

   $$v = -11.11 \text{ cm}$$

   Image will form at 11 cm in front of lens.

   Magnification, $m = \frac{h_{image}}{h_{object}} = \frac{-v}{u}$

   $$\Rightarrow h_{image} = \frac{-(-11.11)}{25} \times 10 = 4.44 \text{ cm}$$

   Image formed will be virtual and not possible to capture on a screen.

6. (d)

7. (b) Because P lens is have minimum focal length and power is inversely related to focal length. The lens with shortest focal length has the maximum power.

8. No, he is not correct because concave lens produces highly diminished, virtual and erect image.

9. When the printed piece of paper is moved near the both lenses, if the letters appear as
   (i) erect and diminished, the lens is concave lens.
   (ii) erect and magnified, the lens is convex lens.

10. (i) When a ray of light passes through the optical centre of a lens, then the ray coming out from the lens will be undeviated.
    (ii) A real and inverted image of an object can be produced by using convex lens or converging lens.

11. (i) The convex lens is used.

(ii) The ray diagram is shown below

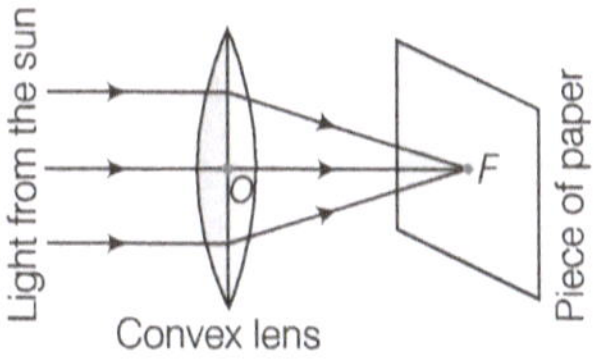

12.

Type of Lens	Position of Object	Nature of Image	Size of Image
Convex	At F	Real and inverted	Highly magnified
Concave	At infinity	Virtual and erect	Highly diminished

13. The ray diagram to show the formation of the image is shown below

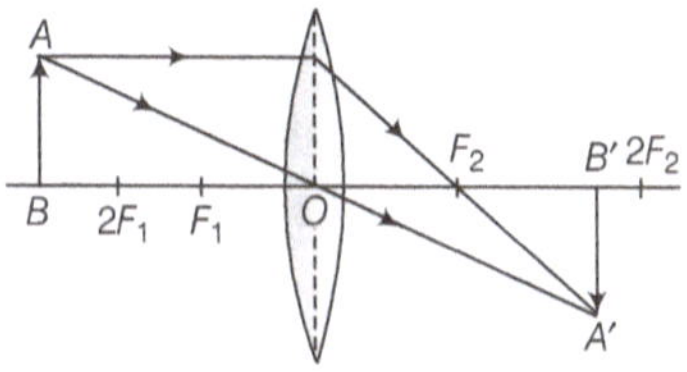

14. The ray diagram to show the formation of the image having same size as that of object is shown below

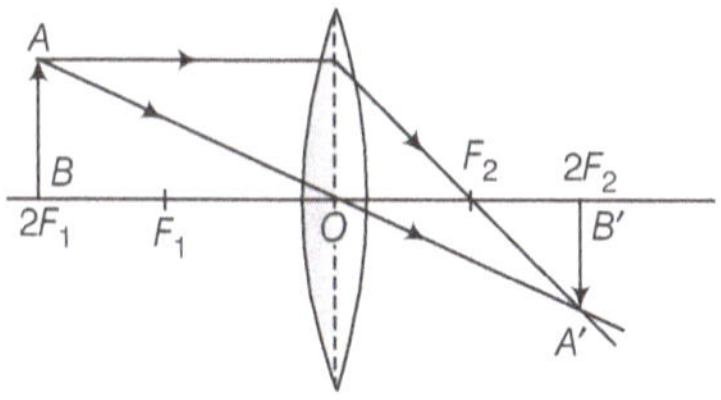

15. (i) In a reading glass, the object is placed between lens and its focus i.e., near the convex lens because convex lens acts as a magnifying lens for this position of object.

(ii) We cannot use concave lens for reading because image formed by the concave lens is virtual erect and highly diminished.

16. (i) No, because concave lens always produce a diminished image.

(ii) If a part of the lens is covered with an opaque paper, the effective aperture of the lens will be reduced, causing a change in amount of light that can pass through lens. This will cause a change in the way the lens focuses light, leading to a change in the effective focal length of the lens.

17. (i) The refractive index of water is more than air.

The formula of focal length,

$$\frac{1}{f}=\left(\frac{n_2}{n_1}-1\right)\left(\frac{1}{R_1}-\frac{1}{R_2}\right)$$

where, f = focal length,

n_2 = refractive index of lens

and n_1 = refractive index of water.

Here, if n_1 is greater than that of air.

So, if n_1 increases, then ratio of refractive index $\frac{n_2}{n_1}$ decreases, which gives us decrease in $\frac{n_2}{n_1}-1$.

So, as $\frac{1}{f}$ decreases, then focal length f increases.

(ii) A thin lens has greater focal length.

18. Given, power of a lens = −5 D

(i) We know that,

Power of lens $P=\dfrac{1}{f\text{ (focal length)}}$

or $f=\dfrac{1}{P} \Rightarrow f=\dfrac{1}{-5}$

$= -0.2\text{ m} = -20\text{ cm}$

(ii) The power of lens is negative, therefore lens is concave.

19. (i) To get real and same size image, object is placed at $2F$.

(ii) To use a converging lens as magnifying lens object must be placed between lens and first focus.

20. A convex lens of small focal length can be used as a reading glass or a magnifying glass. When an object is placed within the focal length of the lens, then a virtual, erect and magnified image is formed.

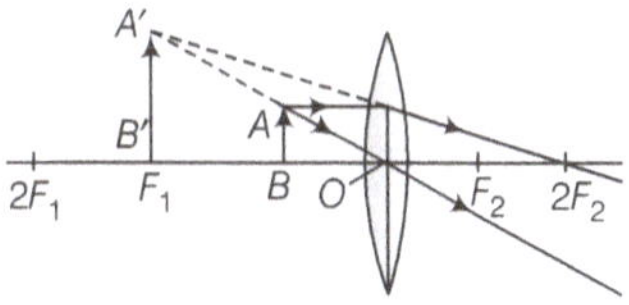

21. The concave lenses will always form virtual and erect images.

22. Given, $u=-36$ cm

$v=72$ cm

$$\frac{1}{f}=\frac{1}{v}-\frac{1}{u} \Rightarrow \frac{1}{f}=\frac{1}{72}-\frac{1}{(-36)}=\frac{1}{72}+\frac{1}{36}$$

$$\frac{1}{f}=\frac{1+2}{72}=\frac{3}{72} \Rightarrow \frac{1}{f}=\frac{1}{24} \Rightarrow f=24\text{ cm}$$

Power, $P = \frac{100}{f} = \frac{100}{24} = 4.16\text{ D}$

23. Given, $f = 10$ cm

$v = 60$ cm

$u = ?$

Using lens formula, $\frac{1}{f} = \frac{1}{v} - \frac{1}{u}$

$\Rightarrow \quad \frac{1}{10} = \frac{1}{60} - \frac{1}{u}$

$\Rightarrow \quad \frac{1}{u} = \frac{1}{60} - \frac{1}{10}$

$\Rightarrow \quad \frac{1}{u} = \frac{1-6}{60}$

$\Rightarrow \quad \frac{1}{u} = -\frac{5}{60}$

$\Rightarrow \quad \frac{1}{u} = -1/12$

$u = -12$ cm

The negative sign shows that the distance is measured in the opposite direction of the incident light.

The lens should be placed at 12 cm to obtain a real image.

Common Mistake In such type of questions, some students do not apply the correct sign convention, so they got wrong values v, u and f.

24. (i) It is concave lens because only concave lens makes virtual and diminished image.

(ii) Lens formula, $\frac{1}{f} = \frac{1}{v} - \frac{1}{u}$

$\frac{1}{f} = \frac{1}{-15} - \frac{1}{-50}$

$= \frac{-20+6}{300} = \frac{-14}{300}$

$\Rightarrow \quad f = \frac{300}{-14} = \frac{-150}{7}$

$\therefore \quad f = -21\frac{3}{7}$

In case of concave lens, u and v both are negative.

25. (i) When an object is placed between the optical centre and the principal focus of a concave lens, then virtual and diminished image of object is formed.

(ii) **Ray diagram**

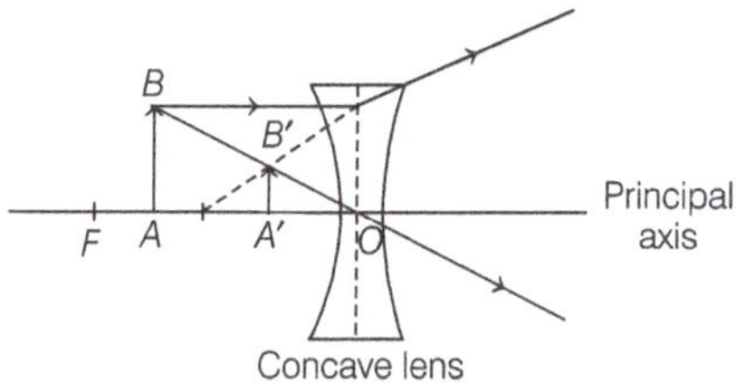

where, f = principal focus

and O = optical centre of lens.

26.

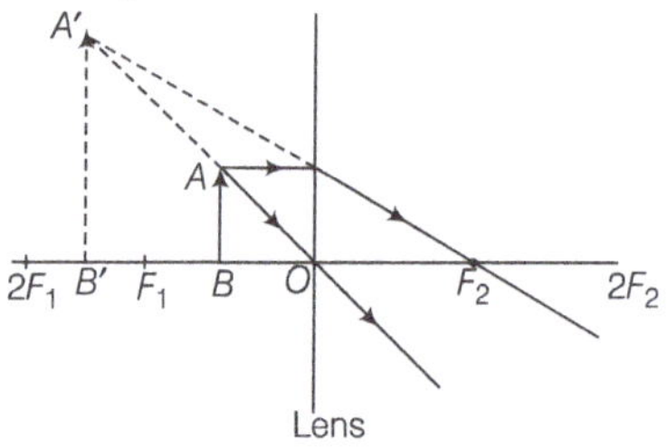

27. (i) Refer to text on page 77 (Power of lens).

(ii) Negative sign shows that child is using a concave lens in spectacle that is, the child has short sightedness.

(iii) Power $(P) = \frac{1}{\text{Focal length}}$

$P = \frac{1}{f}$

$\Rightarrow -25\text{ D} = \frac{1}{f}$

$\Rightarrow \quad f = \frac{1}{-25} = -0.4\text{m} = -40\text{ cm}$

28. Given, $u = -15$ cm

$f = 10$ cm

$v = ?$

Applying lens formula,

$\frac{1}{f} = \frac{1}{v} - \frac{1}{u}$

$\Rightarrow \quad \frac{1}{v} = \frac{1}{10} - \frac{1}{15}$

$\Rightarrow \quad \frac{1}{v} = \frac{3-2}{30}$

$\Rightarrow \quad \frac{1}{v} = \frac{1}{30}$

$\Rightarrow \quad v = 30$ cm

Image is formed at a distance of 30 cm on the other side.

Characteristics of image are

(i) real

(ii) inverted

(iii) magnified

29. (i) Concave lens.

(ii) Ray diagram

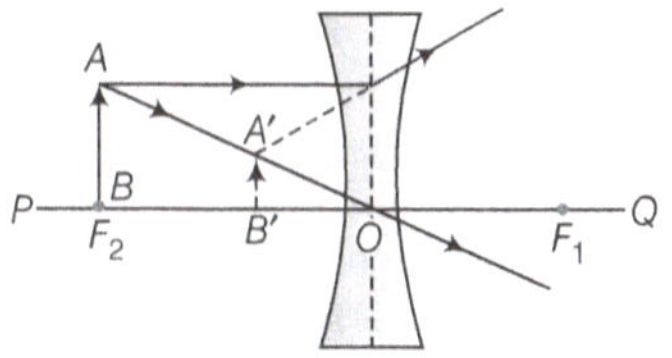

where, AB = object, $A'B'$ = image.

30. (i) Concave lens is the lens which produces a virtual image between the object and the lens.

(ii) The ray diagram is given below

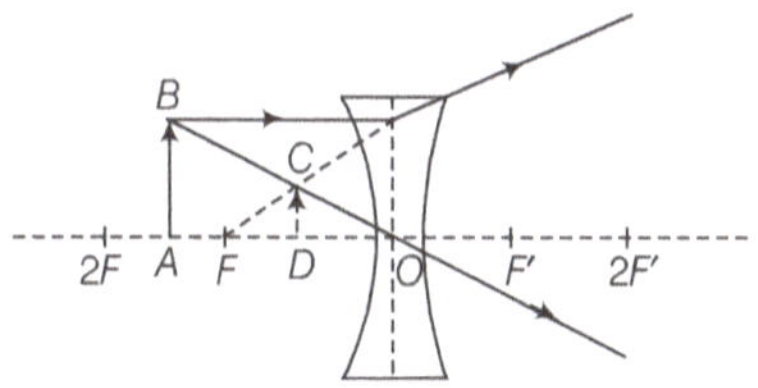

31. (i) In order to obtain a real, inverted and same size image as that of object, an object should be placed at $2F$ of the convex lens.

(ii) Ray diagram for an object located at $2F$.

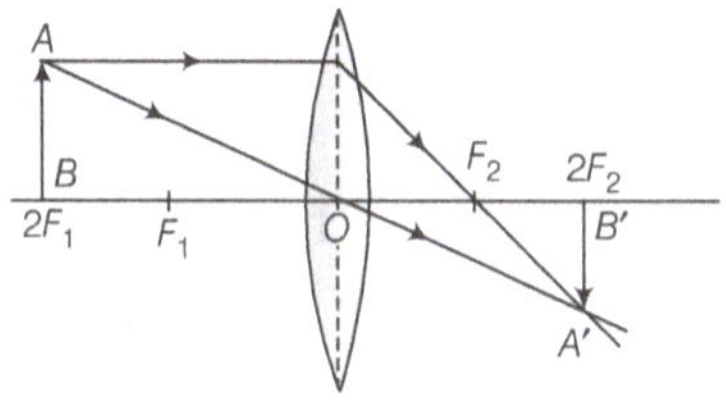

32. (i) The convex lens forms an erect, magnified and virtual image of an object.

(ii) The labelled diagram is shown below

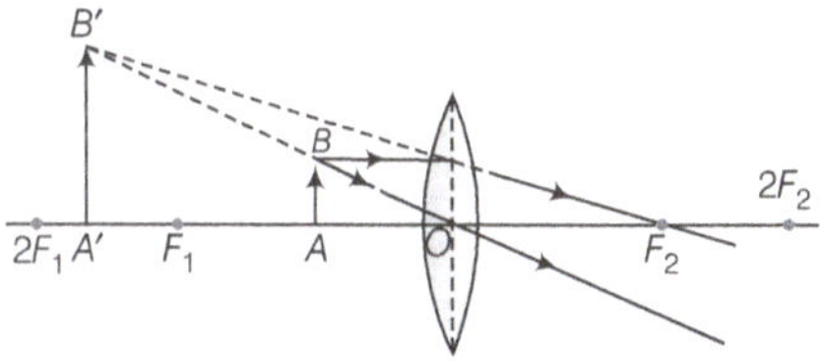

In this case, object is between optical centre (O) and focus (F_1) of a lens.

33. (i) Refer to text on page no. 77 (Power of lens).

(ii) Given, focal length $f = 25\text{ cm} = 0.25\text{ m}$

Power $P = ?$

$$\therefore \quad P = \frac{1}{f} = \frac{1}{0.25} = 4\text{ D}$$

34. (i) The ray diagram showing the formation of the image ($A'B'$) of the object AB is shown below

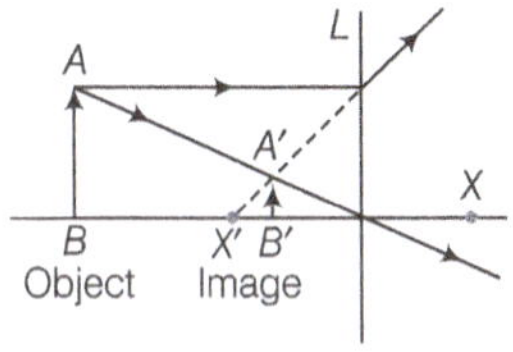

(ii) X is the principal focus.

35. (i) The lens is concave lens.

(ii) The ray diagram showing the formation of image is shown below

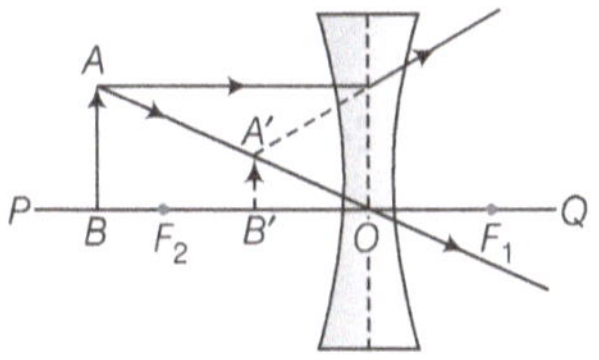

where, AB = object, $A'B'$ = image

The object is placed between focus (F) and $2F$.

36. (a) It is convex lens

(b)

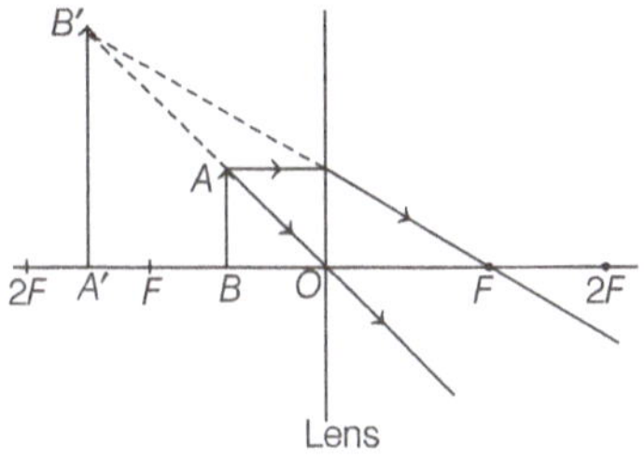

(c) Simple microscope (Magnifying glass)

37. (i) (d) Focal length, $f = +20$ cm

Object distance, $u = -30$ cm

Using lens formula, $\frac{1}{v} - \frac{1}{u} = \frac{1}{f}$

$$\frac{1}{v} = \frac{1}{f} + \frac{1}{u}$$

$$\Rightarrow \quad \frac{1}{v} = +\frac{1}{20} - \frac{1}{30}$$

$$v = +60\text{ cm}$$

Image formed will be real and magnified.

(ii) (a) As, it is a type of convex lens. So, it is used to correct hypermetropia.

(iii) (b) $u = -60$ cm, $f = +20$ cm

Using lens formula, $\frac{1}{v} - \frac{1}{u} = \frac{1}{f}$

$$\frac{1}{v} = \frac{1}{f} + \frac{1}{u}$$

$$\Rightarrow \quad \frac{1}{v} = \frac{1}{20} - \frac{1}{60}$$

$$\Rightarrow \quad \frac{1}{v} = \frac{3-1}{60}$$

$$\Rightarrow \quad v = +30 \text{ cm}$$

(iv) (c) Object distance $= -60$ cm

Image distance $= +30$ cm

Magnification, $m = -\frac{v}{u}$

$$m = +\frac{30}{60} = 0.5$$

38. (i) (c) Between 12 to 24 cm from the lens

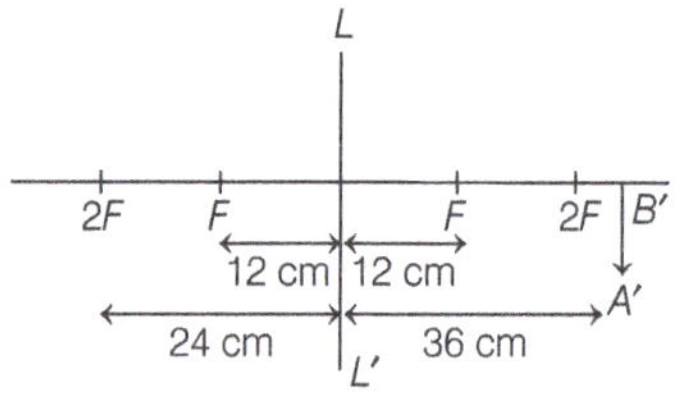

(ii) (c) $P = \frac{1}{f \text{(in m)}} = \frac{1}{12/100} = \frac{100}{12} = 8.33$ D

Positive sign as it is convex lens.

(iii) (a) Given, $f = 12$cm, $v = 36$cm, $u = ?$

using lens formula, $\frac{1}{f} = \frac{1}{v} - \frac{1}{u}$

$$\frac{1}{u} = \frac{1}{36} - \frac{1}{12}$$

$$u = -18 \text{ cm}$$

(iv) (b) The size of image increases because if focal length increases, then size of image increases.

39. (i) A convex lens forms both erect and inverted images while a concave lens always forms erect image, hence the lens must be of convex type.

(ii) Given, $v = 60$ cm, $f = 20$ cm

By lens formula, $\frac{1}{v} - \frac{1}{u} = \frac{1}{f}$

$$\Rightarrow \quad \frac{1}{60} - \frac{1}{u} = \frac{1}{20}$$

$$\Rightarrow \quad \frac{1}{u} = \frac{1}{60} - \frac{1}{20}$$

$$= -\frac{2}{60} = -\frac{1}{30}$$

$$\Rightarrow \quad u = -30 \text{ cm}$$

Hence, lens is at a distance of 30 cm in front of the object.

(iii) Magnification of the image, $m = \frac{v}{u} = \frac{60}{(-30)} = -2$

40. Given,

Object distance, $u = -24$ cm (for convex lens)

Focal length of lens, $f = 8$ cm

(i) As for convex lens, if $|u| > |f|$ then real and inverted image is formed and as $|u| > 2|f|$, then it will be diminished.

(ii) As we know that, $\frac{1}{f} = \frac{1}{v} - \frac{1}{u}$

where, v is the image distance from lens.

$$\frac{1}{v} = \frac{1}{f} + \frac{1}{u}$$

$$v = \frac{uf}{f+u} = \frac{(-24)(8)}{(8)+(-24)}$$

$$v = \frac{(-24) \times 8}{-16} = 12 \text{ cm}$$

(iii) As we know that,

Magnification, $m = \frac{v}{u} = \frac{12}{-24} = -0.5$

Here, negative sign indicates that the image is inverted.

41. Given, distance of object $u = -12$ cm

Focal length of lens $f = 8$ cm

(i) We know that, $\frac{1}{f} = \frac{1}{v} - \frac{1}{u}$

$$\Rightarrow \quad \frac{1}{8} = \frac{1}{v} - \frac{1}{(-12)}$$

$$\Rightarrow \quad \frac{1}{v} = \frac{1}{8} - \frac{1}{12}$$

$$\Rightarrow \quad \frac{1}{v} = \frac{3-2}{24}$$

$$\Rightarrow \quad \frac{1}{v} = \frac{1}{24}$$

$$\Rightarrow \quad v = 24 \text{ cm}$$

(ii) Real, inverted and magnified.

42. The formation of image is shown below

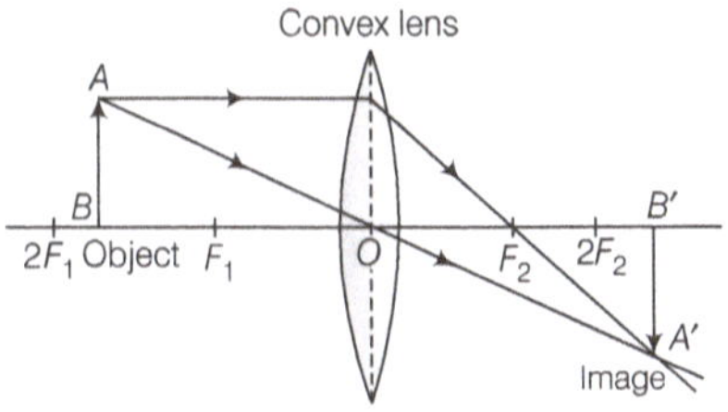

43. (i) The object is placed beyond $2F_1$.

(ii) The ray diagram to illustrate the formation of the image is shown below

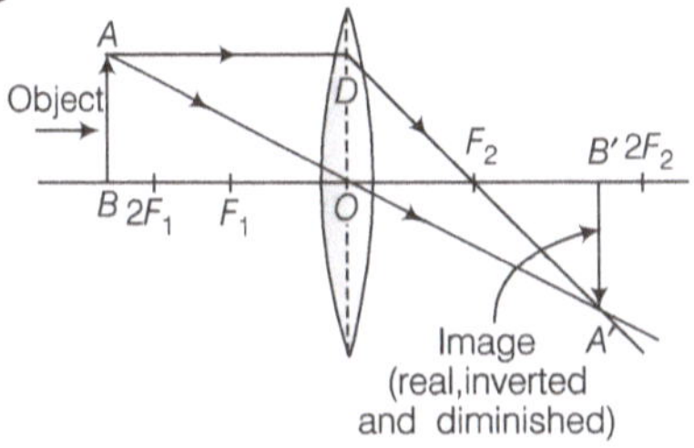

44. (i) This image is formed by using concave lens.

(ii) The ray diagram to show the formation of the image is shown below

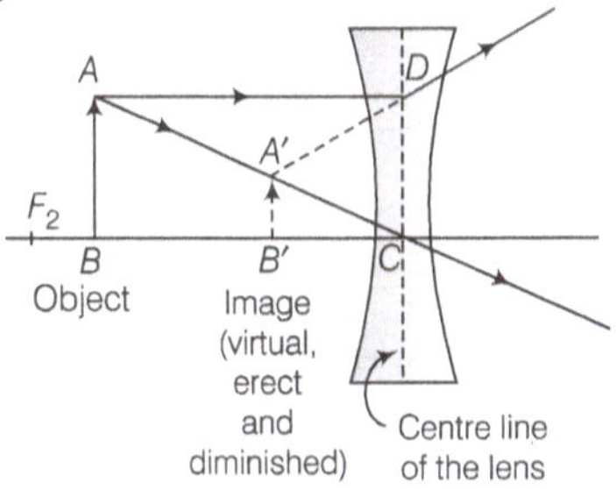

45. (i) The lens used is convex lens.

(ii) The ray diagram to show the formation of the image with the above characteristics is shown below

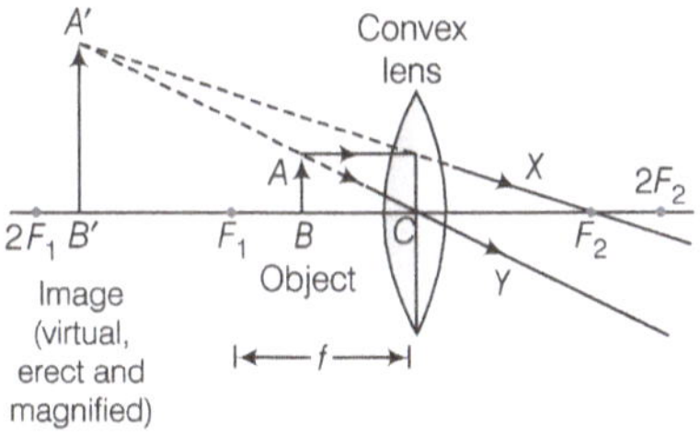

46. The ray diagram is shown below

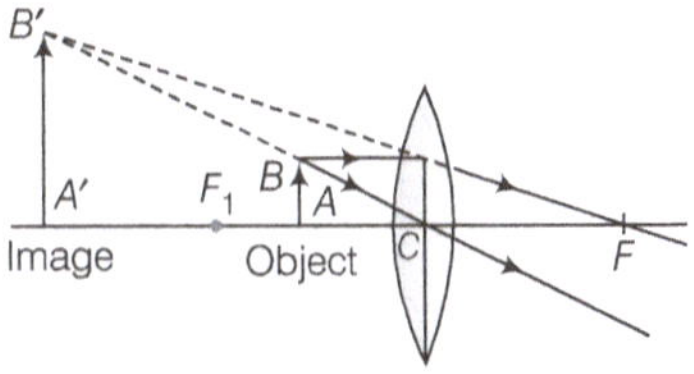

The lens used is convex lens.

47. (i) The type of lens used is concave lens.

(ii) The ray diagram showing the formation of image is shown as below

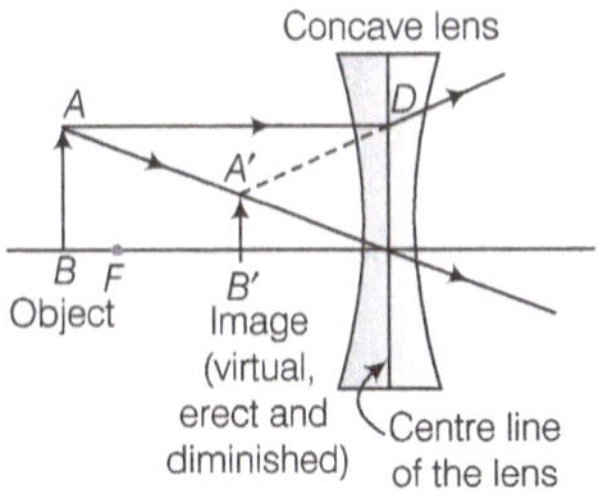

48. A convex lens of small focal length can be used as a reading glass or a magnifying glass. When an object is placed within the focal length of the lens, then a virtual, erect and magnified image is formed.

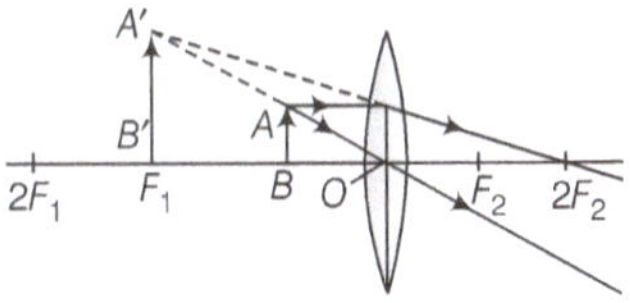

49. Given, focal length $f = -15$ cm

Image distance $v = -10$ cm

By lens formula,

$$\frac{1}{f} = \frac{1}{v} - \frac{1}{u}$$

or

$$\frac{1}{u} = \frac{1}{v} - \frac{1}{f} = \frac{1}{-10} - \frac{1}{(-15)}$$

$$= \frac{1}{15} - \frac{1}{10} = \frac{-1}{30}$$

$\therefore \quad u = -30$ cm from the lens.

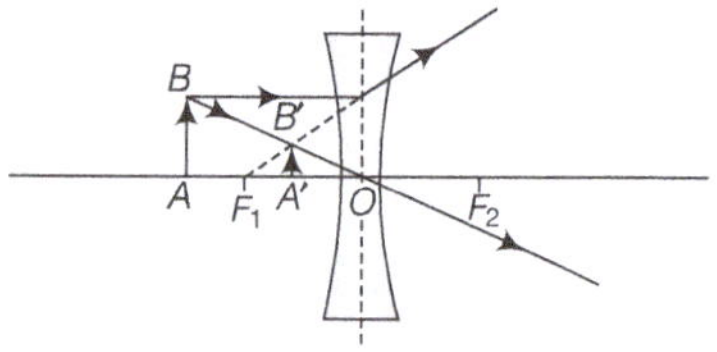

Thus, the object is placed at 30 cm from the concave lens.

50.

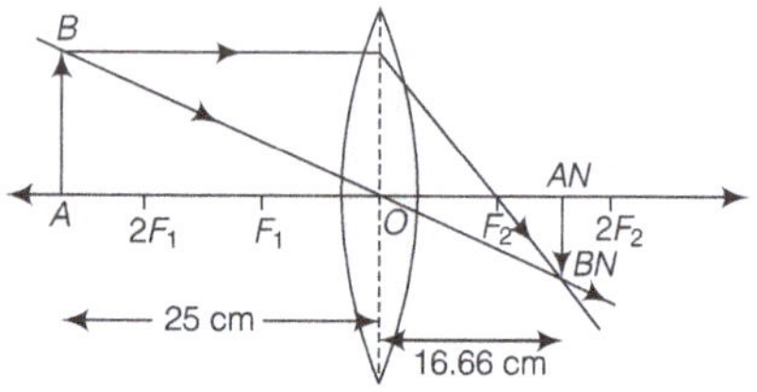

Given, object size $h_o = 5$ cm

Image size $h_i = ?$

Object distance $u = -25$ cm

Image distance $v = ?$

Focal length $f = 10$ cm

From lens formula, $\frac{1}{f} = \frac{1}{v} - \frac{1}{u}$

or $\frac{1}{v} = \frac{1}{f} + \frac{1}{u} = \frac{1}{10} + \frac{1}{(-25)} = \frac{3}{50}$

or $v = \frac{50}{3} = 16.66$ cm from the lens.

Size of image $h_i = h_o \times \frac{v}{u}$

$$= 5 \times \frac{50}{3 \times (-25)} = -3.33 \text{ cm}$$

[diminished inverted image]

The image is real in nature.

51. Given, focal length of lens $f = 18$ cm

Distance of image $v = \pm 36$ cm

[$\because \pm$ sign as an image can be on either side of lens]

Distance of object $u = ?$

Magnification produced $m = ?$

From lens formula,

$$\frac{1}{v} - \frac{1}{u} = \frac{1}{f}$$

$$\Rightarrow \quad \frac{1}{u} = \frac{1}{v} - \frac{1}{f}$$

$$= \frac{1}{\pm 36} - \frac{1}{18} = \frac{1}{36} - \frac{1}{18}$$

and $\frac{1}{-36} - \frac{1}{18} = \frac{1-2}{36}$

and $\frac{-1-2}{36} = \frac{-1}{36}$ and $\frac{-3}{36}$

$\therefore \quad u = -36$ cm and -12 cm

If $u = -36$ cm and $v = 36$ cm, then

$$m = \frac{v}{u} = \frac{36}{-36} = -1$$

Image is real and inverted.

If $u = -12$ cm and $v = -36$ cm, then

$$m = \frac{v}{u} = \frac{-36}{-12} = 3$$

Image is virtual and erect.

Concept Enhancer When image is virtual, it is erect and forms on the same side of lens. Thus, it can be said that convex lens gives positive linear magnification for virtual image and negative linear magnification for real image.

52.

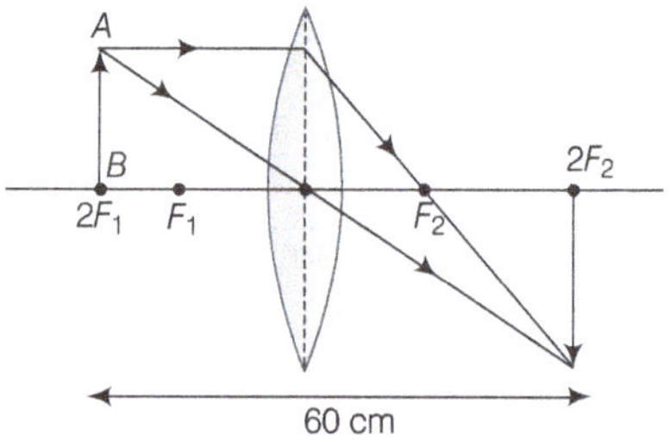

Given, $m = -1$, negative sign shows that image is real and inverted.

$\therefore \; |m| = 1$, it means that $h_i = h_o$

and this is possible in convex lens.

It implies that, object and image both will be at $2F$.

So, $\quad v = u$.

Object distance $\quad u = -30$ cm

Image distance $\quad v = +30$ cm

According to lens formula,

$$\frac{1}{f} = \frac{1}{v} - \frac{1}{u}$$

$$\Rightarrow \quad \frac{1}{f} = \frac{1}{30} - \left(\frac{-1}{30}\right)$$

$\Rightarrow \qquad f = 15\text{ cm}$

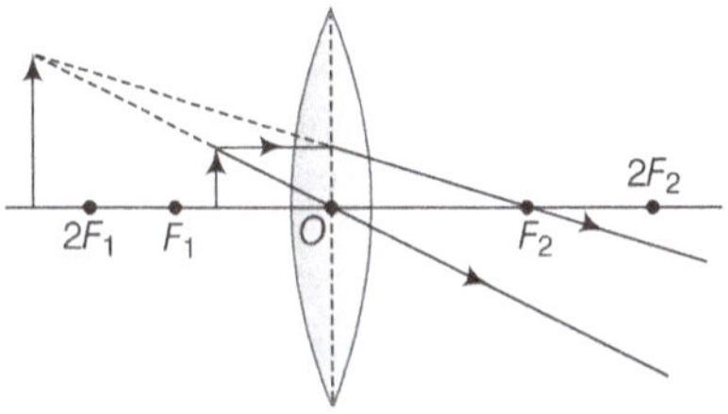

Now, object is moved 20 cm towards the lens.

$\because$ Object distance $u = -10\text{ cm}$

Focal length $f = +15\text{ cm}$

Again, using lens formula,

$$\frac{1}{v} - \frac{1}{u} = \frac{1}{f}$$

$$\Rightarrow \quad \frac{1}{v} = \frac{1}{15} + \frac{1}{(-10)}$$

$$\Rightarrow \quad \frac{1}{v} = \frac{1}{15} - \frac{1}{10} = \frac{2-3}{30}$$

$$\Rightarrow \quad v = -30\text{ cm}$$

53. Given, height of object $h_o = 6$ cm

Focal length of lens $f = 25$ cm

Distance of object $u = -40$ cm

(i) Using lens formula,

$$\frac{1}{f} = \frac{1}{v} - \frac{1}{u}$$

$$\Rightarrow \quad \frac{1}{v} = \frac{1}{f} + \frac{1}{u}$$

$$= \frac{1}{25} + \frac{1}{(-40)}$$

$$= \frac{8-5}{200} = \frac{3}{200}$$

$$\Rightarrow \quad v = \frac{200}{3} = 66.67\text{ cm}$$

(ii) $\therefore$ Magnification

$$m = \frac{h_i}{h_o} = \frac{v}{u}$$

$$\Rightarrow \quad h_i = \frac{v}{u} \times h_o$$

$$= \frac{200}{3 \times (-40)} \times 6$$

$$= -10\text{ cm}$$

54. (i) (a) Object is placed between F and $2F$.

(b) Object is placed between optical centre and F.

(ii) The ray diagrams are as follows

Part (a)

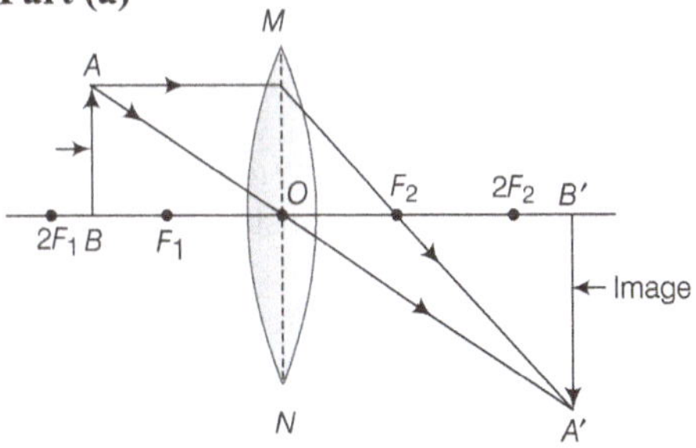

Part (b)

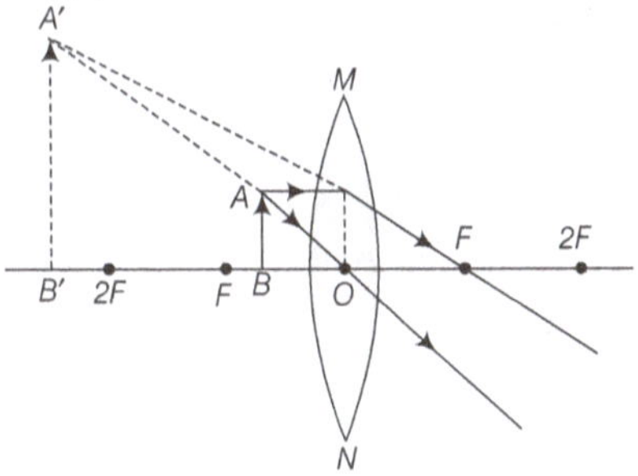

(iii) (a) There will be no change in focal length.

(b) Intensity will become one-fourth.

55. Yes, a lens can form a complete image but of less intensity and brightness.

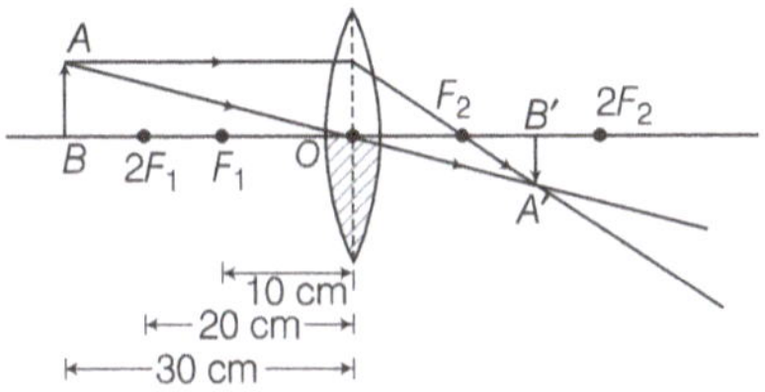

Given, height of object $h_o = 4$ cm,

Focal length $f = 20$ cm and

Distance of object $u = -15$ cm

Using lens formula, $\dfrac{1}{f} = \dfrac{1}{v} - \dfrac{1}{u}$

$$\Rightarrow \quad \frac{1}{v} = \frac{1}{f} + \frac{1}{u} = \frac{1}{20} + \frac{1}{(-15)} = \frac{15-20}{300} = \frac{-5}{300}$$

$$\therefore \quad v = -60\text{ cm}$$

As we know that, magnification, $m = \dfrac{h_i}{h_o} = \dfrac{v}{u}$

$$\Rightarrow \quad h_i = h_o \times \frac{v}{u} = 4 \times \frac{-60}{-15} = 16\text{ cm}$$

Image formed is virtual, erect and magnified.

CHAPTER TEST

01 Mark Questions

1 First focal length and second focal length of a thin are equal.

(a) only if the media on both sides of the lens are same

(b) even if the media on both side of the lens are not same

(c) only if medium on both side of the lens is air

(d) only if the material of the medium is glass

2 A ray of light directed towards the optical centre of a lens suffers

(a) 0° deviation

(b) 90° deviation

(c) 180° deviation

(d) None of the above

3 If a lens is immersed in water, its focal length.

(a) decreases

(b) increases

(c) remains same

(d) may increases or decrease depending on the refractive index of liquid.

4 For which object position, the image formed by a convex lens is of equal size of the object?

(a) At *F*

(b) At 2*F*

(c) At ∞

(d) Between *F* and 2*F*

5 According to sign convention, the focal length of concave lens is

(a) positive (b) negative

(c) zero (d) one

02 Marks Questions

6 What is a lens?

7 Name the two kinds of lens. Draw diagrams to illustrate them.

8 State difference between a convex and a concave lens in their

(i) appearance and

(ii) action on the incident light.

9 Define the term focal length of a lens.

10 Draw a diagram to represent the second focus of a concave lens.

03 Marks Questions

11 Define the term principal foci of a concave lens and show them with the help of proper diagrams.

12 Explain the optical centre of a lens with the help of proper diagrams.

13 What is the difference between double convex and a bi-convex lens?

Structured Questions

14 (i) Show by a diagram, the refraction of two light rays incident parallel to the principal axis on a concave lens by treating it as a combination of a glass slab and two triangular glass prisms. **(3)**

(ii) A beam of light incident on a convex lens parallel to its principal axis converges at a point *F* on the principal axis. Name the point *F*. Draw a ray diagram to show it. **(3)**

(iii) A concave lens forms the image of an object kept at a distance 20 cm in front of it, at a distance 10 cm on the side of the object.

(a) What is the nature of the image?

(b) Find the focal length of the lens. **(4)**

15 (i) The focal length of a convex lens is 25 cm. At what distance from the optical centre of the lens, an object be placed to obtain a virtual image of twice the size. **(3)**

(ii) The focal length of a convex lens is 25 cm. Express its power with sign. **(3)**

(iii) An object is placed at a distance of 20 cm in front of a concave lens of focal length 20 cm. Find

(a) position of image and

(b) the magnification of image. **(4)**

Answers

1. (a) **2.** (a) **3.** (b) **4.** (b) **5.** (b)

14. (iii) (a) virtual image (b) $f = -20$ cm

15. (i) (a) $u = -12.5$ cm (ii) $P = +4.0$ D

(iii) (a) $v = -10$ cm (b) $+0.5$

05

Spectrum of Light

TREND ANALYSIS 4 YEARS

Average No. of Questions Across all Sets

	Types of Questions	2024	2023	2020	2019
Spectrum of Light	1 Mark	1	1	–	–
	2 Marks	–	–	1	1
	3 Marks	1	–	–	–
	4 Marks	–	2	–	–

Prism

A prism is a transparent refracting medium bounded by two plane surfaces inclined to each other at certain angle.

Deviation Produced by a Triangular Prism

The given figure shows the deviation produced by a triangular prism.

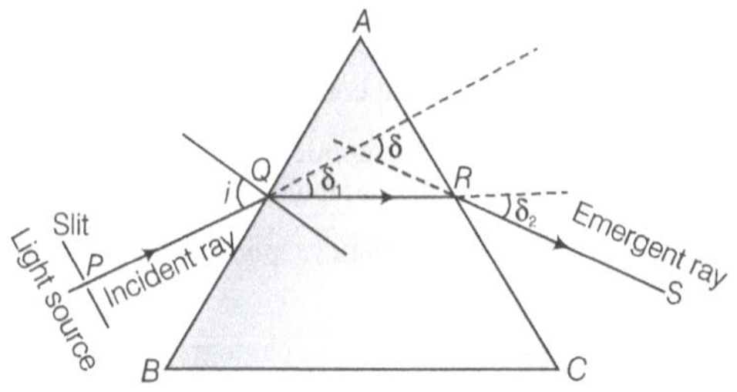

When a light ray PQ of single colour enters a triangular prism ABC, it gets deviated by an angle δ_1 towards the base BC at the first surface AB of the prism and travels straight as QR inside the prism. δ_1 depends on the angle of incidence and the refractive index of material of prism w.r.t. air.

On striking the second surface AC, the ray QR further deviated by an angle δ_2 towards BC and travels RS outside the prism. δ_2 depends on the angle of incidence at the second surface and the refractive index of air w.r.t. glass. For emergent ray RS, the total deviation δ w.r.t. the incident ray PQ is given by

$$\delta = \delta_1 + \delta_2$$

Dependence on Colour (Wavelength) of a Light

The light entering the prism is a mixture of several colours and the emergent beam also has different colours arranged in a definite order, because the light of different colours have different speeds in medium.

Dispersion of White Light by a Glass Prism

The phenomenon of splitting of white light into its component colours when it passes through a prism is called **dispersion of light**. Thus, band of seven colours, so obtained the VIBGYOR (V = violet, I = indigo, B = blue, G = green, Y = yellow, O = orange and R = red) is called **spectrum**.

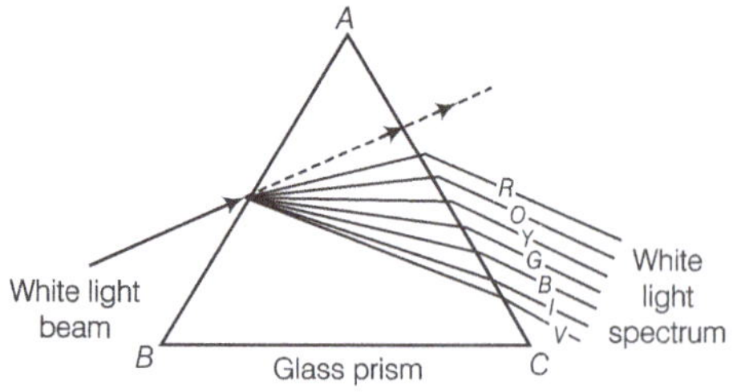

NOTE Isaac Newton was the first one to use a glass prism to obtain the spectrum of light.

Cause of Dispersion

Light rays of different colours travel with the same speed in vacuum and air but in any other medium, they travel with different speeds and bend through different angles, which leads to the formation of spectrum.

Spectrum The band of seven colours formed on a white screen when a beam of white light is passed through a glass prism is called spectrum.

Scattering of Light

It means to throw light in various random directions. When white light from the sun enters into the earth's atmosphere, the light gets scattered by the dust particles and air molecules present in the atmosphere. The scattering of light by the air molecules was first studied by the scientist Rayleigh.

Electromagnetic Spectrum

The orderly distribution of electromagnetic radiations according to their wavelength or frequency is known as electromagnetic spectrum. The portion of the spectrum which lies between the red and the violet regions is called **visible spectrum** and the portion of the spectrum which lies beyond the red and violet regions is called **invisible spectrum.**

Actually, the waves of wavelength longer than the red part of the visible spectrum in increasing order of wavelength are the infrared radiations, microwaves and radio waves, while the waves of wavelength shorter than the violet part of the visible spectrum in decreasing order of wavelength are the ultraviolet rays, X-rays and gamma rays.

These are all electromagnetic waves of different wavelength with properties similar to the light rays. Each wave travels with the same speed equal to $3 \times 10^8 \text{ ms}^{-1}$ in vacuum (in air). The speed (c), frequency (ν) and wavelength (λ) of the electromagnetic waves are related as

$$c = \nu\lambda$$

Broad Classification and Approximate Ranges of Wavelength

The table given below shows the various parts of the electromagnetic spectrum with approximate wavelength range, frequency range, their sources of production and detection.

Type	Wavelength Range (m)	Frequency Range (Hz)	Production	Detection
Radio wave	0.3 to 6×10^2	10^9 to 5×10^5	Oscillating circuit or rapid acceleration and retardation of electrons in aerials	Receiver's aerial
Microwave	10^{-3} to 0.3	3×10^{11} to 1×10^9	Klystron valve or magnetron valve	Point contact diodes
Infrared	8×10^{-7} to 1×10^{-3}	4×10^{14} to 3×10^{11}	Vibrations of atoms and molecules	Thermopile, bolometer, infrared photographic films
Visible light	4×10^{-7} to 8×10^{-7}	8×10^{14} to 4×10^{14}	Excitation of valency electrons in atoms	Human eye, photocells, photographic plate
Ultraviolet	6×10^{-9} to 4×10^{-7}	5×10^{16} to 8×10^{14}	Excitation of atoms spark and arc lamp	Photocells, photographic film
X-rays	1×10^{-13} to 3×10^{-8}	3×10^{21} to 1×10^{16}	X-rays tubes or excitation of inner shell electron	Photographic film, geiger tubes
Gamma rays	0.6×10^{-14} to 1×10^{-10}	5×10^{22} to 3×10^{18}	Nuclear origin	Photographic film, ionisation chamber

Properties Common to all Electromagnetic Spectrum

The properties common to all electromagnetic spectrum are as follows

(i) The electromagnetic waves of entire wavelength range do not require any material medium for their propagation.

(ii) They all travel with the same speed in vacuum which is same as the speed of light in vacuum, i.e. 3×10^8 m/s.

(iii) They exhibit the properties of reflection and refraction.
(iv) These waves are not deflected by the electric and magnetic fields.
(v) These waves are transverse waves.

Properties and Uses of Different Rays

Ultraviolet Radiation

It was discovered by the Ritter in 1801. They are produced by some special lamps and very hot bodies. Ultraviolet rays coming from the sun are absorbed by the ozone layer in the earth's atmosphere. The wavelength range varies from 10 nm to 400 nm.

Properties of ultraviolet radiation are as follows

(i) They can pass through quartz but are absorbed by glass.
(ii) They obey the laws of reflection and refraction.
(iii) These radiations travel in a straight line with a speed of 3×10^8 m/s in air (or vacuum).
(iv) It can be scattered by dust particles in the atmosphere.
(v) They cause health hazards like skin cancer, if our body is exposed for a long period.

Uses of ultraviolet radiation are as follows

(i) For sterilising purposes.
(ii) For detecting the purity of golds, eggs, ghee, etc.
(iii) For producing vitamin D in food of plants and animals.

Infrared Radiation

It was discovered by Herschell. They are sometimes called **heat waves**, because their absorption causes of the heating effect in the bodies and surroundings. They are produced by hot bodies and molecules. Its range is from 700 nm to 1 mm.

Properties of infrared radiation are as follows

(i) They do not affect the ordinary photographic film.
(ii) They obey the laws of reflection and refraction.
(iii) They are absorbed by glass but are not absorbed by rock salt.
(iv) They are detected by their heating property.
(v) They are less scattered by the atmosphere.

Uses of infrared radiation are as follows

(i) They are used in photography at night and also in mist and fog.
(ii) They are used for therapeutic purposes.
(iii) They are used in remote control of TV and other gadgets.
(iv) They are used as signals during war.

PYQs Previous Years Questions

1 Mark Questions

1. Why do we use red colour as a danger signal on the top of a skyscraper ? **(ICSE 2024)**

2. Speed of blue light in water is **(ICSE 2023)**

   (a) more than green light (b) more than orange light
   (c) more than violet light (d) more than red light

3. When seven spectral colours passes through a glass block from air, then which one of the following statements is correct? **(ICSE SQP 2023)**

   (a) In the glass block, speed of blue light > speed of yellow light.
   (b) In the glass block, speed of green light > speed of orange light
   (c) In the glass block, speed of violet light > speed of red light.
   (d) In the glass block, speed of orange light > speed of indigo light.

4. The wavelength range of visible light is **(ICSE 2022 Sem-I)**

   (a) 40 nm to 80 nm (b) 4000 nm to 8000 nm
   (c) 4 nm to 8 nm (d) 400 nm to 800 nm

5. The deviation produced by an equilateral prism does not depend on the **(ICSE 2022 Sem-I)**

   (a) angle of incidence (b) size of the prism
   (c) material of the prism (d) colour of light used

6. The colour of white light which is deviated least by a prism is **(ICSE 2022 Sem-I)**

   (a) green (b) yellow
   (c) red (d) violet

7. Which characteristic property of light is responsible for the blue colour of the sky? **(ICSE 2011)**

8. Fill in the blanks.

A piece of red cloth appears red in white light, because it .... blue and green colours .... only red colour. **(ICSE 2000)**

2 Marks Questions

9. The wavelengths for the light of red and blue colours are nearly 7.8×10^{-7} m and 4.8×10^{-7} m, respectively.
   (i) Which colour has the greater speed in a vacuum?
   (ii) Which colour has a greater speed in glass? **(ICSE 2020)**

10. An electromagnetic radiation is used for photography in fog. **(ICSE 2019)**
   (i) Identify the radiation.
   (ii) Why is this radiation mentioned by you, ideal for this purpose?

11. (i) Define scattering.
   (ii) The smoke from a fire looks white.
   Which of the following statements is true?
   I. Molecules of the smoke are bigger than the wavelength of light.
   II. Molecules of the smoke are smaller than the wavelength of light. **(ICSE 2018)**

12. A boy uses blue colour of light to find the refractive index of glass. He then repeats the experiment using red colour of light. Will the refractive index be the same or different in the two cases? Give a reason to support your answer. **(ICSE 2016)**

13. (i) Name the high energetic invisible electromagnetic waves, which help in the study of the structure of crystals.
   (ii) State an additional use of the waves mentioned in part (i). **(ICSE 2015)**

KEY idea

Student should learn the concept "properties and uses of different rays" to answer this question.

14. (i) Name a prism required for obtaining a spectrum of ultraviolet light.
   (ii) Name the radiations which can be detected by a thermopile. **(ICSE 2014)**

15. Why is the red colour used as a sign of danger? **(ICSE 2014)**

16. (i) What is meant by dispersion of light?
   (ii) In the atmosphere, which colour of light gets scattered the least? **(ICSE 2012)**

17. (i) Why is the white light considered to be polychromatic in nature?
   (ii) Give the range of the wavelength of those electromagnetic waves which are visible to us. **(ICSE 2009)**

18. Why are infrared radiations preferred over ordinary visible light for taking photographs in fog? **(ICSE 2007)**

19. A particular type of high energy invisible electromagnetic rays help us to study the structure of crystals. Name these rays and give another important use of these rays. **(ICSE 2007)**

20. Explain briefly, what causes the twinkling of stars at night? **(ICSE 2005)**

21. Name any two electromagnetic waves, which have a frequency higher than that of violet light. State one use of each. **(ICSE 2005)**

3 Marks Questions

22. Below is an incomplete table showing the arrangement of electromagnetic spectrum in the increasing order of their wavelength. Complete the table. **(ICSE 2024)**

Gamma ray
X-rays
UV - rays
Visible rays
Infrared
A
Radio waves

   (i) Identify the radiation *A*.
   (ii) Name the radiation used to detect fracture in bones.
   (iii) Name one property common to both *A* and radio waves.

23. The diagram below shows the extreme colours of a visible spectrum (*X* and *Y*). **(ICSE SQP 2023)**

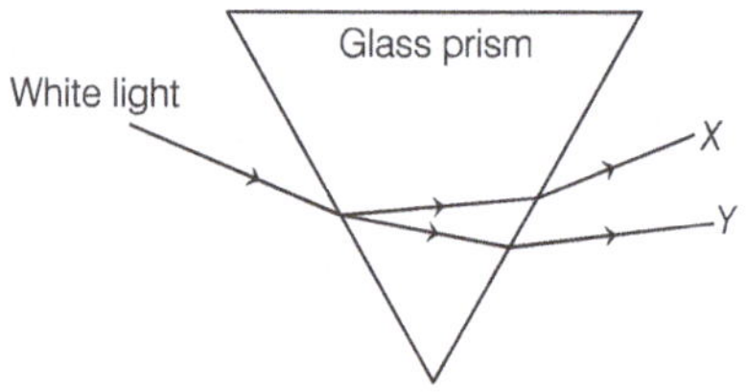

(i) Identify the colours *X* and *Y*.

(ii) Which colour has greater speed in vacuum?

24. (i) Why does the sun appear red at sunrise?

(ii) Name the subjective property of light related to its wavelength. **(ICSE 2015)**

25. A type of electromagnetic wave has wavelength 50 Å.

(i) Name the wave.

(ii) What is the speed of the wave in vacuum?

(iii) State one use of this type of wave. **(ICSE 2014)**

26. Name the radiations

(i) that are used for photography at night.

(ii) used for detection of fracture in bones.

(iii) whose wavelength range is from 10 nm to 400 nm. **(ICSE 2013)**

27. (i) Suggest one way in each case by which we can detect the presence of

(a) infrared radiations

(b) ultraviolet radiations

(ii) Give one use of infrared radiations. **(ICSE 2011)**

28. Two parallel rays of red and violet light travelling through air, meet the air glass boundary as shown in the given figure.

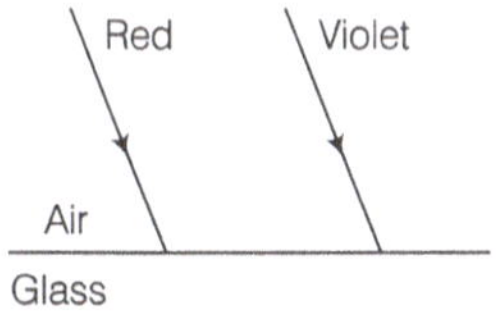

(i) Will their paths inside the glass be parallel? Give a reason for your answer.

(ii) Compare the speeds of the two rays inside the glass. **(ICSE 2010)**

29. Give one use of each of the electromagnetic radiations given below.

(i) Microwave

(ii) Ultraviolet radiation

(iii) Infrared radiation **(ICSE 2006)**

30. (i) A glass slab is placed over a page on which the word VIBGYOR is printed with each letter in its corresponding colour.

(a) Will the image of all the letters be in the same place?

(b) If not, state which letter will be raised to the maximum. Give a reason for your answer.

(ii) What will be the colour of an object which appears green in white light and black in red light? **(ICSE 2005)**

4 Marks Questions

31. The diagram below shows two parallel rays *A* (orange) and *B* (blue) incident from air, on air-glass boundary.

(i) Copy and complete the path of the rays *A* and *B*.

(ii) How do the speeds of these rays differ in glass?

(iii) Are the two refracted rays in glass parallel? Give a reason. **(ICSE 2023)**

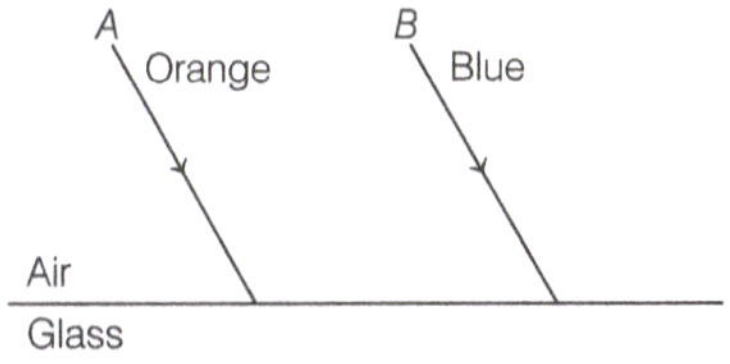

32. (i) Infrared radiations are used in warfare. Explain with reason. Why?

(ii) A ray of light is incident at 45° on an equilateral prism in the diagram below.

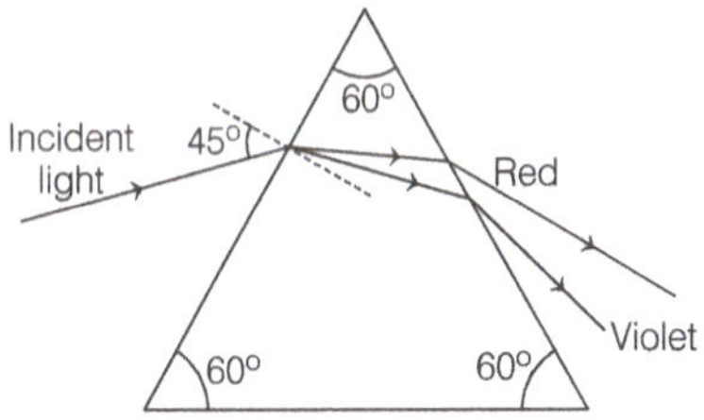

(a) Name the phenomenon exhibited by the ray of light when it enters and emerges out of the prism.

(b) State the cause of the above phenomenon mentioned by you. **(ICSE 2023)**

33. What do you understand by the term 'scattering of light'? Which colour of white light is scattered the least and why? **(ICSE 2016)**

> **KEY idea**
> Student should learn the concept "scattering of the light" to answer this question.

34. Name any four regions of electromagnetic spectrum (other than visible light) in increasing order of their wavelength. **(ICSE 2002)**

35. (i) Explain, why in daylight an object appears red when seen through a red glass and black when seen through a blue glass?

(ii) Name the extreme colours in pure spectrum of light. **(ICSE 2001)**

Explanations

1. Red light is the least scattered by fine particles, fog, or smoke present in the atmosphere. Therefore, it can reach to a longer distance.
2. (c)
3. (d)
4. (d)
5. (b)
6. (c) Red colour of white light deviates least by a prism as it has longer wavelength.
7. The scattering of light is the characteristic property of light responsible for the blue colour of the sky.
8. absorbs, reflect.
9. Given, wavelength of light for red colour,

$$\lambda_R = 7.8 \times 10^{-7} \text{ m}$$

Wavelength of light for blue colour,

$$\lambda_B = 4.8 \times 10^{-7} \text{ m}$$

$$\therefore \quad \lambda_R > \lambda_B$$

(i) Speed of light in vacuum is independent to the wavelength of light. Hence, red colour of light has equal speed in vacuum as the blue colour of light.

(ii) For same medium, speed of light is directly proportional to its wavelength. Therefore, speed of red colour of light is greater than speed of blue colour of light as $\lambda_R > \lambda_B$.

10. (i) Infrared radiations are used in photography in fog and mist and also at night.

(ii) Because infrared radiation have long wavelength. As they are having low frequency the energy associated with them is also low. So, they do not scatter much and can penetrate appreciably through fog.

Concept Enhancer Infrared radiation is used for photography in fog. This radiation is ideal for this purpose because it can penetrate fog.

11. (i) The process of absorption and then re-emission of light energy is called scattering of light. When sunlight passes through the earth's atmosphere, most of the light gets scattered (i.e. the light spreads in all directions) by the fine dust particles and air molecule in it.

(ii) As molecules of the smoke are bigger than the wavelength of light, as a result, they scatter all wavelengths which overlaps to give white colour.

Statement I is correct.

12. Since, the refractive index of the medium is always inversely proportional to the wavelength of light. Moreover, it is known that wavelength of the red colour is more than that of the blue colour. So, the refractive index in case of blue colour of light will be greater than that of red colour of light.
13. (i) X-rays are used to study the structure of a crystal.

(ii) Uses of X-rays are

I. In surgery for the detection of fractures foreign bodies like bullets, stones in human body, etc.

II. For detecting faults, cracks, flaws and holes in the final products of metals.

III. To cure untrackable skin diseases and malignant growths.

14. (i) Quartz prism is required for obtaining a spectrum of ultraviolet light.

(ii) Infrared radiations can be detected by a thermopile.

Concept Enhancer Thermopiles are used for contactless temperature sensing. It does not respond to absolute temperature.

15. The scattering of light is found to be inversely proportional to the fourth power of the wavelength of light. Thus, the scattering of red light is very much less than that of yellow light. Therefore, red colour signals can be seen upto a longer distance, so it is used as a sign of danger.
16. (i) The phenomenon of splitting of white light by a prism into its constituent colours is known as dispersion of light.

(ii) In the atmosphere, red colour of light gets scattered the least.

17. (i) Polychromatic light consists of many colours each having its characteristic wavelength. White colour is polychromatic light, because white light is made up of seven colours, i.e. VIBGYOR.

(ii) The range of 4000 Å to 7800 Å wavelength of electromagnetic wave is visible to us.

18. Infrared radiations are used for photography in fog, because they are not much scattered by mist or fog and can penetrate through fog, so photography can be done easily.
19. The rays discussed are X-rays. The important use of X-rays is to detect the fracture of bone, teeth, etc.

20. The twinkling of a star is due to atmospheric refraction of starlight.
As the light from the star enters the earth's atmosphere, it undergoes refraction due to varying optical densities of air at various altitudes. The continuously changing atmosphere refracts the light by different amounts.

In this way, the starlight reaching our eyes increases and decreases continuously and the star appears to twinkle at night.

21. The two electromagnetic waves which have a higher frequency than that of violet light and its uses are

(i) X-rays having the frequency of 3×10^{16} Hz. They are used for detection of fracture.

(ii) γ-rays having the frequency of 3×10^{19} Hz. They are used in medical sciences to kill cancer cells.

22. (i) Radiation A is microwaves

(ii) X - rays

(iii) Radiowaves and microwaves at the same speed through a vacuum.

23. (i) X is violet colour and Y is red colour.

(ii) In prism all the colours have same speed, while when they passes through the another vacuum like water the red light have the greatest speed.

24. (i) During sunrise, the sun is near the horizon, so the rays have to travel a larger part of the atmosphere. Therefore, light other than red is mostly scattered away. Most of the red light, which is the least scattered, enters our eyes. Hence, the sun appears red during sunrise.

> **Concept Enhancer** Rayleigh law states that the intensity of scattered light is inversely proportional to the fourth power of wavelength.

(ii) The subjective property of light related to its wavelength is the colour of light.

25 (i) The wave is X-rays as its range is 0.1 Å to 100 Å.

(ii) The speed of wave in vacuum is 3×10^{8} m/s.

(iii) X-rays are used for detection of fractures in bone, teeth, etc.

26. (i) Infrared radiations are used for photography at night.

(ii) X-rays are used for detection of fracture in bones.

(iii) Ultraviolet rays which have wavelength in range from 10 nm to 400 nm.

27. (i) (a) **Infrared radiations** By using a thermopile or a blackened bulb thermometer.

(b) **Ultraviolet radiations** By using silver chloride solution.

(ii) They are used in muscular therapy and for taking photographs in fog.

28.

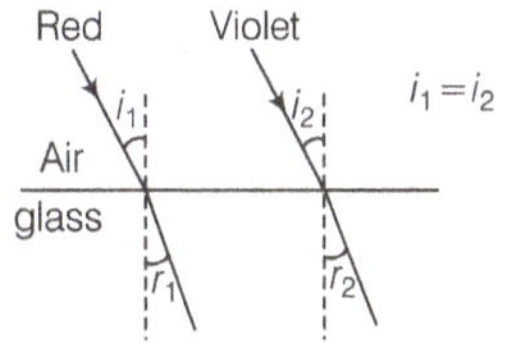

(i) No, the paths of two parallel rays of red and violet colours travelling through glass will not be parallel, because on entering the glass both the rays deviate to different extents, i.e. $r_1 > r_2$.

(ii) The red colour deviates less, while violet colour deviates more. Therefore, the speed of red colour in glass is more than the speed of violet colour in glass, i.e. $v_{\text{violet}} < v_{\text{red}}$.

29. (i) Microwaves are used for satellite communication and radar communication.

(ii) Ultraviolet radiations are used for sterilising purposes and detecting the purity.

(iii) Infrared radiations are used for photography at night in mist or fog.

30. (i) (a) No, the image of all the letters are not in the same place, because the letter of each colour have different frequency.

(b) The letter V for violet is raised more, because λ is least for violet colour.

(ii) The colour of an object which appears green in white light and black in red light will be green.

31. (i) The refractive index of glass is less for orange light, while it is more for blue light ($\mu_O < \mu_B$). So, orange is deviated less, while the blue is deviated more.

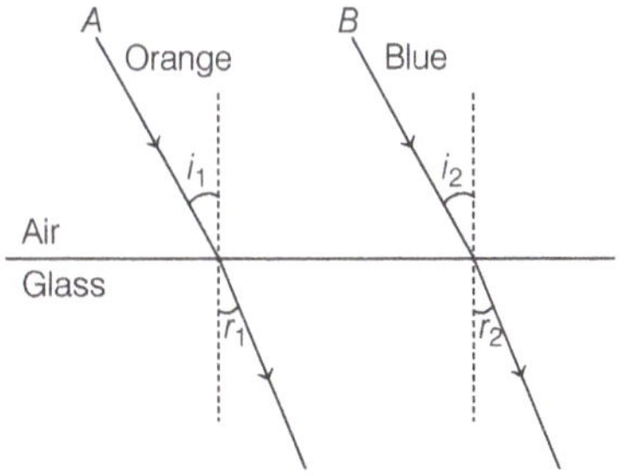

(ii) Since, the refractive index of glass is less for orange light. While it is more for blue light

($\mu_O < \mu_B$) in glass, the orange light travels faster than blue light.

(iii) The two refracted rays inside glass are not parallel. The reason is that the speed of orange light in glass is more. While it is less for the blue light, so the orange ray bends less. While the blue ray bends more (i.e. angle of refraction r_1 for orange is more than angle of refraction r_2 for blue ray).

32. (i) Infrared radiations are used as signals during warfare as they are not visible and they are not absorbed much in the medium. Therefore, they can be used as signals on distant objects obscured by atmospheric haze.

(ii) (a) When white light ray passes through a prism, it disperses into seven different colours and this phenomenon is called dispersion.

(b) When white light ray passes through a glass prism, its constituent colours (red, orange, yellow, green, blue, indigo, violet) travel with different speeds in the prism because the refractive index is colour dependent. This causes the dispersion of light.

33. The process, in which light rays get diffused or deflected by collision with particles of the medium that it traverses is called scattering of light. Red colour of white light is scattered the least and violet colour is scattered the most. It is because violet colour has shorter wavelength than red colour.

34. The four regions of electromagnetic spectrum in increasing order of wavelengths are γ-rays, X-rays, ultraviolet rays and infrared rays.

35. (i) In day or white light, when an object is seen through a red glass, it transmits only red light, because it reflects only red light. But when the same object is seen through blue glass, the red light reflects by the object is not transmitted through the blue glass and the object appears black, since no light reaches to our eyes.

(ii) The extreme colours of a pure spectrum are violet at one end and red at the other end.

Concept Enhancer In the spectrum obtained by the dispersion of white light through prism, speed of red colour of light is maximum whereas that of violet colour of light is minimum.

CHAPTER TEST

01 Mark Questions

1 When a white light ray falls on a prism, the ray at its first surface suffers
(a) only refraction
(b) only dispersion
(c) only deviation
(d) both deviation and dispersion.

2 Which of the following is correct?
(a) $\lambda_{blue} > \lambda_{yellow} > \lambda_{green}$
(b) $\lambda_{yellow} > \lambda_{green} > \lambda_{blue}$
(c) $\lambda_{yellow} > \lambda_{blue} > \lambda_{green}$
(d) $\lambda_{green} > \lambda_{blue} > \lambda_{yellow}$

3 The wavelength range of visible part of electromagnetic spectrum is
(a) 800 Å to 10^7 Å
(b) 4000 Å to 8000 Å
(c) 100 Å to 8000 Å
(d) 100 Å to 4000Å

4 Dispersion of light by a prism is due to the change in
(a) frequency of light
(b) scattering
(c) speed of light for different colour
(d) none of the above

5 Which of the following rays is used for night photography?
(a) Infrared (b) Ultraviolet
(c) Visible light (d) All of these

02 Marks Questions

6 Explain the cause of dispersion of white light through a prism.

7 The clouds are seen white. Give reason.

8 What is meant by scattering of light?

9 Why is white light considered to be polychromatic in nature?

10 Why is it difficult to drive on a foggy day?

11 Calculate the frequency of yellow light of wavelength 5500Å. The speed of light is 3×10^8 ms^{-1}.

12 Give useful and harmful effect of ultraviolet radiation on the human body.

13 The frequency range of visible light is from 3.75×10^{14} Hz to 7.5×10^{14} Hz. Calculate its wavelength range. (Take, speed of light $= 3 \times 10^8$ ms^{-1})

Structured Questions

14 (i) Explain how can you produce deviation with dispersion? **(4)**
(ii) Why is it difficult to drive on a foggy day? **(3)**
(iii) Why do we see a rainbow in the sky only after rainfall? **(3)**

15 (i) Explain how scattering of light depends upon particle size. **(3)**
(ii) Name three radiations and their wavelengths range, which are visible and beyond the violet end of the visible spectrum. **(3)**
(iii) How can we explain the reddish appearance of the sun at sunrise or sunset? Why does it not appear red at noon? **(4)**

Answers

1. (d) **2.** (b) **3.** (b) **4.** (c) **5.** (a)
11. 5.45×10^{14} Hz **13.** 4000Å to 8000Å

06

Sound

TREND ANALYSIS 4 YEARS

Average No. of Questions Across all Sets

Topic	Types of Questions	2024	2023	2020	2019
TOPIC 01 Sound Waves and Vibrations	1 Mark	1	2	–	–
	2 Marks	1	1	2	–
	3 Marks	1	1	–	1
	4 Marks	1	1	1	–
TOPIC 02 Characteristics of Sound	1 Mark	–	1	–	–
	2 Marks	–	–	–	3
	3 Marks	–	–	1	1
	4 Marks	–	–	–	–

Waves is a form of energy in a pattern of periodic disturbances.

Wave motion is a process of energy transfer in a medium in the form of disturbance due to the repeated periodic motion of the particles of the medium about their mean position.

In this process, energy is handed over from one particle to another without actual movement of the particles, they only vibrate about their mean positions.

On the basis of the requirement of the medium, waves can be classified as follows

Mechanical or Elastic Waves These waves which require material medium for their propagation. e.g. Waves on water surface, waves on coiled springs and on stretched springs, sound waves, etc.

Electromagnetic Waves These waves which do not require material medium for their propagation. e.g. Light waves, X-rays, microwaves, etc.

TOPIC 1

Sound Waves and Vibrations

Production of Sound

Sound is produced by vibrating objects. Vibration means a kind of rapid to and fro motion of an object. The sound of human voice is produced due to vibrations in the vocal cords. We can produce sound by striking the tuning fork, by plucking, scratching, rubbing, blowing or shaking different objects. They all produce sound due to vibrations.

Types of Waves

Mainly there are two types of waves

1. Longitudinal Waves

In longitudinal waves, the individual particles of the medium move in a direction parallel to the direction of propagation of the disturbance. The particles do not move from one place to another but they simply oscillate back and forth about their mean position. This is exactly how a sound wave propagates, hence sound waves are longitudinal waves.

2. Transverse Waves

In transverse waves, the individual particles of the medium moves about its mean position in a direction perpendicular to the direction of wave propagation.
e.g. Light is a transverse wave (but it is not a mechanical wave). Transverse waves can be produced only in solids and liquids but not in gases.

Terms Related to Sound Waves

Sound waves can be described by its

Wavelength

The distance between the two consecutive compressions (C) or two consecutive rarefactions (R), is called the wavelength. Wavelength is the minimum distance in which sound wave repeats itself. In other words, it is the combined length of a compression and an adjacent rarefaction. It is represented by a Greek letter lambda (λ). Its SI unit is metre (m).

Frequency

The number of complete waves (or oscillations) produced in one second is called frequency of the wave. It is the number of vibrations that occur per second.
If we can count the number of the compressions or rarefactions that crosses per unit time, we will get the frequency of sound wave. The frequency of a wave is fixed and does not change even when it passes through different substances. It is denoted by ν (Greek letter, nu). Its SI unit is hertz (Hz) named in honour of **Heinrich Rudolf Hertz**, who discovered photoelectric effect.

1 hertz is equal to 1 vibration per second.

$$1 \text{ kHz} = 1000 \text{ Hz}$$

Time Period

The time taken by two consecutive compressions or rarefactions to cross a fixed point is called the time period of the sound wave. In other words, the time required to produce one complete wave (or oscillations) is called time period of the wave. It is denoted by symbol T. Its SI unit is second (s). The time period of a wave is the reciprocal of its frequency, i.e.

$$\text{Time period} = \frac{1}{\text{Frequency}} \quad \text{or} \quad \boxed{T = \frac{1}{\nu}}$$

or

$$\boxed{\text{Frequency} = \frac{1}{\text{Time period}}}$$

Amplitude

The maximum displacement of the particles of the medium from their original mean positions on passing a wave through the medium, is called amplitude of the wave. It is used to describe the size of the wave.

It is usually denoted by the letter A. Its SI unit is metre (m). The amplitude of a wave is the same as the amplitude of the vibrating body producing the wave.

Speed

The distance travelled by a wave in one second is called speed of the wave or velocity of the wave. Under the same physical conditions, the speed of sound remains same for all frequencies. It is represented by letter v.

Its SI unit is metre per second (m/s or ms^{-1}).

Relationship among Speed, Frequency and Wavelength of a Wave

$$\text{Speed} = \frac{\text{Distance travelled}}{\text{Time taken}}$$

Suppose distance travelled by a wave is λ (wavelength) in time T, then the speed is given by

$$\boxed{v = \frac{\lambda}{T}}$$

We know that, $\nu = \dfrac{1}{T}$

Therefore, $v = \lambda \times \nu$ or $\boxed{v = \nu\lambda}$

or Speed (or velocity) = Frequency × Wavelength

Range of Hearing

The average frequency range over which the human ear is sensitive is called **audible range**. The audible range of sound for human beings is from 20 Hz to 20000 Hz.

Children under the age of 5 years and some animals, such as dogs can hear upto 25000 Hz. As people grow older, their ears become less sensitive to higher frequencies.

Infrasonic Sound

The sound of frequencies lower than 20 Hz are known as infrasonic sounds or infrasound, which cannot be heard by human beings.

Ultrasonic Sound

The sounds of frequencies higher than 20000 Hz are called as ultrasonic sounds or ultrasound, which cannot be heard by human beings.

Dogs can hear ultrasonic sounds of frequency upto 50000 Hz. This is why dogs are used for detective work by the police. Monkeys, bats, cats, dolphins, leopard and tortoise can also hear ultrasonic sound.

Bats can hear ultrasonic sounds having frequencies upto 120000 Hz. Bats, dolphins, tortoise and rats can also produce ultrasonic sounds as well as hear ultrasonic sound.

Reflection of Sound Waves

The returning back of the sound wave on striking a surface such as wall, metal sheet, etc., is known as reflection of sound waves. It does not require a smooth and shining surface like mirror. The only condition for reflection of sound wave is that the size of the reflecting surface must be bigger than the wavelength of the sound wave.

Echo

It is the reflection of sound, arriving at the listener sometime after the direct sound. e.g. The echoes are produced by the bottom of a well, by a building or by the walls of an enclosed room and an empty room.

Conditions for formation of echo

(i) The size of the obstacle/reflector must be large as compared to the wavelength of the incident sound (for reflection of sound to take place).

(ii) The distance between the source of sound and the reflector should be atleast 17 m (so that the echo is heard distinctly after the original sound is over).

(iii) The intensity or loudness of the sound should be sufficient for the reflected sound reaching the ear to be audible. The original sound should be of short duration.

Production of Echoes

Imagine a pool of water. If you drop a piece of rock in the water you would see ripples that would travel out evenly in all directions. When one of those ripples hits a wall, you can see that the ripples bounces back from the wall.

Sound works in the same way. Sound is basically just ripples in the air, i.e. vibrations. Echoes are produced when a sound hits back on an object. It is very common in hilly areas. Many bats use this technique to chase and catch their prey.

Uses of Echoes

Uses of echoes by bats, dolphins, fishermen, medical field and in SONAR are given below

The method used by some animals like bats, tortoises and dolphins to locate the objects by hearing the echoes of their ultrasonic squeaks is known as **echolocation**. They search out prey and fly in dark night by emitting and detecting reflections of ultrasonic waves.

Bats

Bats emit high frequency of high pitched ultrasonic squeaks while flying and listen to the echoes produced by reflection of their squeaks from the obstacles or prey in their path.

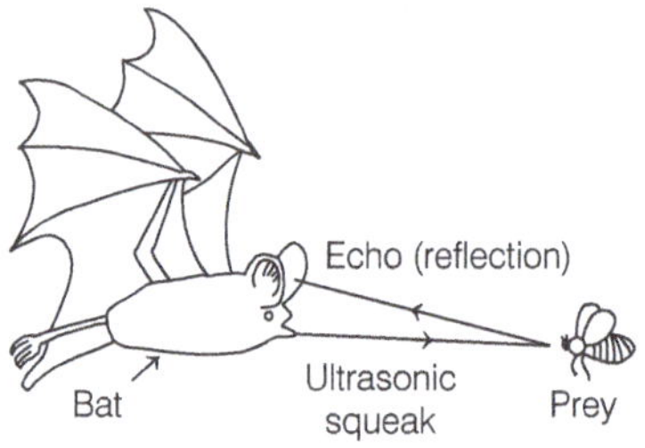

Bats can search their prey in the darkness of night by the method of echolocation

Dolphins

Dolphins uses the same method as used by bats, in order to locate the obstacles or prey. They also emit the ultrasonic waves and hear their echoes to detect their enemy and obstacles or for hunting their prey.

Fishermen or Trawlermen

Initially, they send ultrasonic waves from a source. These waves are then received and reflected by the fish.

After that, the receiver of the fisherman receive the echo and the total time t of the to and fro journey of the wave is recorded. The distance of fish is then calculated by using the relation $d = \frac{vt}{2}$, where v is speed of ultrasonic waves (near 1400 m/s in water).

This helps them to catch the fishes easily.

Medical Field

In the medical field, echoes of the ultrasound is used to investigate the internal organs of human body such as liver, gall bladder, pancreas, kidneys, uterus, heart, etc.

These waves can penetrate through the human body and different type of tissues and get reflected in different ways from a region, where there is a change in tissue density.

Expression for Echo

Let d is the distance between the observer and the obstacle and v is the speed of sound, then the total distance travelled by the sound to reach the obstacle and then to come back is $2d$; and the time taken is given by

$$t = \frac{\text{Total distance travelled}}{\text{Speed of sound}} = \frac{2d}{v} \quad \text{or} \quad \boxed{d = \frac{vt}{2}}$$

SONAR

The word SONAR stands for **Sound Navigation And Ranging.** Sonar is an apparatus used to find the depth of a sea or to locate the underwater things like shoals of fish, shipwrecks and enemy submarines. It uses ultrasonic waves to measure the distance, direction and speed of underwater objects.

SONAR consists of three parts

(i) a transmitter

(ii) a detector

(iii) a receiver (for detecting ultrasonic waves), as shown in figure.

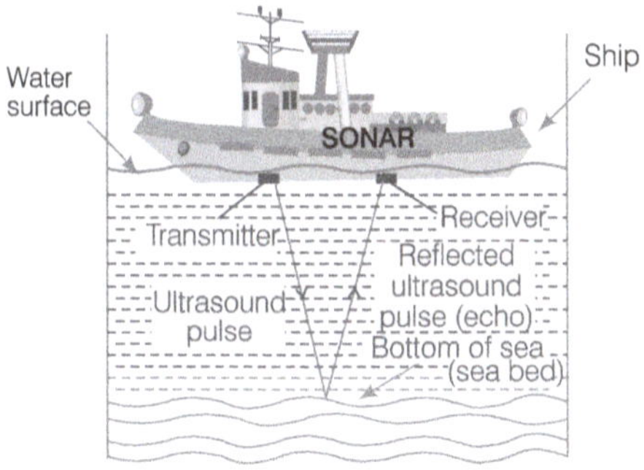

To measure the depth of a sea by using SONAR

The **transmitter** produces and transmits ultrasonic waves. These waves travel down the sea-water towards the bottom of the sea. When the ultrasonic sound pulse strikes the bottom of the sea, it is reflected back in the form of echo and are sensed by the detector.

The **detector** converts the ultrasonic waves into electrical signals which are appropriately interpreted. The distance of the object that reflected the sound wave can be calculated by knowing the speed of sound wave in water and the time interval between transmission and reception of the ultrasound.

This will give us the depth of the sea. Let the time interval between transmission and reception of ultrasound signal be t and the speed of sound through sea-water be v. The total distance $2d$ travelled by the ultrasound is $2d = v \times t$.

This method is called **echo-ranging.** SONAR is used to determine the depth of the sea and to locate underwater hills, valleys, submarine, ice-bergs, sunken ship, etc.

Natural Vibrations

If a body vibrates with its natural frequency without the help of any external periodic forces, it is said to have natural or free vibrations.

e.g. If a tuning fork is struck against a hard rubber pad, it vibrates with it natural frequency.

Forced Vibrations

When a body vibrates under the influence of an external periodic force with a frequency equal to that of the external periodic force, its vibrations are called forced vibrations.
e.g.

(i) The vibrations produced in the diaphragm of a microphones sound box with frequencies corresponding to the speech of the speaker are the forced vibrations.

(ii) While playing a guitar, the artist forces the strings of the guitar to execute forced vibrations.

Damped Vibrations

The periodic vibrations of a body of decreasing amplitude in the presence of resistive force are called the damped vibrations.

The displacement-time graph for the damped oscillation is shown in the figure.

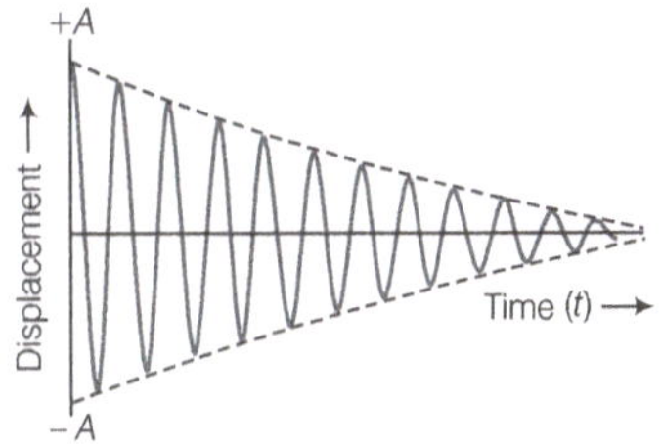

The amplitude/displacement decreases exponentially with time.

Resonance

It is a special case of forced vibration, when the frequency of an externally applied periodic force on a body is equal to its natural frequency, the body readily begins to vibrate with an increased amplitude. e.g.

(i) Sympathetic vibrations of pendulums.
(ii) Resonance in radio and TV receiver.
(iii) Resonance in bridge.
(iv) Frequency heard by tuning fork due to resonance with air.

Sympathetic Vibrations of Pendulums

As shown in the figure, pendulums A and D are of the same length, therefore their frequencies of the vibrations are the same. Now, if pendulum A is displaced from its mean position, let it performs natural vibrations which causes the flexible support to vibrate with the frequency of A.
Through the support, these vibrations are transferred to the other pendulums due to which other pendulums also begin to vibrate with the natural frequency of A.

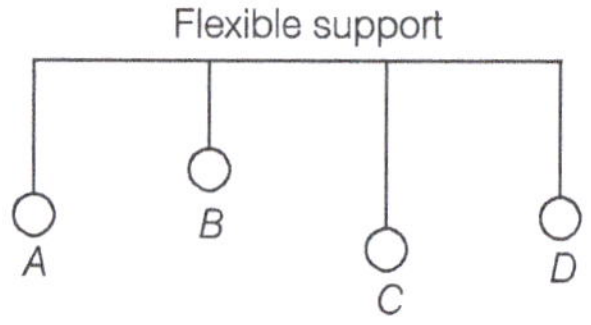

Pendulums B and C vibrate with smaller amplitude than that of A but with the same frequency as that of A. Pendulums B and C are in the state of forced vibrations. Pendulum D also starts vibrating and ultimately acquires the same amplitude as that of A. Pendulum D being of the same length attains the state of resonance.

Vibration of a Stretched String

Consider a string of length l is stretched under tension T between two fixed points.

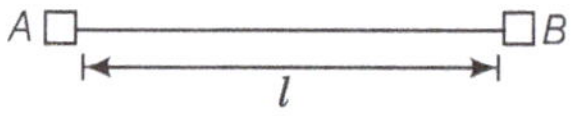

Then, speed of the wave,

$$v = \sqrt{\frac{T}{m}}$$

where, m = linear mass density of the string
and frequency of the wave,

$$\nu = \frac{1}{l} \cdot \sqrt{\frac{T}{m}}$$

PYQs Previous Years Questions

1 Mark Questions

1. When the stem of vibrating tuning fork is pressed on a table, the tabletop starts vibrating. These vibrations are definitely an example of **(ICSE 2024)**

(a) resonance
(b) natural vibrations
(c) forced vibrations
(d) damped vibrations

2. When a body vibrates under a periodic force, the vibrations of the body are always **(ICSE 2023)**

(a) natural vibrations
(b) damped vibrations
(c) forced vibrations
(d) resonant vibrations

3. Two notes are produced from two different musical instruments, such that they have same loudness and same pitch. The produced notes differ in their **(ICSE 2023)**

(a) Waveform (b) Frequency
(c) Wavelength (d) Speed

4. The ratio of the (wavelength of I) : (wavelength of II) is **(ICSE SQP 2023)**

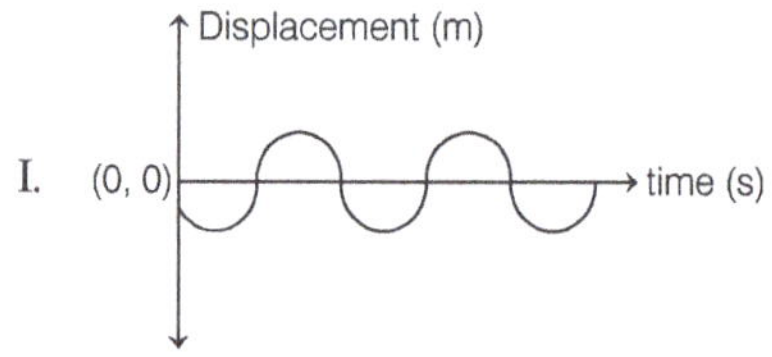

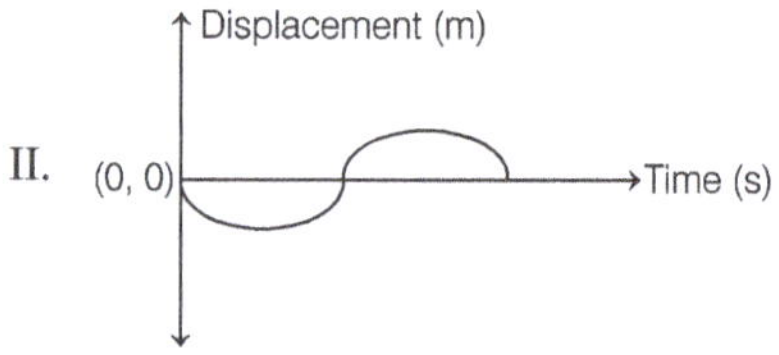

(a) 5 : 2 (b) 1 : 2 (c) 2 : 1 (d) 2 : 3

5. Free vibrations are **(ICSE 2022 Sem-I)**

(a) the vibrations under the influence of a periodic force
(b) the vibrations with larger amplitude
(c) the vibrations when the frequency continuously decreases
(d) the vibrations with a constant frequency and constant amplitude

6. Which one of the following diagnostic methods use reflection of sound? **(ICSE 2022 Sem-I)**
(a) CT scan (b) Electrocardiogram
(c) Echocardiogram (d) MRI

7. Select a correct option with respect to echo depth sounding. **(ICSE 2022 Sem-I)**
(a) Infrasonic waves are used
(b) The frequency of the waves used is between 20 Hz and 20000 Hz
(c) Ultrasonic waves are used
(d) Supersonic waves are used

8. Identify the conditions required to hear a clear and distinct echo by humans, in air **(ICSE SQP 2022 Sem-I)**
(i) The reflecting surface should be rough.
(ii) The size of the reflecting surface should be smaller than the wavelength of sound.
(iii) Sound should not be reflected back within 0.1 s.
(iv) The incident sound should have frequency more than 25000 Hz.
(v) The size of the reflecting surface should be larger than the wavelength of sound.

9. Pendulums *A, B, C* and *D* are tied to a flexible string *PQ* and are at rest. Pendulum *C* is disturbed. Which of the following statements is true? **(ICSE SQP 2022 Sem-I)**

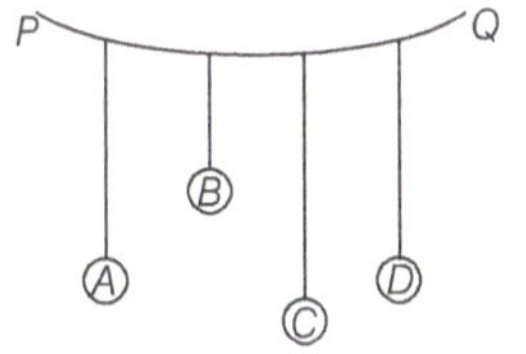

(a) Only pendulum *C* will start vibrating.
(b) Pendulums *A, B* and *D* will also start vibrating but *A* and *D* will vibrate with the maximum amplitude.
(c) Pendulums *A, B* and *D* will also start vibrating.
(d) Vibrations of pendulum *C* are forced vibrations.

10. Why does the amplitude of a vibrating body continuously decrease during damped vibrations? **(ICSE 2018)**

11. What do you understand by the free vibrations of a body? **(ICSE 2018)**

2 Marks Questions

12. Rohan conducted experiments on echo in different media. He observed that a minimum distance of *x* metres is required for the echo to be heard in oxygen and *y* metres in benzene. Compare *x* and *y* and justify your answer.
Speed of sound in oxygen = $340\ ms^{-1}$
Speed of sound in benzene = $200\ ms^{-1}$ **(ICSE 2024)**

13. A freely suspended pendulum in air is disturbed once and left to oscillate on its own
(i) Name the type of vibrations.
(ii) State one way to decrease the frequency of this vibration. **(ICSE 2023)**

14. Draw a graph between displacement from mean position and time for a body executing free vibration in a vacuum. **(ICSE 2020)**

15. A sound wave travelling in water has wavelength 0.4 m. Is this wave audible in air?
(The speed of sound in water = $1400\ ms^{-1}$) **(ICSE 2020)**

16. Displacement-distance graph of two sound waves *A* and *B*, travelling in a medium are as shown in the diagram below

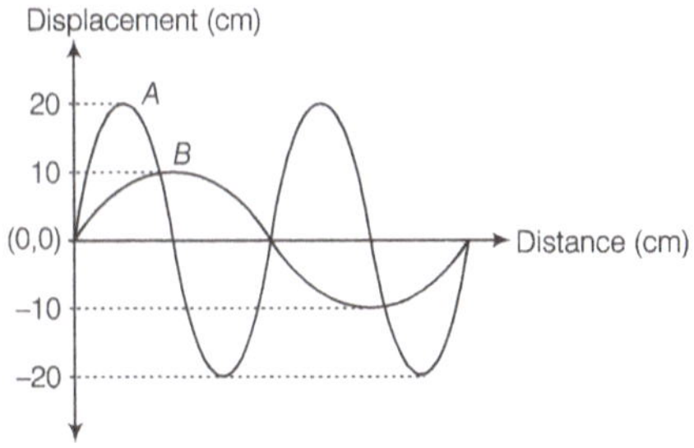

Study the two sound waves and compare their
(i) amplitudes
(ii) wavelengths **(ICSE 2018)**

17. The human ear can detect continuous sounds in the frequency range from 20 Hz to 20000 Hz. Assuming that the speed of sound in air is $330\ ms^{-1}$ for all frequencies, calculate the wavelengths corresponding to the given extreme frequencies of the audible range. **(ICSE 2017)**

18. An enemy plane is at a distance of 300 km from a radar. In how much time, the radar will be able to detect the plane?
(Take, velocity of radio waves as 3×10^8 $^{-1}$) **(ICSE 2017)**

> **KEY idea**
> In this case, time will be calculated by using, $t = \frac{2d}{v}$.

19. A certain sound has a frequency of 256 Hz and a wavelength of 1.3 m.
(i) Calculate the speed with which this sound travels.

(ii) What difference would be felt by a listener between the above sound and another sound travelling at the same speed, but of wavelength 2.6 m? **(ICSE 2017)**

20. How is the frequency of a stretched string related to
(i) its length? (ii) its tension? **(ICSE 2017)**

21. Calculate the wavelength of an electromagnetic wave of frequency 15 MHz. **(ICSE SQP 2017)**

22. State two ways by which the frequency of transverse vibrations of a stretched string can be increased. **(ICSE 2016)**

23. (i) Draw a graph between displacement and the time for a body executing free vibrations.
(ii) Where can a body execute free vibrations? **(ICSE 2015)**

24. (i) What are mechanical waves?
(ii) Name one property of waves that do not change when the wave passes from one medium to another. **(ICSE 2014)**

25. A bucket kept under a running tap is getting filled with water. A person sitting at a distance is able to get an idea, when the bucket is about to be filled.
(i) What change takes place in the sound to give this idea?
(ii) What causes the change in the sound? **(ICSE 2013)**

26. A sound made on the surface of a lake takes 3s to reach a boatman. How much time will it take to reach a diver inside the water at the same depth?
(Take, velocity of sound in air $= 300\ \text{ms}^{-1}$, velocity of sound in water $= 1440\ \text{ms}^{-1}$) **(ICSE 2013)**

27. Name one factor which affects the frequency of sound emitted due to vibrations in an air column. **(ICSE 2012)**

28. (i) Three musical instrument give out notes at the frequencies listed below.
Flute: 400 Hz, Guitar: 200 Hz, Trumpet: 500 Hz.
Which one of these has the highest pitch?
(ii) With which of the following frequencies does a tuning fork of 256 Hz resonate? 288 Hz, 341 Hz, 333 Hz, 512 Hz **(ICSE 2011)**

29. State two differences between light waves and sound waves. **(ICSE 2010)**

30. An ultrasonic wave is sent from a ship towards the bottom of the sea. It is found that the time interval between the sending and the receiving of the wave is 1.5 s. Calculate the depth of the sea, if the velocity of sound in sea water is $1400\ \text{ms}^{-1}$. **(ICSE 2009)**

KEY idea
Depth of the sea can be determineD by half of the distance travelled by ultrasonic wave during 1.5 s.

31. A radar sends a signal to an aeroplane at a distance 45 km away with a speed of $3 \times 10^8\ \text{ms}^{-1}$. After how long is the signal received back from the aeroplane? **(ICSE 2008)**

32. State two ways by which the frequency of transverse vibrations of a stretched string can be decreased. **(ICSE 2005)**

33. What is SONAR? State the principle in which it is based. **(ICSE 2004)**

34. An observer stands at a distance of 850 m from a cliff and fires a gun. After what time gap will he hear the echo, if sound travels at a speed of $350\ \text{ms}^{-1}$ in air? **(ICSE 2002)**

3 Marks Questions

35. (i) Name the waves used in SONAR.
(ii)

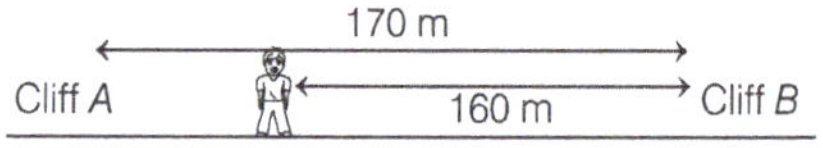

In the above diagram, Lata stands between two cliffs and claps her hands. Determine the time taken by her to hear the first echo. Speed of sound in air $320\ \text{ms}^{-1}$. **(ICSE 2024)**

36. (i) Which characteristic of sound is affected due to the larger surface of a school bell?
(ii) Calculate the distance covered by the ultrasonic wave having a velocity of $1.5\ \text{kms}^{-1}$ in 14 s, when it is received after reflection by the receiver of the SONAR. **(ICSE 2023)**

37. A person standing in front of a cliff fires a gun and hears its echo after 3s. If the speed of sound in air is $336\ \text{ms}^{-1}$.
(i) Calculate the distance of the person from the cliff.
(ii) After moving a certain distance from the cliff he fires the gun again and this time the echo is heard 1.5 s later than the first. Calculate distance moved by the person. **(ICSE SQP 2023)**

38.

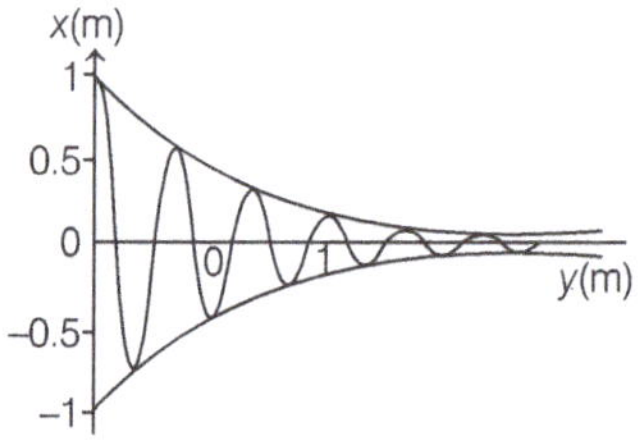

Study the above figure and answer the following.

(i) What type of vibration does the above figure represent?

(ii) State one reason for which the amplitude of the vibration decreases with time.

(iii) Write an example of natural vibrations.

(ICSE 2022 Sem-II)

39. The diagram shows a vibrating tuning fork *E* mounted on a sound box *X*. When the vibrating tuning forks, *A*, *B*, *C* and *D* are placed on the sound box *Y* one-by-one, it is observed that a louder sound is produced when the tuning fork *B* is placed on *Y*.

(2022 Sem-II)

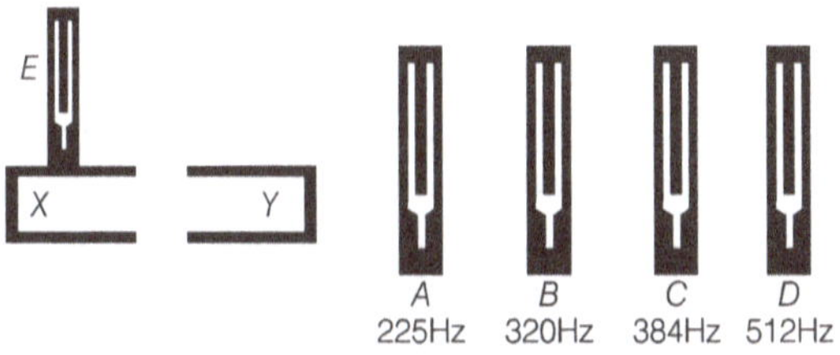

(i) What is the frequency of tuning fork *E*?

(ii) Why does *B* produce a louder sound?

40. (i) Which one of the following graphs *A* or *B* shows free vibrations in vacuum and which one shows free vibrations in a medium?

(ii) How did you come to this conclusion.

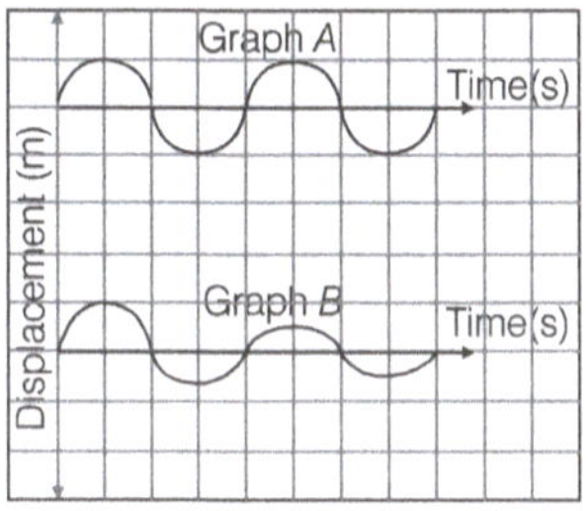

(ICSE SQP 2022 Sem-II)

41. A pendulum has a frequency of 4 vibrations per second. An observer starts the pendulum and fires a gun simultaneously. He hears the echo from the cliff after 6 vibrations of the pendulum. If the velocity of sound in air is 340 m/s, find the distance between the cliff and the observer. **(ICSE 2019)**

> **KEY idea**
>
> Distance can be calculated by half of the value of product of velocity and time.

42. The diagram below shows a wire stretched over a sonometer. Stems of two vibrating tuning forks *A* and *B* are touched to the wooden box of the sonometer. It is observed that the paper rider (a small piece of paper folded at the centre) present on the wire flies off when the stem of vibrating tuning fork *B* is touched to the wooden box but the paper just vibrates when the stem of vibrating tuning fork *A* is touched to the wooden box.

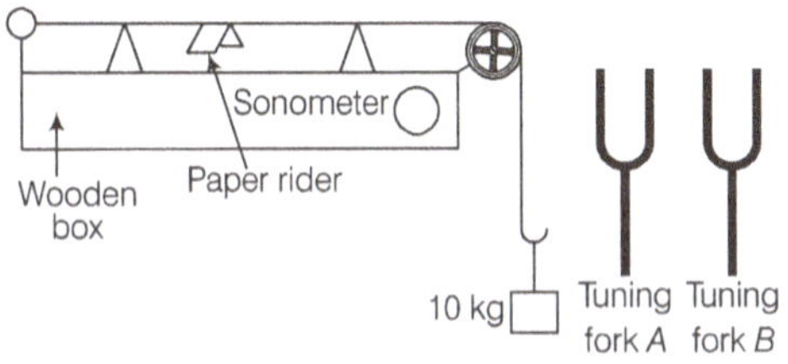

(i) Name the phenomenon when the paper rider just vibrates.

(ii) Name the phenomenon when the paper rider flies off.

(iii) Why does the paper rider fly off when the stem of tuning fork *B* is touched to the box? **(ICSE 2018)**

43. A vibrating tuning fork is placed over the mouth of a burette filled with water.

The tap of the burette is opened and the water level gradually starts falling. It is found that the sound from the tuning fork becomes very loud for a particular length of the water column.

(i) Name the phenomenon taking place when this happens.

(ii) Why does the sound become very loud for this length of the water column? **(ICSE SQP 2018, 13)**

44. (i) What are damped vibrations?

(ii) Give one example of damped vibration.

(iii) Name the phenomenon that causes a loud sound when the stem of a vibrating tuning fork is kept pressed on the surface of a table. **(ICSE 2017)**

45. (i) Draw a displacement-distance graph for two waves *A* and *B* such that the amplitude of wave *A* is three times that of wave *B*.

(ii) Give one example of forced vibration.

(iii) State two necessary conditions for hearing a distinct echo. **(ICSE SQP 2017)**

46. John fires a gun towards a hill and hears its echo after 5 s. He then moves 320 m towards the hill and fires his gun again. This time he hears the echo after 3 s. Calculate the velocity of sound. **(ICSE SQP 2017)**

> **KEY idea**
> Distance covered by the sound will double, because the sound will have to travel and source to reflecting surface and back from it. Hence, distance will be $2d$.

47. (i) Name the waves used for echo depth sounding.
(ii) Give one reason for their use for the above purpose.
(iii) Why are the waves mentioned by you not audible to us? **(ICSE 2016)**

48. (i) What is an echo?
(ii) State two conditions for an echo to take place. **(ICSE 2016)**

49. (i) Name the phenomenon involved in tuning a radio set to a particular station.
(ii) Define the phenomenon named by you in part (i) above.
(iii) What do you understand by loudness of sound?
(iv) In which units is the loudness of sound measured? **(ICSE 2016)**

50. A person standing between two vertical cliffs and 480 m from the nearest cliff shouts. He hears the first echo after 3s and the second echo after 2s later. Calculate
(i) the speed of sound.
(ii) the distance of the other cliff from the person. **(ICSE 2015)**

51. In the diagram below, A, B, C, D are four pendulums suspended from the same elastic string PQ. The length of A and C are equal to each other while the length of pendulum B is smaller than that of D. Pendulum A is set into a mode of vibrations.

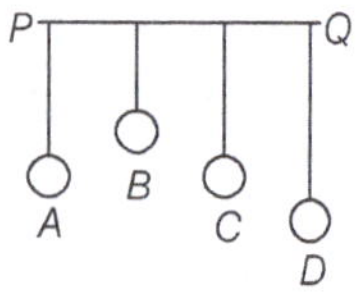

(i) Name the type of vibrations taking place in pendulums B and D.
(ii) What is the state of pendulum C?
(iii) State the reason for the type of vibrations in pendulums B and C. **(ICSE 2015)**

52. The adjacent diagram shows three different modes of vibrations P, Q and R of the same string.

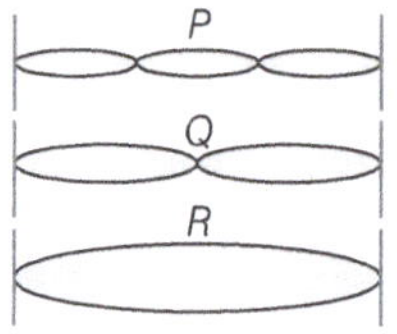

(i) Which vibrations will produce a louder sound and why?
(ii) The sound of which string will have maximum shrillness?
(iii) State the ratio of wavelengths of P and R. **(ICSE 2014)**

53. (i) What is the principle on which SONAR is based?
(ii) An observer stands at a certain distance away from a cliff and produces a loud sound. He hears the echo of the sound after 1.8 s. Calculate the distance between the cliff and the observer, if the velocity of sound in air is 340 ms^{-1}. **(ICSE 2013)**

54. (i) What is meant by resonance?
(ii) State two ways in which resonance differs from forced vibrations. **(ICSE 2012)**

55. (i) A man standing between two cliffs produces a sound and hears two successive echoes at intervals of 3 s and 4 s, respectively. Calculate the distance between the two cliffs. The speed of sound in the air is 330 ms^{-1}.
(ii) Why will an echo not be heard, when the distance between the source of sound and the reflecting surface is 10 m? **(ICSE 2012)**

> **KEY idea**
> Calculate the distance between first and second cliff, then by adding both, get the total distance between the cliffs.

56. (i) Name the type of waves which are used for sound ranging.
(ii) Why are these waves mentioned in (i) above, not audible to us?
(iii) Give one use of sound ranging. **(ICSE 2011)**

57. A man standing 25 m away from a wall produces a sound and receives the reflected sound.
(i) Calculate the time after which he receives the reflected sound, if the speed of sound in air is 350 ms^{-1}.

(ii) Will the man be able to hear a distinct echo? Give a reason for your answer. **(ICSE 2011)**

58. (i) A man stands at a distance of 68 m from a cliff and fires a gun. After what time interval will he hear the echo, if the speed of sound in air is 340 ms^{-1}?

(ii) If the man had been standing at a distance of 12 m from the cliff would he have heard a clear echo? **(ICSE 2010)**

59. (i) What is the principle on which SONAR is based?

(ii) Calculate the minimum distance at which a person should stand in front of a reflecting surface, so that he can hear a distinct echo.
(Take, speed of sound in air $= 350 \text{ ms}^{-1}$) **(ICSE 2009)**

60. (i) What is meant by an echo? Mention one important condition that is necessary for an echo to be heard distinctly.

(ii) Mention one important use of echo. **(ICSE 2008)**

61. A man standing in front of a vertical cliff fires a gun. He hears the echo after 3 s. On moving closer to the cliff by 82.5 m, he fires again. This time, he hears the echo after 2.5 s. Calculate

(i) the distance of the cliff from the initial position of the man.

(ii) the velocity of sound. **(ICSE 2007)**

62. When a tuning fork, struck by a rubber pad, is held over a length of air column in a tube, it produces a loud sound for a fixed length of the air column.

(i) Name the above phenomenon.

(ii) How does the frequency of the loud sound compare with that of the tuning fork?

(iii) State the unit for measuring loudness. **(ICSE 2006)**

63. A radar is able to detect the reflected waves from an enemy aeroplane, after a time interval of 0.02 ms. If the velocity of the waves is $3 \times 10^8 \text{ ms}^{-1}$, calculate the distance of the plane from the radar. **(ICSE 2005)**

64. (i) Sound made in front of a tall building 18 m away, is repeated. Name the phenomenon and briefly explain it.

(ii) A tuning fork, held over an air column of a given length, produces a distinct audible sound. What do you call this phenomenon? How does it occur? **(ICSE 2003)**

65. A sound wave of wavelength 0.332 m has a time period of 10^{-3} s. If the time period is decreased to 10^{-4} s, calculate the wavelength and frequency of the new wave. **(ICSE 2003)**

KEY idea
The frequency of new wave is inversely proportional to the time period.

4 Marks Questions

66. In the given diagram, a vibrating tuning in is kept near the mouth of burette filled with water. The length of the column is adjusted by opening the tap of the burette. At a length of 5 cm of the air column, a sound is heard. **(ICSE 2024)**

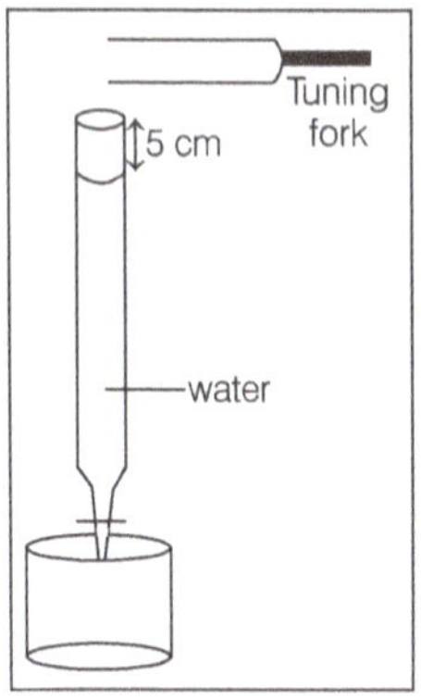

(a) Name the phenomenon illustrated by the above experiment.

(b) Why is a loud sound heard at this particular length.

(c) If the present tuning fork is replaced with a tuning fork of higher frequency, should the length of the air column increase or decrease to produce a loud sound? Give a reason.

67. We are able to see the TV channels clearly when we set TV on auto-tuning. **(ICSE 2023)**

(i) Which phenomenon led to the clear visibility of the channels, due to auto-tuning?

(ii) Define the above phenomenon mentioned by you.

(iii) Give any one more example of this phenomenon.

68. A boy tunes a radio channel to radio station 93.5 MHz.

(i) Name and define the scientific wave phenomenon involved in tuning the radio channel.

(ii) Now, what is the frequency of the channel? Convert this frequency into SI unit. **(ICSE SQP 2023)**

69. A boy standing in front of a wall produces two whistles per second. He notices that the sound of his whistling coincides with the echo. The echo is heard

only once when whistling is stopped. Calculate the distance between the boy and the wall.
(The speed of sound in air = 320 m/s) **(ICSE 2022 Sem-I)**

(i) The time in which the boy hears the echo is
(a) 1 s (b) 0.5 s (c) 1.5 s (d) 2 s

(ii) The distance at which the boy is standing from the wall
(a) 160 m (b) 240 m
(c) 320 m (d) 80 m

(iii) If the speed of sound is increased by 16 ms^{-1} and the boy moves 4 m away from the wall, then in how much time will he hear the echo of the first whistle?
(a) 0.525 s (b) 0.5 s (c) 0.48 s (d) 0.3 s

(iv) In which of the following timings of reflection of the whistle, the echo cannot be heard?
(a) 0.05 s (b) 0.12 s
(c) 0.2 s (d) 0.11 s

70. (i) When a tuning fork (vibrating) is held close to ear, one hears a faint hum. The same (vibrating tuning fork) is held such that its stem is in contact with the table surface, then one hears a loud sound. Explain.

(ii) A man standing infront of a vertical cliff fires a gun. He hears the echo after 3.5 s. On moving closer to the cliff by 84 m, he hears the echo after 3 s. Calculate the distance of the cliff from the initial position of the man. **(ICSE 2020)**

71. A person is standing at the sea shore. An observer on the ship which is anchored in between a vertical cliff and the person on the shore fires a gun. The person on the shore hears two sounds, 2 s and 3 s after seeing the smoke of the fired gun.

If the speed of sound in the air is 320 ms^{-1}, then calculate

(i) the distance between the observer on the ship and the person on the shore.

(ii) the distance between the cliff and the observer on the ship.

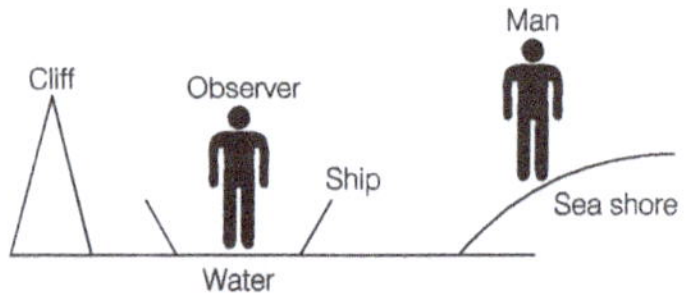

(ICSE 2018)

72. A man standing in front of a wall produces a sound and hears an echo after 3 s. He walks x m away from the wall and produces the same sound. Now he hears an echo after 5.25 s. Calcualte the distance he walked away form the wall. (Speed of sound in air is 340 m/s) **(ICSE SQP 2018)**

73. (i) What is meant by the terms (a) amplitude (b) frequency of a wave?

(ii) Explain, why stringed musical instruments, like the guitar, are provided with a hollow box? **(ICSE 2013, 06)**

74. The diagram alongside shows the displacement-time graph for a vibrating body.

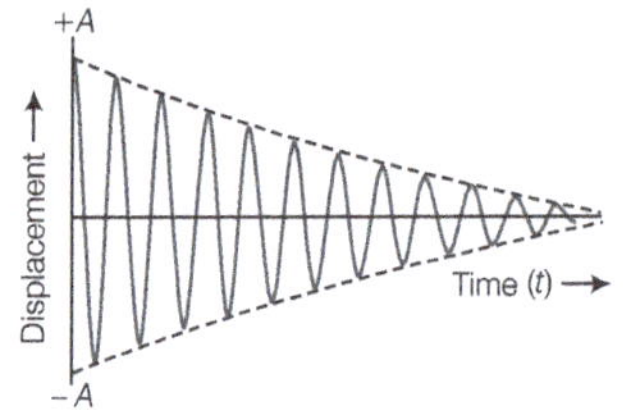

(i) Name the type of vibrations produced by the vibrating body.

(ii) Give one example of a body producing such vibrations.

(iii) Why is the amplitude of the wave gradually decreasing?

(iv) What will happen to the vibrations of the body after sometime? **(ICSE 2012)**

75. (i) A person is tuning his radio set to a particular station. What is the person trying to do to tune it?

(ii) Name the phenomenon involved, in tuning the radio set.

(iii) Define the phenomenon named by you in part (ii). **(ICSE 2009)**

76. (i) Sometimes when a vehicle is driven at a particular speed, a rattling sound is heard. Explain briefly, why this happens and give the name of the phenomenon taking place?

(ii) Suggest one way by which the rattling sound could be stopped. **(ICSE 2008)**

77. (i) Differentiate between resonance and forced vibrations.

(ii) The wavelength of waves produced on the surface of water is 20 cm. If the wave velocity is 24 ms^{-1}, calculate

(a) the number of waves produced in one second and

(b) the time required to produce on wave. **(ICSE 2004)**

78. (i) Give one example each of natural vibration, forced vibration and resonance.

(ii) Mention one practical use of echoes. **(ICSE 2001)**

Explanations

1. (c) When the stem of vibrating tuning fork is pressed on a table, the tabletop starts vibrating. These vibrations are definitely an example of forced vibration.

2. (c) When the external periodic force is applied to the vibrating body, the body gradually acquires the frequency of the applied periodic force.

3. (a) Two notes of the same pitch and loudness, played from different instruments do not sound the same because the waveforms are different and therefore differ in quality or tone.

4. (a)

5. (d) Free vibrations are the vibrations with a constant frequency and constant amplitude. It occurs when no external force acts on the body which causes the motion.

6. (c) Echocardiogram is the diagnostic method which is based on reflection of sound using ultrasound.

7. (c) Ultrasonic waves are used to measure the distance, direction of underwater object and also to measure echo depth.

8. (v) The size of the reflecting surface should be larger than the wavelength of sound.

> **Concept Enhancer** The human ear cannot distinguish between two successive sound, if the period between them is less than 0.1 s. But the size of reflecting surface should be larger than the wavelength of sound.

9. (b) Pendulums A, B and D will also start vibrating but A and D will vibrate with the maximum amplitude.

10. A body continuously losses its energy due to the presence of frictional force by the surrounding medium in damped oscillations, therefore amplitude of a vibrating body continuously decreases.

11. Free vibrations are the periodic vibrations of a body in the absence of any external force on it.

12. The minimum distance for an echo to be heard is shorter in oxygen than in benzene because the speed of sound is faster in oxygen compared to benzene. Therefore, $x < y$.

13. (i) Damped vibration
    (ii) Increasing the length of pendulum frequency decreases.

14. The amplitude and frequency of a freely vibrating body in vacuum remains constant with respect to time. The displacement-time graph of a body executing free vibration in vacuum is given as

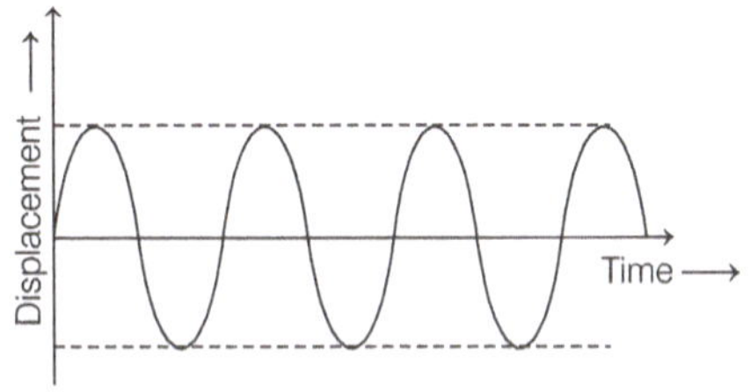

15. Given, speed of sound in water, $v = 1400 \text{ ms}^{-1}$

Wavelength of sound wave in water, $\lambda = 0.4$ m

If f be the frequency of sound wave, then

$$v = f\lambda$$

$$\Rightarrow \quad f = \frac{v}{\lambda} = \frac{1400}{0.4} = 3500 \text{ Hz}$$

Since, frequency of sound wave remains same in water and air. Hence, $f_{water} = f_{air} = 3500$ Hz.

Since, $20 \text{ Hz} < f_{air} < 20 \text{ kHz}$, hence given sound wave is audible in air.

16. (i) Amplitude of sound wave, $A = 20$ cm
    Amplitude of sound wave, $B = 10$ cm
    $\therefore$ Amplitude of sound wave A is twice than that of sound wave B.
    (ii) From the graph, it can be seen that wavelength of sound wave A is half of the wavelength of sound wave B.

17. Applying the formula,

where, v = Velocity of sound $= 330 \text{ ms}^{-1}$,

ν = Frequency, λ = Wavelength of sound.

We have, range of frequencies from 20 Hz to 20000 Hz.

Hence, for frequency $\nu = 20$ Hz, we have

$$330 = \lambda \times 20$$

$$\Rightarrow \quad \lambda = \frac{330}{20} = 16.5 \text{ m}$$

For frequency $\nu = 20000$ Hz, we have

$$330 = \lambda \times 20000$$

$$\Rightarrow \quad \lambda = \frac{330}{20000} = 16.5 \times 10^{-3} \text{ m}$$

18. As we know, speed $= \frac{\text{distance}}{\text{time}}$

Given, distance from the radar to the plane,
$d = 300 \text{ km} = 3 \times 10^5 \text{ m}$

Velocity of radar, $v = 3 \times 10^8 \text{ ms}^{-1}$

According to the formula, $d = \frac{v \times t}{2}$

$$\Rightarrow \quad t = \frac{2 \times d}{v} = \frac{2 \times 3 \times 10^5}{3 \times 10^8}$$

$$= \frac{2}{1000} = 0.002 \text{ s}$$

19. Given, $\nu = 256 \text{ Hz}, \lambda = 1.3 \text{ m}$

(i) Using the formula,

$$v = \nu \lambda = 256 \times 1.3 = 332.8 \text{ m/s}$$
$$\simeq 333 \text{ m/s}$$

(ii) Now, new wavelength = 2.6 m

$$\therefore \quad v = \nu \times \lambda \Rightarrow 333 = \nu \times 2.6$$

$$\Rightarrow \quad \nu = \frac{333}{2.6} = 128.07 \text{ Hz}$$

Frequency of above sound is 256 Hz, whereas frequency of this calculated sound is 128 Hz, because speed of sound is same.

20. (i) Frequency of stretched string related with its length

as $\quad \nu \propto \frac{1}{\text{length}}$

(ii) Frequency of stretched string is related to tension in string as

$$\nu \propto \text{tension}$$

This means, frequency is inversely proportional to the length of the string and directly proportional to its tension.

21. From the formula,

$$\lambda = \frac{v}{f}$$

$$v = 3 \times 10^8 \text{ m/s}$$

$$f = 15 \text{ MHz} = 15 \times 10^6 \text{ Hz}$$

So, $\quad \lambda = \frac{v}{f} = \frac{3 \times 10^8}{15 \times 10^6}$

$$= \frac{300}{15} = 20 \text{ m}$$

22. The frequency of transverse vibrations of a stretched string can be increased by

(i) decreasing the length of the string $\left(\text{as } \nu \propto \frac{1}{l}\right)$.

(ii) decreasing the mass per unit length of string $\left(\text{as } \nu \propto \frac{1}{\sqrt{m}}\right)$.

23. (i) The displacement-time graph for a freely vibrating body is given by

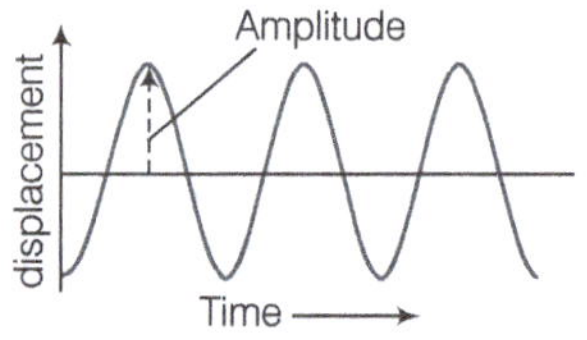

(ii) For a body to execute free vibrations, the body should be in complete vacuum, so as to make it an independent system and the frictional forces of the medium will not affect the vibrations of the body.

24. (i) The waves that travel in the medium through the vibrations of the medium particles about their mean positions are known as mechanical waves.

(ii) It is the frequency of the waves that do not change when the wave passes from one medium to another.

25. (i) The frequency of the sound appears to be increased as the air column of bucket is filled with water.

(ii) The changes in the sound is caused, because air column is decreased in filling the water in bucket.

26. First calculate the distance between boatman and source, then by using this, calculate the time taken to reach the sound to the diver.

Given, time of sound to reach at boatman $t = 3$ s

Velocity of sound in air $v_a = 300$ m/s

Velocity of sound in water $v_w = 1440$ m/s

Time taken by diver $t_d = ?$

$\therefore$ Depth of lake $d_l = v_a \times t$ (as given in question)

$$= 300 \times 3 = 900 \text{ m}$$

Time taken by sound in water to reach diver

$$t_w = \frac{d_l}{v_w} = \frac{900}{1440} = 0.62 \text{ s}$$

27. The frequency of sound emitted due to vibrations in air column is affected by the length of air column.

28. (i) Trumpet having highest frequency of 500 Hz have highest pitch, because pitch is directly proportional to the frequency.

(ii) The frequency 512 Hz will resonate a tuning fork of 256 Hz as 512 Hz is an integral multiple of the natural frequency of the tuning fork.

29. The differences between sound waves and light waves are

Sound waves	Light waves
Sound waves are mechanical waves.	Light waves are electromagnetic waves .
They are longitudinal in nature.	They are transverse in nature.
They require medium for propagation.	They do not require medium for propagation.
Speed of sound waves is 330 m/s in air.	Speed of light waves is 3×10^8 m/s in air.

30. Given, time interval, $t = 1.5\,s$,

d = Distance travelled by ultrasonic waves during 1.5 s.

Velocity $v = 1400$ m/s

So, $d = v \times t = 1400 \times 1.5 = 2100$ m

As, the depth of the sea will be given by

$$= \frac{d}{2} = \frac{2100}{2} = 1050\text{ m}$$

31. Given, distance $d = 45$ km $= 45000$ m

Total distance travelled by radar signal is

$$2d = 45000 \times 2 = 90000\text{ m}$$

Speed $v = 3 \times 10^8$ m/s

So, time taken $t = ?$

$$\therefore \quad t = \frac{2d}{v} = \frac{2 \times 45000}{3 \times 10^8} = 3 \times 10^{-4}\text{ s}$$

32. The two ways by which the frequency of transverse vibrations of a stretched string can be decreased are

(i) by increasing the length (l), where tension (T) and mass (m) are kept constant.

(ii) by decreasing the tension (T), when length (l) and mass (m) are kept constant.

33. SONAR is an abbreviation for Sound Navigation and Ranging. It uses ultrasonic waves to detect and locate objects under water. It is based on the principle of echo and states that the sound heard after reflection from a distant obstacle after the original sound has ceased.

34. Given, distance between sound source and cliff, $d = 850$ m

Total distance travelled by the sound $= 2d$

Speed $v = 350$ m/s, Time $t = ?$

$$\therefore \quad v = \frac{2d}{t} \Rightarrow t = \frac{2d}{v} = \frac{2 \times 850}{350} = 4.86\text{ s}$$

35. (i) Ultrasonic waves

(ii) 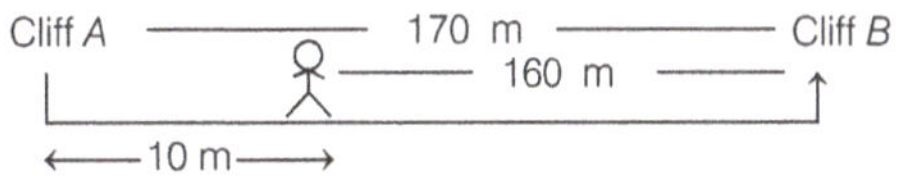

Echo will be heard, if the minimum distance between the source of sound and obstacle is 17m. Therefore, echo can be heard by cliff B.

So, time taken to hear the first echo

$$t = \frac{\text{Total distance travelled by the sound}}{\text{Speed of sound}}$$

$$= \frac{2d}{v} = \frac{2 \times 160}{320} = 1\text{ s}$$

36. (i) The larger surface area of a school bell can affected the amplitude or loudness of the sound produced by the bell. When the surface area of a bell is increased, it allows for a larger amount of air to be displaced when the bell is struck, resulting in a larger sound wave and a louder sound.

(ii) Distance covered by the ultrasonic wave can be calculated using formula.

Distance = Velocity × Time

Here, velocity of the ultrasonic wave is given as 1.5 km/s

Time taken for it to travel to the target and back is 14 s.

Since, the actual distance covered will be half of the total distance travel by the wave.

So, we can calculate the distance covered by the ultrasonic wave as

$$\text{Distance} = \frac{\text{Velocity} \times \text{Time}}{2} = \frac{1.5 \times 14}{2} = 10.5\text{ km}$$

∴ The distance covered by ultrasonic wave is 10.5 km when it is received after reflection by the receiver of the SONAR.

37. (i) If the distance of the cliff is d, then

$$3 = \frac{2d}{v} \text{ or } 3 = \frac{2d}{336}$$

$$d = 504\text{ m}$$

(ii) If now the distance of the cliff be d, then

$$(3 + 1.5)\,s = \frac{2d'}{v}$$

Or, $4.5\,s = 2d/336$

$$d' = 756\text{ m}$$

So, the person moved a distance$(756 - 504)$ $= 252$ m from the cliff.

38. (i) The vibration which is represented in the above figure is damped vibration.

(ii) The amplitude of vibration decreases with time due to the presence of resistive force.

(iii) If a tuning fork is struck against a hard rubber pad, it vibrates with its natural frequency.

39. (i) As the tuning fork B produces louder sound when placed on Y, then the frequency of tuning fork $E = 320$ Hz.

(ii) B produces louder sound due to the condition which is known as resonance.

In resonance, when the frequency of an externally applied periodic force on a body is equal to its natural frequency, the body readily begins to vibrate with an increased amplitude.

40. (i) Graph A, shows free vibration in vacuum.

Graph B, shows free vibration in medium.

(ii) In Graph A, amplitude is constant but in Graph B amplitude is decreasing.

41. Given, frequency of pendulum, $\nu = 4$ Hz

Velocity of sound in air, $v_s = 340$ m / s

As we know that,

Time period, $T = \dfrac{1}{\text{Frequency}} = \dfrac{1}{4}$ s

Time in which echo is heard, $t = 6 \times \dfrac{1}{4} = 1.5$ s

According to the question, $2d = v_s \times t$

$$\Rightarrow \quad d = \frac{v_s \times t}{2} = \frac{340 \times 1.5}{2} = 255 \text{ m}$$

42. (i) Forced vibration

(ii) Resonance

(iii) The paper rider flies off, because the natural frequency of vibration of wire matches the frequency of the tuning fork. This result is increase in magnitude of amplitude of vibrations.

43. (i) The phenomenon taking place is called resonance.

(ii) The sound becomes very loud for this length of water column because this happens when the frequency of the air column becomes equal to the frequency of the tuning fork.

44. (i) The periodic vibrations of a body of decreasing amplitude in presence of resistive force are called the damped vibrations.

(ii) Simple pendulum's oscillation.

(iii) **Resonance** It is a special case of forced vibration, when the frequency of an externally applied periodic force on a body is equal to its natural frequency, the body readily begins to vibrate with an increased amplitude.

e.g. Sympathetic vibrations of pendulums, frequency heard by tuning fork due to resonance with air, etc.

45. (i) The displacement equation of wave A is

$$y_a = a \sin(\omega t)$$

The displacement equation of wave B is

$$y_b = (3a) \sin(\omega t)$$

$\therefore$ The displacement-time graph of two wave is

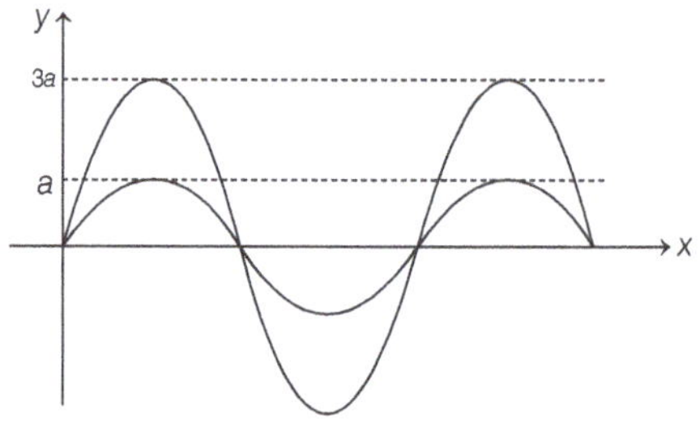

(ii) **For example** When guitar is played, the artist forces the strings of the guitar to execute forced vibrations.

(ii) The two conditions for echo to be heard are

(a) The minimum distance between source and reflecting surface should be 17.2m.

(b) To hear a distinct echo, the interval between original and reflected sound must be 0.1 s.

46. At position-I

$(\text{Distance})_1 = d$ m

$$t_1 = 5 \text{ s}$$

$$v_1 = \frac{2d}{5}$$

At position-II

$(\text{Distance})_2 = (d - 320)$m

$$t_2 = 3 \text{ s}$$

$$v_2 = \frac{2(d - 320)}{3}$$

$$v_1 = v_2$$

(as velocity of sound in air is the same)

$$\frac{2d}{5} = \frac{2(d - 320)}{3}$$

$$3d = 5(d - 320)$$

$$3d = 5d - 1600$$

$$2d = 1600$$
$$d = 800 \text{ m}$$

$\therefore$ Velocity of sound $= \dfrac{2 \times 800}{5} = 320 \text{ ms}^{-1}$ in air.

47. (i) Ultrasonic waves

(ii) These waves can be confined into a narrow beam and are not easily absorbed in the medium and can travel a long distance.

(iii) The frequency of ultrasonic waves is above 20000 Hz which is beyond the audibility range of humans.

48. (i) Echo is the sound heard after it gets reflected from a rigid surface.

(ii) Two conditions for an echo to take place are given below

(a) There should be a minimum distance of 17.2m between the listener and the reflecting body.

(b) Reflecting body should be big as compared to the wavelength of sound.

49. (i) Resonance

(ii) Resonance is the phenomenon in which vibration takes place under the influence of periodic force, where frequency of the applied force is equal to the natural frequency of the vibrating body.

(iii) Loudness is the sensation produced in the ear which enables to distinguish between a loud and a faint sound.

(iv) Loudness of sound is measured in units called decibels (dB).

50. (i)

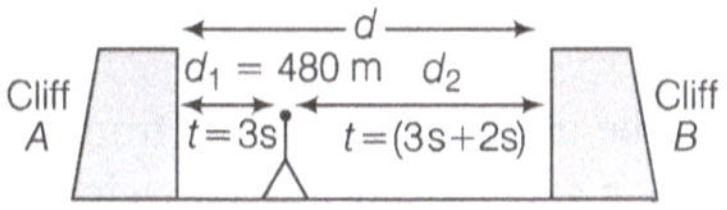

For the first echo,

Let d_1 be the distance of the nearest cliff A from the person.

$\therefore$ Total distance travelled by the sound in going and coming back

$$= 2d_1 = 2 \times 480 \text{ m} = 960 \text{ m}$$

Time taken $t_1 = 3$ s

$\therefore$ Speed of sound

$$= \frac{\text{Total distance travelled}}{\text{Total time taken}}$$
$$= \frac{960}{3} = 320 \text{ m/s}$$

(ii) The second echo is heard from the farther cliff B.

Time taken to reach second echo

$$= 3 + 2 = 5 \text{ s}$$
$$v = \frac{2d}{t}$$

Distance from the other cliff,

$$d = \frac{vt}{2} = \frac{320 \times 5}{2} = 800 \text{ m}$$

51. (i) B and D will exhibit forced vibrations.

(ii) Pendulum C is in the state of resonant vibrations.

(iii) The vibrations produced in pendulum A are passed onto pendulums B, C and D through the rubber string as forced vibrations. The pendulums B and D remain in the state of forced vibrations while the pendulum C comes into resonant vibrations, because the natural time period of pendulum C is equal to that of pendulum A.

52. (i) The mode of vibration R will produce a louder sound, because its amplitude is more than that of P and Q.

(ii) The sound of P string will have maximum shrillness, because its frequency is more than that of P and Q.

(iii) Frequency $f_P = 3f$ and frequency $f_R = f$

$$\lambda = \frac{v}{f}$$

$\therefore$ The ratio of wavelengths of P and R is given by

$$\frac{\lambda_P}{\lambda_R} = \frac{v/f_P}{v/f_R}$$
$$= \frac{f_R}{f_P} = \frac{f}{3f} = \frac{1}{3}$$

Concept Enhancer Wavelength of mode of vibration is inversely proportional to the frequency and directly proportional to the velocity.

53. (i) The SONAR is based on the principle of echo.

(ii) Given, time $t = 1.8$ s

Velocity of sound in air $v_a = 340$ m/s

Distance travelled $d = ?$

Distance = Speed × Time $\Rightarrow$ $2d = v_a \times t$

$$\Rightarrow \quad d = \frac{v_a \times t}{2} = \frac{340 \times 1.8}{2} = 306 \text{ m}$$

54. (i) The phenomenon in which body vibrates under the influence of periodic force, where frequency of the applied periodic force is equal to the natural frequency of the vibrating body. The body beings to vibrate with increased amplitude.

(ii) The two ways in which resonance differs from forced vibrations are as

Resonance	Forced vibrations
The phenomenon of setting a body A into vibration with the help of another body B, where frequency of B is equal to the natural frequency of A.	A body A is set into vibrations under the influence of periodic force of body B. Frequency of vibration of body B is different from the natural frequency of the body A.
Vibrations are of large amplitude.	Vibrations are of small amplitude.

55. (i) Given, time taken from nearer cliff $t_1 = 3\,s$

Time taken from another cliff $t_2 = 4\,s$

Velocity of sound in air $v_a = 330$ m/s

Total distance, $d = ?$

Distance of man from nearer cliff,

$$d_1 = \frac{v_a \times t_1}{2} = \frac{330 \times 3}{2} = 495\,\text{m}$$

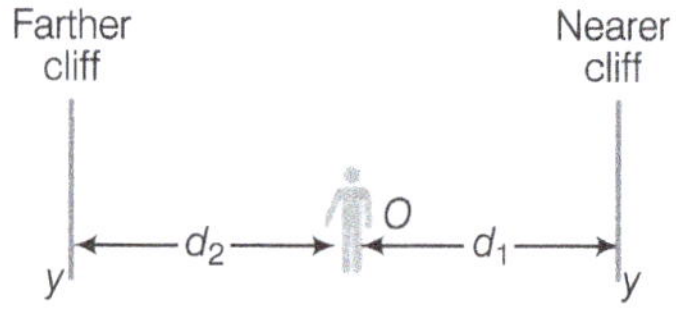

Distance of man from another cliff,

$$d_2 = \frac{v_a \times t_2}{2} = \frac{330 \times 4}{2} = 660\,\text{m}$$

Total distance between two cliffs,

$$d = d_1 + d_2 = 495 + 660 = 1155\,\text{m}$$

(ii) An echo will not be heard, when the distance between the source of sound and the reflecting surface is 10 m, because to hear the echo distinctly, the minimum distance of the obstacle from the observer should be 17 m.

56. (i) Ultrasonic waves are used for sound ranging as the frequency is greater than 20 kHz.

(ii) As the frequency of ultrasonic is above 20 kHz while the audible range of human is below 20 kHz.

(iii) Sound ranging is used to find the depth of the sea.

57. Given, distance between man and wall $d = 25$ m

(i) $t = ?$

Velocity of sound $v = 350$ m/s

$\therefore \quad v = \frac{2d}{t}$

$\Rightarrow \quad t = \frac{2d}{v} = \frac{2 \times 25}{350} = 0.14\,\text{s}$

(ii) Yes, the man will be able to hear a distinct echo, because the least time for distinct echo to be heard is 0.1 s as 0.14 s > 0.1 s.

NOTE As the distance travelled by the sound wave is twice the distance between man and wall, so take distance as $2d$.

58. (i) Given, Distance between man and cliff $d = 68$ m

Total distance travelled by the sound $= 2d$

Velocity of sound $v = 340$ m/s

Time $t = ?$

$\therefore \quad t = \frac{2d}{v} = \frac{2 \times 68}{340} = 0.4\,\text{s}$

(ii) No, he has not heard a clear echo, because to hear a clear echo distinctly, the reflecting surface in air should be at a minimum distance of 17 m from the listener.

59. (i) SONAR is based on the principle of echo.

(ii) Given, speed of sound $v = 350$ m/s

Distance $d = ?$, Time $t = 0.1\,s$

[$\because$ persistence of hearing]

$\therefore \quad d = \frac{v \times t}{2} = \frac{350 \times 0.1}{2} = 17.5\,\text{m}$

60. (i) **Echo** The sound heard after reflection from a distant obstacle after the original sound has ceased.

Condition To hear echo distinctly, the reflecting surface in air should be at a minimum distance of 17 m from the listener.

(ii) The uses of echo are SONAR.

61. As the velocity of sound remains constant for both the cases, so equate the two equation by keeping v constant.

(i) Let d be the distance of cliff from the initial position of man and v be the velocity of sound.

So, the distance travelled by sound in 3 s $= 2d$ metre

$\therefore$ Speed of sound $v = \frac{2d}{\text{time}} = \frac{2d}{3}$ ...(i)

On moving closer to the cliff by a distance of 82.5 m, then distance

$= 2(d - 82.5)$ m

So, $\quad v = \frac{\text{distance}}{t} = \frac{2(d - 82.5)}{2.5}$ ...(ii)

From Eqs. (i) and (ii), we have

$$\frac{2d}{3} = \frac{2(d - 82.5)}{2.5}$$

$\Rightarrow \quad 2.5d = 3d - 247.5$

$0.5d = 247.5$

$$\Rightarrow \quad d = \frac{247.5}{0.5} = \frac{2475}{5} = 495 \text{ m}$$

(ii) Substituting the value of d in Eq. (i), we get

$$v = \frac{2 \times 495}{3} = 330 \text{ m/s}$$

62. (i) The above phenomenon is based on resonance.

(ii) The frequency of the loud sound is equal or integral multiple of the frequency of the tuning fork.

(iii) The unit for measuring loudness is decibel (dB).

63. Given, time $t = 0.02 \text{ ms} = 0.02 \times 10^{-3}$ s

Velocity $v = 3 \times 10^8$ m/s

As the distance travelled by the wave is twice of the distance between energy and source.

So, $v = \frac{2d}{t} \Rightarrow d = \frac{v \times t}{2} = \frac{3 \times 10^8 \times 0.02 \times 10^{-3}}{2}$

$= 3000 \text{ m} = 3 \text{ km}$

64. (i) As we know, the minimum distance between source and reflector is 17 m and here the distance is 18 m, so the phenomena due to which sound is repeated is echo.

(ii) We call the phenomenon as resonance. This occurs when the frequency of forced vibrations produced by the tuning fork becomes equal to the natural frequency of the air column.

65. First of all calculate frequency, then after by putting its value calculate wavelength.

Given, wavelength $\lambda_1 = 0.332$ m

Time period $T_1 = 10^{-3}$ s

Time period $T_2 = 10^{-4}$ s

Wavelength $\lambda_2 = ?$

Frequency f_1 and $f_2 = ?$

$$\therefore \quad f_1 = \frac{1}{T_1} = \frac{1}{10^{-3}} = 10^3 \text{ Hz}$$

and $f_2 = \frac{1}{T_2} = \frac{1}{10^{-4}} = 10^4$ Hz

$$\therefore \quad \lambda_2 = \frac{v}{f_2} \qquad [\because v = f_1\lambda_1 = 10^3 \times 0.332 = 332 \text{ m/s}]$$

$$= \frac{332}{10^4} = 0.0332 \text{ m}$$

66. (i) Resonance

(ii) A loud sound is heard this particular length because the frequency of the air column becomes equal to the frequency of the tuning fork.

(iii) The frequency of air column is inversely proportional to the length of air column, i.e.,

$$f \propto \frac{1}{l}$$

When the present tuning fork is replaced with a tuning fork of higher frequency, the length of air column should be decreased to produce loud sound (or higher frequency).

67. (i) The phenomenon led to the clear visibility of the channels due to auto-tuning is called resonance.

(ii) Resonance is a phenomenon that occurs when an object is subjected to an external force at its natural frequency, causing it to vibrate with a large amplitude in the context of TV channels, the phenomenon of resonance is not directly related to the clear visibility of TV channels due to auto-tuning.

(iii) Example of resonance is in musical instruments, where the natural frequency of the instruments components, such as strings or air columns, can resonate with the applied force of the musician playing the instrument, creating the characteristic sound of the instrument.

68. (i) The phenomenon involved is resonance, It is forced vibration. When the frequency of an externally applied periodic force on a body is equal to the natural frequency, then the body begins to vibrate with higher amplitude.

(ii) Frequency of the channel is 93.5 MHz

In SI unit,

$93.5 \text{ MHz} = 93.5 \times 10^6 \text{ Hz}$

69. (i) (b) Echo heard by the boy is only once when whistle stops.

$$t = \frac{1}{2} \text{ s} = 0.5 \text{ s}$$

(ii) (d) Time $= \frac{2d}{v}$

Distance between the boy and the wall,

$$d = \frac{\text{time} \times v}{2}$$

$$d = \frac{0.5 \times 320}{2} = 80 \text{ m}$$

(iii) (b) If speed of sound $= (320 + 16) \text{ ms}^{-1} = 336$ m/s

Distance between boy and wall

$= d + 4 = 84$ m

Time of echo, $t = \frac{2(d+4)}{v} = \frac{2 \times 84}{336} = 0.5$ s

(iv) (a) Time of hearing an echo $t \geq 0.1$ s.
So, correct option is (a) when echo cannot be heard.

70. (i) When a tuning fork is held close to ear, then one hears a faint hum because it produces damped vibration. When the stem of vibrating tuning fork is in contact with the table surface, then table surface starts vibrating with same frequency of tuning fork. Hence, loud sound is produced due to resonance.

(ii) If v be the speed of sound and x be the distance of cliff from initial position of man, then according to first condition of man

$$\frac{2x}{v} = 3.5 \Rightarrow v = \frac{2x}{3.5} \quad \ldots\text{(i)}$$

When man is moved closer to the cliff by 84 m, then

$$\frac{2(x-84)}{v} = 3$$

$$\Rightarrow \quad v = \frac{2(x-84)}{3} \quad \ldots\text{(ii)}$$

From Eqs. (i) and (ii), we have

$$\frac{2x}{3.5} = \frac{2(x-84)}{3}$$

$$6x = 7x - 588$$

$$\Rightarrow \quad x = 588 \text{ m}$$

71.

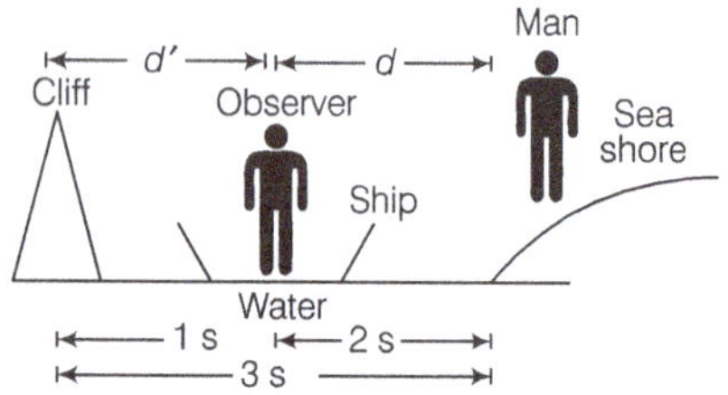

(i) Observer hears direct sound in 2s.

As, velocity $= \frac{\text{distance}}{\text{time}}$

$$320 = \frac{d}{2}$$

$$\Rightarrow \quad d = 320 \times 2 = 640 \text{m}$$

∴ Distance between person and observer = 640 m.

(ii) Observer hears reflected sound in 3s. This means sound goes to cliff and reflect back in remaining one second.

i.e. $\quad t = 1\text{ s} \Rightarrow v = \frac{2d'}{t}$

$$\Rightarrow \quad 320 = \frac{2d'}{1}$$

$$\Rightarrow \quad \frac{320}{2} = d' \Rightarrow d' = 160 \text{ m}$$

72. Applying $2d = v \times t$

$$2d = 340 \times 3$$

$$2d = 1020$$

$$d = 510$$

Again, $2(d + x) = 340 \times 5.25$

$$\Rightarrow \quad 2d + 2x = 1785$$

$$\Rightarrow 2(510) + 2x = 1785$$

$$\Rightarrow \quad 2x = 1785 - 1025$$

$$\Rightarrow \quad 2x = 765 \Rightarrow x = 382.5 \text{ m}$$

73. (i) (a) The maximum displacement of the particle of medium on either side of its mean position is known as amplitude of wave. It is denoted by A.

(b) The number of vibrations made by the particle in one second is known as frequency of wave. It is denoted by f or ν.

(ii) The musical instruments like guitar is provided with a hollow box, because vibrating strings of the instrument produce a very weak sound which cannot be heard. But strings set into vibration produce forced vibration, the large volume of air filled in hollow box and the loud sound of the frequency matching with the frequency of the vibrating string is produced.

74. (i) Damped vibrations

(ii) A simple pendulum oscillating in air, tuning fork vibrating in air are examples of a body producing such vibrations.

(iii) The amplitude of the wave gradually decreasing due to friction as energy is continuously losing.

(iv) Its amplitude decreases and finally stops.

75. (i) The person is trying to change the frequency of his radio set to a particular station.

(ii) The phenomenon of resonance is involved in tuning the radio set.

(iii) Refer to page 103 (Resonance)

76. (i) Sometimes when a vehicle is driven at a particular speed, a rattling sound is heard, because the frequency of movement of piston in the engine becomes equal to the natural frequency of the part which is rattling. The phenomenon taking place is resonance.

(ii) The rattling sound can be stopped by changing the speed of the vehicle.

77. (i) Refer to Ans. 54 (ii) on page 116.

(ii) Given, wavelength $\lambda = 20\,\text{cm} = 0.2\,\text{m}$

Wave velocity $v = 24\,\text{m/s}$

(a) Number of waves/s

$$f = \frac{v}{\lambda} = \frac{24}{0.2}$$

$$= 120\ \text{waves/s}$$

(b) Time, $t = \frac{1}{f} = \frac{1}{120}\,\text{s}$

78. (i) **For natural vibration** A tuning fork struck against a hard rubber pad.

For forced vibration Vibration produced in the board of a guitar when its string is made to vibrate.

For resonance While tuning a wireless receiver, we adjust its natural frequency equal to that of the incoming wireless carries waves, so that a loud sound of incoming signal is heard.

(ii) The practical use of echoes is to determine distance between two object.

$$v = \frac{2d}{t} \Rightarrow d = \frac{vt}{2}$$

where, d is the distance (not less than 17 m) between the source of sound and reflecting surface t is time taken.

Common Mistake Usually, students think that the every vibration in the system produce sound but not all vibrations produce sound.

TOPIC 2

Characteristics of Sound

A sound have four characteristics such as loudness, pitch, quality (or timbre) and intensity by which two sound waves can be distinguished from one another.

Loudness

It is the property by virtue of which a loud sound can be distinguished from a faint one, both having the same pitch and intensity. The loudness of sound is measured in decibel (dB). It depends on the sensitivity or the response of our ears.

The following sketches shows soft and loud notes

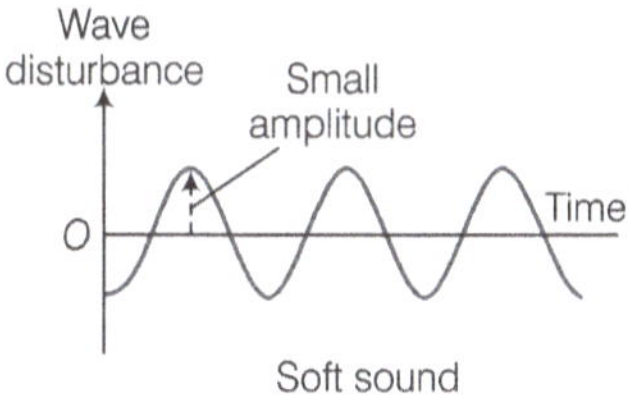

Soft sound

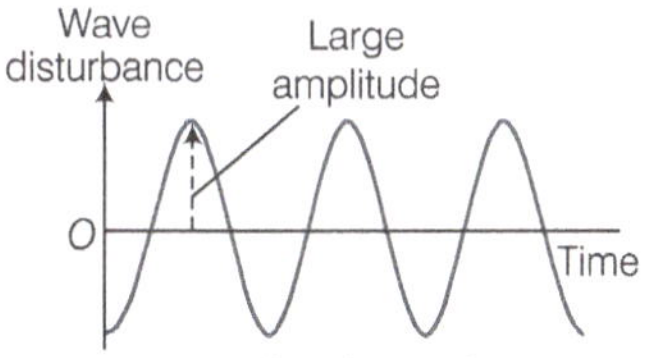

Loud sound

Factors Affecting the Loudness of Sound

The factors affecting the loudness of sound are

(i) It is proportional to the square of the amplitude.
(ii) It is inversely proportional to the square of the distance.
(iii) It depends on the surface area of the vibrating body.
(iv) It depends on the density of the medium.
(v) It depends on the presence of resonating body.

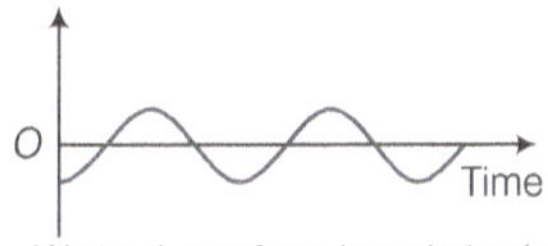

Wave shape for a low pitched sound

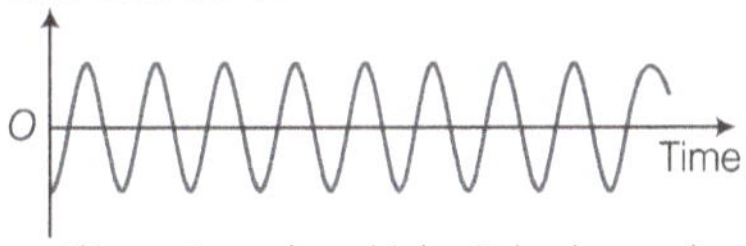

Wave shape for a high pitched sound

Intensity

The amount of sound energy passing each second through unit area is known as the intensity of sound. The

SI unit of intensity is watt per square metre (W/m^2). The intensity of a sound wave in air is proportional to

(i) the square of the amplitude of vibration.
(ii) the square of the frequency of vibration.
(iii) the density of air.

Pitch and Frequency

It is that characteristic of sound by which we can distinguish between different sounds of the same loudness. Due to this characteristic, we can distinguish between a man's voice and woman's voice of the same loudness without seeing them. Low pitch sound has low frequency and high pitch of sound has high frequency.

Examples

- Pitch of a sound depends on the frequency of vibration. Greater the frequency of a sound, the higher will be its pitch.
- In other words, the faster the vibration of the source, the higher is the frequency and hence higher is the pitch, as shown in figure.

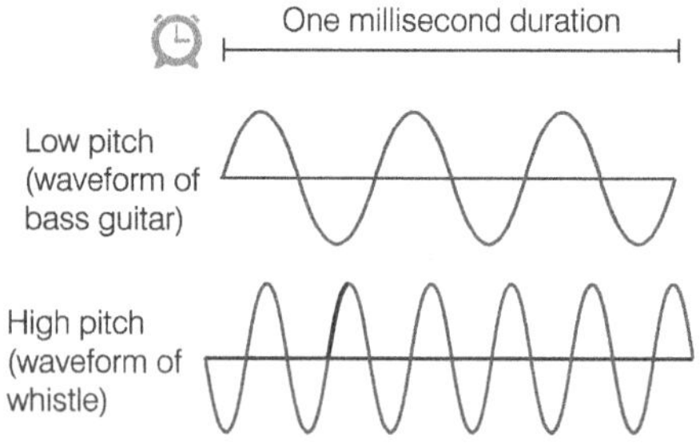

Thus, a high pitch sound corresponds to more number of compressions and rarefactions passing a fixed point per unit time.

Quality and Waveforms

The quality of sound is that characteristic of sound which enable us to distinguish one sound from another having the same pitch and loudness.

The pleasant sound is said to be of a rich quality. A sound of single frequency is called a **tone**. The sound produced due to a mixture of several frequencies is called a **note** and is pleasant in listening too. Noise is unpleasant to ear, music is pleasant to ear and is of rich quality.

The sound produced by the different musical instruments like flute, violin, sitar, tanpura, etc., and similarly, sound produced by different singers, like Kumar Sanu, Mohammad Rafi, Udit Narayan, etc., can be distinguished from one another on the basis of their quality.

(a) Shape of sound waves produced by a note played on flute

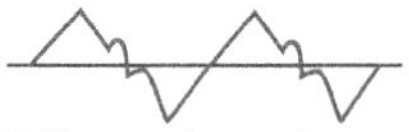

(b) Shape of sound waves when the same note is played on violin

The quality of musical instrument depends on

(i) the shaft of the sound wave produced.
(ii) mixture of frequencies present.

Sound Level in Decibel (dB)

The unit of loudness is phons. The level of sound is expressed in decibel (dB). Thus, the loudness of a sound in phons is the loudness in decibel of an equally loud pure sound of frequency 1 kHz. 60 phons is as loud as a 60 dB.

Noise Pollution

The disturbance caused in the environment due to undesirable loud and harsh sound of level above 120 dB from different sources such as loudspeaker, siren, moving vehicles, etc., is known as noise pollution. It causes headache and permanent damage to the ears of listener.

PYQs Previous Years Questions

1 Mark Questions

1. The characteristics of sound which enables to differentiate between two sounds of different intensity is (ICSE SQP 2023)

   (a) quality (b) amplitude
   (c) pitch (d) loudness

2. The diagram below shows four sound waves. Which sound has the highest pitch? (ICSE 2022 Sem-II)

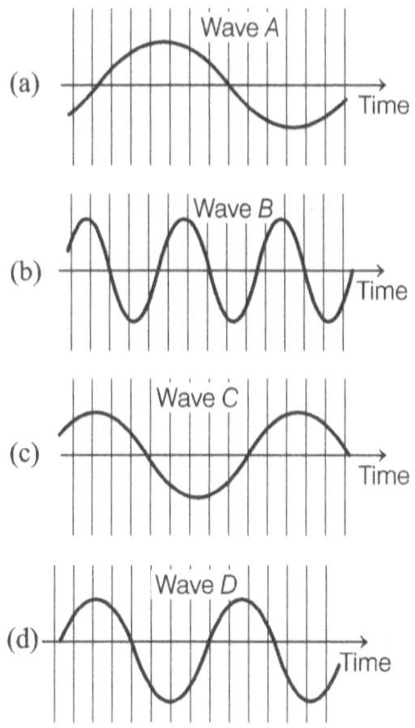

3. The ratio of the amplitudes of two waves is 4 : 9. What is the ratio of their intensities? (ICSE 2003)

2 Marks Questions

4. (i) Define resonant vibrations.

   (ii) Which characteristic of sound, makes it possible to recognise a person by his voice without seeing him? (ICSE 2019)

5. A man playing a flute is able to produce notes of different frequencies. If he closes the holes near his mouth, will the pitch of the note produced, increase or decrease? Give a reason for your answer. (ICSE 2019)

> **KEY idea**
> The frequency of sound is inversely proportional to the wavelength.

6. Two waves of the same pitch have amplitudes in the ratio 1: 3. What will be the ratio of their
   (i) intensities and
   (ii) frequencies ? (ICSE 2019)

7. What characteristics of sound would change, if there is a change in its (ICSE 2018)
   (i) amplitude and
   (ii) waveform?

8. The ratio of amplitude of two waves from same source is 3 : 4. What is the ratio of their
   (i) loudness? (ii) frequencies? (ICSE 2016)

9. What is meant by noise pollution? Name one source of sound causing noise pollution. (ICSE 2016)

10. Name the unit used for measuring the sound level. (ICSE 2012)

11. Which characteristics of sound will change, if there is a change in its
    (i) amplitude? (ii) waveform? (ICSE 2012)

12. When acoustic resonance takes place a loud sound is heard. Why does this happen? Explain. (ICSE 2011)

> **KEY idea**
> The loudness of the sound is directly proportional to the square of the amplitude.

13. Two waves of the same pitch have their amplitudes in the ratio 2 : 3.
    (i) What will be the ratio of their loudness?
    (ii) What will be the ratio of their frequencies? (ICSE 2010)

14. What change, if any, would you expect in the characteristics of a musical sound when we increase
    (i) its frequency?
    (ii) its amplitude? (ICSE 2002)

3 Marks Questions

15. Rohit playing a flute and Anita playing a piano emit sounds of same pitch and loudness. (ICSE 2022 Sem-II)
    (i) Name one characteristic that is different for waves from the two different instruments.

(ii) If now the loudness of the sound from flute becomes four times that of the sound from piano, then write the value of the ratio $A_F : A_P$ (where, A_F = amplitude of sound wave from flute, A_P = amplitude of sound wave from piano)

(iii) Define pitch of a sound.

16. (i) Define pitch.

(ii) Two wires AB and CD of same length are stretched by same amount. Which wire will produce sound of greater pitch on plucking?

(iii) Given a reason for your answer

(ICSE SQP 2022 Sem-II)

17. A change in amplitude of a sound wave is noticed.

(ICSE SQP 2022 Sem-II)

(i) Which characteristic of sound is affected due to the above change?

(ii) How is amplitude related to your answer to part (i) above?

(iii) What happens to the quality of the sound?

18. (i) Name the system which enables us to locate underwater objects by transmitting ultrasonic waves and detecting the reflecting impulse.

(ii) What are acoustically measurable quantities related to pitch and loudness? **(ICSE 2020)**

19. It is observed that during march past we hear a base drums distinctly from a distance compared to the side drums.

(i) Name the characteristic of sound associated with the above observation.

(ii) Give a reason for the above observation. **(ICSE 2019)**

4 Marks Questions

20. Name the factor that determines the

(i) loudness of the sound heard

(ii) quality of the note

(iii) pitch of the note **(ICSE 2017)**

21. (i) State the safe limit of sound level in terms of decibel for human hearing.

(ii) Name the characteristic of sound in relation to its waveform. **(ICSE 2015)**

22. (i) Name the characteristic of sound which enables a person to differentiate between two sounds with equal loudness but having different frequencies.

(ii) Define the characteristic named by you in (i).

(iii) Name the characteristic of sound which enables a person to differentiate between two sounds of the same loudness and frequency but produced by different instruments. **(ICSE 2009)**

23. A vibrating tuning fork is placed over the mouth of a burette filled with water. The tap is opened and the water level gradually falls. It is observed that the sound becomes the loudest for a particular length of air column.

(i) What is the name of the phenomenon taking place when this happens?

(ii) Why does the sound become the loudest?

(iii) What is the name of the phenomenon taking place, when sound is produced for another length of air column is not the loudest? **(ICSE 2002)**

24. (i) State three characteristics of a musical sound.

(ii) How does the musical sound differ from noise? **(ICSE 2001)**

25. (i) Two friends were playing on their identical guitars whose string were adjusted to give notes of the same pitch. Will the quality of the two notes be the same? Give a reason for your answer.

(ii) Give the relation among wavelength, time period and wave velocity of a wave motion. **(ICSE 2000)**

Explanations

1. (a) Quality is a characteristic of a sound which enables us to distinguish between the sounds of same loudness (intensity) or pitch.

2. (b) Wave B has the highest pitch due to more number of compressions and rarefactions per unit time. The frequency of wave B is highest, hence wave B has the highest pitch.

3. As intensity is directly proportional to the square of amplitude, so putting the value of amplitude you get the ratio of intensities.

   Ratio of amplitudes of two waves

   $$\frac{a_1}{a_2} = \frac{4}{9}$$

   As, intensity $(I) \propto$ amplitude $(A)^2$

   So, ratio of intensities $\frac{I_1}{I_2} = \frac{a_1^2}{a_2^2} = \frac{16}{81}$

4. (i) The increase in amplitude of oscillation of an electric or mechanical system exposed to a periodic force whose frequency is equal or very close to the natural undamped frequency of the system, called resonant vibrations.

   (ii) The quality (timbre) of sound.

5. If we close the hole near the mouth, the wavelength of the sound wave will decrease. Since, frequency of the sound wave is inversely proportional to wavelength, so frequency will increase. Greater the frequency of a sound, the higher will be its pitch. Hence, pitch will increase.

6. (i) Given, amplitude of two waves,

   $$\frac{a_1}{a_2} = \frac{1}{3} \quad \text{...(i)}$$

   $\because$ We know that, intensity is proportional to amplitude square, i.e. $I \propto a^2$

   $\therefore$ Ratio of intensity, $\frac{I_1}{I_2} = \left(\frac{1}{3}\right)^2 = \frac{1}{9}$

   (ii) Frequency of the sound wave has no effect on amplitude, so ratio of frequency remains same, i.e. 1 : 3.

7. (i) Loudness will change on changing the amplitude of the sound.

   (ii) Quality or timbre will change on changing the waveform of the sound.

8. (i) Ratio of loudness will be 9:16 as loudness depends upon intensity which is directly proportional to the square of amplitude.

   (ii) Ratio of frequencies will be 1:1 as frequency remains same for the two waves.

9. Noise pollution is the disturbance or unpleasant sound that may harm the activity or balance of human or animal life.

   The noise pollution is mainly caused by machines, transportation systems, etc.

10. Decibel (dB)

11. (i) Loudness of sound will change, if there is a change in its amplitude.

    (ii) Quality of sound will change, if there is a change in its waveform.

12. When acoustic resonance takes place a loud sound is heard, because the amplitude of the sound is increased. As loudness of the sound is directly proportional to the square of the amplitude, i.e. $L \propto A^2$. So, loudness of sound increases.

13. (i) As, loudness $\propto$ (amplitude)^2

    $\therefore$ Its ratio $\left(\frac{2}{3}\right)^2$ becomes $\frac{4}{9}$.

    (ii) The ratio of frequencies is 1 : 1 as pitch depends upon the frequency.

14. (i) If the frequency is increased, the pitch of the sound increases.

    (ii) If the amplitude is increased, the loudness of the sound increases.

15. (i) The quality of sound is that characteristic of sound which enables us to distinguish one sound from another having the same pitch and loudness.

    (ii) Given, $(\text{Loudness})_{\text{flute}} = 4 \times (\text{Loudness})_{\text{piano}}$

    We know that,

    Loudness $\propto$ (Amplitude)^2

    $$\Rightarrow \frac{(\text{Loudness})_{\text{flute}}}{(\text{Loudness})_{\text{piano}}} = \frac{(\text{Amplitude})^2_{\text{flute}}}{(\text{Amplitude})^2_{\text{piano}}}$$

    $$\Rightarrow \frac{(\text{Amplitude})_{\text{flute}}}{(\text{Amplitude})_{\text{piano}}} = \frac{A_F}{A_P} = \sqrt{4}$$

    $$\Rightarrow \frac{A_F}{A_P} = 2 \text{ or } A_F : A_P = 2:1$$

(iii) Refer to text 22 on page 120 (Pitch frequency).

16. (i) Refer to text on page no. 120 (Pitch and frequency)

(ii) When both wires are stretched by same amount, wire AB will produce sound of greater pitch on plucking.

(iii) Pitch depends upon the frequency of the wave. More the frequency of the wave, higher is its pitch. In the given case, both the wires are of same length but wire AB is thinner than wire CD. So, wire AB will vibrate faster and have higher frequency than wire CD. Thus, pitch of wire AB is more compared to wire CD.

> **Concept Enhancer** Pitch depends on frequency. Thinner wire can vibrate faster than thicker wire, so thinner wire can produce greater pitch.

17. (i) Loudness

(ii) Loudness is proportional to the square of its amplitude i.e. $L \propto (a)^2$.

(iii) The quality of the sound does not change because quality is dependent on the waveform.

18. (i) Refer to text on page no. 103 [SONAR]

(ii) Refer to text on pages 119 and 120 (Loudness and Pitch) .

19. (i) Pitch and timbre

(ii) Side drums and base drums are made up of different material, so they have different frequency, hence the pitch. The quality (timbre) of sound enables us to distinguish between two sounds. Base drums and side drums have different quality due to different material.

20. (i) Loudness – amplitude

(ii) Quality – (timbre) nature of waveform

(iii) Pitch of note – frequency

21. (i) Sound level of below 120 dB is safe for human beings.

(ii) Quality or timbre of a sound depends on the waveform.

22. (i) Pitch or shrillness is the characteristic of sound which enables a person to differentiate between two sounds with equal loudness but having different frequencies.

(ii) Pitch is that characteristic of sound by which an acute (or shrill) note can be distinguished from a grave or flat note.

(iii) Quality is that characteristic of sound which enables a person to differentiate between two sounds of the same loudness and frequency but produced by different instruments.

23. (i) The phenomenon taking place is resonance in air column.

(ii) The frequency of vibrating tuning fork becomes equal to the frequency of vibrating air column. As a result, amplitude of the sound produced increases. Since, loudness is proportional to the square of amplitude, so sound is loudest.

(iii) Forced vibrations, i.e. frequency of forced vibration is not equal to the frequency of the vibrating air column.

24. (i) The three characteristics of a musical sound are

Pitch It is the frequency of a sound perceived by human ear. A high frequency gives rise to a high pitch note and a low frequency produces a low pitch note.

Loudness (Intensity) It is the property by virtue of which a loud sound can be distinguished from a faint one. It depends upon the amplitude of wave ($I \propto A^2$).

Quality (Timbre) It is the characteristics of musical sound which distinguish between two sounds of same loud and same pitch but emitted by two different instruments.

(ii) The musical sound differ from noise in the following ways

Musical sound	Noise
It is produced by vibrations which are periodic.	It is produced by irregular or non-periodic disturbances in succession.
It is pleasant and smooth to ear. 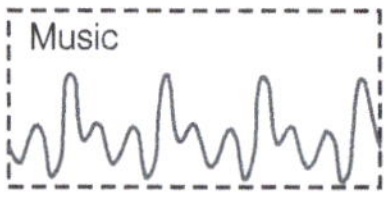	It is discordant and unpleasant to ear. 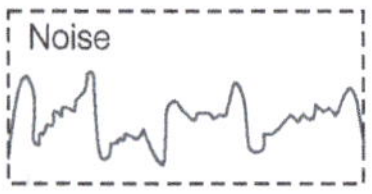

25. (i) Yes, the quality of the two notes will be same. Quality of a wave depends on the wavelength and the number of subsidiary notes. Since, both guitars are identical and have same pitch, the notes will have an identical quality.

(ii) The relation between wavelength (λ), time period (T) and wave velocity (v) of a wave motions is given by

$$v = \frac{\lambda}{T}$$

CHAPTER TEST

01 Mark Questions

1 Two sounds of same loudness and same pitch produced by two different instruments differ in their
(a) amplitudes (b) frequencies
(c) waveforms (d) All of these

2 The unit of quantity on which pitch of the sound depends is
(a) hertz (b) metre
(c) metre/second (d) second

3 Pitch of high frequency sound is
(a) low (b) zero
(c) infinite (d) high

4 By reducing the amplitude of a sound wave, its
(a) pitch decreases (b) loudness decreases
(c) pitch increases (d) loudness increases

5 The minimum distance between the source and the obstacle for an echo to take place is (speed of sound is 340 m/s)
(a) 172 m (b) 18 m
(c) 17 m (d) 34 m

02 Marks Questions

6 Distinguish between transverse wave and longitudinal wave.

7 Define echo and state its uses.

8 State the conditions for the formation of echo.

9 Define the term intensity of a sound wave. State the unit in which it is measured.

Structured Questions

10 (i) (a) Name the waves used for echo depth sounding.
(b) Give one reason of their use for the above purpose.
(c) Why are the waves mentioned by you not audible to us? **(3)**

(ii) Differentiate between forced vibrations and resonance. **(3)**

(iii) A person standing between two vertical cliffs and 640 m away from the nearest cliff shouted. He heard the first echo after 4 s and the second echo after 3 s later. Calculate
(a) the velocity of sound in air.
(b) the distance between the cliffs. **(4)**

11 (i) Name the factor that determines
(a) loudness of the sound heard.
(b) quality of the note.
(c) pitch of the note.

(ii) Explain why musical instruments like the guitar are provided with a hollow box?

(iii) A sound wave of wavelength 0.332 m has a time period of 10^{-3} s, If the time period is decreased to 10^{-4} s, calculate the wavelength and frequency of the new wave.

Answers

1. (c) **2.** (a) **3.** (d) **4.** (b) **5.** (c)

10. (iii) (a) 320 m/s (b) 1760 m

11. (iii) 0.0332 m

07

Current Electricity

TREND ANALYSIS 4 YEARS

Topic	Types of Questions	2024	2023	2020	2019
TOPIC 01 Electricity and Resistance	1 Mark	2	1	–	–
	2 Marks	1	–	1	2
	3 Marks	1	1	–	–
	4 Marks	1	1	1	1
TOPIC 02 Electrical Power and Energy	1 Mark	–	1	–	–
	2 Marks	–	1	1	–
	3 Marks	–	–	1	–
	4 Marks	–	–	–	–
TOPIC 03 Domestic Circuits	1 Mark	1	–	–	–
	2 Marks	1	–	1	–
	3 Marks	–	–	–	–
	4 Marks	–	–	–	–

Average No. of Questions Across all Sets

TOPIC 1

Electricity and Resistance

Electric Current

It is defined as the rate of flow of charge. If a charge Q flows through the cross-section of a conductor in time t, then current I through it is given by

$$I = \frac{Q}{t} = \frac{ne}{t} \qquad [\because Q = ne]$$

where, n is the number of electrons and e is charge on an electron $(1.6 \times 10^{-19}\ \text{C})$.

The SI unit of current is ampere (A).

Electric Potential Difference

Potential at a point is defined as the amount of work done (W) in bringing a unit positive charge (Q) from infinity to that point. It is denoted by V. It is expressed as $V = \frac{W}{Q}$

Its SI unit is volt. It is a scalar quantity.

Potential difference between two points A and B is given by

$$\Delta V = V_B - V_A = \frac{W}{Q}$$

Ohm's Law

According to this law, the electric current I flowing through a conductor is directly proportional to the potential difference V applied across its ends, providing the physical conditions (such as temperature) remain unchanged.

If V is the potential difference applied across the ends of a conductor through which current I flows, then according to Ohm's law,

i.e. $V \propto I$ [at constant temperature]

or $V = IR$ or $I = \frac{V}{R}$

where, R is the constant of proportionality called **resistance** of the conductor at a given temperature.

V-I Graph

The V-I graph is given as

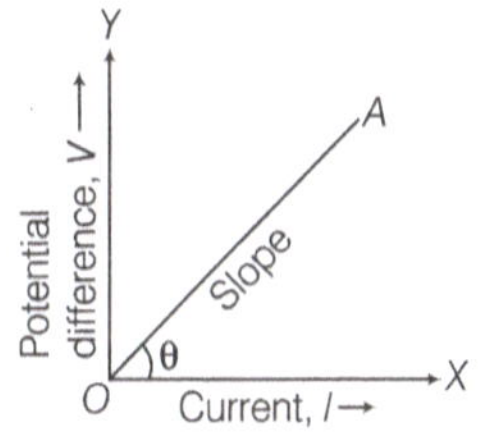

V-I graph for metal conductor

Slope of V-I graph, gives resistance, i.e. slope.

$$= \tan\theta = \frac{\Delta V}{\Delta I}$$

$$= \frac{V}{I} = \text{resistance}$$

Resistance

It is the property of a conductor by virtue of which it opposes/resists the flow of charges through it.

Resistance of a conductor is given by $R = \frac{V}{I}$. The SI unit of resistance is ohm (Ω).

Factors on which the Resistance of a Conductor Depends

The electrical resistance of a conductor depends on the following factors

(i) **Length of the Conductor** The resistance of a conductor R is directly proportional to its length l.

i.e. $R \propto l$

(ii) **Area of Cross-Section of the Conductor** The resistance of a conductor R is inversely proportional to its area of cross-section A.

i.e. $R \propto \frac{1}{A}$

(iii) **Nature of the Material of the Conductor** The resistance of a conductor depends on the nature of the material of which it is made. Some materials have low resistance, whereas other have high resistance.

(iv) **Effects of Temperature**

(a) Resistance of a conductor increases linearly with increase in temperature.

(b) Resistance of a semiconductor decreases with increase in temperature.

(c) Resistance of insulators (non-conductors) decreases with increase in temperature.

(d) Resistance of electrolytes decreases with increase in temperature.

(e) Resistance of alloy increases with increase in temperature.

From the above relation (i) and (ii), we can write $R \propto \frac{l}{A}$ or $R = \rho\frac{l}{A}$

where, ρ is the constant of proportionality called **resistivity** or **specific resistance** of the conductor.

Ohmic and Non-ohmic Resistors

The conductors which obeys Ohm's law are called **ohmic resistors** (or **linear resistances**). e.g. Silver, nichrome, copper, iron, etc. The graph between voltage across the conductor and current through it is a straight line (as shown in V-I graph). The conductors which do not obey Ohm's law are known as **non-ohmic resistors** (or **non-linear resistances**). e.g. Triode valve, junction diode, transistor, etc.

Specific Resistance (Resistivity)

It is defined as the resistance of a conductor of unit length and unit area of cross-section. Its SI unit is ohm-metre (Ω-m). It depends on nature and temperature of the material.

Conductivity

It is defined as the reciprocal of resistivity of a conductor. It's SI unit is mho per metre ($\Omega^{-1}\text{m}^{-1}$) or siemen per metre (S/m). It is expressed as $\sigma = \frac{1}{\rho}$.

Electromotive Force (emf) of a Cell (ε)

The work done by the cell in moving unit positive charge through the whole circuit (including the cell) is called the electromotive force (emf) of the cell.

emf of the cell, $\varepsilon = \dfrac{W}{q}$

Its unit is joule/coulomb or volt.

Internal Resistance (r)

It is defined as the resistance offered by the electrolyte of the cell to the flow of current through it. It is denoted by r. Its unit is also ohm.

Terminal Potential Difference (V)

Terminal potential difference of a cell is defined as the potential difference between the two terminals of the cell in a closed circuit (i.e., when current is drawn from the cell). Its unit is volt. It is always less than the emf of the cell.

Relationship among emf, Terminal Voltage and Internal Resistance

In the given circuit,

- Total resistance of circuit $= R + r$
- Current drawn from the cell, $I = \dfrac{E}{R+r}$
- emf of the cell can be calculated by $E = I(R + r)$.

where, r is the internal resistance, R is external resistance and I is current through the circuit.

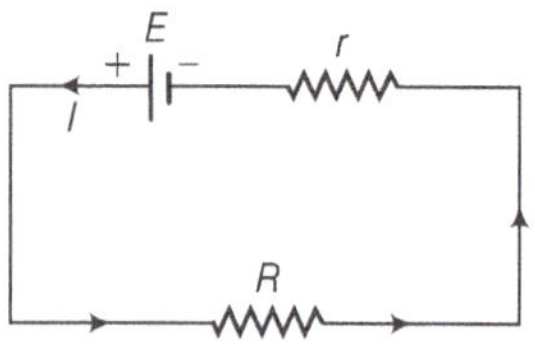

- Terminal voltage of the cell,

$$V = IR = E - Ir$$

- Voltage drop due to internal resistance $= Ir$
- Internal resistance,

$$r = \frac{E - V}{I} = \frac{E - V}{V/R} = \left(\frac{E}{V} - 1\right)R$$

Series Combination of Resistors

When two or more resistors are connected end to end, they are said to be connected in series. This is also known as **maximum effective resistance.**

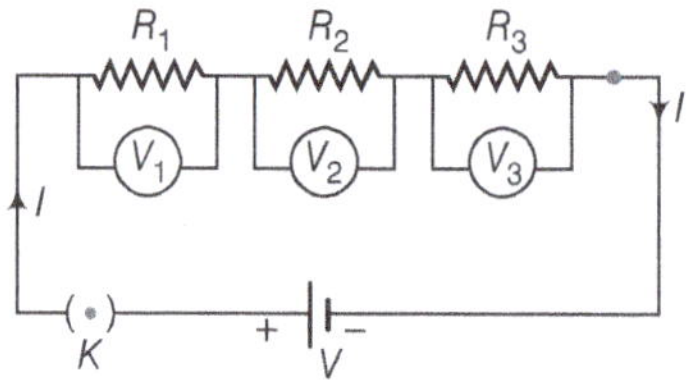

The equivalent resistance in series combination is given as

$$\boxed{R = R_1 + R_2 + R_3}$$

Parallel Combination of Resistors

When one end of the given resistors is connected at one point and other end is connected to other point of a resistance, then it is called parallel combination.

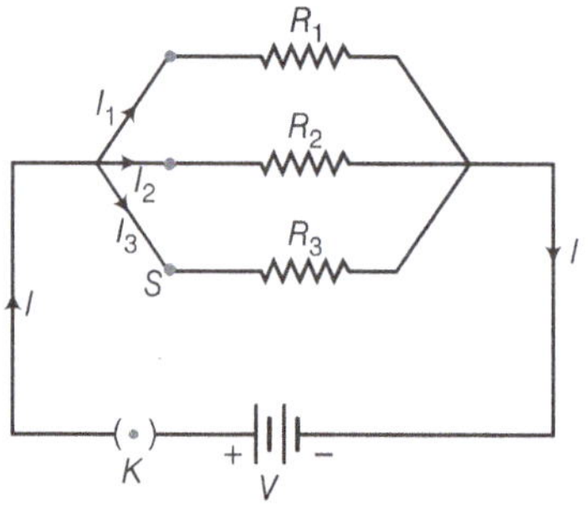

This is also known as **minimum effective resistance.**

The equivalent resistance of parallel combination of resistors is given as

$$\Rightarrow \quad \boxed{\frac{1}{R} = \frac{1}{R_1} + \frac{1}{R_2} + \frac{1}{R_3}}$$

PYQs Previous Years Questions

1 Mark Questions

1. The specific resistance of a conductor depends on its **(ICSE 2024)**
   (a) length (b) material
   (c) area of cross-section (d) radius

2. The potential difference between terminals of a cell in a closed electric circuit is **(ICSE 2024)**
   (a) terminal voltage (b) electromotive force
   (c) voltage drop (d) None of these

3. Choose the correct relation for emf (E) and terminal voltage V. **(ICSE 2023)**
   (a) $E = V$ (always)
   (b) $V > E$ (always)
   (c) $V < E$ (when the cell is in use)
   (d) None of the above

4. The graph shows I against V relation for three conductors A, B and C. Choose the correct relation for the resistors of A, B and C. **(ICSE SQP 2023)**

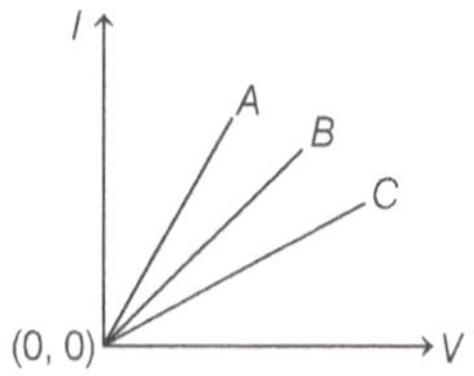

   (a) $R_A > R_B > R_C$
   (b) $R_B > R_C < R_A$
   (c) $R_C > R_B < R_A$
   (d) $R_C > R_B > R_A$

5. The graph plotted for potential difference (V) against current (I) for ohmic resistors is **(ICSE 2022 Sem-II)**
   (a) a curve passing through the origin
   (b) a straight line not passing through origin
   (c) a straight line passing through origin
   (d) a circle centred at the origin.

6. Which of the following is not a characteristic of parallel combination of resistors? **(ICSE 2022 Sem-II)**
   (a) If one resistor is fused, the circuit does not become open.
   (b) The total resistance R is given by the formula $\frac{1}{R} = \frac{1}{R_1} + \frac{1}{R_2} + \frac{1}{R_3}$........
   (c) The total resistance becomes less than the least resistor, present in the combination.
   (d) The current through each resistor always remains the same.

2 Marks Questions

7. 5 bulbs are connected in series in a room. One bulb is fused. It is removed and remaining 4 bulbs are again connected in series to the same circuit. What will be the effect on the following physical quantities? (Increases, decreases, remain same) **(ICSE 2024)**
   (a) Resistance (b) Intensity of light

8. Calculate the total resistance across AB. **(ICSE 2020)**

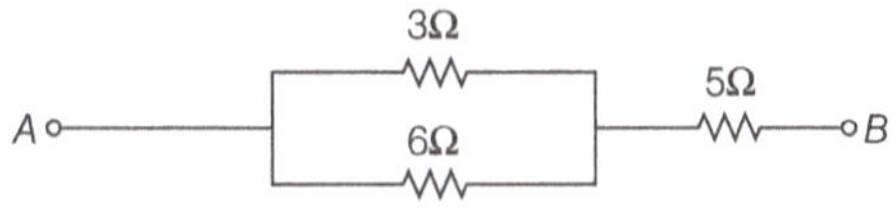

9. Calculate the effective resistance across AB.

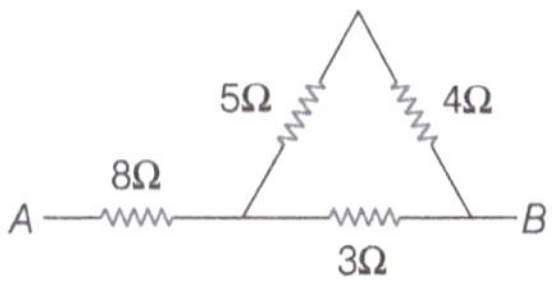

(ICSE 2019)

10. How does an increase in the temperature affect the specific resistance of a **(ICSE 2019)**
    (i) metal ?
    (ii) semiconductor?

11. You have three resistors of values $2\,\Omega$, $3\,\Omega$ and $5\,\Omega$. How will you join them, so that the total resistance is more than $7\,\Omega$?
    (i) Draw a diagram for the arrangement.
    (ii) Calculate the equivalent resistance. **(ICSE 2018)**

12. A metal wire has a resistance of $60\,\Omega$. It is cut into three equal lengths. Find the equivalent resistance when two parts are connected in parallel and the third part is in series with them. **(ICSE SQP 2018)**

13. Draw a well labelled circuit diagram for the verification of Ohm's law. **(ICSE SQP 2018)**

14. Define specific resistance and state its SI unit. **(ICSE 2017)**

15. Mention two factors on which the resistance of a wire depends. **(ICSE 2017, 07)**

16. A music system draws a current of 400 mA, when connected to a 12 V battery.

(i) What is the resistance of the music system?

(ii) The music system is left playing for several hours and finally the battery voltage drops and the music system stops playing when the current drops to 320 mA. At what battery voltage does the music system stop playing? **(ICSE 2016)**

17. The *V-I* graph for a series combination and for a parallel combination of two resistors is shown in the figure below. Which of the two *A* or *B*, represents the parallel combination? Give a reason for your answer.

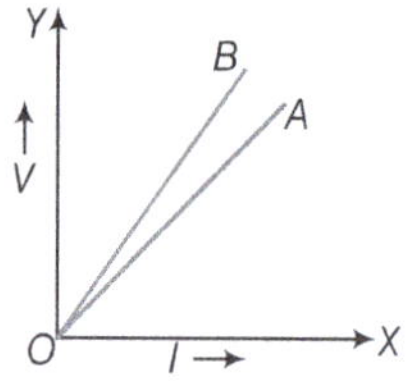

(ICSE 2016, 07)

18. Find the equivalent resistance between points *A* and *B*. **(ICSE 2015)**

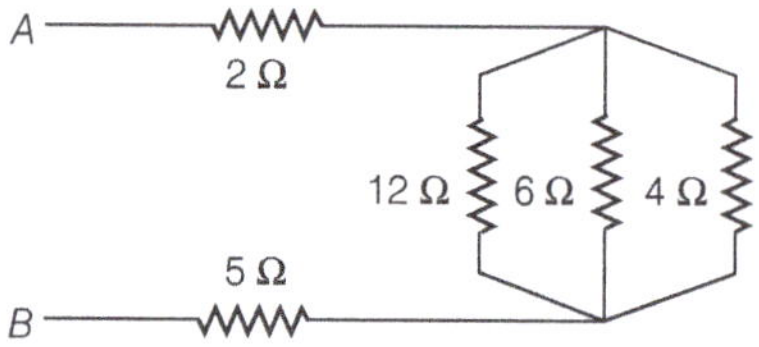

19. Find the equivalent resistance between points *A* and *B*.

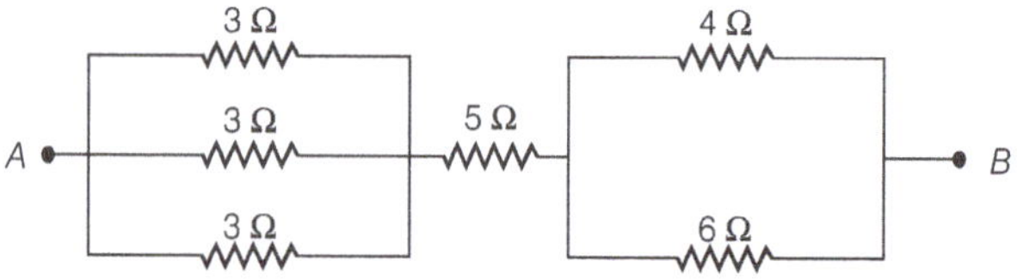

(ICSE 2014)

20. Calculate the equivalent resistance between the points *A* and *B* for the following combination of resistors.

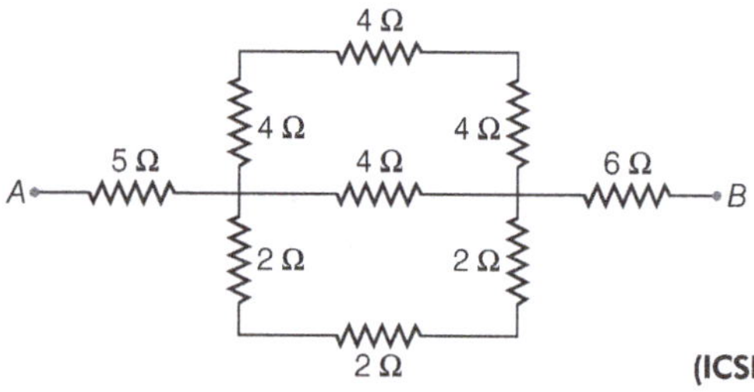

(ICSE 2013)

21. Calculate the equivalent resistance between *P* and *Q* from the following diagram.

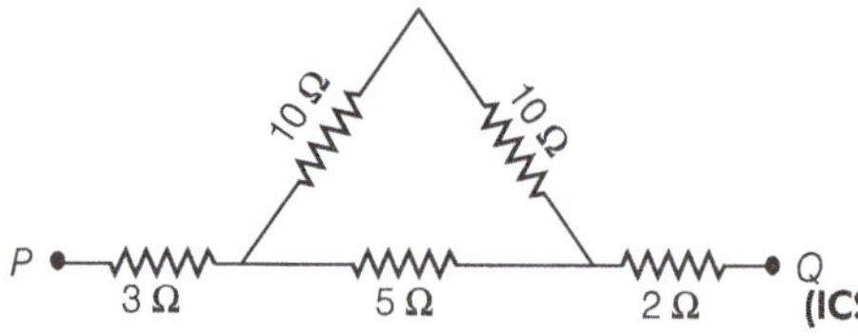

(ICSE 2012)

22. Calculate the equivalent resistance between *A* and *B* from the following diagram.

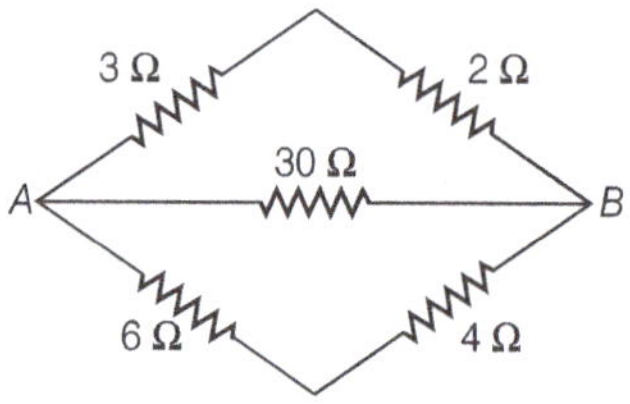

(ICSE 2011)

23. Six resistances are connected together as shown in the figure. Calculate the equivalent resistance between the points *A* and *B*.

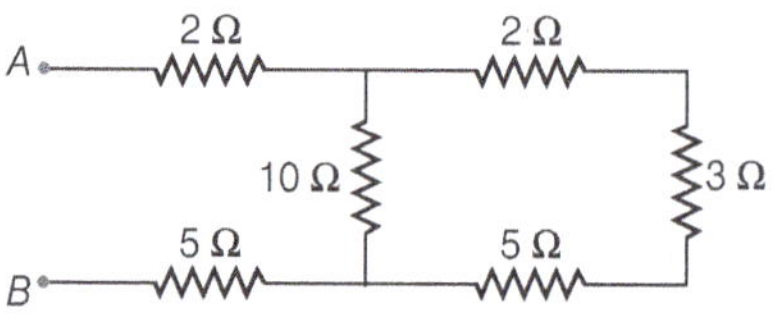

(ICSE 2010)

24. The equivalent resistance of the following circuit diagram is 4 Ω. Calculate the value of *x*. **(ICSE 2009)**

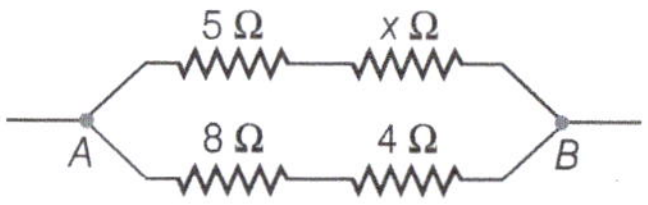

25. (i) Sketch a graph to show the change in potential difference across the ends of an ohmic resistor and the current flowing in it. Label the axes of your graph.

(ii) What does the slope of the graph represent? **(ICSE 2008)**

26. A wire of a uniform thickness with a resistance of 27 Ω is cut into three equal pieces and they are joined in parallel. Find the resistance of the parallel combination. **(ICSE 2006)**

27. Four resistances of 2.0 Ω each are joined end to end, to form a square *ABCD*. Calculate the equivalent resistance of the combination between any two adjacent corners. **(ICSE 2005)**

28. Mention two factors on which the internal resistance of a cell depends. **(ICSE 2004)**

3 Marks Questions

29. The voltage-current readings of a certain material are shown in the table given below. **(ICSE 2024)**

Voltage (V)	10V	20V	30V
Current (I)	2A	3A	4A

Study the table.

(a) State whether the conductor used is ohmic or non-ohmic

(b) Justify your answer.

(c) State Ohm's law.

30. (i) Define specific resistance.

(ii) What happens to the specific resistance of a conductor, if its length is doubled?

(iii) Name a substance whose specific resistance remains almost unchanged with the increase in its temperature. **(ICSE 2023)**

31. (i) Calculate the total resistance across AB.

(ii) If a cell of emf 2.4 V with negligible internal resistance is connected across AB, then calculate the current drawn from the cell. **(ICSE 2022 Sem-II)**

32. (i) Find the equivalent resistance between A and B.

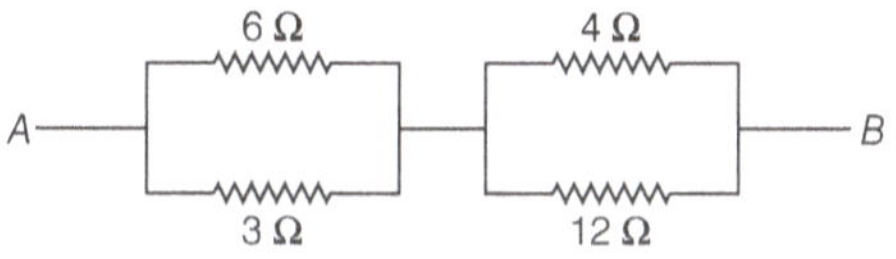

(ii) State whether the resistivity of a wire changes with the change in the thickness of the wire. **(ICSE 2018)**

33.

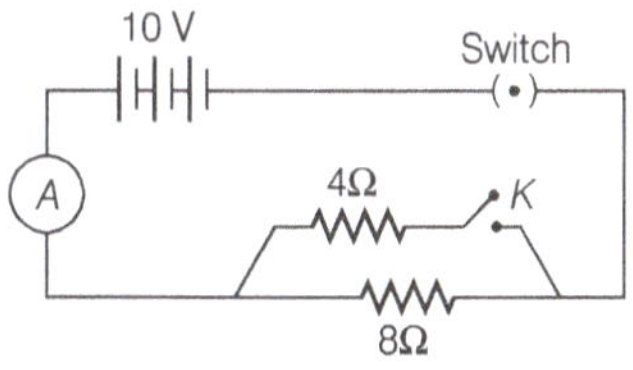

(ICSE 2017)

Calculate the reading of A when

(i) K is closed.

(ii) K is open.

34. The relationship between the potential difference and the current in a conductor is stated in the form of a law. **(ICSE 2015)**

(i) Name the law.

(ii) What does the slope of V-I graph for a conductor represent?

(iii) Name the material used for making the connecting wire.

35. (i) State Ohm's law.

(ii) A metal wire of resistance 6 Ω is stretched, so that its length is increased to twice its original length. Calculate its new resistance. **(ICSE 2013)**

> **KEY idea**
>
> Resistivity of a material is given by $R = \rho \frac{l}{A}$, where ρ is resistivity, l is the length of wire and A is area of the wire.

36. (i) What is an ohmic resistor?

(ii) Two copper wires are of the same length, but one is thicker than the other.

(a) Which wire will have more resistance?

(b) Which wire will have more specific resistance? **(ICSE 2014)**

37. (i) Draw a graph of potential difference (V) *versus* current (I) for an ohmic resistor.

(ii) How can you find the resistance of the resistor from this graph?

(iii) What is a non-ohmic resistor? **(ICSE 2011)**

38. (i) A substance has nearly zero resistance at a temperature of 1K. What is such a substance called?

(ii) State any two factors which affect the resistance of a metallic wire. **(ICSE 2010)**

39. (i) State Ohm's law.

(ii) Diagrammatically illustrate how you would connect a key, a battery, a voltmeter, an ammeter, an unknown resistance R and a rheostat, so that it can be used to verify the above law. **(ICSE 2009)**

40. Three resistors of 6.0 Ω, 2.0 Ω and 4.0 Ω respectively, are joined together as shown in the figure. The resistors are connected to an ammeter and to a cell of emf 6.0 V.

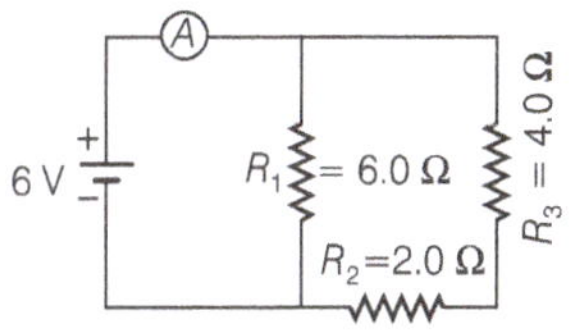

Calculate

(i) the effective resistance of the circuit.

(ii) the current drawn from the cell. **(ICSE 2008)**

4 Marks Questions

41. Study the diagram **(ICSE 2024)**

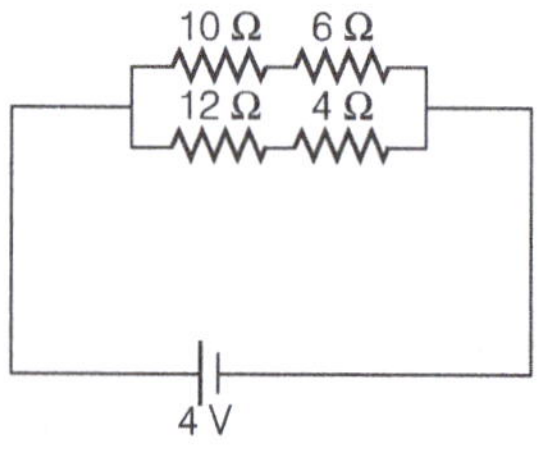

(a) Calculate the total resistance of the current .

(b) Calculate the current drawn from the cell.

(c) State whether the current through 10Ω resistor is greater than, less than or equal to the current through the 12Ω resistor.

42. Find the value of current I drawn from the cell. **(ICSE 2023)**

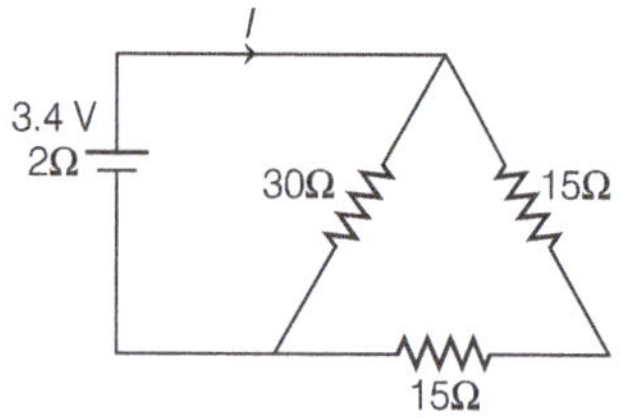

(i) Calculate the current I.

(ii) Calculate the terminal voltage.

43. Observe the given circuit diagram and answer the questions that follows. **(ICSE SQP 2023)**

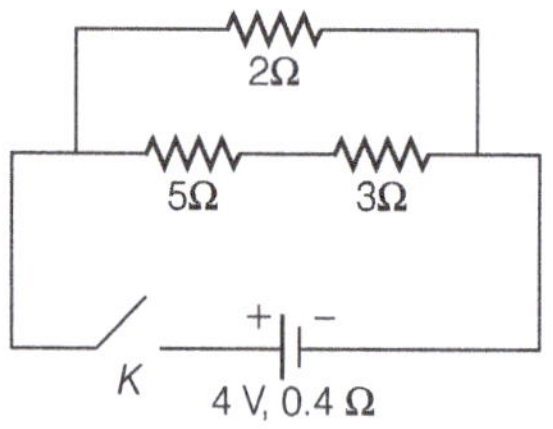

(i) Calculate the resistance of the circuit when the key K completes the circuit.

(ii) Calculate the current through 3 Ω resistance.

KEY idea

The equivalent resistance, can be calculate the current by the formula, $I = \frac{V}{R_{eq}}$

44.

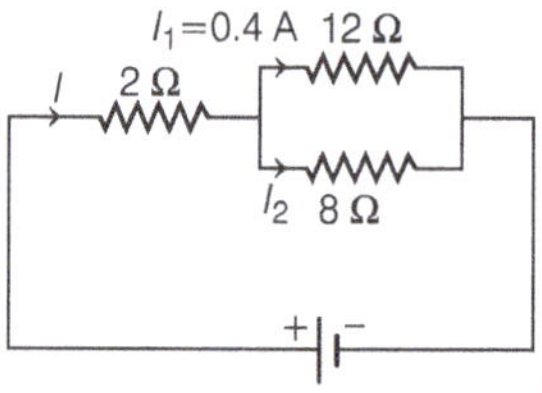

(ICSE 2022 Sem-II)

In the above circuit diagram, calculate

(i) the external resistance of the circuit

(ii) the current I_2

(iii) the current I

45. If a wire of resistance 2 Ω gets stretched to thrice its original length. **(ICSE 2022 Sem-II)**

(i) Calculate the new resistance of the wire.

(ii) What happens to the specific resistance of the wire?

46.

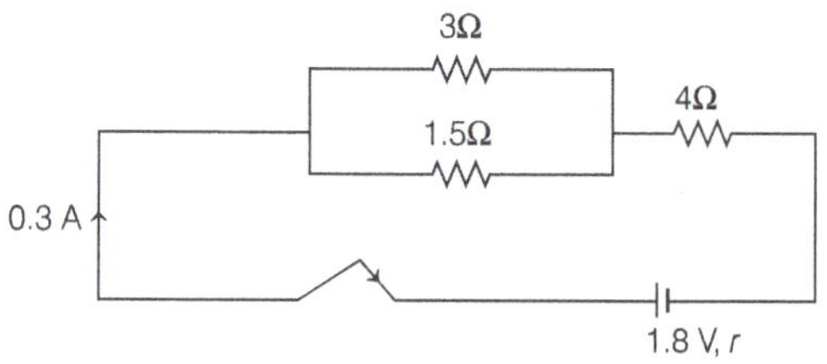

The diagram above shows three resistors connected across a cell of emf 1.8 V and internal resistance r.

Calculate **(ICSE 2020)**

(i) current through 3 Ω resistor

(ii) and the internal resistance r.

47.

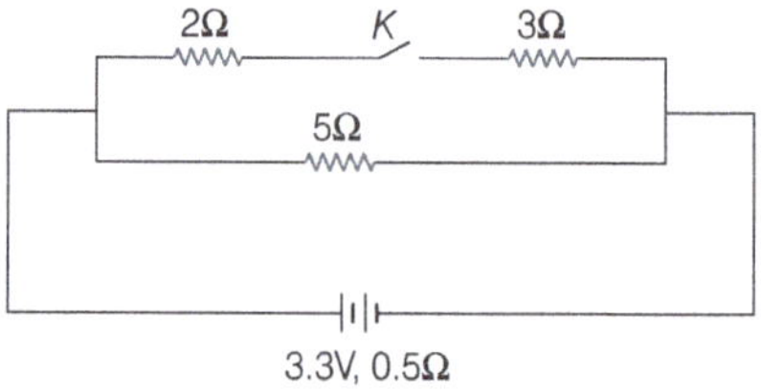

The above figure shows a circuit with the key K open. Calculate

(i) the resistance of the circuit when the key K is open.

(ii) the current drawn from the cell when the key K is open.

(iii) the resistance of the circuit when the key K is closed.

(iv) the current drawn from the cell when the key K is closed. **(ICSE 2019)**

48. In the circuit diagram given below, a cell of 9V and internal resistance 0.5 Ω is connected across a resistor *A* of 2 Ω in series and two resistors 2 Ω and 6 Ω which are in parallel.

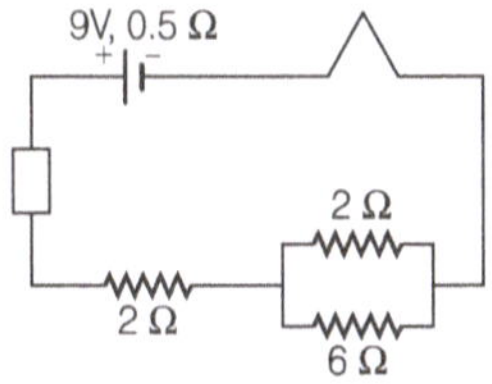

Find,
(i) the total resistance,
(ii) the total current,
(iii) the current in the 6 Ω resistor and
(iv) the potential difference across the terminals of the cell. **(ICSE SQP 2018)**

49. The diagram shows an electrical circuit used for the verification of Ohm's law. Label *A*, *B* *C*, *D* and *E*. Draw a sketch to show how the value of current varies for different values of voltage across *C*. **(ICSE SQP 2017)**

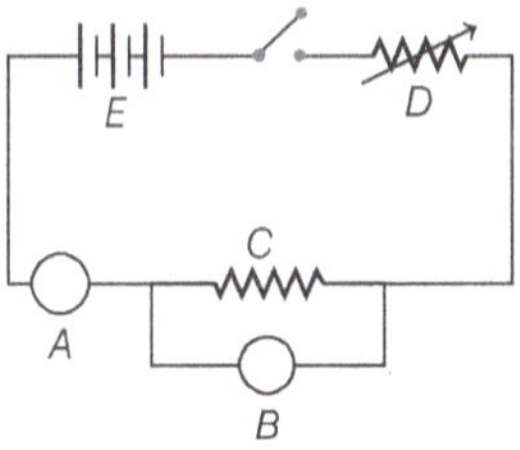

50. A cell of emf 2V and internal resistance 1.2 Ω is connected with an ammeter of resistance 0.8 Ω and two resistors of 4.5 Ω and 9 Ω as shown in the diagram below

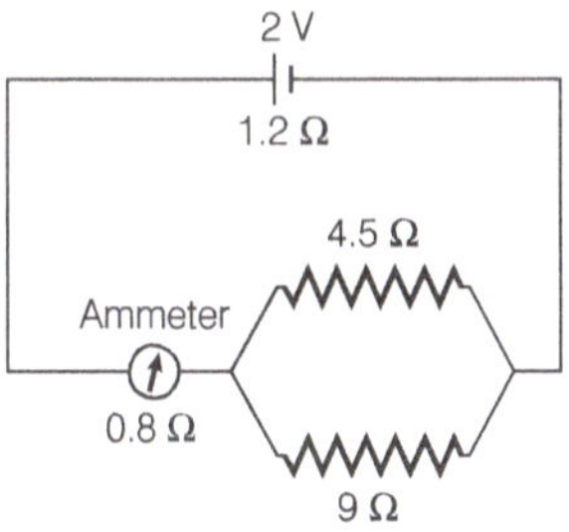

(i) What would be the reading on the ammeter?
(ii) What is the potential difference across the terminals of the cell? **(ICSE 2015)**

KEY idea

The potential difference across the terminals of the cells is determine by $V = IR_{eq}$.

51. Two resistors of 4Ω and 6Ω are connected in parallel to a cell to draw 0.5 A current from the cell.
(i) Draw a labelled circuit diagram showing the above arrangement.
(ii) Calculate the current in each resistor. **(ICSE 2014)**

52. Three resistors are connected to a 6 V battery as shown in the figure.

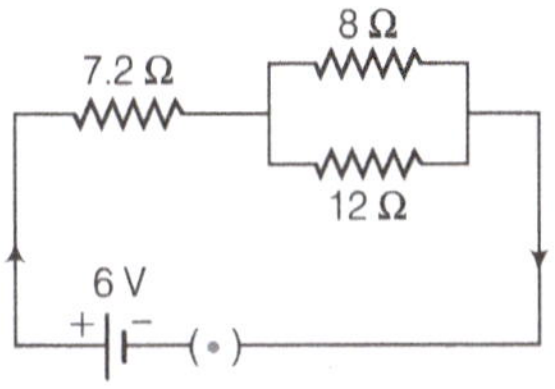

Calculate
(i) the equivalent resistance of the circuit,
(ii) total current in the circuit and
(iii) potential difference across the 7.2 Ω resistor. **(ICSE 2012)**

53. Three resistors are connected to a 12 V battery as shown in the figure given here.

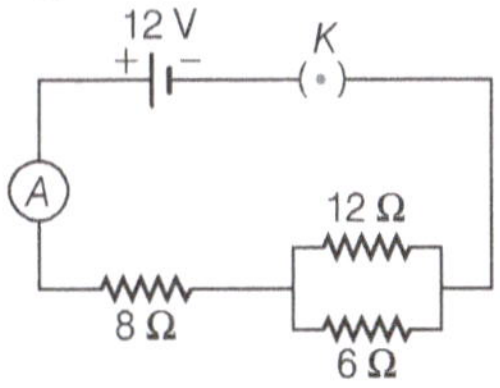

(i) What is the current through the 8 Ω resistor?
(ii) What is the potential difference across the parallel combination of 6 Ω and 12 Ω resistors?
(iii) What is the current through the 6 Ω resistor? **(ICSE 2011)**

54. Five resistors of different resistances are connected together as shown in the figure. A 12 V battery is connected to the arrangement.

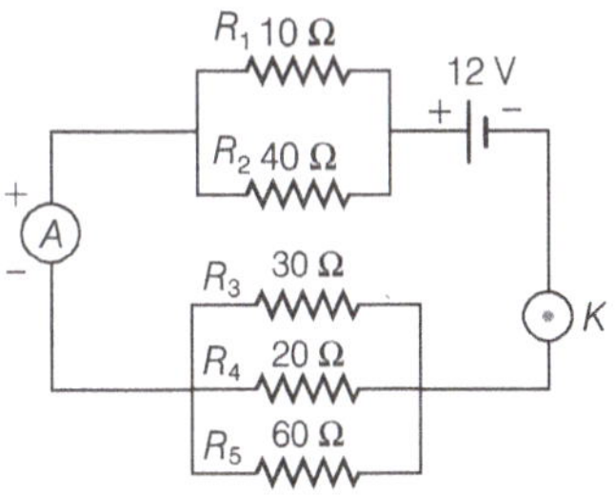

Calculate
(i) the total resistance in the circuit.
(ii) the total current flowing in the circuit. **(ICSE 2010)**

55. A cell of emf 1.5 V and internal resistance 1.0 Ω are connected to two resistors of 4.0 Ω and 20.0 Ω in series as shown in the figure.

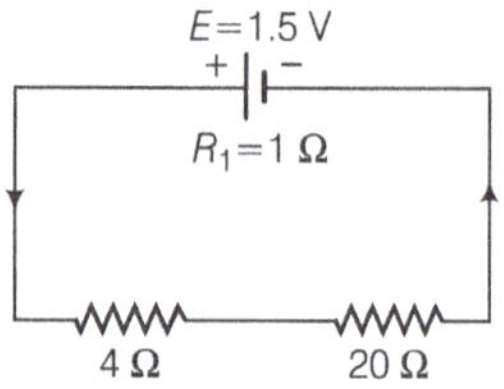

Calculate the

(i) current in the circuit.

(ii) potential difference across the 4.0Ω resistor.

(iii) voltage drop across internal resistance when the current is flowing.

(iv) potential difference across the cell. **(ICSE 2007)**

56. In the figure given below, the ammeter A reads 0.3 A.

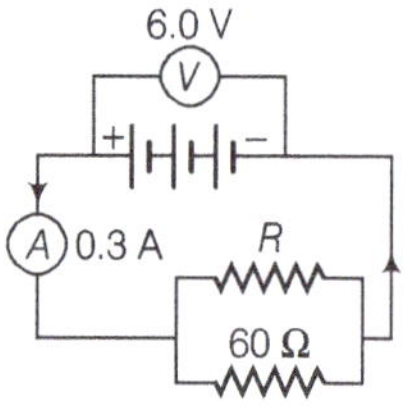

Calculate

(i) the total resistance of the circuit.

(ii) the value of R.

(iii) the current flowing through R. **(ICSE 2006)**

57. In the figure given below A, B and C are three ammeters. The ammeter B reads 0.5 A. (All the ammeters have negligible resistance).

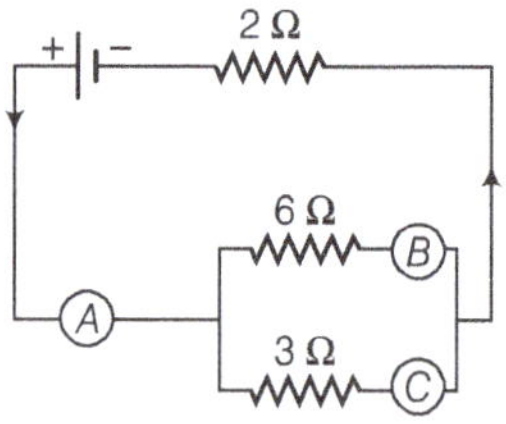

Calculate

(i) the readings in the ammeters A and C.

(ii) the total resistance of the circuit. **(ICSE 2005)**

58. (i) Which of the two wires of similar dimensions, copper or nichrome, would you use for the electric heater element? Give reasons to justify your answer.

(ii) Two fuse wires of the same length are rated 5 A and 20 A. Which of the two fuse wires is thicker and why? **(ICSE 2003)**

59. Four cells, each of emf 1.5 V and internal resistance 2.0 Ω are connected in a parallel. The battery of the cells is connected to an external resistance of 2.5 Ω. Calculate

(i) the total resistance of the circuit.

(ii) the current flowing in the external circuit.

(iii) the drop in potential across the terminals of the cells. **(ICSE 2002)**

Explanations

1. (b) Specific resistance is a characteristic property of the material of a conductor. Hence, specific resistance of conductor depends on its material.

2. (a) The potential difference terminals of a cell in closed electric circuit is terminal voltage. Its unit is volt.

3. (c)

4. (d) $R_C > R_B > R_A$

$$\text{Slope} = \frac{1}{V} = \frac{1}{R} \text{ is least for } R_C$$

A is the best conductor, as it has the least resistance among A, B and C.

Common Mistake Generally, students are taking slope as simply resistance (R) without observing I and V axes.

5. (c)

6. (d)

7. (a) Resistance decreases

(b) Intensity of light increases

8.

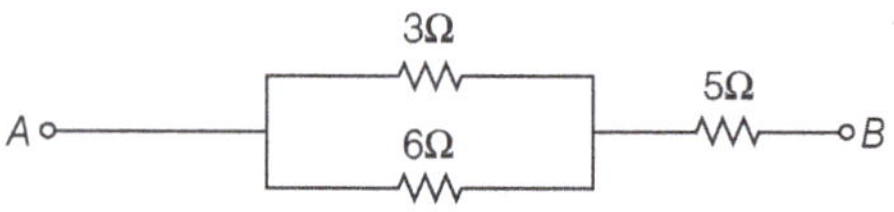

Total resistance between A and B.

$$R_{AB} = (3 || 6) + 5$$

$$= \frac{3 \times 6}{3+6} + 5$$

$$= 2 + 5 = 7\,\Omega$$

9.

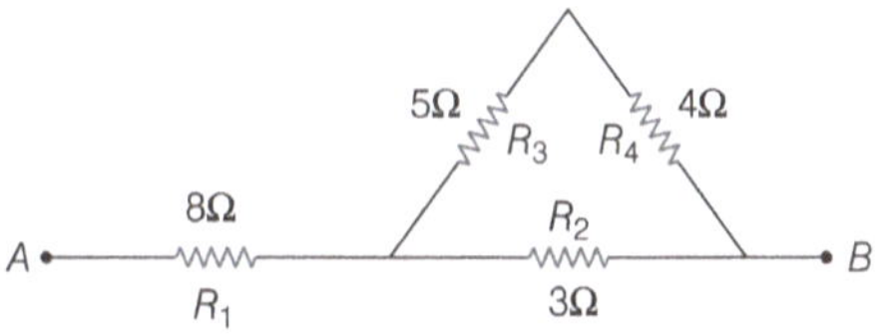

Here, R_3 and R_4 are in series combination, so total resistance,

$$R_5 = R_3 + R_4 = 5 + 4 = 9\,\Omega$$

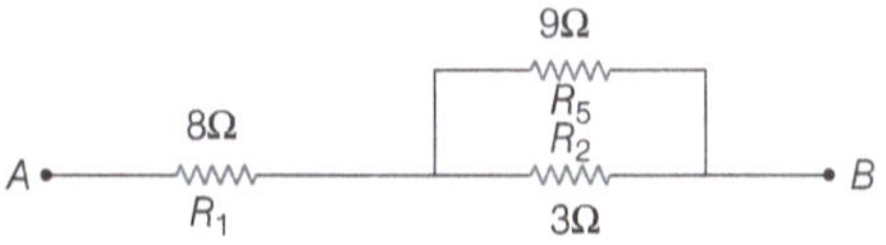

Here, R_5 and R_2 are in parallel combination, so total resistance,

$$\frac{1}{R_6} = \frac{1}{R_2} + \frac{1}{R_5} = \frac{1}{3} + \frac{1}{9}$$

$$\frac{1}{R_6} = \frac{4}{9}$$

$$\therefore \quad R_6 = \frac{9}{4}\,\Omega$$

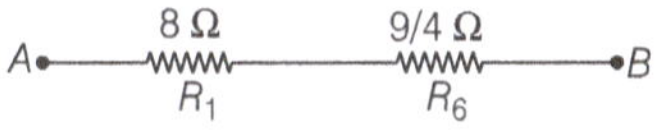

Here, R_1 and R_6 are in series combination, so resultant resistance across AB.

Now, equivalent resistance,

$$R_{eq} = R_1 + R_6 = 8 + \frac{9}{4} = \frac{41}{4}\,\Omega$$

> **Concept Enhancer** Equivalent resistance in parallel combination is always less than individual resistance.

10. (i) If the temperature of the metal is raised, the atom vibrate more strongly and the electrons make more violent collisions with them, so the resistance of the metal increase. Hence, resistivity will increases.

Thus, specific resistance of the metal increase.

(ii) In case of semiconductor as the temperature increases, the electrons in the valence band get excited and jump into the conduction band and hence, the conductance increases resulting in the decreasing of resistance. As resistance is directly proportional to resistivity.

Hence, resistivity of semiconductor decreases rapidly with rise in temperature.

11. To get total resistance more than 7Ω, we can connect 2Ω, 3Ω and 5Ω in series.

(i)

(ii) $R_{eq} = R_1 + R_2 + R_3$ [For series combination]

$R_{eq} = 2 + 3 + 5 = 10\,\Omega$

12. Resistance of wire $= 60\,\Omega$

When cut into three equal parts.

Resistance of each part $= \frac{60}{3} = r = 20\,\Omega$

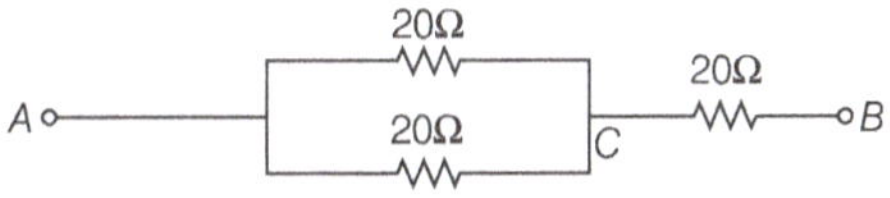

Resistance between A and C is given by

$$\frac{1}{R'} = \frac{1}{20} + \frac{1}{20} = \frac{2}{20} = \frac{1}{10}$$

$$R' = 10\,\Omega$$

Now resistance between A and B is

$$R'' = 10 + 20 = 30\,\Omega$$

13.

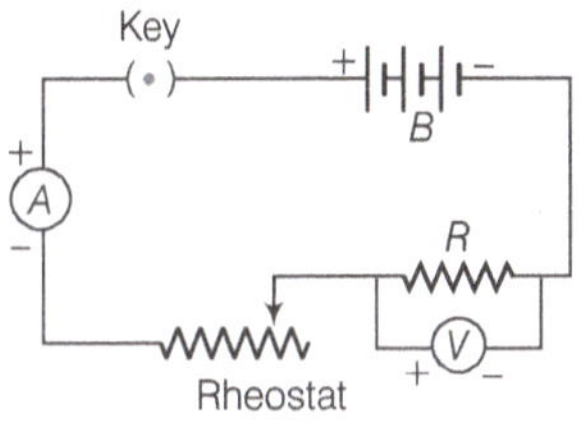

where, B is the battery, V is the voltmeter and A is the ammeter.

14. Specific resistance or resistivity (ρ) of a conductor is defined as the resistance of a conductor of unit length and unit area of cross-section.

From the factors affecting the resistance of a conductor, the resistance is given by

$$R = \rho \frac{l}{A}$$

$$\Rightarrow \quad \rho = \frac{RA}{l} = \frac{\Omega\text{-}m^2}{m} = \Omega\text{-}m$$

Its SI unit is ohm-metre (Ω - m).

Specific resistance or resistivity is the characteristic property of a conducting material and it depends only on the nature of that material and temperature.

15. The resistance of a wire depends on the following factors

(i) Length of the wire.

(ii) Area of cross-section of the wire.

16. Given, current, $I = 400 \text{ mA} = 400 \times 10^{-3} \text{ A} = 0.4 \text{ A}$

Voltage, $V = 12 \text{ V}$

(i) Resistance of the music system is

$$R = \frac{V}{I} = \frac{12}{0.4} = \frac{120}{4} = 30\Omega$$

(ii) Resistance of music system, $R = 30\Omega$,

Current, $I = 320 \text{ mA} = 0.32 \text{ A}$

By Ohm's law, $R = \frac{V}{I} \Rightarrow V = IR$

$\Rightarrow \quad V = 0.32 \times 30$

$\Rightarrow \quad V = 9.60 \text{ V}$

17. In parallel combination, resultant resistance becomes less than the resultant resistance in series combination. According to graph, slope of line A is less than the slope of line B. So, line A represents the parallel combination.

18.

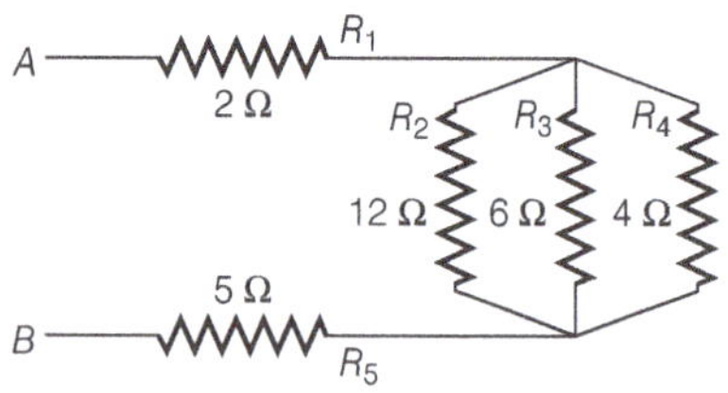

R_2, R_3 and R_4 are in parallel.

So, equivalent resistance corresponding to them

$$R_p = \frac{R_2R_3R_4}{R_3R_2 + R_3R_4 + R_4R_2}$$

$$= \frac{12 \times 6 \times 4}{6 \times 12 + 6 \times 4 + 4 \times 12}$$

$$R_p = \frac{288}{144} = 2\Omega$$

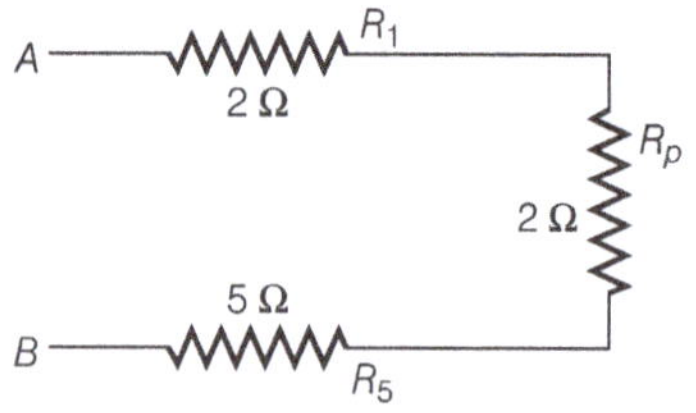

R_1, R_p and R_5 are in series.

Now, equivalent resistance will be given by

$$R = R_1 + R_p + R_5$$

$$= 2 + 2 + 5$$

$$R = 9\Omega$$

19. The three resistances each of 3Ω are in parallel.

$$\frac{1}{R_1} = \frac{1}{3} + \frac{1}{3} + \frac{1}{3} = \frac{3}{3} = 1\Omega \Rightarrow R_1 = 1\Omega$$

The resistance 4Ω and 6Ω are in parallel.

$$\frac{1}{R_3} = \frac{1}{4} + \frac{1}{6} = \frac{3+2}{12} = \frac{5}{12}\Omega$$

$$\Rightarrow \quad R_3 = \frac{12}{5} = 2.4\Omega$$

The resistances R_1, 5Ω and R_3 are in series. So, total resistance

$$R = R_1 + 5 + R_3$$

$$= 1 + 5 + 2.4 = 8.4\Omega$$

20. The three resistances each of 4Ω are in series.

$\therefore \quad R_1 = 4 + 4 + 4 = 12\Omega$

The three resistances each of 2Ω are in series.

$\therefore \quad R_2 = 2 + 2 + 2 = 6\Omega$

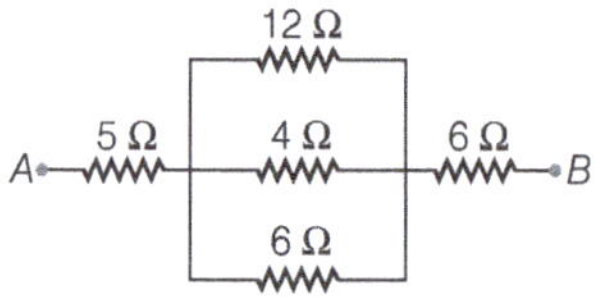

The resistances 4Ω, 12Ω and 6Ω are in parallel.

$$\therefore \quad \frac{1}{R_3} = \frac{1}{4} + \frac{1}{12} + \frac{1}{6}$$

$$= \frac{3+1+2}{12} = \frac{6}{12} = \frac{1}{2}\Omega$$

$$\Rightarrow \quad R_3 = 2\Omega$$

The resistances 5Ω, 2Ω and 6Ω are in series.

$\therefore \quad R_{eq} = 5 + 2 + 6 = 13\Omega$

21. The two resistances $10\,\Omega$ and $10\,\Omega$ are in series.

$$R = 10 + 10 = 20\,\Omega$$

The resistances $5\,\Omega$ and R are in parallel.

$$\therefore \quad \frac{1}{R_1} = \frac{1}{5} + \frac{1}{20}$$

$$= \frac{4+1}{20} = \frac{5}{20} = \frac{1}{4}$$

$$\Rightarrow \quad R_1 = 4\Omega$$

The resistances 3Ω, 4Ω and 2Ω are in series.

$\therefore$ Equivalent resistance,

$$R_{eq} = 3 + 4 + 2 = 9\,\Omega$$

22. Resistances 3Ω and 2Ω are in series.

$\therefore \quad R_1 = 3 + 2 = 5\Omega$

Also, resistances 6Ω and 4Ω are in series.

$\therefore \quad R_2 = 6 + 4 = 10\Omega$

Equivalent resistance between A and B is

$$\frac{1}{R_{eq}} = \frac{1}{5} + \frac{1}{30} + \frac{1}{10}$$

$$= \frac{6+1+3}{30} = \frac{10}{30} = \frac{1}{3}$$

$\therefore \quad R_{eq} = 3\Omega$

23. Resistance between the points C and D,

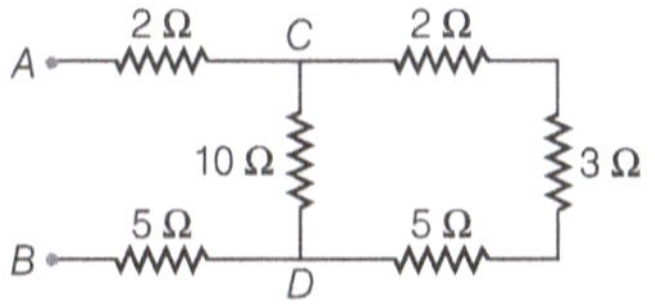

$$\frac{1}{R_{CD}} = \frac{1}{10} + \frac{1}{2+3+5} = \frac{1}{10} + \frac{1}{10}$$

$$= \frac{2}{10} = \frac{1}{5}$$

$\therefore \quad R_{CD} = 5\Omega$

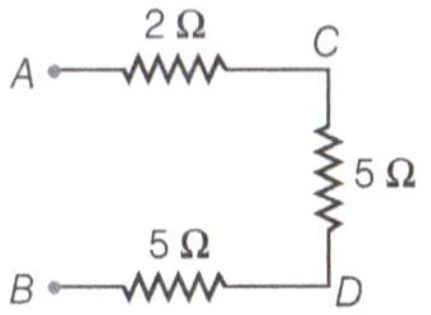

Now, equivalent resistance between the points A and B.

$$R_{AB} = R_{AC} + R_{CD} + R_{BD}$$

$$= 2 + 5 + 5 = 12\,\Omega$$

24. According to the question,

$$\frac{1}{R_{AB}} = \frac{1}{R_1} + \frac{1}{R_2}$$

$$\Rightarrow \quad \frac{1}{4} = \frac{1}{5+x} + \frac{1}{8+4} \Rightarrow \frac{1}{4} = \frac{1}{5+x} + \frac{1}{12}$$

$\Rightarrow \quad x = 1\Omega$

25. (i)

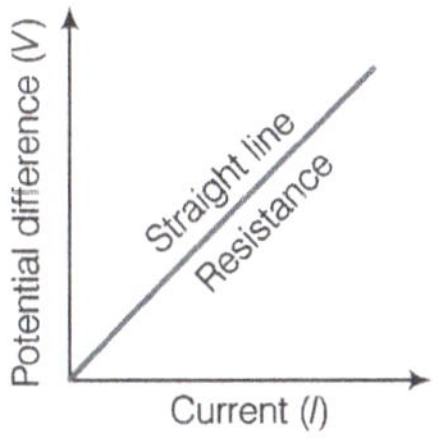

(ii) The slope of the graph represents resistance of the resistor.

Common Mistake Students are confused to plot V and I either of X-axis or Y-axis. Here, variable (V) is taken on Y-axis and variable (I) is taken on X-axis.

26. Given, resistance of given wire $= 27\Omega$

$\therefore$ Resistance of small wire

$$= \frac{\text{Resistance of wire}}{\text{Number of pieces of wire}} = \frac{27}{3} = 9\Omega$$

Now, the each wire of resistance 9Ω are connected in parallel.

$$\therefore \quad \frac{1}{R_{eq}} = \frac{1}{9} + \frac{1}{9} + \frac{1}{9} = \frac{3}{9} = \frac{1}{3}$$

$$R_{eq} = 3\Omega$$

27. Resistance between two adjacent corners A and B is

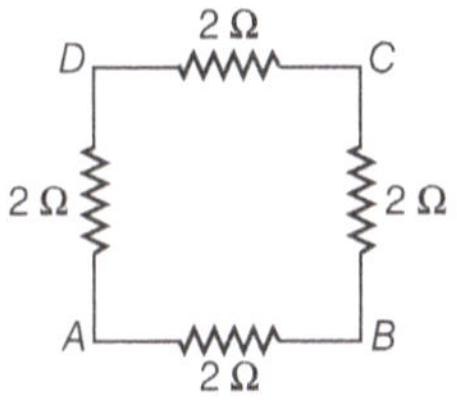

$$\frac{1}{R} = \frac{1}{R_{AB}} + \frac{1}{R_{BC} + R_{CD} + R_{AD}}$$

$$\Rightarrow \quad \frac{1}{2} + \frac{1}{2+2+2} = \frac{1}{2} + \frac{1}{6} \Rightarrow \frac{3+1}{6} = \frac{4}{6} = \frac{2}{3}$$

$$\Rightarrow \quad R = \frac{3}{2} = 1.5\,\Omega$$

28. The internal resistance of a cell depends on following factors

(i) Surface area of the electrode.

(ii) Concentration of the electrolyte.

29. (a) Non-ohmic

(b) Resistance of material is variable.

(c) Refer to text Ohm's law on Page 127.

30. (i) Refer to text on page No. 127 (Specific resistance)

(ii) The specific resistance do not depend on the length or cross-section area of a conductor. It depends on the internal properties of that conductor. Hence, it remains same.

(iii) The resistance of alloys like german-silver, manganin, constantan practically does not change with rise in temperature.

31. (i) Resistors $3\,\Omega$ and $5\,\Omega$ are in series, the equivalent resistance of these two is $8\,\Omega$.

Now, this 8 Ω is connected with another 8 Ω resistor in parallel.

The equivalent resistance of these two are,

$$= \frac{8 \times 8}{8+8} = \frac{64}{16} = 4\,\Omega$$

Thus, the total resistance across AB is 4 Ω.

(ii) $I = \frac{\text{Voltage }(V)}{\text{Equivalent resistance }(R)} = \frac{2.4}{4} = 0.6\text{ A}$

32. (i)

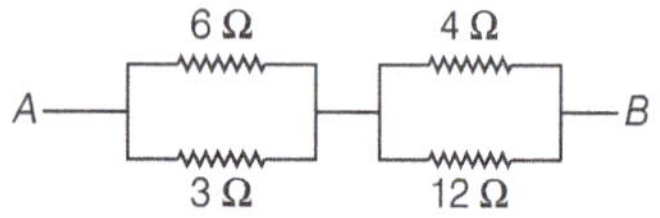

In the given circuit, 6Ω and 3Ω resistances are in parallel combination.

$$\therefore \quad \frac{1}{R_{p_1}} = \frac{1}{R_1} + \frac{1}{R_2}$$

$$R_{p_1} = \frac{R_1 \times R_2}{R_1 + R_2} = \frac{6 \times 3}{6+3} = \frac{18}{9} = 2\Omega$$

Similarly, 4Ω and 12Ω resistances are in parallel combination.

$$\therefore \; R_{p_2} = \frac{R_3 \times R_4}{R_3 + R_4} = \frac{4 \times 12}{4+12} = \frac{48}{16} = 3\Omega$$

Now, we get new circuit as

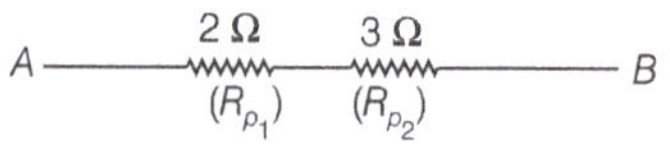

Here, 2Ω and 3Ω resistances are in series combination.

So, total resistance of circuit,

$$R_T = R_{p_1} + R_{p_2} = 2 + 3 = 5\Omega$$

(ii) Resistivity is a material property, it does not change with change in thickness of wire.

33. (i) When K is closed, 4 Ω and 8 Ω are in parallel.

$$\text{Net resistance} = \frac{8 \times 4}{8+4} = \frac{8}{3}\Omega$$

$$I = \frac{V}{R} = \frac{10}{8/3} = \frac{15}{4}\text{A}$$

(ii) When K is open

Net resistance = 8 Ω

$$I = \frac{V}{R} = \frac{10}{8} = 1.25\text{ A}$$

34. (i) Ohm's law gives the relationship between the potential difference and the current in a conductor.

(ii) The slope of V-I graph for a conductor gives the resistance of the conductor.

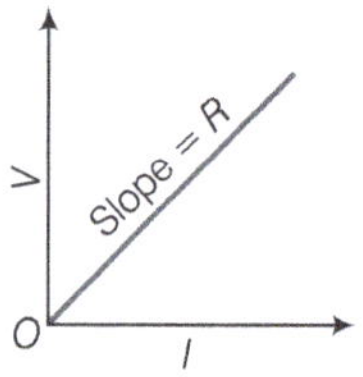

(iii) Copper is used for making the connecting wire.

35. (i) Ohm's law states that the current flowing through a conductor is directly proportional to the potential difference across its ends provided that the physical conditions and the temperature of the conductor remains constant.

(ii) Given, $R_1 = 6\Omega, l_1 = l,$

$$l_2 = 2l_1 = 2l, R_2 = ?$$

$$\therefore \; R_1 = \rho \frac{l_1}{A_1} \quad \text{and} \quad R_2 = \rho \frac{l_2}{A_2}$$

The volume of metal wire remains same.

$$\therefore \quad A_1 l_1 = A_2 l_2 \Rightarrow \frac{l_2}{l_1} = \frac{A_1}{A_2} \quad \ldots\text{(i)}$$

$$\text{Now, } \frac{R_2}{R_1} = \frac{l_2}{A_2} \times \frac{A_1}{l_1} = \frac{l_2}{l_1} \times \frac{l_2}{l_1} \qquad \left[\because \frac{A_1}{A_2} = \frac{l_2}{l_1}\right]$$

$$\Rightarrow \quad R_2 = R_1 \left(\frac{l_2}{l_1}\right)^2 = 6\left(\frac{2l}{l}\right)^2 = 24\,\Omega$$

36. (i) The conductor which obeys Ohm's law is called ohmic resistor or linear resistance. e.g. Silver, aluminium, copper, nichrome, etc.

(ii) (a) Thin wires will have more resistance, because the resistance of the wire varies inversely to the area of the wire, i.e. $R \propto \frac{1}{A}$.

(b) Both wires will have same specific resistance because it depends on the internal properties of the material and not on the dimensions.

37. (i) The graph of potential difference (V) *versus* current (I) for an ohmic resistor is shown below

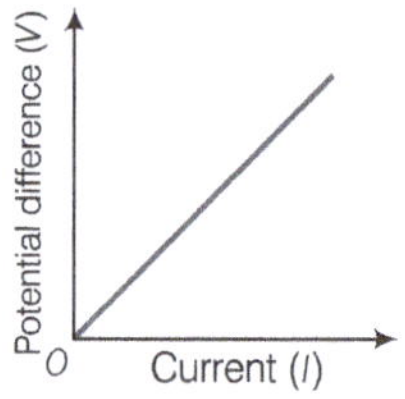

(ii) The resistance of the resistor is given by the slope of the straight line in the V-I graph.

(iii) The conductor which does not obey Ohm's law is known as non-ohmic resistor.

38. (i) The substance which has nearly zero resistance at a temperature of 1K is called as superconductor.

(ii) The two factors which affect the resistance of a metallic wires are

(a) Length of the wire (l), i.e. $R \propto l$.

(b) Area of cross-section (A), i.e. $R \propto \frac{1}{A}$.

39. (i) Refer to text on page no 127.

(ii) To illustrate the Ohm's law, we draw the following circuit.

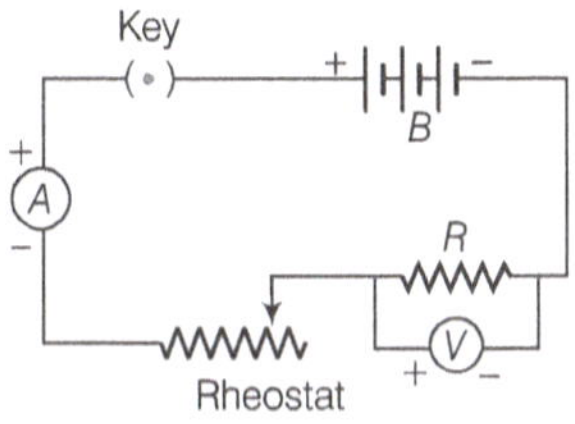

where, B is the battery, V is voltmeter and A is the ammeter.

40. According to the question as shown in the figure,

(i) $R_s = R_2 + R_3 = 2 + 4 = 6\Omega$

$$\therefore \quad \frac{1}{R_{eq}} = \frac{1}{R_1} + \frac{1}{R_s} = \frac{1}{6} + \frac{1}{6} = \frac{1}{3}$$

$$R_{eq} = 3\,\Omega$$

(ii) $\therefore \quad I = \frac{E}{R} = \frac{6}{3} = 2\text{ A}$

41.

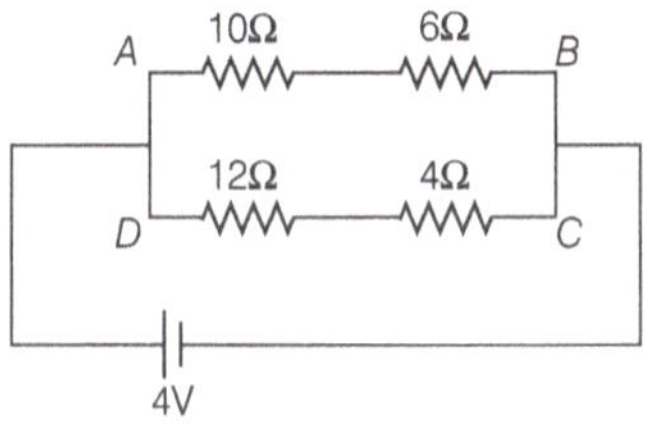

(a) Resistances 10Ω and 6Ω are in series

$R_1 = 10 + 6 = 16\Omega$

Resistances 12Ω and 4Ω are in series

$R_2 = 12 + 4 = 16\Omega$

Now, resistances 16Ω and 16Ω are in parallel, so

$$\frac{1}{R} = \frac{1}{16} + \frac{1}{16} = \frac{2}{16}$$

$$R = \frac{16}{2} = 8\Omega$$

(b) Current, $I = \frac{V}{R} = \frac{4}{8} = 0.2\text{ A}$

(c) The current through $10\,\Omega$ resistor is equal to the current through $12\,\Omega$ resistor because the equivalent resistance of both arms AB and CD are same.

42. (i)

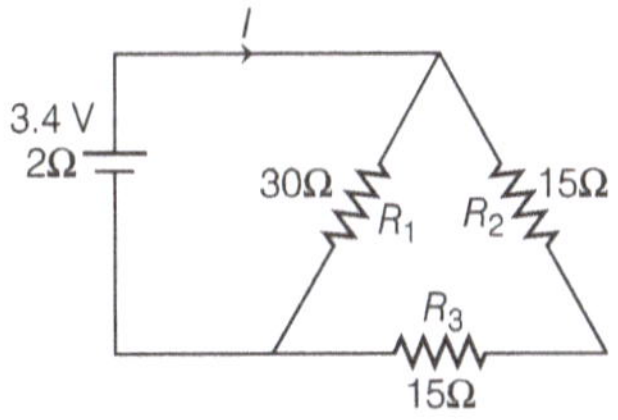

Both R_2 and R_3 are in series hence, their combined resistance is $15\,\Omega + 15\,\Omega = 30\,\Omega$, $R_2, R_3\,(30\,\Omega)$ and $R_1\,(30\,\Omega)$ are parallel.

Hence, combine resistance will be $\frac{30}{2} = 15\,\Omega$

Total resistance of circuit $= 15\,\Omega + 2\,\Omega = 17\,\Omega$

$$I = \frac{\text{emf}}{\text{total resistance}} = \frac{3.4}{17} = 0.2\text{A}$$

(ii) Terminal voltage, $V = \varepsilon - Ir$

$$= 3.4 - (0.2)\,(2) = 3\text{ V}$$

43. (i) $R_1 = 5\Omega + 3\Omega = 8\Omega$

$$R = \frac{(R_1)\,(2)}{R_1 + 2}$$

$$R = \frac{8 \times 2}{8 + 2} = \frac{16}{10} = 1.6\,\Omega$$

(ii) Total current $= \frac{V}{R + r} = \frac{4}{1.6 + 0.4} = 2\text{A}$

Voltage across resistance combination

$$V = IR = 2 \times 1.6 = 3.2\text{ V}$$

Current in $3\,\Omega$ resistance $= \frac{3.2}{5 + 3} = 0.4\text{ A}$

44. (i) External resistance of the circuit,

$$R_S = R_2 + (R_{12} || R_8)$$

$$= R_2 + \left(\frac{R_{12} \times R_8}{R_{12} + R_8}\right)$$

$$= 2 + \left(\frac{12 \times 8}{20}\right) = 2 + 4.8 = 6.8\,\Omega$$

(ii) Voltage across $12\,\Omega$ and $8\,\Omega$ is equal due to parallel combination.

Voltage across

$$12\,\Omega = I_1 \times R = 12 \times 0.4$$

$$V = 4.8\text{ V}$$

Current, $I_2 = \frac{V}{R_2} = \frac{4.8}{8}$

$$I_2 = 0.6\text{ A}$$

(iii) Current, $I = I_1 + I_2$

$$= 0.4 + 0.6 = 1\text{ A}$$

45. (i) In both the cases, the volume of the wire remains unchanged.

$$V = V'$$

$$Al = A'l' \text{ or } A' = \frac{Al}{l'}$$

$$A' = \frac{lA}{3l} = \frac{A}{3}$$

Now, $r = \dfrac{\rho l}{A}$

and $R' = \dfrac{\rho l'}{A'} = \dfrac{\rho 3l}{A/3}$

$$R' = \frac{9\rho l}{A} = 9R$$

$$R' = 9 \times 2 = 18\,\Omega$$

(ii) Since, the specific resistance (resistivity) depends on the nature of material of the wire and it is independent of the dimensions of wire, so specific resistance will not change.

46. (i) The given circuit diagram is as shown below

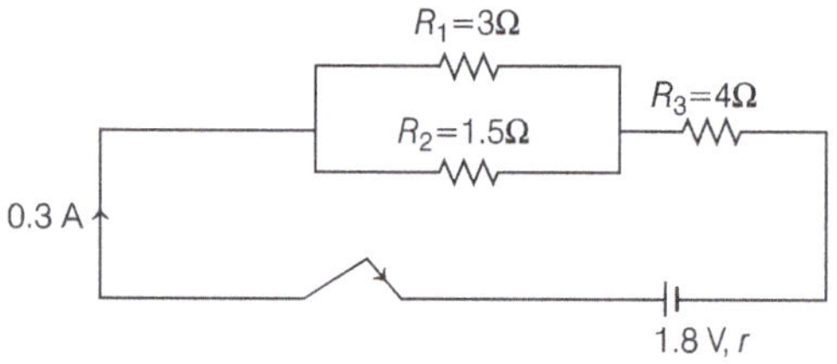

According to current division rule, current through 3 Ω resistance,

$$I' = I \cdot \frac{R_2}{R_1 + R_2} = 0.3 \times \frac{1.5}{3 + 1.5}$$

$$= \frac{0.45}{4.5} = 0.1 \text{ A}$$

(ii) From circuit diagram, equivalent resistance of circuit is given as

$$R = (3 \,||\, 1.5) + 4 + r$$

$$= \frac{3 \times 1.5}{3 + 1.5} + 4 + r = \frac{4.5}{4.5} + 4 + r$$

$\Rightarrow$ $R = 5 + r$

$\therefore$ Current drawn through battery,

$$I = \frac{V}{R} \Rightarrow 0.3 = \frac{1.8}{5 + r}$$

$\Rightarrow$ $5 + r = \dfrac{1.8}{0.3}$

$\Rightarrow$ $5 + r = 6$

$\Rightarrow$ $r = 6 - 5 = 1\,\Omega$

47.

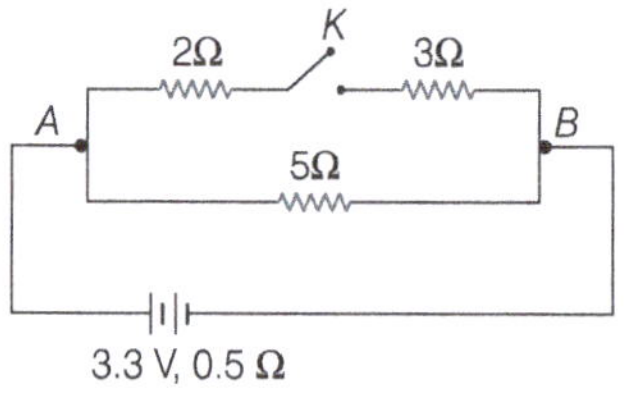

(i) When the key K is open, then 2 Ω and 3 Ω resistances are not in the circuit, i.e. this branch is not accounted in the circuit.

Now, equivalent resistance,

$$R_{eq} = 5 + 0.5 = 5.5\,\Omega$$

(ii) According to the Ohm's law, $V = I\,R_{eq}$

$$I = \frac{V}{R_{eq}}$$

Here, $V = 3.3$ V and $R_{eq} = 5.5\,\Omega$

So, current, $I = \dfrac{3.3}{5.5} = 0.6$ A

(iii)

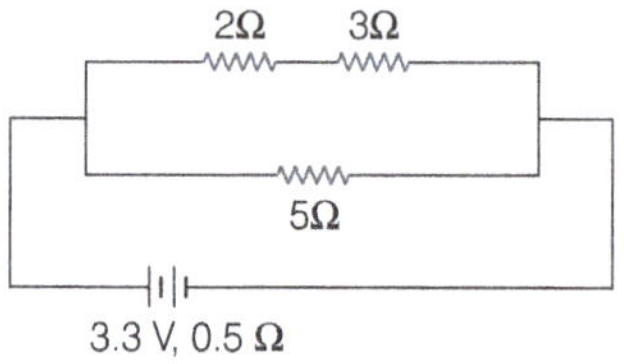

When the key K is closed, then resistance of the circuit is

$$= 2\Omega + 3\Omega$$

$$= 5 \,||\, (0.5 + 5) = 5 \,||\, 5.5$$

$$= \frac{5.5 \times 5}{5.5 + 5} = \frac{27.5}{10.5}$$

$$R_{eq} = 2.62\,\Omega$$

(iv) The current drawn form the cell when the key K is closed,

$$V = IR_{eq}$$

$$3.3 = I\,(2.62)$$

$$I = \frac{3.3}{2.62} = 1.26 \text{ A}$$

48. (i) Here, 6 Ω and 2 Ω resistors are in parallel so,

$$R_{eq} = \frac{R_1 R_2}{R_1 + R_2} = \frac{6 \times 2}{6 + 2} = \frac{12}{8} = 1.5\,\Omega$$

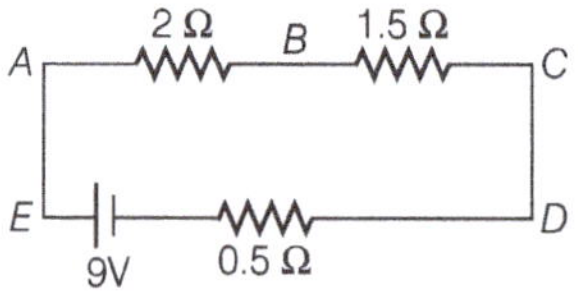

(ii) $R_{eq} = 2 + 1.5 + 0.5 = 4\,\Omega$

$$I = \frac{V}{R} = \frac{9}{4} = 2.5 \text{ A}$$

(iii) $V_{BC} = 1.5 \times \frac{9}{4} = \frac{27}{8} \text{ V}$

$$I_{6\,\Omega} = \frac{27}{8 \times 6} = \frac{9}{16} \text{ A} = 0.5625 \text{A}$$

(iv) $V_{\text{Battery}} = 9 - IR$

$$= 9 - \left(\frac{9}{4}\right)(0.5)$$

$$= 7.875 \text{ V}$$

49.

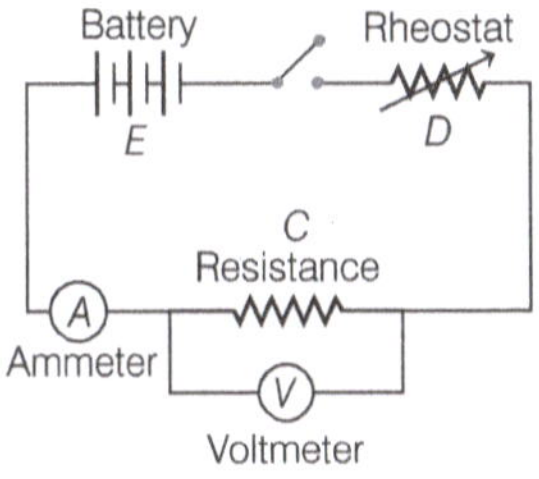

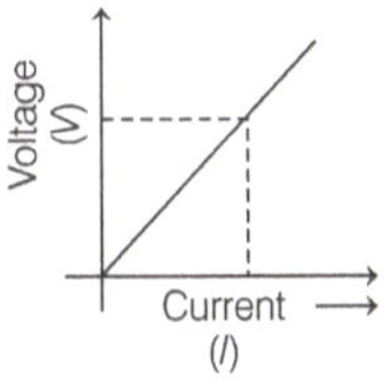

50. (i)

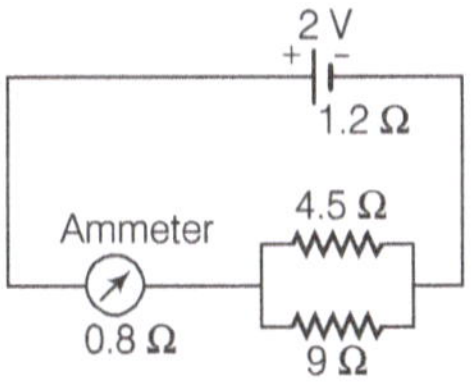

Given, emf of a cell, $E = 2$ V

Internal resistance, $r = 1.2\Omega$

Resistance of ammeter $= 0.8\,\Omega$

Two resistances connected in parallel are 4.5Ω and 9Ω.

$$\therefore \quad R = \frac{4.5 \times 9}{(4.5 + 9)}$$

We know,

$$E = I\,(R + r) = I \times \left\{\left(\frac{4.5 \times 9}{4.5 + 9}\right) + 0.8 + 1.2\right\}$$

$$2 = I\,[3 + 0.8 + 1.2] \;\Rightarrow\; 2 = 5\,I$$

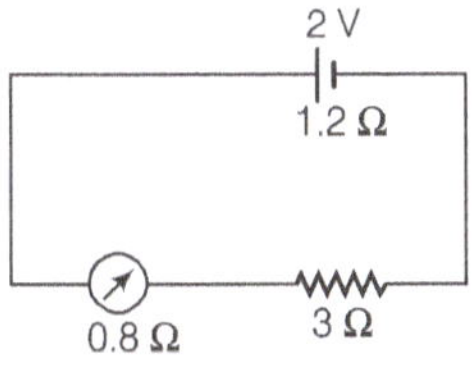

$$\Rightarrow \quad I = \frac{2}{5}$$

$$\therefore \quad I = 0.4 \text{ A}$$

(ii) Potential difference across the terminals of the cell is given by

$$V = I R_{\text{external}} = 0.4 \times [3 + 0.8]$$

$$= 0.4 \times 3.8 = 1.52 \text{ V}$$

51. (i) The circuit diagram is shown below

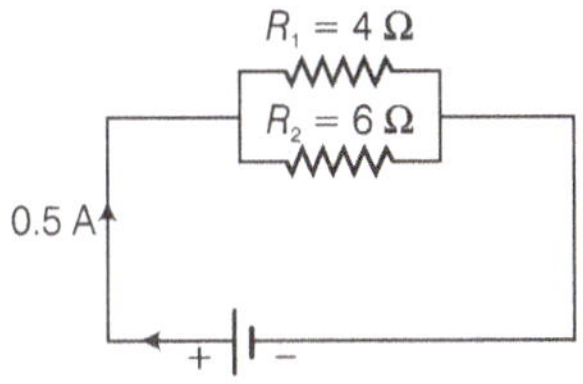

(ii) Let the current flowing through resistance R_1 is I and current flowing through R_2 resistance is $0.5 - I$.

$$\therefore \quad I \times 4 = (0.5 - I) \times 6$$

$$\Rightarrow \quad 4I = 3 - 6I$$

$$\Rightarrow \quad 10I = 3$$

$$\Rightarrow \quad I = 0.3 \text{ A}$$

$\therefore$ Current flowing through $R_1 = 4\Omega$ is 0.3 A and current flowing through $R_2 = 6\Omega$ is

$$0.5 - 0.3 = 0.2 \text{ A}$$

52. (i) Resistances 8 Ω and 12 Ω are in parallel.

$$\therefore \quad \frac{1}{R_1} = \frac{1}{8} + \frac{1}{12}$$

$$= \frac{3 + 2}{24} = \frac{5}{24}$$

$$\Rightarrow \quad R_1 = \frac{24}{5} = 4.8\Omega$$

Now, resistances R_1 and 7.2 Ω are in series.

$$\therefore \quad R_{eq} = 4.8 + 7.2 = 12\Omega$$

(ii) $I = ?$

$$\therefore \quad I = \frac{V}{R_{eq}} = \frac{6}{12} = \frac{1}{2} = 0.5 \text{ A}$$

(iii) Potential difference (PD) across 7.2Ω resistor

$$= 0.5 \times 7.2 = 3.6 \text{ V}$$

53. (i) Resistances 12Ω and 6Ω are in parallel. So,

$$\frac{1}{R_1} = \frac{1}{12} + \frac{1}{6} = \frac{3}{12} = \frac{1}{4}$$

$$R_1 = 4\Omega$$

Equivalent resistance of the circuit,

$$R_{eq} = 4 + 8 = 12\Omega$$

$$\therefore \quad I = \frac{V}{R_{eq}} = \frac{12}{12} = 1 \text{ A}$$

The current through 8Ω resistor is 1A.

(ii) Potential difference (PD) across the parallel combination of resistances 6Ω and 12Ω is

$$V = I \times R_1 = 1 \times 4 = 4\text{ V}$$

(iii) Current through the 6Ω resistor is

$$= \frac{4}{6} = 0.67\text{ A}$$

54. (i) The net resistance of R_1 and R_2,

$$\frac{1}{R_{12}} = \frac{1}{10} + \frac{1}{40} = \frac{4+1}{40} = \frac{5}{40} = \frac{1}{8}$$

$$\Rightarrow \quad R_{12} = 8\Omega$$

The net resistance of R_3, R_4 and R_5,

$$\frac{1}{R_{345}} = \frac{1}{30} + \frac{1}{20} + \frac{1}{60}$$

$$= \frac{2+3+1}{60}$$

$$\frac{1}{R_{345}} = \frac{6}{60} = \frac{1}{10}$$

$$\Rightarrow \quad R_{345} = 10\Omega$$

Total resistance of the circuit

$$R = R_{12} + R_{345} = 8 + 10 = 18\Omega$$

(ii) Total current, $I = \frac{V}{R} = \frac{12}{18} = \frac{2}{3} = 0.67\text{ A}$

55. Given, $E = 1.5\text{ V}$, $r = 1\Omega$,

$$R_1 = 4\Omega, R_2 = 20\Omega$$

The net external resistance of the circuit,

$$R = R_1 + R_2 = 4 + 20 = 24\Omega$$

(i) Current in the circuit,

$$I = \frac{E}{R+r} = \frac{1.5}{24+1} = \frac{1.5}{25} = 0.06\text{ A}$$

(ii) Potential difference across the 4Ω resistor

$$V = IR_1 = 0.06 \times 4 = 0.24\text{ V}$$

(iii) Voltage drop across internal resistance

$$V_r = Ir = 0.06 \times 1 = 0.06\text{ V}$$

(iv) Terminal voltage V

= Potential difference across the cell

$$= E - Ir = 1.5 - 0.06 = 1.44\text{ V}$$

56. (i) $R_{\text{total}} = \frac{V}{I} = \frac{6.0}{0.3} = 20\Omega$

(ii) Resistances are in parallel, then

$$\frac{1}{20} = \frac{1}{R} + \frac{1}{60}$$

$$\Rightarrow \quad \frac{1}{R} = \frac{1}{20} - \frac{1}{60} = \frac{3-1}{60} = \frac{1}{30}$$

$$\Rightarrow \quad R = 30\Omega$$

(iii) $V = IR$

Since, potential at two ends are equal.

So, $I_1R_1 = I_2R_2$

$$I_1 \times 30 = (0.3 - I_1) \times 60$$

$$I_1 = 0.6 - 2I_1 = \frac{0.6}{3} = 0.2\text{ A}$$

57. (i) As 6Ω and 3Ω resistances are in parallel, so the potential difference across these resistances will be same.

So, $\quad I_B \times 6 = I_C \times 3$

$$\Rightarrow \quad 0.5 \times 6 = I_C \times 3$$

$$\Rightarrow \quad I_C = 1.0\text{ A}$$

Reading of ammeter at C, $I_C = 1.0\text{ A}$

Reading of ammeter at A, I_A

$$= I_B + I_C = 0.5 + 1.0 = 1.5\text{ A}$$

(ii) Total resistance of the circuit

$$R = 2 + \frac{6 \times 3}{6+3} = 2 + \frac{18}{9} = 4\Omega$$

58. (i) Nichrome wire is used for electric heater, because it has high melting point and high resistivity.

(ii) A wire rated 20 A is thicker, because it carries large current and its cross-sectional area will be large.

59. Given, number of cells, $n = 4$, emf of each cell $E = 1.5\text{ V}$, $r = 2.0\,\Omega$, $R = 2.5\Omega$

(i) Total internal resistance of cells

$$\frac{1}{r'} = \frac{1}{2} + \frac{1}{2} + \frac{1}{2} + \frac{1}{2} = \frac{4}{2}$$

$$r' = 0.5\,\Omega$$

Total resistance of the circuit $= r' + R$

$$= 0.5 + 2.5 = 3.0\,\Omega$$

(ii) $I = \frac{E}{r'+R} = \frac{1.5}{3} = 0.5\text{ A}$

(iii) Potential drop $= E - \frac{I}{4}r = 1.5 - \frac{0.5}{4} \times 2$

$$= 1.5 - 0.25 = 1.25\text{ A}$$

TOPIC 2

Electrical Power and Energy

Electrical Energy

Electrical energy is converted into heat energy, light energy, mechanical energy, chemical energy, sound energy and magnetic energy.

e.g.

(i) When an electric current is passed through a metallic wire, it gets heated up due to its resistance and the electrical energy is converted into heat energy.

(ii) When an electric current is passed through an electric motor, its coil begin to rotate and simultaneously the coil gets heated slightly. The electrical energy is converted into mechanical energy and sometimes into heat energy.

(iii) When an electric current is passed through an electric lamp, the filament of the bulb gets heated and it glows. Thus, electrical energy is converted into heat and light energy.

(iv) When the output of a microphone which is in the form of electric pulses is passed to a loud speaker, the electrical energy is converted into sound energy.

Measurement of Electrical Energy

$$W = QV = VIt = I^2Rt = \frac{V^2t}{R}$$

[$\because Q = It$ and $V = IR$ by Ohm's law]

The SI unit of electrical energy is joule (J).

Electrical Power

The rate at which work is done in maintaining the current (I) in an electric circuit is called electrical power. It is expressed as

$$P = \frac{W}{t} = VI = \frac{V^2}{R} = I^2R \qquad \left[\because W = VIt \text{ and } I = \frac{V}{R}\right]$$

Its unit is watt (W) or volt-ampere (V-A) or J/s.

Its other unit is horse power (HP).

1 horse power (1 HP) = 746 W

Commercial Unit of Electrical Energy (kWh)

One kilowatt-hour (1 kWh) is the electrical energy consumed by an electrical appliance of power 1 kW when it is used for 1 hour.

$$1 \text{ kilowatt-hour (1 kWh)} = 1 \text{ kilowatt} \times 1 \text{ hour}$$
$$= 1000 \text{ watt} \times 1 \text{ hour}$$
$$= 1000 \text{ Js}^{-1} \times (60 \times 60 \text{s})$$

[$\because 1 \text{ h} = 60 \times 60 \text{s}$]

$$= 3.6 \times 10^6 \text{ J}$$

The electrical energy for electricity consumed in our houses (or industries) is measured in this unit and electricity bill is paid to the electric company accordingly.

Power Rating of Common Appliances

The electrical appliances such as electric bulb, geyser bulb, heater, etc., are rated with power and voltage. We calculate the two quantities such as

(i) Resistance of the filament of the bulb (coil)

$$R = \frac{V^2}{P} = \frac{(\text{Voltage rating of appliance})^2}{\text{Power rating of appliance}}$$

(ii) Safe limit of current through the filament of the bulb (coil)

$$I = \frac{P}{V} = \frac{\text{Power rating of appliance}}{\text{Voltage rating of appliance}}$$

Household Consumption of Electrical Energy

The electrical energy consumed by a household appliance in a certain time (t) is calculated in kWh using the following relation.

Energy (in kWh)

$$= \text{Power (in kW)} \times \text{Time (in hour)}$$

$$= \frac{\text{Power (in watt)} \times \text{Time (in hour)}}{1000}$$

$$= \frac{V \text{(volt)} \times I \text{ (ampere)} \times t \text{ (hour)}}{1000}$$

Cost of electricity = Energy consumed (in kWh) $\times$ Rate in rupees per unit.

Heating Effect

The heat produced in a wire on passing current through it is called heating effect of current. It is expressed by

$H = I^2Rt$ (in joule) $= 0.24I^2Rt$ (in cal)

This is known as **Joule's law of heating**.

PYQs Previous Years Questions

1 Mark Questions

1. When a current I flows through a wire of resistance R for time t, then the electrical energy produced is given by **(ICSE 2023)**
   (a) I^2Rt (b) IR^2t
   (c) IRt (d) IRt^2

2. One horse power is equal to **(ICSE SQP 2022 Sem-II)**
   (a) 100 W (b) 735 W
   (c) 764 W (d) 746 W

3. Name the physical quantity measured in terms of horse power. **(ICSE 2015)**

4. 1 kWh = _____ J. **(ICSE 2015)**

5. What is consumed using different electrical appliances, for which electricity bills are paid? **(ICSE 2014)**

2 Marks Questions

6. 'A geyser is rated 240 W-220 V'. Explain the meaning of this statement. **(ICSE 2023)**

7. Define a kilowatt hour. How is it related to joule? **(ICSE 2020)**

8. An electric bulb of resistance 500 Ω, draws a current of 0.4A. Calculate the power of the bulb and the potential difference at its end. **(ICSE 2017)**

9. Calculate the quantity of heat produced in a 20 Ω resistor carrying 2.5 A current in 5 min. **(ICSE 2016)**

10. An electrical appliance is rated at 1000 kW, 220 V. If the appliance is operated for 2 h, calculate the energy consumed by the appliance in
    (i) kWh (ii) joule **(ICSE 2012)**

11. Two bulbs are marked 100 W, 220 V and 60 W, 110 V. Calculate the ratio of their resistances. **(ICSE 2011)**

12. (i) Write an expression for calculating electrical power in terms of current and resistance.
    (ii) State a relation between electrical power, resistance and potential difference in an electrical circuit. **(ICSE 2011, 10)**

13. An electric heater is rated 1000 W - 200 V. Calculate
    (i) the resistance of the heating element.
    (ii) the current flowing through it. **(ICSE 2009)**

14. An electrical heater is rated 4 kW, 220 V. Find the cost of using this heater for 12 h, if one kWh of electrical energy costs ₹ 3.25. **(ICSE 2008)**

> **KEY idea**
> To determine the cost of energy consumed. First calculate the energy consumption and then the cost of energy consumed.

15. How does the heat produced in a wire or a conductor depend upon the
    (i) current passing through the conductor?
    (ii) resistance of the conductor? **(ICSE 2008)**

16. An electric kettle is rated 2.5 kW, 250 V. Find the cost of running the kettle for two hours at 60 paise per unit. **(ICSE 2003)**

17. A geyser has a label 2 kW, 240 V. What is the cost of using it for 30 min, if the cost of electricity is ₹ 3 per commercial unit? **(ICSE 2002)**

> **KEY idea**
> The cost of electrical energy consumed by appliance is equal to the product of cost of one unit to the total unit.

18. A family uses a light bulb of 100 W, a fan of 100 W and a heater of 1000 W, each for 8 h a day. If the cost of electricity is ₹ 2 per unit, what is the expenditure for the family per day on electricity? **(ICSE 2001)**

19. Calculate the electrical energy in SI units consumed by a 100 W bulb and a 60 W fan connected in parallel for 5 min. **(ICSE 2000)**

3 Marks Questions

20. An appliance rated 440 W, 220 V is connected across 220 V supply. **(ICSE 2022 Sem-II)**
    (i) Calculate the maximum current that the appliance can draw.
    (ii) Calculate the resistance of the appliance.

21. (i) what are superconductors?
    (ii) Calculate the current drawn by an appliance rated 110 W, 220 V when connected across 220 V supply.
    (iii) Name a substance whose resistance decreases with the increase in temperature. **(ICSE 2020)**

22. (i) A fuse is rated 8 A. Can it be used with an electrical appliance rated 5 kW, 200 V? Give a reason.
(ii) An electric iron is rated 220 V, 2 kW. If the iron is used for 2 h daily, find the cost of running it for one week, if its cost ₹ 4.25 per kWh. **(ICSE 2018)**

23. In Mrs. Pinto's flat there are 6 bulbs of 100 W each, a heater of 2 kW and 5 fans of 50 W each. If these are used everyday as shown below, calculate the cost of energy consumption for a month of 30 days at the rate of Rs. 3.50 per kWh.

6 bulbs of 100 W each used 8 h per day

1 heater of 2 kW used half hour daily

5 fans of 50 W each are used 6 h everyday. **(ICSE SQP 2017)**

24. (i) Write an expression for the electrical energy spent in the flow of current through an electrical appliance in terms of *I*, *R* and *t*.
(ii) At what voltage is the alternating current supplied to our houses?
(iii) How should the electric lamps in a building be connected? **(ICSE 2012)**

25. (i) An electric bulb is marked 100 W, 250 V. What information does this convey?
(ii) How much current will the bulb draw, if connected to a 250 V supply? **(ICSE 2011)**

26. Calculate the quantity of heat that will be produced in a coil of resistance 75 Ω, if a current of 2 A is passed through it for 2 min. **(ICSE 2010)**

27. Find the cost of operating an electric toaster for two hours, if it draws 8 A current on a 110 V circuit. The cost of electrical energy is ₹ 2.50 per kWh. **(ICSE 2006)**

28. An electrical appliance is rated 1500 W, 250 V. This appliance is connected to 250 V mains. Calculate
(i) the current drawn.
(ii) the electrical energy consumed in 60 h.
(iii) the cost of electrical energy consumed at ₹ 2.50 per kWh. **(ICSE 2005)**

29. Make a table with the names of three electrical appliances used in your home in one column, their power, voltage rating and approximate time for which each one is used in one day in the other columns. **(ICSE 2002)**

4/5/6 Marks Questions

30. An electric bulb is rated '240 V, 100 W'.
(i) What information can you get from the above statement?
(ii) What will happen, if this bulb is connected across 220 V?
(iii) Calculate the resistance of the bulb.
(iv) Also, find the energy consumed by the bulb in 10 minutes. **(ICSE 2022 Sem-II)**

31. A battery of emf 12V and internal resistance 2 Ω is connected with two resistors *A* and *B* of resistance 4 Ω and 6 Ω respectively, joined in series.

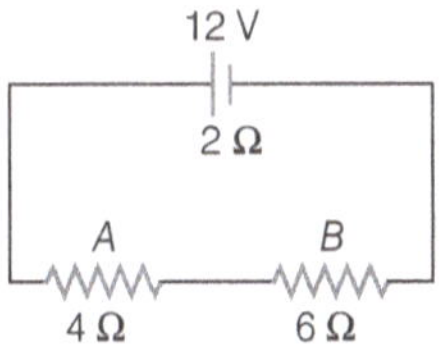

Find
(i) current in the circuit.
(ii) the terminal voltage of the cell.
(iii) the potential difference across 6 Ω resistor.
(iv) electrical energy spent per minute for 4 Ω resistor. **(ICSE 2016)**

32. The figure shows a circuit, when the circuit is switched ON, the ammeter reads 0.5 A.

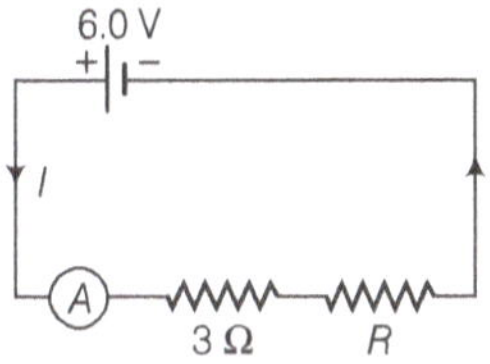

(i) Calculate the value of the unknown resistor *R*.
(ii) Calculate the charge passing through the 3 Ω resistor in 120 s.
(iii) Calculate the power dissipated in the 3 Ω resistor. **(ICSE 2013)**

KEY idea

Power dissipated in any circuit or non-circuit diagram is determine by using $P = V \times I$.

33. With reference to the diagram given below, calculate

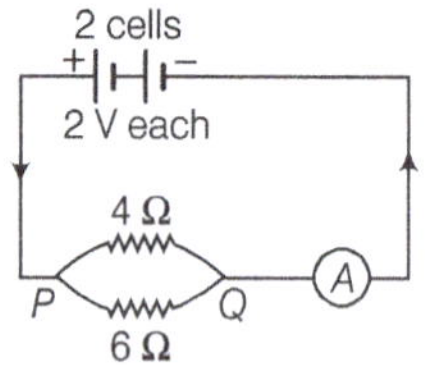

(i) the equivalent resistance between P and Q.

(ii) the reading of an ammeter.

(iii) the electrical power between P and Q. **(ICSE 2003)**

34. Electrical power P is given by an expression

$$P = \frac{(Q \times V)}{\text{time}}$$

(i) What do the symbols Q and V represent?

(ii) Express 'power' in terms of current and resistance explaining the symbols used there in. **(ICSE 2003)**

35. An electric bulb rated 220 V, 60 W is working at full efficiency.

(i) State the resistance of the coil of the bulb.

(ii) Another identical bulb is connected in series with the first one and the system is connected across the mains as shown alongside.

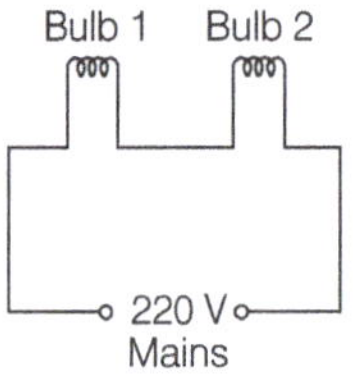

(a) State the rate of conversion of energy in each bulb.

(b) Calculate the total power.

(c) What will be the total power, if the bulbs are connected in parallel? **(ICSE 2004)**

36. A bulb is marked 100 W, 220 V and an electric heater is marked 2000 W, 220 V.

(i) What is the ratio between the resistances of these two devices?

(ii) How does the power-voltage rating of a device help us to decide about the type of loads (connecting wires) to be used for it?

(iii) In which of the two devices, a thicker connecting wire or load is required? **(ICSE 2001)**

Explanations

1. (a)

2. (d)

3. Electrical energy is measured in terms of horse power.

4. $1\text{kWh} = 3.6 \times 10^6 \text{J}$

5. Electrical energy is consumed using different electrical appliances, for which electricity bills are paid.

6. A geyser is rated 240 W-220 V means that the geyser operates at 240 W when connected to a 220 V source.

7. Refer to text on Page no. 143 (Commercial unit of electrical energy)

8. Given, resistance of bulb, $R = 500\,\Omega$

Current, $I = 0.4$ A

Power, $P = ?$

Potential difference, $V = ?$

As we know power, $P = I^2R = (0.4)^2 \times 500$

Power, $P = 80$ W

$\therefore$ Potential difference, $V = IR$

$$= 0.4 \times 500 = 200 \text{ V}$$

9. Given, resistance, $R = 20\Omega$

Current, $I = 2.5$ A

Time, $t = 5 \text{ min} = 5 \times 60 = 300$

According to Joule's law of heating,

$$H = I^2Rt = (2.5)^2 \times 20 \times 300$$

$$= \frac{625}{100} \times 20 \times 300$$

$$= 625 \times 20 \times 3$$

$$H = 37500 \text{ J}$$

10. Given, $P = 1000$ kW, $t = 2$ h

(i) Energy consumed in kWh is

$$E = P \times t = 1000 \times 2$$

$$= 2000 \text{ kWh}$$

(ii) Energy consumed in joule is

$$E = 2000 \times 3.6 \times 10^6 \text{ J} = 7.2 \times 10^9 \text{ J}$$

11. Given, $P_1 = 100$ W, $P_2 = 60$ W, $V_1 = 220$ V,

$$V_2 = 110 \text{ V}, \quad \frac{R_1}{R_2} = ?$$

We know that, power is given by

$$P = \frac{V^2}{R}$$

$$\therefore \quad R_1 = \frac{V_1^2}{P_1} \text{ and } R_2 = \frac{V_2^2}{P_2}$$

$$\Rightarrow \quad R_1 = \frac{(220)^2}{100} \text{ and } R_2 = \frac{(110)^2}{60}$$

$$\therefore \quad \frac{R_1}{R_2} = \frac{\frac{(220)^2}{100}}{\frac{(110)^2}{60}} = \frac{(220)^2 \times 60}{(110)^2 \times 100} = \frac{12}{5}$$

12. (i) The expression for calculating electrical power (P) in terms of current (I) and resistance (R) is given by $P = I^2R$.

(ii) The relation between electrical power, resistance and potential difference in an electrical circuit is given by

$$P = \frac{V^2}{R}$$

13. Given, $P = 1000$ W, $V = 200$ V

(i) $R = \frac{V^2}{P} = \frac{200 \times 200}{1000} = 40\,\Omega$

(ii) $I = \frac{P}{V} = \frac{1000}{200} = 5$ A

14. Given, $P = 4$ kW, $V = 220$ V, $t = 12$ h

$\therefore \quad E = P \times t = 4 \times 12 = 48$ kWh

$\therefore$ Cost of energy consumed $= 48 \times 3.25 =$ ₹156

15. (i) Heat produced in a wire is directly proportional to the square of the current (I^2) flowing through the conductor.

(ii) Heat produced in a wire is directly proportional to the resistance (R) of the conductor.

16. Given, power $P = 2.5$ kW,

Voltage, $V = 250$ V

Rate per unit = 60 paise = ₹ 0.6

Time, $t = 2$ h

$\therefore$ Energy, $E = P \times t = 2.5 \times 2 = 5$ kWh

$\therefore$ Cost of energy consumed $= 5 \times 0.6 =$ ₹ 3.00

17. Given, $P = 2$ kW, $V = 240$ V,

$t = 30 \text{ min} = \frac{30}{60} = 0.5$ h

Rate = ₹ 3/unit, Cost = ?

$\therefore$ Energy, $E = P \times t = 2 \times 0.5 = 1$ kWh

$\therefore$ Cost of energy consumed $= 1 \times 3 =$ ₹ 3

18. Given, $P_b = 100$ W, $P_f = 100$ W, $P_h = 1000$ W

$t = 8$ h (each), Rate = ₹ 2/unit

$$\therefore \quad P = P_b + P_f + P_h = 100 + 100 + 1000 = 1200 \text{ W} = 1.2 \text{ kW}$$

$$\therefore \quad E = P \times t = 1.2 \times 8 = 9.6 \text{ kWh}$$

$\therefore$ Cost of energy consumed per day $= 9.6 \times 2 =$ ₹ 19.20

19. Given, $P_b = 100$ W, $P_f = 60$ W

$t = 5 \text{ min} = \frac{5}{60} = \frac{1}{12}$ h, $E = ?$

$$\therefore \quad P = P_b + P_f = 100 + 60 = 160 \text{ W}$$

$$\therefore \quad E = P \times t = 160 \times \frac{1}{12} \times \frac{1}{1000} = 0.013 \text{ kWh}$$

$$= 0.013 \times 3.6 \times 10^6 \text{ J} = 46800 \text{ J}$$

20. (i) Given, power = 440 W

Voltage applied, $V = 220$ V

$$\text{Current} = \frac{\text{Power}}{\text{Voltage}}$$

$$I = \frac{440}{220} \text{ A} \Rightarrow I = 2 \text{ A}$$

(ii) Resistance of the appliance, power $= \frac{V^2}{R}$

$$R = \frac{V^2}{P} = \frac{220 \times 220}{440}$$

$$R = 110\,\Omega$$

21. (i) The conductor with infinite conductivity or zero resistivity are called superconductors.

(ii) Given, power of appliance, $P = 110$ W

Supply voltage, $V = 220$ V

We know that,

$$P = VI \Rightarrow I = \frac{P}{V} = \frac{110}{220} = 0.5 \text{ A}$$

(iii) Semiconductor

22. (i) Given, power, $P = 5 \text{ kW} = 5 \times 10^3$ W

Voltage, $V = 200$ V

We know that, $I = \frac{P}{V} = \frac{5 \times 10^3}{200}$

$\Rightarrow \quad I = 25$ A

$\therefore \quad I = 25 \text{ A} > 8$ A

Thus, it cannot be used as the appliance will get fused.

(ii) Given, power, $P = 2\text{ kW} = 2\times10^3$ W

Voltage, $V = 220$ V

Time, $t = 2$h daily for 1 week

$= 2\times7 = 14$

$\therefore$ Electrical energy (in kWh)

$= P\times t = 2\times 14 = 28$ kWh

$\therefore$ Running cost $= 28\times4.25 =$ ₹119.

23. Electrical energy consumed by bulbs in one month

$= (6\times100\text{W})\times(8\text{h}\times30)/1000\text{ kWh}$

$= 144$ kWh

Electrical energy consumed by heater in one month

$= 2\text{kW}\times(0.5\times30) = 30$ kWh

Electrical energy consumed by fans in one month.

$= (5\times50)\times(6\times30)/1000 = 48$ kWh

Total energy consumed $= (144+30+48)$ kWh

$= 222$ kWh

Cost of electricity = ₹ (222×3.50) = ₹ 777.

24. (i) The expression for the electrical energy, $E = I^2Rt$.

(ii) Alternating current supplied to our houses is at voltage 220 V.

(iii) The electric lamps in a building should be connected in parallel.

25. (i) It conveys that when the bulb is lighted on 250 V supply, it consumes 100 W electrical power, i.e. 100 J of electrical energy is consumed in 1 s.

(ii) Current drawn, $I = \frac{P}{V} = \frac{100}{250} = 0.4$ A

26. Given, $R = 75\Omega$, $t = 2\text{ min} = 2\times60 = 120$ s, $I = 2$ A

Heat produced, $H = ?$

$\therefore\ H = I^2Rt = (2)^2\times75\times120 = 36000$ J

27. Given, $t = 2$ h, $I = 8$ A, $V = 110$ V

Cost = ` 2.50/kWh

$\therefore$ Energy, $E = VIt = \frac{110\times8\times2}{1000} = 1.76$ kWh

Cost of 1.76 kWh $= 2.5\times1.76 =$ ₹ 4.40

28. Given, $P = 1500$ W, $V = 250$ V

(i) $I = \frac{P}{V} = \frac{1500}{250} = 6$ A

(ii) $E = P\times t = \frac{1500\times60}{1000} = 90$ kWh

(iii) Cost of energy $= 90\times2.50 =$ ₹ 225

29.

Electrical Appliances	Power	Voltage Rating	Time
CFL	15 W	220 V	8 h
Television	120 W	220 V	6 h
Refrigerator	150 W	220 V	16 h

30. (i) The above statement gives the information that when the electric bulb is put at 240 V of a potential difference it consumes 100 W of power.

(ii) The bulb will consume less power.

(iii) $R = \frac{V^2}{P} = \frac{240\times240}{100}$

$R = 576\,\Omega$

(iv) Electrical energy (kWh) = kW × h

$= \frac{100}{100}\times\frac{10}{60} = \frac{1}{60}$ kWh

31. According to the question,

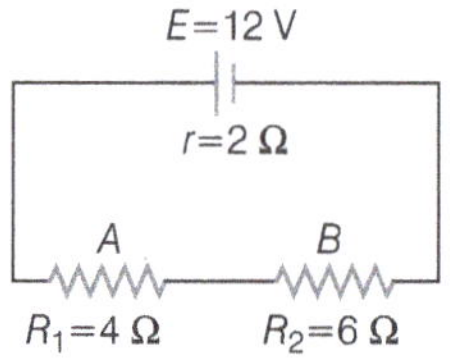

(i) Current in the circuit is given by

$V = IR_{eq}$

$I = \frac{V}{R_{eq}} = \frac{12}{4+6+2} = 1$ A

[$\because R_{eq} = R_1 + R_2 + R_3$, for series combination]

(ii) Terminal voltage of the cell is given by

TPD $= E - Ir = 12 - 1\times2 = 10$ V

(iii) Potential difference across 6 Ω resistance is given by

$V = IR_2 = 1\times6 = 6$ V

(iv) Electrical energy spent per minute is given by

$E = I^2Rt = 1^2\times4\times60$ [$\because$ 1 = 60]

$= 240$ J

32. (i) $\because\quad I = \frac{V}{R}$

$\Rightarrow\quad 0.5 = \frac{6.0}{3+R}$

$\Rightarrow\quad 3+R = \frac{6}{0.5}$

$$\Rightarrow \quad R = \frac{60}{5} - 3 = 9\,\Omega$$

(ii) $Q = I \times t = 0.5 \times 120 = 60\text{ C}$

(iii) $P = VI = I^2R = (0.5)^2 \times 3$

$$= 0.25 \times 3 = 0.75\text{ W}$$

33. (i) $\frac{1}{R_{eq}} = \frac{1}{4} + \frac{1}{6} = \frac{3+2}{12} = \frac{5}{12}$

$$\Rightarrow \quad R_{eq} = \frac{12}{5} = 2.4\,\Omega$$

(ii) emf, $E = 2 \times 2 = 4\text{ V}$, $E = IR_{eq}$

$$\Rightarrow \quad I = \frac{E}{R_{eq}} = \frac{4}{2.4} = 1.67\text{ A}$$

(iii) Power, $P = I^2R_{eq}$

$$= (1.67)^2 \times 2.4 = 6.67\text{ W}$$

34. (i) In the given expression, $P = \frac{Q \times V}{\text{time}}$

Q represents electric charge flowing through the conductor and V represents potential difference.

(ii) The expression of power in terms of current and resistance is given by

$$P = I^2R$$

where, I is the current in ampere and R is the resistance in ohm.

35. (i) Given, $V = 220\text{ V}$, $P = 60\text{ W}$

We know that, $P = \frac{V^2}{R}$

$$\Rightarrow R = \frac{V^2}{P} = \frac{220 \times 220}{60} = 806.7\,\Omega$$

(ii) When another identical bulb is connected in series. Then,

(a) Energy conversion in each bulb

Total resistance $= 806.7 + 806.7$

$$R_{total} = 1613.4\,\Omega$$

$$\because \quad V = IR$$

$$\Rightarrow \quad I = \frac{V}{R_{total}} = \frac{220}{1613.4} = 0.136\text{ A}$$

$$P = I^2R = (0.136)^2 \times 806.7$$

$$= 14.92\text{ W}$$

$$\approx 15\text{ W}$$

(b) Total power $= 15 + 15 = 30\text{ W}$

(c) In parallel, each bulb will consume the power 60 W.

$\therefore$ Total power $= 60 + 60 = 120\text{ W}$

36. Given, $P_1 = 100\text{ W}$, $V_1 = 220\text{ V}$

$P_2 = 2000\text{ W}$, $V_2 = 220\text{ V}$

(i) $P = \frac{V^2}{R} \Rightarrow R = \frac{V^2}{P}$

$$R_1 = \frac{(220)^2}{100}$$

and $R_2 = \frac{(220)^2}{2000}$

$$\therefore \quad \frac{R_1}{R_2} = \frac{\frac{(220)^2}{100}}{\frac{(220)^2}{2000}} = \frac{2000}{100} = \frac{20}{1}$$

(ii) $I_1 = \frac{P_1}{V_1} = \frac{100}{220} = 0.45\text{ A}$

and $I_2 = \frac{P_2}{V_2} = \frac{2000}{220} = 9.1\text{ A}$

A wire having current 9.1 A is required for a heater.

(iii) The current flowing through the bulb is only 0.45 A, while through heater is 9.1 A. Hence, a heavy load is needed for the heater while for a bulb an ordinary thin connecting wire is required.

TOPIC 3

Domestic Circuits

House Wiring System

In a house, the wiring is commonly done by the ring system. The ring system of wiring is shown below.

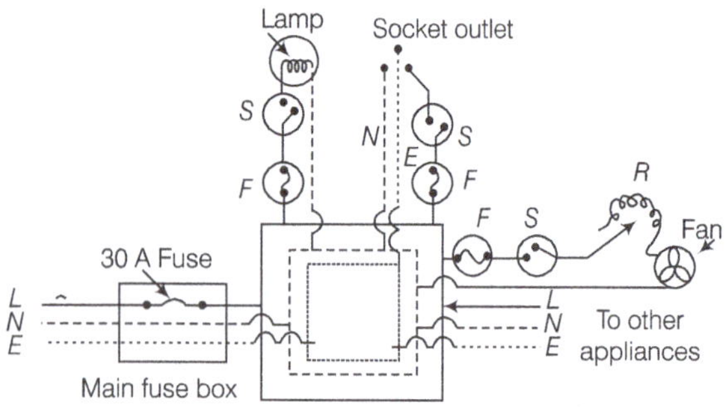

In this system, the wires starting from the main fuse box run around all the rooms of the house and then come back to the fuse box again forming the ring. The fuse box contains a fuse of rating about 30 A.

Power Distribution

The distribution of power from the generating station is shown below

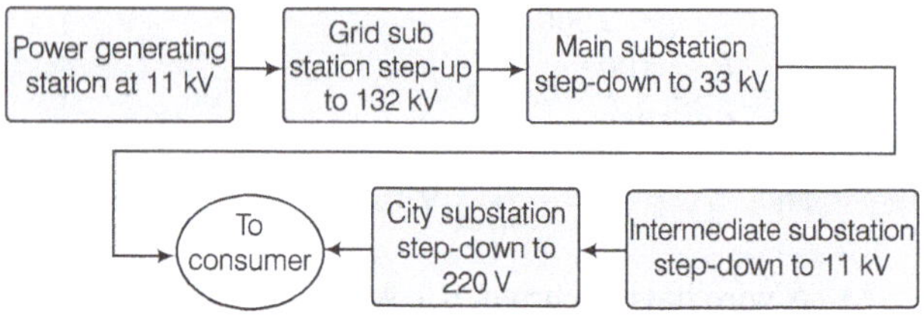

Main Circuit

The main circuit has three wires such as live (or phase) wire (*L*), neutral wire (*N*) and the earth wire (*E*). The neutral and the earth wires are connected together at the local substation, so that the neutral and the earth wires are at the same potential.

The live wire carries current from the source to the distribution board, while the neutral wire is for the return path of current. The connections are made to the distribution board through a **main fuse** and a **main switch.**

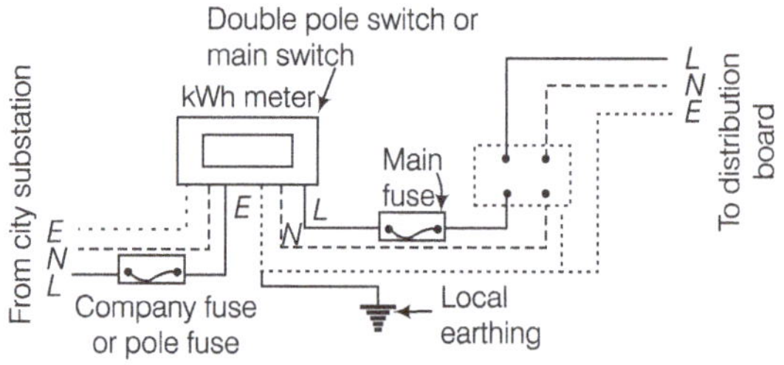

Two-Way Switch

It means two or more switches in different locations to control one lamp. They all wired, so that operation of either switch will control the lights. This given figure illustrate that lights to be controlled from both locations.

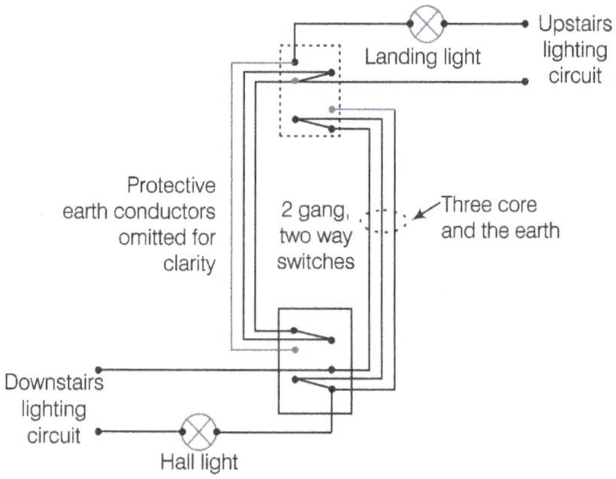

Staircase Wiring

It is a dual control switch system in which the double pole type switches are used at the top and bottom of a staircase.

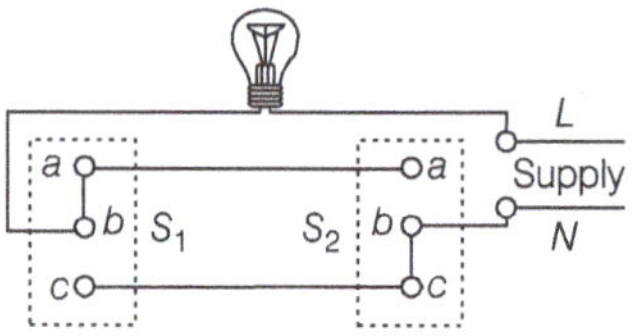

(a) Bulb OFF

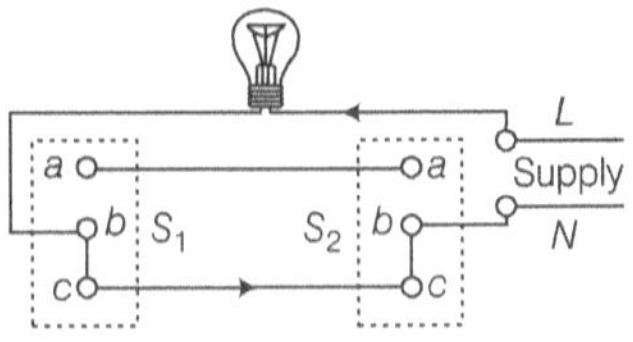

(b) Bulb ON through switch S_1

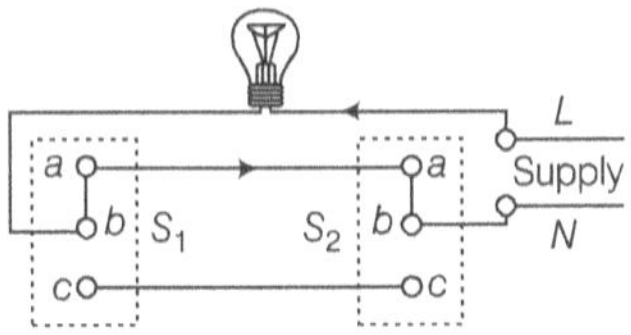

(c) Bulb ON through switch S_2

Need for Earthing

To avoid the risk from electrical shock, the metal body of appliances is earthed. Earthing means to connect the metal case of the appliance to the earth (i.e. zero potential) by means of a metal wire called the **earth wire** (in green insulation cover).

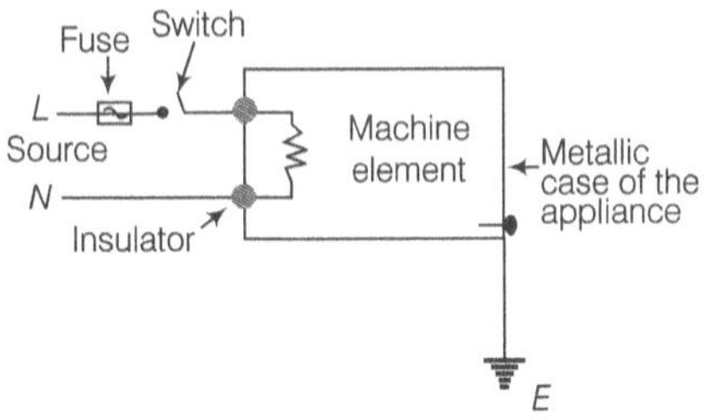

The symbol ⏚ is used for earthing appliances.

Fuse

It is a safety device having short length of thin wire made up of tin (25%) and lead (75%) alloy having low melting point around 200°C. The fuse wire is of chosen thickness, so as to fix its resistance and hence amount of heating on passage of a particular amount of current.

Whenever current through the fuse exceeds the set limit, the fuse wire melts and breaks the circuit. This saves the main circuit components from damage.

MCB : Miniature Circuit Breaker

In these days, instead of a fuse, a MCB is used for each individual circuit. If due to short circuiting (or some fault), a heavy current flow in the circuit, the MCB falls down to switch OFF the circuit in a very short time (≈ 25 ms). After repairing the fault in the circuit, the MCB is raised up.

Thus, the use of MCB is more convenient and safe in comparison to a fuse.

(i) It avoids the inconvenience of connecting a new fuse and wire.

(ii) It is much safer due to its quick response.

Three-Pin Plug and Socket with Conventional Location of Wires

In a three-pin plug, the top pin is for earthing, the left pin is for live and the right pin is for neutral.

Socket

A socket is a fixture in an electric circuit in which the plug is inserted. It has three holes whose inner walls are made up of hollow metallic tubes, i.e. brass and are converted to the live, neutral and the earth wires of the line.

The upper bigger hole in the socket is for the earth connection, while the hole on the right side is for connection to live wire and the hole on left side is for connection to the neutral wire of electric supply.

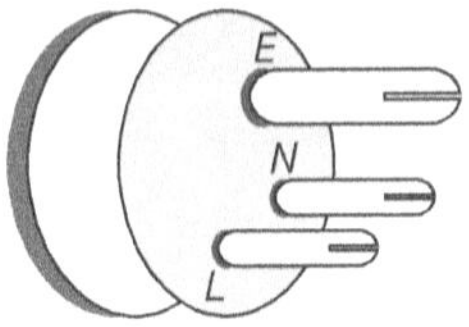

Three-pin plug

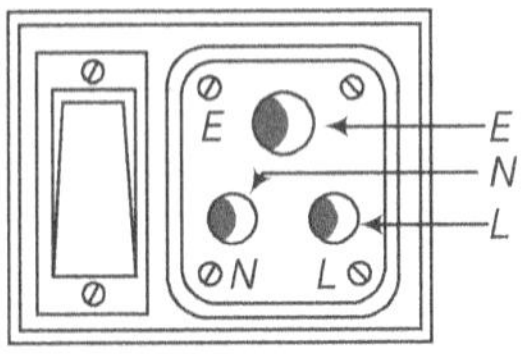

Socket

Safety Precautions

The safety precautions are as

- A switch should not be touched with wet hands.
- The switch should always be connected in the live wire.
- Electrical appliances should be properly earthed.
- Always use appropriate fuse rating in the live wire of the circuit.

Conventional Colour Coding of Wires

The colour coding of wires in a cable are as

Wires	Colour	
	Old Convention	New Convention
Live	Red	Brown
Neutral	Black	Light blue
Earth	Green	Green or Yellow

PYQs Previous Years Questions

1 Mark Questions

1. Identify the option that displays the correct wiring with correct colour code **(ICSE 2024)**

(a)

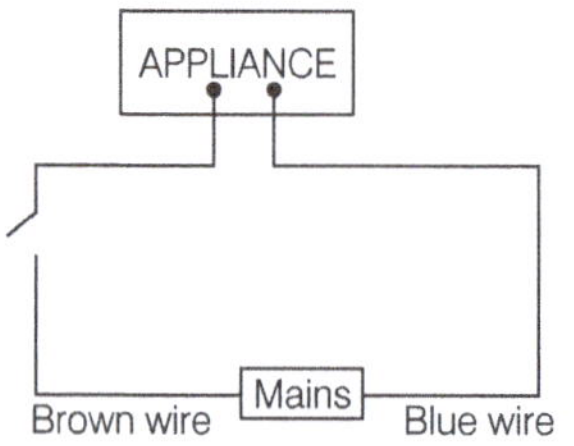

(b)

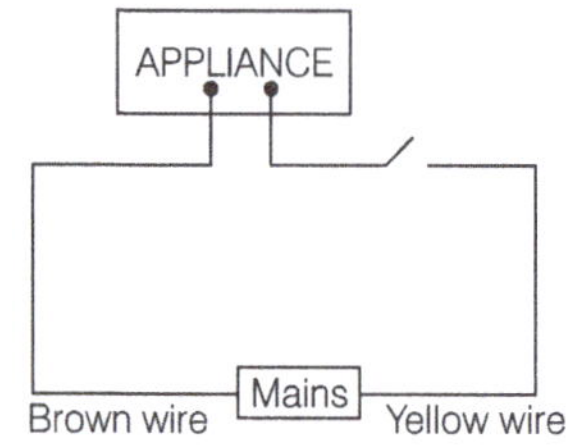

(c)

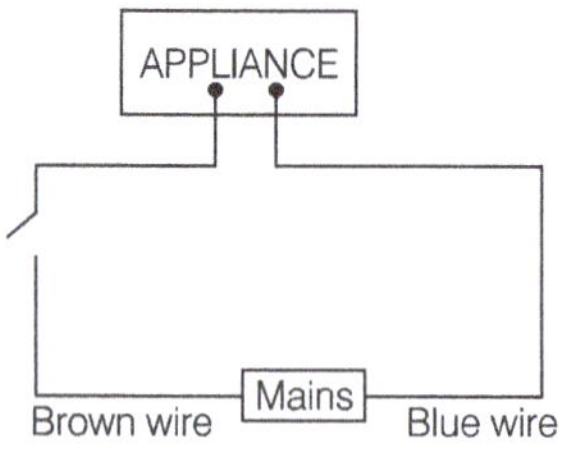

(d)

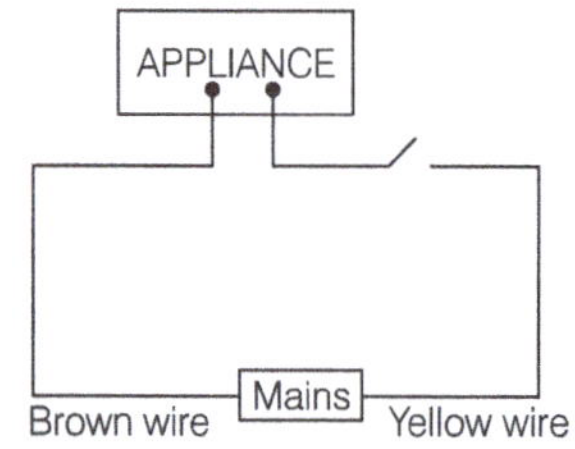

2. Which of the following is the correct colour code of the three wires live, neutral and earth? **(ICSE SQP 2023)**

(a)	Live : Green	Neutral : Red	Earth : Yellow
(b)	Live : Brown	Neutral : Red	Earth : blue
(c)	Live : Brown	Neutral : Blue	Earth : Yellow
(d)	Live : Blue	Neutral : Brown	Earth : Green

3. A main switch in the main distribution board is present in **(ICSE 2022 Sem-II)**

(a) a live wire
(b) a neutral wire
(c) a live as well as neutral wire
(d) an earth wire

4. Which one of the following statements is correct? **(ICSE 2022 Sem-II)**

(a) Live wire has zero potential.
(b) Fuse is connected in a neutral wire.
(c) Potential of live and earth wire is always the same.
(d) Earth wire is used to prevent electric shock.

2 Marks Questions

5. A fuse is rated 5 A. Can it be used with a geyser rated 1540 W, 220 V. Write **yes** or **no**. Give supporting calculations to justify your answer. **(ICSE 2024)**

6. Why is it not advisable to use a piece of copper wire as fuse wire in an electric circuit? **(ICSE 2020)**

7. Identify the following wires used in a household circuit. **(ICSE 2018)**

(i) The wire is also called as the phase wire.
(ii) The wire is connected to the top terminal of a three-pin socket.

8. Why is the earth pin of a three-pin plug made longer and thicker? **(ICSE SQP 2018)**

9. Explain the meaning of the statement 'current rating of a fuse is 5A'. **(ICSE 2017)**

10. (i) To which wire of a cable in a power circuit, should the metal case of a geyser be connected?
(ii) To which wire, should the fuse be connected? **(ICSE 2017, 16)**

11. Name the material used for **(ICSE 2017)**

(i) Electric fuse.
(ii) Connecting wire
(iii) Filament of an electric bulb.
(iv) Heating element of an electric toaster.

12. State the characteristics required in a material to be used as an effective fuse wire. **(ICSE 2016)**

13. (i) At what frequency is AC supplied to residential houses?
(ii) Name the wire in a household electrical circuit to which the switch is connected. **(ICSE 2015)**

14. (i) Name the device used to protect the electric circuits from overloading and short circuits.
(ii) On what effect of electricity does the above device work? **(ICSE 2013)**

15. (i) What is the colour code for the insulation on the earth wire?
(ii) Which part of an electrical appliance is earthed? **(ICSE 2011, 10)**

16. (i) Give two characteristic properties of copper wire which make it unsuitable for use as fuse wire.
(ii) Name the material which is used as a fuse wire. **(ICSE 2009, 2000)**

17. The electrical gadgets used in a house such as bulbs, fans, heater, etc., are always connected in parallel, not in series. Give two reasons for connecting them in parallel. **(ICSE 2008)**

18. On the three connecting wires in a household circuit
(i) Which two of the three wires are at the same potential?
(ii) In which of the three wires should the switch be connected? **(ICSE 2007)**

19. What is meant by earthing of an electrical appliance? Why is it essential? **(ICSE 2007)**

20. Draw a labelled diagram of a three-pin socket. **(ICSE 2006)**

21. State the purpose of a fuse in an electric circuit. Name the material used for making a fuse wire. **(ICSE 2004)**

22. Explain in briefly about the function of the following in the household wiring
(i) a three-pin plug.
(ii) main switch. **(ICSE 2002)**

23. Draw the diagram of the ring main circuit. **(ICSE 2001)**

24. How does earthing prevent electrical shock? **(ICSE 2001)**

3 Marks Questions

25. (i) What is the meaning of the statement 'the power rating of an appliance is 60 W, 220 V'?
(ii) In which wire is the fuse connected in a circuit?
(iii) State the function of main switch in an electric circuit. **(ICSE SQP 2023)**

26. Three wires with proper colour coding are connected to the three terminals of a three pin socket. Match the colour of the wire with the proper terminals *A*, *B* and *C* of the socket. **(ICSE 2022 Sem-II)**

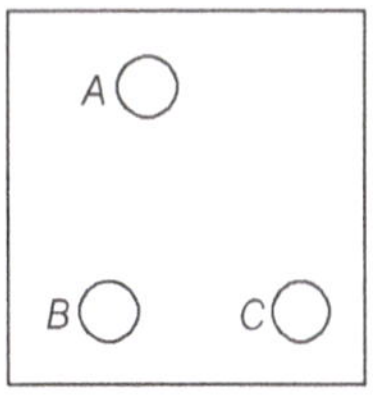

(i) Brown (ii) Green (iii) Light blue

27. (i) Name the safety devices which are connected to the live wire of a household electric circuit.
(ii) An electric iron is rated 220 V, 2 kW. Why is the fuse absolutely necessary in a power circuit? **(ICSE 2018)**

28. What is an electrical fuse? State two characteristics of an electrical fuse. **(ICSE SQP 2018)**

29 (i) Name the colour code of the wire which is connected to the metallic body of an appliance.
(ii) Draw the diagram of a dual control switch when the appliance is switched 'ON'. **(ICSE 2017)**

30. (i) Two sets *A* and *B* of three bulbs each, are glowing in two separate rooms. When one of the bulbs in set *A* is fused, the other two bulbs also cease to glow. But in set *B*, when one bulb fuses, the other two bulbs continue to glow. Explain, why this phenomenon occurs?
(ii) Why do we prefer arrangements of set *B* for house circuiting? **(ICSE 2014)**

31. (i) An electrical gadget can give an electric shock to its user under certain circumstance. Mention any two of these circumstances.
(ii) What preventive measure provided in a gadget can protect a person from an electric shock? **(ICSE 2013)**

32. (i) A cell is sending current in an external circuit. How does the terminal voltage compare with the emf of the cell?
(ii) What is the purpose of using a fuse in an electrical circuit?
(iii) What are the characteristic properties of a fuse wire? **(ICSE 2012)**

4/5 Marks Questions

33. (i) Name two safety devices which are connected to the live wire of a household electrical circuit.
(ii) Give one important function of each of these two devices. **(ICSE 2011)**

34. (i) In what unit, does the domestic electric meter measure the electrical energy consumed? State the value of this unit in SI unit.

(ii) Why should switches always be connected to the live wire?

(iii) Give one precaution that should be taken while handling switches. **(ICSE 2010)**

35. (i) The diagram (a) and (b) given below are of a plug and a socket with arrow marked as 1, 2, 3 and 4, 5, 6 respectively on them. Identify and write live (L), neutral (N) and the earth (E) against the correct number.

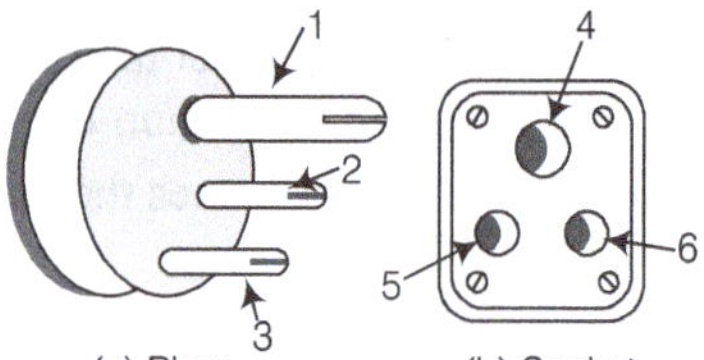

(a) Plug (b) Socket

(ii) Calculate the electrical energy consumed when a bulb of 40 W is used for 12.5 h everyday for 30 days. **(ICSE 2009)**

36. (i) Under what circumstances does one get an electric shock from an electric gadget?

(ii) What is meant by earthing of an electrical appliance? How does earthing offer protection? **(ICSE 2000)**

Explanations

1. (a) The live wire is represented with brown colour, the neutral wire is represented as blue colour. Fuse or key is connected in live wire. So, option a is correct.

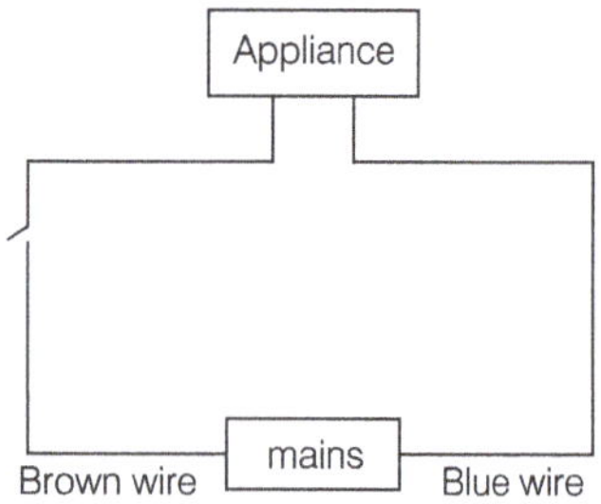

2. (c)

3. (c)

4. (d)

5. No, a 5A fuse cannot be used with a geyser rated at 1540 W, 220 V. The current drawn by the geyser is 7A, which exceeds the rating of the 5A fuse. Hence, there will be a risk of fire when the geyser is used with a 5A fuse.

Alternate

Current drawn by geyser, $I = \frac{P}{V} = \frac{1540}{220} = 7\text{A}$

The current drawn by the geyser is 7A, which exceed the rating of 5A fuse. So, there will be a risk of fire when the geyser is used with a 5A fuse.

No, a 5A fuse cannot be used with a geyser rated at 1540 W, 220 V.

6. Resistance of copper wire is very low and its melting point is very high but fuse wire must have high resistance and low melting point.

Therefore, fuse wire is not made of copper.

7. (i) Live wire is also called as the phase wire.

(ii) Earth wire is connected to the top terminal of three-pin socket.

8. Because when you insert the plug, the earth pin will first come in contact with the power supply before the other two (live and neutral). So, that any unwanted charges which may be in the circuit will be removed (grounded) before the other two pins go inside the terminals. This ensures that you connect the earth first which increases your safety in the events of an equipment failure.

9. Current rating of a fuse is 5A means, it is a safety device having short length of thin wire having low melting point of a particular amount of current 5A. Whenever current through this fuse exceeds to the 5A limit, it will melt and break the circuit and save the main circuit components from damage.

10. (i) Earth wire

(ii) Live wire of the circuits

11. (i) Copper

(ii) Copper

(iii) Tungsten

(iv) Nichrome

12. Characteristics required in a material to be used as an effective fuse wire are given below

(i) High resistance

(ii) Low melting point.

> **Concept Enhancer** Fuses are made up of tin (25%) and lead (75%) alloy having low melting point around 200°C.

13. (i) The frequency of AC supplied to residential houses is 50 Hz.

(ii) An electrical switch is always connected to live wire.

14. (i) Electric fuse is used to protect the electric circuits from overloading and short circuits.

(ii) Heating effect of electric current.

15. (i) The colour code for the insulation on the earth wire is green or yellow.

(ii) Metallic body of an electrical appliance is earthed.

16. (i) The two characteristic properties of copper wire are as

(a) It should be of low melting point and high resistivity.

(b) It should be a good conductor of electricity.

(ii) The alloy of tin and lead is used as fuse wire.

17. The electrical gadgets are always connected in parallel, because of the following

(i) Each appliance works at the same voltage.

(ii) If one appliance stop working, the other appliance continue to work.

18. (i) Neutral and the earth wires are at the same potential, because the earth wire and neutral wire are connected together.

(ii) Switch should be connected in live wire.

19. Earthing of an electrical appliance is a process in which the appliance is connected to thick copper wire, which is buried deep in the earth and its ends are connected to a copper plate surrounded by a mixture of charcoal and salt. If the live wire touches the metal body, it prevents us to touching the appliance from electric shock.

20. The three-pin socket diagram is shown below

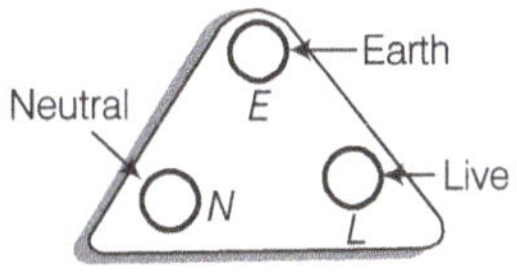

21. The purpose of a fuse in an electric circuit is to safeguard the circuit from an excessive flow of current in the circuit. The alloys of lead and tin are used for making a fuse wire.

22. (i) In three-pin plug, the left pin has live wire, the right pin has neutral wire and the stop pin has earthing wire. All the pins have split ends to provide the spring action.

(ii) It is used to switch OFF or ON the main current supply.

23. The diagram is shown below

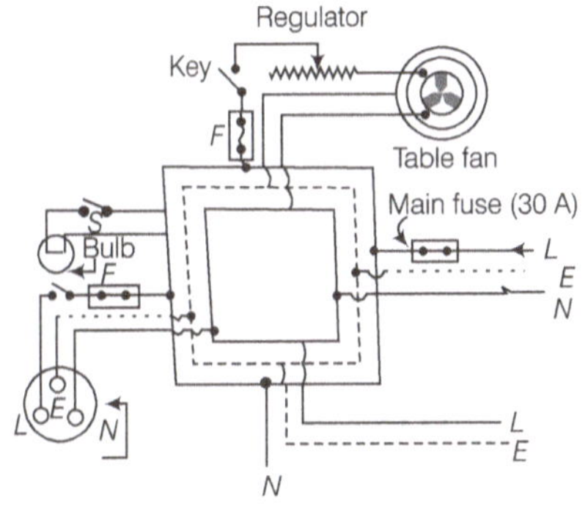

24. Refer to text on page no 151 (Need for earthing).

25. (i) A bulb having marking of 60 W, 220 V over it, indicates that the bulb will consume across the main supply of voltage 220V.

(ii) The fuse wire is always connected E_0 the live wire of the circuit.

(iii) The function of main switch in an electric circuit is to either make or break the electric circuit. A switch is used to turn current to an electrical appliance either ON or OFF.

26. (i) Colour of the wire Brown-Terminal C (Live)

(ii) Colour of the wire Green- Terminal A (Earth)

(iii) Colour of the wire Light blue- Terminal B (Neutral)

27. (i) Fuse, MCB

(ii) The purpose of using a fuse in an electrical circuit is to limit the electric current in a electric circuit. It prevents overheating or overloading in the circuit when a short circuit occurs.

28. The electrical fuse is a safety device in electric circuits used to limit the current and thus, it acts as a safeguard for the household circuit and any electric appliance connected in the circuit from being damaged.

Its characteristics are

(i) It has a low melting point of about 200° C and is usually made from an alloy of 50% tin and 50% lead.

(ii) It has a high resistance so that its temperature rises rapidly and soon exceeds its melting point and thus breaks it, when current passing through it exceeds the permissible limits.

In such a case it acts as a switch.

29. (i) The colour coding of wires in a cable are as follow

Wires	Colour	
	Old Convention	**New Convention**
Live	Red	Brown
Neutral	Black	Light blue
Earth	Green	Green or Yellow

(ii) **Two-Way or Dual Way Switch** It means two or more switches in different locations to control one lamp. This figure illustrates that lights to be controlled from both locations.

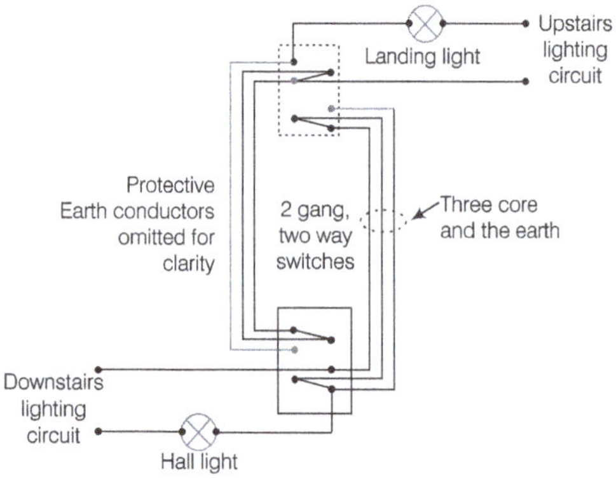

30. (i) The bulbs of set A are connected in series. Therefore, when one bulb fuse the current stop flowing.

Whereas, the bulbs of set B are connected in parallel. When one bulb fuse, then current flows through the other bulbs.

(ii) We prefer arrangement of set B for house circuiting, because the potential difference in it is same.

31. (i) The two circumstances, which give electric shock are as

(a) An electric shock may be caused due to poor insulation of wires.

(b) When wires of electric appliances are touched with wet hands.

(ii) To prevent from electric shocks, the insulation of wires must be of good quality and it should be checked from time to time, particularly when they become old.

32. (i) Terminal voltage is less than that of emf of the cell.

(ii) The purpose of using a fuse in an electrical circuit, to limit the electric current in an electric circuit, when there is overheating or overloading in the circuit. A fuse is used as safety device.

(iii) The characteristic properties of a fuse wire are low melting point and high resistance.

33. (i) The two safety devices which are connected to the live wire of a household electrical circuit are fuse and switch.

(ii) The important functions are as

Fuse It is used to limit the current in a circuit and safeguard the appliances.

Switch It is used for switching ON or OFF the circuit.

34. (i) The domestic electric meter measure electrical energy in kilowatt-hour (kWh).

(ii) Switches should always be connected to the live wire, because on switching OFF, the live and neutral wires will be at the zero potential. On the other hand, if the switch is connected to the neutral wire, on switching OFF, the appliance remains connected to the live wire and it will be at supply voltage.

(iii) Switches should not be touched with wet hands.

35. (i) 1–Earth (E), 2–Neutral (N)
3–Live (L), 4–Earth (E)
5–Neutral (N)
6–Live (L)

(ii) Given, $P = 40$, $t = 12.5$

Number of days = 30

Electrical energy, $E = ?$

$$\therefore \quad E = P \times t \times \text{number of days}$$

$$= \frac{40}{1000} \times 12.5 \times 30$$

$$= 15 \text{ kWh}$$

Common Mistake Mostly students think that the grounding of wire will not change the circuit value but this thought is wrong.

36. (i) Refer to ans. 31 (i).

(ii) Refer to text on page 151 (Need for earthing)

CHAPTER TEST

01 Mark Questions

1 1 coulomb is equal to

(a) 1 ampere × 1 second (b) 1 joule × 1 second
(c) 1 joule × 1 ampere (d) None of these

2 Identify the ohmic resistor.

(a) Silver (b) Silicon
(c) Germanium (d) None of these

3 Which of the following relation is not correct?

(a) $R \propto L$ (b) $R \propto A$
(c) $R = \frac{V}{I}$ (d) $I = \frac{Q}{t}$

4 Which of the following represent Ohm's law?

(a) $V \times R = I$ (b) $I = \frac{R}{V}$
(c) $\frac{V}{I} = R$ (d) $\frac{1}{V} = R$

5 In a house two 60 W lamps glow for 5 h a day and a fan of 100 W runs for 10 h a day. What is the energy consumption per day?

(a) 1.6 kWh (b) 1600 kWh
(c) 16 kWh (d) 160 kWh

02 Marks Questions

6 Define the term resistance. State its SI unit.

7 Distinguish between ohmic and non-ohmic resistors.

8 Find the specific resistance of a wire of length 1.1m, 0.4 m in diameter and having a total resistance of 4.2 Ω.

9 An electric bulb is connected in an electric circuit. 10 C charge flows through this bulb in 5 s. Find the current flowing through this bulb.

10 Electric fuse is an important component of all domestic circuits. Why? Also, name two common materials used as heating elements.

Structured Questions

11 (i) (a) Name two devices based on Joule's heating effect.

(b) Name two safety devices used in domestic circuiting.

(c) A bulb is rated at 110V, 80 W. What does this mean?

(ii) (a) Draw a *V-I* graph for a conductor obeying Ohm's law.

(b) What does the slope of *V-I* graph for a conductor represent?

(iii) Three 4 Ω resistors, *A*, *B* and *C* are connected as shown in figure. Each of them dissipates energy and can with stand a maximum power of 36 W without melting. Find the maximum current that can flow through the three resistors.

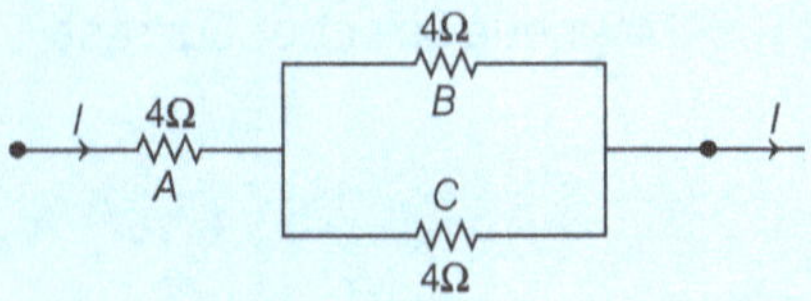

12 (i) (a) Draw a graph of potential difference (*V*) *versus* current (*I*) for an ohmic resistor.

(b) How can you find the resistance of the resistor from this graph?

(c) What is a non-ohmic resistor?

(ii) (a) A fuse is rated 8A. Can it be used with an electrical appliance rated 5 kW, 200 V? Give a reason.

(b) Name the safety devices which are connected to the live wire of a household electric circuit.

(iii) A heater coil connected to 200 V has a resistance of 80 Ω. If the heater is plugged in for the time *t* such that 1 kg of water at 20° C attains a temperature of 60° C. Find

(a) the power of heater.

(b) the heat absorbed by water.

(c) the value of *t* in seconds.

Answers

1. (a) **2.** (a) **3.** (b) **4.** (c) **5.** (a)

8. 0.48 Ω-m

9. $I = 2A$

11. (iii) 2.45 A

12. (iii) (a) 500 Js^{-1} (b) 167.2 kJ
(c) 334.4 s

08

Magnetic Effect of Current

TREND ANALYSIS 4 YEARS

Average No. of Questions Across all Sets

Topic	Types of Questions	2024	2023	2020	2019
TOPIC 01 Magnetic Effect of Current	1 Mark	–	1	–	–
	2 Marks	1	1	2	–
	3 Marks	1	–	–	–
	4 Marks	–	1	–	–
TOPIC 02 Electromagnetic Induction	1 Mark	1	–	–	–
	2 Marks	–	–	–	1
	3 Marks	1	–	–	–
	4 Marks	–	–	–	–

TOPIC 1

Magnetic Effect of Current

Oersted's Experiment on the Magnetic Effect of Electric Current

In 1820, Hans Oersted observed that when an electric current is passed through a conducting wire, a magnetic field is produced around it. The presence of magnetic field at a point around a current carrying wire can be detected with the help of a compass needle.

Magnetic Field

The region surrounding a magnet in which its effect can be experienced, i.e. its force can be detected is called magnetic field. It is denoted by B. It is a vector quantity. Its SI unit is tesla (T).

Magnetic Field Lines due to Current in a Straight Wire

The magnetic field lines form concentric circles around the wire with their plane perpendicular to the straight wire and with their centres lying on the wire. When the direction of current in the wire is reversed, it is observed that the pattern of iron filings do not change, but the direction of deflection of the compass needle gets reversed. Hence, the direction of magnetic field is reversed.

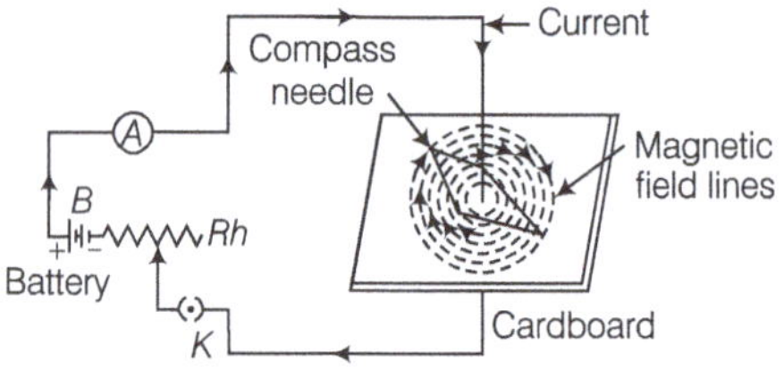

On increasing the current in the wire, the magnetic field lines become denser and the iron filings get arranged in circles upto a larger distance from the wire showing that the magnetic field strength has increased.

Maxwell's Right Hand (Clasp) Rule

It states that, if we hold the current carrying conductor in right hand such that the thumb points in the direction of the current, then the fingers incircle the wire in the direction of the magnetic field lines.

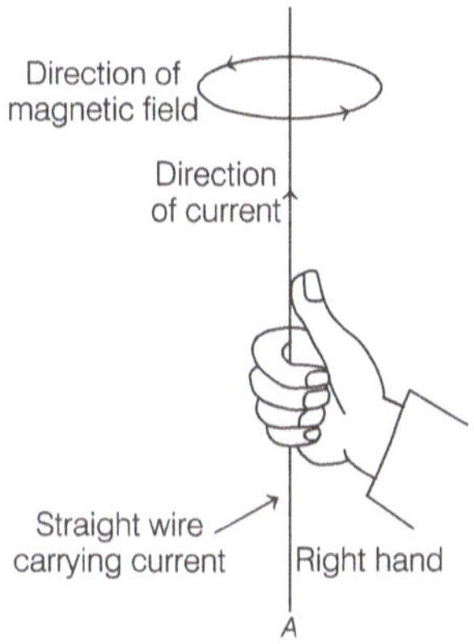

Magnetic Field Lines due to Current in a Loop

The following figure shows the magnetic field due to current in a loop.

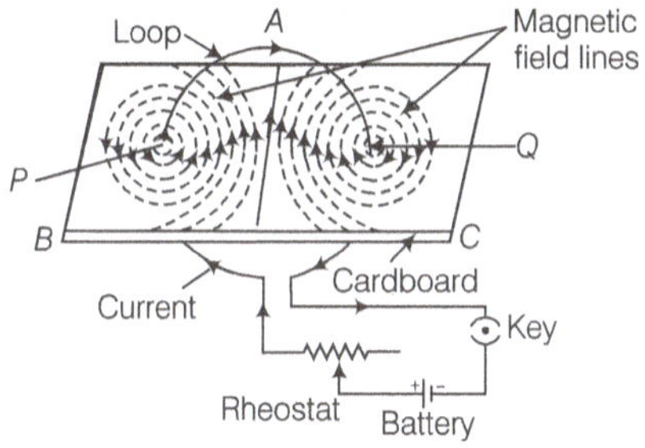

The pattern of magnetic field lines observed from the above figure are as

(i) In the vicinity of wire at P and Q, the magnetic field lines are nearly concentric circular.

(ii) Within the space enclosed by the wire, the magnetic field lines are in the same direction.

(iii) Near the centre of loop, the magnetic field lines are nearly parallel and the magnetic field may be assumed to be nearly uniformed in a small region near the centre.

(iv) At the centre, the magnetic field lines are along the axis of the loop and normal to the plane of the loop.

(v) The magnetic field lines become denser, if

- the strength of current in the loop is increased.
- the number of turns in the loop are increased.

Electromagnet

It is a temporary strong magnet made from a piece of soft iron when current flows in the coil wound around it. It is an artificial magnet.

The strength of an electromagnet increases with

(i) increase in number of turns in the coil

(ii) increase in the amount of current flowing through the coil.

(iii) decrease in the air gap between poles.

Comparison of Electromagnet and Permanent Magnet

Electromagnet	Permanent Magnet
It is made of soft iron.	It is made of steel.
It produces the magnetic field so long as current flows in its coils, i.e. it produces the temporary magnetic field.	It produces a permanent magnetic field.
The magnetic field strength can be changed.	The magnetic field strength cannot be changed.
The electromagnets can produce a very strong magnetic field.	The magnetic field due to permanent magnets are not so strong.
The polarity of an electromagnet can be reversed.	The polarity of a permanent magnet cannot be reversed.
It can easily be demagnetised by switching off the current.	It cannot be demagnetised.

Uses of Electromagnet

(i) It is used for lifting and transporting the large masses of iron scrap, girder, plates, etc.

(ii) It is used for loading the furnace with iron.

(iii) It is used for separating the magnetic substances such as iron from debris and raw materials.

(iv) It is used for removing pieces of iron from wounds.

Fleming's Left Hand Rule

This rule provides us the direction of force on a current carrying wire placed in a magnetic field. It states that, if the forefinger, thumb and middle finger of left hand are stretched mutually perpendicular to each other, such that the forefinger points along the direction of external magnetic field, middle finger indicates the direction of current, then the thumb points towards the direction of force acting on the conductor.

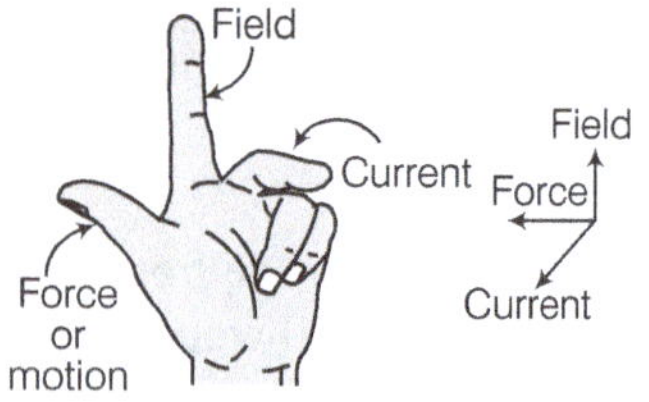

Fleming's left hand rule

Electric Motor

It is a device, which converts the electrical energy into the mechanical energy.

Principle A motor works on the principle when an electric current is passed through a conductor placed normally in a magnetic field. A force acts on the conductor as a result of which the conductor begins to move and the mechanical energy (or work) is obtained. The direction of force is obtained with the help of Fleming's left hand rule.

Construction and its main parts The basic structures of an electric motor are shown in the given figure.

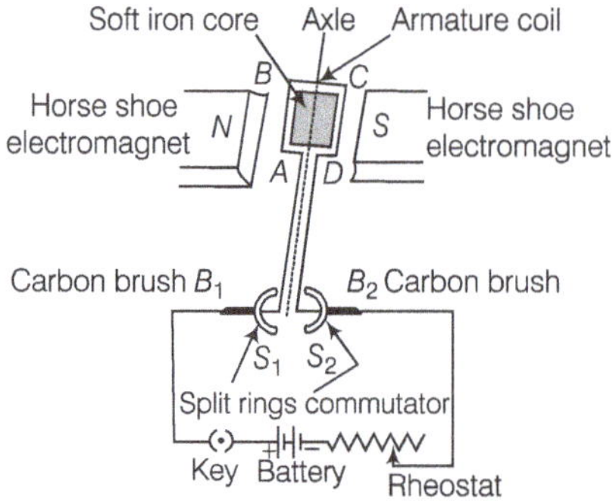

The main parts of an electric motor are as

(i) The armature coil *ABCD* mounted on an axle.

(ii) The split parts S_1 and S_2 of ring (i.e. a slip ring made of copper is divided in two parts S_1 and S_2) which is also known as commutator.

(iii) A pair of carbon brushes B_1 and B_2.

(iv) A horse shoe electromagnet N-S.

(v) A DC source (i.e. battery).

PYQs Previous Years Questions

1 Mark Questions

1. If the strength of the current flowing through a wire is increased, the strength of the magnetic field produced by it **(ICSE 2023)**

(a) decreases
(b) increases
(c) remains the same
(d) first increases then decreases

2. When a conductor carrying current is placed in a magnetic field, perpendicular to it, then the direction of the force experienced can be found out using **(ICSE SQP 2023)**

(a) Lenz's law
(b) Fleming's left hand rule
(c) Fleming's right hand rule
(d) right hand thumb rule

3. A coil wound around a piece of soft iron can become an electromagnet only when **(ICSE 2022 Sem-II)**

(a) the circuit is open
(b) a magnetic compass is present in the vicinity
(c) a galvanometer is connected to the circuit
(d) a current flows in the circuit

4. A conductor *AB* is kept along North-South direction of the earth above a magnetic needle as shown below. When the key *K* is closed, then **(ICSE 2022 Sem-II)**

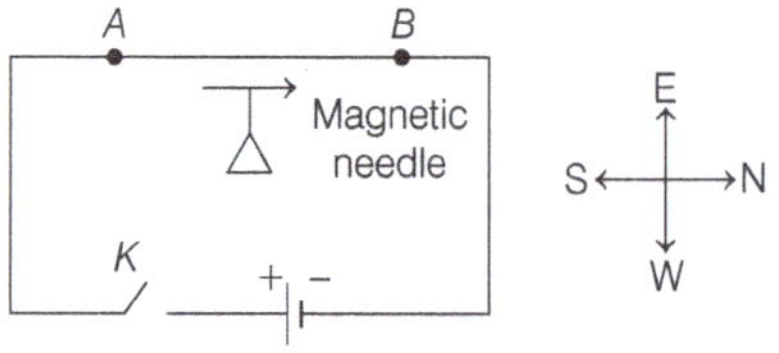

(a) the needle will not show any deflection
(b) the needle will deflect towards East
(c) the needle will turn in the opposite direction i.e. towards South
(d) the needle will deflect towards West.

5. The diagram below shows a free conductor *AB* is kept in a magnetic field and is carrying current from *A* to *B*. (To avoid confusion complete path of the circuit is not

shown) The direction of the force experienced by the conductor will be **(ICSE SQP 2022 Sem-II)**

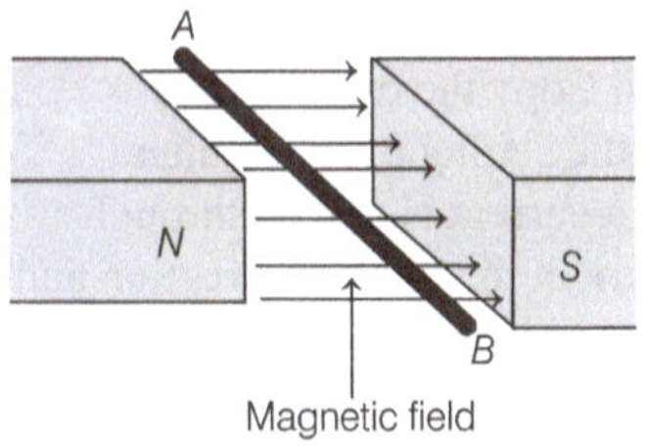

(a) up (b) down (c) towards N (d) towards S

6. Name a common device that uses electromagnet. **(ICSE 2014)**

7. What energy conversion take place during the working of a DC motor? **(ICSE 2006)**

8. State the function of a split ring in a DC motor. **(ICSE 2005)**

2 Marks Questions

9. State two factors affecting the speed of rotation of the coil in a DC motor. **(CBSE 2024)**

10. A copper conductor is placed over two stretched copper wires whose ends are to a DC supply as shown in the diagram. **(ICSE 2023)**
    (i) What should be the magnetic poles at the points *A* and *B* lying on either side of the conductor to experience the force in the upward direction?
    (ii) Name the law used to find these polarities

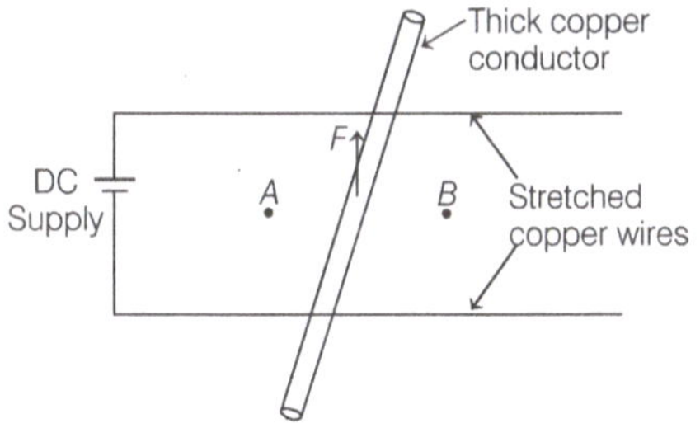

11. When a current carrying conductor is placed in a magnetic field, it experiences a mechanical force. What should be the angle between the magnetic field and the length of the conductor, so that the force experienced is **(ICSE 2020)**
    (i) zero (ii) and maximum?

12. The diagram below shows a loop of wire carrying current *I*.

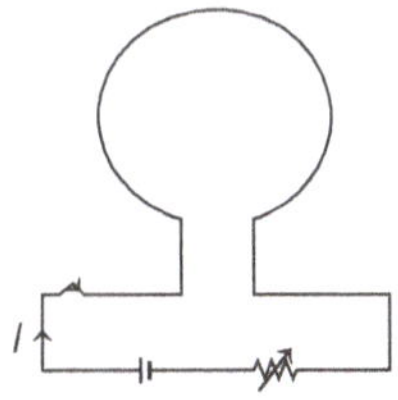

    (i) What is the magnetic polarity of the loop that faces us?
    (ii) With respect to the diagram, how can we increase the strength of the magnetic field produced by this loop? **(ICSE 2020)**

13. State any two advantages of an electromagnet over a permanent magnet. **(ICSE 2018)**

14. Mention two ways to increase the strength of an electro-magnet. **(ICSE SQP 2018)**

15. (i) Why does a current carrying, freely suspended solenoid rest along a particular direction?
    (ii) State the direction in which it rests. **(ICSE 2015)**

16. You have been provided with a solenoid *AB*.

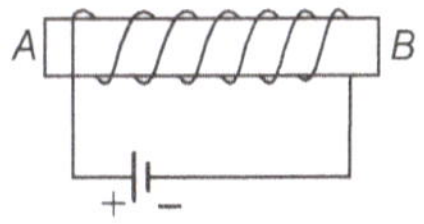

    (i) What is the polarity at end *A*?
    (ii) Give one advantage of an electromagnet over a permanent magnet. **(ICSE 2013)**

17. The figure given below shows an electromagnet.

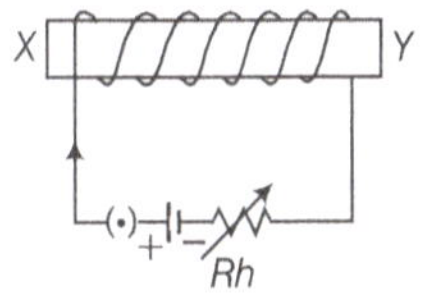

    (i) What will be the polarity at the end *X*?
    (ii) Suggest a way by which the strength of the electromagnet referred to in the question, may be increased. **(ICSE 2009)**

18. State two advantages of an electromagnet over a permanent magnet. **(ICSE 2006, 02)**

3 Marks Questions

19. Given below is a current to study the magnetic effect of electtric current . $ABCD$ is a cardboard kept perpendicular to the conductor XY.

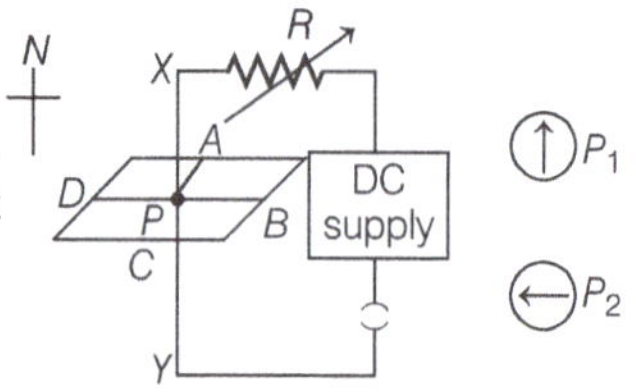

A magnetic compass is placed at the point P of the cardboard. P_1 and P_2 are the positions of the magnetic compass, before and after passing a current through XY, respectively.

(i) Name the rule that is used to predict the direction of deflection of the magnetic compass.

(ii) State the direction of current in the conductor (X to Y or Y to X) when the circuit is complete.

(iii) If resistance R is increased. Then, what will be the effect on the magnetic lines of force around the conductor ? **(ICSE 2024)**

20. (i) Name two factors on which the force experienced by a conductor carrying current, placed in a magnetic field, depends. Also state how these factors affect the force.

(ii) With the help of which rule you can determine the direction of force acting on a current carrying conductor placed in a magnetic field? **(ICSE 2022 Sem-II)**

21. The diagram shows a coil wound around a U-shape soft iron bar AB.

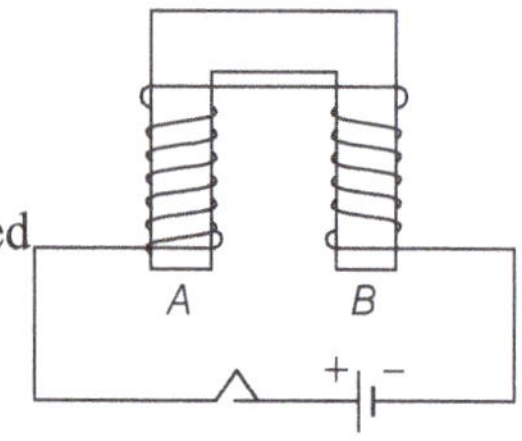

(i) What is the polarity induced at the ends A and B when the switch is pressed?

(ii) Suggest one way to strengthen the magnetic field in the electromagnet.

(iii) What will be the polarities at A and B, if the direction of current is reversed in the circuit? **(ICSE 2018)**

22. The diagram given shows a current carrying loop or a circular coil passing through a sheet of cardboard at the points M and N. The sheet of cardboard is sprinkled uniformly with iron filings.

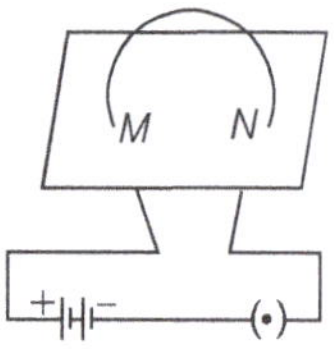

(i) Copy the diagram and draw an arrow on the circular coil to show the direction of current flowing through it.

(ii) Draw the pattern of arrangement of the iron filings when current is passed through the loop. **(ICSE 2012)**

23. (i) A straight wire conductor passes vertically through a piece of cardboard sprinkled with iron filings as shown in the figure below. Copy the diagram and show the setting of iron filings when a current is passed through the wire in the upward direction and the cardboard is tapped gently.

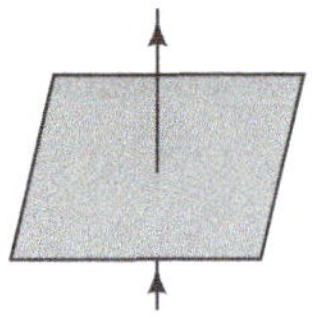

Draw arrows to represent the direction of the magnetic field lines.

(ii) Name the law which helped you to find the direction of the magnetic field lines. **(ICSE 2010)**

24. (i) Why does a magnetic needle shows a deflection when brought close to a current carrying conductor?

(ii) A wire bent into a circle carries current in an anti-clockwise direction. What polarity does this face of the coil exhibit? **(ICSE 2008)**

25. Explain briefly, how a magnet can be demagnetised using an alternating current. **(ICSE 2004)**

4/5 Marks Questions

26. The diagram below shows a cardboard on which iron filings are kept. A wire bent in the form of a loop is seen passing through the cardboard. When current flows through it the iron filings arrange themselves as shown below. **(ICSE 2023)**

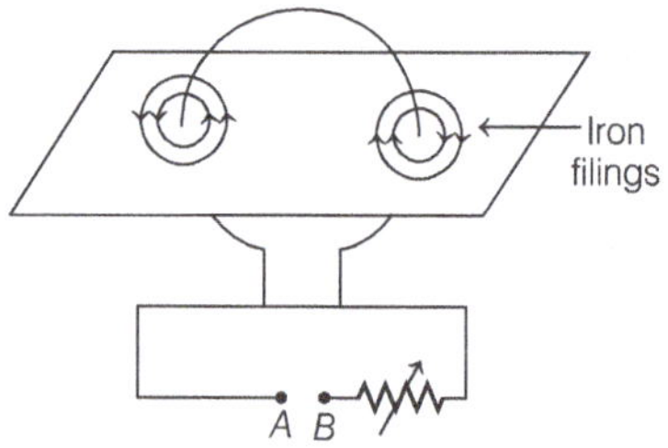

(i) State the polarities of the battery at A and B.

(ii) State the effect on the magnetic field if an iron rod is held along the axis of the coil.

(iii) State one way to

(a) Change the polarity of the coil.

(b) Decrease the strength of the magnetic field around the coil.

> **KEY idea**
> Use right hand thumb rule to Judge the polarities of the battery A and B.

27. (i) Draw a simple labelled diagram of a DC electric motor.
(ii) What is the function of the split rings in a DC motor?
(iii) State one advantage of AC over DC. **(ICSE 2013)**

28. (i) State two ways by which the magnetic field of a solenoid can be made stronger.
(ii) What material is used for making the armature of an electric bell? Give reason for using this material. **(ICSE 2010)**

29. Draw a representative diagram of a DC motor. Label the following in your diagram.
(i) The field magnet (ii) The armature
(iii) Commutator (iv) Wire brushes
What is the energy change in this case? **(ICSE 2011)**

Explanations

1. (b) 2. (b)

3. (d) A coil wound around a piece of soft iron becomes electromagnet only when a current flows in the circuit.

4. (d) From the figure we can see that the magnetic needle is kept below the conductor *AB* which is kept at North-South direction. We can see that the current is in clockwise direction and from the right hand thumb rule the direction of magnetic field will be from East to West. Hence, according to Fleming's left hand rule, the deflection produced will be towards East.

5. (a) Up
Applying Fleming's left hand rule the direction of force may be obtained.

6. Electric bell uses electromagnet.

7. During the working of a DC motor, electrical energy is converted into mechanical energy.

8. The function of a split ring in a DC motor is to flow the current in armature coil in such a way that it always keep on rotating in the same manner.

9. Two factors that affect the speed of rotation of the coil in DC motor are given below.
(i) **Voltage** The speed of rotation of the coil in a DC motor is directly proportional to the voltage applied to the motor terminals.
(ii) **Strength of the magnetic field** The strength of the magnetic field produced by the motor's magnet also affects the speed of rotation.

10. (i) The magnetic poles at *A* and *B* should be of opposite polarity. Specifically, the pole at point *A* should be North (N) and the pole at point *B* should be South (S).
(ii) The law used to find these polarities is the Fleming's left-hand rule for DC electric motors.
This rule relates the direction of force on current-carrying conductor in magnetic field to the direction of current and the direction of magnetic field.

Concept Enhancer Fleming's right hand palm rule is also used to find the direction of magnetic field and hence polarities at *A* and *B*.

11. (i) A current carrying conductor placed in uniform magnetic field experiences no force (zero force), if the angle between the magnetic field and the length of the conductor is 0° and 180°.
(ii) A current carrying conductor placed in uniform magnetic field experiences maximum force, if the angle between the magnetic field and the length of conductor is 90°.

Common Mistake There may be a confusion that when the current carrying conductor inclined to magnetic field, then what will be the force on it. So, the current carrying conductor also experience force in this condition.

12. (i) The direction of current flowing through the loop is shown below.

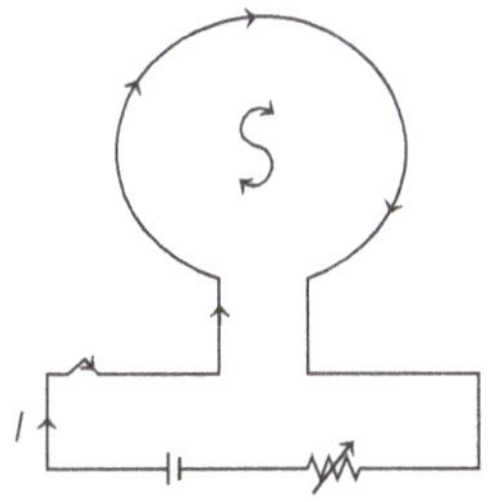

Since, direction of current in the loop is clockwise, hence it behaves as a South pole.
(ii) The strength of magnetic field produced by the loop is increased by decreasing the resistance

(or increasing the current) with the help of rheostat.

> **Concept Enhancer** If the direction of current in the loop is reversed, then the polarity facing to us will be North(N) pole.

13. The two advantages of an electromagnet over a permanent magnet are

(i) The polarity of an electromagnet can be changed by reversing the direction of current in the solenoid while polarity of a permanent magnet can never be changed.

(ii) An electromagnet can produce a stronger magnetic field than permanent magnet.

14. There are two methods by which we can increase strength of an electromagnet are

(i) By increasing the turn of wire in the coil.

(ii) By increasing the current flowing through the coil.

15. (i) A current carrying solenoid behaves as a temporary bar magnet having North pole towards the positive terminal of the DC supply. When a current carrying solenoid is suspended freely it aligns itself along the geographical North-South directions.

(ii) The North pole of the solenoid aligns, itself towards the geographical North direction and the South pole of the solenoid aligns itself towards the geographical South direction.

16. (i) The polarity at end A is North polarity.

(ii) An advantage of an electromagnet over a permanent magnet is that an electromagnet can produce a strong magnetic field.

17. (i) The polarity at end X is North polarity.

(ii) The strength of the electromagnet can be increased by increasing the strength of the current or by decreasing the resistance in the rheostat.

18. The two advantages of an electromagnet over a permanent magnet are

(i) The polarity of an electromagnet can be changed by reversing the direction of current in the solenoid while polarity of a permanent magnet can never be changed.

(ii) An electromagnet can produce a stronger magnetic field than permanent magnet.

19. (i) Right hand thumb rule

(ii) X to Y

(iii) Magnetic field is inversely proportional to the resistance R. So, if resistance R is increased, the magnetic lines of force decreases.

20. (i) Factors on which the force experienced by conductor carrying current depends

(a) Magnetic field strength

(b) The magnitude of the current flowing through the conductor and the length of the conductor.

(ii) By using Fleming's left hand rule, we can determine the direction of force acting on a current carrying conductor placed in a magnetic field.

> **Common Mistake** Students are confused in between Maxwell's right hand rule and Fleming's left hand rule. Maxwell's right hand rule is used to determine the direction of current and Fleming's left hand rule is used to determine the direction of force.

21. (i) Current enters at point A (clockwise rotation) and leaving from point B (anti-clockwise rotation). Hence, A will be South pole and B will be North pole.

(ii) Increasing the number of turns of coils, increases current.

(iii) A = North, B = South.

22. The direction of current is from M to N.

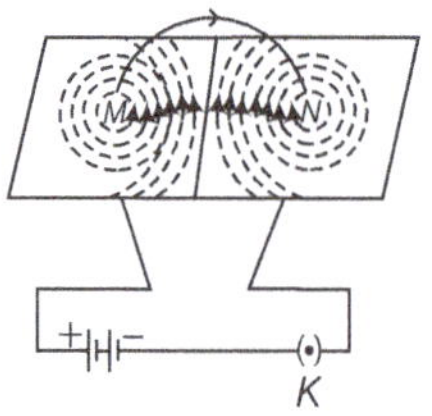

23. (i) The following diagram shows the magnetic field lines.

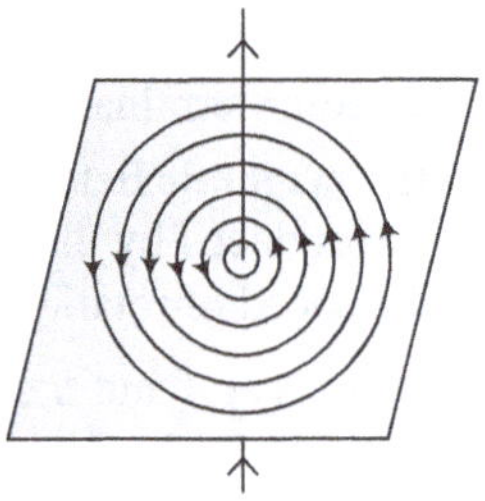

(ii) The right hand thumb rule helps to find the direction of the magnetic field lines.

24. (i) A magnetic needle shows a deflection when brought close to a current carrying conductor, because the magnet of the current carrying conductor exerts a force on the magnetic needle.

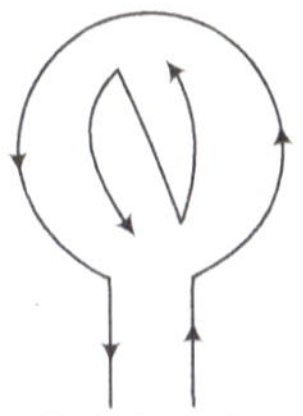

(ii) The face of the coil exhibits North polarity.

25. To demagnetise a magnet, place it inside a long solenoid with its length in East-West direction. A 12 V AC supply is connected with a rheostat in series. Switch on the current when AC is passed, its polarity changes due to which magnetic domains are reversed.

Thus, it becomes randomly oriented and the bar loses its magnetism to a greater extent. Gradually, the current is reduced to zero by rheostat which makes the re-alignment of domains most difficult. Thus, the bar of magnet is demagnetised.

26. (i) A is +ve terminal and B is – ve terminal. At A current is upward so magnetic field line is anti-clockwise and it has North polarity. At B current is downward so magnetic field line is clockwise and it has South polarity.

(ii) If an iron is held along axis of the coil, the strength of the magnetic field is increased.

(iii) (a) The polarity of the coil can be changed by reversing the direction of the current.

(b) The strength of the magnetic field around the coil can be decreased by decreasing the current which can be achieved by increasing the resistance.

27. (i)

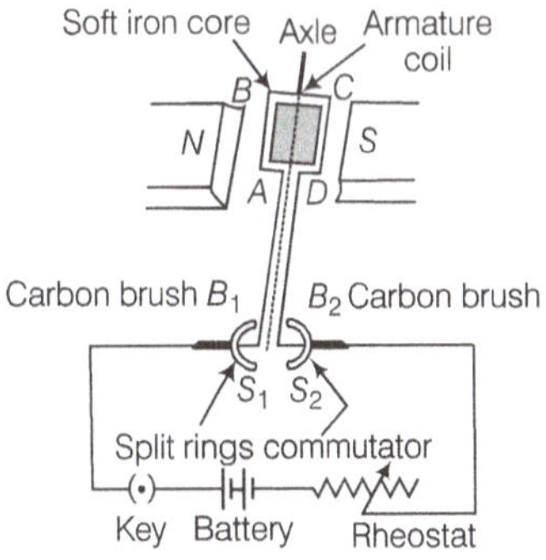

(ii) In a DC motor, when the coil rotates, the split ring rotate with it to flow the current in the armature coil in such a way that it always keep on rotating in the same manner.

(iii) AC can be transported to a large distance without much loss.

28. (i) Magnetic field of a solenoid can be made stronger by increasing

(a) the current in the solenoid.

(b) the number of turns in the solenoid.

(ii) Soft iron is used for making the armature of an electric bell, because soft iron is magnetised easily on passing the current and completely demagnetised easily on withdrawing the current through the solenoid.

29. The labelled diagram of DC motor is as shown below

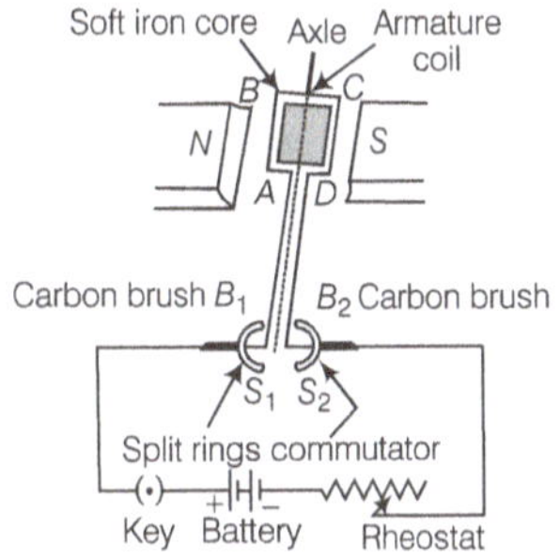

(i) The magnetic field is labelled as N-S. It is an electromagnet with concave pole pieces.

(ii) The armature coil mounted on an axle is labelled as $ABCD$.

(iii) The commutator is labelled as S_1, S_2.

(iv) Wire brushes are labelled as B_1, B_2 .

In an electric DC motor, the electrical energy is converted into mechanical energy.

TOPIC 2

Electromagnetic Induction

Electromagnetic induction is the phenomenon in which an emf is induced in the coil, if there is a change in the magnetic flux linked with the coil. Faraday formulated the two laws of electromagnetic induction such as

(i) Whenever, there is a change in the magnetic flux linked with a coil, an emf is induced.

(ii) The magnitude of the emf induced is directly proportional to the rate of change of the magnetic flux linked with the coil.

The factors affecting the magnitude of induced emf are

- change in the magnetic flux.
- time in which the magnetic flux changes.

The direction of induced emf can be obtained by

- Fleming's right hand rule
- Lenz's law.

Fleming's Right Hand Rule

Stretch the thumb, middle finger and forefinger of your right hand such that they are mutually perpendicular to each other.

If the forefinger indicates the direction of magnetic field and the thumb indicates the direction of motion of conductor, then the middle finger will indicate the direction of induced current.

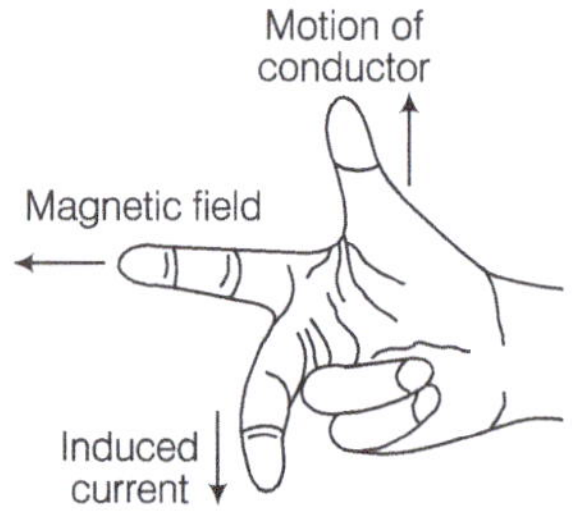

Lenz's Law

It states that the direction of induced emf always tends to oppose the cause which produces it.

Electric Generator

It is a device which converts the mechanical energy into the electrical energy using the principle of electromagnetic induction.

Principle

In a generator, a coil is rotated in a magnetic field. Due to rotation, the magnetic flux linked with the coil changes and therefore an emf is induced between the ends of the coil. Thus, a generator acts like a source of current, if an external circuit containing load is connected between the ends of its coil.

Construction and its Main Parts

The basic construction of an electric generator is shown in the adjacent figure.

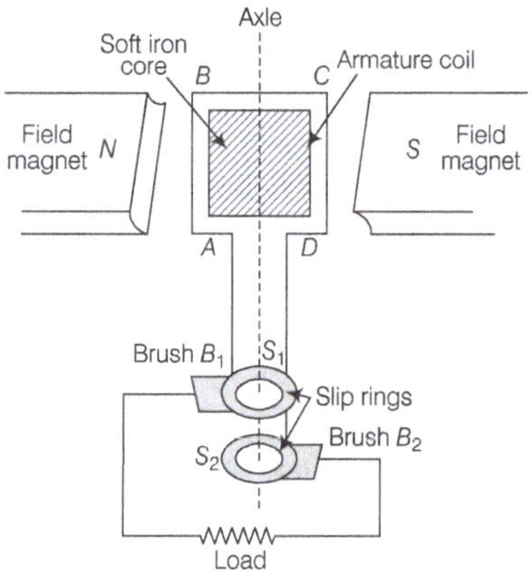

The main parts of an AC generator are

(i) **Field Magnet** It is a strong horse shoe permanent magnet N-S. An electromagnet run by a DC source can also be used as a field magnet.

(ii) **Armature Coil** There is a soft iron core on which a coil *ABCD* having a large number of turns of insulated copper wire is wound. The coil is rotated rapidly in the magnetic field of the field magnet by the axle fixed to it.

(iii) **Slip Rings** There are two coaxial metallic rings S_1 and S_2. They rotate alongwith the coil. One end of the coil is connected to the slip ring S_1 and the other end of the coil is connected to the slip ring S_2. Each slip rings against the brush which is stationary.

(iv) **Brushes** There are two brushes B_1 and B_2 made of carbon, which press gently against the slip rings S_1 and S_2, respectively. The other ends of brushes act as terminals of the generator for the external circuit. The external circuit (i.e. load) is connected between the other ends of brushes. The brushes B_1 and B_2 do not rotate alongwith the coil and the slip rings.

Frequency of Alternating Current (AC)

The alternating current has the frequency equal to the frequency of rotation of the coil. If the coil makes n rotations per second, the magnitude of induced current is given by

$$i = i_0 \sin 2\pi nt$$

and the emf is expressed as $e = e_0 \sin 2\pi nt$

where, e_0 and i_0 represent the maximum values of emf and current.

Differences between AC Generator and DC Motor

AC Generator	DC Motor
An AC generator is a device which converts mechanical energy into electrical energy.	A DC motor is a device which converts electrical energy into mechanical energy.
An AC generator works on the principle of electromagnetic induction.	A DC motor works on the principle of force acting on a current carrying conductor placed in a magnetic field.
In a generator, the coil is rotated in a magnetic field so as to produce electric current.	In a DC motor, the current from a DC source flows in the coil placed in a magnetic field due to which the coil rotates.
A generator makes use of two separate coaxial slip rings.	A DC motor makes use of two parts of split rings which act as a commutator.

Advantages of AC over DC

(i) AC generator is easy and economical.

(ii) It can be easily converted in DC with the help of rectifier.

(iii) In AC, energy loss is minimum, so it can be transmitted over long distances.

Disadvantages of AC over DC

(i) AC shock is attractive while DC shock is repulsive, so AC is more dangerous.

(ii) AC cannot be used in electroplating process, because here need of constant current and it is given by DC.

Transformer

It is a device which is used to increase or decrease the amplitude of an alternating emf.

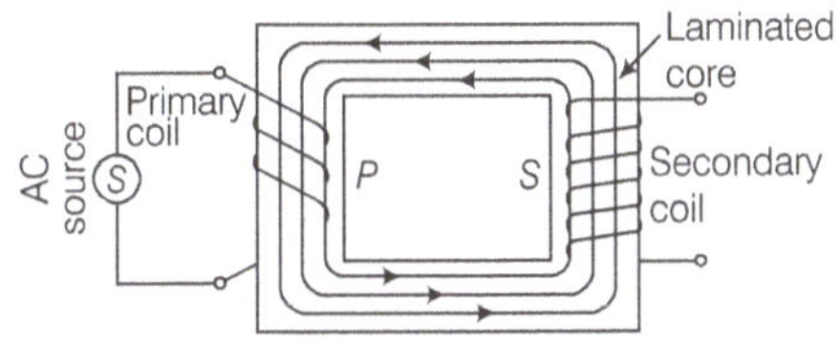

The transformers are of following types

(i) Step-up transformer

(ii) Step-down transformer.

Principle

Transformer is based on the principle of mutual induction.

Construction

It consists of two coils primary coil (p) and secondary coil (s), insulated from each other wounded on soft iron core often the primary coil is the input coil and secondary coil is the output coil. These soft iron cores are laminated to minimise eddy current loss.

The following figures shows step-up and step-down transformers

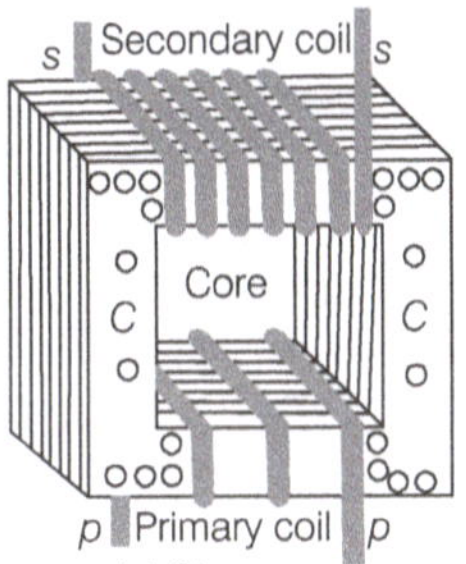

(a) Step-up transformer

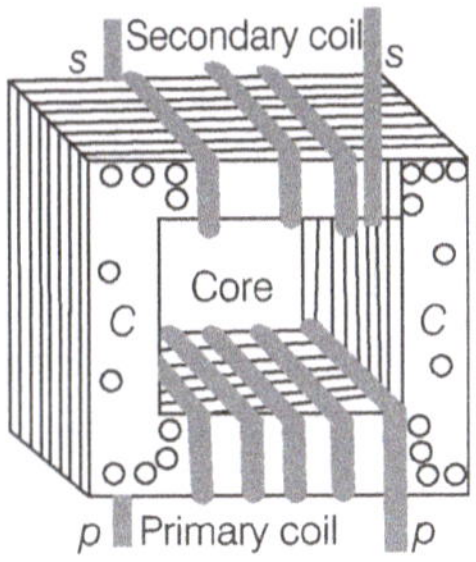

(b) Step-down transformer

Uses of Transformers

In our houses, both type of transformers are used with electrical appliances which operate at a voltage other than the voltage supplied by the mains (e.g. a door bell needs
6 V, while a TV requires nearly 10000 V).

Uses of step-up transformers

(i) In transmission of electric power at the power generating station to step-up the voltage.

(ii) With television.

(iii) With wireless sets.

(iv) With X-ray machines to provide a high accelerating voltage.

Uses of step-down transformers

(i) With electric bells, night electric bulbs, mobile phones, computers, etc.

(ii) At the power sub-stations to step-down the voltage before its distribution to the consumers.

PYQs Previous Years Questions

1 Mark Questions

1. State one factor the affects the magnitude of induced current in an AC generator . **(ICSE 2024)**

2. The diagram below shows a magnet moved near a coil along its axis. Which of the diagram shows correct flow of current during this motion? **(ICSE SQP 2022 Sem-II)**

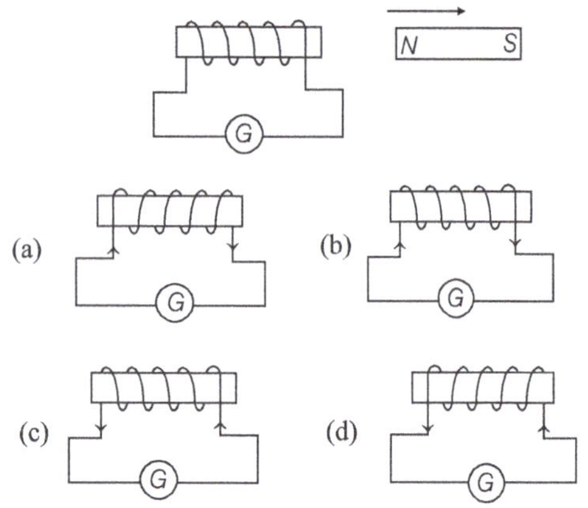

2 Marks Questions

3. A magnet kept at the centre of two coils *A* and *B* is moved to and fro as shown in the figure given below. The two galvanometers show deflection. **(ICSE 2019)**

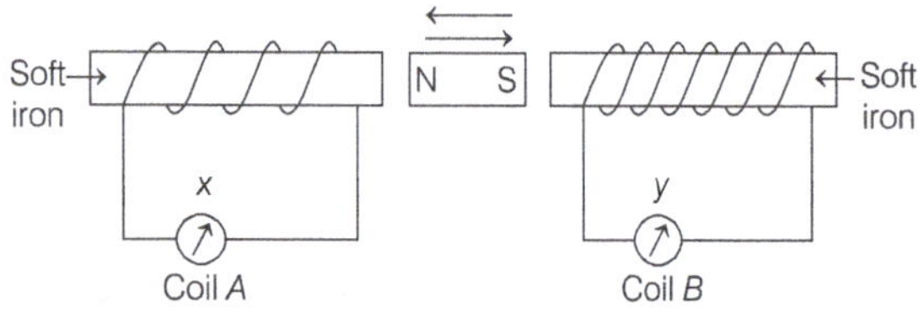

4. (i) How is the emf across primary and secondary coils of a transformer related with the number of turns of coil in them?
   (ii) On which type of current do transformers work? **(ICSE 2018)**

5. State any two advantages of an electromagnet over a permanent magnet. **(ICSE 2018)**

6. State two causes of energy loss in a transformer. **(ICSE 2017)**

7. In the transmission of power, the voltage of power generated at the generating stations is stepped up from 11kV to 132kV before it is transmitted. Why? **(ICSE 2017)**

8. Which coil of a step-up transformer is made thicker and why? **(ICSE 2016)**

9. Give two similarities between an AC generator and a DC motor. **(ICSE 2015)**

10. (i) What is an AC generator or dynamo used for?
    (ii) Name the principle on which it works. **(ICSE 2012)**

11. Give two differences between a DC motor and an AC generator. **(ICSE 2010)**

12. A device is used to transform 12 V AC to 200 V AC.
    (i) What is the name of this device?
    (ii) Name the principle on which it works. **(ICSE 2010)**

13. State one point of similarity and one point of difference between an AC generator and a DC motor. **(ICSE 2008)**

14. Draw a simple sketch of a step-down transformer. Label the different parts in the diagram. **(ICSE 2008)**

15. Draw a labelled diagram of an AC generator. **(ICSE 2005)**

16. State the energy change which takes place when a magnet is moved inside a coil having a galvanometer at its ends. Name this phenomenon. **(ICSE 2005)**

17. Mention two reasons, why a soft iron core is used within the coil of a moving coil galvanometer? **(ICSE 2005)**

18. State two ways by which the emf in an AC generator can be increased. **(ICSE 2004)**

19. State two dissimilarities between a DC motor and an AC generator. **(ICSE 2002)**

3 Marks Questions

20. Below is the diagram of a transformer

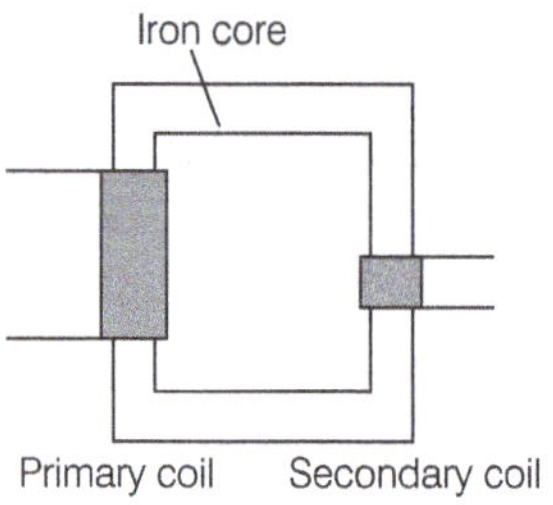

(i) Identify the type of transformer.

(ii) In this type of transformer, which of the wire is thicker, the primary or the secondary? Give a reason . **(ICSE 2024)**

21. The diagram below shows a magnetic compass kept closer to a coil AB wound around a hollow cylindrical cardboard. **(ICSE 2022 Sem-II)**

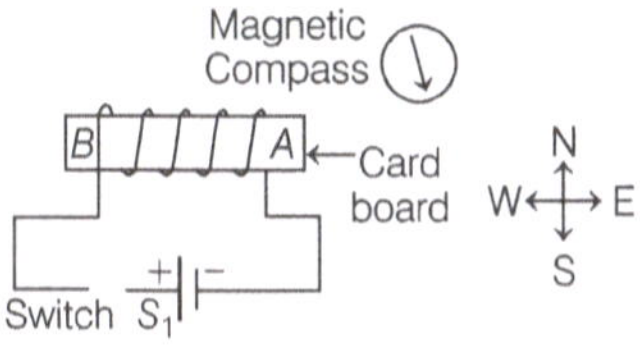

(i) After studying the circuit and the magnetic compass carefully, state whether the switch S_1 is open or closed.

(ii) How did you arrive at the conclusion in part (i) ?

(iii) What is the purpose of placing the magnetic compass in the above setup?

22. (i) State the Faraday's laws of electromagnetic induction.

(ii) Name one electrical device which works on this principle. **(ICSE 2022 Sem-II)**

23. (i) Name the transformer used in the power transmitting station of a power plant.

(ii) What type of current is transmitted from the power station?

(iii) At what voltage is this current available to our household? **(ICSE 2016)**

24. (i) Draw a neat and labelled diagram to show the structure of an AC generator.

(ii) State the energy conversion taking place in the AC generator when it is working. **(ICSE 2009)**

4/5 Marks Questions

25. The diagram below shows an insulated copper wire wound around a hollow card board cylindrical tube. Answer the questions that follow **(ICSE SQP 2022 Sem-II)**

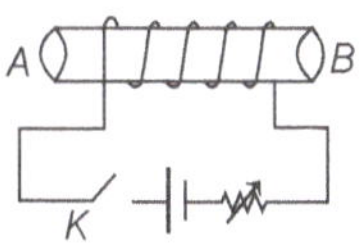

(i) What are the magnetic poles at A and B when the key K is closed?

(ii) State two ways to increase the strength of the magnetic field in this coil without changing the coil.

(iii) If we place a soft iron bar at the centre of the hollow cardboard and replace the DC source by an AC source, then will it attract small iron pins toward itself when the current is flowing through the coil?

26. (i) Name two factors on which the magnitude of an induced emf in the secondary coil depends.

(ii) In the following diagram an arrow shows the motion of the coil towards the bar magnet.

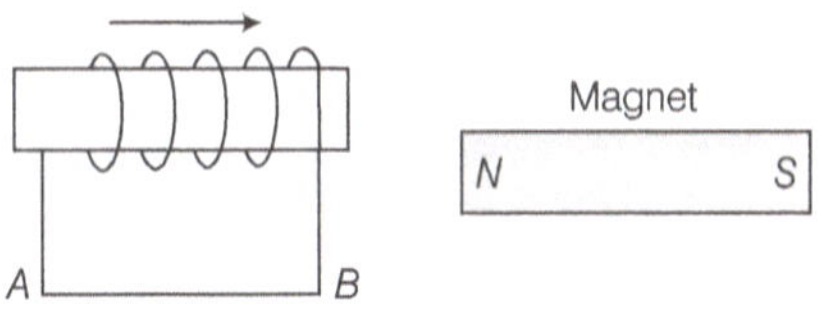

(a) State in which direction the current flows, A to B or B to A?

(b) Name the law used to come in the conclusion. **(ICSE 2014)**

27. (i) Draw a labelled diagram to show the various components of a step- down transformer.

(ii) State the main difference between a step-up and step-down transformer. **(ICSE 2004)**

28. The diagram shows a coil connected to a galvanometer G. The galvanometer shows a deflection to the right when the N-pole of a powerful magnet is moved to the right as shown.

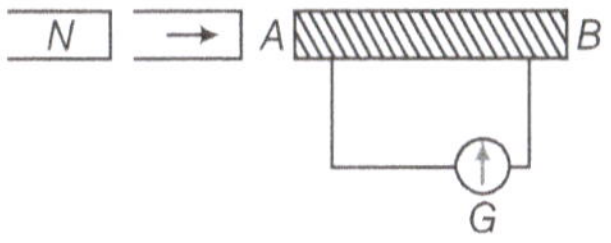

(i) Explain, why the deflection occur in the galvanometer?

(ii) Does the direction of the current in the coil appear clockwise or anti-clockwise, when viewed from the end A?

(iii) State the observation in G when the coil is moved away from N.

(iv) State the observation in G when both the coil and the magnet are moved to the right at the same speed. **(ICSE 2003)**

Explanations

1. Speed of rotation of coil.

2. (a) and (c)

Since, N of magnet is moving away from the coil the pole S will be formed at the right end of the coil (clockwise current flow).

Concept Enhancer When seen from the side of the magnet, we can use Fleming's right hand rule to find direction of movement of current. It is seen to be in the clockwise direction.

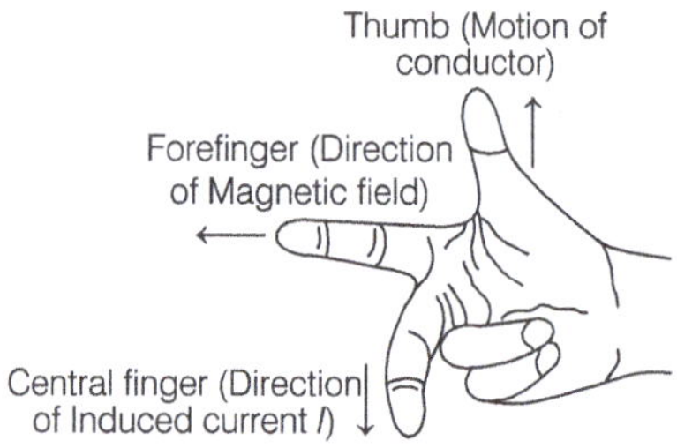

3. In the figure, the number of turns in coil B is greater than coil A. Hence, deflection in coil B will be greater than deflection in coil A. i.e. $y > x$.

4. (i) Let the emf across primary and secondary coils are E_s and E_p respectively.

$$\therefore \quad \frac{E_s}{E_p} = \frac{N_s}{N_p}$$

where, N_s = number of turns in secondary coil and N_p = Number of turns in primary coil.

Hence, emf is directly proportional to the number of turns in coil.

(ii) Transformer works with alternating current (AC).

5. The two advantages of an electromagnet over a permanent magnet are

(i) The polarity of an electromagnet can be changed by reversing the direction of current in the solenoid while polarity of a permanent magnet can never be changed.

(ii) An electromagnet can produce a stronger magnetic field than permanent magnet.

6. The two causes of energy loss in a transformer are as follow

(i) **Eddy Currents** The alternating magnetic flux induces eddy currents in the iron core and causes heating.

(ii) **Resistance of the windings** The wire used for the windings has some resistance and so energy is lost due to heat produced in the wire (I^2R).

7. Step–up transformer increases the amplitude of alternating voltage from 11 kV to 132 kV before it is transmitted to get better efficiency with less loss of energy.

8. Primary coil of a step-up transformer is made thicker, because it carries heavy current at low voltage.

9. Similarities between an AC generator and a DC motor are

(i) Both AC generator and DC motor works on magnetic effect of electric current.

(ii) In both the cases, a coil rotates in a magnetic field between the pole pieces of a strong electromagnet.

10. (i) An AC generator or dynamo is used to convert mechanical energy into electrical energy.

(ii) It works on the principle of Faraday's law of electromagnetic induction.

11. The two differences between a DC motor and an AC generator are

DC Motor	AC Generator
It converts electrical energy into mechanical energy.	It converts mechanical energy into electrical energy.
It is based on the principle that when a coil carrying current is held in a magnetic field, it experiences a torque which rotates the coil.	It is based on the phenomenon of electromagnetic induction.

12. (i) The name of this device is step-up transformer.

(ii) It is based on Faraday's law of electromagnetic induction.

13. **Similarity** In both the coil or armature moves or rotate in a uniform magnetic field.

Difference Refer to Ans. 11.

14. The sketch of step-down transformer is shown below

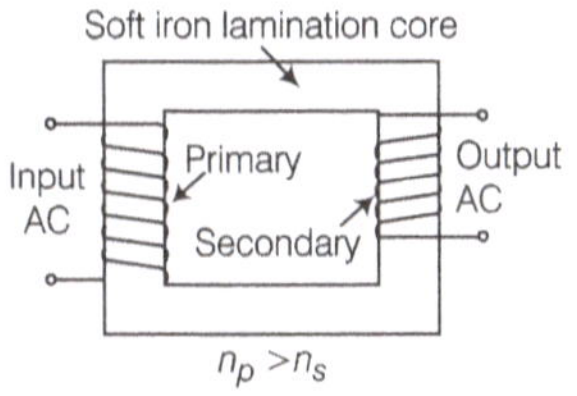

15. The labelled diagram of an AC generator is shown below

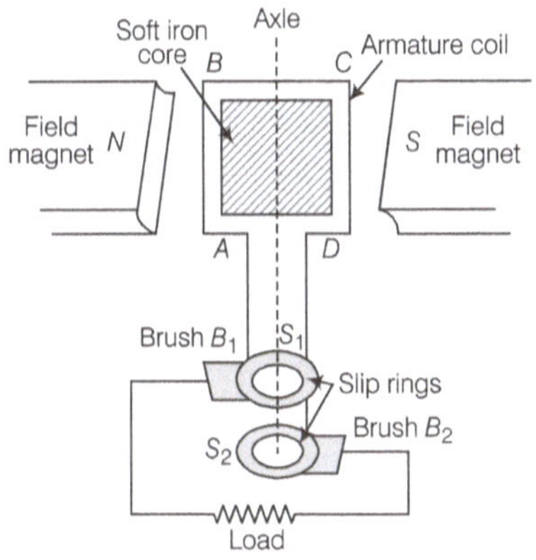

16. When a magnet is moved inside a coil having a galvanometer at its ends, the mechanical energy is converted into electrical energy. This phenomenon is known as electromagnetic induction.

17. A soft iron core is used within the coil of a moving coil galvanometer, because of the following reason

(i) To make the field radial.

(ii) To concentrate the magnetic lines of force.

18. The emf in an AC generator can be increased by

(i) increasing the speed of rotation of the coil.

(ii) increasing the strength of magnetic field.

19. Refer to Ans. 11.

20. (i) Step-down transformer

(ii) Secondary coil

The reason is that, secondary coil of a step-down transformer has greater current than primary. So, secondary coil is thicker as compared to its primary coil .

21. (i) The switch S_1 is open because no current was going through the circuit. (Compass is not showing any deflection)

(ii) As the switch does not have a wire connected to the circuit. Thus, we can say that the circuit is open or the switch is open.

(iii) The purpose of placing a magnetic compass is to study the deflection and to measure the direction of current.

22. (i) Faraday's laws of electromagnetic induction

First Law When a conductor is placed in a varying magnetic field, an EMF is induced in it.

If the conductor circuit is closed, a current flows through it, known as induced current.

Second Law The induced emf in a coil is equal to the rate of change of magnetic flux linkage with the coil.

(ii) Electric generator is a device which works on the principle of electromagnetic induction.

23. (i) In the power transmission station, step-up transformer is used to minimise the loss of electrical energy in transmission.

(ii) Alternating Current (AC) is transmitted from the power station.

(iii) At our household 220V of current is supplied by the step-down transformer.

24. (i) Refer to Ans. 15.

(ii) In the AC generator, mechanical energy of the rotation of the coil converts into electrical energy.

25. (i) As the anti-clockwise flow of current will occur at *A*, North pole will be produced at *A*; and as clockwise flow of current will occur at *B,* the South pole will be produced at *B*.

(ii) Two ways to increase the strength of the magnetic field in this coil

(a) By increasing the turn of wire in the coil.

(b) By increasing the current flowing the coil.

(iii) This is because AC will not create any magnetic effect, though it is a flow of free charged particles.

Concept Enhancer The copper wire wound around a hollow cardboard acts as solenoid which is also equivalent to a bar magnet due to its polarity on left and right side.

26. (i) The two factors on which the magnitude of an induced emf in the secondary coil depends are

(a) The change in magnetic flux.

(b) The time in which magnetic flux changes.

(ii) (a) The current flows from B to A.

(b) The law used to come to the conclusion is Lenz's law.

Common Mistake Many students are not aware with Lenz's law and they are also confused with the number turns of coil.

27. (i) Refer to Ans. 14.

(ii) The difference between step-up and step-down transformer are

Step-up Transformer	Step-down Transformer
It is used to change a low voltage alternating emf to high voltage alternating emf.	It is used to change a high voltage alternating emf to low voltage alternating emf.
The number of turns in primary coil is less than the number of turns in secondary coil.	The number of turns in primary coil is greater than the number of turns in secondary coil.

Concept Enhancer Transformer does not work for DC supply because there is no mutual induction in DC as its direction does not change.

28. (i) The deflection in the galvanometer occurs due to the motion of the magnet, these happen when change in magnetic flux is linked with the coil.

As a result, emf is induced across its ends due to which induced current flows in the coil.

(ii) The direction of the current in the coil is anti-clockwise, when viewed from the end A.

(iii) When the coil is moved away from N, the needle of galvanometer shows deflection to its left side.

(iv) When both the coil and magnet are moved to the right at the same speed, we observe no deflection as there is no change in magnetic flux linked with the coil.

CHAPTER TEST

01 Mark Questions

1 Magnetic field lines determine
(a) the shape of magnetic field
(b) Only the direction of magnetic field.
(c) Only the relative strength of magnetic field.
(d) Both the direction and the relative strength of magnetic field

2 The magnetic field near a long straight wire is described by
(a) straight field lines parallel to the wire
(b) straight field lines perpendicular to the wire
(c) connective circle centred on the wire
(d) radial field lines starting from the wire

3 A device for producing electric current is called a
(a) motor (b) generator
(c) galvanometer (d) ammeter

4 The direction of induced current obtained by
(a) Fleming's left hand rule
(b) right hand thumb rule
(c) Fleming's right hand rule
(d) clock rule

5 The current induced in a coil may be increased
(a) by the rapid motion of the magnet (or coil)
(b) by the use of a strong magnet
(c) by increasing the area of the coil
(d) All of the above

02 Marks Questions

6 In which position, the force on conductor is maximum is placed in uniform magnetic field?

7 What is the function of a step-up and step-down transformers?

8 Write two properties of magnetic field lines.

9 State Fleming's right-hand rule.

10 What is the significance of the current magnetic effect?S

Structured Questions

11 (i) A power transmission line feeds input power at 2300 V to a step-down transformer with its primary winding having 4000 turns. What should be the number of turns in the secondary winding in order to get output power at 230 V? **(3)**

(ii) What is the principle of electric motor? State the function of
(a) split ring
(b) field magnet used in electric motor **(3)**

(iii) A step-up transformer operated on a 2.5 kV line. It supplies a load with 20A. The ratio of the primary winding to the secondary is 10 : 1. If the transformer is 100% efficient, then calculate
(a) the power output
(b) the voltage and
(c) the current is the secondary. **(4)**

12 (i) The input and output voltage of a transformer are 220 V and 44V respectively. Find
(a) the turns ratio.
(b) the current in input circuit, if the output current is 2A. **(4)**

(ii) (a) Name two device which work on the magnetic effect of current.
(b) Name the essential parts of a DC motor. **(3)**

(iii) The primary coil of a transformer has 800 turns and the secondary coil 8 turns. It is connected to a 220 V AC supply. What will be the output voltage ? **(3)**

Answers

1. (d) **2.** (c) **3.** (b) **4.** (c) **5.** (d)

11. (i) 400 (iii) (a) 5×10^4 W (b) 250 V (c) 200 A

12. (i) (a) 1 : 5 (b) 0.4 A (iii) 2.2 V

09

Heat

TREND ANALYSIS 4 YEARS

Average No. of Questions Across all Sets

Topic	Types of Questions	2024	2023	2020	2019
TOPIC 01 Specific Heat Capacity	1 Mark	1	–	–	–
	2 Marks	–	1	2	2
	3 Marks	–	–	1	1
	4 Marks	–	–	–	–
TOPIC 02 Latent Heat	1 Mark	1	–	–	–
	2 Marks	1	–	–	1
	3 Marks	2	1	2	1
	4 Marks	–	–	1	1

TOPIC 1

Specific Heat Capacity

Temperature

It is the measure of degree of hotness or coldness of any body. Heat flows from a body at higher temperature to another body at lower temperature, until they reach to equal temperature. The SI unit of temperature is kelvin (K). Other units of temperature are celsius (°C) and fahrenheit (°F).

$$T\,(\mathrm{K}) = T\,(^\circ\mathrm{C}) + 273.15$$

Heat

It is the form of energy which flows from one part to other part of the system without any mechanical work involved (by virtue of temperature difference only). It measures the total internal energy possessed by the molecules. It is represented by Q.

Different Units of Heat Energy

One calorie It is the amount of heat required to raise the temperature of 1 g of pure water by 1°C.

$$1\ \text{cal} = 4.186\ \text{J} = 4.2\ \text{J}$$

One kilocalorie It is the amount of heat required to raise the temperature of 1 kg of pure water by 1°C.

$$1\ \text{kcal} = 10^3\ \text{cal} = 4.2 \times 10^3 0\text{J}$$

Thermal Capacity or Heat Capacity

It is defined as the total amount of heat required to raise the temperature of a body by 1°C. It is represented by C.

$$\text{Heat capacity } (C) = \frac{\text{Heat supplied to the body } (Q)}{\text{Change in temperature } (\Delta t)}$$

Its SI unit is joule/°C or joule/K. Its older unit is cal/°C or cal/K or kcal/°C.

Specific Heat Capacity

It can be defined as the amount of heat energy required to raise the temperature of unit mass by 1°C. It is dependent on nature of the substance. It is represented by c.

Specific heat capacity (c)

$$= \frac{\text{Heat energy supplied } (Q)}{\text{Mass of the body or substance } (m) \times \text{Change in temperature } (\Delta T)}$$

Relationship between Heat Capacity and Specific Heat Capacity

The relationship between the quantities thermal (heat) capacity C' and specific heat capacity (c) can be given as

$$C' = \text{mass } (m) \times c \text{ or } c = C'$$

The SI unit of specific heat capacity is J/kg-K. The other units which is useful in calculation of specific heat is cal/g°C or kcal/kg°C.

Values of Specific Heat Capacity for Some Common Substances

Material	cal/g°C	J/kg-K
Water	1	4186
Ethanol	0.55	2302
Paraffin	0.51	2135
Ice	0.50	2093
Steam	0.46	1926
Aluminium	0.215	900
Glass	0-0.2	419-837
Iron	0.112	470
Copper	0.093	389
Lead	0.031	130

Natural Phenomena and High Specific Heat Capacity of Water

(i) Water is used in cold countries as heat reservoir for wine and juice bottles to prevent their freezing. This is because of its high specific heat capacity. So, it imparts a large amount of heat before reaching to the freezing temperature.

(ii) Almost, all the plants and animals have a high water content in their bodies (i.e. nearly 80% to 90%). It is because of high specific heat capacity of water, the body temperature nearly same in all the seasons.

(iii) For fomentation, the hot water bottles are used. It is because of the high specific heat capacity of water, it does not get cool quickly. So, due to this, a hot water bottle provides the heat energy for fomentation for a longer period of time.

(iv) In car radiators, water is used as coolant. This is because it can absorb a large amount of heat energy from the engine of a car, but itself does not rise to very high temperature.

(v) During a cold winter night, if the atmospheric temperature falls below 0°C, then the chances of destroying of crops becomes high. So, in order to save the crop on such cold nights, farmers fill their fields with water.

Consequences of High Specific Heat of Water

- We feel cool after hot water bath.
- Heat in summer get very oppressive just after rainfall.
- Water is used as a coolant in car radiator.
- Farmer fill their fields with water to protect the crops from frost.
- These all facts are occurred due to high specific heat of water.

Thermal Equilibrium

It is the condition between the two bodies, when they are in contact with each other, there is no flow of heat from one body to another.

Principle of Calorimeter or Method of Mixture Use

Calorimeter is the copper vessel in which the measurement of heat transfer takes place. According to the principle of calorimeter, ''when a hot body is mixed or kept in contact with cold body, there is a heat energy transfer from hot body to cold body until they reach to the same temperature. i.e. We can say heat gained by cold body is equal to heat lost by hot body''. It is based on law of **conservation of energy**.

Mathematical statement of calorimeter

Heat lost by the hot body is always equals to the heat gained by the cold body.

$\Rightarrow$ Heat lost (Q_L) = Heat gained (Q_G)

PYQs Previous Years Questions

1 Mark Questions

1. The graph given below shows heat energy supplied against change in temperature when no energy is lost to the surrounding. **(ICSE 2024)**

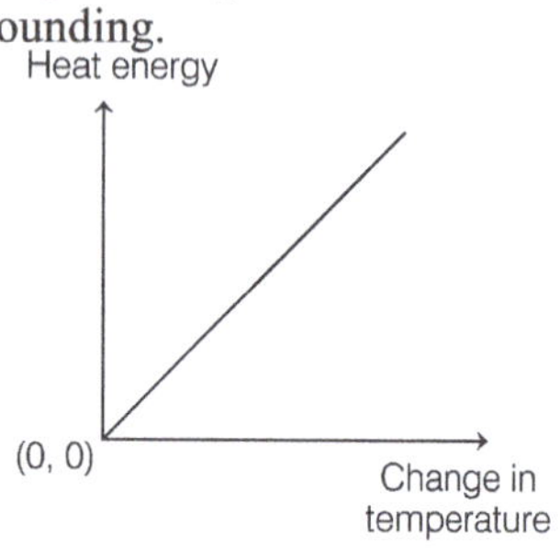

The slope of this graph will give
(a) specific heat capacity
(b) latent heat of fusion
(c) latent heat of vaporisation
(d) heat capacity

2. Which of the following liquids is most suitable for radiators in cars? **(ICSE SQP 2023)**
(a) Liquid P with specific heat capacity 4000 $Jkg^{-1}K^{-1}$
(b) Liquid Q with specific heat capacity 2000 $Jkg^{-1}K^{-1}$
(c) Liquid R with specific heat capacity 1500 $Jkg^{-1}K^{-1}$
(d) Liquid S with specific heat capacity 2100 $Jkg^{-1}K^{-1}$

3. If water absorbs 4000 J heat to increase the temperature of 1 kg of water through $1\,°C$, then the specific heat capacity of water is **(ICSE 2022 Sem-II)**
(a) 4 $Jkg^{-1}\,°C^{-1}$ (b) 400 $Jg^{-1}\,°C^{-1}$
(c) 4 $Jg^{-1}\,°C^{-1}$ (d) 4.2 $Jg^{-1}\,°C^{-1}$

4. Water is used in car radiators because **(ICSE 2022 Sem-II)**
(a) it is a good conductor of heat
(b) it conducts heat faster as compared to the other substances and cools the engine quickly
(c) its specific heat capacity is very low
(d) its specific heat capacity is very high, so it can cool the engine without a greater increase in its own temperature.

5. The meaning of the statement 'Specific heat capacity of water is 4200 $Jkg^{-1}\ K^{-1}$' is **(ICSE 2022 Sem-II)**
(a) Water needs 4200 J heat to raise its temperature by 1 K.
(b) To raise the temperature of water 4200 J of heat is absorbed.
(c) 1 kg water absorbs 4200 J heat to increase its temperature by 1 K.
(d) 1 kg water needs 1 K temperature to absorb 4200 J heat.

6. Which property of water makes it an effective coolant? **(ICSE 2015)**

7. What is the principle of calorimetry? **(ICSE 2015)**

8. Name the law on which the principle of calorimetry is based. **(ICSE 2015)**

2 Marks Questions

9. Calculate the heat absorbed by 200 g ice at $0°$ C to change to water at $60°$ C. [Specific heat capacity of ice $= 2100\ J\ kg^{-1}\ K^{-1}$, Specific heat capacity of water $= 4200\ J\ kg^{-1}\ K^{-1}$, Specific latent heat of ice $= 336000\ Jkg^{-1}$] **(ICSE 2023)**

10. Two metallic blocks P and Q having masses in ratio 2 : 1 are supplied with the same amount of heat. If their temperatures rise by same degree, compare their specific heat capacities. **(ICSE 2020)**

11. Why does stone lying in the sun get heated up much more than water lying for the same duration of time? **(ICSE 2020)**

12. (i) Name the physical quantity which is measured in calories.
(ii) How is calorie related to the SI unit of that quantity? **(ICSE 2019)**

13. The specific heat capacity of a substance A is 3800 $Jkg^{-1}K^{-1}$ and that of a substance B is 400 $Jkg^{-1}K^{-1}$. Which of the two substances is a good conductor of heat? Give a reason for your answer. **(ICSE 2019)**

14. (i) How can a temperature in degree celsius be converted into SI unit of temperature?
(ii) A liquid X has the maximum specific heat capacity and is used as a coolant in car radiators. Name the liquid X. **(ICSE 2018)**

15. Name a metal commonly used to make a calorimeter. Give a reason to support your answer. **(ICSE SQP 2018)**

16. State the SI unit of specific heat capacity and heat capacity. **(ICSE SQP 2018)**

17. Define heat capacity and state its SI unit. **(ICSE 2017, 13)**

18. Why is the base of a cooking pan generally made thick? **(ICSE 2017)**

> **KEY idea**
>
> Always remember that heat capacity depends on mass. So, as mass increases heat capacity also increases.

19. A solid of mass 50 g at 150°C is placed in 100 g of water at 11°C, when the final temperature recorded is 20°C. Find the specific heat capacity of the solid. (Take, specific heat capacity of water = 4.2 J/g°C) **(ICSE 2017)**

> **KEY idea**
>
> To solve this, you should use the following formula,
>
> $$\text{Specific heat capacity} = \frac{\text{Specific heat of solid}}{\text{Specific heat capacity of water}}$$

20. What do you understand by the following statements?

(i) The heat capacity of the body is 60 JK^{-1}.

(ii) The specific heat capacity of lead is 130 $Jkg^{-1}K^{-1}$. **(ICSE 2016)**

21. State two factors upon which the heat absorbed by a body depends. **(ICSE 2016)**

22. 50 g of metal piece at 27°C requires 2400 J of heat energy so as to attain a temperature of 327°C, calculate the specific heat capacity of the metal. **(ICSE 2014)**

23. Differentiate between heat capacity and specific heat capacity. **(ICSE 2012)**

24. A hot solid of mass 60 g at 100°C is placed in 150 g of water at 20°C. The final steady temperature recorded is 25°C. Calculate the specific heat capacity of the solid. (Take, specific heat capacity of water $= 4200\ J\ kg^{-1}\,°C^{-1}$) **(ICSE 2012)**

> **KEY idea**
>
> To solve this question, you should use the principle of calorimetry.
>
> i.e. Heat gain = Heat lost.

25. Differentiate between heat and temperature. **(ICSE 2011)**

26. Define calorimetry. **(ICSE 2011)**

27. 200 g of hot water at 80°C is added to 300 g of cold water at 10°C. Calculate the final temperature of the mixture of water. Consider the heat taken by the container to be negligible. (Take, specific heat capacity of water is $4200\ J\ kg^{-1}\,°C^{-1}$) **(ICSE 2011)**

28. (i) Give one example, where high specific heat capacity of water is used as a heat reservoir.

(ii) Give one example, where high specific heat capacity of water is used for cooling purposes. **(ICSE 2011)**

29. 40 g of water at 60°C is poured into a vessel containing 50 g of water at 20°C. The final temperature recorded is 30°C. Calculate the thermal capacity of the vessel. (Take, specific heat capacity of water is $4.2\ J\,g^{-1}\,°C^{-1}$). **(ICSE 2009)**

30. Some hot water was added to three times its mass of cold water at 10°C and the resulting temperature was found to be 20°C. What was the temperature of the hot water? **(ICSE 2007)**

31. Give two reasons, why copper is preferred over other metals for making calorimeter? **(ICSE 2006)**

32. (i) Does land cool at a slower or faster rate than water? Give one reason.

(ii) Explain, why steam pipes warm a building more effectively than hot water pipes in cold countries? **(ICSE 2003)**

3 Marks Questions

33. A metal piece present at 120° C is quickly dropped in a calorimeter of mass 80 g containing 200 g of water at 30° C. The final temperature attained by the mixture is 40° C. Calculate the thermal capacity of the metal piece. [Specific heat capacity of water = $4.2\ Jg^{-1}\,°C^{-1}$, Specific heat capacity of calorimeter = $0.4\ Jg^{-1}\,°C^{-1}$] **(ICSE 2022 Sem-II)**

34. (i) Give an important reason for copper to be used as a material for a calorimeter.

(ii) Calculate the thermal capacity of 40 g of water. [Specific heat capacity of water = $4200\ Jkg^{-1}\,°C^{-1}$] **(ICSE 2022 Sem-II)**

35. (i) Why does it become colder after a hailstorm than during or before the hailstorm?

(ii) 'If two bodies have the same specific heat capacities, then they will always absorb the same amount of heat if their temperature increases by the same amount'. State whether the given statement is true or false. **(ICSE 2022 Sem-II)**

36. (i) Define heat capacity of a substance.

(ii) Write the SI unit of heat capacity.

(iii) What is the relationship between heat capacity and specific heat capacity of a substance? **(ICSE 2020)**

37. (i) Define calorimetry.

(ii) Name the material used for making a calorimeter.

(iii) Why is a calorimeter made up of thin sheets of the above material answered in (ii)? **(ICSE 2019)**

38. The temperature of 170 g of water at 50°C is lowered to 5°C by adding certain amount of ice to it. Find the mass of ice added.

(Take, specific heat capacity of water = 4200 J kg^{-1} $°C^{-1}$ and specific latent heat of ice = 336000 J kg^{-1}) **(ICSE 2018, 2009)**

39. Two liquids *A* and *B* have specific heat capacities 2.5 $Jg^{-1}°C^{-1}$ and 3.2 $Jg^{-1}°C$ respectively.

(i) Which liquid is a good conductor of heat? Why?

(ii) Which liquid is more suitable as a liquid in radiators for cooling? **(ICSE SQP 2018)**

40. A body of mass m_1 of a substance of specific heat capacity c_1, at a temperature t_1 is mixed with another body of mass m_2 of specific heat capacity c_2 at a lower temperature t_2. Deduce an expression for the temperature of the mixture t_3. **(ICSE SQP 2017)**

41. (i) What is the principle of method of mixtures?

(ii) What is the other name given to it?

(iii) Name the law on which the principle is based. **(ICSE 2016)**

42. Specific heat capacity of substance *A* is 3.8 J/gK, whereas the specific heat capacity of substance *B* is 0.4 J/gK.

(i) Which of the two is good conductor of heat?

(ii) How is one led to the above conclusion?

(iii) If substances *A* and *B* are liquid, then which one would be more useful in car radiators? **(ICSE 2014)**

43. How is the heat capacity of the body related to its specific heat capacity? **(ICSE 2013)**

44. A certain amount of heat *Q* will warm 1 g of material *X* by 3°C and 1 g of material *Y* by 4°C. Which material has a higher specific heat capacity? **(ICSE 2013)**

45. (i) Name the liquid which has the highest specific heat capacity.

(ii) Name two factors on which the heat absorbed or given out by a body depends.

(iii) An equal quantity of heat is supplied to two substances *A* and *B*. The substance *A* shows a greater rise in temperature. What can you say about the heat capacity of *A* as compared to that of *B*? **(ICSE 2010)**

46. (i) Define heat capacity of a given body. What is its SI unit?

(ii) What is the relation between heat capacity and specific heat capacity of a substance? **(ICSE 2008)**

47. Explain, why water is used in hot water bottles for fomentation and also as a universal coolant? **(ICSE 2006)**

48. Water falls from a height of 50 m. Calculate the rise in temperature of water, when it strikes the bottom. (Take, $g = 10\ ms^{-2}$, specific heat capacity of water = 4200 J/kg°C) **(ICSE 2005)**

49. (i) Define specific heat capacity of a substance. State its SI unit.

(ii) Give one example of each, where high specific heat capacity of water is used

(a) in cooling (b) as heat resistor. **(ICSE 2002)**

4 Marks Questions

50. A metal piece of mass 420g present at 80°C is dropped in 80g of water present at 20°C in a calorimeter of mass 84g. If the final temperature of the mixture is 30°C, then calculate the specific heat capacity of the metal piece.

[Specific heat capacity of water = 4.2 $Jg^{-1}°C^{-1}$, Specific heat capacity of the calorimeter = 200 $Jkg^{-1}°C^{-1}$] **(ICSE 2022 Sem-II)**

51. Two metals *A* and *B* have specific heat capacities in the ratio 2 : 3. If they are supplied same amount of heat, then **(ICSE 2022 Sem-II)**

(i) Which metal piece will show greater rise in temperature given their masses are the same?

(ii) Which metal piece will have greater mass, if the rise in temperature is the same for both metals?

(iii) If the mass ratio of metal *A* and metal *B* is 3:5, then calculate the ratio in which their temperatures rise.

(iv) If specific heat capacity of metal *A* is 0.26 $Jg^{-1}°C^{-1}$, then calculate the specific heat capacity of metal *B*. **(ICSE SQP 2022 Sem-I)**

52. (i) State two differences between heat capacity and specific heat capacity.

(ii) Give a mathematical relation between heat capacity and specific heat capacity. **(ICSE 2018)**

53. A calorimeter of mass 60 g contains 180 g of water at 29° C. Find the final temperature of the mixture, when 37.2 g of ice at − 10° C is added to it (specific heat capacity of water = 4200 J / kg K,

Latent heat of ice $= 336 \times 10^3$ J/kg

Specific heat capacity of ice = 2100 J/kg K,

Specific heat capacity of the calorimeter $= 0.42\ \text{Jg}^{-1}\text{°C}^{-1}$)

54. (i) How is the transference of heat energy by radiation prevented in a calorimeter?

(ii) You have a choices of three metals *A*, *B* and *C*, of specific heat capacities $900\ \text{J kg}^{-1}\text{°C}^{-1}$, $380\ \text{J kg}^{-1}\text{°C}^{-1}$ and $460\ \text{J kg}^{-1}\text{°C}^{-1}$, respectively. To make a calorimeter, which material will you select? Justify your answer.

(ICSE 2017)

55. A copper vessel of mass 100 g contains 150 g of water at 50°C. How much ice is needed to cool it to 5°C?

(Take, specific heat capacity of copper $= 0.4\ \text{Jg}^{-1}\ \text{°C}^{-1}$

Specific heat capacity of water $= 4.2\ \text{Jg}^{-1}\text{°C}^{-1}$

Specific latent heat of fusion of ice $= 336\ \text{Jg}^{-1}$)

(ICSE 2016)

56. A refrigerator converts 100 g of water at 20°C to ice at −10°C in 35 min.

Calculate the average rate of heat extraction in terms of watts.

(Take, specific heat capacity of ice $= 2.1\ \text{J g}^{-1}\ \text{°C}^{-1}$

Specific heat capacity of water $= 4.2\ \text{Jg}^{-1}\text{°C}^{-1}$

Specific latent heat of fusion of ice $= 336\ \text{J g}^{-1}$)

(ICSE 2015)

57. A calorimeter of mass 50 g and specific heat capacity $0.42\ \text{J g}^{-1}\text{°C}^{-1}$ contains some mass of water at 20°C. A metal piece of mass 20 g at 100°C is dropped into the calorimeter. After stirring, the final temperature of the mixture is found to be 22°C. Find the mass of water used in the calorimeter.

(Take, specific heat capacity of the metal piece $= 0.3\ \text{J g}^{-1}\text{°C}^{-1}$, specific heat capacity of water $= 4.2\ \text{J g}^{-1}\text{°C}^{-1}$)

(ICSE 2013)

58. In a laboratory experiment to measure specific heat capacity of copper, 0.02 kg of water at 70°C was poured into a copper calorimeter with a stirrer of mass 0.16 kg initially at 15°C. After stirring, the final temperature reached to 45°C. Specific heat of water is taken as 4200 J/kg°C.

(i) What is the quantity of heat released per kg of water per 1°C fall in temperature?

(ii) Calculate the heat energy released by water in the experiment in cooling from 70°C to 45°C.

(iii) Assuming that the heat released by water is entirely used to raise the temperature of calorimeter from 15°C to 45°C, calculate the specific heat capacity of copper. **(ICSE 2007)**

59. A piece of iron of mass 2.0 kg has a thermal capacity of 966 J/°C.

(i) How much heat is needed to warm it by 15°C?

(ii) What is its specific heat capacity in SI unit?

(ICSE 2006)

Explanations

1. (d) $\Delta Q = C' \Delta T$

Heat capacity, $C' = \dfrac{\Delta Q}{\Delta T}$

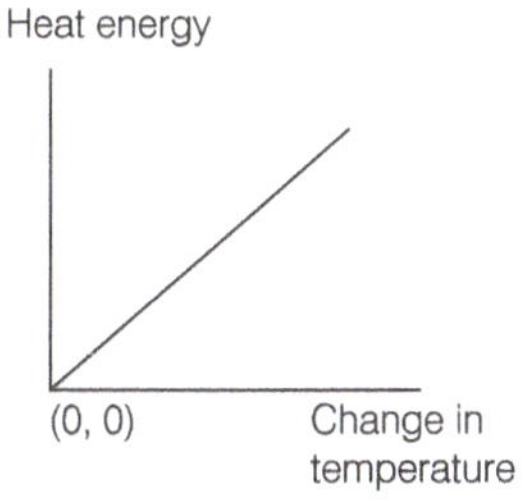

Hence, the slope of this graph will give heat capacity.

2. (a) Liquid *P* with specific heat capacity $4000\ \text{Jkg}^{-1}\text{K}^{-1}$.

High specific heat capacity means, gain a great amount of heat to get hot as compared to other liquids.

3. (c) Heat gained $= m \cdot c \cdot \Delta T$

$$4000 = 1000\text{g} \times c \times 1\text{° C}$$

$$4\ \text{Jg}^{-1}\text{°C}^{-1} = c$$

$\Rightarrow$ Specific heat capacity of water $= 4\ \text{Jg}^{-1}\text{°C}^{-1}$

4. (d) Water is used in car radiators as coolant because water becomes hot by gaining a large amount of heat due to its high specific heat capacity.

5. (c) 1 kg water absorbs 4200 J heat to increase its temperature by 1 K.

   Specific heat is the amount of heat required to raise the temperature of unit mass of a substance by 1 K or 1° C.

6. The high specific heat capacity of water, which makes it an effective coolant.

7. The principle of calorimetry states that, "when two or more bodies at different temperatures are brought into thermal contact and if no heat is allowed to escape to the surroundings, then the total heat lost by hot bodies must be equal to the total heat gained by cold bodies".

8. The principle of calorimetry is based on law of conservation of energy.

9. Latent heat of ice $(L_i) = 336000 \text{ Jkg}^{-1}$

   Specific heat of the water $(C_w) = 4200 \text{ Jkg}^{-1}$

   Heat absorbed = Heat absorbed from ice at 0° C to water at 0° C + Heat absorbed from water at 0° C to water at 60° C.

   So, heat absorbed $= mL_i + mC_wT$

   $$= 200 \times 336000 + 200 \times 4200 \times 60$$
   $$= 67200000 + 50400000$$
   $$= 11,76,00,000 = 1.76 \times 10^8 \text{ J}$$

10. Ratio of masses of blocks P and Q,

   $$m_P : m_Q = 2:1$$
   $$\Rightarrow \quad \frac{m_Q}{m_P} = \frac{1}{2} \quad \ldots \text{(i)}$$

   We know that, heat supplied is given as

   $$H = ms\Delta T$$

   where, s is specific heat.

   But $$H_P = H_Q$$
   $$\Rightarrow \quad m_P s_P \Delta T = m_Q s_Q \Delta T$$
   $$\Rightarrow \quad \frac{s_P}{s_Q} = \frac{m_Q}{m_P} = \frac{1}{2} \quad \text{[from Eq. (i)]}$$
   $$\Rightarrow \quad s_P : s_Q = 1:2$$

11. The water does not get heated up so quickly as compared to stone. It is because water requires about five times more heat energy than stone for the same rise in temperature, i.e. water has higher specific heat capacity than stone.

12. (i) Heat

   (ii) The SI unit of heat is joule and it is represented by J.

   1 cal = 4.186 J

13. The substance B is a good conductor of heat comparative to the substance A, because it needs less amount of heat to get heated quickly.

14. (i) The SI unit of temperature is kelvin. To convert temperature in degree celsius to kelvin 273.15 is added to celsius. $T(\text{in K}) = T(°\text{C}) + 273.15$

   (ii) Liquid X will be water as water has a high value of specific heat capacity.

15. Copper is preferably used to making of a calorimeter because it is a good conductor of heat and it takes the least amount of heat from its contents to attain the temperature of the content because specific heat capacity of the copper is quite low as compared to other metals.

16. Refer to text on page No-174 and 175.

17. The quantity of heat given to any substance depends on its mass m, the change in temperature ΔT and the nature of substance which is being warmed. To change the temperature of substance, a given quantity of heat is absorbed or rejected by it, which is characterised by a quantity known as heat capacity or thermal capacity.

   So, thermal capacity is defined as the total amount of heat required to raise the temperature of a body by 1° C. It is represented by S.

   $$\text{Heat capacity } (C) = \frac{\text{Heat supplied to the body } (Q)}{\text{Change in temperature } (\Delta T)}$$

   Its SI unit is joule/°C or joule/K. Its older unit is cal/°C or cal/K or kcal/°C.

18. Thinner base pans definitely transmit heat from the burner to the food, as the base is made up of metal, which is good conductor of heat. But, when it comes to even cooking and maintaining regular heating without hot spots around the pans, it is convenient to use thicker base pans.

   Also, it has more thermal mass and it also retain its temperature, i.e. the pan will stay at high temperature above and beyond the amount of heat that can immediately supplied by the heat source.

19. According to the question,

   Mass of solid = 50 g,
   Temperature of solid = 150° C,
   Mass of water = 100 g
   Temperature of water = 11° C,
   Final temperature of mixture = 20°C
   Specific heat of water = 1 cal/g°C
   Let specific heat capacity of solid = x

According to the principle of thermal equilibrium,

Q_L (heat lost) $= Q_C$ (heat gained)

$\Rightarrow 50 \times x \times (150-20) = 100 \times 1 \times (20-11)$

$$\Rightarrow \quad x = \frac{100 \times 9}{50 \times 130}$$

$\therefore$ Specific heat of solid $= \frac{9}{65} = 0.138$ cal/g/°C

Specific heat capacity of solid

$$= \frac{0.138}{4.2 \text{ J/g°C}} = 0.033 \text{ J/g°C}$$

20. (i) The heat capacity of the body is 60 K. It means that 60J of heat is required to raise the temperature of the body by 1°C. The temperature change is the difference between the final and initial temperature.

(ii) The specific heat capacity of lead is 130J/kg-K. It means that 130J of heat is required to raise the temperature of 1kg of mass by 1°C. The temperature change is the difference between the final and the initial temperature.

Concept Enhancer Heat capacity depends on mass, whereas specific heat capacity is a mass independent quantity.

21. Heat absorbed by a body depends on

(i) mass of the body.

(ii) specific heat of the body.

22. Given, mass $m = 50$ g

$\Delta T = 327°\text{C} - 27°\text{C} = 300°\text{C}$

Heat $Q = 2400$ J

As we know that, $Q = mc\,\Delta T$

$$\Rightarrow \quad c = \frac{Q}{m\,\Delta T} = \frac{2400}{50 \times 300} = 0.16 \text{ J/g°C}$$

23. Specific heat capacity is defined for the unit mass of the body, whereas heat capacity is defined as for entire mass of the body.

24. According to principle of calorimeter,

Heat gained = Heat lost

So, heat gained $= 150 \times 4.2 \times (25-20)$ ...(i)

Heat lost $= 60 \times c \times (100-25)$ ...(ii)

So, from Eqs. (i) and (ii), we get

$60 \times c \times 75 = 150 \times 4.2 \times 5$

$$\Rightarrow \quad c = \frac{150 \times 4.2 \times 5}{60 \times 75} = 0.7 \text{ J/g°C}$$

25. Differentiate between heat and temperature are given below

Heat	Temperature
It is the internal energy of a body.	It is the degree of hotness and coldness of a body.
Its SI unit is joule.	Its SI unit is kelvin.
Other unit of heat is cal or kcal	Its other unit is °C and °F

26. **Calorimetry** It is the principle through which we can understand that heat flows from higher temperature to lower temperature and heat lost by a body is equal to the heat gained by another body when kept in contact.

27. As given in question and from principle of calorimety,

Heat lost by hot water = Heat gained by cold water

So, $200 \times 4.2 \times (80 - T) = 300 \times 4.2 \times (T - 10)$

where, T is final temperature.

$\Rightarrow \quad 2(80 - T) = 3(T - 10)$

$160 - 2T = 3T - 30$

$\Rightarrow \quad 5T = 190 \Rightarrow T = 38°\text{C}$

28. (i) High specific heat capacity of water is used in hot water bottles for fomentation.

(ii) High specific heat capacity of water is used for cooling radiators in cars.

29. As from principle of calorimeter,

Heat gained = Heat lost

So, heat lost by hot water = heat gained by cold water + heat gained by vessel

$\Rightarrow 40 \times 4.2 \times 30 = 50 \times 4.2 \times 10 + (\text{Heat capacity} \times 10)$

$\Rightarrow$ Heat capacity

$$= \frac{(40 \times 4.2 \times 30) - (50 \times 4.2 \times 10)}{10}$$

$= 294$ J/°C

30. Let mass of hot water be m kg, so mass of cold water will be $= 3m$ kg

Let temperature of hot water is t°C.

So, by principle of calorimetry,

Heat taken by cold water = Heat given by hot water

$mc\,\Delta t = 3\,mc\,\Delta t$

$\Rightarrow m \times c \times (t - 20) = 3\,m \times c \times (20 - 10)$

$\Rightarrow \quad t - 20 = 3 \times 10$

$\Rightarrow \quad t = 50°\text{C}$

31. The two factors by which copper is preferred for calorimeter are

(i) It has low specific heat than other metal.

(ii) It takes least amount of heat from its contents to attain the temperature of the contents.

32. (i) Because water has high specific heat capacity (4200 J/kg°C), so land cools faster than water.

(ii) As steam losses considerable amount of heat and converts into hot water. So, steam pipes warm a building more effectively in colder countries.

33.

Substance	Mass	SHC	Initial temp	Final temp = 40° C
Metal piece	?(*m*)	? (*c*)	120° C	80° C
Calorimeter	80g	$0.4\ Jg^{-1}\ °C^{-1}$	30° C	$\theta_F = 120 - 40 = 80°C$
Water	200g	$4.2\ Jg^{-1}°C^{-1}$	30° C	$\theta_R = (40 - 30) = 10°C$

Let C_1 is the thermal capacity of metal piece such that $C_1 = mc$.

Heat given out by metal piece

$$= mCQ_f = C_1 \times 80°C$$

Heat absorbed by calorimeter

$$= m_c Q_R = 80 \times 0.4 \times 10 = 320\ J$$

Heat absorbed by water

$$= mcQ_R = 200 \times 4.2 \times 10 = 8400\ J$$

∴ Total heat absorbed

$$= (8400 + 320)\ J = 8720\ J$$

By the principle of calorimetry,

Heat given out by metal = Total heat absorbed

$$\Rightarrow \quad C_1 \times 80°C = 8720\ J$$

$$C_1 = \frac{8720\ J}{80°C} = 109\ J/°C$$

34. (i) As copper has low specific heat capacity, so it can be used as a material for a calorimeter.

(ii) Thermal capacity $= m \times c$

$$= 40 \times 4.2\ Jg^{-1}°C^{-1}$$

$$= 168\ Jg^{-1}°C^{-1}$$

35. (i) Before and during the hailstorm, there is plenty amount of heat present in the atmosphere. But after the hailstorm, ice absorbs heat energy required for melting from the surrounding.

So, the temperature of surroundings fall and we feel cold.

(ii) The given statement is false as the heat absorbed also depends on the mass of the two bodies.

Concept Enhancer Hailstroms typically occur in areas with thunderstorm activity, particularly in summer months. They are most common in regions with a high frequency of severe thunderstorm, such as great plains of the unified states.

36. (i) and (ii) Refer to text on page no. 174 and 175.

(iii) Refer to text on page no. 175.

[Relationship between heat capacity and specific heat capacity].

37. (i) Calorimetry is the science associated with determining the change in energy of a system by measuring the heat exchanged with surroundings.

(ii) Copper and wood

(iii) It is because copper is a good conductor of heat, so it soon acquires the temperature of its contents and thin copper sheet has low heat capacity, so it takes only small amount of heat from its contents.

38. Given, $M_w = \frac{170}{1000}$ kg, $s_w = 4200\ J\ kg^{-1}C^{-1}$,

$$\Delta T = 5°C,\ L_f = 336000\ J/kg$$

According to the principle of calorimetry,

amount of heat given by water = amount of heat absorbed by ice

$$M_w S_w\ \Delta T = M_{ice} \times L_f + M_{ice} \times S_w \times \Delta T'$$

$$\frac{170}{1000} \times 4200 \times (50 - 5) = M_{ice} \times 336000 + M_{ice} \times 4200 \times (5 - 0)$$

$$32130 = 357000 \times M_{ice}$$

$$M_{ice} = \frac{32130}{357000} = 0.09\ kg$$

$$M_{ice} = 90\ g$$

39. (i) Liquid *A* is good conductor of heat as it has low specific heat capacity.

(ii) Liquid *B* is more suitable as a liquid in radiators for cooling as it has high specific heat capacity.

40. Heat is lost by body at higher temperature

Heat lost $= mc\Delta t = m_1 c_1 (t_1 - t_3)$

Heat will be gained by body at lower temperature.

Heat gained $= mc\Delta t = m_2 c_2 (t_3 - t_2)$

According to principle of calorimetry,

Heat lost = Heat gained

$$m_1c_1(t_1 - t_3) = m_2c_2(t_3 - t_2)$$
$$m_1c_1t_1 + m_2c_2t_2 = (m_1c_1 + m_2c_2)t_3$$
$$t_3 = \frac{m_1c_1 + m_2c_2t_2}{m_1c_1 + m_2c_2}$$

41. (i) According to the principle of mixtures, heat lost by the hot body must be equal to heat gained by the cold body, provided there is no heat loss to the surroundings.

(ii) The other name of principle of mixtures is principle of calorimetry.

(iii) Principle of mixture is based on the principle of conservation of energy.

42. (i) As the specific heat capacity of *B* is much less than *A*, so *B* is good conductor of heat.

(ii) Since, the specific heat capacity of *B* is less than *A*. So, *B* is good conductor of heat.

(iii) Since, the specific heat capacity of *A* is higher than that of *B*, so it can absorb more heat, therefore it is useful in car radiator.

43. Heat capacity (Q) of the body is related as follows

$$Q = mc\,\Delta t$$

(where, c = Specific heat capacity,
m = Mass of body,
Δt = Change in temperature)

44. As we know that,

$$\text{Specific heat } c = \frac{Q}{m\,\Delta T} \Rightarrow c \propto \frac{1}{\Delta T}$$

So, material *X* has a higher specific heat capacity than *Y*.

45. (i) Water has highest specific heat capacity.

(ii) Factors on which heat given out or absorbed depends upon

(a) Temperature of the body with respect to surrounding.

(b) Specific heat capacity of the body.

(iii) As substance *A* has greater rise in temperature, so heat capacity of *A* is less than heat capacity of *B*.

46. (i) Refer to text on pages no 174 and 175.

(ii) The relation between heat capacity and specific heat capacity is

Heat capacity = Mass × Specific heat capacity

47. Since, water has large specific heat capacity, so it is used hot water bottles for fomentation. Water is used as a universal coolant, because it has large specific heat capacity. So, it can absorb large amount of heat.

48. From energy conservation,

Heat energy = Potential energy

$$mc\,\Delta t = mgh$$
$$\Rightarrow \quad c\,\Delta t = gh$$
$$\Rightarrow \quad \Delta t = \frac{gh}{c} = \frac{10 \times 50}{4200}$$
$$= \frac{5}{42} = 0.119°\text{C} = 0.12°\text{C (approx)}$$

49. (i) Specific heat capacity can be defined as the total amount of heat required to raise the temperature of unit mass of substance by 1°C.

Its SI unit is J/kg°C.

(ii) (a) Water is used as cooler.

(b) Heat resistor is used in car radiator.

50. Heat energy given by metal piece,

$$= m \cdot c \cdot \Delta T_1$$
$$= 420 \times c \times (80 - 30) = 21000 \times c$$

Heat energy gained by water,

$$= m_w \times c_w \times \Delta T_2$$
$$= 80 \times 4.2 \times (30 - 20) = 3360\text{ J}$$

Heat energy gained by calorimeter

$$= m_c \times c_c \times \Delta T_2$$
$$= 84 \times \frac{200}{1000} \times (30 - 20) = 168\text{ J}$$

By principle of calorimeter, Heat lost = Heat gained

Heat energy given by metal

= Heat gained by water + Heat gained by calorimeter.

$21000 \times c = 3360 + 168$

Specific Heat, $c = 0.168\text{ Jg}^{-1}°\text{C}^{-1}$

Common Mistake The specific heat capacity of a substance may vary with tempeature. It is important to take this into account when solving problems that involve temperature changes.

51. (i) The metal piece which has specific heat is less will show greater rise of temperature. So, in this case, the metal piece *A* will show greater rise of temperature.

(ii) The metal piece which has specific heat is less will have greater mass. So, the metal piece *A* will have greater mass.

(iii) $m_Ac_A\,\Delta t_A = m_Bc_B\,\Delta t_B$

or $$\frac{m_A}{m_B} \times \frac{c_A}{c_B} = \frac{\Delta t_B}{\Delta t_A}$$

or $\frac{3}{5} \times \frac{2}{3} = \frac{\Delta t_B}{\Delta t_A}$ or $\frac{\Delta t_B}{\Delta t_A} = \frac{2}{5}$

$\therefore \quad \frac{\Delta t_A}{\Delta t_B} = \frac{5}{2}$

(iv) $\frac{c_A}{c_B} = \frac{2}{3}$

$\therefore \quad c_B = \frac{3}{2} \times 0.26 = 0.39 \text{ Jg}^{-1}\,^\circ\text{C}^{-1}$

52. (i)

Heat capacity	**Specific heat capacity**
It is defined as the total amount of heat required to raise the temperature of a body by 1 °C.	It can be defined as the total amount of heat energy required to raise the temperature of unit mass by 1 °C.
Heat capacity $= \frac{\text{Heat supplied to the body}}{\text{Change in temperature}}$	Specific heat capacity $= \frac{\text{Heat energy supplied}}{\text{Mass of the body} \times \text{Change in temperature}}$

(ii) The relation between specific heat capacity and heat capacity is heat capacity = mass × specific heat capacity.

53. Final temperature of mixture be T° C

Heat lost by calorimeter $= 60 \times 0.42 \times (29 - T)$

Heat lost by water $= 180 \times 4.2 \times (29 - T)$

Total heat lost

$= 180 \times 4.2 \times (29 - T) + 6 \times 4.2 \times (29 - T)$

$= 186 \times 4.2\,(29 - T)$

Heat gained by ice is given by

$= 37.2 \times 2.1 \times 10 + 37.2 \times 336 + 37.2 \times 4.2 \times (T - 0)$

$= 37.2\,(21 + 336 + 4.2\,T)$

According to principle of mixtures

$186 \times 4.2\,(29 - T) = 37.2 \times (357 + 4.2\,T)$

$\Rightarrow 781.2\,(29 - T) = 37.2\,(357 + 4.2\,T)$

$\Rightarrow \quad 21\,(29 - T) = 372\,(4.2\,T)$

$\Rightarrow \quad 609 - 21\,T = 357 + 4.2\,T$

$\Rightarrow \quad 252 = 25.2\,T$

$\therefore \quad T = 10^\circ$C

54. (i) Calorimeter surface (outer) is highly polished, so that to minimise the heat loss due to radiation as polished metallic surfaces are poor absorber and poor emitter of heat. Calorimeters are made up of copper, which has highly polished surface.

(ii) We shall select C whose specific heat capacity is 460 J/kg°C to make a calorimeter, because of its low specific heat capacity. Specific heat capacity means the total amount of heat required to raise the temperature of unit mass by 1°C. For C, the heat required is less to increase temperature of calorimeter. Hence, C should be selected.

55. According to question,

Mass of Cu vessel $= 100$ g

Mass of water $= 150$ g

Initial temperature of water $= 50^\circ$ C

Final temperature of water $= 5^\circ$ C

From principle of calorimetry,

Heat gained by ice = Heat lost by Cu vessel and water

So, $M \times 336 = (100 \times 0.4) + (150 \times 4.2 \times 45)$

$= 40 + 28350$

$\Rightarrow \quad M = \frac{40 + 28350}{336}$ (where, M = Mass of ice)

$= \frac{28390}{336} = 84.49$ g

84.49 g ice is required.

56. Here, $m = 100$ g, $t_1 = 20$ °C $t_2 = -10$°C

Heat released

$= mc_w\,(t_1 - 0) + m\,L_{\text{ice}} + mc_{\text{ice}}\,(0 - t_2)$

$Q = (100 \times 4.2 \times 20) + (100 \times 336) + (100 \times 2.1 \times 10)$

$= 8400 + 33600 + 2100 = 44100$ J

$\therefore$ Power, $P = \frac{Q}{t} = \frac{44100}{35 \times 60} \Rightarrow P = 21$ W

57. As from the question,

Amount of heat given by metal $= mc\Delta T_1$

$= 20 \times 0.3 \times (100 - 22) = 468$ J

Amount of heat gained by water

$= m_w \times c_w \times \Delta t_2$

$= m_w \times 4.2 \times (22 - 20) = 8.4 m_w$ J

Heat energy gained by calorimeter

$= m_c \times c_c \times \Delta T_2$

$= 50 \times 0.42 \times (22 - 20) = 42$ J

Heat loss = Heat gained

$468 = 8.4 m_w + 42$

$m_w = \frac{468 - 42}{8.4} = 50.7$ g

(i) Quantity of heat released per kg of water per °C fall in temperature is given by 4200° J/kg°C.

(ii) Quantity of water released on cooling is given by $Q = mc\Delta t$

$= 0.02 \times 4200 \times 25 = 2100$ J

(iii) By assuming no loss of heat by principle of calorimetry,

Heat gained = Heat taken up by calorimeter

So, $2100 \text{ J} = 0.16 \times s \times 30$

$$\Rightarrow \quad s = \frac{2100}{0.16 \times 30} = 437.5 \text{ J/kg°C}$$

59. As given in question, mass $m = 2$ kg

Thermal capacity = 966 J/°C

Rise in temperature $\Delta t = 15°C$

(i) Thermal capacity $= \dfrac{\text{Heat required}}{\Delta t}$

So, heat required $= 966 \times 15 = 14490$ J

(ii) As we know, specific heat capacity

$$= \frac{\text{amount of heat}}{\text{mass} \times \Delta t} = \frac{14490}{2 \times 15} = \frac{14490}{30}$$

$= 483$ J/kg°C

TOPIC 2

Latent Heat

Interconversion of States of Matter

In your daily life, you come across various substances which exist in three states, i.e. solid, liquid and gas. e.g. Water, wax, ghee, etc. Water is the most commonly observed example that exists as ice (solid), water (liquid) as well as steam (gas). It means that the three states of matter are interconvertible.

The phenomenon of change of matter from one state to another and back to original state by altering the conditions of temperature and pressure is called the interconversion of states of matter.

Latent Heat

It is the hidden amount of heat that is given out or taken by the unit mass of any substance to change its state without the change in temperature.

Specific Latent Heat of Fusion

It can be defined as the amount of heat required to convert a unit mass of solid into liquid without any change in the temperature.

Mathematical expression

$$\text{Specific latent heat } (L) = \frac{\text{Heat given } (Q)}{\text{Total mass of the substance } (m)}$$

i.e. $Q = mL$

Latent heat of fusion of ice is $3.36 \times 10^5 \text{ J kg}^{-1}$.

Specific Latent Heat of Vaporisation

It is defined as the amount of heat required to convert a unit mass of liquid into vapour without any change in temperature.

Mathematical expression

Specific latent heat of vaporisation (L)

$$= \frac{\text{Heat given } (Q)}{\text{Total mass of substance } (m)}$$

i.e. $Q = mL$

The SI unit of specific latent heat of fusion/vaporisation is same and is J/kg. Other units of specific latent heat are J/g, cal/g, kcal/kg, etc. Latent heat of vaporisation of water is $2.25 \times 10^6 \text{ J kg}^{-1}$.

Heating Curve for Water

To evaluate the heating curve for water, the following steps must be followed first

(i) First of all, take some water in a flask (at room temperature nearly about 25°C) and suspend a thermometer in it.

(ii) By keeping the flask over a bunsen burner, try to heat it and record its temperature after every half minute till the time, it starts boiling and the flask contains vapours.

Now, by taking the temperature along Y-axis and the time on X-axis, the graph can be plotted. It is called the heating curve for water.

If we see the graph (given below), we will observe that water is at 25°C at C (i.e. room temperature) and the water in a liquid state rises continuously in part CD with the absorption of heat energy.

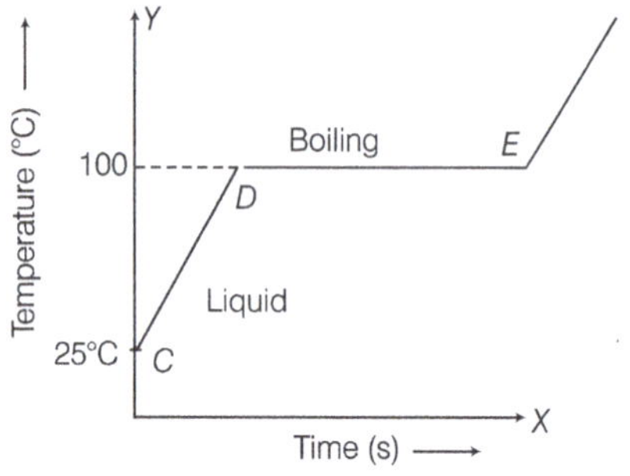

Heating curve of water

At point D, the boiling starts and the temperature does not rise further as shown in part DE.

It can be explained as, at point D, the water starts to convert into gaseous state from liquid state, so it require latent heat of vaporisation, all the heat being provided here is used in converting the state of water from liquid to gas, so temperature does not rise till all the water converts into vapour.

So, temperature along DE remains constant. Again, from point E, temperature starts to increase, because the heat being provided now is not used as latent energy (there is no change of state now), so it increases the temperature.

PYQs Previous Years Questions

1 Mark Questions

1. During melting of ice at 0°C, the **(ICSE 2024)**
   (a) energy is released and temperature remains constant
   (b) energy is absorbed and temperature remains constant
   (c) energy is released and temperature decreases
   (d) energy is absorbed and temperature increases

2. Choose the correct statement.
   Latent heat absorbed **(ICSE SQP 2023)**
   (a) is independent of the mass of the substance.
   (b) is directly proportional to the increase in the temperature of the substance.
   (c) is directly proportional to the specific heat capacity of the substance.
   (d) is directly proportional to the specific latent heat of the substance.

3. 200 g of ice at 0° C needs _____ heat to melt. [Specific latent heat of ice = 336000 J kg^{-1}] **(ICSE SQP 2022 Sem-II)**
   (a) 6720 J (b) 67200 J (c) 672000 J (d) 67.2 J

2 Marks Questions

4. How much heat is required to convert 500 g of ice at 0°C to water at 0°C .The latent heat of fusion of ice 330 Jg^{-1}. **(ICSE 2024)**

5. From the graph of heating curve given below, state the melting point and boiling point of the substance. **(SQP 2022 Sem-II)**

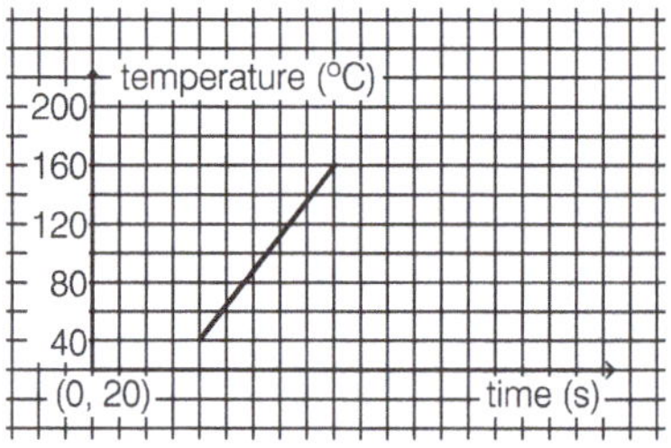

6. (i) State whether the specific heat capacity of a substance remains same, when its state changes from solid to liquid.
   (ii) Give one example to support your answer. **(ICSE 2019)**

7. A solid metal weighing 150 g melts at its melting point of 800 °C by providing heat at the rate of 100 W. The time taken for it to completely melt at the same temperature is 4 min. What is the specific latent heat of fusion of the metal? **(ICSE 2018)**

8. Calculate the mass of ice required to lower the temperature of 300 g of water at 40°C to 0°C. **(ICSE 2016)**

9. Rishi is surprised, when he sees water boiling at 115°C in a container. Give reasons as to why water can boil at the above temperature. (Take, specific latent heat of ice = 336 J/g, specific heat capacity of water = 4.2 J / g°C) **(ICSE 2015)**

10. How much heat energy is released, when 5 g of water at 20°C changes to ice at 0°C? **(ICSE 2013)**

11. Explain, why the weather becomes very cold after a hailstorm? **(ICSE 2011)**

12. Why do pieces of ice added to a drink, cool it much faster than ice cold water added to it? **(ICSE 2009)**

13. Why are burns caused by steam more severe than those caused by boiling water at the same temperature? **(ICSE 2007)**

14. Calculate the amount of heat released, when 5.0 g of water at 20°C is changed into ice at 0°C. (Take, specific heat capacity of water = 4.2 J/g°C, specific latent heat of fusion of ice = 336 J/g) **(ICSE 2006)**

15. Why does the temperature of the surroundings start falling, when the ice of a frozen lake starts melting? **(ICSE 2005)**

16. Calculate the heat energy that will be released, when 5.0 kg of steam at 100°C condenses to form water at 100°C. Express your answer in SI unit. (Take, specific latent heat of vaporisation of steam is 2268 J/kg) **(ICSE 2005)**

17. Explain, why one feels icecream at 0°C colder than water at 0°C? **(ICSE 2001)**

3 Marks Questions

18. 85g of water at 30°C is cooled to 5°C by adding certain mass of ice, find the mass of ice required.
[Specific heat capacity of water = 4.2 $Jg^{-1}\,°C^{-1}$.
Specific latent heat of fusion = 336 J/g **(ICSE 2024)**

19. (a) Why does it become pleasantly warm when the lakes start freezing.
(b) Water freezes to form ice. What change would you expect in the average kinetic energy of the molecules?
(c) Which will contain more heat energy 1 g of ice at 0° C or 1 g water at 0°C? **(ICSE 2024)**

20. The diagram below shows a cooling curve for a substance
(i) State the temperatures at which the substance condenses and solidifies respectively.
(ii) The temperature range in which the substance is in liquid state. **(ICSE 2023)**

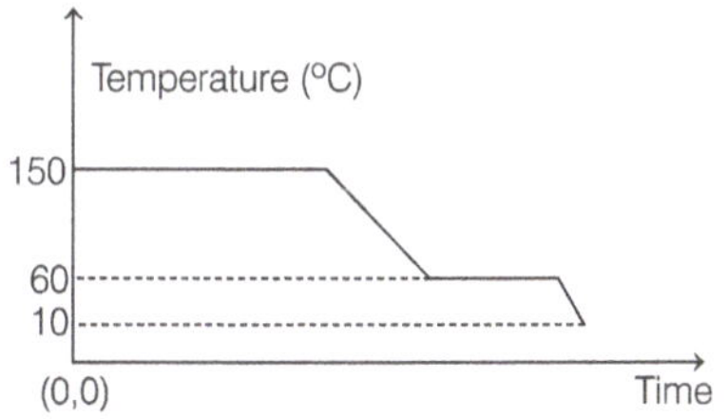

(iii) Why do we prefer ice to ice-cold water for cooling a drink?

21. The diagram below shows a cooling curve for 200 g of water. The heat is extracted at the rate of 100 Js^{-1}. **(ICSE 2022 Sem-II)**

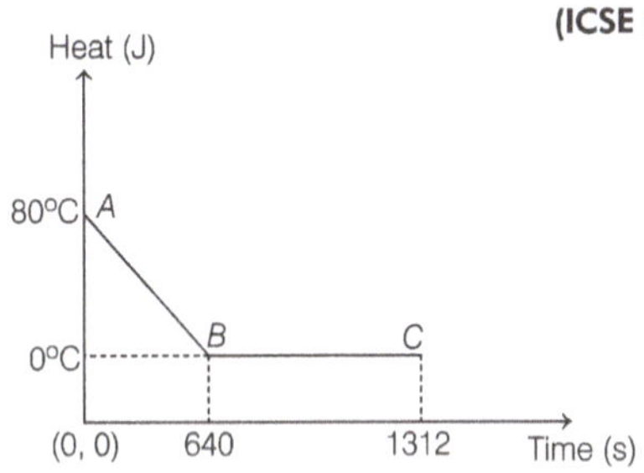

Calculate
(i) specific heat capacity of water.
(ii) heat released in the region *BC*.

22. (i) Which will absorb more heat, 10 g of ice at 0° C or 10 g of water at 0° C?
(ii) For the same mass of ice and ice-cold water, does ice produce more cooling than ice-cold water? **(ICSE 2022 Sem-II)**

23. The diagram below shows the change of phases of a substance on a temperature *versus* time graph on heating the substance at a constant rate. **(ICSE 2020)**

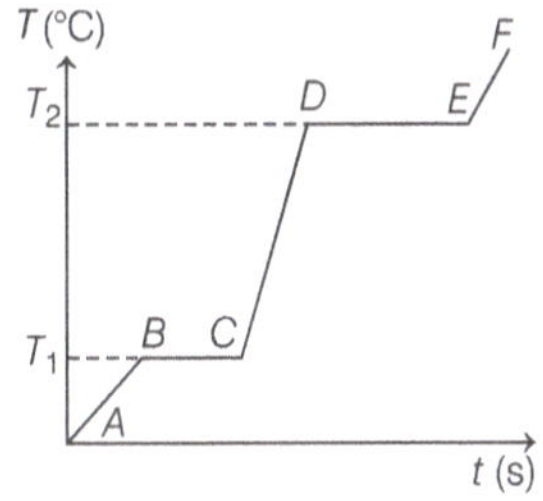

(i) Why is the slope of *CD* is less than slope of *AB*?
(ii) What is the boiling and melting points of the substance? **(ICSE 2020)**

24. The melting point of naphthalene is 80 °C and the room temperature is 30°C. A sample of liquid naphthalene at 100°C is cooled down to the room temperature. Draw a temperature-time graph to represent this cooling. In this graph, mark the region which corresponds to the freezing process. **(ICSE 2019)**

25. (i) Heat supplied to a solid changes it into liquid. What is this change in phase called?
(ii) During the phase change, does the average kinetic energy of the molecules of the substance increase?
(iii) What is the energy absorbed during the phase change called? **(ICSE 2018)**

26. (i) Define specific latent heat of fusion of ice.

(ii) What happens to the heat supplied to the substance when the heat supplied causes no change in the temperature of the substance?

27. Calculate the mass of ice needed to cool 150 g of water contained in a calorimeter of mass 50 g at 32°C such that the final temperature is 5°C.

(Take, specific heat capacity of calorimeter = 0.4 J/g°C,

Specific heat capacity of water = 4.2 J/g°C

and latent heat capacity of ice = 330 J/g) **(ICSE 2017)**

28. Calculate the amount of heat given out while 400 g of water at 30° C is cooled and converted into ice at −2° C.

Specific heat capacity of water = 4200 J / kg K

Specific heat capacity of ice = 2100 J / kg K

Specific latent heat of fusion of ice = 336000 J / kg **(ICSE SQP 2017)**

29. Some ice is heated at a constant rate and its temperature is recorded after every few seconds, till steam is formed at 100°C. Draw a temperature-time graph to represent the change. Label the two phase changes in your graph. **(ICSE 2016)**

30. It is observed that the temperature of the surrounding starts falling, when the ice in a frozen lake starts melting. Give a reason for the observation. **(ICSE 2013, 08)**

31. (i) Write an expression for the heat energy liberated by a hot body.

(ii) Some heat is provided to a body to raise its temperature by 25°C. What will be the corresponding rise in temperature of the body as shown on the kelvin scale?

(iii) What happens to the average kinetic energy of the molecules as ice melts at 0°C? **(ICSE 2012)**

32. A piece of ice at 0°C is heated at a constant rate and its temperature recorded at regular intervals till steam is formed at 100°C. Draw a temperature-time graph to represent the change in phase. Label the different parts of your graph. **(ICSE 2012)**

33. (i) What happens to the heat supplied to a substance, when the heat supplied causes no change in the temperature of the substance?

(ii) When 1 g of ice at 0°C melts to form 1 g of water at 0°C, then is the latent heat absorbed by the ice or given out by it? **(ICSE 2011)**

34. State in brief, the meaning of each of the following

(i) The heat capacity of a body is 50 $J°C^{-1}$.

(ii) The specific latent heat of fusion of ice is 336000 $J\ kg^{-1}$.

(iii) The specific heat capacity of copper is 0.4 $J g^{-1} °C^{-1}$. **(ICSE 2009)**

35. (i) What is meant by specific heat capacity of a substance?

(ii) Why does the heat supplied to a substance during its change of state not cause any rise in its temperature? **(ICSE 2007)**

4 Marks Questions

36. A piece of ice of mass 60 g is dropped into 140 g of water at 50°C. Calculate the final temperature of water when all the ice has melted.

(Assume, no heat is lost to the surrounding)

Take, specific heat capacity of water = 4.2 $J\ g^{-1}K^{-1}$

and specific latent heat of fusion of ice = 336 Jg^{-1}) **(ICSE 2020)**

37. 104 g of water at 30°C is taken in a calorimeter made of copper of mass 42 g. When a certain mass of ice at 0°C is added to it, the final steady temperature of the mixture after the ice has melted, was found to be 10°C. Find the mass of ice added.

[Take, specific heat capacity of water = 4.2 $Jg^{-1}\,°C^{-1}$;
Specific latent heat of fusion of ice = 336 Jg^{-1}; Specific heat capacity of copper = 0.4$Jg^{-1}\,°C^{-1}$.] **(ICSE 2019)**

38. Heat energy is supplied at a constant rate to 100 g of ice at 0°C. The ice is converted into water at 0°C in 2 min. How much time will be required to raise the temperature of water from 0°C to 20°C? (Take, specific heat capacity of water = 4.2 $J\ g^{-1}°C^{-1}$, latent heat of ice = 336 J/g) **(ICSE 2014)**

39. 40 g of ice at 0°C is used to bring down the temperature of a certain mass of water at 60°C to 10°C. Find the mass of water used.

(Take, specific heat capacity of water $= 4200 \text{ J kg}^{-1}\text{°C}^{-1}$, specific latent heat of fusion of ice $= 336 \times 10^3 \text{ J kg}^{-1}$) **(ICSE 2012)**

> **KEY idea**
> To know mass of the water, you should use principle of calorimetry.

40. 250 g of water at 30°C is present in a copper vessel of mass 50 g. Calculate the mass of ice required to bring down the temperature of the vessel and its contents to 5°C. (Take, specific latent heat of fusion of ice $= 336 \times 10^3 \text{ J kg}^{-1}$, specific heat capacity of copper vessel $= 400 \text{ J kg}^{-1}\text{°C}^{-1}$, specific heat capacity of water $= 4200 \text{ J kg}^{-1}\text{°C}^{-1}$) **(ICSE 2011)**

41. (i) Define the term specific latent heat of fusion of a substance.

(ii) What energy change would you expect to take place in the molecules of a substance when it undergoes

(a) a change in its temperature?

(b) a change in its state without any change in its temperature? **(ICSE 2010)**

42. 50 g of ice at 0°C is added to 300 g of a liquid at 30°C. What will be the final temperature of the mixture when all the ice has melted? The specific heat capacity of the liquid is $2.65 \text{ J g}^{-1}\text{°C}^{-1}$, while that of water is $4.2 \text{ J g}^{-1}\text{°C}^{-1}$. (Take, specific latent heat of fusion of ice $= 336 \text{ J g}^{-1}$) **(ICSE 2010)**

43. Calculate the amount of ice which is required to cool 150 g of water contained in a vessel of mass 100 g at 30°C, such that the final temperature of the mixture is 5°C. (Take, specific heat capacity of material of vessel $= 0.4 \text{ J g}^{-1}\text{°C}^{-1}$, specific latent heat of fusion of ice $= 336 \text{ J g}^{-1}$, specific heat capacity of water $= 4.2 \text{ J g}^{-1}\text{°C}^{-1}$) **(ICSE 2009)**

44. A piece of ice of mass 40 g is dropped into 200 g of water at 50°C. Calculate the final temperature of water after all the ice has melted. (Take, specific heat capacity of water = 4200 J/kg°C, specific latent heat of fusion of ice $= 336 \times 10^3$ J/kg) **(ICSE 2008)**

45. A substance is in the form of a solid at 0°C. The amount of heat added to this substance and the temperature of the substance are plotted on the following graph

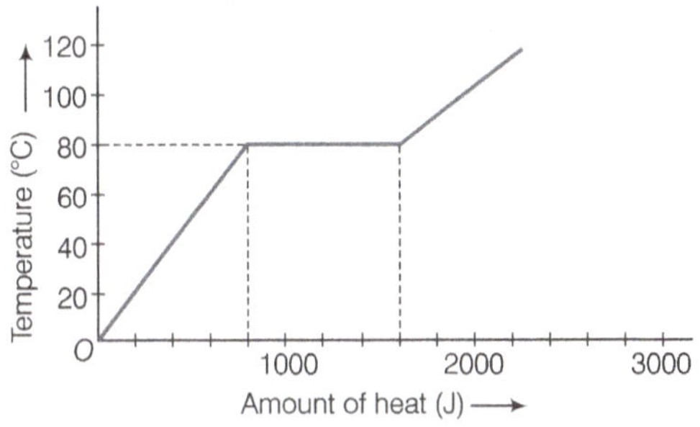

If the specific heat capacity of the solid substance is 500 J/kg°C, find from the graph

(i) The mass of the substance.

(ii) The specific latent heat of fusion of the substance in the liquid state. **(ICSE 2007)**

46. If there is no heat loss to the surroundings, the heat released by the condensation of m_1 gram of steam at 100°C into water at 100°C can be used to convert m_2 gram of ice at 0°C into water at 0°C.

(i) Find (a) the heat lost by steam in terms of m_1.

(b) the heat gained by ice in terms of m_2.

(ii) Form a heat equation to find the ratio of $m_2 : m_1$.

(Take, specific latent heat of vaporisation of steam = 2268 kJ/kg, specific latent heat of fusion of ice = 336 kJ/kg, specific heat capacity of water = 4200 J/kg°C) **(ICSE 2005)**

47. (i) In winter, the weather at forecast for a certain day was 'severe frost'. A wise farmer watered his fields the night before to prevent from damage to his crops. Why did he water his field?

(ii) 10125 J of heat energy boils of 4.5 g of water at 100°C to steam at 100°C. Find the specific latent heat of steam. **(ICSE 2004)**

48. A thermo flask of negligible heat capacity contains 100 g of ice and 30 g of water.

(i) Calculate

(a) the mass of steam at 100°C needed to condense in the flask to just melt the ice.

(b) the amount of water in the flask after condensation.

(Take, specific latent heat of vaporisation of steam = 2260 J/g, specific latent heat of fusion of ice = 336 J/g, specific heat capacity of water = 4.2 J/g°C)

(ii) Is it possible to condense the water formed, back to ice by adding ice at 0°C? Explain, giving a suitable reason to justify your answer. **(ICSE 2004)**

49. (i) State the principle of calorimetry.

(ii) Express 1 kWh in terms of SI unit of energy.

(iii) Which of the two, 1 g of ice at 0°C or 1 g of water at 0°C contains more heat? Give reason for your answer. **(ICSE 2004)**

50. In a laboratory experiment for finding specific latent heat of ice, 100 g of water at 30°C was taken in calorimeter made of copper and of mass 10 g.

When 10 g of ice at 0°C was added to the mixture and within the liquid till the ice melted completely, the final temperature of the mixture was found to be 20°C.

(i) What is the total quantity of water in the calorimeter at 20°C?

(ii) Specific heat capacities of water and copper being 4.2 J/g°C and 0.4 J/g°C respectively, what quantity of heat would each release in cooling down to 20°C from the initial stage?

(iii) Write an expression for the heat gained by ice on melting.

(iv) Calculate the value of the latent heat of fusion of ice from the data discussed above. **(ICSE 2003)**

51. A vessel of negligible heat capacity contains 40 g of ice at 0°C, 8 g of steam at 100°C is passed into ice to melt it. Find the final temperature of the contents of the vessel. (Take, specific latent heat of vaporisation of steam = 2268 J/g, specific latent heat of fusion of ice = 336 J/g, specific heat capacity of water = 4.2 J/g°C) **(ICSE 2002)**

52. (i) It takes a much longer time to boil off (change to steam) a certain quantity of water, rather than bring it to its boiling point from room temperature, say 25°C. Explain the reason for this.

(ii) A hot solid of mass 60 g at 100°C is placed in 100 g of water at 18°C. The final steady temperature recorded is 20°C. Find the specific heat capacity of the solid. **(ICSE 2000)**

53. Calculate the mass of steam at 100°C that must be passed into 8.4 kg of water at 30°C to raise the temperature of water to 80°C. (Take, specific heat capacity of water = 4.2 J/g°C, specific latent heat of vaporisation of steam = 2268 J/g) **(ICSE 2000)**

Explanations

1. (b) During melting of ice at 0°C, the energy is absorbed and temperature remains constant.

2. (b)

3. (b)

$$Q = mL$$
$$m = 200\text{g}$$
$$L = 336000 \text{ J kg}^{-1}$$
$$Q = mL = \left(\frac{200}{1000}\right) \times 336000 = 67200 \text{ J}$$

4. Given, mass of ice = 500 g

Later heat of fusion = 330 J/g

Heal, $Q = mL = 500 \times 330 = 165000$ J

So, 165000 J of heat are required to convert 500 g of ice at 0°C to water at 0°C.

5. The melting point of the given heating curve is 40°C.

The boiling point of the given heating curve is 160°C.

6. (i) Specific heat does not change when a substance is undergoing the phase change because specific heat causes temperature change during phase change.

So, when substance's state changes from solid to liquid, then no temperature changes. So, specific heat capacity will be same.

(ii) Specific heat capacity of ice and specific heat capacity of water are same.

7. Given, $m = 150\text{g} = 150 \times 10^{-3}$ kg $= 0.15$ kg

Power $P = 100$ W

Time $t = 4 \text{ min} = 4 \times 60 = 240$ s

The amount of heat supplied in 4 min is given as heat energy

$$= P \times t = 100 \times 240 = 24000 \text{ J}$$

This heat energy is used in melting.

Let L be the latent specific heat.

$$\therefore \quad mL = 24000 \quad \Rightarrow L = \frac{24000}{0.15} = 16 \times 10^4 \text{ J kg}^{-1}$$

8. According to question,

Mass of water $m_w = 300$ g

Temperature of water = 40°C

From principle of calorimetry,

Heat loss by the water at 40°C

= Heat gain by the ice at 0°C

$$\Rightarrow \quad m_w \times s \times \Delta t = m_{ice} (\text{mass of ice}) \times L$$

$$\Rightarrow \quad m_{ice} = \frac{m_w \times s \times \Delta t}{L}$$

$$= \frac{300 \times 4.2 \times 40}{336} = 150 \text{g} \qquad [\because \Delta t = 40°]$$

150 g of ice is required.

9. The boiling point of water is 100°C at 76 mm of mercury, i.e. atmospheric pressure. The boiling point increases with the increase in pressure. Since, the water is boiling at 115°C, so the pressure is greater than atmospheric pressure.

10. Given, $m = 5\text{ g}, \Delta t = t_2 - t_1 = 20° - 0° = 20°\text{C}$

$c = 4.2$ J/g°C,

$L = 336$ J/g

So, according to the question,

$$Q = mc\,\Delta t + mL = m[(4.2 \times 20) + 336]$$

$$= 5 \times (84 + 336) = 2100 \text{ J}$$

11. After the hailstorm, the ice balls begin to melt and require 336 J of heat energy per gram to melt which is taken from the atmosphere thereby decreasing the temperature of atmosphere.

12. Due to extra latent heat of fusion of ice, i.e. 336 J/g, each gram of ice takes 336 J of extra heat from drink. The soft drinks cools much faster in ice as compared to cold water.

13. As the latent heat of vaporisation is more than specific heat of boiling water, so burn caused by steam are more painful than boiling water.

14. Amount of heat released during the conversion of 5 g of water at 20°C to 5 g of ice at 0°C is as following

5 g water at 20°C to 5 g water at 0°C

$$= mc\,\Delta t = 5 \times 4.2 \times (20 - 0)$$

$$= 84 \times 5 = 420 \text{ J}$$

5 g water at 0°C to 5 g ice at 0°C

$$= mL = 5 \times 336 = 1680$$

So, total heat released

$$= 1680 + 420$$

$$= 2100 \text{ J}$$

15. When frozen lake starts melting, it takes the amount of energy per gram equal to the latent heat from surrounding. So, there is fall in temperature of surrounding.

16. As given in question,

Mass $m = 5$ kg

Latent heat $L = 2268$ J/kg

As we know that, $Q = mL = 5 \times 2268 = 11340$ J

17. Icecream at 0°C extracts heat (latent heat of fusion) and freeze to water at 0°C. As we know, icecream is able to extract more heat, so it produces more cooling effect.

18. Given ,

The mass of water = 85 g

Initial temperature of water = 30°C

Final temperature of water = 5°C

Latent heat capacity of ice = 336 J/g

Heat gain by the ice = Heat loss by water

$$m_i L + m_i C_w \Delta T = m_w C_w \Delta T$$

$$m_i [L + C_w (\Delta T)] = m_w C_w \Delta T$$

$$m_i [336 + 4.2 \times (30 - 5)] = 85 \times 4.2 \times (30 - 5)$$

Mass of ice, $m_i = 24.72$ g

19. (a) When the water changes from liquid into ice, it releases heat into the surrounding. So, when the lakes starts freezing, it become pleasantly warm.

(b) The average kinetic energy is proportional to the temperature of water. When water freezes, the temperature of water molecules reduce. Hence, the average kinetic energy of the water molecules also reduces.

(c) 1 g water at 0°C contains more heat.

20. (i) The part AB represents at 150° C. It means the substance condenses.

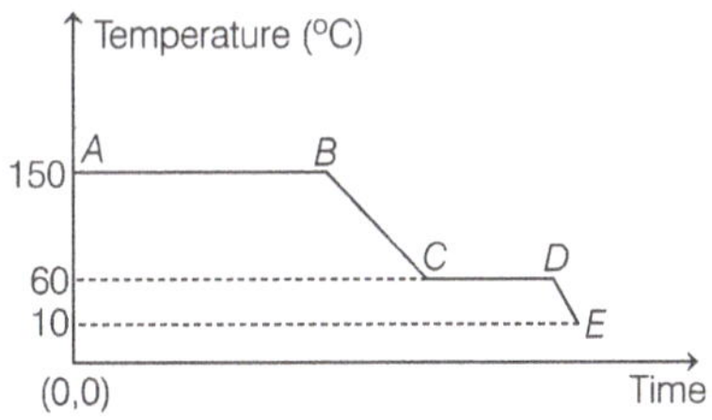

The part CD represents solidifies at 60° C.

(ii) The range of liquid state

$= 150°\text{ C} - 60°\text{ C} = 90°\text{ C}$

(iii) Because ice takes heat equal to its latent heat without raising temperature.

21. (i) In the part of AB,

Temperature change $= \Delta t = 80°C$

Mass of water $m = 200g$

The rate of heat extraction $= 100 \ Js^{-1}$

Heat extraction in 640s $(H) = 640 \times 100 = 64000$

From the relation,

$$H = mc\Delta t$$

$$100 \times 640 = 200 \times c \times 80$$

$$c = \frac{100 \times 640}{200 \times 80} = 4 \ J/g°C$$

(ii) Heat lost in the part BC

$$= 100 \times (1312 - 640) = 67200 \ J$$

22. (i) 10 g ice at 0° C will absorb more heat because it has 80 cal/g less heat compared to water at 0° C. After that, both the samples will absorb the same amount of energy, since they will be in the same state.

(ii) Ice produces more cooling because It has 80 cal/g less heat as compared to water at 0° C.

23. (i) According to given diagram, substance is at lowest temperature in the initial state A, when temperature is given to the substance in its initial stage, then its temperature rises quickly with respect to time, i.e. less specific heat capacity. In the state BC, substance melts. Therefore, its temperature rises slowly with respect to time, i.e. high specific heat capacity. Hence, slope of CD is less than slope of AB.

(ii) From given diagram, at point B, the melting of substance starts. Hence, melting point $= T_1$ °C. At point D, substance starts boiling, hence boiling point $= T_2$ °C.

24. Temperature-time graph of naphthalene is given below.

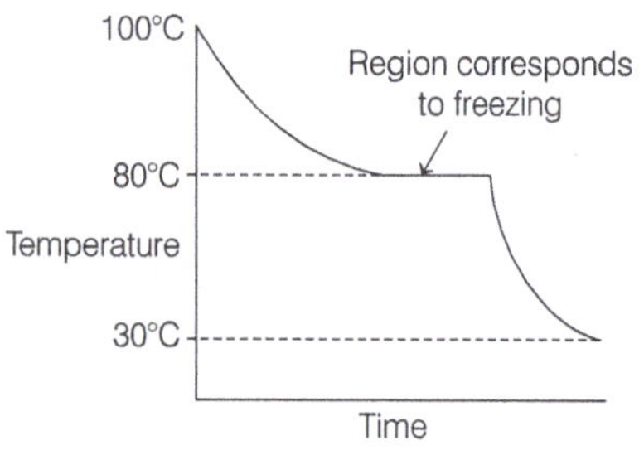

25. (i) Heat supplied to solid changes it into liquid. This change in phase is called melting.

(ii) During the phase change, average kinetic energy of the molecules does not change, because the temperature remains constant.

(iii) The energy absorbed during the phase change is called latent heat of fusion.

26. (i) Refer to text on page no. 185 (Specific latent heat of fusion).

(ii) When the heat supplied causes no change in the temperatures of the substance. The heat supplied to the substance is utilised to change the state by separating the molecules and overcoming intermolecular forces of attractions. This heat absorb is called latent heat.

Concept Enhancer Latent heat cannot be measured by a thermometer. It is an intensive property.

27.

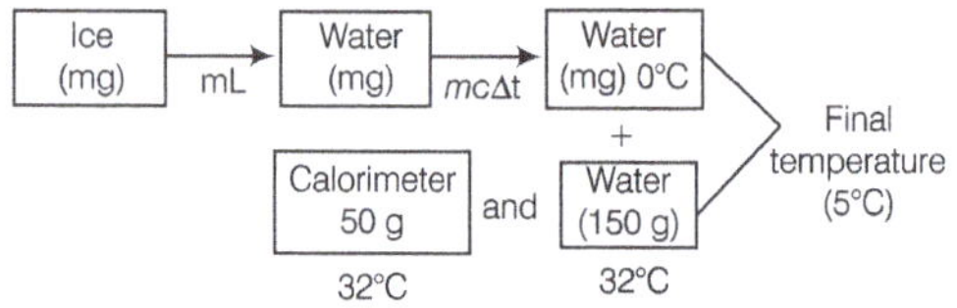

From the principle of calorimetry,

Heat gained by ice = Heat lost by water + Heat lost by calorimeter

$$mL + mc\,\Delta t = m_w C_w \,\Delta t + m_{cal}\, c_{cal}\, \Delta t \qquad \ldots(i)$$

where, m = Mass of ice (suppose),

L = Latent heat of ice $= 330$ J/g,

Δt = Change in temperature $= (5 - 0) = 5°C$,

Final temperature $= 5°C$,

c_w = Specific heat of water $= 4.2$ J/g°C,

m_w = mass of water $= 150$ g,

m_{cal} = mass of calorimeter $= 50$ g

and c_{cal} = specific heat of calorimeter $= 0.4$ J/g°C

Now, heat lost by water and calorimeter will be

$$= 150 \times 4.2 \times (32 - 5) + 150 \times 0.4 \times (32 - 5)$$

$$= 150 \times 4.2 \times 27 + 150 \times 0.4 \times 27$$

$$= 150 \times 27 \ (4.2 + 0.4) = 150 \times 27 \times 4.6$$

Now, according to Eq. (i), we have

$$m \times 330 + m \times 4.2 \times 5 = 150 \times 27 \times 4.6$$

$$\Rightarrow m \ (330 + 21) = 150 \times 27 \times 4.6$$

$$\Rightarrow m \times 351 = 150 \times 27 \times 4.6$$

$$\Rightarrow \quad m = \frac{150 \times 27 \times 4.6}{351} = \frac{18630}{351} = 53.07 \approx 53.1 \ g$$

28. $m_w = 400g$

$t_1 = 30°C$

$t_2 = 0°C$

$C_w = 4200 \ J/kg \ K$

$C_{ice} = 2100 \text{ J / kg K}$

$L_f = 336000 \text{ J / kg}$

Heat given out on reducing the temperature of 400 g of water from 30° C to 0° C $= mc_w \, \Delta t$

$$= \frac{400}{1000} \times 4200 \times 30 = 50,400 \text{ J}$$

The amount of heat given out on converting water at 0° C to ice at 0° C $= mL_f$

$$= \frac{400}{1000} \times 336000 = 1,34,400 \text{ J}$$

The amount of heat given out on reducing the temperature of ice at 0° C to −2°C $= m\,C_{ice}\Delta t$

$$= \frac{400}{1000} \times 2100 \times 2 = 1680 \text{ J}$$

Total heat given out in three stages

$$= 50400 + 134400 + 1680 = 1,86,480 \text{ J}$$

29. According to question, the heating curve of ice is given below

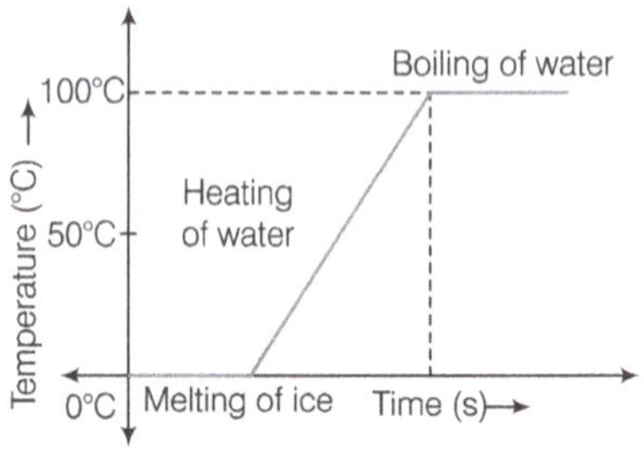

Concept Enhancer By calculating the slope of the graph, we can calculate the heat released or heat gained by the substances.

30. During the conversion of ice to water, a large amount of heat is required. So, this heat taken from the surrounding environment. As a result, temperature of surrounding fall.

31. (i) As from the question,

$\Delta Q = mc\,\Delta t$

where, m = Mass of substance,

c = Specific heat of substance,

Δt = Change in temperature,

ΔQ = Heat given or lost.

(ii) The temperature rise will be same in both celsius and kelvin scale, as it is the change in temperature (Δt) only.

(iii) The average KE of molecules increases when ice melts as temperature of body increases.

32. The temperature-time graph is shown below

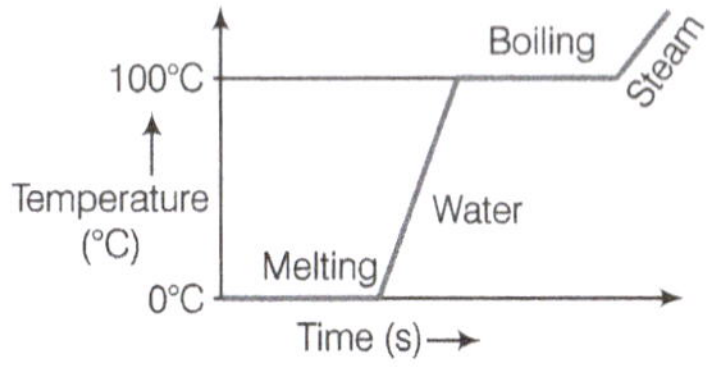

Concept Enhancer Temperature and time graphs can be used to calculate the various properties of a system, such as its specific heat capacity, the heat of fusion or vaporisation and the rate of heat transfer.

33. (i) This process is called isothermal process. Heat is stored as latent heat, which is used in change the state of the substance.

(ii) During the melting of ice, the heat given out is equal to latent heat.

34. (i) The heat capacity of body is 50 J/°C, it means 50 J of heat is required to raise the temperature of body by 1°C.

(ii) It means the amount of heat is required to change the state of body from ice to water without change in temperature.

(iii) This means that 0.4 J of heat is required to raise the temperature of 1 g of copper by 1°C.

35. (i) Specific heat capacity is defined as the amount of heat required to raise the temperature of unit mass by 1°C.

(ii) Because heat supplied to the substance is used to raise the potential energy of the substance, so there is no change in temperature.

36. Given, specific heat capacity of water,

$c = 4.2 \text{ J g}^{-1}\text{K}^{-1}$

$= 4.2 \times 10^3 \text{ J kg}^{-1}\text{K}^{-1}$

Specific latent heat of fusion of ice

$= 336 \text{ J g}^{-1} = 336 \times 10^3 \text{ J kg}^{-1}$

Mass of ice, $m_i = 60 \text{ g} = 0.06 \text{ kg}$ and mass of water,

$m_w = 140 \text{ g} = 0.14 \text{ kg}$

Suppose T be the final temperature, then

Heat lost by 0.14 kg of water, when its temperature falls from 50°C to T°C

$= m_w c_w (50 - T)$

$= 0.14 \times 4.2 \times 10^3 \; (50 - T)$

$= 588 \; (50 - T)$

Heat required to melt 0.06 kg of ice into water at 0°C

$= m_i L = 0.06 \times 336 \times 10^3 = 20.16 \times 10^3$ J

Heat required to raise temperature of 0.06 kg of water from 0°C to T°C

$= mC_w (T - 0) = 0.06 \times 4.2 \times 10^3 T = 252\,T$

By the principle of calorimetry,

Heat gained = Heat lost

$20.16 \times 10^3 + 252T = 580\,(50 - T)$

$20160 + 252T = 29000 - 580T$

$832T = 8840$

$\Rightarrow \; T = \frac{8840}{832} = 10.625°\,C$

Common Mistake There are different equations to calculate the heat transferred and the temperature change depending on the specific scenario. It is important to choose the correct equation and to use it correctly.

37. Given,

Mass of water, $m_w = 104$ g

Temperature of water, $T_w = 30°$ C,

Mass of copper, $m_c = 42$ g

Temperature of ice, $T_1 = 0°C$

Let mass of ice be m_i.

Final temperature of mixture, $T = 10°C$

According to the principle of calorimetry

Heat lost = Heat gained

$m_w s_w (T_w - T) + m_c s_c (T_w - T)$
$= m_i s_i + m_i s_w (T - T_i)$

Here,

s_w = Specific heat capacity of water = 4.2 Jg^{-1} °C^{-1}

s_c = Specific heat capacity of copper
= 0.4 Jg^{-1} °C^{-1}

s_i = Specific latent heat of fusion of ice
= 336 Jg^{-1}°C^{-1}

$104 \times 4.2 \times (30 - 10) + 42 \times 0.4(30 - 10)$
$= m_i (336) + m_i \times 4.2 \times (10 - 0)$

i.e., $8736 + 336 = m_i [336 + 42]$

Mass of ice, $m_i = \frac{9072}{378} = 24$ g

38. As given in question,

Mass $m = 100$ g,

Time $t = 2$ min $= 2 \times 60 = 120$ s

Heat energy taken by ice at 0°C to convert it into water at 0°C,

$Q = mL = 100 \times 336 = 33600$ J

As we know that,

Power $P = \frac{Q\,(\text{Energy})}{t\,(\text{Time})} = \frac{33600}{2 \times 60} = 280$ J/s ...(i)

Heat energy required to raise the temperature from 0°C to 20°C,

$Q = mc\,\Delta t = 100 \times 4.2 \times 20 = 8400$ J ...(ii)

[c of water = 4.2 J/g/°C]

Now, from Eqs. (i) and (ii), we get

$Q = Pt = 8400$ J

$t = \frac{8400}{P} = \frac{8400}{280} = 30$s

$= \frac{30}{60}$ min $= 0.5$ min

39. As given in question,

Mass of water used $m = 40$ g

Temperature of water $t_1 = 0°C$

$L = 336$ J/g, $c = 4.2$ J/g°C

Mass of the another water = M gram

Change in temperature

$\Delta t = (60 - 10) = 50°C$

So, by principle of calorimetry,

Heat gained = Heat lost

$\Rightarrow M \times 4.2 \times (60 - 10)$
$= (40 \times 336) + 40 \times 4.2 \times (10 - 0)$

$\Rightarrow \; M = \frac{13440 + 1680}{42 \times 5} = \frac{15120}{210} = 72$ g

40. According to the principle of calorimetry,

Heat lost = Heat gained by water
+ Heat gained by copper vessel

So, $M \times L_f = m_1 c_w \Delta t + m_2 c_c \Delta t$

$\Rightarrow M \times 336 \times 10^3 = \frac{250}{1000} \times 4200 \times (30 - 5)$
$+ \frac{50}{1000} \times 400 \times (30 - 5)$

$\Rightarrow M \times 336 \times 10^3 = 26250 + 500$

$\Rightarrow M = \frac{26750}{336 \times 10^3} = 79.61$ g $= 0.07961$ kg

41. (i) Specific latent heat of fusion is the heat required to change the state of substance from ice to liquid without change in temperature.

(ii) (a) Kinetic energy changes which defines specific heat capacity of the substance.

(b) Intermolecular or space charges defines latent heat of the substance.

42. From the question, we consider

Mixture reach a final temperature = T°C

So, heat absorb by ice = $mL + mc\Delta t$

$= 50 \times 336 + 50 \times 4.2 \times T$ ...(i)

Again, heat release by liquid to come to t °C = $mc\Delta t$

$= 300 \times 2.65 \times (30 - T)$ ...(ii)

According to the principle of calorimetry, (Heat gained = Heat lost) and from Eqs. (i) and (ii), we have

$50 \times 336 + 50 \times 4.2 \times T = 300 \times 2.65 \times (30 - T)$

$\Rightarrow \quad 1005T = 7050$

$\Rightarrow \quad T = 7.014°C \Rightarrow T = 7.02°C$

43. According to the principle of calorimetry,

Heat gained by ice = Heat lost by water + Heat lost by vessel

$\Rightarrow mL + mc\Delta T = m_w c_w \Delta T + m_v c_v \Delta T$

$\Rightarrow m \times 336 + m \times 4.2 \times 5 = 150 \times 4.2 \times 25 + 100 \times 4 \times 25$

$\Rightarrow \quad m = 30.67$ g

44. As given in question,

Mass of ice $m_i = 40\text{ g} = 40 \times 10^{-3}$ kg

Mass of water $m_w = 200$ g $= 200 \times 10^{-3}$ kg

Temperature (water) = 50°C

Let final temperature be t.

According to the principle of calorimetry,

Heat lost by water = Heat taken by ice

$m_w c\Delta t = m_i L + m_i c\Delta t$

$\Rightarrow 200 \times 10^{-3} \times 4.2 \times 10^3 \times (50 - t)$

$= 40 \times 10^{-3} \times 33.6 \times 10^4 + 40 \times 10^{-3} \times 4.2 \times 10^3 \times t$

$\Rightarrow \quad 200 \times 4.2 \times (500 - t) = 40 \times 33.6 + 40 \times 4.2t$

$\Rightarrow 21(50 - t) = 33.6 + 4.2\,t \Rightarrow 25.2t = 714$

$\Rightarrow \quad t = \dfrac{714}{25.2} = 28.33°C$

45. (i) According to the question,

Suppose, mass of substance be m kg

As we know that, $Q = mc\Delta t$ from the graph

$Q = 800$ J, $\Delta t = 80°C$, $c = 500$ J/kg°C

$\Rightarrow 800 = m \times 500 \times 80$

So, $m = \dfrac{800}{500 \times 80} = \dfrac{1}{50}$ kg $= 20$ g

(ii) Latent heat of fusion, i.e. $Q = mL$

$\Rightarrow (1600 - 800) = L \times \dfrac{1}{50}$

$\Rightarrow L = 800 \times 50 = 40000$ J/kg

46. (i) (a) The heat lost by the steam is given by $m_1 L_s$ (where, L_s = Latent heat of steam)

(b) The heat gained by the ice is given by $m_2 L_i$ (where, L_i = Latent heat of ice)

(ii) According to the principle of calorimetry,

Heat taken by ice = Heat given by steam

$m_2 L_i = m_1 L_s$

$\Rightarrow \quad \dfrac{m_2}{m_1} = \dfrac{L_s}{L_i} = \dfrac{2268}{336} = \dfrac{27}{4}$

$\Rightarrow \quad m_2 : m_1 = 27 : 4$

47. (i) To increase the temperature of surrounding as we know that water has high specific heat, so it liberates very large heat when temperature falls and ice forms water.

(ii) Given, heat $Q = 10125$ J

Mass $m = 4.5\text{ g} = 4.5 \times 10^{-3}$ kg

$\therefore \; Q = mL \Rightarrow L = \dfrac{Q}{m} = \dfrac{10125}{4.5 \times 10^{-3}} = 225 \times 10^4$ J/kg

48. (i) (a) According to the principle of calorimetry,

Heat lost by steam = Heat gained by ice

$(M_{\text{steam}} \times L_{\text{steam}}) + (M_{\text{steam}} \times C_{\text{water}} \times \Delta\theta) = M_{\text{ice}} \times L_{\text{ice}}$

$\Rightarrow (M \times 2260) + M \times 4.2 \times 100 = 100 \times 336$

$\Rightarrow M\,(2260 + 420) = 33600$

$\Rightarrow \quad M = \dfrac{33600}{2680} = 12.54$ g

(b) The amount of water present after condensation $= 30 + 100 + 12.54 = 142.54$ g

(ii) Water will not freeze, only ice added will melt, because water and ice used are at the same temperature.

49. (i) It states that heat gained by one body is equal to heat lost by another body till they attain equal temperature.

(ii) SI unit of energy is joule (J), i.e. 1 kWh $= 1000\text{W} \times 3600\text{ s} = 3.6 \times 10^6$ J

(iii) 1 g of water at 0°C contains more heat, because latent heat of water is 80 cal/g.

50. (i) Given, $m_1 = 100\,g$, $m_2 = 10\,g$

Total mass $= m_1 + m_2 = 100\,g + 10\,g = 110\,g$

(ii) Total heat released

$$= m_1 c_1 \Delta t + m_2 c_2 \Delta t$$
$$= 100 \times 4.2 \times (30-20) + 10 \times 0.4 \times (30-20)$$
$$= 4200 + 40 = 4240\,J$$

(iii) As we know,

Latent heat of fusion,

i.e. $Q_2 = mL \Rightarrow Q_2 = 10 \times L$

(iv) As from the question,

$10L + 10 \times 4.2 \times (20-0) = 4240$

So, $10L + 840 = 4240 \Rightarrow 10L = 4240 - 840$

$$\Rightarrow L = \frac{3400}{10} = 340\,J/g$$

51. Let the final temperature θ°C.

According to principle of calorimetry,

Heat gained by ice at 0°C to water at 0°C + Heat gained by water at 0°C to water at θ°C = Heat lost by steam at 100°C to water at 100°C + Heat lost by water at 100°C to water at θ°C

$\therefore mL_f + mc\,\Delta\theta = m' L_V + m' c\,\Delta\theta$

$(40 \times 336) + 40 \times 4.2 \times (\theta - 0)$

$= 8 \times [2268 + 4.2 \times (100 - \theta)]$

$\Rightarrow 13440 + 168\theta = 18144 + 3360 - 33.6\theta$

$\Rightarrow 168\theta + 33.6\theta = 8064$

$\Rightarrow 201.6\theta = 8064 \Rightarrow \theta = 40°C$

52. (i) Amount of heat required to bring water of its boiling point $= m \cdot s \cdot (100-25) = 75\,m$ cal (as $s = 1$ cal/g°C for water)

As we know, latent heat of steam is 540 cal/g. So, it required much longer time to boil.

(ii) Let the specific heat capacity of solid be s.

So, according to the principle of calorimetry,

Heat taken by water = Heat given by solid

$\Rightarrow 100 \times 1 \times (20-18) = 60 \times c \times (100-20)$

$$\Rightarrow c = \frac{100 \times 2}{60 \times 80}$$

$$\Rightarrow c = \frac{1}{24} = 0.041\,cal/g°C$$

Specific heat capacity of the solid, i.e.

$= 0.041$ cal/g°C

53. Let the mass of steam be m gram

(i) Heat given out,

i.e. Latent heat of steam (Q)

$= mL = m \times 2268 = 2268\,m$ J

(ii) Heat given out by water $= ms\Delta t$

$= m \times 4.2 \times (100-80) = 84\,m$ J

$\therefore$ Total heat given out of system

$= (2268\,m + 84\,m)\,J = 2352\,m$ J

Heat taken by 8.4 kg $= ms\Delta t$

$= 8400 \times 4.2 \times 50°C = 1764000$ J

According to the principle of calorimetry,

$$m = \frac{1764000}{2352} = 750\,g$$

CHAPTER TEST

01 Mark Questions

1 The SI Unit of heat capacity is
(a) J kg^{-1} (b) JK^{-1}
(c) J $kg^{-1}K^{-1}$ (d) cal° C^{-1}

2 The specific heat capacity of water is
(a) 4200 J kg^{-1} K^{-1} (b) 420 J g^{-1} K^{-1}
(c) 0.42 J g^{-1} K^{-1} (d) 4.2 J kg^{-1} K^{-1}

3 *m* gram hot water at *t*° C is added to 3*m* gram of cold water at 10° C. If the final temperature of the mixture is 20° C, then the value of *t* is
(a) 30° C (b) 40° C
(c) 50° C (d) 60° C

4 The specific latent heat of fusion of water is
(a) 80 cal g^{-1} (b) 2260 J g^{-1}
(c) 80 J g^{-1} (d) 336 J kg^{-1}

5 Amount of heat energy required to melt 5 kg of ice at 0° C is (Specific latent heat of ice = 336 Jg^{-1})
(a) 1680000 J
(b) 1680 J
(c) 168×10^2 J
(d) 168 kJ

02 Marks Questions

6 Define the term calorie. How is it related to joule?

7 Define temperature and its SI unit.

8 Name a liquid which has the highest specific heat capacity.

9 Differentiate between heat capacity and specific heat capacity.

10 Determine the specific heat capacity of lead of mass 0.5 kg, if 1300 J of heat is supplied to raise its temperature from 20° C to 40° C.

Structured Questions

11 (i) Define the following
(a) Melting point
(b) Latent heat
(c) Vaporisation **(3)**

(ii) What do you mean by the following statements
(a) The heat capacity of a body is 50 JK^{-1}?
(b) The specific heat capacity of copper is 0.4 J $g^{-1}K^{-1}$? **(4)**

(iii) What is the effect of presence of impurity on the melting point of ice? Mention one use of it. **(3)**

12 (i) (a) What is the principle of method of mixtures?
(b) What is the other name given to it?
(c) Name the law on which the principle is based. **(3)**

(ii) The temperature of 170 g of water at 50° C is lowered to 5° C by adding certain amount of ice to it. Find the mass of ice added.
(Take, specific heat capacity of water = 4200 J kg^{-1} °C^{-1} and specific latent heat of ice = 336000 J kg^{-1}) **(3)**

(iii) (a) Define the term "specific latent heat of fusion of a substance."
(b) What energy change would you expect to take place in the molecules of a substance when it undergoes
I. a change in its temperature?
II. a change in its state without any change in its temperature? **(4)**

Answers

1. (b) **2.** (a) **3.** (c) **4.** (a) **5.** (a)

10. 130 J$kg^{-1}K^{-1}$

12. (ii) 90 g

10

Radioactivity and Nuclei

TREND ANALYSIS 4 YEARS

Average No. of Questions Across all Sets

	Types of Questions	2024	2023	2020	2019
Radioactivity and Nuclei	1 Mark	2	–	1	1
	2 Marks	2	1	1	2
	3 Marks	1	2	–	–
	4 Marks	–	–	1	–

The discovery of electrons by JJ Thomson and scattering experiments by Rutherford and others led to the structure of atom and its nucleus.

Atoms These are the smallest part of any substance, which consists of a centralised dense part called **nucleus**.

Nucleus It is that part of atom which consists of neutron and proton. Most of the mass of atom is situated inside nucleus.

Atomic Number (Z) Atomic number of an atom is the number of proton present in its nucleus (which is same as the number of electrons in that atom). It is denoted by Z.

Mass Number (A) The total number of proton and neutron present in the nucleus is called atomic mass number of that atom. It is denoted by A. Hence, number of neutrons $(N) = A - Z$

Isotopes The atoms belonging to the same element, having same atomic number (Z), but different mass numbers are called isotopes. e.g. Protium ($_1^1\text{H}$) and deuterium ($_1^2\text{H}$) are isotopes having same atomic number ($Z = 1$) and different mass number 1 and 2.

Isotones Atoms (nuclei) with the same neutron number N but different atomic number Z are called isotones. e.g. $_{11}^{23}\text{Na}$ and $_{12}^{24}\text{Mg}$ are isotones having same neutron numbers (12).

Isobars Atoms (nuclei) with the same mass number A but different atomic numbers Z are called isobars. e.g. $_{11}^{23}\text{Na}$ and $_{12}^{23}\text{Mg}$ are the isobars having same mass number 23 and different atomic numbers 11 and 12.

Radioactivity

Radioactivity is the spontaneous process by which a nucleus of an unstable atom decay by emitting radiations such as α, β and γ.

Radioactive Substances

A material that spontaneously emits α (alpha particle), β (beta particle) and γ (gamma rays) is known as radioactive substance. Example of radioactive substances are uranium, plutonium, thorium, etc.

Properties of α-Particles

- α-particle consists of a helium nuclei. It is denoted by $_2He^4$ (atomic number 2 and mass number 4). It is a positively charged particle.
- It has least penetration power and highest ionisation power.
- They cannot penetrate skin but is harmful for human body.
- α-particles effect a photographic plate.
- α-particles cause fluorescence on striking a fluorescent material.
- These are affected by electric and magnetic fields.

Properties of β-Particles

- β-particles are highly energetic electrons, which are released from inside of a nucleus. It is denoted by $_{-1}\beta^0$(atomic number -1 and mass number 0) and $_{+1}\beta^0$.
- β-particles are negatively and positively charged and they have negligible mass.
- For the emission of negative β-particle, a neutron divides into a proton and an electron, inside the nucleus and for $+\beta$-particle proton converts into neutron.
- β-particle has greater penetration power as compared to α-particle.
- It has less ionisation power but is still harmful.
- β-particles effect a photographic plate.
- β-particles cause fluorescence on striking a fluorescent material.
- These are affected by electric and magnetic fields.

Properties of γ-Rays

- The waves from the high frequency end of electromagnetic spectrum which do not have mass are called γ-rays.
- It is neutral in nature and denoted by $_0\gamma^0$. They are chargeless and massless.
- It is highly penetrating in nature as compared with α and β-particles. It is very harmful to the living cell and cause mutation.
- These radiations effect a photographic plate.
- These radiations cause fluorescence, when they strike a fluorescent material.
- These rays are not affected by electric and magnetic fields.

Changes within the Nucleus During α, β and γ-decay

Atomic number and mass number of the nucleus changes during the process of α, β-decay.

α-decay

As α-particle consist of helium nuclei, i.e. ($_2He^4$). On α-decay, the parent nucleus loses its atomic number by 2 and mass number by 4.

General equation for α-decay is

$$\underset{\text{(Parent nucleus)}}{_ZX^A} \xrightarrow{-\alpha\text{-particle}} \underset{\text{(Daughter nucleus)}}{_{Z-2}Y^{A-4}} + \underset{(\alpha\text{-particle})}{^4_2He}$$

e.g. $$\underset{\text{Uranium}}{_{92}U^{238}} \xrightarrow{-\alpha\text{-particle}} \underset{\text{Thorium}}{_{90}Th^{234}} + {^4_2He}$$

β-decay

As β-particle has -1 as atomic number. So, on β-decay, a new element formed having atomic number increased by 1 and same mass number as of the initial element.

General equation for negative β-decay is

$$\underset{\text{(Parent nucleus)}}{_ZX^A} \xrightarrow{-\beta} \underset{\text{(Daughter nucleus)}}{_{Z+1}Y^{A-0}} + {^0_{-1}e}$$

e.g. $$_6C^{14} \longrightarrow {_7N^{14}} + \underset{(\beta\text{-particle})}{^0_{-1}e}$$

NOTE When an unstable nucleus contains more neutrons than the protons, a neutron changes into a proton by emitting an electron. This emitted electron at a high speed is called a negative β-particle.

i.e. $$\underset{\text{(Neutron)}}{^1_0n} \longrightarrow \underset{\text{Proton}}{^1_1p} + \underset{(\beta\text{-particle})}{^0_{-1}e}$$

γ-decay

During γ-decay, there is no change in the mass number and atomic number of the nucleus.

General equation for γ-decay is

$$^A_ZX \longrightarrow {^A_ZX} + \underset{\text{(Gamma radiation)}}{\gamma}$$

Uses of Radioactivity- Radioisotopes

There are some elements with atomic number $Z < 82$, whose isotopes are also radioactive. These isotopes are called **radioisotopes**.

e.g. Potassium $^{40}_{19}K$ (atomic number $=19$, mass number

$= 40$) and Carbon ${}^{14}_{6}C$ (atomic number $= 6$, mass number $= 14$), etc., are the radioisotopes.

Radioisotopes has its applications in different fields, they are discussed as follows

Medical Uses

(i) Diseases like leukemia, cancer, etc., can be cured by radioisotopes.

(ii) γ-rays emitted by ${}^{60}_{27}Co$ are used to kill the cells in malignant tumour of patient.

(iii) The weak radioactive tracers of isotopes such as radioisotopes of NaCl, I, etc., are used to diagnose the brain tumour, blood clots before they become dangerous.

Industrial Uses

(i) To avoid the accumulation of charge on moving parts of machine due to friction, radioactive isotopes are used. Due to ionisation effect, charges accumulated on moving parts will be taken.

(ii) The radioactive isotopes have such an ionisation effect that they can be used in making luminescent signs.

(iii) Radioactive tracers are used to check the underground pipelines.

(iv) Radioisotopes in the form of nuclear fuel are used to produce power.

Scientific Uses

(i) The radioisotopes are used in determining the age of rocks containing carbon, by measuring the percentage of C^{12} and C^{14} in them.

(ii) The age of old objects not containing carbon can be determined by measuring the percentage of isotopes atom in them.

(iii) These are used in α-**particle gold foil experiment** in order to study the structure of an atom.

(iv) Radioactive sources of elements N, P, K are used in agriculture science to study the growth of plants with respect to manure.

X-Rays

It was discovered by German professor Roentgen. Its frequency ranges from 10^{16} to 3×10^{20} Hz. These are electromagnetic waves travels with speed of light (3×10^8 m/s).

Uses of X-rays are given below

(i) Used in surgery to detect the fracture, diseased organs, stones in the body, etc.

(ii) Used in engineering to detect fault, crack on bridges, testing of welds, etc.

(iii) Used for security purposes to detect metal or explosive material.

(iv) Used in scientific research.

Sources of Harmful Radiation

Radioactive or nucleus radiations are very harmful for human being, they can cause diseases likes sore throat, loss of hair, cancer, leukemia, etc.

Along within they have affect on genetics which can appear in later generation.

There are three main sources from where we get the radiations

Radioactive Fall out from Nuclear Power Plants and Other Resources

In case any accident occurred in the reactor of these plants, radioactive radiations will escape into the atmosphere in a large amount. It will not only affect the population around the plant but also affect the life at far off places, where they can reach with air currents.

Nuclear Waste

When the activity of the fuel rods used in nuclear power reactor decreases, they get rejected. But still, these rods are quite radioactive in nature.

Cosmic Radiations

Cosmic radiations from the sun enter the earth's atmosphere from outer space. Out of these radiations, substantial amount of uncharged radiations such as γ-ray and X-ray, etc., enter the earth's atmosphere.

These radiations are also very harmful for human beings.

Background Radiations

All the radiations which are present in the atmosphere, even if there is no radioactive source present are called background radiations.

The sources of these radiations are

(i) cosmic radiations.

(ii) natural and artificial radioactive isotopes.

(iii) products after nuclear explosion.

(iv) traces of radioactive substances present in earth, i.e. rocks.

Safety Precautions while Using Nuclear Energy

Some of the safety precautions which are required to be undertaken while using nuclear energy are as follows

Safety Measures for Handling the Radioactive Materials

(i) Each type of radiations should have some safety limits and that should be known to each and everyone, so that no one get exposed beyond the safety limit in any case.

(ii) People working with radioactive materials should wear special lead lined aprons and lead gloves.

(iii) In order to stop radiations from spreading all around, the radioactive substances must be kept in thick lead containers with a very narrow opening.

Safety Measures for Establishment of Nuclear Plants

When a nuclear power plant is going to be established to generate the electricity, proper care must be taken, so that the working people in it are not exposed to the nuclear radiations.

Given below are some safety measures which are to be followed during the establishment of nuclear power plants.

(i) The housing of nuclear reactor must be done in an air-tight building of strong concrete structure which can with stand earthquakes, fires and explosion.

(ii) For backup, the cooling system must be there for the reactor core for safety in case of failure.

Safe Disposal of Nuclear Waste

Nuclear wastes are the wastes found after use of radioactive material. It is obtained from different places like laboratories, power plants, hospitals, scientific establishment.

So, it must be first kept them in thick casks and then must be buried in the specially constructed deep under ground stores.

Nuclear Energy

Nuclear energy is the energy released during the transformation of nuclei to another nuclei.

Two distinct ways of obtaining nuclear energy from nucleus are as follows

(i) Nuclear fission

(ii) Nuclear fusion

Nuclear Fission

Nuclear fission is the phenomenon of splitting of a heavy nucleus (usually $A > 230$) into two or more lighter nuclei by the bombardment of proton, neutron, α-particle, etc. In fission, a heavy nucleus like $^{235}_{92}\text{U}$ breaks into two smaller fragments by the bombardment of thermal neutron (low energy or slow moving).

e.g.

$$^{235}_{92}\text{U} + ^{1}_{0}n \longrightarrow ^{141}_{56}\text{Ba} + ^{92}_{36}\text{Kr} + 3\,_0n^1 + Q$$

(Energy released)

Nuclear Fusion

Nuclear fusion is the phenomenon of fusing two or more lighter nuclei forming a single heavy nucleus.

e.g.

$$_1\text{H}^1 + _1\text{H}^1 \longrightarrow _1\text{H}^2 + _1e^+ + \nu + 0.42 \text{ meV}$$

$$_1\text{H}^2 + _1\text{H}^2 \longrightarrow _2\text{He}^3 + _0n^1 + 3.27 \text{ meV}$$

$$_1\text{H}^2 + _1\text{H}^2 \longrightarrow _1\text{H}^3 + _1\text{H}^1 + 4.03 \text{ meV}$$

Fusion of hydrogen nuclei into helium nuclei is the source of energy of most of the stars including the sun.

PYQs Previous Years Questions

1 Mark Questions

1. A radioactive nucleus containing 128 nucleons emits αβ-particle. After β-emission, the number of nucleons present in the nucleus will be **(ICSE 2024)**

(a) 128 (b) 129 (c) 124 (d) 127

2. A radioactive element is placed in an evacuated chamber. Then , the rate of radioactive decay will **(ICSE SQP 2024)**

(a) decrease
(b) increase
(c) remain unchanged
(d) depend on the surrounding temperature

3. Which of the following nuclear radiations can be stopped by a sheet of paper? **(ICSE SQP 2023)**

(a) Alpha (b) Beta
(c) Gamma (d) None of these

4. A radioactive nucleus emits a beta particle. Does the position of daughter nucleus change in a periodic table as compared to the parent nucleus? **(ICSE SQP 2023)**

5. To which electrically charged plate the beta radiations will deflect, while passing through an electric field? **(ICSE SQP 2023)**

6. The heaviest nuclear radiation is **(ICSE 2022 Sem-II)**

(a) X-radiation (b) α -radiation
(c) γ-radiation (d) β-radiation.

7. To study the age of excavated material of archaeological significance we study the rate of decay of an isotope of **(ICSE 2022 Sem-II)**

(a) uranium (b) cobalt (c) carbon (d) chlorine

8. The radiation with maximum penetrating power is **(ICSE SQP 2022 Sem-II)**

(a) γ (b) β (c) X-radiation (d) α

9. The nuclear radiation which gets deflected towards negatively charged plate in an electric field is **(ICSE SQP 2022 Sem-II)**

(a) gamma (b) ultraviolet
(c) beta (d) alpha

KEY idea
In beta decay, atomic number of nucleus increases by one unit, whereas mass number remain same.

10. State one safety precaution in the disposal of nuclear waste. **(ICSE 2020)**

11. Complete the reaction.

$$^{3}He_{2} + {}^{2}H_{1} \rightarrow {}^{4}He_{2} + \ldots\ldots + \text{Energy}$$ **(ICSE 2019)**

2 Marks Questions

12 Copy and complete the nuclear reaction by filling in the blanks.

$${}_{92}U^{235} + {}_{0}n^{1} \longrightarrow {}_{56}Ba^{\cdots\cdots} + {}_{\cdots\cdots}Kr^{92} + 3\,{}_{0}n^{1}$$

(ICSE 2024)

13 In the following atoms. Which one is radioisotope ? Give one use of this isotope.

$$O^{16}, C^{14}, N^{14}, He^{4}$$ **(ICSE 2024)**

14. How is the radioactivity of a radio isotope affected, if it undergoes a chemical change? Give a reason for your answer. **(ICSE 2023)**

15. What are background radiations? **(ICSE SQP 2023)**

16. Complete and rewrite the following nuclear reaction by filling the blanks.

$${}^{235}_{\cdots}U \rightarrow {}^{\cdots}_{90}Th + {}^{4}_{2}He$$ **(ICSE 2022 Sem-II)**

KEY idea
In α-decay, mass number of nucleus decreased by four while atomic number decreases by two.

17. A nucleus ${}_{84}X^{202}$ of an element emits an α-particle followed by a β-particle. The final nucleus is ${}_{a}Y^{b}$. Find the values of *a* and *b*. **(ICSE 2020)**

18. It is possible for a hydrogen $({}^{1}_{1}H)$ nucleus to emit an alpha particle? Give a reason for your answer. **(ICSE 2019)**

19. Rewrite and complete the following nuclear reaction by filling in the atomic number of Ba and mass number of Kr. **(ICSE 2019)**

$${}^{235}_{92}U + {}^{1}_{0}n \longrightarrow {}^{144}_{\cdots}Ba + {}_{36}Kr^{\cdots} + 3{}^{1}_{0}n + \text{Energy}$$

20. (i) What do you understand by the term nuclear fusion?
(ii) Nuclear power plants use nuclear fission reaction to produce electricity. What is the advantage of producing by fusion reaction? **(ICSE 2018)**

21. (i) What are isobars? (ii) Give one example of isobars. **(ICSE 2018)**

22. State any two properties of α-radiation. **(ICSE SQP 2018)**

23. Why is radioactivity considered to be a nuclear phenomenon? **(ICSE SQP 2018)**

> **KEY idea**
> When some unstable nuclei may emit a quantity of energy and spontaneous emission lead to most to light in radioactivity.

24. State two precautions that should be taken, while handling radioactive substances. **(ICSE SQP 2018)**

25. When does the nucleus of an atom tend to be radioactive? **(ICSE 2017)**

26. Show by equations, the effect on the proton number Z and mass number A of the parent nucleus brought about by the two types of radioactive decay. **(ICSE SQP 2017)**

27. State one industrial use of α, β and γ radiations. **(ICSE SQP 2017)**

28. A radioactive substance is oxidised. Will there be any change in the nature of its radioactivity? Give a reason for your answer. **(ICSE 2016)**

29. An element ${}_ZS^A$ decays to ${}_{85}R^{222}$ after emitting 2α-particles and β-particle. Find the atomic number and atomic mass of the element S. **(ICSE 2016)**

30. Which of the radioactive radiations occurs in the following cases
(i) Can cause severe genetical disorder?
(ii) Are deflected by an electric field? **(ICSE 2013)**

31. A radioactive nucleus undergoes a series of decays according to the sequence.

$$X \xrightarrow{\beta} X_1 \xrightarrow{\alpha} X_2 \xrightarrow{\alpha} X_3$$

If the mass number and atomic number of X_3 are 132 and 69 respectively, what is the mass number and atomic number of X? **(ICSE 2012)**

32. A mixture of radioactive substances gives off three types of radiations.
(i) Name the radiation which travels with the speed of light.
(ii) Name the radiation which has the highest ionising power. **(ICSE 2011)**

33. The nucleus ${}_{84}X^{202}$ emits an α-particle and forms the nucleus Y. Represent this change in the form of an equation. **(ICSE 2011)**

34. Complete the following nuclear changes.
(i) ${}_{11}\text{Na}^{24} \longrightarrow {}_{\dots}\text{Mg}^{\dots} + {}_{-1}\beta^0$
(ii) ${}_{92}\text{U}^{238} \longrightarrow {}_{90}\text{Th}^{234} + \dots + \text{Energy}$ **(ICSE 2010)**

35. (i) Which radiation produces maximum biological damage?
(ii) What happens to the atomic number of an element, when the radiation named by you in part (i) above are emitted? **(ICSE 2010)**

36. A certain radioactive nucleus emits a particle that leaves its mass unchanged but increases its atomic number by one identify the particle and write its symbol. **(ICSE 2006)**

37. How many α and β-particles are emitted when uranium nucleus ${}_{92}\text{U}^{238}$ decays to lead ${}_{82}\text{Pb}^{206}$? **(ICSE 2006)**

3 Marks Questions

38. (a) Complete the following radioactive reaction

$$X \rightarrow Y + {}_2^4\text{He} \longrightarrow {}_{91}^{234}Z + {}_{-1}^{0}e$$

(b) Uranium is available in two forms U - 235 and - U-238. Which of the two isotopes of uranium is more fissionable? **(ICSE 2024)**

39. (i) Complete the following nuclear changes **(ICSE 2023)**

$${}_{92}^{238}P \rightarrow =Q + {}_2^4\text{He} \rightarrow =R + {}_{-1}^{0}\text{e}$$

(ii) Name the nuclear radiation which has the highest ionising power.

40. (i) Which nuclear radiation will travel undeviated in an electric field?
(ii) How can one stop the radiations escaping from a nuclear reactor in a nuclear power plant?
(iii) Name one internal source of background radiations. **(ICSE 2023)**

41. (i) A radioactive nucleus X emits an alpha particle followed by two beta particles and forms nucleus Y. What is the general name of the elements X and Y?
(ii) If the atomic number of Y is 80, then what is the atomic number of X?

(iii) If the atomic mass number of Y is 189, then what is the atomic mass number of X? **(ICSE SQP 2023)**

42. (i) Copy and complete the following nuclear reaction.

$$_{86}^{\;\_}Rn \rightarrow {}_{\_}^{218}Po + {}_{2}^{4}\alpha$$

(ii) What will be the effect on the radiation emitted in the above reaction when it is allowed to pass through an electric field? [Be specific in your answer] **(ICSE SQP 2023)**

43. A beam of α, β and γ rays are travelling through a certain region in space.

(i) Arrange them in ascending order of ionising power.

(ii) Which of the above will pass undeviated, if subjected to an electric field?

(iii) With respect to your answer to part (ii) above, what will be the change in the nucleus of an atom after such a ray is emitted. **(ICSE SQP 2022 Sem-II)**

44. The ore of uranium found in nature contains $_{92}U^{238}$ and $_{92}U^{235}$.

Although both the isotopes are fissionable, it is found out experimentally that one of the two isotopes is more easily fissionable.

(i) Name the isotope of uranium which is easily fissionable.

(ii) Give a reason for your answer.

(iii) Write a nuclear reaction when uranium 238 emits an alpha particle from a thorium (Th) nucleus. **(ICSE 2018)**

45. (i) (a) What are background radiations?

(b) Write an equation of an α emission from U_{92}^{238}.

(c) What will be the change in the rate of radioactivity, if the temperature of the radioactive substance is raised to four times the initial temperature?

(ii) What is nuclear fusion? Write an equation for it. **(ICSE SQP 2018)**

46. (i) Define radioactivity.

(ii) A radioactive substance is oxidised. What change would you expect to take place in the nature of its radioactivity? Give a suitable reason. **(ICSE SQP 2017)**

47. Arrange α, β and γ-rays in ascending order with respect to their

(i) penetrating power

(ii) ionising power

(iii) biological effect **(ICSE 2016)**

48. An atomic nucleus A is composed of 84 protons and 128 neutrons.

(i) The nucleus A emits an α-particle and is transformed into nucleus B. What is the composition of nucleus B?

(ii) The nucleus B emits a β-particle and is transformed into a nucleus C. What is the composition of nucleus C?

(iii) Does the composition of nucleus C change, if it emits gamma radiations? **(ICSE 2015)**

49. A nucleus $_{11}Na^{24}$ emits a β-particle to change into magnesium (Mg).

(i) Write the symbolic equation for the process.

(ii) What are numbers 24 and 11 called?

(iii) What is the general name of $_{12}Mg^{24}$ with respect to $_{11}Na^{24}$? **(ICSE 2014)**

50. (i) What is meant by radioactivity?

(ii) What is meant by nuclear waste?

(iii) Suggest one effective process for the safe disposal of nuclear waste. **(ICSE 2013)**

51. (i) Define radioactivity.

(ii) What happens inside the nucleus, that causes the emission of β-particle?

(iii) Express the above change in the form of an equation. **(ICSE 2011)**

> **KEY idea**
>
> If a nucleus is unstable, then it lead to become stable by using β or α-decay.

52. (i) Name the radioactive radiations which have the least penetrating power.

(ii) Give one use of radio isotopes.

(iii) What is meant by background radiation? **(ICSE 2009)**

53. (i) When does the nucleus of an atom become radioactive?

(ii) How is the radioactivity of an element affected, when it undergoes a chemical change to form a chemical compound?

(iii) Mention one use and one harmful effect of radioactivity. **(ICSE 2008)**

4/5 Marks Questions

54. (i) What is nuclear energy?

(ii) After emission of a nuclear radiation, the atomic number of the daughter nucleus increases by 1. Identify the nuclear radiation.

(iii) Write a nuclear reaction indicating the nuclear change mentioned in (ii).

(iv) What is the special name given to the parent and daughter nucleus when this radiation is emitted? **(ICSE 2022 Sem-II)**

55. A nucleus $^{194}_{82}X$ emits an alpha particle.

(i) What will be the atomic number of the daughter nucleus Y?

(ii) What will be the number of neutrons in the daughter nucleus Y?

(iii) Write a nuclear reaction showing the emission of this particle. **(ICSE SQP 2022 Sem-II)**

56. (i) Why is water used as a coolant in radiators of a car?

(ii) Name the radioactive isotope used to find the age of fossils. Name the radioactive radiation which it emits? **(ICSE SQP 2022 Sem-II)**

57. An atomic nucleus A is composed of 84 protons and 128 neutrons. The nucleus A emits an α-particle and is transformed into a nucleus B.

(i) What is the composition of B?

(ii) The nucleus B emits a β-particle and is transformed into a nucleus C. What is the composition of C?

(iii) What is mass number of the nucleus A?

(iv) Does the composition of C change, if it emits γ-radiations? **(ICSE 2020)**

58. Radiations given out from a source when subjected to an electric field in a direction perpendicular to their path are shown below in the diagram. The arrows show the path of the radiation A, B and C. Answer the following questions in terms A, B and C.

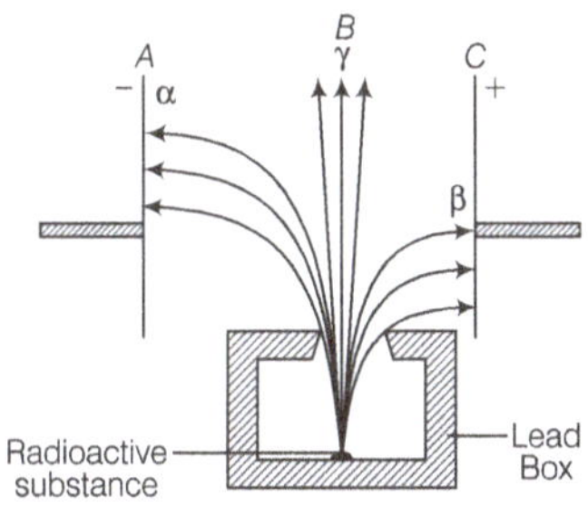

(i) Name the radiation B which is unaffected by the electrostatic field.

(ii) Why does the radiation C deflect more than A?

(iii) Which among the three causes the least biological damage externally?

(iv) Name the radiation which is used in carbon dating. **(ICSE 2018)**

59. 'Radioactive materials as an alternative source of energy must be used wisely'. Give reasons to justify this statement. **(ICSE SQP 2017)**

60. (i) Represent the change in the nucleus of a radioactive element when a β-particle is emitted.

(ii) What is the name given to elements with same mass number and different atomic numbers?

(iii) Under which conditions does the nucleus of an atom tend to be radioactive? **(ICSE 2016)**

61. A certain nucleus X has a mass number 14 and atomic number 6. The nucleus X changes to ${}_7Y^{14}$ after the loss of a particle.

(i) Name the particle emitted.

(ii) Represent this change in the form of an equation.

(iii) A radioactive substance is oxidised. What change would you expect to take place in the nature of its radioactivity? Give a reason for your answer. **(ICSE 2012)**

62. A nucleus ${}_ZX^A$ emits an alpha particle followed by γ-emission, thereafter it emits two β-particles to form X_B.

(i) Copy and complete the values of A and Z for X_3

$$^A_ZX \xrightarrow{-\alpha} X_1 \xrightarrow{-\gamma} X_2 \xrightarrow{-2\beta} X_3$$

(ii) Out of α, β and γ-radiations,

(a) which radiation is the most penetrating?

(b) which radiation is negatively charged? **(ICSE 2009)**

63. (i) What happen to the atomic number of an element, when it emits

(a) an α-particle (b) a β-particle.

(ii) Explain, why α and β-particles are deflected in an electric or a magnetic field but γ-rays are not deflected in such a field. **(ICSE 2007)**

64. (i) Name the particles given out during radioactive decay.

(ii) Show by equation, the effect on the proton number Z and mass number A of the parent nucleus brought about by the two types of radioactive decay.

(iii) What is carbon-14 dating? **(ICSE 2007)**

65. The isotope of $_{92}U^{238}$ decays by α-emission to an isotope of thorium (Th). The thorium isotopes decays by β- emission to an isotope of protactinium (Pa). Write down the equations to represents these two nuclear charges. **(ICSE 2003)**

66. Describe briefly, two properties of each of α and β-particles. **(ICSE 2002)**

67. $_{12}Mg^{24}$ α, β Al γ

In the above nuclear reaction,

(i) $_{12}Mg^{24}$ emits α, β-particles and is transformed to aluminium. What is the mass number and the atomic number of aluminium?

(ii) Aluminium emits γ-rays. What is the resulting nucleus?

(iii) (a) Which radiation or particle from radioactivity produces maximum biological damage?

(b) State three precautions that must be taken while handling a radioactive source. **(ICSE 2001)**

68.

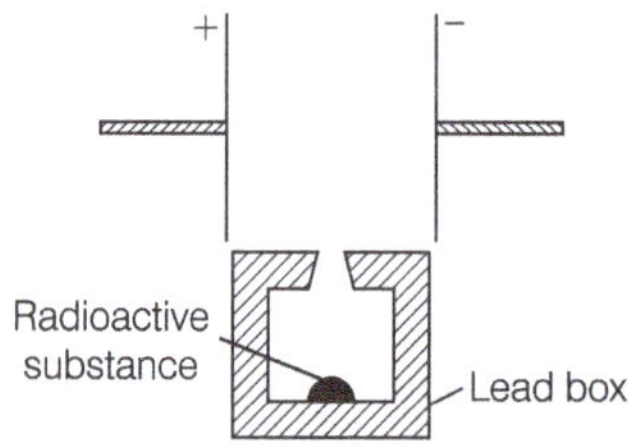

(i) Complete the diagram as given above by drawing the deflection of radioactive radiations in an electric field.

(ii) State any two precautions to be taken while handling radioactive substances. **(ICSE 2015)**

Explanations

1. (a) In this case, the radioactive nucleus contains 128 nucleons. When it emits a β-particle, a neutron is converted into a proton. the number of protons increases by one but neutrons decreases by one. Therefore, the number of nucleons will still be 128.

2. (c) The rate of radioactive decay will remain unchanged as the rate of disintegration is a nuclear phenomenon and does not depend upon environmental factors.

3. (a) Alpha particles can easily be shielded by a single sheet of paper and cannot penetrate the outer dead of skin.

4. When beta decay occurs, the atomic number of nucleus will increase by one unit and mass number will remain same. Thus, here after beta decay, the daughter nucleus has same mass number as product nuclei and one unit atomic number will increase than parent nuclei.

5. The beta particles are attracted to the positively charged plate.

> **Concept Enhancer** Beta particles have negative charge. In cathode rays experiment, these rays have negative charge, so deflected towards the positive plate or anode.

6. (b) The heaviest nuclear radiation is the α-radiation. It is the helium nuclei.

7. (c) The age of excavated material is determined by archaeologists with the help of an isotope of carbon (Carbon-14).

8. (a) γ-particles have highest penetrating power than α, β and X-rays.

9. (d) α-particles are positively charged particle. That's why, it is deflected towards the negatively charged particles.

10. Disposal of nuclear waste should be grounded in deep mines because there is a risk of nuclear accidents causing due to leakage of nuclear radiation.

11. $^3He_2 + {}^2H_1 \rightarrow {}^4He_2 + {}^1H_1 + \text{Energy}$

12. $_{92}U^{235} + {}_0n^1 \longrightarrow {}_{56}Ba^{141} + {}_{36}Kr^{92} + 3\,{}_0n^1$

For balancing, $235 + 1 = x + 92 + 3 \times 1$

$$236 = x + 95$$

$$x = 236 - 95 = 141$$

Again, $92 + 0 = 56 + y + 3 \times 0$

$$y = 92 - 56 = 36$$

13. C^{14} is a radioisotope and it is used in agriculture to increased the yield of crop seeds.

14. Radioactivity of an element is not affected by the chemical change as radioactivity is a nuclear phenomenon and does not involve extranuclear electrons.

15. Refer to text on page 200 (Background radiations).

16. General equation for α-decay is

$$_{Z}X^{A} \xrightarrow{\alpha\text{-particle}} {}_{Z-2}Y^{A-4} + {}_{4}^{2}\text{He}$$

(Thorium) (α-particle)

$$Z_{LHS} = Z_{RHS}$$
$$x = 90 + 2$$
$$x = 92$$
$$A_{LHS} = A_{RHS}$$
$$235 = y + 4$$
$$235 - 4 = y$$
$$231 = y$$

Now, complete reaction is

$$^{235}_{92}\text{U} \longrightarrow {}^{231}_{90}\text{Th} + {}^{4}_{2}\text{He}$$

17. When an α-particle is emitted by a nucleus, then mass number of nucleus is decreased by 4 units, while atomic number is decreased by 2 units. Similarly, for β-particle emission, atomic number is increased by one unit while mass number remains same.

$$\therefore \quad {}_{84}X^{202} \xrightarrow{-\alpha} {}_{82}Z^{198} \xrightarrow{-\beta} {}_{83}Y^{198}$$
$$\therefore \quad {}_{a}Y^{b} = {}_{83}Y^{198}$$
$$\Rightarrow \quad a = 83 \text{ and } b = 198$$

18. No, it is not possible because alpha particle consists of two protons and two neutrons. However, none of the isotopes of hydrogen has the same or more number of protons and neutrons in its nuclei. Thus, they cannot emit an alpha particle.

19.
$$Z_{LHS} = Z_{RHS}$$
$$92 = 36 + x + 0$$
$$92 - 36 = x \Rightarrow x = 56$$
$$A_{LHS} = A_{RHS}$$
$$235 + 1 = 144 + y + 3$$
$$y = 236 - 147 = 89$$

Now, the complete reaction is

$$^{235}_{92}\text{U} + {}^{1}_{0}n \rightarrow {}^{144}_{56}\text{Ba} + {}^{89}_{36}\text{Kr} + 3{}^{1}_{0}n + \text{Energy}$$

Common Mistake Students think that the nuclear reaction products remain same for $^{235}_{92}\text{U}$ but nuclear reaction depends upon the neutron nature

20. (i) In nuclear fusion, two light nuclei are combined to form a heavy nucleus with release of energy.
(ii) In fusion per unit mass more energy is released than fission, therefore it will be more useful in producing electricity.

21. (i) The atoms of different elements which have the same mass number (A), but different atomic number (Z) are called isobars.
(ii) $^{23}_{11}\text{Na}$ and $^{23}_{11}\text{Mg}$ are isobars having same mass number 23 and different atomic numbers.

22. Refer to text on page 199.
(Properties of α-particles).

23. Radioactivity is the spontaneous random emission of particles from within the nucleus of atom. Radiations are emitted from nucleus of an atom, thus the radioactivity considered to be a nuclear phenomenon.

24. (i) One should put on special lead-lined aprons and hand gloves.
(ii) One should handle radioactive materials with long lead tongs.

25. Atoms with unstable nuclei are constantly changing as a result of the imbalance of energy within the nucleus. Instability of an atoms nucleus may result from an excess of either neutrons or protons. Radioactivity is the release of energy and matter. This means, when the nucleus loses a neutron, it gives off energy and becomes radioactive.

26. Two types of radioactive decay are
(i) Emission of α-ray
(ii) Emission of β-ray

Equation of emission of α-ray

$$^{A}_{Z}X \longrightarrow {}^{A-4}_{Z-2}Y + {}^{4}_{2}\text{He}$$

Equation of emission of β-ray

$$^{A}_{Z}X \longrightarrow {}^{A}_{Z+1}Y + {}^{0}_{-1}e$$

27. **α-radiation** As smoke detectors for industrial purpose.
β-radiation Monitoring paper thickness in industries.
γ-radiation As tracers for detecting leakage in pipes.

28. There will be no change in the nature of its radioactivity, because radioactivity is a nuclear phenomenon and oxidation does not affect the nucleus of the substance.

29. $_{88}S^{230} \longrightarrow {_{85}R^{222}} + 2\alpha \longrightarrow {_{+1}^{0}e} + \nu_e$

Therefore, atomic number, $Z = 88$

Mass number, $A = 230$

30. (i) Gamma radiation can cause severe genetical disorder.

(ii) Since α, β are charged particles, so it gets deflected by an electric field.

31. According to the question, $_{72}X^{140} \xrightarrow{_{-1}\beta^0} {_{73}X_1^{140}}$

$\xrightarrow{\alpha(_2He^4)} {_{71}X_2^{136}} \xrightarrow{\alpha(_2He^4)} {_{69}X_3^{132}}$

32. (i) γ- radiation.

(ii) α ($_2He^4$) particle.

33. The equation for the given nuclear reaction is

$$_{84}X^{202} \xrightarrow{_2He^4} {_{82}Y^{198}} + \alpha\text{-particle}$$

34. (i) $_{11}Na^{24} \longrightarrow {_{12}Mg^{24}} + {_{-1}\beta^0}$

(ii) $_{92}U^{238} \longrightarrow {_{90}Th^{234}}$

$+ {_2He^4}$ (α-particle) Energy

35. (i) γ-radiation produces maximum biological damage.

(ii) There is no change in atomic and mass number of element formed after γ- radiation or emission.

36. As β-particle consists of $_{-1}\beta^0$ and after its emission, atomic number increases by 1 and mass number remains as it is. Its symbol is $_{-1}\beta^0$.

37. As from the question, change in mass number is $238 - 206 = 32$ and change in atomic number is $92 - 82 = 10$.

As mass number is decreased by 32, so there is emission of 8α-particle ($_2He^4$). Since, the change in atomic number is only 10, so there must be 6 β-particle emission.

38. (a) $_AX^B \rightarrow {_CY^D} + {_2He^4} \rightarrow {_{91}Z^{234}} + {_{-1}e^0}$

On balancing,

$$D + 4 = 234 + 0$$
$$D = 234 - 4 = 230$$
$$C + 2 = 91 - 1 = 90$$
$$C = 90 - 2 = 88$$

Again, $B = 234$

$$A = 91 - 1 = 90$$

So, complete equation

$$_{90}X^{234} \rightarrow {_{88}Y^{230}} + {_2He^4} \rightarrow {_{91}Z^{234}} + {_{-1}e^0}$$

(b) Refer to answer of question 44 on the page 209.

39. (i) Nuclear reaction was accompanied with release of a particle having mass number and atomic number equal to 4 and 2, respectively. Hence, emitted atom is an alpha particle.

$$^{238}_{92}U \rightarrow {^{234}_{90}Th} + {^4_2He} + \text{Energy}$$

Secondly, parent nucleus Q changes into daughter nucleus R due to beta decay. When a beta particle is emitted, the atomic number increased by 1 but the mass number of the parent nuclei remains the same.

$$^{234}_{90}Th \rightarrow {^{234}_{91}Pa} + {^0_{-1}e}$$

(ii) Alpha particles have the highest ionisation power than the other two types of radiations owing to the fact that an α-particle is double ionised helium nucleus. i.e. He^{2+}.

40. (i) Gamma radiations will travel undeviated in an electric field.

(ii) The steel containment vessel serves as a barrier to prevent leakage of any radioactive gases or fluids from the plant. An outer concrete building serves as final layer, protecting the steel containment vessel.

(iii) All people have internal radiation, mainly from radioactive potassium-40 and carbon-14 inside their bodies from birth.

41. (i) $_ZX^A \xrightarrow{-\alpha} {_{Z-2}B^{A-4}} \xrightarrow{-2\beta} Y^{A-4}$

X and Y are isotopes.

(ii) 80 isotopes have same atomic number.

(iii) $A - 4 = 189 \Rightarrow A = 189 + 4 = 193$

42. (i) $^{222}_{86}Rn \rightarrow {^{218}_{84}Po} + {^4_2\alpha}$

$$\Rightarrow Z + 84 = 86$$
$$Z = 2$$
$$\Rightarrow A + 218 = 222$$
$$\Rightarrow A = 222 - 218$$
$$A = 4$$

(ii) α-particles are positively charged particles. It is deflected towards negative plate or terminals.

43. (i) $\gamma < \beta < \alpha$

(ii) γ-rays pass undeviated, if subjected to an electric field.

(iii) The nucleus of the atom has no change in the mass number and atomic number during γ-emission. So, γ-rays take no mass and no electrical charge from the nucleus.

44. (i) $_{92}U^{235}$ is easily fissionable.

(ii) Fission of uranium with mass number of 238 is possible by only fast neutron but the fission of uranium with mass number of 235 is also possible by slow neutron.

(iii) $^{238}_{92}U \longrightarrow ^{234}_{90}Th + ^{4}_{2}He$ (α-particle)

45. (i) (a) Refer to text on page no 200 (Background radiation).

(b) $^{238}_{92}U \xrightarrow{\alpha\text{-emission}} ^{234}_{90}X + ^{4}_{3}He + \text{Energy}$

(c) No change, radioactivity does not depend on temperature.

(ii) Refer to text on page 201 (Nuclear fusion).

46. (i) Refer to text on page 198 (Radioactivity).

(ii) If a radioactive substance is oxidised, then it will no affect its radioactivity because oxidation is a chemical process involving electrons presents outside the nucleus and radioactivity is the process happening inside the nucleus and it affects the protons and neutrons.

47. Ascending order arrangement of α, β and γ-particles with respect to their

(i) penetrating power: α-particle, β-particle, γ-particle.

(ii) Ionising power: γ-particle, β-particle, α-particle.

(iii) Biological effect: γ-particle, β-particle, α-particle.

48. (i) Emission of α-particle implies loss of 1 helium nuclei. So, the composition of nucleus *B* is 82 protons and 124 neutrons.

$$^{128}A_{84} \longrightarrow ^{124}B_{82} + ^{4}He_{2}$$

(ii) β-emission implies loss of 1 fast moving electron. So, the composition of nucleus *C* is

$$^{124}B_{82} \longrightarrow ^{124}C_{83} + ^{0}e_{-1}$$

(iii) In case of gamma emission, electromagnetic waves are emitted and there will be no change in the composition of nucleus *C*.

49. (i) The symbolic equation of this process is

$$_{11}Na^{24} \longrightarrow _{12}Mg^{24} + _{-1}e^{0}$$

(ii) 24 is the mass number and 11 is the atomic number.

(iii) $_{11}Na^{24}$ and $_{12}Mg^{24}$ are isobars.

Concept Enhancer $^{24}_{11}$Na is less stable, so it goes in beta decay to form stable magnesium nuclei and release a neutron. This neutron on decomposition gives proton and beta particles.

50. (i) Refer to text on page 198 in radioactivity.

(ii) Nuclear waste are the material which remains after the use of radioactive element such as α, β and γ-particles in the form of radiation.

(iii) Nuclear waste must be put in a thick casks (dumbell shaped structure), then after burried in the specially constructed deep underground stores.

51. (i) Refer to text on page 198 (radioactivity).

(ii) Inside the nucleus, to attain stability neutrons may changes to a proton and emits a β-particle.

(iii) $_{Z}X^{A} \xrightarrow{_{-1}\beta^{0}} _{Z+1}Y^{A} + _{-1}e$

where, A = mass number

and Z = atomic number.

52. (i) α-particle ($_{2}He^{4}$).

(ii) Radioactive isotopes are used in fuel for atomic energy reactor.

(iii) These are the invisible radioactive radiations such as α, β and γ produced during nuclear decay.

53. (i) If the atomic number of an element is more than 82, then after it becomes radioactive. Atomic number between 82 to 92 are good radioactive elements.

(ii) There is no change in the radioactivity during the chemical reaction, because chemical reaction involves electrons of shell, whereas radioactivity involves nucleons (i.e. neutron and protons).

(iii) Uses of radioactivity is in production of electricity in nuclear reactor and in carbon dating by (C^{14}) and in harmful effect, it can cause skin cancer and eye diseases.

Concept Enhancer The average life of radioactive element is determine with the help of carbon (C^{14}).

54. (i) Nuclear energy is the energy released during the transformation of nuclei to another nuclei.

(ii) The atomic number of the daughter nucleus increases by 1 in the β-decay.

(iii) Nuclear reaction for β-decay.

$$ {}^{1}_{0}n \longrightarrow {}^{1}_{1}p + \underset{(\beta\text{-particle})}{{}^{0}_{-1}e} $$

(iv) Parent nucleus is known as neutron and daughter nucleus is known as proton.

55. (i) ${}^{194}_{82}X$ emits an alpha particle.

We know, an alpha particle consists of two protons and two neutrons (${}^{4}_{2}\alpha$).

On emitting an alpha particle, the atomic number will reduce by 2 and the mass number will reduce by 4.

Thus, atomic number of the daughter nucleus Y

$$= 82 - 2 = 80$$

Mass number of the daughter nucleus Y

$$= 194 - 4 = 190$$

(ii) Number of protons in daughter nucleus $Y = 80$

Thus, number of neutrons in daughter nucleus Y

$$= 190 - 80 = 110$$

(iii) Nuclear reaction showing the emission of this particle is ${}^{194}_{-82}X \xrightarrow{-({}^{4}_{2}\alpha)} {}^{190}_{80}Y$

56. (i) Water is used as a coolant in car radiators because of its high specific heat capacity.

(ii) Carbon-14 is a radioactive isotope which is used to find the age of fossils. It is β-radiation. When carbon-14 emits a beta particle, it becomes nitrogen-14.

57. (i) Number of proton in atomic nucleus, $A = 84$

∴ Atomic number of $A = 84$

Number of neutron, $N = 128$

∴ Mass number of A,

$$M = Z + N = 84 + 128 = 212$$

∴ When an α-particle is emitted from a nucleus, then its mass number is decreased by 4 units and atomic number is decreased by 2 units.

$$\therefore \qquad {}_{84}A^{212} \xrightarrow{\alpha} {}_{82}B^{208}$$

(ii) When a β-particle is emitted from a nucleus, then atomic number is increased by one unit and mass number is unaffected.

$$\therefore \qquad {}_{82}B^{208} \xrightarrow{\beta} {}_{83}C^{208}$$

(iii) Mass number of nucleus A

$$= Z + N = 84 + 128 = 212$$

(iv) There is no change in the composition of C by the emission of γ-radiations.

58. (i) Gamma radiations.

(ii) The radiation C deflect more than A, because the mass of β-particles is less than that of α-particle hence radiation deflects more than A.

(iii) γ-rays

(iv) β-radiation is used in carbon dating.

59. Ratioactive materials as an alternative source of energy must be used wisely because of the following reasons

(i) Radioactive materials are available in nature as a conservative amount due to which they are found very less amount in nature.

(ii) The radioactive materials emit a large amount of energy in the process, if nuclear reaction which is used in nuclear power plants to generate energy.

(iii) Radioactive materials also emit harmful rays like α, β and γ-rays.

(iv) These rays damage the human body due to which various diseases occur in the body lke cancer and skin diseases.

Therefore, radioactive material is an alternative source of energy that must be used wisely.

Hence, that's why radioactive materials are used wisely.

60. (i) The emission of β-particle by the nuclei of radioactive substance does not change the mass number of the atom, but increases its atomic number by one.

$$ {}^{A}_{Z}X \longrightarrow {}^{A}_{Z+}Y + {}^{0}_{-1}e $$

(ii) Isobar is the name given to the elements with the same mass number and different atomic numbers.

(iii) If the neutron to proton ratio of an atom is greater than 1.5 or atoms of atomic number greater than 82, this atom tends to become radioactive.

61. (i) Since, during the ${}_{-1}\beta^{0}$-emission, there is gain in atomic number.

(ii) $ {}_{6}X^{14} \xrightarrow{{}_{-1}\beta^{0}} {}_{7}Y^{14} + {}_{-1}e^{0} $

(iii) There is no change in the nature of radioactivity during oxidation. Because oxidation is a phenomena in which involvement of electrons takes place, whereas in radioactivity nucleons takes part in reaction.

62. (i) $_ZX^A \xrightarrow{-\alpha(_2He^4)} {}_{Z-2}X_1^{A-4} \xrightarrow{-_0\gamma^0}$

$_{Z-2}X_2^{A-4} \xrightarrow{-2\beta(_{-1}\beta^\circ)} {}_ZX_3^{A-4}$

(ii) (a) The penetration power of γ is maximum.

(b) As β is $_{-1}\beta^0$, so it is negatively charged particle in the radiation during radioactivity.

63. (i) (a) When an α-particle is emitted, then atomic number decreases by 2 and mass number decreases by 4.

(b) During β-emission, atomic number increases by 1 as it consists of $_{-1}\beta^0$.

(ii) Since, alpha particle is a helium nuclei ($_2He^4$) and is positively charged particle and β-particle is ($_{-1}\beta^\circ$), negatively charged particle.

So, in an electric field, it experiences some force, to get deflected.

64. (i) The particle given out in nuclear reaction are α-particle ($_2He^4$), β-particle ($_{-1}\beta$) and γ-particle ($_0\gamma^0$).

(ii) As the parent nucleus be X, so after

α-decay is $_ZX^A \xrightarrow{-\alpha(_2He^4)} {}_{Z-2}X^{A-4}$

and β-decay is $_ZP^A \xrightarrow{-\beta(_{-1}\beta^0)} {}_{Z+1}P^A$

(iii) Carbon 14 dating, is a scientific method that can accurately determine the age of rocks containing carbon.

65. The equation for α-emission is as follows

$$_{92}U^{238} \xrightarrow{-\alpha(_2He^4)} {}_{90}Th^{234}$$

The equation for β-emission is as follows

$$_{90}Th^{234} \xrightarrow{-\beta(_{-1}\beta^0)} (\text{Protactinium})\ _{91}Pa^{234}$$

66. Refer to text on page no 199.

67. The equation for radioactive reaction is

$$_{12}Mg^{24} \xrightarrow{-1\alpha,\ -1\beta} {}_{11}Al^{22}$$

(i) The mass number will be 22 and atomic number will be 11.

(ii) When aluminium emits γ-rays, there will be no effect in the nucleus formed.

(iii) (a) The radiation of γ-particles give most damage to the biological system.

(b) Three protective measures to handle radioactive material are as follows

I. Person should put on special lead lived aprons, lead gloves, etc.

II. Nucleus materials must be kept in lead box.

III. The workers must wear special film badges which can absorb nuclear radiations and they must have compulsory medical check up.

68. (i)

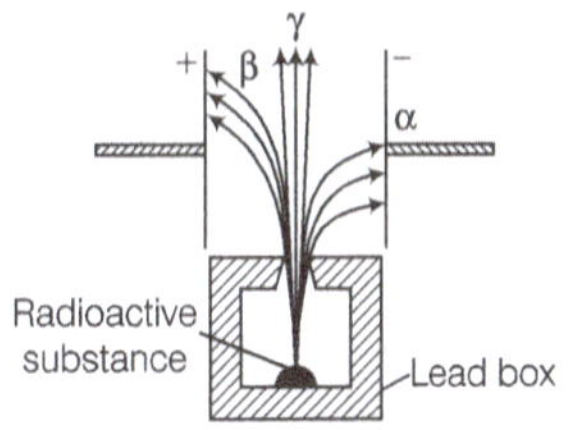

(ii) While handling the radioactive materials following precautions must be taken

(a) Radioactive substance must be kept in a thick lead box.

(b) One should wear special protective lead coats and lead gloves while handling a radioactive substance.

CHAPTER TEST

01 Mark Questions

1 A radioactive substance emits radiations
(a) α ,β and γ simultaneously
(b) in the order α ,β and γ one-by-one
(c) X-rays and γ-rays
(d) α or β

2 The least penetrating radiation is
(a) α-particles
(b) β-particles
(c) X-rays
(d) γ-radiations

3 In fission of one U-235 nucleus, the loss in mass is 0.2 amu. Calculate the energy released.
(a) 186.2 MeV
(b) 182.6 MeV
(c) 156.4 MeV
(d) 189.1 MeV

4 Which of the following are the radioactive elements?
(a) Uranium, radium
(b) Polonium, thorium
(c) Plutonium, actinium
(d) All of the above

5 In emission of gamma radiation, there is
(a) change in number of proton
(b) change in number of neutron
(c) change in energy of nucleus
(d) change in number of protons and neutrons

02 Marks Questions

6 Define the following terms
(i) Atomic number
(ii) Mass number

7 Define the term isotopes. Give an example.

8 What are isobars?

9 When does nucleus of an atom, tend to be radioactive?

10 What is nuclear fission?

Structured Questions

11 (i) What is meant by radioactivity? Name the radioactive substances. **(3)**
(ii) Differentiate between nuclear fission and nuclear fusion. **(3)**
(iii) Describe briefly two properties of each α, β and γ-radiations. **(4)**

12 (i) Explain in brief the given statement:
Radioactivity is a nuclear phenomenon. **(3)**
(ii) Write a comparison between α, β and γ-radiations. **(3)**
(iii) (a) Briefly explain the two main sources of nuclear radiations.
(b) How are these radiations harmful? **(4)**

Answers

1. (d) **2.** (a) **3.** (a) **4.** (d) **5.** (c)

ICSE

SAMPLE PAPER 01

Time : 2 hrs
Marks : 80

Physics
Paper 1

General Instructions

1. You will not be allowed to write during the first 15 minutes. This time is to be spent in reading the question paper.
2. The time given at the head of this paper is the time allowed for writing the answers.
3. Section A is compulsory. Attempt any four questions from Section B.
4. The intended marks for questions or parts of questions are given in brackets [ ].

Section-A [40 Marks]

(Attempt all questions from this section)

1. Choose the correct answers to the questions from the given options. **[15]**

(i) A pump of 200 W power is lifting 2 kg water per second from an average depth of 10m. The velocity with which water comes out of the pump is (Take, $g = 9.8\ ms^{-2}$)

(a) $2\ ms^{-1}$ (b) $2.5\ ms^{-1}$
(c) $4\ ms^{-1}$ (d) $10.2\ ms^{-1}$

(ii) Moment is said to be positive when it is

(a) in opposite direction
(b) anti-clockwise
(c) clockwise
(d) in same direction

(iii) Pendulums A, B, C and D are tied to a flexible string PQ and are at rest.

Pendulum C is disturbed. Which of the following statements is true?

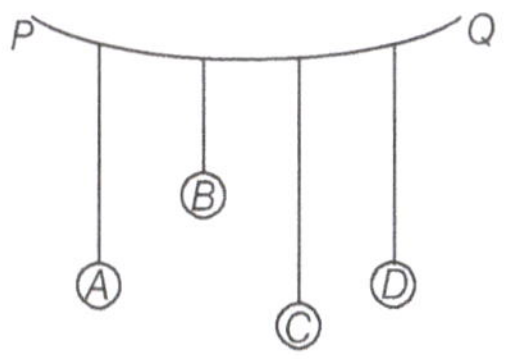

(a) Only pendulum C will start vibrating.
(b) Pendulums A, B and D will also start vibrating but A and D will vibrate with the maximum amplitude.
(c) Pendulums A, B and D will also start vibrating.
(d) Vibrations of pendulum C are forced vibrations.

(iv) Kinetic energy of an object increases which is due to

(a) change in momentum
(b) change in position
(c) change in distance
(d) None of the above

(v) The radiation with maximum energy is

(a) γ-rays (b) β- rays
(c) X-rays (d) α- ray

(vi) **Assertion** (A) Reflection of light is the phenomenon of bouncing back of light in the same medium on striking the surface of any object.

Reason (R) Light particle possess elastic property.

(a) Both A and R are true.
(b) A is true but R is false.
(c) A is false but R is true.
(d) Both A and R are false.

(vii) To determine the equivalent resistance of two resistors when connected in series. A student arranged the circuit components as shown in the figure but he did not succeed to achieve the objective.

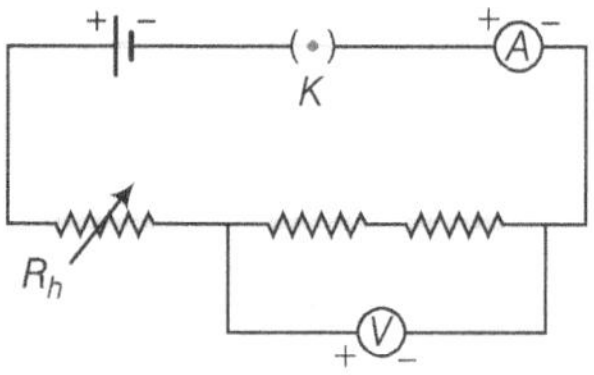

Which of the following mistakes has been committed by him in setting up the circuit?
(a) Position of ammeter is incorrect
(b) Position of voltmeter is incorrect
(c) Terminals of ammeter are wrongly connected
(d) Terminals of voltmeter are wrongly connected

(viii) What will be the power of the combination of lenses given below?

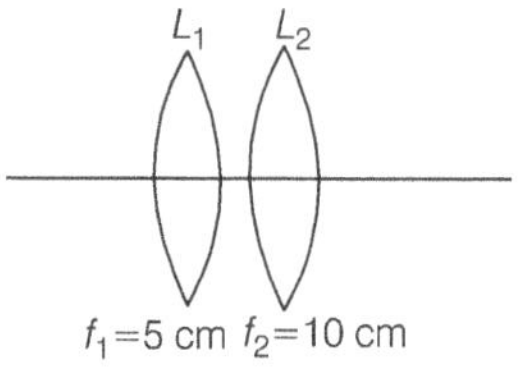

(a) 10 D (b) 20 D
(c) 30 D (d) 40 D

(ix) Resonance is a forced vibration, in which
(a) amplitude remains constant
(b) frequency of forced vibration is greater than the frequency of free vibrations of the body
(c) frequency of forced vibration is equal to the frequency of free vibrations of the body
(d) frequency of forced vibration is less than the frequency of free vibrations of the body

(x) For the given circuit, name the components which are connected in parallel.

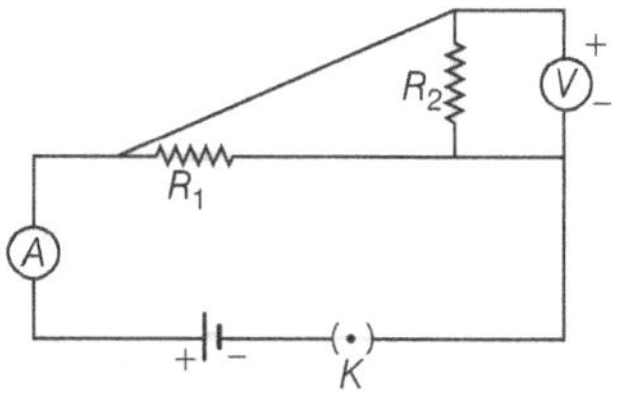

(a) Both R_1 and R_2 (b) R_1, R_2 and V
(c) Both R_2 and V (d) Both R_1 and V

(xi) Apparent depth is due to
(a) reflection of light
(b) diffuse reflection of light
(c) refraction of light
(d) None of the above

(xii) Which of the following is not true for refraction?
(a) The light rays bend towards normal in denser medium.
(b) The light rays bend away from normal in rarer medium.
(c) The frequency of the light ray does not change.
(d) The wavelength of the ray does not change.

(xiii) Two identical calorimeters A and B contain equal quantity of water at 20° C. A 5 g piece of metal X of specific heat 0.2 cal $g^{-1}°C^{-1}$ is dropped into A and a 5 g piece of metal Y into B. The equilibrium temperature in A is 22°C and in B is 23°C. The initial temperature of both the metals is 40° C. The quantity of water used is
(a) 9 g (b) 10 g (c) 12 g (d) 14 g

(xiv) How many grams of ice at –14°C are needed to cool 200 g of water from 25°C to 10°C? (Take, specific heat of ice = 0.5 cal g^{-1} $°C^{-1}$ and latent heat of ice = 80 cal g^{-1})
(a) 20 g (b) 27 g (c) 30 g (d) 31 g

(xv) A small bar magnet is slowly inserted in the solenoid with uniform velocity and taken out from other end as shown in figure.

Which of the following represent the graph of induced emf ?

(a)
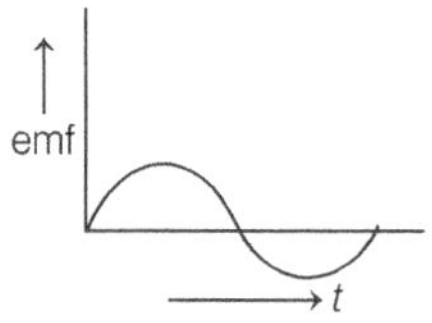

(b)
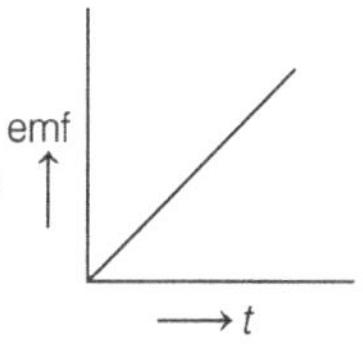

(c)
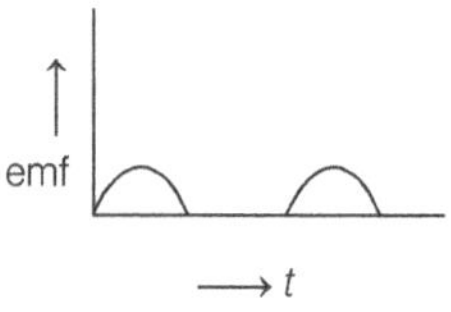

(d)
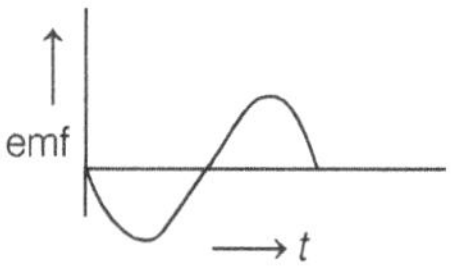

2. (i) Complete the following by choosing the correct answers from the bracket. [6]

(a) In class ……… (I/II/III) lever, the effort is situated between the load and the fulcrum.

(b) The energy change during photosynthesis in plants is …… (heat to chemical/light to chemical/chemical to heat).

(c) Speed of light ……… (increases/decreases/reamins same) when light passes from a denser to a rarer medium.

(d) If the mass as well as the velocity of the body is tripled, then the kinetic energy of the body…… (is doubled/becomes twenty seven times/becomes four times) the initial kinetic energy.

(e) Optical fibre is based upon the principle of ……… [Reflection/Total internal reflection/Refraction].

(f) The centre of gravity of a uniform ball is at its…… (geometrical centre/bottom/topmost point).

(ii) An erect, diminished and virtual image is formed when an object is placed between the optical centre and principal focus of a lens.
Draw a ray diagram to show the formation of the image with the above characteristics. [2]

(iii) What are the factors on which the internal resistance of a cell depends? [2]

3. (i) P, Q and R are three coplanar forces which acts at a distance x_1, x_2 and x_3 respectively from point O as shown in the figure. A point O lies in the same plane $P = Q = R = 6$ N.
If $x_1 = 4$ m, $x_2 = 3$ m and $x_3 = 1$ m, [2]

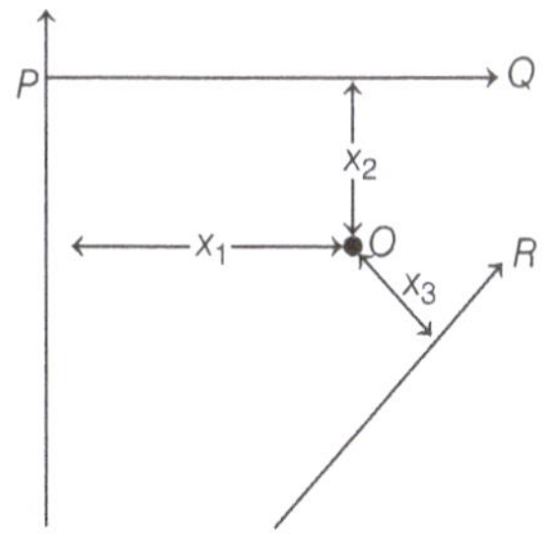

(a) which force has the least moment about O?

(b) which force has the greatest moment about O?

(ii) (a) Derive the relation between CGS and SI unit of power. [1]

(b) A man is holding a suitcase in his hand at rest. What is the work done by him? [1]

(iii) (a) A baby recognises her mother by her voice. Name the characteristic of sound involved. [1]

(b) A human heart beats 72 times in 1 min. Calculate its frequency. [1]

(iv) (a) A torch bulb when cold has 1 Ω resistance. It draws a current 0.3 A when glowing from a source of 3V. Calculate the resistance of the bulb when glowing. [1]

(b) Explain the reason for the difference in resistance. [1]

(v) Water is used in cold countries as heat reservoir for wine and juice bottles to prevent their freezing. Why? [2]

(vi) A mixture of radioactive substances gives off three types of radiations.

(a) Name the radiation which travels with the speed of light. [1]

(b) Name the radiation which has the highest ionising power. [1]

(vii) (a) Why is it easier to draw water from a well when the rope passes over a pulley?
Following equations reflect the nuclear reactions described incompletely. Fill the gaps in these equations.

(b) $^{210}_{93}\text{Bi} \longrightarrow ^{\cdots}_{\cdots}\text{Po} + ^{-1}_{0}\beta\text{-particle}$

(c) $^{39}_{19}\text{K} + _{\cdots} \longrightarrow ^{42}_{20}\text{Ca} + ^{1}_{1}\text{H}$ [3]

Section-B [40 Marks]

(Attempt any four questions from this section)

4. (i) (a) State the conditions required for total internal reflection of light to take place.

(b) The diagram shows the refraction of a ray light from air to a liquid is as shown in the figure below. Write the values of angle of incidence and refraction. [3]

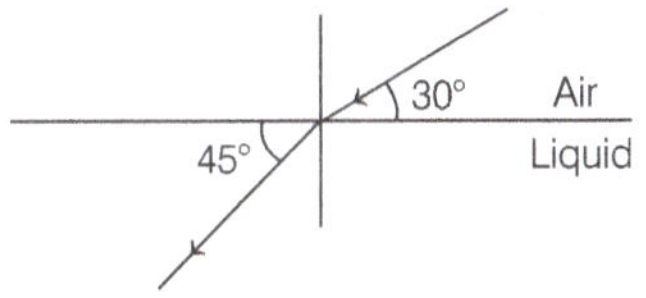

(ii) A 6 cm tall object is placed perpendicular to the principal axis of a convex lens of focal length 25 cm. The distance of the object from the lens is 40 cm.
By calculation, determine

(a) the position and

(b) the size of the image formed. [3]

(iii) (a) When does a ray of light falling on a lens pass through it undeviated?

(b) Copy and complete the ray diagram to show the formation of the image of the object PQ.

I. Name the lens LL'.

II. What is the name given to point X? **[4]**

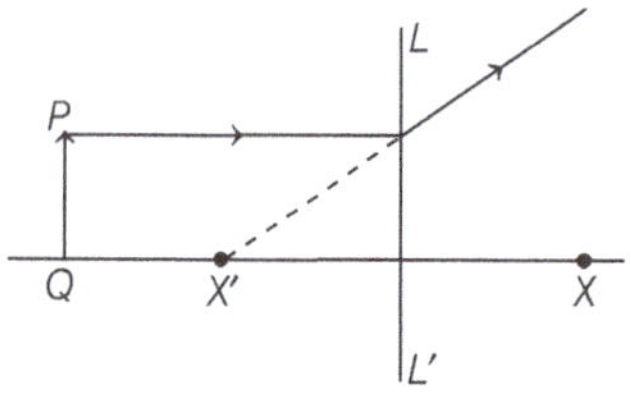

5. (i) From the diagram given below, answer the questions that follow

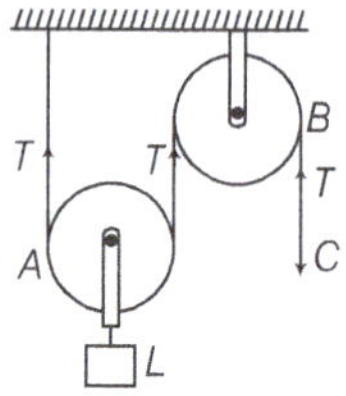

(a) What kind of pulleys are A and B?

(b) State the purpose of pulley B.

(c) What effort has to be applied at C to just raise the load $L = 20$ kgf ? (Neglect the weight of pulley A and friction) **[3]**

(ii) A uniform meter scale can be balanced at the 70.0 cm mark when a mass of 0.05 kg is hung from the 94.0 cm mark.

(a) Draw a diagram of the arrangement.

(b) Find the mass of the meter scale. **[3]**

(iii) (a) A man having a box on his head climbs up a slope and another man having an identical box walks the same distance on a levelled road. Who does more work against the force of gravity and why?

(b) Calculate the kinetic energy of a body of mass 0.5 kg and momentum 30 kg-m/s. **[4]**

6. (i) (a) Write the parameters on which the intensity of sound wave depends.

(b) Give one example of forced vibrations.

(c) In which unit, is the loudness of sound measured? **[3]**

(ii) (a) Briefly explain the term radiation hazards.

(b) Define the causes of radiations. **[3]**

(iii) The figure shows the displacement-time graph of a vibrating body.

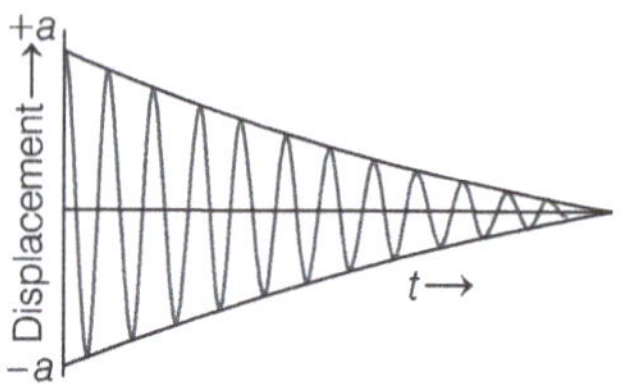

(a) Name the kind of vibrations and give one example of such vibrations.

(b) Why is the amplitude of vibrations gradually decreasing?

(c) What happens to the vibrations of the body after sometime? **[4]**

7. (i) (a) A thorium isotope $^{223}_{90}Th$ undergoes an α-decay and changes into radium. What is the atomic number and mass number of the radium produced?

(b) If the radium undergoes a further disintegration and emits two β particles, represent this reaction in the form of an equation.

(c) What is the source of energy released during the decay? **[3]**

(ii) (a) Write an expression for the heat energy liberated by a hot body.

(b) Some heat is provided to a body to raise its temperature by 25°C. What will be the corresponding rise in temperature of the body as shown on the Kelvin scale?

(c) What happens to the average kinetic energy of the molecules as ice melts at 0°C? **[3]**

(iii) The figure below shows a magnetic needle kept just below the conductor AB which is kept in North-South direction.

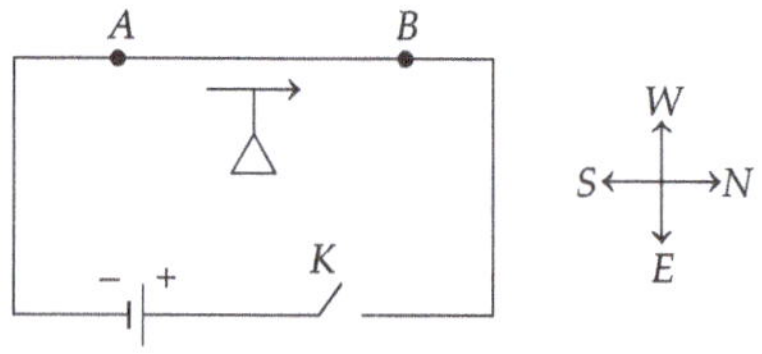

(a) In which direction will the needle deflect when the key is closed?

(b) Why is the deflection produced?

(c) What will be the change in the deflection, if the magnetic needle is taken just above the conductor AB?

(d) Name one device which works on this principle. **[4]**

8. (i) (a) Name the new and old colour codes of the wire which is connected to the switch of an appliance.
(b) Draw the diagrams of a dual control switch when the bulb is switched ON and OFF.
(c) Calculate the electrical energy consumed when a bulb of 40 W is used for 12.5 h everyday for 30 days. **[3]**

(ii) A piece of ice of mass 100 g is dropped into 450 g of water at 45°C. Calculate the final temperature of water after all of the ice has melted. (Specific heat capacity of water = 4200 J/kg°C, specific heat of fusion of ice $= 336 \times 10^3$ J/kg) **[3]**

(iii) (a) Draw a labelled diagram to make an electromagnet from a soft iron bar. Mark the polarity at its ends in your diagram.
(b) What is the nature of magnetic field inside a long straight solenoid carrying current?
(c) Consider a circular loop of wire lying in the plane of table. The current passing through the loop clockwise.
Draw the magnetic field lines inside and outside the loop. **[4]**

9. (i) A metal piece of mass 20 g is heated to a constant temperature of 100°C. Then, it is dropped in a calorimeter of mass 50 g and specific heat capacity 0.42 J $g^{-1}K^{-1}$, containing 50 g of water at 20°C. After stirring the water, the highest temperature recorded is 22°C. Calculate the specific heat capacity of metal. (Specific heat capacity of water is 4.2 J$g^{-1}K^{-1}$) **[3]**

(ii) A piece of ice is heated at a constant rate. The variation in the temperature with time is shown in the graph below.

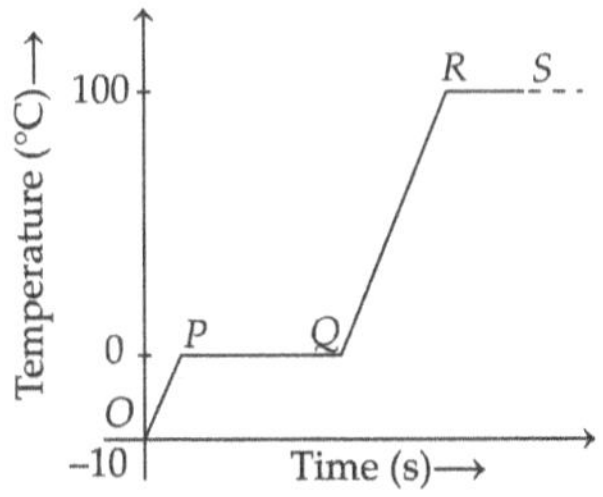

(a) Identify the different phases present in the graph above.
(b) Compare the lengths of *PQ* and *RS* and explain the difference.
(c) What does the slope of the graph between the phase changes indicate? **[3]**

(iii) Monika has drawn the electric circuit to study Ohm's law as shown in figure. Her teacher told that the circuit diagram require correction.

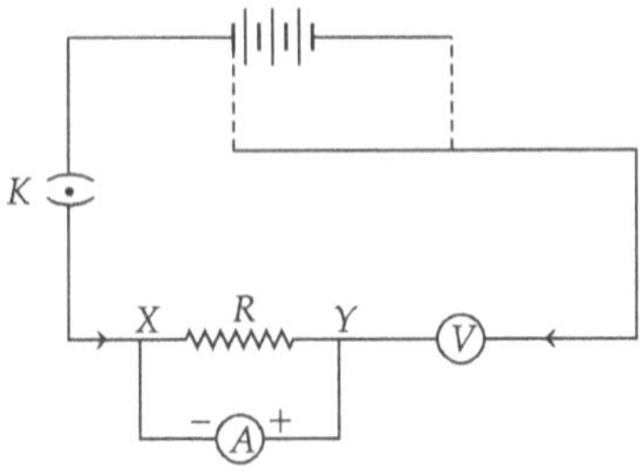

(a) What corrections Monika should do in above circuit to be correct?
(b) Redraw the correct circuit.
(c) Can you explain why a voltmeter is connected the way it is in part (b)? **[4]**

Answer

1. (i) (d) (ii) (b) (iii) (b) (iv) (a) (v) (a) (vi) (c) (vii) (c) (viii) (c) (ix) (c) (x) (b) (xi) (c) (xii) (d) (xiii) (a) (xiv) (d) (xv) (d)
2. (i) (a) III (b) light to chemical (c) increases (d) becomes twenty seven times
(e) Total Internal Reflection (f) geometric centre.
3. (i) (a) *R* (b) *P* (iii) (b) 1.2 Hz (iv) (a) 10 Ω
4. (i) (b) 60° and 45° (ii) (a) $v = 66.67$ cm (b) $h_i = -10$ cm
5. (i) (a) Fixed pulley (c) $E = 10$ kgf (ii) (a) $w = 0.06$ kg (iii) (a) zero (b) KE = 900 J
6. (i) (b) Microphones (c) decibels (iii) (a) Damped vibration.
7. (ii) (b) 25 K (iii) (a) East (d) Galvanometer
8. (i) (c) 15 kWh (ii) 22.27°C

ICSE

SAMPLE PAPER 02

Time : 2 hrs
Marks : 80

Physics
Paper 1

General Instructions

1. You will not be allowed to write during the first 15 minutes. This time is to be spent in reading the question paper.
2. The time given at the head of this paper is the time allowed for writing the answers.
3. Section A is compulsory. Attempt any four questions from Section B.
4. The intended marks for questions or parts of questions are given in brackets [ ].

Section-A [40 Marks]

(Attempt all questions from this section)

1. Choose the correct answers to the questions from the given options. **[15]**

(i) A boy of mass 40 kg walks up a flight of stairs to a vertical distance of 12 m in a time interval of 40 s. Rate at which the boy is doing work against the force of gravity is
(a) 500 W
(b) 400 W
(c) 120 W
(d) 100 W

(ii) A magnetic field is applied perpendicular to the path of α and β-rays. The curvature of the path of the two types of rays in the field are
(a) equal in same direction
(b) unequal in same direction
(c) equal in opposite directions
(d) unequal in opposite directions

(iii) Essential characteristic of equilibrium is
(a) momentum equals to zero
(b) acceleration equals to zero
(c) KE equals to zero
(d) velocity equals to zero

(iv) A boy *P* has a mass of 20 kg and is moving with a velocity of 5 ms^{-1}. Another boy *Q* has a mass of 5 kg and is moving with a velocity of 20 ms^{-1}. Calculate the ratio of the momentum of *P* and *Q*.
(a) 2 : 1 (b) 1 : 1
(c) 1 : 2 (d) 3 : 2

(v) A bat sends sound waves and it gets reflected by a small insect within 0.3 s.

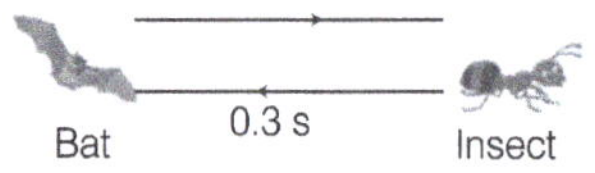

How far is the insect from the bat? (Take, speed of sound in air = 340 m/s)
(a) 17 m (b) 35 m (c) 51 m (d) 68 m

(vi) A submarine produces an ultrasonic wave of speed 1500 ms^{-1}. A man sends a signal from transmitter and it detects an object 1600 m below the submarine .

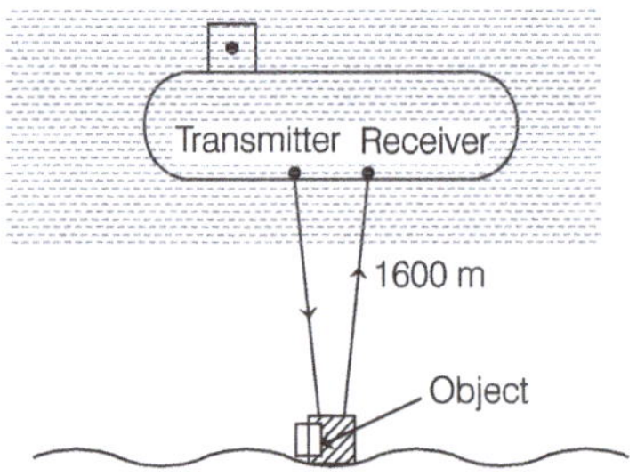

What will be the time taken for receiver to receive signal sent from transmitter?

(a) 2.5 s (b) 2.4 s
(c) 2.1 s (d) 2.0

(vii) A double convex lens made of a material of refractive index μ_1, is placed inside two liquids of refractive indices μ_2 and μ_3 as shown $\mu_2 > \mu_1 > \mu_3$. A wide and parallel beam of light is incident on the lens from the left. The lens will give rise to

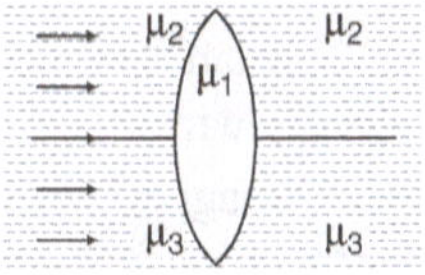

(a) a single convergent beam
(b) two different convergent beams
(c) two different divergent beams
(d) a convergent and a divergent beam

(viii) When white light is dispersed by a prism, then compared with blue light, the red light is
(a) slowed down less and refracted less
(b) slowed down less and refracted more
(c) slowed down more and refracted less
(d) slowed down more and refracted more

(ix) In total internal reflection, the value of critical angle will be maximum when light passes
(a) from glass to air
(b) from diamond to air
(c) from glass to water
(d) from water to air

(x) **Assertion** (A) ENT specialist use a concave mirror as a head mirror to concentrate light on the body parts like eye, ear, nose, etc.

Reason (R) A concave mirror is more cost effective and easily available.
(a) Both A and R are true.
(b) A is true but R is false.
(c) A is false but R is true.
(d) Both A and R are false.

(xi) A certain substance of mass 50 g/mol having 300 J heat is added to 25 g of the same material. If its temperature rises from 25°C to 45°C, then thermal capacity is
(a) 5 J/°C (b) 10 J/°C
(c) 15 J/°C (d) 20 J/°C

(xii) The diagram below shows a free conductor AB is kept in a magnetic field and carrying current from A to B (to avoid confusion, complete path of the circuit is not shown). The direction of the force experienced by the conductor will be

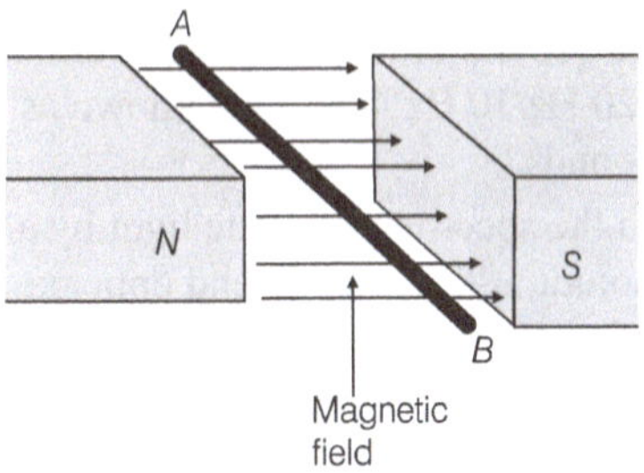

(a) up (b) down
(c) towards N (d) towards S

(xiii) A vessel from which the air is rapidly being pumped out contains 100 g of water at 0°C. The intensive evaporation causes a gradual freezing of water. What part of the original water can be converted into ice by this method? [Take, latent heat of vaporisation at 0°C, $L_1 = 2.1 \times 10^6$ J/kg and latent heat of fusion of ice, $L_2 = 3.36 \times 10^5$ J/kg]
(a) 60% (b) 62%
(c) 70% (d) 86%

(xiv) The V-I graph for four metallic conductors is given

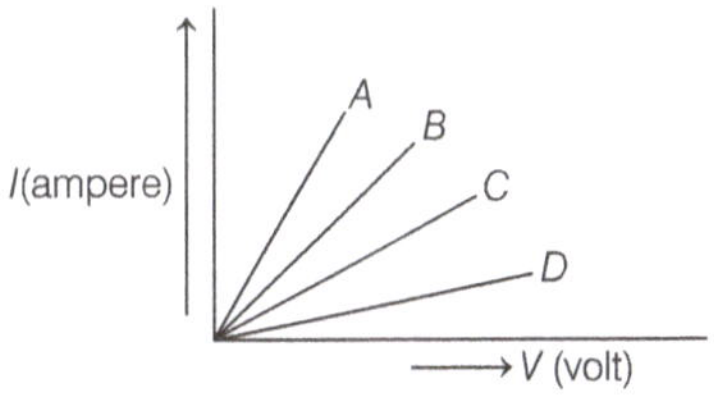

Which of the following will be useful for making heating element?
(a) D (b) C
(c) B (d) A

(xv) Which one of the following statements is correct?
(a) Live wire has zero potential.
(b) Fuse is connected in a neutral wire.
(c) Potential of live and earth wires is always same.
(d) Earth wire is used to prevent electric shock.

2. (i) (a) A totally reflecting right angled isosceles prism can be used to deviate a ray of light through .... (90°/ 30°/ 60°).
(b) The direction of force on a current carrying conductor in a magnetic field is given by .... (Fleming's left hand rule/ Fleming's right hand rule/ Right hand thumb rule)
(c) If the speed of a moving particle is tripled, then the ratio of its kinetic energy to its momentum will be ...... (doubled/tripled /quadrupled).

(d) The sound of frequencies lower than ...... (20 Hz/10 Hz/40Hz) are known as infrasonic sounds.

(e) In the spectrum of white light by a prism, the colour at the extreme end opposite to the base of prism is ...... (red/blue/violet).

(f) A wire stretched between two fixed supports, is plucked exactly in the middle then released, it executes ....(natural/damped/forced) vibration.

(ii) Observe the given figure and write the location of centre of gravity for both objects. **[2]**

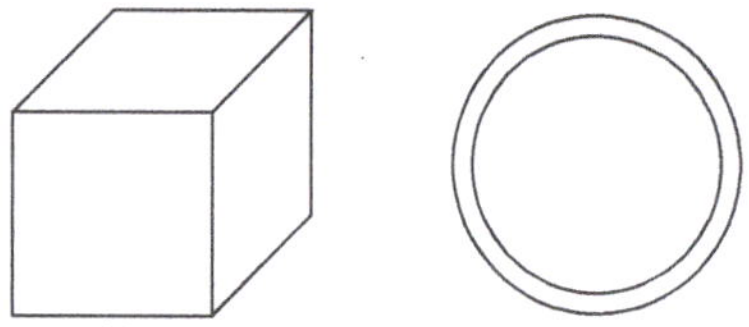

(a) (b)

(iii) State one example which demonstrates that when liquid evaporates, it takes heat from the surroundings. **[2]**

3. (i) (a) A body of mass 1.5 kg is dropped from second floor of a building which is at height of 12 m. What is the force acting on it during its fall ? (Take, $g = 9.8 \text{ ms}^{-2}$)

(b) A meter scale is balanced in horizontal position as shown in figure. Find the value of w.

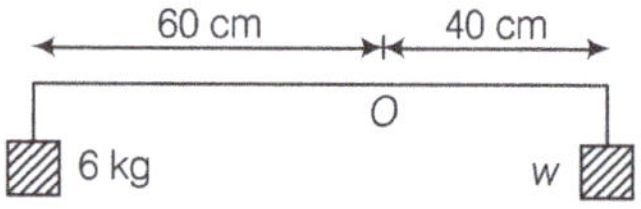

[2]

(ii) A force of 20 N displaces a body by a distance of 4 m.

Find the amount of work done when the displacement

(a) is in the direction of force.

(b) at an angle 60° with the force. **[2]**

(iii) (a) A substance has nearly zero resistance at a temperature of 1 K. What is such a substance called? **[1]**

(b) What are the special characteristics of a fuse wire? **[1]**

(iv) (a) When does a ray of light falling on a lens pass through its focus ? **[1]**

(b) Which lens can produce a real and inverted image of an object? **[1]**

(v) The electrical resistivities of five substances A, B, C, D and E are given below

$A = 520 \times 10^{-8}\ \Omega\text{-m}$, $B = 110 \times 10^{-8}\ \Omega\text{-m}$,

$C = 2.60 \times 10^{-8}\ \Omega\text{-m}$, $D = 10 \times 10^{-8}\ \Omega\text{-m}$ and

$E = 1.70 \times 10^{-8}\ \Omega\text{-m}$

(a) Which substance is the best conductor of electricity? **[1]**

(b) Which two substances should be used for making electric wires? **[1]**

(vi) What is an electromagnet? Why do we prefer a U-shape soft iron piece for stronger electromagnet? **[2]**

(vii) Figure shows a uniform meter rule weighing 100 gf pivoted at its centre O. Two weights 150 gf and 250 gf hang from the meter rod as shown in the figure.

Calculate **[3]**

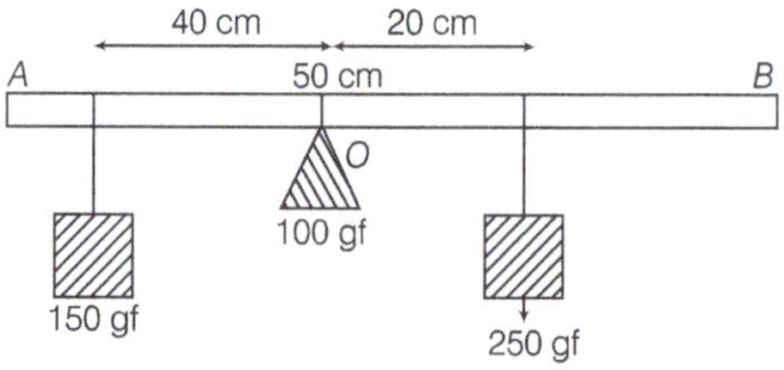

(a) the total anti-clockwise moments about O.

(b) the total clockwise moments about O.

(c) the distance O, where a 100 gf weight should be placed to balanced the meter rule.

Section-B [40 Marks]

(Attempt any four questions from this section)

4. (i) (a) Draw a neat labelled diagram to show the formation of image by a magnifying glass.

(b) What are the uses of convex lens? **[3]**

(ii) It is seen that the white light splits into bands of seven colours when passed through the glass prism. With reference to this observation, answer the following questions.

(a) State the conclusion that you draw about the white light. Name the sequence of colours from the base of the prism.

(b) Do all the bands are of same width? If not, then why? **[3]**

(iii) (a) An object of height 5 cm is placed perpendicular to the principal axis of a concave lens of focal length 10 cm. If the distance of the object from the optical centre of the lens is 20 cm, determine the position, nature and size of the image formed using the lens formula.

(b) Name the type of lens used for burning a piece of paper by focusing the sun rays. **[4]**

5. (i) (a) Define the term dispersion and spectrum of light.

(b) In the diagram shown below, a ray of light PQ is incident normally on one face AB of an equilateral glass prism. What are the angles of incidence at the faces AB and AC ?

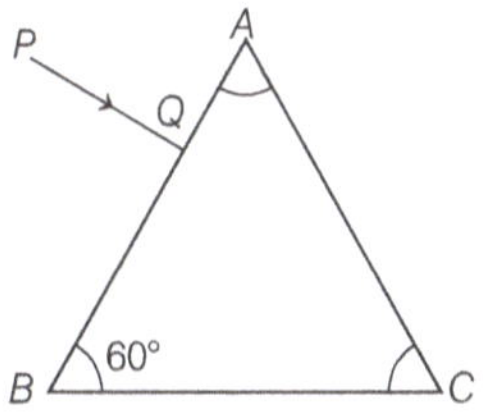

(c) Complete the ray diagram showing its emergence into air after passing through the prism. **[3]**

(ii) (a) Write any two common properties of electromagnetic waves.

(b) Is it possible that a glass disperse the light? If not, why? **[3]**

(iii) The diagram shows below two parallel rays of red and violet light incident from air on air-glass boundary. Complete the diagram showing the refracted rays for them in the glass.

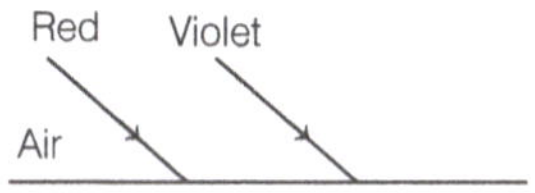

(a) Are the two refracted rays in the glass parallel? Give reasons and compare the speed of the rays in glass.

(b) A ray of light strikes a glass slab at an angle of incidence equal to 30°. Find the refractive index of glass such that the angle of refraction is 19.5°.

(Take, $\sin 19.5° = \frac{1}{3}$ and $\sin 30° = \frac{1}{2}$) **[4]**

6. (i) A pump is used to lift 500 kg of water from a depth of 80 m in 10 s. Calculate

(a) weight of lifting water **[1]**

(b) work done by the pump **[1]**

(c) the power at which the pump works and the power rating of the pump, if its efficiency is 40%. **[1]**

(ii) Maya is climbing a hill from point A to point C as shown in the figure below. The distance between each point is 100 m and the hill has a constant slope of 30°. Maya has a mass of 50 kg. Assume negligible friction throughout the climb. **[3]**

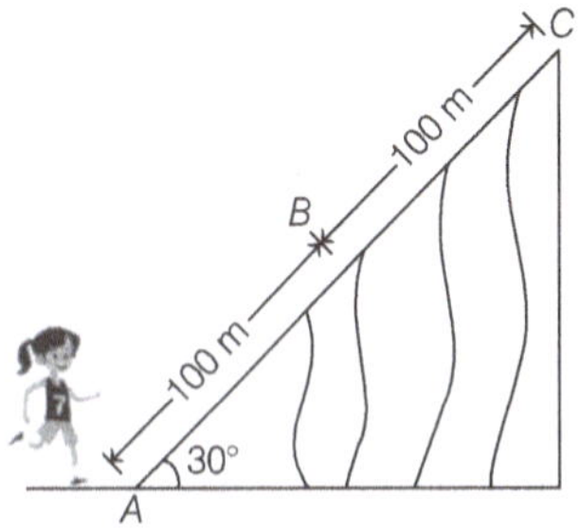

(a) Calculate the total work done by Maya in climbing from point A to C. **[2]**

(b) Determine the potential energy gained by Maya at point C relative to point A. **[2]**

(iii) (a) A half-metre ruler is suspended by a thread from the mid-point of the ruler as shown in the figure **[3]**

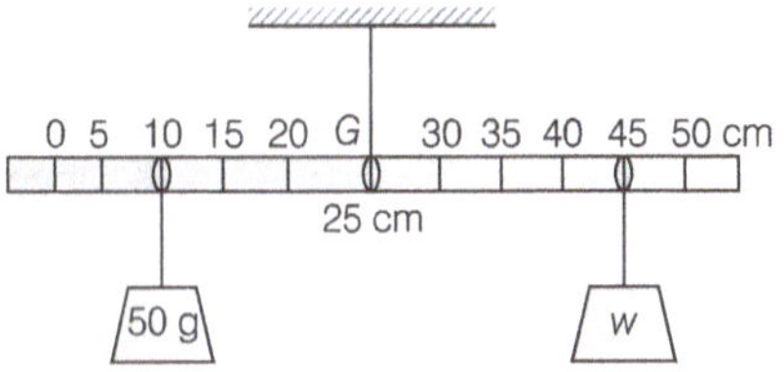

It balances horizontally when a 50 g and an unknown weight w are suspended respectively from 10 cm and 45 cm mark. Calculate the magnitude of weight w.

(b) What is the nature of centripetal force on the planet revolving around the sun in circular path?

7. (i) A person standing between the two vertical cliffs. When he was 640 m away from the nearest cliff, he shouted, he heard the first echo after 4 s and the second echo 3 s later. Find

(a) the speed of the sound in air and

(b) the distance between the cliffs.

(c) What is an echo? **[3]**

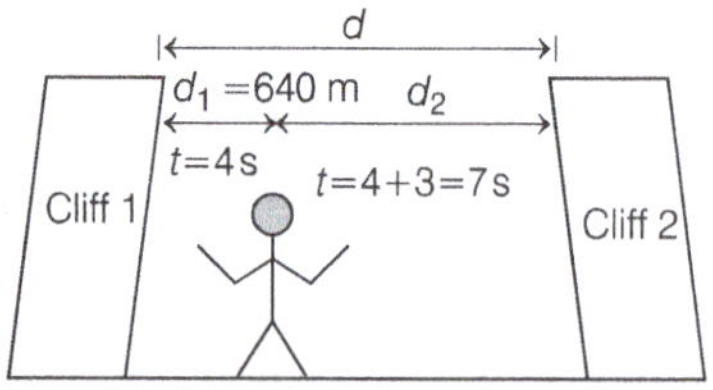

(ii) (a) Explain, how are nuclear wastes generated.

(b) Why do they pose a threat to the environment?

(c) State one way for the safe disposal of these wastes. **[3]**

(iii) (a) An electromagnetic wave has a frequency of 500 MHz and a wavelength of 60 cm. Calculate time period and velocity of electromagnetic waves.

(b) An enemy plane is at a distance of 300 km from a RADAR. In how much time, the RADAR will be able to detect the plane? (Take, velocity of radio waves as $3\times10^8\ ms^{-1}$) **[4]**

8. (i) A block of lead mass 250 g at 27°C was heated in a furnace till it completely melted. Find the quantity of heat required **[3]**

(a) to bring the block to melting point

(b) to completely melt the block at its melting point.

(Take, melting point of lead = 327°C, specific heat capacity = 0.13 J/g-K, specific latent heat of fusion = 26 J/g)

(ii) A solid is heated at constant rate. The variation of temperature with heat input is shown graphically in the given figure.

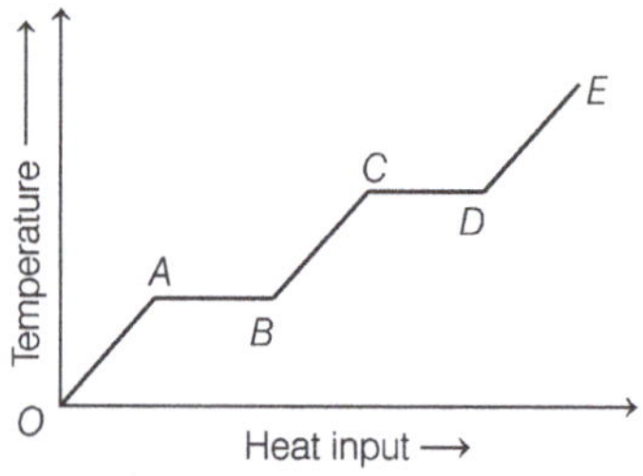

(a) What is represented by AB and CD? **[1]**

(b) What conclusion would you draw, if $CD = 2AB$? **[1]**

(c) What conclusion would you draw from the fact that the slope of OA is greater than the slope of BC? **[1]**

(iii) The diagram shows a coil connected to a galvanometer G. The galvanometer shows a deflection to the right when the N-pole of a powerful magnet is moved to the right as shown in below figure.

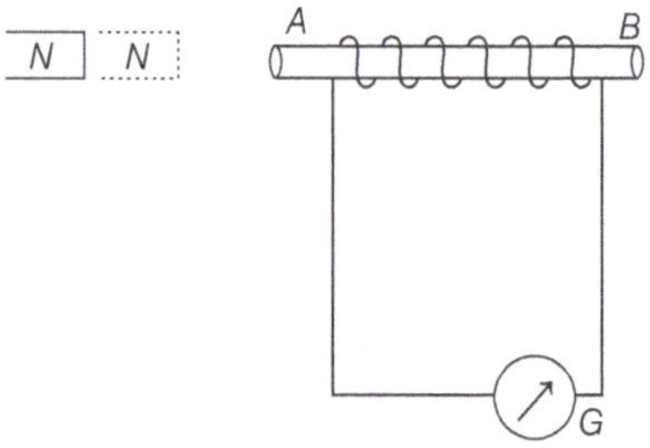

(a) Explain, why the deflection occurs in the galvanometer? **[1]**

(b) Does the direction of the current on the coil appear clockwise or anti-clockwise when viewed from the end A? **[1]**

(c) State the observation in G when the coil is moved away from N. **[1]**

(d) State the observation in G when both the coil and the magnet are moved to the right at the same speed. **[1]**

9. (i) Hema uses two appliances in her home. One appliance is rated at 100 W and operates at 220 V, while the other appliance is rated at 60 W and also operates at 220 V. These appliances are connected to the electrical main supply in both series and parallel configurations as shown in the figure 1 and 2.

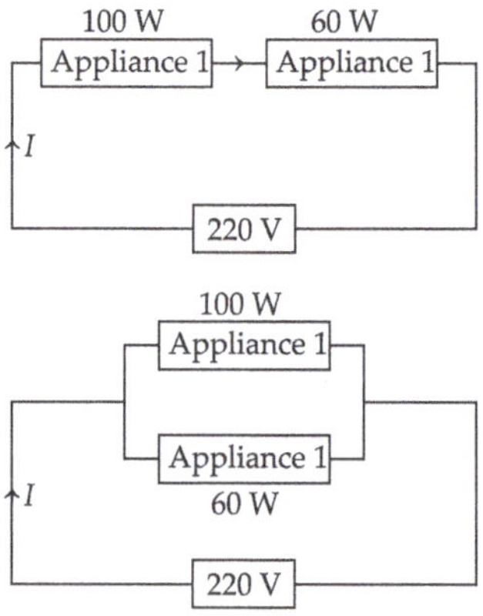

(a) Calculate the total power consumption when the two appliances are connected in series.

(b) Calculate the total power consumption when the two appliances are connected in parallel.

(c) Which configuration results in higher total power consumption, series or parallel? **[3]**

(ii) (a) State two common properties of γ-rays and X-rays.

(b) Explain, why radium paint, consisting of zinc sulphide and a trace of radium salt, glows in the dark. **[3]**

(iii) Five resistors of different resistances are connected together as shown in the figure.

A 12 V battery is connected to the arrangement.

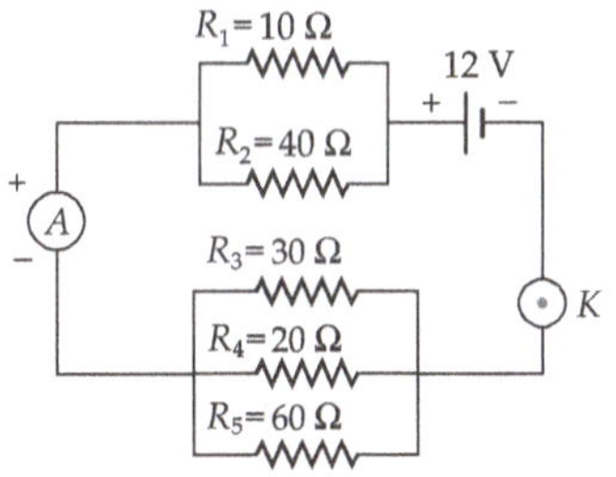

Calculate

(a) the total resistance in the circuit.

(b) the total current flowing in the circuit. **[4]**

Answer

1. (i) (c) (ii) (d) (iii) (b) (iv) (b) (v) (c) (vi) (c) (vii) (d) (viii) (a) (ix) (c) (x) (b) (xi) (c) (xii) (a) (xiii) (d) (xiv) (a) (xv) (d)

2. (i) (a) 90° (b) Fleming's left hand rule (c) tripled (d) 20 Hz

(e) red (f) natural

3. (i) (a) 1407 N (b) 9 kg (ii) (a) 80 J (b) 40 J (v) (a) E (b) C and E (vii) (a) 6000 gf-cm (b) 5000 gf-cm (c) 10 cm to the right of O.

4. (iii) (a) $v = -6.67$ cm

5. (i) (b) $AB \rightarrow$ Zero $AC \rightarrow 60°$ (iii) (b) 1.5

6. (i) (a) 5000 N (b) 4×10^5 J (c) 100 kW (ii) (a) 49000 J (b) 49000 J (iii) (a) 37.5 g

7. (i) (a) 320 m/s (b) 1760 m

(iii) (a) $T = 0.2 \times 10^{-5}$ s, $v = 3 \times 10^8$ m/s (b) 0.002 s

ICSE

SAMPLE PAPER 03

Time : 2 hrs
Marks : 80

Physics
Paper 1

General Instructions

1. You will not be allowed to write during the first 15 minutes. This time is to be spent in reading the question paper.
2. The time given at the head of this paper is the time allowed for writing the answers.
3. Section A is compulsory. Attempt any four questions from Section B.
4. The intended marks for questions or parts of questions are given in brackets [ ].

Section-A [40 Marks]

(Attempt all questions from this section)

1. Choose the correct answers to the questions from the given options. **[15]**

(i) A body is moved along a straight road by a machine delivering constant power. The distance moved by the body in time t is proportional to

(a) $t^{1/2}$ (b) $t^{3/4}$ (c) $t^{3/2}$ (d) t^2

(ii) A radioactive nucleus is represented by $^{227}_{85}X$. It emits a beta particle and forms a different nucleus of element Y. Which of the following represents this new nucleus?

(a) $^{223}_{83}Y$ (b) $^{228}_{85}Y$
(c) $^{225}_{84}Y$ (d) $^{227}_{86}Y$

(iii) Before playing the orchestra in a musical concert, a sitarist adjust the tension and pluck the strings suitably. In doing this, he adjusted which characteristics of sound?

(a) Intensity of sound only
(b) Amplitude of sound only
(c) Frequency of sitar with other instruments
(d) Loudness of sound

(iv) Which of the following is not a representation of moment?

(a) $\mathbf{r} \times \mathbf{F}$
(b) $\mathbf{F} \cdot \mathbf{r}$
(c) Both (a) and (b)
(d) Neither (a) nor (b)

(v) Three similar bulbs A, B and C are connected to a voltage source as shown in the figure. If C is removed, how will the illumination of A and B affected?

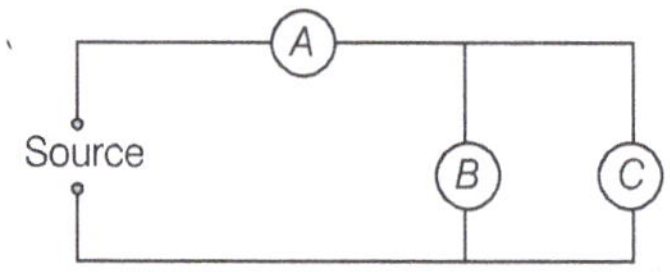

(a) Both A and B will become dimmer.
(b) Both A and B will become brighter.
(c) A will become dimmer and B will become brighter.
(d) A will become brighter and B will become dimmer.

(vi) Which of the following does not remain constant in the phenomenon of refraction?

(a) Phase
(b) Frequency
(c) Both (a) and (b)
(d) Neither (a) nor (b)

(vii) An electric kettle with a 2 kW heater contains 0.25 kg of boiling water. It will take time of ......

before all the water to boil away.
(Take, specific latent heat for steam = 2.0 MJ/kg)
(a) 250 s (b) 400 s
(c) 600 s (d) 850 s

(viii) The diagram represents two block of copper A and B. The mass of A is two times that of B. When same amount of heat is supplied, the temperature of A rises to half that of rise in B.

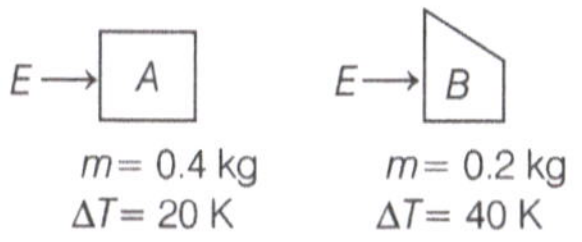

Which statement is correct about above information?
(a) The specific heat capacity of A is twice that of B.
(b) The heat capacity of A is same that of B.
(c) The heat capacity of A is half that of B.
(d) The heat capacity of A is twice that of B.

(ix) If a swimmer inside water looks at an aeroplane in the sky, then which one of the following conditions is fulfilled?

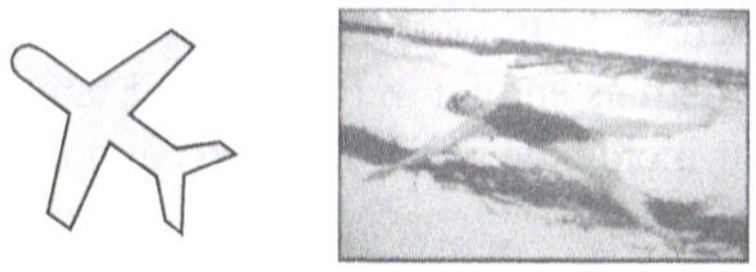

(a) For the swimmer, the aeroplane will appear to be lower than it actually is.
(b) For the swimmer, the aeroplane will appear to be higher than it actually is.
(c) For the swimmer, the aeroplane will appear at its actual height.
(d) For the pilot, the swimmer will appear to be at greater depth than it actually is.

(x) Kinetic energy of a freely falling body
(a) continuously decreases
(b) continuously increases
(c) remains constant
(d) None of the above

(xi) A convex lens of focal length 40 cm, a concave lens of focal length 40 cm and a concave lens of focal length 15 cm are placed in contact. The power of the combination in dioptre is
(a) + 1.5 (b) – 1.5
(c) + 6.67 (d) – 6.67

(xii) Which of the following phenomena is due to refraction?
(a) Lateral shift (b) Dispersion of light
(c) Twinkling of stars (d) All of these

(xiii) **Assertion** (A) Heater wire must have high resistance and high melting point.
Reason (R) If resistance is high, the electric conductivity will be less.
(a) Both A and R are true.
(b) A is true but R is false.
(c) A is false but R is true.
(d) Both A and R are false.

(xiv) The diagrams below represent sound waves displayed on the screen of same oscilloscope with the same control settings.
Which of the following diagram represents softest sound with highest pitch?

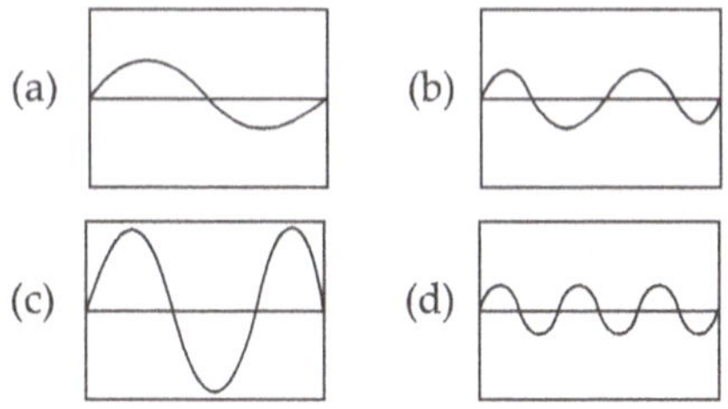

(xv) A compass needle is placed near one end A of a solenoid. When a current is passed through the coil, the compass shows a deflection as the figure given below.

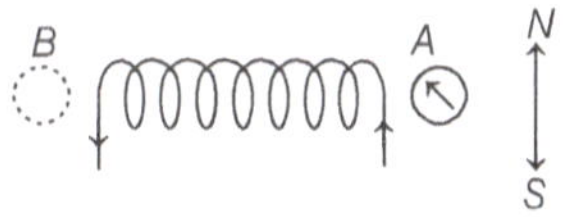

The needle points closer to magnetic north when the
(a) current in the coil is increased
(b) current in the coil is decreased
(c) compass is moved nearer to the coil
(d) compass is moved to position B

2. (i) Complete the following by choosing the correct answer from the bracket.
(a) The ...... (mechanical advantage/efficiency/velocity ratio) of a machine is the ratio of the work done on the load by the machine to the work done on the machine by the effort.
(b) A ray of light incident on a lens parallel to its principal axis, after refraction passes through or appears to come from .... (second focus/optical centre/first focus).
(c) When a body vibrates under a periodic force. the vibrations of the body are always (forced/natural/damped) vibrations.

(d) Speed of blue light in water is more than ...... (green/orange/violet light).

(e) When the force and displacement are in perpendicular direction, work done is said to be...... (negative/positive/zero).

(f) The strength of magnetic field produced by a straight current carrying wire is directly proportional to the .... (current/distance/voltage).

(ii) If the moment of F about the centre of square is 15 N-m, then find the moment of F about A. **[2]**

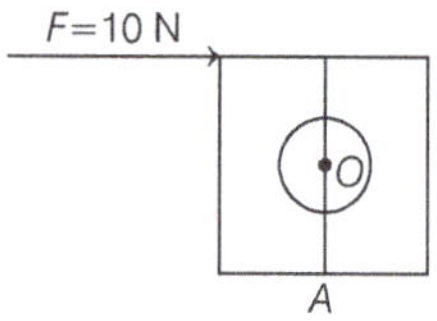

(iii) An observer stands at a distance of 850 m from a cliff and fires a gun. After what time gap will he hear the echo, if sound travels at a speed of 350 m/s in air? **[2]**

3. (i) (a) If the lens is placed in water instead of air, how does its focal length change? **[1]**

(b) Which lens, thick or thin has greater focal length? **[1]**

(ii) (a) State Ohm's law. **[1]**

(b) Diagrammatically illustrate how you would connect a key, a battery, a voltmeter, an ammeter, an unknown resistance R and a rheostat, so that it can be used to verify the above law? **[1]**

(iii) It is established that an electric current through a metallic conductor produces a magnetic field around it. Is there a similar magnetic field produced around a thin beam of moving (a) α-particles, (b) neutrons? Justify your answer. **[2]**

(iv) Which of the radioactive radiations occurs in the following cases

(a) That can cause severe genetical disorder. **[1]**

(b) Are deflected by an electric field? **[1]**

(v) Define the term calorie. State its relation with joule. **[2]**

(vi) (a) A body is acted upon by a force. State two conditions under which the work done could be zero. **[1]**

(b) What is the work done by the moon when it revolves around the earth? **[1]**

(vii) The diagram below shows two parallel rays-A (orange) and B (blue) incident from air, on air-glass boundary.

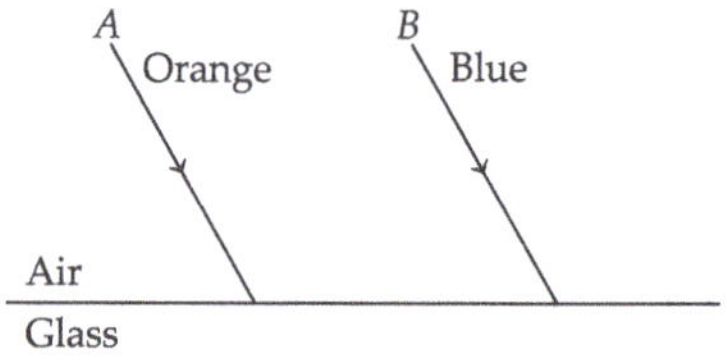

(a) Copy and complete the path of the rays A and B.

(b) How do the speeds of these rays differ in glass ?

(c) Are the two refracted rays in glass parallel ? Give reason. **[3]**

Section-B [40 Marks]

(Attempt any four questions from this section)

4. (i) (a) What do you understand by term "spectrum of light"? Name one natural spectrum formed by sunlight after rain. Can a monochromatic light show dispersion?

(b) If a ray of light passes from medium I to medium II without any change of direction. What can be said about the refractive indices of these media (Angle i is not zero)? **[4]**

(ii) (a) A ray of light passes through a right angled prism as shown in the figure. State the angles of incidence at the faces AC and BC.

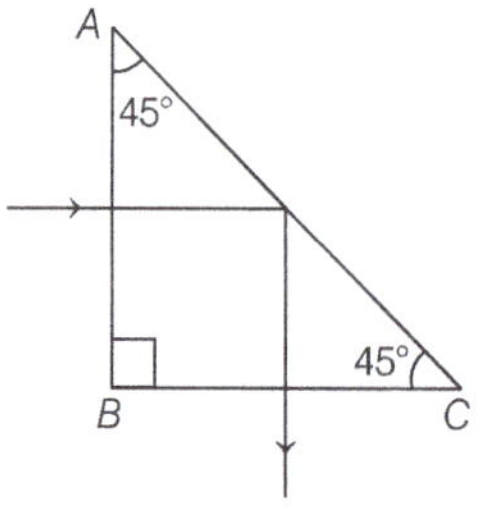

(b) Name the phenomenon which the ray suffers at the face AC. **[3]**

(iii) (a) What is meant by refraction? **[1]**

(b) Express the refractive index μ of a medium

I. in terms of the velocity of light.

II. in terms of the angle of incidence (i) in air and the angle of refraction (r) in a denser medium. **[3]**

5. (i) The given ray diagram illustrates the experimental set up for the determination of the focal length of a converging lens using a plane mirror.

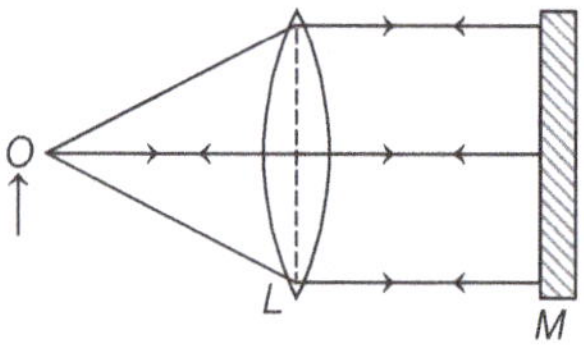

(a) State the magnification of the image formed.
(b) Write any two characteristics of image formed. **[3]**

(ii) A glass slab is placed over a page on which the word VIBGYOR is printed with each letter in its corresponding colour.
(a) Will the image of all the letters be in the same place?
(b) If not, state which letter will be raised to the maximum. Give a reason for your answer.
(c) What will be the colour of an object which appears blue in white light and black in red light? **[3]**

(iii) An object is placed 25 cm away from a converging lens of focal length 10 cm.
(a) Draw the ray diagram. Find the position of image and what will be the nature of the image?
(b) Obtain its magnification. **[4]**

6. (i) A pulley system with a velocity ratio of 4 is used to lift a load of 150 kgf through a vertical height of 20 m. The effort required is 50 kgf in the downward direction.

Calculate
(a) the distance moved by the effort. **[1]**
(b) the mechanical advantage. **[1]**
(c) the efficiency of the pulley system. **[1]**

(ii) Rahul and Priya are playing on a multistorey building. Suddenly Rahul throws a toy of mass 1 kg the toy is falling under the affect of gravity and after sometimes, it reaches on the ground.

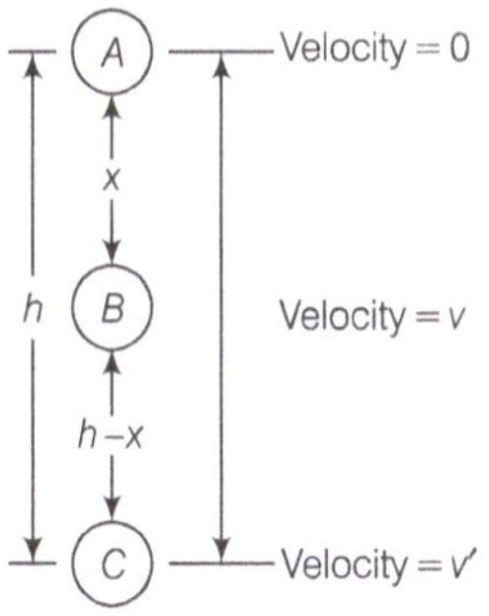

(a) What is the momentum of the toy after 5 s?
(b) What is the height of the freely falling body? **[3]**

(iii) (a) Why does a rope walker hold a long pole in his hands?
(b) The passengers in a boat are not allowed to stand while crossing a river. Why? **[4]**

7. (i) (a) Define staircase wiring.
(b) An electric heater is rated at 2 kW. Calculate the cost of using it for 2 h daily for the month of september, if each unit costs ₹ 4. **[3]**

(ii) Write the two properties of each of
(a) an α-particle,
(b) a β-particle and
(c) a γ-radiation **[3]**

(iii) A ceiling fan is rotating and Rahul is observing that fan. He thought to calculate how much electrical energy is being converted into mechanical energy by the fan.

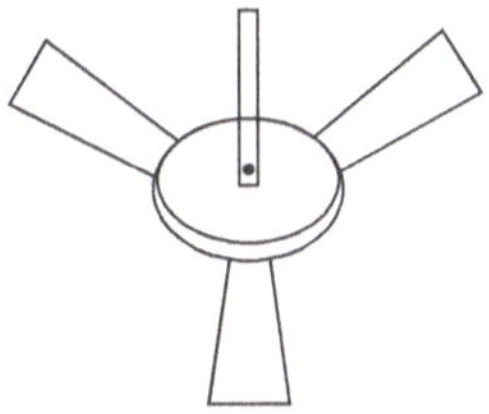

(a) If input voltage is 220 V and current is 0.5 A, then at what rate the electrical energy is transformed by the fan?
(b) How much energy is transformed in 2 min?
(c) If cost of energy is ₹ 4.5 per kWh, then how much it will cost in 30 days. (The fan is operated 6 h/day) **[4]**

8. (i) A metal piece present at 120°C is quickly dropped in a calorimeter of mass 80 g containing 200 g of water at 30°C. The final temperature attained by the mixture is 40°C. Calculate the thermal capacity of the metal piece. [Specific heat capacity of water $= 4.2\ Jg^{-1}{}^{\circ}C^{-1}$, specific heat capacity of calorimeter $= 0.4\ Jg^{-1}{}^{\circ}C^{-1}$] **[3]**

(ii) The diagram below shows a cooling curve for a substance. **[3]**
(a) State the temperatures at which the substance condenses and solidifies, respectively.
(b) The temperature range in which the substance is in liquid state.

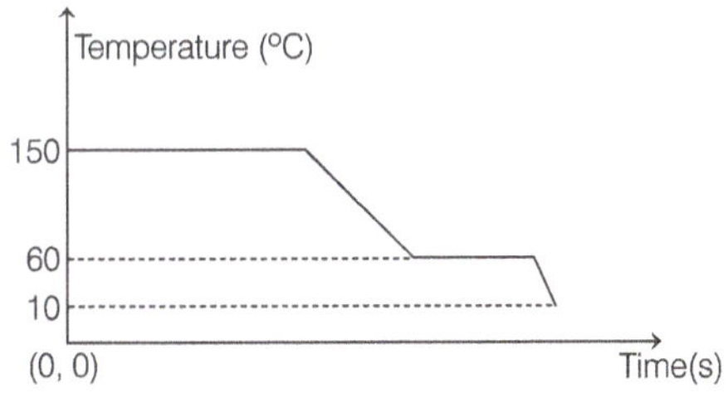

(c) Why do we prefer ice to ice-cold water for cooling a drink?

(iii) The diagram below shows a magnet placed between two coils A and B. The magnet is moved along the axis towards coil B. **[4]**

(a) State the polarities induced at the ends Q and R of the coil due to the motion of the magnet.

(b) Name the phenomenon due to which the current is induced in the coils.

(c) Name the law which helps to find the polarities at the ends Q and R.

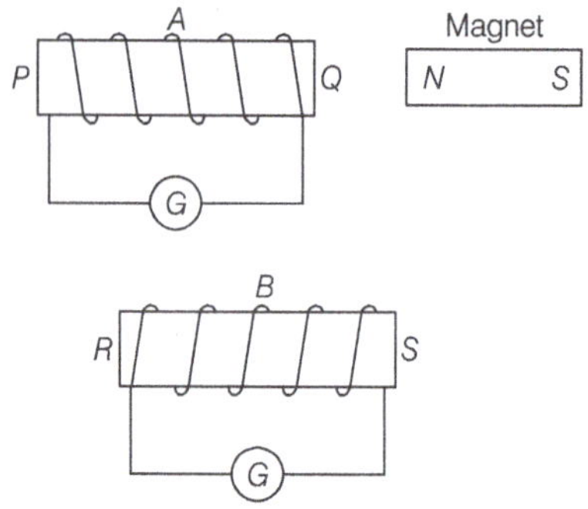

(d) If the magnet do not move, then which polarities will be induced at the ends Q and R?

9. (i) A man standing in front of vertical cliff fires a gun. He hears the echo after 4 s. On moving 50 m towards cliff, he fires again and hears after 3.6 s.

Calculate the

(a) distance of cliff from the initial position of man.

(b) speed of sound. **[3]**

(ii) The nucleus $^{15}_{7}P$ losses

(a) one proton,

(b) one β-particle and

(c) one α-particle.

Write the symbol of the new nucleus in each case and express each change by a reaction. **[3]**

(iii) Two pendulums C and D are suspended from a wire as shown in the figure given below. Pendulum C is made to oscillate by displacing it from its mean position. It is seen that D also starts oscillating. **[4]**

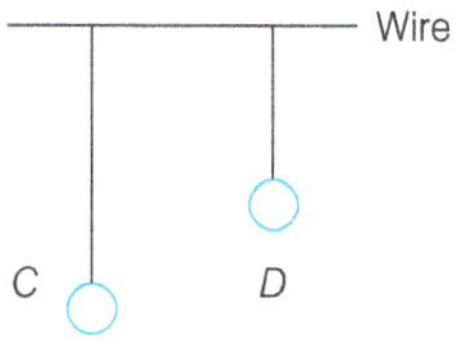

(a) Name the type of oscillation, C will execute.

(b) Name the type of oscillation, D will execute.

(c) If the length of D is made equal to C, then what difference will you notice in the oscillations of D?

(d) What is the name of the phenomenon when the length of D is made equal to C?

Answer

1. (i) (c) (ii) (d) (iii) (c) (iv) (b) (v) (c) (vi) (d) (vii) (a) (viii) (d) (ix) (b) (x) (b) (xi) (d) (xii) (d) (xiii) (a) (xiv) (d) (xv) (b)

2. (i) (a) efficiency (b) second focus (c) forced (d) violet (e) zero (f) current

(ii) 30 N-m

(iii) 4.857 s

5. (iii) (a) 16.68 cm (b) $-\frac{2}{3}$

6. (i) (a) 80 cm (b) 3 (c) 75%

(ii) (a) 50 kg m/s (b) 125 m

7. (i) ₹ 480 (iii) (a) 110 W (b) 13200 J (e) ₹ 89

8. (i) 10^9 J/kg (ii) (b) 90°C

9. (i) (a) 1500 m (b) 750 m/s

ICSE

Latest Specimen Question Paper

Time : 2 hrs
Marks : 80

Physics
Paper 1

General Instructions

1. Answer to this paper must be written on the paper provided separately.
2. You will not be allowed to write during first 15 minutes. This time is to be spent in reading the question paper.
3. The time given at the head of this paper is the time allowed for writing the answers.
4. Section A is compulsory. Attempt any four questions from Section B.
5. The intended marks for questions or parts of questions are given in brackets [ ].

Section-A

(Attempt all questions from this section)

1. Choose the correct answers to the questions from the given options. **[15]**

(i) A moment of couple has a tendency to rotate the body in an anti-clockwise direction. Then, the moment of couple is taken as *Recall*

(a) positive (b) negative
(c) maximum (d) zero

(ii) The kinetic energy of a given body depends on the *Understanding*

(a) position
(b) centre of gravity of the body
(c) momentum
(d) displacement

(iii) For burning of coal in a thermoelectric station, the energy conversion taking place is *Recall*

(a) chemical to heat to mechanical
(b) chemical to heat to mechanical to electrical
(c) chemical to heat to light
(d) heat to chemical to mechanical

(iv) The adjacent diagram shows the movable block of a block and tackle system with effort in a convenient direction. From the diagram, we can conclude that the number of pulleys used in the fixed block are......... *Analysis & Application*

(a) 1 (b) 3
(c) 2 (d) 4

(v) White light is dispersed by a prism. Inside the prism, compared to the blue light, the red light *Analysis & Application*

(a) slows down less and refracts more
(b) slows down more and refracts less
(c) slows down more and refracts more
(d) slows down less and refracts less

(vi) An endoscope uses optic fiber to transmit high resolution images of internal organs without loss of information. The principle of light that is used by the optic fiber is based on *Recall*

(a) refraction (b) reflection
(c) scattering (d) total internal reflection

(vii) A convex lens has focal length 12 cm with an object at a distance of 20 cm in front of the lens. He obtains a blurred image on the screen placed at a distance of 23 cm in front of the lens. In order to obtain the clear image, he has to move the screen *Application*

(a) towards the lens
(b) away from the lens
(c) to a position very far away from the lens
(d) either towards or away from the lens

(viii) **Assertion** (A) Infrared radiations travel long distances through a dense fog and mist.

Reason (R) Infrared radiations undergo minimal scattering in the earth's atmosphere. *Understanding & Recall*

(a) Both A and R are true and R is the correct explanation of A.
(b) Both A and R are true and R is not the correct explanation of A.
(c) A is false but R is true.
(d) A is true but R is false.

(ix) Two sound waves X and Y have the same amplitude and the same wave pattern but their frequencies are 60 Hz and 120 Hz respectively, then *Understanding*

(a) X will be shriller and Y will be grave
(b) X will be grave and Y will be shriller
(c) X will differ in quality than Y
(d) X is louder than Y

(*x*) The graph of voltage *versus* current for four different materials is shown below.

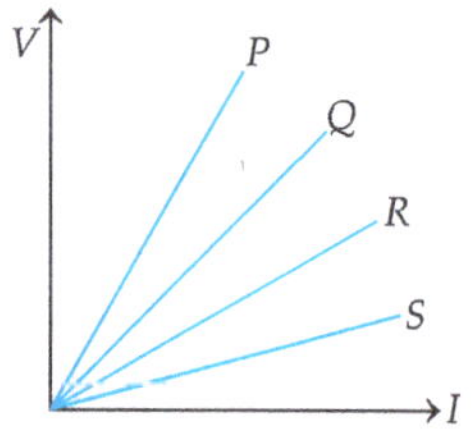

Which of these four materials would be used for making filament of a bulb? *Understanding & Recall*

(a) Q (b) S
(c) P (d) R

(*xi*) According to the old convention, the colour of the earth wire is *Recall*

(a) black (b) green
(c) yellow (d) red

(*xii*) Current is flowing through a coil as shown in the figure. Which one of the given figures will correctly depict the magnetic polarity and the direction of the lines of force along the axis of the coil. *Application*

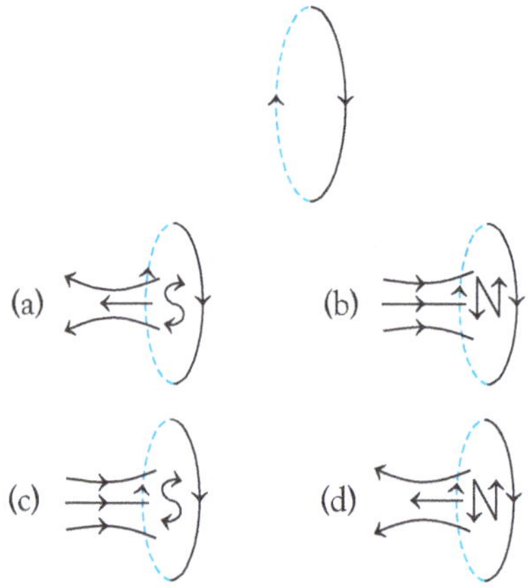

(xiii) Heat capacity of a body is the *Recall*

(a) energy needed to melt a body without change in its temperature.
(b) energy needed to raise the temperature of a body by 1°C.
(c) increase in volume of the body when its temperature increases by 1°C.
(d) total amount of internal energy that is constant.

(xiv) The amount of heat energy required to melt a given mass of a substance at its melting point without any rise in its temperature is called as the

(a) specific heat capacity *Recall*
(b) specific latent heat of fusion
(c) latent heat of fusion
(d) specific latent heat of freezing

(xv) A nucleus of an atom consists of 146 neutrons and 95 protons. It decays after emitting an alpha particle. How many protons and neutrons are left in the nucleus after an alpha emission?

(a) Protons = 93, neutrons = 142 *Understanding*
(b) Protons = 95, neutrons = 144
(c) Protons = 93, neutrons = 144
(d) Protons = 95, neutrons = 42

2. (i) Complete the following by choosing the correct answers from the bracket. **[6]**

(a) A ………… [class I/class II/class III] lever will always have MA > 1.

(b) In a block and tackle system, increase in the weight of the movable block ……… [decreases/does not affect/increases] the efficiency of the pulley system.

(c) If the mass as well as the velocity of a body is doubled, then the kinetic energy of the body ……… [is doubled/becomes eight times/becomes four times] the initial kinetic energy.

(d) Unit of power used in mechanical engineering is .... [watt/horse power/erg per second].

(e) Two copper wires can have the different .... [resistivity/resistance] but will have same .... [resistance / resistivity].

Recall & Understanding

(ii) Draw a graph of potential energy *versus* height for a body thrown vertically upwards. [Assume no friction is present]. *Understanding* [2]

(iii) (a) Name the waves used for echo depth sounding.

(b) Give one reason for their use in the above purpose. *Recall* [2]

3. (*i*) (a) Refer to the diagram given below. A lens with two different refractive indices is shown. If the rays are coming from a distant object, then how many images will be seen ? *Understanding*

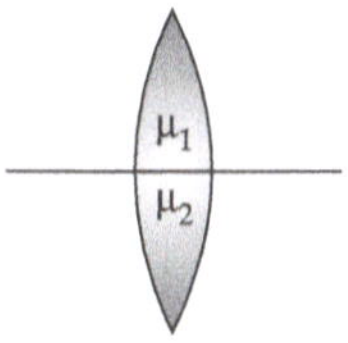

(b) A glass lens always forms a virtual, erect and diminished image of an object kept in front of it. Identify the lens. *Recall* [2]

(*ii*) If live wire makes an accidental contact with the metal case, which circuit (*A* or B) in the diagram, illustrating an electric iron, is considered to be safe for the user (assuming the fuse is present in the live wire in both circuits)? Justify your answer. **[2]**

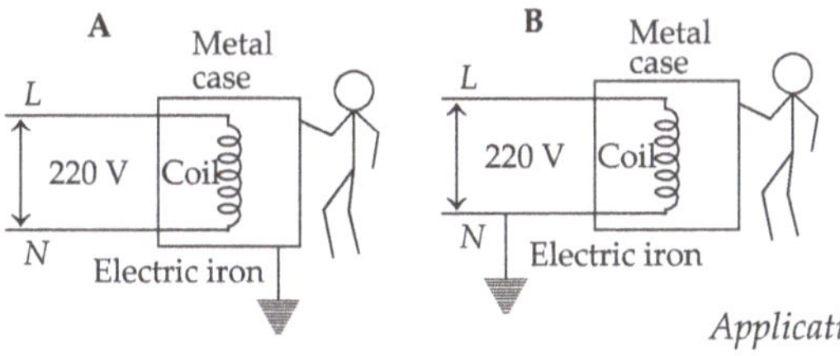

Application

(*iii*) A transformer is used to change a high alternating emf to a low alternating emf of the same frequency.

(a) Identify the type of transformer used for the above purpose. *Understanding*

(b) State whether the turns ratio of the above transformer is $=1$ or >1 or <1. *Recall* [2]

(*iv*) A solid of mass 60 g at 100°C is placed in 150 g of water at 20°C. The final steady temperature is 25°C. Calculate the heat capacity of solid. [Specific heat capacity of water = 4.2 $Jg^{-1}K^{-1}$] *Understanding & Evaluate* [2]

(*v*) (a) Name the principle of AC generator.

(b) State its one use. *Recall* [2]

(*vi*) (a) Name the radiations that are emitted during the decay of a nucleus, which have the highest penetrating power? *Recall*

(b) Does the emission of the above-mentioned radiation result in a change in the mass number? *Understanding* [2]

(*vii*) The graph (Fig. A) illustrates the correlation between the number of protons (*X*-axis) and the number of neutrons (*Y*-axis) for elements *A*, *B*, *C*, *D* and *E* in the periodic table. These elements are denoted by the letters rather than their conventional symbols. When the element *C*, depicted in the graph, undergoes radioactive decay, it releases radioactive rays. When these rays are directed into the plane of the paper in the presence of a magnetic field, as indicated in the (Fig. B), they experience deflection, causing them to move upwards.

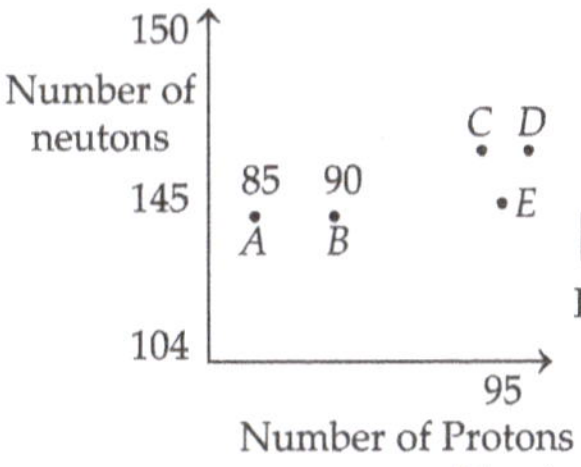

Fig. A

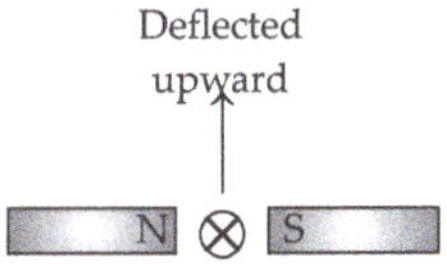

Ray passed into the plane of the paper

Fig. B

(a) Name the radioactive radiations emitted by the element *C*.

(b) Identify the daughter element from the graph.

(c) Name the law used to identify the radioactive radiations emitted by the element.

Application [3]

Section-B

(Attempt any four questions from this section)

4. (i) The diagram given below shows a fish in the tank and its image is seen on the surface of water. **[3]**

(a) Name the phenomenon responsible for the formation of this image. *Understanding & Recall*

(b) A double convex lens with refractive index μ_1 inside two liquids of refractive indices μ_2 and μ_3 are shown in the diagrams below. The refractive indices are such that $\mu_2 > \mu_1$ and $\mu_1 > \mu_3$.

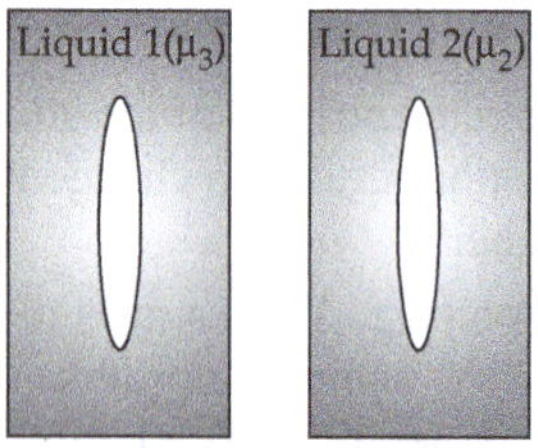

Fig. A Fig. B

How would a parallel incident beam of light refract when it comes out of the lens in each of the cases shown above? *Application*

1. In Fig. A. 2. In Fig. B.

(ii) The refractive index of water is 1.33 at a certain temperature. When the temperature of water is increased by 40 °C, the refractive index changes to x. [3]

(a) State whether $x < 1.33$ or $x > 1.33$. *Understanding*

(b) State two differences between normal reflection and total internal reflection. *Recall*

(iii) (a) Mixture of red+blue+green colours is passed through a convex lens as shown in the diagram below. State whether the ray passes through a single point or through different points on the principal axis after refraction. *Understanding*

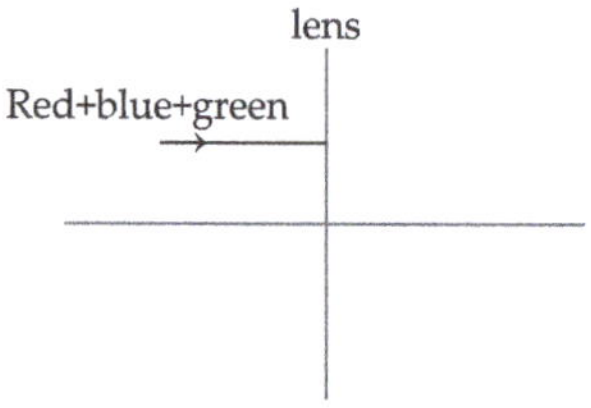

(b) Name the invisible radiations which are studied using the quartz prism. *Recall*

(c) State one use of these radiations. *Recall*

(d) Name one radiation having the wavelength longer than the wavelength of these radiations. *Recall* [4]

5. (i) An object is placed at a distance 24 cm in front of a convex lens of focal length 8 cm.

(a) What is the nature of the image so formed?

(b) Calculate the distance of the image from the lens. *Understanding & Evaluate* [3]

(ii) When sunlight passes through water droplets in the atmosphere, it gets dispersed into its constituent colours forming a rainbow. A similar phenomenon is observed when white light passes through a prism. **[3]**

(a) Which colour will show the maximum angle of deviation and which colour will show the minimum angle of deviation? *Recall*

(b) If instead of sunlight, a green-coloured ray is passed through a glass prism. What will be the colour of the emergent ray? *Understanding*

(*iii*) O is a luminescent particle trapped inside a glass block. A student traces the path of rays coming out of it and reflecting over a plane mirror as shown in the figure below.

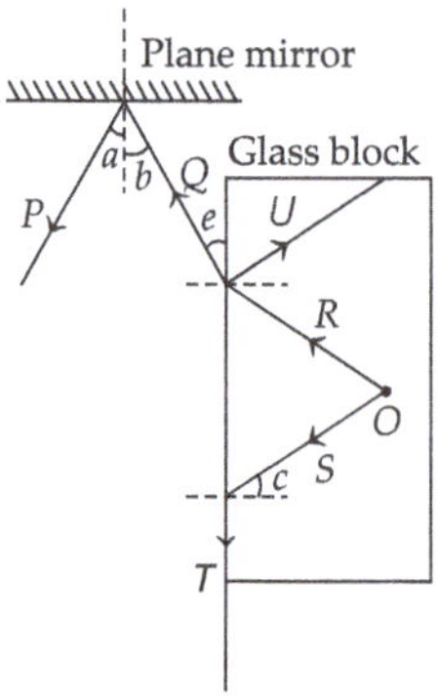

Complete the table using the labels from the figure. The first label is done for you.

Sr. No.	Description	Label
a.	an angle of reflection on the mirror	*a*
b.	a partially reflected ray in the glass slab	
c.	a critical angle	
d.	refracted rays	
e.	an angle of refraction of the ray *R*	

Understanding & Application [4]

6. (i) A metal rod *AB* of length 80 cm is balanced at 45 cm from the end A with 100 gf weights suspended from the two ends.

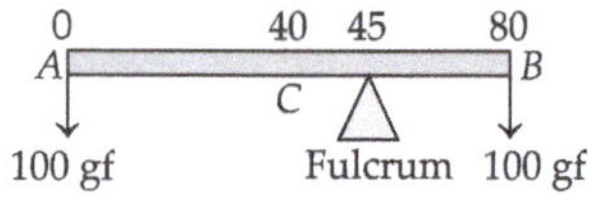

[3]

(a) If this rod is cut at the centre C, then compare the weight of AC to the weight of BC. *Understanding & Application*

(b) Give a reason for your answer in (a).

(ii) For each of the following scenarios, state whether the work done by gravity is positive, negative or zero. **[3]**

(a) A person walks on a levelled road.
(b) A person climbs a ladder.
(c) A car in neutral gear is coming down the slope.

Understanding & Recall

(iii) The figure below shows a simple pendulum of mass 200 g. It is displaced from the mean position *A* to the extreme position *B*. The potential energy at the position *A* is zero. At the position *B*, the pendulum bob is raised by 5 m. **[4]**

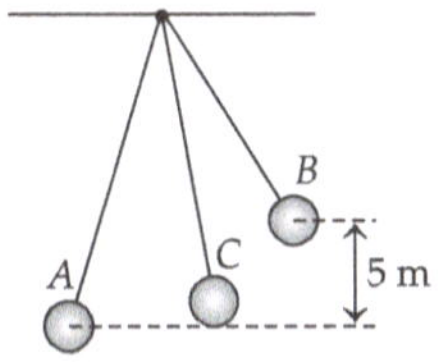

(a) What is the potential energy of the pendulum at the position *B* ? *Recall*

(b) What is the total mechanical energy at point *C* ? *Recall*

(c) What is the speed of the bob at the position *A* when released from *B* ? *Application & Evaluate*

(Take, $g = 10\ ms^{-2}$ and given that there is no loss of energy).

7. (i) A block and tackle system of pulleys has velocity ratio 4. **[3]**

(a) Draw a labelled diagram of the system indicating clearly the direction of the load and effort. *Recall*

(b) Calculate the potential energy of the load 100 kgf lifted by this pulley to a height 5 m. (Take, $g = 10\ ms^{-2}$) *Understanding & Evaluate*

(ii) A person standing in front of a cliff fires a gun and hears its echo after 3 s. If the speed of sound in air is $336\ ms^{-1}$, **[3]**

(a) calculate the distance of the person from the cliff.

(b) After moving a certain distance from the cliff, he fires the gun again and this time the echo is heard 1.5 s later than the first. Calculate the distance that the person moved.

Understanding & Evaluate

(iii) The above picture shows a mother pushing her daughter sitting on a swing. The swing is going through the positions *A*, *B*, *C* where *A* and *C* are extreme positions and *B* is the mean position. **[4]**

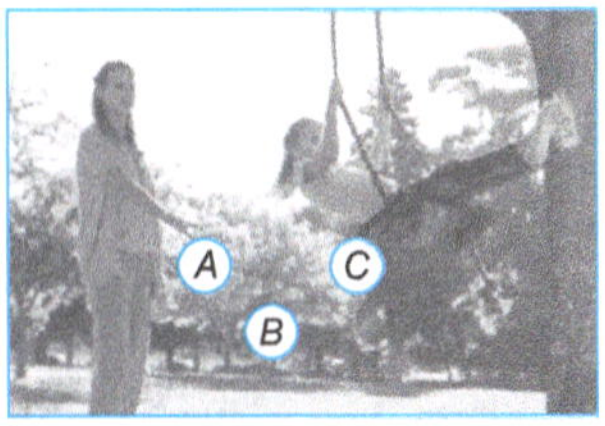

(a) Which is the right position, i.e. at *A*, *B* or *C*, for the mother to give a constant periodic push to the swing every time in the forward direction to increase the amplitude of the swing?

(b) Name the phenomenon involved in this.

(c) Explain with this example, how this phenomenon helps to increase the amplitude of the swing. *Application*

8. (*i*) The circuit depicted in the figure is employed for studying Ohm's Law. Instead of using a standard resistor, a student opts for a glass tube filled with mercury (tube 1), connected to the circuit through two electrodes E_1 and E_2. He records the readings of the ammeter and voltmeter, thereby calculates the resistance. The student repeats the experiment by substituting tube 1 with tube 2, where the same amount of mercury fills the tube 2.

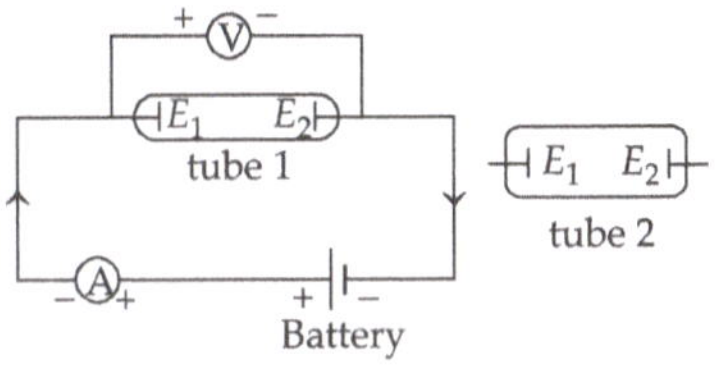

Neglecting internal resistance of the cell use (> or < or =) to compare

(a) the resistance in both the cases.
(b) the voltmeter readings in both the cases.
(c) the specific resistance in both the cases.

Understanding & Application [3]

(ii) A radioactive nucleus *X* emits an alpha particle followed by two beta particles to form nucleus *Y*.

(a) With respect to the element *X*, where would you position the element *Y* in the periodic table?

(b) What is the general name of the elements *X* and Y?

(c) If the atomic number of *Y* is 80, then what is the atomic number of *X*?

Understanding & Recall [3]

(iii) Observe the given circuit diagram and answer the questions that follow.

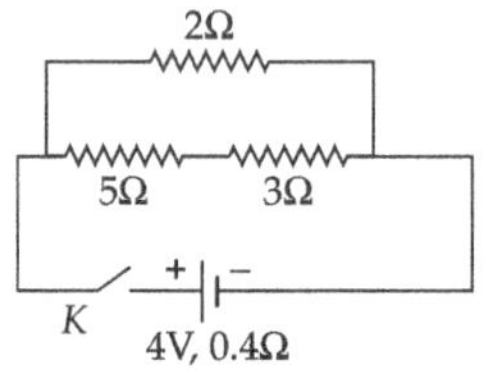

(a) Calculate the resistance of the circuit when the key K completes the circuit.

(b) Calculate the current through 3Ω resistance when the circuit is complete. *Understanding & Evaluate* [4]

9. (i) What mass of ice at 0°C added to 2.1 kg water, will cool it down from 75°C to 25°C? [Given, specific heat capacity of water = 4.2 Jg^{-1} $°C^{-1}$, specific latent heat of ice = 336 Jg^{-1}]. *Understanding & Evaluate* [3]

(ii) The diagram below shows a cooling curve for a substance. **[3]**

(a) State the temperature at which the substance condenses.

(b) The temperature range in which the substance is in liquid state.

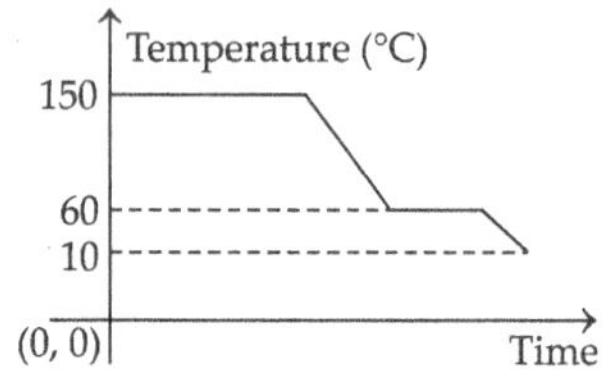

(c) Why do we prefer ice to ice-cold water for cooling a drink? *Understanding & Recall*

(iii) The diagram below shows a cardboard on which iron filings are kept. A wire bent in the form of a loop is seen passing through the cardboard. When current flows through it, the iron filings arrange themselves as shown below with the direction of magnetic field. **[4]**

(a) State the polarities of the battery at A and B.

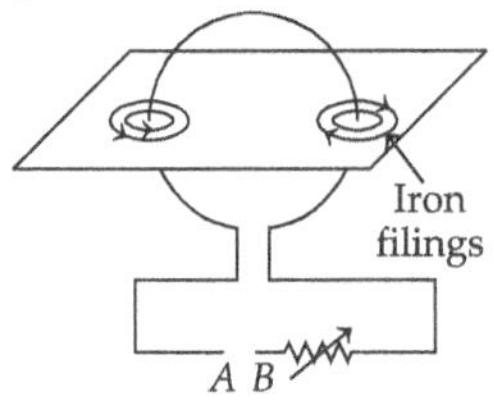

(b) State the effect on the magnetic field, if an iron rod is held along the axis of the coil. *Understanding & Application*

(c) State one way to

1. change the polarity of the coil.
2. decrease the strength of the magnetic field around the coil.

Understanding & Recall

Explanations

1. (i) (a) The anti-clockwise couple is taken as positive and clockwise couple is taken as negative.

(ii) (c) The kinetic energy of a body is

$$KE = \frac{p^2}{2m}$$

$$KE \propto (\text{momentum})^2$$

(iii) (b) In thermoelectric station, the energy conversion taking place is chemical to heat to mechanical to electrical.

(iv) (c) From the diagram, we can conclude that the number of pulleys used in the fixed block are 2.

(v) (d) Inside the prism, compared to the blue light, the red light slows down less and refracts less because the wavelength of red colour is maximum.

(vi) (d) The phenomenon of light governing in optical fibre is based on total internal reflection.

(vii) (b) By lens formula,

For convex lens, $f = +12$ cm

$u = -20$ cm

$$\frac{1}{f} = \frac{1}{v} - \frac{1}{u}$$

$$\Rightarrow \quad \frac{1}{12} = \frac{1}{v} - \frac{1}{(-20)} \quad \Rightarrow \quad \frac{1}{12} = \frac{1}{v} + \frac{1}{20}$$

$$\Rightarrow \quad \frac{1}{v} = \frac{1}{12} - \frac{1}{20} \quad \Rightarrow \quad \frac{1}{v} = \frac{5-3}{60} = \frac{2}{60}$$

$$\Rightarrow \quad \frac{1}{v} = \frac{1}{30} \quad \Rightarrow \quad v = 30 \text{ cm}$$

Image will be formed at a distance 30 cm. So, in order to obtain a clear image, he has to move the screen away from the lens.

(viii) (a) Both A and R are true and R is the correct explanation of A.

The infrared radiations have long wavelengths, so they undergo minimal scattering in earth's atmosphere and travel long distances in dense fog and mist.

(ix) (b) The pitch or shrillness of a sound is directly proportional to its frequency.

$\therefore$ X will be grave and Y will be shriller.

(x) (c) Resistance, R = Slope of V-I graph = $\tan\theta$

As, $\theta_P > \theta_Q > \theta_R < \theta_S$

$\Rightarrow \quad R_P > R_Q > R_R > R_S$

The filament of a bulb is made up of high resistance material. So, material P is used to make its filament.

(xi) (b) According to old convention, the colour of live, neutral and earth wires are red, black and green respectively.

(xii) (c) According to Maxwell's right hand thumb rule, the figure given in option (c) will be correct.

(xiii) (b) Heat capacity of a body is the heat or energy required to raise its temperature by 1°C.

(xiv) (c) The amount of heat energy required to melt a given amount of substance at its melting point is called as the latent heat of fusion.

(xv) $p = 95$, $n = 146$

$A = p + n = 95 + 146 = 241$

Now, ${}_{95}X^{241} \longrightarrow {}_{93}X^{237} + {}_{2}He^{4}$

Number of neutrons $= A - Z = 237 - 93 = 144$

Number of protons, $Z = 93$

Hence, option (c) is correct.

2. (i) (a) class II (b) decreases
(c) becomes eight times (d) horse power
(e) resistance, resistivity

(ii) The potential energy of a body at height h,

$$U = mgh$$

$$U \propto h$$

$\therefore$ The graph of U *versus* h is given below

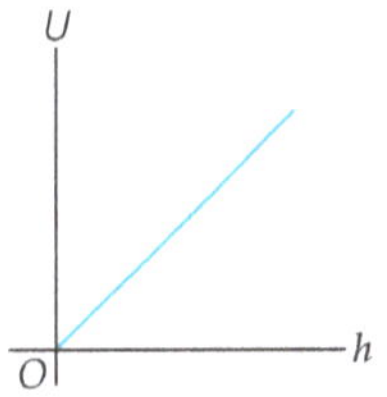

(iii) (a) The waves used for echo depth sounding are ultrasonic waves.

(b) Ultrasonic waves are used in echo depth sounding because these waves have very high frequency and short wavelength. So, these waves can penetrate undeviated through long distances in sea water.

3. (i) (a) As, the lens is made of two different refractive indices material so number of images formed will be two.

(b) In a concave lens, the image formed is always virtual, erect and diminished.

(ii) In circuit A, metal case is earthed. So, the person would not get electric shock but in circuit B, metal case is not earthed. So, the circuit will be completed through the body of the person giving him a shock. Therefore, circuit A is safe for the user.

(iii) (a) The transformer used to change a high alternating emf to a low alternating emf of same frequency is called step-down transformer.

(b) As, turns ratio, $r = \frac{N_s}{N_p} = \frac{E_s}{E_p}$

For step-down transformer,

$$E_s < E_p$$

$$\Rightarrow \quad \frac{E_s}{E_p} < 1$$

$$\therefore \quad r < 1 \text{ (less than 1)}$$

(iv) Given, $s_w = 4.2 \text{ Jg}^{-1} \text{ K}^{-1}$

For solid, $m_s = 60$ g, $T_s = 100°C$

For water, $m_w = 150$ g, $T_w = 20°C$

Final temperature, $T_f = 25°C$

By principle of calorimetry,

Heat lost by solid = Heat gained by water

$$\Rightarrow \quad m_s \cdot s_s (T_s - T_f) = m_w s_w (T_f - T_w)$$

$\therefore$ Heat capacity of solid, $m_s s$

$$= \frac{m_w c_w (T_f - T_w)}{(T_s - T_f)}$$

$$= \frac{150 \times 4.2 \times (25 - 20)}{(100 - 25)} = 42 \text{ JK}^{-1}$$

(v) (a) Faraday's first law or principle of electromagnetic induction.

(b) AC generator is used as a power source in major power stations like wind turbines.

(vi) (a) Gamma radiations

(b) No

(vii) (a) Beta

(b) Daughter element E

(c) Fleming's left hand rule

4. (i) (a) The image formed of fish on the water surface is based on the phenomenon of total internal reflection.

(b) 1. Converge 2. Diverge

(ii) (a) As, refractive index $\propto \frac{1}{\text{temperature}}$

$$\therefore \quad x < 1.33$$

(b) Two differences between normal reflection and total internal reflection :

Normal reflection	Total internal reflection
In this reflection, light rays can be incident at any angle.	In this reflection, light rays must be incident at an angle greater than critical angle.
The energy of reflected rays is less than that of incident rays, i.e. there is loss of energy.	The energy of reflected rays is same as that of incident rays, i.e. there is no loss of energy.

(iii) (a) When mixture of red + blue + green colours is passed through a convex lens, each ray passes through a different points on the principal axis after refraction.

(b) Ultraviolet radiations are obtained by a quartz prism, as they are not absorbed by it.

(c) These radiations are used for killing bacteria.

(d) Visible radiation or infrared or microwaves or radiowaves.

5. (*i*) For convex lens, $f = 8$ cm, $u = -24$ cm

(a) As $u > 2f$, so the image formed is real, inverted and smaller size than object.

(b) By lens formula,

$$\frac{1}{f} = \frac{1}{v} - \frac{1}{u} \quad \Rightarrow \quad \frac{1}{8} = \frac{1}{v} - \frac{1}{(-24)}$$

$$\Rightarrow \quad \frac{1}{v} = \frac{1}{8} - \frac{1}{24} = \frac{1}{12}$$

$$\therefore \quad v = 12 \text{ cm}$$

(*ii*) (a) As, deviation $\propto \frac{1}{\text{wavelength}}$

$\therefore$ Violet colour will show maximum deviation and red colour will show minimum deviation because wavelength of violet colour is minimum and wavelength of red colour is maximum.

(b) When green-coloured ray is passed through a glass prism, then the colour of emergent ray will be also green because green light has not any component of light.

(*iii*)

Sr. No.	Description	Label
a.	an angle of reflection on the mirror	a
b.	a partially reflected ray in glass slab	U
c.	a critical angle	c
d.	refracted rays	Q, T
e.	an angle of refraction of the ray R	$90 - e$

6. (i) (a) Weight of AC < Weight of BC

(b) Since, the rod is balanced at F (fulcrum)

$\therefore \quad w_{AF} = w_{BF}$

Now, $\quad w_{AF} - w_{CF} < w_{CF} \propto w_{BF} + w_{CF}$

[subtracting weight of CF from left and adding to right]

$\Rightarrow \quad w_{AC} < w_{BC}$

(ii) (a) No work is done.

(b) Negative work is done.

(c) Positive work is done

(iii) (a) The potential energy of the pendulum at point B

$$(\text{PE})_B = mgh = 02 \times 10 \times 5 = 10\text{ J}$$

(b) Applying conservation of mechanical energy,

$$E_A = E_B = E_C$$

$\therefore$ Total mechanical energy at point C,

$$E_C = E_B = (\text{KE})_B + (\text{PE})_B$$
$$= 0 + 10 = 10\text{ J}$$

(c) Applying conservation of mechanical energy at points A and B,

$$\frac{1}{2}mv^2 = mgh$$

$$\therefore \quad v = \sqrt{2gh}$$
$$= \sqrt{2 \times 10 \times 5} = 10\text{ m/s}$$

7. (i) (a) A block and tackle system of pulley,

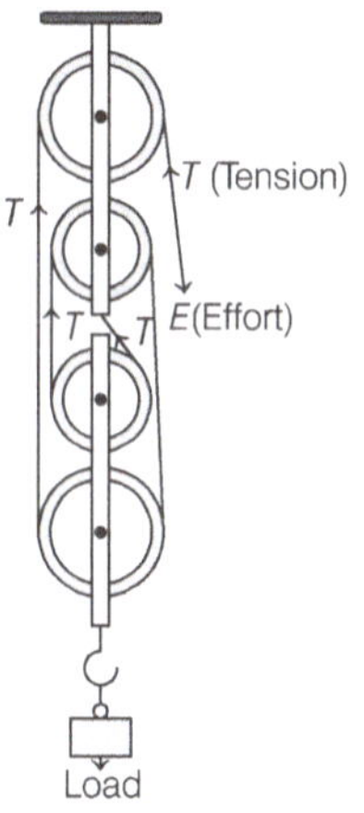

(b) Potential energy,

$$U = mgh = 100 \times 10 \times 5$$
$$U = 5000\text{ J}$$

(ii) (a) Given, $t = 3$ s,

speed of sound, $v = 336$ m/s

Let d = distance of person from cliff.

$\therefore \; 2d = v \times t \;\Rightarrow 2d = 336 \times 3 \;\Rightarrow\; d = 504$ m

(b) Let the extra distance moved by person from the cliff $= x$

$$t = 3 + 1.5 = 4.5\text{ s}$$

$\therefore \quad 2(d + x) = v \times t$

$\Rightarrow \quad 2(504 + x) = 336 \times 4.5$

$\therefore \quad x = 252$ m

(iii) (a) At point A

(b) Resonance

(c) The natural frequency of the swing will equal the frequency of the force applied by mother. Due to which the amplitude of swing will increase.

8. (i) (a) $R_1 < R_2$ (b) $V_1 = V_2$ (c) $S_1 = S_2$

(ii) Atomic number Z and mass number A

$${}^{A}_{Z}X \xrightarrow{\alpha} {}^{A-4}_{Z-2}X \quad \text{and} \quad {}^{A}_{Z}Y \xrightarrow{2\beta} {}^{A-4}_{Z-2}Y$$

(a) As, the atomic number of both the elements X and Y are same, so they are placed at the same position in the periodic table.

(b) X and Y are isotopes.

(c) Atomic number of X = Atomic number of $Y = 80$

(iii) (a) When key K is closed, then the circuit diagram is as shown below.

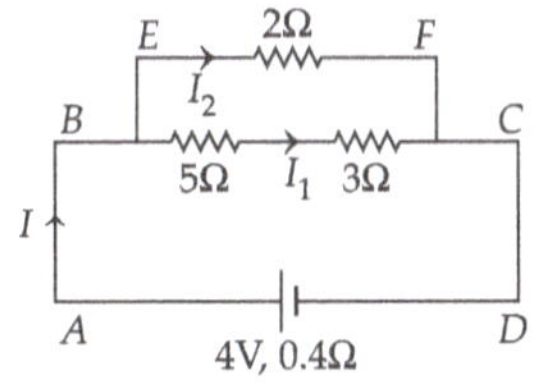

The resistance of the circuit is given by

$$R = \frac{2 \times (5+3)}{2 + (5+3)} + 0.4 = 2\,\Omega$$

(b) Current, $I = \dfrac{\varepsilon}{R + r} = \dfrac{4}{2 + 0.4} = 2$ A

Current in 3 Ω, $I_{3\Omega} = \dfrac{IR_1}{R_1 + R_2}$

$$= \frac{5}{3} \times \frac{2}{[2 + (5+3)]}$$

$$I_{3\Omega} = \frac{1}{3}\text{ A}$$

9. (i) Given, $m_w = 2.1$ kg,

$(\Delta T)_{w,\text{ Heat lost}} = (75 - 25) = 50°\text{C}$

$s_w = 4.2\text{ Jg}^{-1}\,°\text{C}^{-1}$, $L_{\text{ice}} = 336\text{ Jg}^{-1}$

Let m = mass of ice added at 0°C.

∴ By principle of calorimetry,

Heat lost by water from 75° to 25° C = Heat gained by ice at 0°C to water at 0° C + Heat gained by water at 0°C to water at 25°C

$$\Rightarrow \quad m_w s_w (\Delta T)_{w,\ \text{Heat lost}} = mL_i + ms_w (\Delta T)_{w,\ \text{Heat gain}}$$

$$\Rightarrow \quad 21 \times 10^3 \times 42 \times 50 = m[336 + 42 \times 25]$$

∴ Mass of ice, $m = 1000\text{ g} = 1\text{ kg}$

(ii) The cooling curve for the substance is shown below.

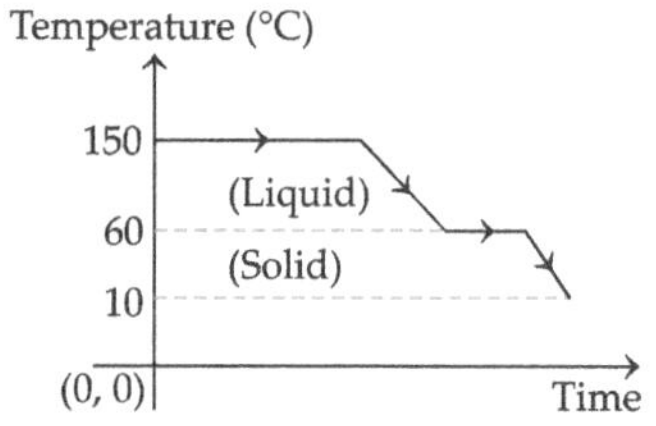

(a) The substance is condensed at the temperature of 150°C.

(b) The temperature range for which the substance is in liquid state is 60°C to 150°C.

(c) When ice melts to water at 0°C, it absorbs heat equal to latent heat of melting of ice and gets converted into water. This is the reason why drinks get even more colder when kept in ice as ice absorbs heat from the drink.

(iii) (a) $A \rightarrow$ Positive terminal

$B \rightarrow$ Negative terminal

(b) Magnetic field will expand in the direction of the held rod.

(c) 1. Reversing the direction of the current.

Or Reversing the direction of the battery.

2. Reduce the potential difference across the coil.

Or Decreasing the strength of the current through the coil.

ICSE Fully Solved

EXAMINATION PAPER 2025

Time : 2 hrs
Marks : 80

Physics

General Instructions

1. You will not be allowed to write during the first 15 minutes. This time is to be spent in reading the question paper.
2. The time given at the head of this paper is the time allowed for writing the answers.
3. **Section-A** is compulsory. Attempt **any four** questions from **Section-B**.
4. The intended marks for questions or parts of questions are given in brackets [].

Section A

[40 Marks]

(Attempt all questions from this section)

1. Choose the correct answers to the questions from the given options. **[15]**

(i) A body is acted upon by two equal and opposite forces, that are not along the same straight line. The body will
(a) remain stationary
(b) have only rotational motion
(c) have only rectilinear motion
(d) have both rectilinear and rotational motion

(ii) Which among the following is a vector quantity?
(a) Work
(b) Power
(c) Energy
(d) Moment of couple

(iii) What is the correct energy transformation during burning of a candle?
(a) Heat $\rightarrow$ Kinetic + Potential
(b) Heat $\rightarrow$ Chemical + Light
(c) Chemical $\rightarrow$ Heat + Light
(d) Mechanical $\rightarrow$ Chemical + Heat

(iv) When a ray of light passes from one optical medium to another, which of the following physical quantities does not change?
(a) Amplitude of the wave
(b) Frequency of the wave
(c) Wavelength of the wave
(d) Speed of the wave

(v) Which one of the following combinations is the correct ascending order of electromagnetic waves in terms of wavelength?
(a) Gamma-rays, visible light, microwaves
(b) Microwaves, visible light, gamma-rays
(c) Gamma-rays, microwaves, visible light
(d) Microwaves, gamma-rays, visible light

(vi) For a lever, a graph is plotted with load on Y-axis and effort on X-axis. Which of the following represents the slope of the graph?
(a) Mechanical advantage
(b) Velocity ratio
(c) 1/ Velocity ratio
(d) 1 Mechanical advantage

(vii) For a real image formed by a convex lens, the ratio of $I : O = 2 : 5$, then the object is I is the height of the image and O is the height of the object)
(a) between O and F
(b) beyond $2F$
(c) at F
(d) between F and $2F$

(viii) A ray of light is incident normally on a face of an equilateral prism. The ray gets totally reflected at the second refracting surface. The total deviation produced in the path of the ray is
(a) 30° (b) 60°
(c) 90° (d) 120°

(ix) In a closed circuit containing a bulb and a cell, the electromotive force (ε) and the terminal voltage (V) is related as
(Given, I is current and r is internal resistance)
(a) $V = \varepsilon + Ir$ (b) $V = \varepsilon - Ir$
(c) $V = \varepsilon \div Ir$ (d) $V = \varepsilon \times Ir$

(x) A metal piece of mass 5 g has thermal capacity 2.5 JK^{-1}. If the mass of the metal is tripled, then its specific heat capacity will be
(a) 7.5 JK^{-1} (b) 2.5 JK^{-1}
(c) 1.5 $Jg^{-1}K^{-1}$ (d) 0.5 $Jg^{-1}K^{-1}$

(xi) **Assertion (A)** As the level of water in a tall measuring cylinder kept under running tap rises, the pitch of sound gradually increases.
Reason (R) Frequency of sound is inversely proportional to the length of the water column.
(a) Both A and R are true and R is correct explanation of A.
(b) Both A and R are true but R is not the correct explanation of A.
(c) A is true but R is false.
(d) A is false but R is true.

(xii) In the given circuits Y and Z, the resistors R_1 and R_2, are connected in

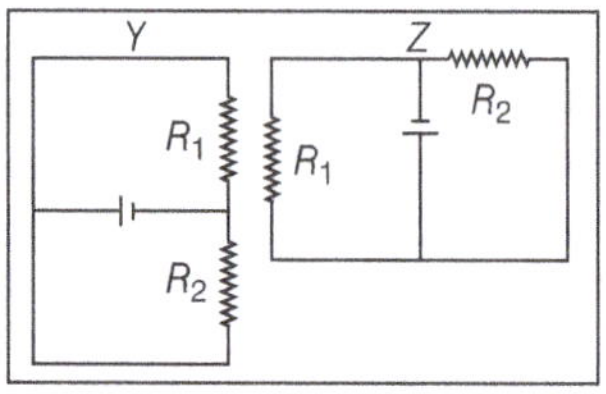

(a) series in both the circuits
(b) parallel in both the circuits
(c) parallel in Y and series in Z
(d) series in Y and parallel in Z

(xiii) A radioactive element P emits one α-particle and transforms to a new element Q. What will be the position of the element Q in the periodic table?
(a) One group to the left of P
(b) One group to the right of P
(c) Two groups to the right of P
(d) Two groups to the left of P

(xiv) Each of the substances given below is supplied with same amount of heat.
Which one will attain the highest temperature?

Substance	Lead	Aluminium	Copper	Iron
Specific heat capacity (cal/g°C)	0.031	0.21	0.095	0.115

(a) Aluminium (b) Copper
(c) Iron (d) Lead

(xv) The following figure shows a small bar magnet falling freely through a copper ring. For the observer at A, the direction of the induced current will be

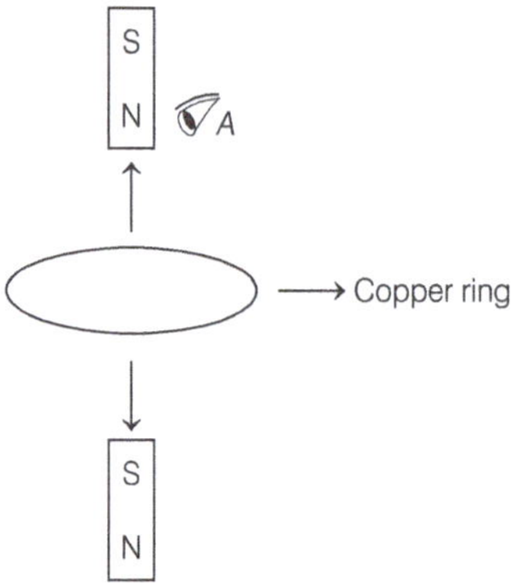

(a) clockwise when magnet is above and below the ring
(b) anti-clockwise when magnet is above and below the ring
(c) anti-clockwise when magnet is above the ring and clockwise when the magnet is below the ring
(d) clockwise when magnet is above the ring and anti-clockwise when the magnet is below the ring

2. (i) Complete the following by choosing the correct answers from the bracket **[6]**
(a) In uniform circular motion the centrifugal force acts ....
(towards the centre/away from the centre/along the tangential direction).
(b) Refractive index of a medium is independent of ....
(temperature/angle of incidence/wavelength of light).
(c) Heat absorbed during change of phase depends on .... (mass/change in temperature/specific heat capacity) of the substance.
(d) Emf of a cell is .... (greater than / less than / equal to) the terminal voltage when the cell is in open circuit.
(e) In a step-up transformer the turns ratio is .... (more than 1/less than 1/equal to 1)
(f) The nuclear radiation with lowest ionising power is .... ($\alpha / \beta / \gamma$).

(ii) A non-uniform kite is hanging freely from the branch of a tree as shown. Study the figure and answer the following **[2]**

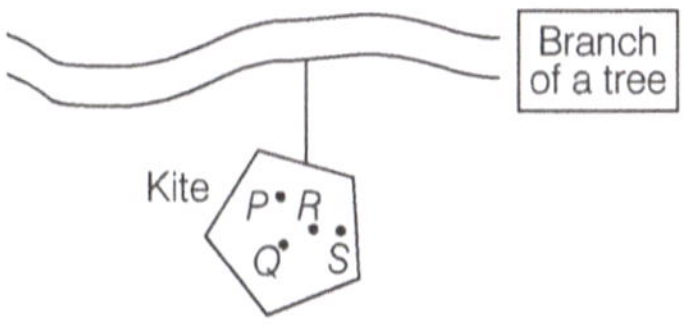

(a) Fill in the blank.
.... (*P*, *Q*, *R* or *S*) is the most probable position of its centre of gravity.
(b) Support your answer to (a) with a reason.

(iii) The displacement-time graph of a sound wave produced by a vibrating wire is shown below. **[2]**

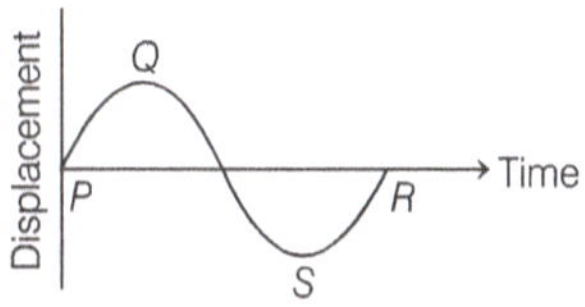

(a) How will you adjust the tension in the wire, to reduce the length of *PR*?
(b) Which characteristic of sound is affected by the reduction in the length of *PR*?

3. (i) A ray of light enters a rectangular glass slab submerged in water at an angle of incidence 55°. Does this ray undergo total internal reflection when it moves from water to glass? Justify your answer. (The critical angle for glass-water interface is 54°.) **[2]**

(ii) According to the new colour convention which colour of wire is connected to **[2]**
(a) the metal body of the appliance
(b) the switch of the appliance?

(iii) (a) Which of the two, alternating current or direct current, produces a varying magnetic field when it flows through a conductor? **[2]**
(b) State the frequency of the alternating current supply in India

(iv) Calculate the amount of heat absorbed by 200 g of paraffin wax to melt completely at its melting point [Specific latent heat of fusion of paraffin wax $= 146\ \text{Jg}^{-1}$] **[2]**

(v) Copper wire is wound around a steel bar *FT*. Current is allowed to pass through the coil for some time and then the bar is removed. **[2]**
(a) Draw only the magnetised bar *FT* and mark its poles.
(b) Trace two magnetic lines of force around *FT* clearly indicating the direction.

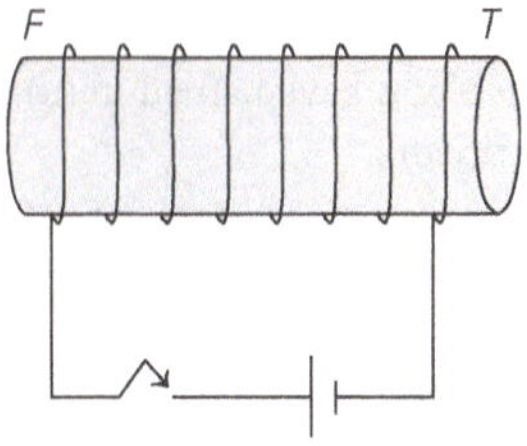

(vi) A current flows through a metallic conductor for a long period of time. State the change you would expect in its **[2]**
(a) Resistance(b) Resistivity

(vii) Curium is a radioactive element with the symbol $^{247}_{96}\text{Cm}$ named in honour of Madam Curie. The graph of number of protons *versus* number of neutrons for some elements are shown below

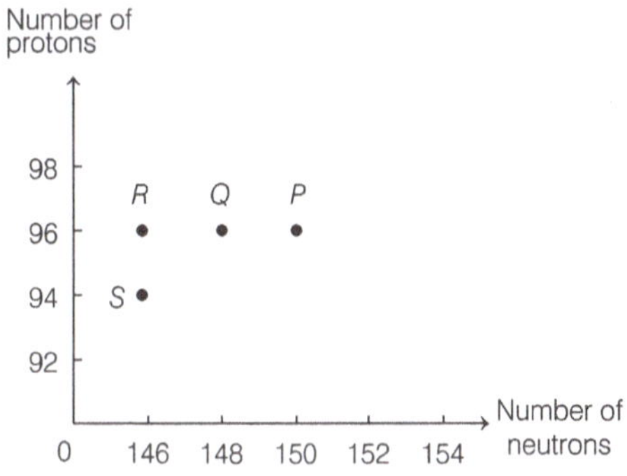

(a) Which point on the graph indicates the element Cm? **[1]**
(b) Which point on the graph indicates daughter nucleus after Cm undergoes radioactive decay of 1α followed by 2β ? **[1]**
(c) State the mass number of the daughter nucleus. **[1]**

Section B

(Attempt any four questions from this section)

4. (i)

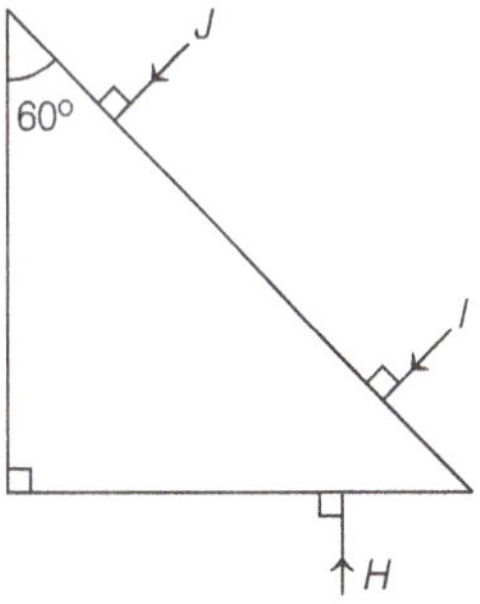

[3]

(a) Out of the three rays (*I*, *J*, *H*) shown in the diagram, which ray will suffer total internal reflection, while inside the prism? (Critical angle of the prism is 42°.)

(b) Copy the diagram to complete the path of the ray which you have named in (a) till it comes out of the prism

(ii) A rectangular glass block of refractive index 1.5 has an air bubble trapped inside it as shown in the diagram. When seen from the surface *AB*, it appears to be 4 cm deep. **[3]**

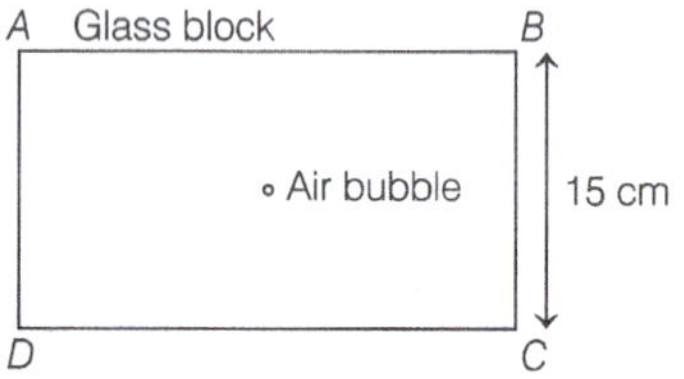

(a) Calculate the actual depth of the air bubble from the surface *AB*.

(b) For which colour of light, blue or yellow, the apparent depth will be greater?

(c) Turning the glass block upside down, does not change the apparent depth of the air bubble. State true or false.

(iii) (a) An object is placed at 2*F* position of a convex lens. Draw a ray diagram -showing the formation of the image.

(b) How will the size of the image change if we, only replace the lens in the above arrangement with another lens of a greater focal length? **[4]**

5. (i) An object is placed in front of a concave lens at a distance of 45 cm from it. If its image is formed at a distance of 30 cm from the lens, calculate the focal length of the lens? **[3]**

(ii) Two rays *PQ* and *RS* are incident on a rectangular glass block as shown in the diagram. Observe the diagram and answer the questions that follow. **[3]**

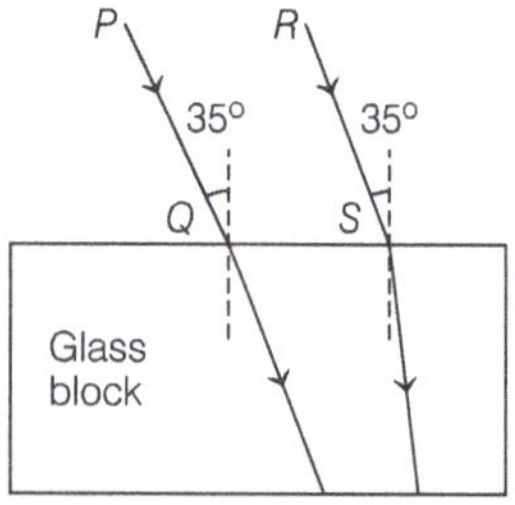

Which of these two rays will

(a) have greater lateral displacement on emerging out of the block?

(b) travel with greater speed in the block?

(c) scatter more in the atmosphere?

(iii) (a) Name the radiations **[4]**

1. for which a quartz prism is used to study the spectrum.
2. which are used in remote sensing devices.
3. which are used in traffic signals m India.

(b) Name one property common to all electromagnetic radiations.

6. (i) Akash takes a uniform meter scale and suspends a weight of 2 N at one end '*X*' and a weight of 5 N on the other end '*Y*'. He then balances the ruler horizontally on a knife edge placed at 70 cm from *X*. Draw a diagram of the arrangement and calculate the weight of the ruler. **[3]**

(ii) Three levers *X*, *Y*, *Z* of equal lengths are shown in the diagram.

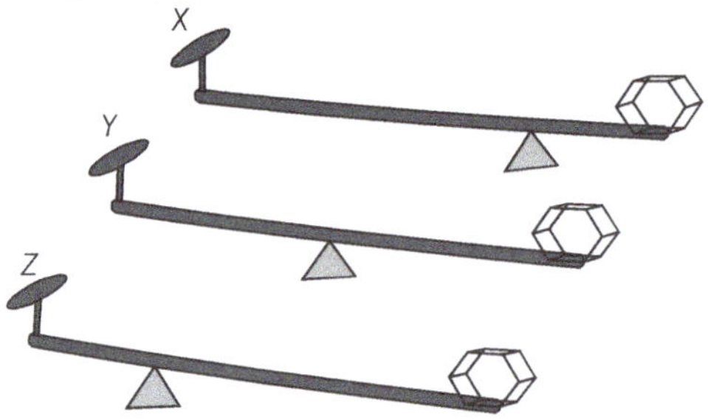

(a) Which class of lever do these belong to?

(b) Among these (*X*, *Y* or *Z*) which one will give the maximum mechanical advantage? Justify your answer. **[3]**

(iii)

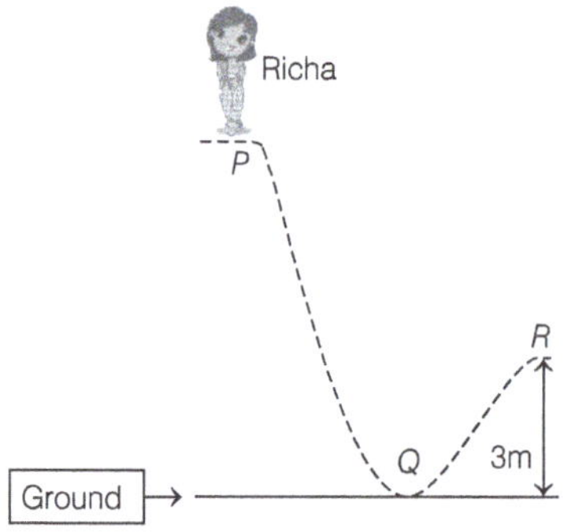

Richa weighing 40 kgf leaves point *P* on her skateboard and reaches point *Q* on the ground with velocity 10 ms^{-1}. Calculate **[4]**

(a) the kinetic energy of Richa at point *Q*.

(b) the vertical height of point *P* above the ground. (Use *g* as 10 m/s^2 and neglect friction

(c) the kinetic energy of Richa at point *R*. (While moving from *Q* to *R*, she loses 500 J of energy against friction)

7. (i) Draw a block and tackle system of pulleys with velocity ratio equal to 3. **[3]**

(ii) A submarine in the sea, sends ultrasonic ping and a stopwatch is started simultaneously. The stopwatch stops on receiving the reflected wave from an obstacle and reads 1 minute 40 seconds. Calculate the distance of the obstacle from the submarine. (Speed of sound in water 1500 ms^{-1}) **[3]**

(iii) The diagrams given below show two sound boxes A and B with wires of same length (l) and tension (10 kgf) but different cross-sectional areas. Simultaneously, vibrating tuning forks of frequency 300 Hz are placed on the boxes A and B. The paper rider falls off in case of B but not in case of A. **[4]**

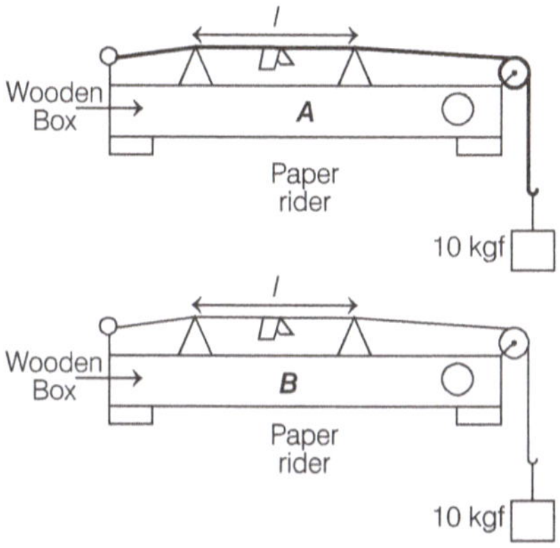

(a) Name and explain the phenomenon responsible for the falling off of the paper rider in B.

(b) The wire A resonates with a tuning fork of frequency f. Is f greater than, less than or equal to 300 Hz? Justify your answer.

8. (i) The diagram shows wiring in a meter room of a building. **[3]**

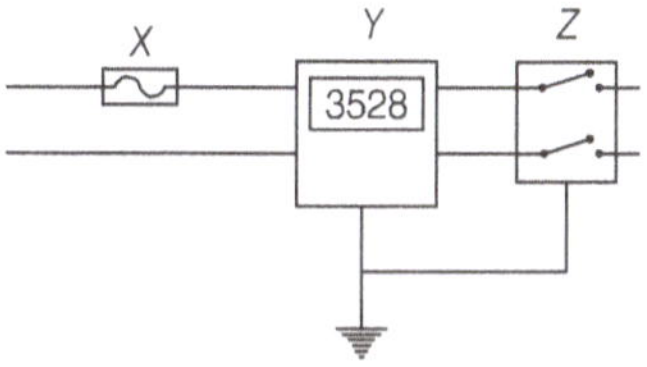

(a) What is the current rating of device X?

(b) What is the difference between the switch Z shown in the diagram and the switches you use to operate different appliances at home?

(c) What is the unit of the physical quantity displayed in Y?

(ii) Study the diagram given below and answer the questions that follow:

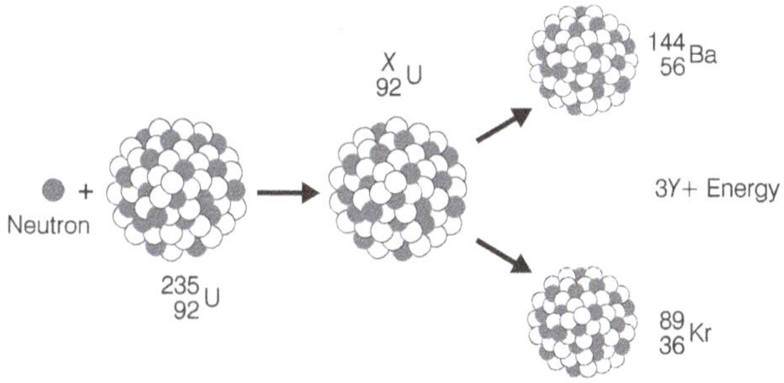

(a) Name the process depicted in the diagram.

(b) What is the value of X?

(c) Identify Y. the missing product of the reaction. **[3]**

(iii)

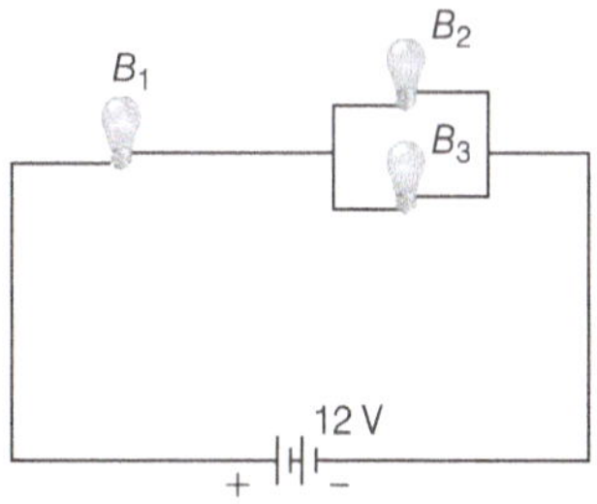

Three identical bulbs B_1, B_2, and B_3 each of power rating 18 W, 12 V are connected to a battery of 12 V. **[4]**

(a) Calculate:

1. the resistance of each bulb
2. the current drawn from the cell

(b) If the bulb B_3 is removed from the circuit, then will the brightness of the bulb B_1 increase, decrease or remain the same?

9. (i) 30 g of ice at 0°C is used to bring down the temperature of a certain mass of water at 70 °C to 20 °C. Find the mass of water (Specific heat capacity of water = $4.2\ Jg^{-1}\ °C^{-1}$ and specific latent heat of ice = $336\ Jg^{-1}$) **[3]**

(ii) (a) A certain amount of heat will warm 1 g of material X by 10 °C and 1 g of material Y by 40°C. Which material has higher specific heat capacity? **[3]**

(b) Which material, X or Y, would you select to make a calorimeter?

(c) The specific heat capacity of a substance remains the same when it changes its state from solid to liquid. State true or false.

(iii) A copper rod PQ carrying-current is kept in a magnetic field as shown in the diagram.

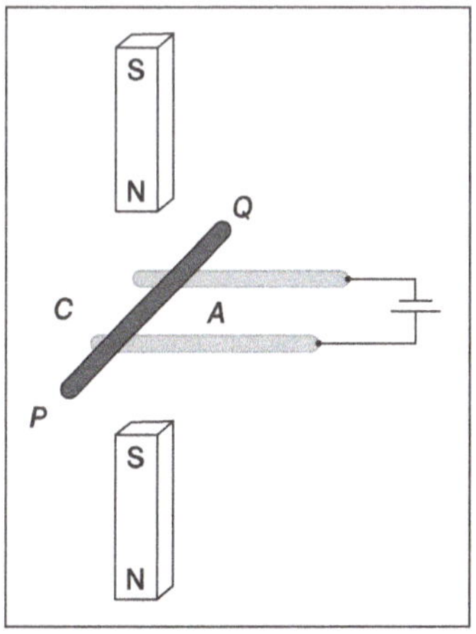

(a) The copper rod PQ will move towards C. State true or false.

(b) Name the law used to determine the direction of motion of PQ.

(c) What will be the effect on the force experienced, if the rod PQ is replaced by another copper rod of same length but of greater cross-sectional area?

(d) Justify your answer in (c). **[4]**

Solutions

1. (i) (b) When two equal and opposite forces not acting along the same line acts on a body, it forms a couple.

A couple is always needed to produce rotation in a body.

(ii) (d)

(iii) (c) When a candle burns, a chemical reaction occurs where wax reacts with oxygen which converts the chemical potential energy into heat and light.

(iv) (b)

(v) (a)

(vi) (a)

$$\text{Mechanical advantage} = \frac{\text{Load}}{\text{Effort}}$$

$$\text{and slope of a graph} = \frac{\Delta Y}{\Delta X}$$

(vii) (b) Here the image formed is real and diminished which depicts that the object is kept beyond $2F$.

(viii) (d)

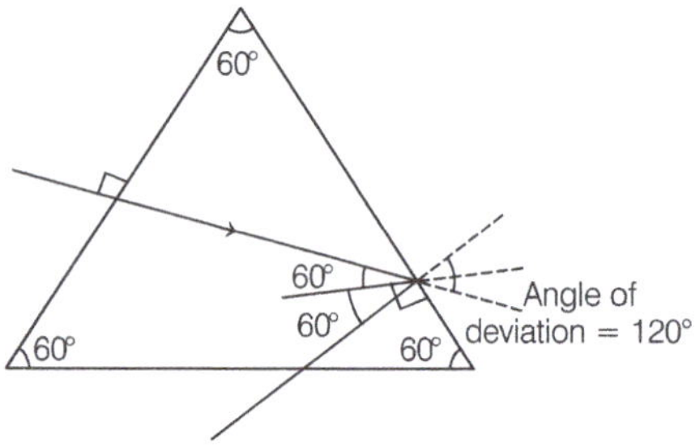

(ix) (b)

(x) (d) Specific heat capacity of the metal piece is

$$\frac{\text{thermal capacity}}{\text{mass}} = \frac{2.5}{5}\,JK^{-1}g^{-1}.$$

$$= 0.5\,JK^{-1}g^{-1}.$$

When the mass of the metal is tripled, the specific heat capacity remains unchanged as it is independent of the mass of the body.

(xi) (a) Both A and R are true and R is the correct explanation of A because as the water level rises, the air column decreases which increases the frequency of vibration of the air column thereby increasing the pitch of the sound.

(xii) (b)

(xiii) (d)

(xiv) (d) Since, lead has the lowest specific heat capacity, so the rise in temperature in case of lead will be the highest.

(xv) (c)

2. (i) (a) away from the centre

(b) angle of incidence

(c) specific heat capacity

(d) equal to

(e) more than 1

(f) γ

(ii) (a) Q.

(b) For a stable equilibrium of a body, the centre of gravity should be as low as possible and also near the geometric centre of the body and in the above case Q is the most appropriate point for the centre of gravity of the kite.

(iii) (a) The frequency of note produced by a stretched string is related to the tension in the string as $f \propto \sqrt{T}$.

When the length PR is reduced, the wavelength of the wave is reduced thereby increasing the frequency of the wave.

So, the tension must be increased in case if PR has to be reduced.

(b) The pitch of the vibration of sound increases when the length PR is reduced.

3. (i) Yes, the ray will undergo total internal reflection as the critical angle of the glass-water interface is less than the angle of incidence of the ray of light.

(ii) (a) Green or Yellow (Earth).

(b) Brown (Live).

(iii) (a) Alternating current would produce a varying magnetic field when it flows through a conductor.

(b) Frequency of alternating current supply in India is 50 Hz.

(iv) Specific latent heat of fusion of paraffin wax = $146\,Jg^{-1}$.

$\therefore$ Amount of heat absorbed by 200 g of paraffin wax to meet completely is = $(146 \times 200)\,J = 29200\,J$.

(v) (a)

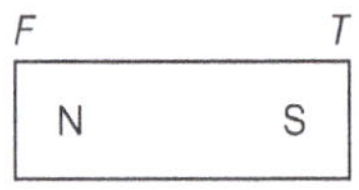

(b)

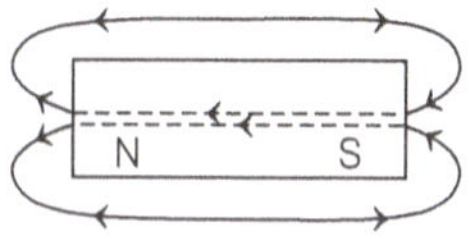

(vi) (a) Since the current flows for a long period of time so the resistance will increase due to the heating effect of current.

(b) Since, resistivity is also dependent on temperature and it increases with the increase in temperature so the resistivity is also affected in the above case.

(vii) (a) Point P

(b) Point R

(c) Mass number of the daughter nucleus is 243.

4. (i) (a) Ray J

(b)

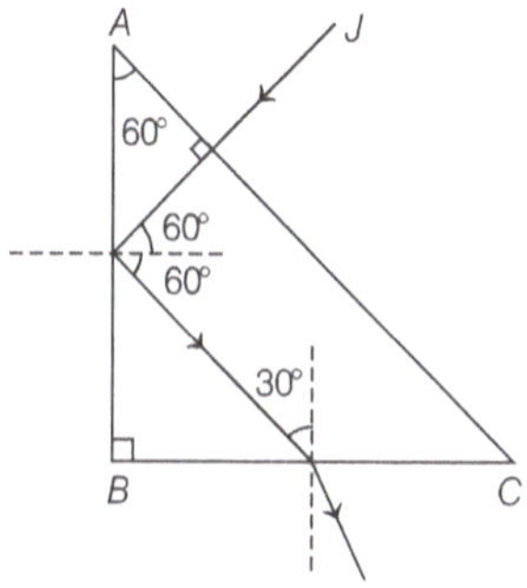

(ii) (a) Refractive index of a medium with respect to air,

$$\mu = \frac{\text{Real depth or actual depth}}{\text{Apparent depth}}$$

$$\therefore \quad 1.5 = \frac{\text{Actual depth}}{4}$$

$\Rightarrow$ Actual depth $= (1.5 \times 4) = 6\,\text{cm}$

(b) Apparent depth $\propto \frac{1}{\text{RI}}$

$\therefore$ The apparent depth will be greater for yellow light, since its refractive index for yellow light is lower.

(c) When the glass block is turned upside down, the real depth of the air bubble becomes 9 cm.

$\therefore$ Apparent depth $= \frac{9}{1.5} = 6\,\text{cm}$.

$\therefore$ The statement is false.

(iii) (a)

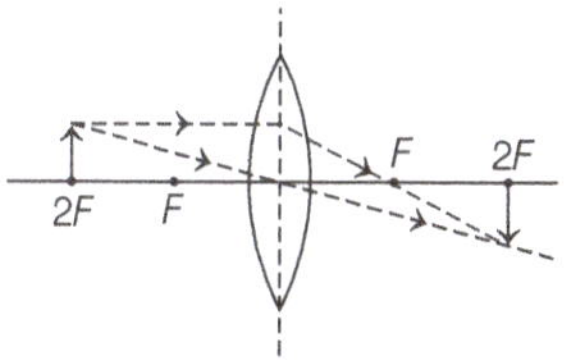

(b) Since the size of the image in the above case is same as that of the object so it will remain same even if the lens is replaced with a lens of a different focal length.

5. (i) From lens formula, we know that $\frac{1}{v} - \frac{1}{u} = \frac{1}{f}$

where v is the image distance, u is the object distance and f is the focal length of the lens.

Here, $v = -30\,\text{cm}$, $u = -45\,\text{cm}$.

$$\therefore \quad \frac{1}{f} = \frac{1}{(-30)} - \frac{1}{(-45)} = \frac{-1}{30} + \frac{1}{45} = \frac{-1}{90}$$

$$\therefore \quad f = -90\,\text{cm}$$

$\therefore$ The focal length of the concave lens is 90 cm.

(ii) (a) Ray RS

Since, it bends more inside the glass block.

(b) Ray PQ.

Since, it bends less inside the glass block and hence has a lower refractive index as compared to ray RS.

(c) The light ray having greater refractive index will suffer less deviation as compared to the light having lower refractive index.

Therefore, PQ having lower refractive index will scatter more.

(iii) (a) 1. Ultraviolet radiation 2. Infrared radiation 3. Visible light

(b) All electromagnetic waves travel with the same speed in vacuum that is 3×10^8 m/s.

6. (i)

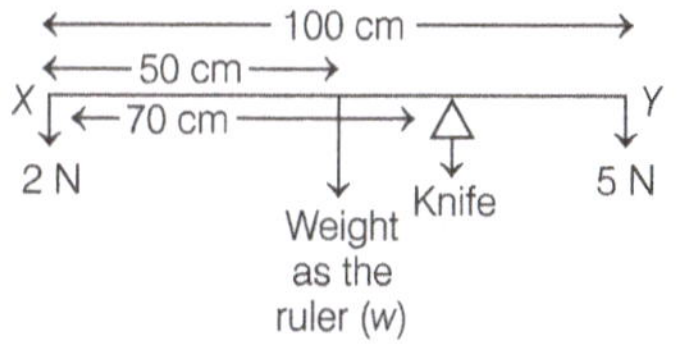

From the principle of moment, we know that sum of anti-clockwise moment = sum of clockwise moment.

$$\therefore \quad (2 \times 70) + w \times 20 = 5 \times 30$$

$$\Rightarrow \quad 140 + 20w = 150$$

$$\Rightarrow \quad w = \frac{150 - 140}{20} = 0.5\,\text{N}$$

$\therefore$ The weight of the ruler is 0.5 N.

(ii) (a) Class I lever.

(b) Mechanical advantage $= \frac{\text{Effort arm}}{\text{Load arm}}$

Since the effort arm is greatest and the load arm is the least for Z, so Z will have the maximum mechanical advantage.

(iii) (a) Weight of Richa $= 40\,\text{kgf} = 40 \times 10\,\text{N} = 400\,\text{N}$

$\therefore$ Mass of Richa $= \frac{400}{10} = 40\,\text{kg}$

$\therefore$ Kinetic energy of Richa when she reaches point $Q = \left(\frac{1}{2} \times 40 \times 10^2\right)\text{J} = 2000\,\text{J}$

(b) From conservation of energy,

we know PE = KE

$$\Rightarrow \quad mgh = \frac{1}{2}mv^2 = 2000\text{ J}$$

where, h = length of PQ.

$$\therefore \quad h = \frac{2000}{400} = 5\text{ m}$$

(c) PE of Richa at point $R = (400 \times 3)\text{ J} = 1200\text{ J}$

Loss of energy = 500 J

∴ KE + 500 = 1200, by law of conservation of energy

∴ KE = 700 J, at point R.

7. (i)

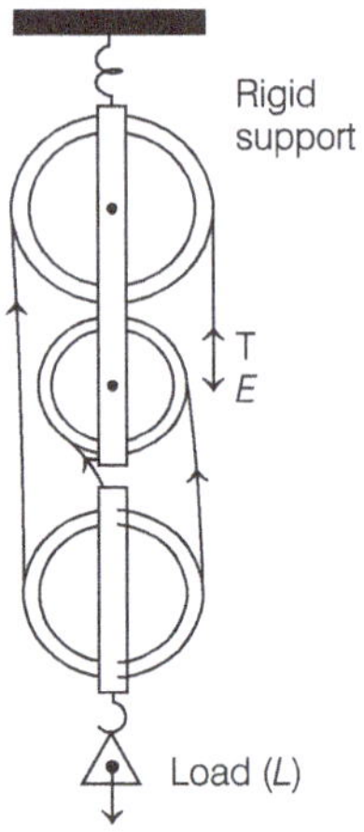

(ii) Let the total distance travelled by the ultrasonic wave from sending to receiving the signal be $2d$ m

Total time taken = 1 m 40 s = 100 s.

Speed of the ultrasonic wave in water = 1500 ms^{-1}.

$$\therefore \quad 2d = (1500 \times 100)\text{ m}$$

$$\Rightarrow \quad d = 75000\text{ m} = 75\text{ km}.$$

∴ The distance of the obstacle from the submarine = 75 km

(iii) (a) The wire B undergoes resonance which is responsible for the falling off of the paper rider in B.

Refer to theory on page 139 (Resonance).

(b) f will be less than 300 Hz. because frequency of a stretched string is inversely proportional to the radius of the string. Since, the string in A has a greater radius, so it will have smaller resonant frequency as compared to the resonant frequency of B.

8. (i) (a) 5 ampere.

(b) Switch Z is the main switch which is a double pole switch which helps in breaking the connection with both neutral and live wires simultaneously from the main supply which is not present in switches used for operating household appliances.

(c) Kilowatt hour (KWh).

(ii) (a) Nuclear fission

(b) 236

(c) ${}^{1}_{0}n$ (neutron)

(iii) (a) 1. Power rating of each bulb = 18 W.

Since, all the bulbs have the same resistance so let each have a resistance of $R\,\Omega$.

The maximum voltage that the bulbs can draw are 12 V.

$$\therefore R = \frac{V^2}{P} = \frac{12 \times 12}{18} = 8\,\Omega$$

2. The effective resistance in the circuit,

$$R_{EF} = R + \frac{R \times R}{R + R}$$

$$= R + \frac{R}{2} = \frac{3R}{2}$$

$$\therefore R_{EF} = 3 \times \frac{8}{2} = 12\,\Omega$$

$$\therefore \text{Current drawn} = \frac{\text{Supplied voltage}}{R_{EF}}$$

$$= \frac{12}{12} = 1\text{ A}$$

(b) If the bulb B_3 is removed from the circuit, then R_{EF} becomes $2R = 2 \times 12\,\Omega$

$$= 24\,\Omega$$

$$\therefore \text{Current drawn} = \frac{12}{24} = 0.5\text{ A}$$

So, the brightness of bulb B_1 will decrease.

9. (i) Let the mass of the water required be m grams.

Heat released by water = Heat absorbed by ice

$$\therefore \quad m \times 4.2 \times (70 - 20) = 30 \times 336$$

$$\Rightarrow \quad m = \frac{30 \times 336}{4.2 \times 50}$$

$$= \frac{10080}{210} = 48\text{ g}$$

∴ The mass of water required = 48 g

(ii) (a) Material X has a higher specific heat capacity.

(b) Material Y

(c) False

(iii) (a) True

(b) Fleming's left hand rule

(c) Remains same

(d) Since $F \propto l$, where l is the length of the rod so it will not be affected due to the increase in cross - sectional area since the length remains same.